L

xamples

Oracle SQL
Jumpstart with Examples

Gavin Powell
Carol McCullough-Dieter

ELSEVIER
DIGITAL
PRESS

AMSTERDAM • BOSTON • HEIDELBERG • LONDON
NEW YORK • OXFORD • PARIS • SAN DIEGO•
SAN FRANCISCO • SINGAPORE • SYDNEY • TOKYO

Elsevier Digital Press
200 Wheeler Road, Burlington, MA 01803, USA
Linacre House, Jordan Hill, Oxford OX2 8DP, UK

Library of Congress Cataloging-in-Publication Data
Application submitted.

ISBN: 1-55558-323-7

British Library Cataloguing-in-Publication Data
A catalogue record for this book is available from the British Library.

For information on all Digital Press publications
visit our Web site at www.digitalpress.com and www.bh.com/digitalpress

04 05 06 07 08 09 10 9 8 7 6 5 4 3 2 1

Printed in the United States of America

Contents at a Glance

Table of Contents

24 Basic PL/SQL   531

Foreword

As a consultant with more than 12 years of experience working with Oracle databases on a daily basis, reviewing this book was a unique and enjoyable experience. The SQL language is without doubt one of the most critical database skills and it is best learned by example. This book addresses that crucial need. Mr. Powell does an excellent job of clarifying the concepts by using meaningful and easy to understand examples. **Frankly, I have not come across any other book on SQL that is as good a compilation of SQL concepts in a single source.**

Oracle SQL Jumpstart with Examples will be a very useful reference and should be a hit for anyone who may be using Oracle SQL. This book should become very popular not only with Developers and DBAs but also Database Managers, Designers and System Managers. Even busy executives can use the book to quickly write queries on an occasional basis. Additionally, the examples in the book provide a good reference for functional people, (such as systems engineers and project leaders,) who want a better understanding of the true capabilities of Oracle SQL, allowing for better articulation and understanding of user and system requirements.

One comes across very few books that make a significant difference in the fundamental understanding of a subject. This is one such book if you want to understand a core database skill – Oracle SQL. This book deserves a place in your secret library and you will find it a great reference not only for learning SQL but also for learning data relationships, data organization, data analysis possibilities and so forth. I feel that the title, Oracle SQL Jumpstart with Examples, might be too simplistic to describe the content. Read on, you will find the real value hidden inside this book.

– Ravi Sharma—Senior Principal Consultant

Preface

Welcome to *Oracle SQL Jumpstart with Examples*!

The title of this book was originally Oracle SQL Reference, but during the writing process, we set our hearts on the new title *Oracle SQL Jumpstart with Examples*. Why "with Examples"? This book is still an Oracle SQL reference manual simply by the nature of its structure and content. However, it is a reference manual with much added usefulness. The book contains an absolute plethora of properly tested example Oracle SQL code.

In my years as a developer and database administrator, I have often found that the quickest solution to a knotty coding problem is resolved by finding simple working examples. Therefore this book is targeted at database administrators (DBAs), developers, designers, and managers, both telling and showing how to solve problems with Oracle SQL. This book is applicable to anyone who uses Oracle SQL on a daily basis or periodically, be it for questions about data, application development, finding problems, fine-tuning those problems, or otherwise.

This book is full of working examples. All examples have been *tested* and *verified* in Oracle Database 10*g* on a Windows 2000 Intel platform. Examples applicable to Oracle Database 9*i* are tested in an Oracle9*i* database as well as an Oracle10*g* database. Because of the nature of Oracle SQL residing and executing from within an Oracle database, there should be no operating system differences or dependencies.

Note: Different operating systems and platforms may require different Oracle database releases, but it is still unlikely that there will be any differences with respect to Oracle SQL.

This book is also written to include Oracle SQL contained in both Oracle Database 10*g* and Oracle Database 9*i*. Whenever you see (10*g*) that indicates an Oracle Database 10*g* update or enhancement. The differences between Oracle Database 10*g* and Oracle Database 9*i* are easy to see in this book. Many Oracle installed sites still run Oracle Database 9*i*, and perhaps even Oracle Database 8*i* and earlier versions. This means you can use this book now and continue to use it when you upgrade to 10*g* in the future.

This book is unique. Because I am an experienced techie myself, I tend to write what I would like to read. Never in my career of pulling Oracle books off a shelf and paging through them have I found a book with as many examples, covering as many different aspects of Oracle SQL. Not to toot my own horn, but this book is written as a book that people like me would want to read because it is written by me, for me and my own personal use. To reiterate, this book is useful not only as a reference manual for Oracle SQL but also as a basis for rapidly solving coding problems. Simply look it up and copy the example!

In addition, this book also contains chapters covering Oracle SQL as applied to XML in Oracle, some PL/SQL basics, Oracle Partitioning, plus both (10*g*) Oracle Expression Filter and (10*g*) Regular Expressions.

All of the scripts written to create the MUSIC database that is used throughout this book are found in Appendix A. In addition, you can find the scripts listed on a simple menu on my website at the following URL:[1]

```
www.oracledbaexpert.com/oracle/
OracleSQLJumpstartWithExamples/index.html
```

You will find scripts for other books I have written plus other information as well, and of course, my resume.

So that is the reason for the title. The use of Oracle SQL applies to a wide scope of Oracle products and disciplines falling under the umbrella of Oracle Database 10*g* and 9*i*. Most significant of these disciplines are database administration and programming Oracle SQL code (development), or other disciplines including any type of database access and application programming.

So what is this book about? This book is about all aspects of Oracle SQL, both for DBAs and developers. Essentially this book is all about Oracle SQL with some interesting additions such as XML, basic PL/SQL programming, and the basic facts about Oracle Database underlying architecture.

What is the objective of this book? The objective of this book is to cover as many of the aspects of Oracle SQL as possible, with the intention of providing a source of reference and proven examples to any type of Oracle SQL user. The end result will hopefully make people's jobs a little easier and perhaps a little more productive as well.

What is the approach in this book? The approach in this book is to present syntax, and then explain and prove by example. So there are two ways in which this book is organized and written that make it unique among all other Oracle SQL titles. First, it is organized like an Oracle SQL reference manual. Second, it is chock full of tested, verified, working examples, covering nearly every aspect of Oracle SQL possible. This book is also unique because it does not gloss over details to save paper; it's all here. Readers of computer books are constantly looking for simple examples that actually work so they do not have to spend time thinking about solutions for problems. The examples in this book are all proofed on Oracle Database 10*g*.

Why is this book needed? This book is needed because many Oracle SQL texts simply present facts without adequate example proof. A book containing a thorough analysis of Oracle SQL, plus some of its toys and tricks, is missing from bookshelves and the warehouses of online book retailers. This book fills the void.

Who would benefit from reading this book? Anyone using Oracle software, and specifically Oracle SQL users, would benefit from reading this book. This book contains something for everyone from entry level to more senior experienced Oracle DBAs and programmer/developers, across a whole range of Oracle SQL tools and methods.

What Is in This Book?

Chapter 1. Introduction to Oracle SQL

This chapter discusses relational data modeling history, Normalization, Denormalization, and the origins of SQL and different SQL tools. Also included are Entity Relationship Diagrams for the MUSIC schema. The MUSIC schema is used throughout this book for examples. The MUSIC schema includes both transactional (OLTP) tables plus fact-dimensional data warehouse tables. The database does not contain large amounts of data. Quantity would be important for an Oracle SQL tuning book but not an Oracle SQL book.[2]

Chapter 2. New Features of Oracle SQL

This chapter covers new Oracle SQL and PL/SQL features for both Oracle Database 10*g* and Oracle Database 9*i*.

Chapter 3. Oracle Database Architecture

This chapter examines the basic architecture of Oracle Database, including the Oracle Instance, datafile physical architecture, database startup and shutdown, followed by brief descriptions of some advanced feature options such as Oracle Partitioning and replication.

Chapter 4. The SELECT Statement

Here you will be introduced to the SELECT statement and different query types from the mundane to the obscure. There is also some analysis on some basic queries using simple facets of Oracle SQL such as the DUAL table, DISTINCT, and NULLs.

Chapter 5. Filtering Rows

This chapter looks at filtering using the WHERE clause, including a brief examination of expression conditions, logical operators, and Top-N queries.

Chapter 6. Sorting Rows

The ORDER BY clause is used for sorting data in various different manners.

Chapter 7. Operators, Conditions, and Pseudocolumns

Containing referential facts about operators, conditions, and pseudocolumns in a single chapter is essential. This is necessary not only for reference purposes but also as a way of drawing facts together during the reading process.

Chapter 8. SQL*Plus and iSQL*Plus Reporting

This chapter covers advanced environmental and formatting settings for using SQL*Plus and iSQL*Plus.

Chapter 9. Single Row Functions

Single row functions used in queries operate as expressions once on each row retrieved.

Chapter 10. Joining Tables

The purpose of a join is to retrieve data from a relational structure in a readable or more usable format. The result is that joining tables can be fairly complex, with various different types of joins possible.

Chapter 11. Grouping and Summarizing Data

Grouping and summarizing data is complex, involving various types of grouping functions from simple aggregation to complex statistical analysis, and OLTP type activities and even multidimensional spreadsheet and modeling formats.

Chapter 12. Subqueries

Subqueries are perhaps one of the most complex aspects of Oracle SQL. Subqueries can be used for simplification and tuning of Oracle SQL code.

Chapter 13. Unusual Query Types

Unusual query types encompass less used and specialized types of queries, including composite queries, hierarchical queries, version flashbacks, and parallel queries.

Chapter 14. Expressions

There are many types of simple expressions. Expressions are an integral part of many aspects of Oracle SQL command structure. Additionally, this chapter covers two factors new to Oracle Database 10*g*: Regular Expressions and the Oracle Expression Filter.

Chapter 15. Data Manipulation Language (DML)

DML is the part of Oracle SQL allowing changes to data in an Oracle database. Commands include INSERT, UPDATE, DELETE, MERGE, and special transactional control commands.

Chapter 16. Datatypes and Collections

Datatypes range from simple datatypes containing simple numbers to object reference pointers and collections. Oracle SQL collection functions are also included in this chapter.

Chapter 17. XML in Oracle

Oracle SQL allows for generation and manipulation of XML documents in Oracle Database. This chapter introduces various aspects of using XML in Oracle SQL.

Chapter 18. Tables

Tables are the primary and central structure for containing data in a relational database. As a result, table syntax and use is fairly complex. This chapter begins a series of chapters covering Oracle Database object use and manipulation.

Chapter 19. Views

A view is a logical overlay over one or more tables. A view does not contain data but merely a query for accessing data from underlying tables.

Chapter 20. Constraints

Constraints are used to apply rules to data sets and between data sets. Constraints can be used on tables and to a more limited extent on views.

Chapter 21. Indexes and Clusters

Indexes are special performance-increasing options used as subsets of table data sets, often sorted and organized with special high-speed searching functionality such as binary search trees. Clusters group sets of data together physically for use as preconstructed high-speed access data sources.

Chapter 22. Sequences and Synonyms

A sequence is a special Oracle Database object used to maintain sequential counters. Sequences perform much better than manual counters. Synonyms provide a way to allow reference of database objects across different schemas and even different databases.

Chapter 23. Security

Security can be divided into two sections, namely users (same as a schema) and the way in which users access things in a database. Access is controlled by system and object privileges, sometimes grouped together using roles.

Chapter 24. Basic PL/SQL

This chapter introduces the basics of PL/SQL using syntax and example coding.

Sample Database Used in This Book

The sample database used in this book is called the MUSIC schema. The MUSIC schema contains a small amount of data with both OLTP and client-server type transactional and data warehouse dimensional/fact tables. Details on the MUSIC schema are covered with explanation and entity relationship diagrams (ERDs) in Chapter 1 and schema creation scripts in Appendix A. Scripts are available from a simple menu on my Web site at www.oracledbaexpert.com/oracle/OracleSQLJumpstartWithExamples/index.html.

Let's get started.

Endnotes

1. Universal Resource Locator (Web page address in a browser such as Internet Explorer)

2. Oracle Performance Tuning for 9i and 10g (ISBN: 1-555-58305-9)

Acknowledgements

For my wife and daughter who tolerated my nightly and often daily vigils at the keyboard, and to my favorite cat for not trying to sit on the keyboard too often.

—Gavin Powell

Many thanks to Gavin Powell for spear heading this project. His hard work is evident throughout this fine book. And, as always, thanks to my husband, Patrick, and son, Blue, for putting up with me even when I stay up late and ignore them to meet a deadline.

—Carol McCullough-Dieter

Introduction to Oracle SQL

In this chapter:

- Examine the history and evolution of data models and relational and Oracle Databases.

- What is relational data modeling?

- What is SQL?

- What software do you need to have in order to use this book?

- What are the tools for executing SQL?

- Sample tables you use in the book

This chapter will examine data modeling, the origins of SQL, software requirements, plus SQL tools and how to use them. Finally, we will present the MUSIC schema, which is used throughout this book. Let's begin with a little history.

1.1 A Little History

1.1.1 The Evolution of Database Modeling

The history of databases is essentially the history of different data modeling techniques. Data modeling techniques have evolved over the last 50 years from use of simple file systems to relational, object, and object-relational models. Figure 1.1 shows the evolution of data modeling techniques.

- **File System**. Operating system files or "flat" text files. There is no logical overlay structure.

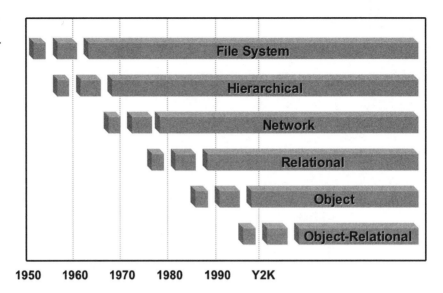

Figure 1.1
The Evolution of Data Modeling.

- **Hierarchical**. A branch-leaf tree structure as shown in Figure 1.2 such that child tables can only have single parent tables. A child table is completely dependent on the existence of its parent table. As a result, one-to-many relationships are supported but not many-to-many relationships. The primary disadvantage of a hierarchical structure is that everything must be accessed from the root node of the tree. In Figure 1.2, accessing a Song would require retrieval of an Artist and all of that artist's songs.

Figure 1.2
The Hierarchical Data Model.

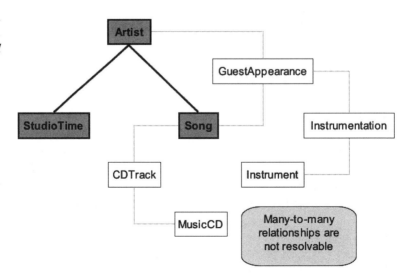

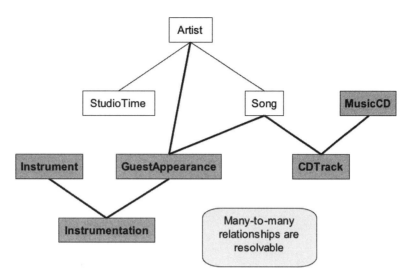

Figure 1.3
The Network Data Model.

- **Network**. Refinement of the hierarchical model where many-to-many relationships are permitted because child tables can have more than a single parent table. This creates a "networked" structure of tables as shown in Figure 1.3. A network structure is an improved hierarchical or branch-leaf tree structure where many-to-many entities can be accessed, but access to a node still requires access to all parent nodes from the root node.

- **Relational**. Any two tables can be linked irrespective of hierarchical placement. Therefore, any table can be accessed directly without having to access child tables through a hierarchy or network of parent tables. Relatively complex and efficient data structures can be created with the relational data model. The operative phrase for use of relational tables is rapid selection of groups of data rather than single items. Relational databases are most effective for reporting. An example relational structure is shown in Figure 1.4 where any table can be retrieved from based on key values. Tables or entities are built from those keys.

- **Object**. Directly addressed hierarchies of collections to any data item within a structure. This assumes that the direct address or pointer is a known value. The relational data model is most efficient for accessing groups of data at once, such as in reporting. On the contrary, the object data model is excellent for access to unique data items within large, highly complex data sets or groups of interlinked objects. In other words, the object data model is much more effective than the

Figure 1.4
*The Relational
Data Model.*

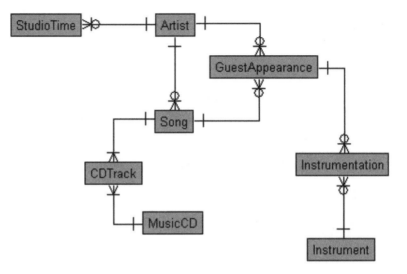

relational model with respect to extremely complex data structures. Figure 1.5 shows an object data model.

- **Object-Relational**. Without losing efficiency, minimal object capabilities can be included in a relational data model. Be warned that relational and object data modeling is completely contrary, and "building too many" objects in a relational database will likely result in serious impact on general application performance. It is usually

Figure 1.5
*The Object Data
Model.*

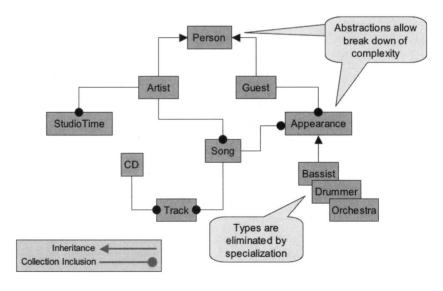

Figure 1.6
*Including
Multimedia in a
Relational
Database.*

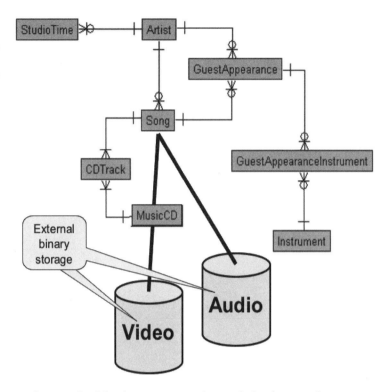

best to build relations in a relational database and reserve complex object structure for application code. Figure 1.6 shows storing of binary images into a relational database.

1.1.2 The History of Relational Databases

Relational databases began with several papers written by Dr. Edgar F. Codd. Numerous other papers followed by various other researchers. Figure 1.7 shows several distinct branches of development. These branches were DB2 from IBM, Oracle Database from Oracle Corporation, and a multitude of relational databases stemming from Ingres, which was initially conceived by two scientists at the University of California at Berkeley.

In Figure 1.7, the most important point to note about the general development path of relational databases is as follows: Development from one database to another resided usually in different companies and was characterized by movement of personnel rather than of database source code. In other words, the people invented the different databases, not the companies, where people moved between different companies. Additionally, numerous object databases have been developed. Object databases generally

Figure 1.7
The Origins of
Databases.

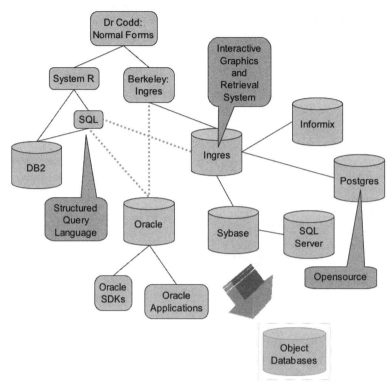

have distinct applications. Some object databases have their roots in relational technology, once again in terms of the movement of personnel skills.

1.1.3   The Evolution of Oracle Database

In the evolution of Oracle Corporation software, certain milestones were significant:

- **1979**. RSI released the first version of Oracle using a version of SQL. RSI is the original name of Oracle Corporation.

- **Early 1980s**. RSI was renamed Oracle Corporation, plus cross-platform capabilities and portable toolsets were introduced.

- **Mid-1980s**. Client-server environments and 4GL were introduced. 4GL is an acronym for a fourth-generation programming language.

- **Late 1980s**. Oracle6 was released. The first application Oracle Financials was introduced, and PL/SQL or Programming Language for SQL was included. PL/SQL allows execution of SQL commands in blocks, where sequentially executed lines of code can depend on previously executed lines of code, much like a programming language. SQL is not a programming language, however. SQL is a coded tool or shorthand method of accessing groups of rows from a relational database.

- **Early 1990s**. Oracle7 was released. Oracle7 included Referential Integrity, cost-based statistics for optimization, and clustering. Referential Integrity is important for automated maintenance of accuracy of related data sets. Cost-based optimization uses statistics, providing a realistic picture rather than one based on "intelligent" rules. Rule-based optimization is a best guess for query performance optimization. Cost-based optimization is vastly superior to rule-based optimization. Finally, clustering allows for fail-over, scalability, and high availability.

- **Mid-1990s**. The release of Oracle8 introduced the concept of the Object-Relational database for Oracle Corporation. Additionally, thin client and application server capabilities were introduced.

- **Late 1990s**. The first Internet database Oracle Database 8*i* was released. Oracle Database 8*i* was specifically designed for database Internet access and performance. In addition, database kernel-executed Java procedures were introduced. Java or Java Virtual Machine (JVM) executed code is much more capable of complex coding than PL/SQL. However, there is something to be said for maintaining simplicity and sticking to only relational methodologies in a relational database. Mixing of relational and object methods can sometimes create more complexity than it solves. Object databases are excellent tools for resolving complexity. Relational databases can become drastically or even disastrously difficult to understand and maintain when attempting to cater for complexity.

- **Y2K**. The second-generation Internet database Oracle Database 9*i* was released. Oracle Database 9*i* has improvements over that of Oracle Database 8*i*. Middle-tier application server and Oracle tools integration were also introduced.

- **2003**. Oracle Database 10*g* is the Oracle Grid database designed for use on grids of large numbers of computers. Grid computing allows for enormously enhanced scalability, performance, versatility, integration, and automation. Oracle Database 10*g* is the first version of Oracle Database to cater to the power of grid computing. Oracle Database 10*g* grid computing capacity is limited with respect to grid technology, but that path has been set as the next leap in the computer revolution. Oracle Corporation is pursuing a grid approach and has always been visionary in the past.

Now let's look at the basics of relational data modeling, which is important because SQL is based on and stems from the relational data model.

1.2   The Basics of Relational Data Modeling

1.2.1   Normalization

Normalization[1,2,3] is a process of removal of duplicated information. Removal of duplication reduces the space used and enforces a logical structure. Relational data modeling utilizes a process called Normalization using what are called Normal Forms. The three most commonly used Normal Forms or NF are called 1NF, 2NF, and 3NF. There are other subsidiary and often overly detailed Normal Forms called 4NF, 5NF, and even beyond those. I always thought of the accepted definitions of the different Normal Forms as being academic and far too complex to make any sense of, unless they are read about five times each. Therefore, I like to simplify the explanations of Normal Forms as follows:

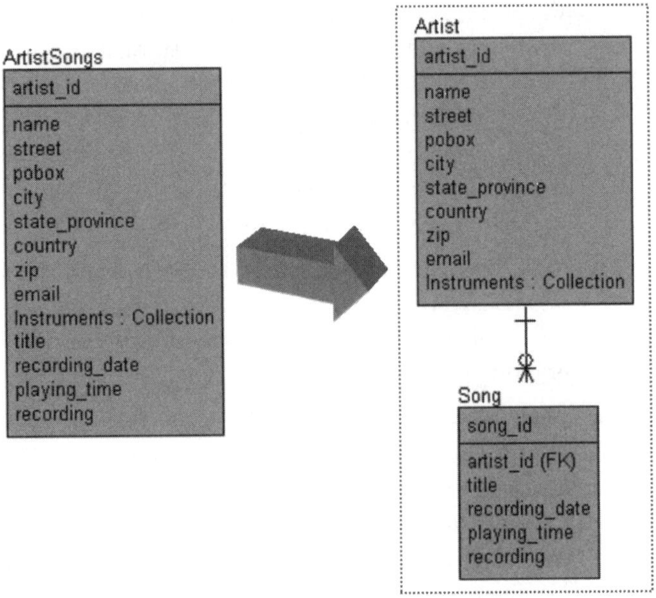

Figure 1.8
First Normal Form (1NF).

- **First Normal Form (1NF).** Removes repetition by creating one-to-many relationships between master and detail entities, as shown in Figure 1.8.

Note: An entity is synonymous with or the same thing as a table.

- **Second Normal Form (2NF).** Creates many-to-one relationships between static and dynamic entities, as shown in Figure 1.9.

- **Third Normal Form (3NF).** Can be used to resolve many-to-many relationships into unique values, as shown in Figure 1.10. This is where Normal Forms begin to become a bit of a gray area. Sometimes many-to-many 3NF entities are what I like to call many-to-many join resolution entities. Many-to-many join resolution entities are often not utilized by applications and are usually superfluous. Always be sure that a many-to-many join resolution entity is actually required. One simple method of being sure that these entities are useful is that they have a meaningful name. The more entities that are created in a data model, the more complex SQL code joins will become. Contrary

Figure 1.9
Second Normal Form (2NF).

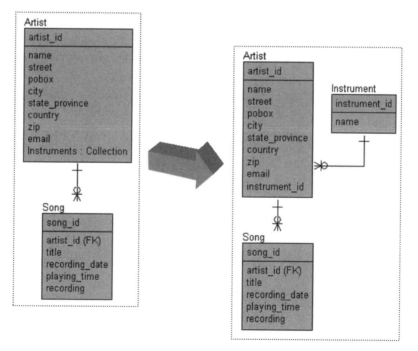

Figure 1.10
*Third Normal
Form (3NF).*

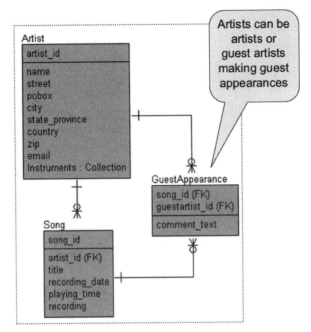

to popular belief, SQL code joins are never tunable in comparison to simple SELECT statements against a single table.

- **Fourth Normal Form (4NF)**. Now the concept of Normal Forms gets even grayer, or perhaps just fuzzier. 4NF entities are often created in order to remove potentially null-valued columns into separate entities, minimizing physical space. Because Oracle Database tables use variable-length records, there is really no point in separating nulls into separate entities because null is nothing anyway. Nothing occupies no space whatsoever, and thus 4NF is even grayer than 3NF, or as I said just fuzzy!

- **Fifth Normal Form (5NF) and Beyond**. As far as performance is concerned, 5NF and beyond should simply be avoided. In fact, 3NF and beyond are often commercially unviable, usually totally impractical, and nearly always detrimental to performance.

1.2.1.1   Referential Integrity

Referential Integrity[2] is a mechanism used to validate data between primary and foreign key columns in related tables. In order to explain Referential Integrity briefly, we need to backtrack a little to both data modeling evolution and Normalization.

What are primary and foreign keys? Going back to Normalization, Normalization separates tables and removes duplicate data values, creating parent and child tables. At the heart of Normal Forms is the creation of unique primary keys and their related child table foreign keys. A primary key uniquely identifies a row in a table, namely a parent table. Thus a table can have only one primary key, identifying each row in that table as being different from every other row in the same table (uniquely). A foreign key is placed in a child table, being a copy of the primary key value in a related parent table. The previous section on the evolution of data modeling stated that the relational data model allows access to any table using key values, where a table can be linked to any number of other tables. Therefore, a child table can contain multiple foreign keys and as a result links to multiple parent table primary keys.

So what is Referential Integrity? Referential Integrity is the process of ensuring the integrity or correctness of data. First, primary key rows in parent tables cannot be deleted unless foreign key child table rows are deleted first. Second, rows cannot be added to child tables unless foreign key values exist in parent tables. An exception to this second rule is where a foreign key value can contain a null value, in the case of a one-to-many-or-zero relationship. In other words, parent table rows must exist in order for the child table row to exist but not always.

Referential Integrity is enforced using Oracle constraints, triggers, or sometimes even at the application level. The most efficient and effective method of enforcing Referential Integrity in an Oracle database is by using constraints, which are centralized and only coded or applied once. Triggers are extremely slow and either generically coded or overcoded. Application level–coded Referential Integrity can be more difficult to maintain than triggers.

1.2.2 Denormalization

Denormalization[4] is often, but not always, the opposite of Normalization. Denormalization should usually be applied to a data model in order to create data warehouse or reporting-only type tables. Unfortunately, Denormalization is often required to revive dying applications caused by dreadful performance. This is often as a result of overzealous use of Normalization in development of data models and applications. So Denormalization will often attempt to reverse granularity created by overapplication of Normal Forms during the Normalization process. Other factors helpful to performance can be classified as Denormalization, however vaguely:

- **Specialized Oracle Database Objects**. Clustering, presorting, and physical preconstruction of data. The objective is to avoid repeating the same tasks, targeting and tuning hard-hitting SQL code.

  - **Clusters**. Duplicate the most commonly used indexing plus part of data column values together in the same place physically, in the desired order. Retrieving from a cluster avoids costly joins and conflict with highly concurrent source tables.
  - **Index-Organized Tables**. A table is constructed including both index and data columns in the same physical space. The table becomes both the index and the data because the table is constructed as a sorted binary tree, rather than just a heap or pile of unorganized bits and pieces.

- **Materialized Views**. Duplicates, preconstructs, and stores the results of grouping SQL statements avoiding repetitive SQL. Materialized views "materialize" or precreate reusable data buckets by storing data physically separated from source tables.

Note: Views are overlays and not duplications of data and will interfere with underlying source tables. Views often cause far more in the way of performance problems than the application design issues they ease.

- **Copy Columns between Tables**. Make copies of columns between tables not directly related to each other. This can help avoid multiple table joins between two tables where other tables must be passed through in order to join the two desired tables.

- **Place Summary Columns in Parent Tables**. This can help avoid costly grouping joins, but real-time updates can cause serious problems with hot blocks.

Note: A hot block is a very busy part of the database accessed much too often by many different sessions.

- **Separate Inactive from Active Data**. Physical separation of historical and perhaps seldom used or completely unnecessary data is often ignored by data model designs. Avoid searching through data that is no longer used in order to reduce the amount of physical space searched through. Historical data can often be destroyed or transferred to a data warehouse or backups.

- **Do Not Mix Heavily and Lightly Accessed Columns**. Much like separating inactive and active data at the table level, tables containing columns with vastly different rates of access can be separated. This avoids continual physical scanning of rarely used data column values, especially when those values do not contain nulls. This is one potentially sensible use of 4NF.

- **Cache Data in Applications and Middle Tiers**. Direct database access of static data values can often be avoided.

1.2.3 Different Forms of the Relational Data Model

The relational data model[2] has evolved from primary keys containing all column values in all subsidiary child tables to modern use of surrogate primary and foreign keys, servicing object-coded online Java applications.

What are surrogate keys? Surrogate keys are abstracted identifying values for table rows where the actual key values are complete abstractions to the semantics or contents of the row values. Phew! I bet you would like that one in English? For example, let's briefly describe a simple table containing customers. Your customers could be identified by long, variable-length customer names or even unwieldy and difficult to remember customer codes. A surrogate key is an extra column added to the Customer table. The surrogate key is a generated integer value created by an Oracle sequence object, whenever a new Customer row is added. Customers are later retrieved using pick lists and transparent access to the surrogate key integer values. In other words, you do not need to type in the number but simply pick the name from a list. No typing of long names or codes is required, which is much easier and more efficient!

So surrogate keys are generated for each row and are usually identifying integers or pointers to table rows, perhaps somewhat similar to object identifiers. However, they are not object identifiers. Addressed object identifiers should never be used in a relational database to identify an object in an application. Surrogate key integers can be generated extremely efficiently in Oracle Database using sequence generators (Oracle sequence objects).

Note: Never use centralized tables to store the latest values of individual sequence counters. This is nice for the application, but your database might meet with its demise (die) from hot blocking that table. Your job might join it!

A surrogate key is the most effective and efficient method of both applying Referential Integrity and accessing single-row data items in OLTP-type, high-concurrency transactional databases. Obviously, complex composite primary key values are suited for data warehouse and reporting tables. Why? Multiple-column indexes are presorted. The exception is where reporting tables are accessed in more than a single sorted order. Of course, specialized goodies such as clusters, index-organized tables, and materialized views can be utilized.

Next we will look at the origins of SQL and what Oracle SQL is.

1.3   Structured Query Language (SQL)

1.3.1   The Humble Origins of SQL

Why are we going backward in time looking at things no longer in use? In order to understand SQL code effectively, we need to understand the most basic forms of SQL, having much to do with why SQL was invented in the first place. In short, SQL database access has evolved with data modeling techniques, Oracle Database, and other databases. SQL is pronounced "sequel" or "ess-queue-ell." The acronym SQL represents the term Structured Query Language.

SQL is a language used to query a structured (Relational) data set in a logically consistent manner.

> **Note:** The query language used to access an Object database is called ODQL. ODQL stands for Object Definitional Query Language. The acronym "QL" thus means "query language," a language used to query a database.

SQL in its most primitive form stems from the idea of a reporting language devised in theory by the inventor of the Relational data model. The roots of SQL lie in retrieval of data sets. What this means is that SQL is intended as a language to retrieve many rows from one or many tables at once, a result set. SQL was not originally intended to retrieve individual rows from a relational database as exact row matches in transactional or OLTP databases. However, SQL can now be used to do precisely that, and fairly efficiently.

What does all of this mean without using another plethora of nasty long words? SQL was developed as a shorthand method of retrieving information from relational databases and has become the industry standard over the last 20 years. Here is an example of a query (a question posed to the database that asks for certain information) written in SQL:

```
SELECT NAME, STREET, CITY, COUNTRY
FROM ARTIST
WHERE COUNTRY IN ('USA','Canada');
```

1.3.2 What Is Oracle SQL?

Like many other relational database products, Oracle SQL is a proprietary and exclusive form of SQL written for Oracle Database. ANSI standards are generally adhered to. Most database vendors have specific characteristics within their exclusive versions of SQL, and Oracle Corporation is no exception.

Oracle SQL consists of three essential parts:

- **SELECT.** The SELECT statement is used to retrieve data from Oracle Database objects such as tables, views, or clusters.

- **DML.** The Data Manipulation Language (DML) changes data in tables in a database. Commands included are INSERT, UPDATE, DELETE, and MERGE. All DML commands are subject to transactional control. Transactional control includes the COMMIT and ROLLBACK commands, which allow changes to be permanently stored or undone, respectively.

- **DDL.** The Data Definition Language (DDL) allows changes to "definitional" data or metadata. Metadata is the data about the data. Metadata is the definition of data objects such as tables along with their column names, sizes, and data types of those column names. In some relational databases, DDL-type commands can be undone using a ROLLBACK command, but not in Oracle Database. DDL commands cannot be committed or rolled back because they are automatically and forcibly committed (permanently changed).

1.3.2.1 ANSI Standards and Oracle

The standard format of SQL was developed by the American National Standards Institute (ANSI). ANSI works with companies like Oracle Corporation to develop its standards, thus helping to gain support among competitors for a unified standard that benefits everyone.

Oracle Database provides full support for ANSI standard SQL and, like most database vendors, adds extra features making SQL more robust and versatile as a database access language. For example, Oracle Database contains a rich set of functions. These functions can be used to alter column data within queries. For instance, the UPPER function can convert all of the letters in a word to capitals, and ADD_MONTH can add a month to a date, among a comprehensive multitude of other function options.

Let's digress a little and examine software that is useful to have for reading this book.

1.4   Software Useful for Reading this Book

Oracle Database 10*g* or Oracle Database 10 Grid is the latest relational database management system (RDBMS) from Oracle Corporation. Oracle Database began in the 1970s and has grown to be the dominating force in the database market.

Oracle Database 10*g* is delivered with an extensive a set of standard utilities, tools, and wizards, some of which help you get going quickly. The Oracle Database 10*g* database engine is set up to run the same way on all platforms. For example, Oracle Database 10*g* running on UNIX has all of the same features as Oracle Database 10*g* running on Windows 2000 or Windows 2003. Oracle Database 10*g* is available on Solaris, Windows NT/2000/XP Pro, Linux, and AIX, to name a few.

Although Oracle Database 10*g* looks the same to you regardless of the platform you use, on the inside each operating system's version of Oracle Database 10*g* is different. Oracle takes advantage of each computer's unique features for storage, reading, writing, and so on, in the programming of the software.

To use this book and run all of the examples, experimenting with SQL commands, you need the following software:

■ **Oracle Database 10*g*.** When you install the software, you will have some choices. First, be sure to select Oracle Database 10*g*. Next, you can select any of the three editions of the database: (1) the Enterprise Edition is for large, multiuser databases; (2) the Standard Edition is for small workgroups; and (3) the Personal Edition is for a single user. All three editions contain the same capabilities for the SQL work you will do in this book. They have different licensing costs. Install whichever edition fits your requirements the best.

- **Internet Browser**. One of the more recent features of Oracle Database is the browser version of its SQL tool, called iSQL*Plus.

That's it! If you need instructions on how to install Oracle Database 10*g*, refer to the online documentation found on Oracle's Technet Web site (otn.oracle.com). The Web site requires you to register, but registration is free. Once registered, you have access to valuable resources.

- **Installation guides**. Go to this Web site and select the installation guide under the database release number and operating system you are using. The documentation is supplemented with an excellent search tool that helps you zoom into areas of interest very quickly.

- **Forums**. Find out what other Oracle users have to say about the database features and get feedback from Oracle technical support personnel for free.

- **Temporarily licensed software**. Download extras and demonstrations to learn all you want about features such as XML in the database, Java applications, and the Oracle Internet File System.

Note: The content of and manner in which online documentation and downloads are accessed can change at any time. Downloads are generally much too large for a modem connection. Temporarily licensed software can usually be ordered on CD-ROM from Oracle Corporation for a nominal shipping fee.

Now let's look at syntax conventions used in this book.

1.5   Syntax Conventions Used in This Book

Syntax diagrams in this book utilize what is known as Backus-Naur Form syntax notation convention. Backus-Naur Form has become the de facto standard for most computer texts. Oracle SQL is used to describe the notation.

- Angle brackets: < ... >

Angle brackets are used to represent names of categories (variable substitution representation). In this example, <table> will be replaced with a table name in a schema as shown:

```
SELECT * FROM <table>;
```

becomes:

```
SELECT * FROM ARTIST;
```

Note: Angle brackets are generally not used in this book unless stated as such at the beginning of a chapter.

- OR: |

  A pipe, or | character, represents an OR conjunction meaning either can be selected. The asterisk (*) and curly braces are explained further on. In this case, all or some columns can be retrieved, some meaning one or more.

  ```
  SELECT { * | { <column>, … } } FROM <table>;
  ```

- Optional: […]

  In a SELECT statement, a WHERE clause is syntactically optional.

  ```
  SELECT * FROM <table> [ WHERE <column> = … ];
  ```

- At least one of: { … | … | … }

  In this example, the SELECT statement retrieval list must include an asterisk (*), retrieving all columns in a table, or a list of one or more columns.

  ```
  SELECT { * | { <column>, … } } FROM <table>;
  ```

Note: This is not a precise interpretation of Backus-Naur Form, where curly braces usually represent zero or more. In this book, curly braces represent one or more iterations, never zero.

It's time to look at some of the tools you can use for executing SQL commands.

1.6   SQL Tools

Oracle has provided a user-friendly interactive tool for running SQL since its first release. The SQL*Plus tool today has four variations from which to choose:

- **SQL*Plus Command Line**. Use this when you don't have a Windows interface, such as when using telnet to reach a remote UNIX database server.
- **SQL*Plus Windows**. Use this in a Windows-capable environment (can be invoked using a network name from a client or directly on the database server, regardless of the operating system).
- **SQL*Plus Worksheet**. This comes as part of Oracle Enterprise Manager, a Windows-like user interface created to support the database administrator and simplify many tasks.
- **iSQL*Plus**. This gives you the same interface as SQL*Plus Windows, except it runs in a Web browser. Use this to run SQL commands and automatically generate a report in HTML format.

The next sections show you how to start up all four of these tools and try them out with some SQL commands. Any of the SQL tools can be used.

1.6.1   SQL*Plus in Command-Line Mode

This is the most basic SQL interface you can use. It requires only a command line to run, which makes it useful for very quick access via a remote dial-up connection or perhaps when a database is shut down.

Before you begin the following steps, you will need these two pieces of information about your database:

- **The database name or network name**. If you are running the database on your own computer, this is the name you gave the database when it was created. If you are not sure what you named it, go to a command prompt (see step 1 to learn how) and then type this command:

  ```
  lsnrctl status
  ```

  Look for a line that begins like this. The word in quotation marks is your database name. In this example, the database SID name is OLTP.

  ```
  Instance "oltp", status READY, ...
  ```

  If you are running from a client computer and using a remote database on the network, you must use the network name defined in your local Oracle Net configuration. The configuration file named TNSNAMES.ORA has all of the network names available to you. The file is located in $ORACLE_HOME/network/admin directory. Here is an example of the text found in the TNSNAMES.ORA file for the OLTP network name:

  ```
  OLTP =
    (DESCRIPTION =
      (ADDRESS_LIST =
        (ADDRESS =
      (PROTOCOL = TCP)
      (HOST = 1300server)
      (PORT = 1521)))
        (CONNECT_DATA =
      (SERVER = DEDICATED)
      (SERVICE_NAME = oltp)))
  ```

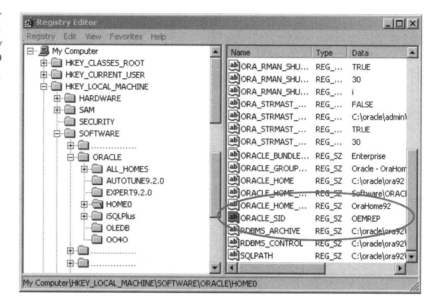

Figure 1.11
*Win2K Registry
ORACLE_SID
Variable.*

- **The password for the users named SYS and SYSTEM**. The Oracle Database Configuration Assistant in Oracle Database 10*g* allows setting of SYS and SYSTEM passwords to the same value.

If you are running a database on your own computer or on a database server, you can reach the database directly by omitting the database name. When you omit the name, Oracle uses the bequeth protocol and the current $ORACLE_SID variable setting to access the database. In Windows the $ORACLE_SID variable is set in the registry, and on UNIX or Linux in a user or root profile. Figure 1.11 shows a Win2K registry location.

When you use the database name, Oracle uses the transmission control protocol (TCP). Follow these steps to start up SQL*Plus Command Line and run an SQL command:

Note: The steps here, and throughout the book, use the sample tables and data created especially for this book. Appendix A contains instructions for locating and installing all of the sample tables.

---

1. Go to a command-line prompt on your computer. If you are using Windows, click on Start/Programs/Accessories/Command Prompt. A window appears with a blinking cursor. This is your

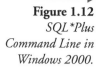

Figure 1.12
*SQL*Plus
Command Line in
Windows 2000.*

SQL*Plus command prompt   Command prompt window

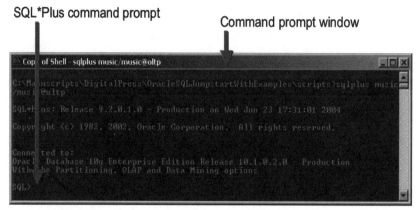

command prompt. If you are using UNIX, you may be at the command prompt when you log in. It looks like a dollar sign ($). If you are not already at the UNIX command prompt, select Terminal Window from your Utilities menu or execute an operating system shell.

2. Type the following command, replacing **pwd** with the password for the SYSTEM user and replacing **name** with your appropriate network name, and press Enter.

```
sqlplus system/pwd@name
```

3. You will see status information about SQL*Plus and the database and a message stating you are connected. Then your display's prompt changes to "SQL>", indicating that you are now in SQL*Plus. Figure 1.12 shows an example of the command prompt window after starting up SQL*Plus.

4. Type the following SQL*Plus commands, and press Enter after each line. These set up the column width displayed for the query that follows. (More on SQL*Plus commands in Chapter 8.)

```
COL PRODUCT FORMAT A35
COL VERSION FORMAT A15
COL STATUS FORMAT A15
```

5. Type the following query and press Enter:

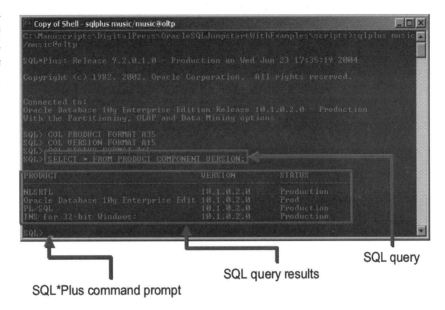

Figure 1.13
*SQL*Plus SQL
Commands Return
Instant Results.*

SQL query

SQL query results

SQL*Plus command prompt

```
SELECT * FROM PRODUCT_COMPONENT_VERSION;
```

The asterisk represents all of the columns. Thus all columns are displayed in this query. Figure 1.13 shows the results. The actual data may be different, depending on the shape of your Oracle Database 10*g* installation.

6. Exit SQL*Plus by typing EXIT and pressing Enter. This returns you to your command prompt.

7. Exit from the command prompt by typing EXIT and pressing Enter.

One of the disadvantages of using the command-line mode of SQL*Plus is the inability to use the mouse to correct your typing. You must erase using the backspace key. Table 1.1 shows the editing commands you can use.

An advantage of the command-line mode is the ability to add parameters to the sqlplus command. For example, you can run a script immediately upon startup, or start SQL*Plus without logging into any database instance (this is useful for issuing SQL commands for starting and stopping the database).

SQL*Plus does have a line editor built into it that you can use instead of starting up an editor.

Table 1.1   *SQL*Plus Line Editing Commands.*

Command	Description
c/old/new	Change old to new characters in current line.
l or **list**	List the SQL in the buffer.
l n	Go to line **n** in the SQL buffer.
del n or **del** * or **del** n m	Delete line **n** in the SQL buffer, or delete the current line (*) or delete lines **n** through **m**.
a text or **append** text	Add **text** to the end of the current line.
i or **input** or **i** text or **input** text	Insert a new line after the current line. Add **text** to the line, if **text** is specified.

Next, you will look at the Windows-like SQL*Plus tool.

1.6.2   SQL*Plus in Windows Mode

This version of SQL*Plus gives you a Windows-like interface with a few environmental options. However, it still requires you to type a single line at a time.

To try out SQL*Plus in Windows mode, follow these steps:

1. If you are using a Windows operating system, start the tool by clicking Start/Programs/Oracle – Orahome10/Application Development/SQL*Plus. If you are using another operating system, go to a command-line prompt, type sqlplusw, and press Enter.

    You will see a Log On window appear. You must log on with valid credentials now.

2. Type SYSTEM in the User Name box, the current password for SYSTEM in the Password box, and your database name in the Host String box. Figure 1.14 shows the Log On window with the information filled in. Notice that the password appears as a line of asterisks. This is to keep your password private.

3. Click OK to log in. The SQL*Plus window appears. Just like the command-line version, you see status information and get

Figure 1.14
*Log into Your
Database as a
Valid User.*

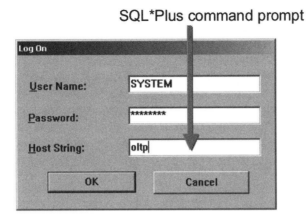

SQL*Plus command prompt

Log On

User Name: SYSTEM

Password: ********

Host String: oltp

OK   Cancel

an SQL> prompt telling you that SQL*Plus is ready to accept commands.

4. Type the following command and press Enter. This is an SQL*Plus command that tells the database to list the structure of the table or view that you name. A view is a query stored with a name in the database. It acts like a table but does not store any data. (Chapter 19 covers views in detail).

```
DESC DBA_USERS
```

5. The screen shows the names and datatypes of all the columns in this view. This is very useful when you are about to write an SQL command and you need a quick reminder of the exact column names in a table. Now type this query and press Enter after each line. Notice that the prompt changed from "SQL>" to "2" on the second line. This indicates that SQL*Plus knows you have started a command and you are continuing it on the next line. The semi-colon at the end of the second line signals to SQL*Plus that the command is complete and should be immediately executed.

```
SELECT USERNAME, ACCOUNT_STATUS, CREATED
FROM DBA_USERS;
```

6. The results scroll by, and you can use the scroll bar on the right side of the window to move up or down and view the results. Figure 1.15 shows the results from the query. The column headings

Figure 1.15
SQL*Plus in Windows Mode Has a Scroll Bar and Menu.

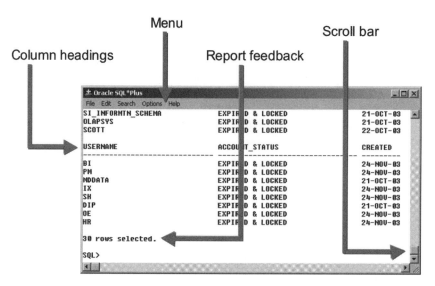

and report feedback are standard parts of every mode of SQL*Plus; however, the scroll bar and the menu are features of the Windows mode and not of the command-line mode. Some operating systems will allow configuration changes to allow addition of scroll bars to command-line windows.

7. Click on Edit in the top menu and invoke the editor. A window appears with an editing program and the text of the query you wrote ready for editing. In Windows, the default editor is Notepad. In UNIX, Linux, and other operating systems, the default editor can be configured in a user profile.

8. The editor can be used to change the command you created while working in SQL*Plus. You can retrieve files with SQL commands in them using the File/Open command on the menu. Selecting the File/Run command from the menu will execute the most recent SQL command. Modify the query by removing the CREATED column from the query.

9. Save the file and exit the editor. The modified query now appears on the screen, ready to run if you choose. Figure 1.16 shows what your SQL*Plus screen should look like now.

10. Before running the command, select File/Spool/Spool File from the menu. A window opens in which you can select the file name and location. This file will contain everything you type and SQL*Plus returns from the moment you return to SQL*Plus

Figure 1.16
*Invoking
(Opening) the
Editor.*

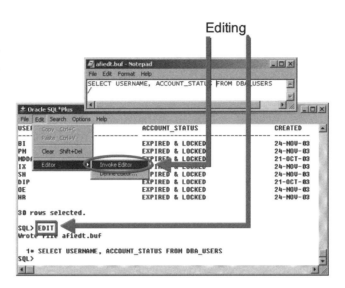

until you turn it off, or until you exit SQL*Plus. This is a handy way to record your work. In addition, in Chapter 8, you will find out how to write reports using this spooling technique. Navigate to a directory of your choosing, such as C:\TEMP in Windows, and then type "testing" as the file name and click Save. The file will automatically receive a suffix of ".LST" on Windows and of ".lis" on UNIX and other operating systems.

11. Type **/** (a forward slash) to run the query. The forward slash and the semi-colon both tell SQL*Plus to execute a command. The forward slash must be used alone on a line by itself, whereas the semi-colon is used at the end of a line of code. The semi-colon terminates and submits a single-line SQL command to the database. The forward slash does the same and additionally compiles and executes blocked sections of PL/SQL code.

12. The results scroll into the window as before.

13. Type the letter L and press Enter. This is the LIST command of SQL*Plus. It displays whatever SQL command is currently in the SQL*Plus buffer.

14. Select File/Spool/Spool off to end the spooling of data to the file. This closes the file that has been receiving data from the SQL*Plus session. Your spool file will be empty until this command is executed or you exit SQL*Plus.

15.   Exit SQL*Plus by typing EXIT and pressing Enter or by clicking the X at the top right corner of the window.

16.   Navigate through Windows Explorer to find the TESTING.LST file that was spooled in the location you chose. If you are using UNIX, use the cd command or your File Directory window to find the testing.lst file. Open the file with your editor and view the results. You should see the forward slash (the first thing you typed after turning on spooling), the query results, the "**L**" command, and the query in this file.

Spooling is useful for saving queries you develop in SQL*Plus. In addition, with a few extra commands, you can create a report (with headings, titles, summaries, and so on) from SQL queries and spool the report to a file ready for printing.

17.   Close the file.

Note: If you make a mistake and press Enter before fixing it, you sometimes get a line number prompt instead of an SQL prompt. This means SQL*Plus has interpreted your line as the beginning of a command and is expecting you to complete the command before executing. To get out of this continuing line mode, type a period (.) alone on a line and press Enter. You will be returned to the SQL prompt so you can begin again.

Another form of the SQL*Plus tool can be found within Oracle Enterprise Manager.

1.6.3   SQL*Plus Worksheet

The Oracle Enterprise Manager (OEM) is a great set of tools for the database administrator (DBA). The OEM Console gives you a bird's-eye view of your database, or many databases if you have access to more than one. The SQL*Plus Worksheet is a standard part of the OEM suite that is installed when you install Oracle Database 10*g* (Enterprise, Standard, or Personal Editions).

To run the worksheet by itself, without going through the OEM Console, follow these instructions:

1. Start SQL*Plus Worksheet from Windows by clicking Start/Programs/Oracle – Orahome10/Application Development/SQL*Plus Worksheet. If you are using UNIX, Linux, or other platforms, go to a command prompt and type:

   ```
   oemapp worksheet
   ```

2. A login window appears. The window title is "Oracle Enterprise Manager Login" because the same login window appears for the OEM Console and other OEM tools. Select the "Connect directly to the database" button.

Note: The Management Server is out of the scope of this book.

   Type SYSTEM in the User Name box, the current password for SYSTEM in the Password box, and your database name in the Service Name box. Leave the Connect As box defaulting to "Normal." Figure 1.17 shows the completed login window; click OK to log into SQL*Plus Worksheet.

3. The SQL*Plus Worksheet window appears. The top windowpane is your area for typing SQL commands. The lower pane displays the results. Click Enter to clear the window.

4. Type the following query in the top pane:

   ```
   SELECT FILE_NAME, BYTES FROM DBA_DATA_FILES;
   ```

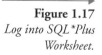

Figure 1.17
*Log into SQL*Plus Worksheet.*

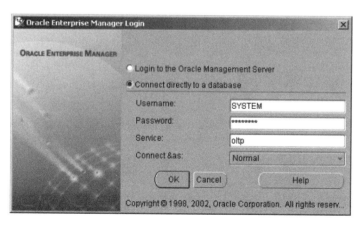

Figure 1.18
*SQL*Plus
Worksheet Has
Useful Windows-
like Functions.*

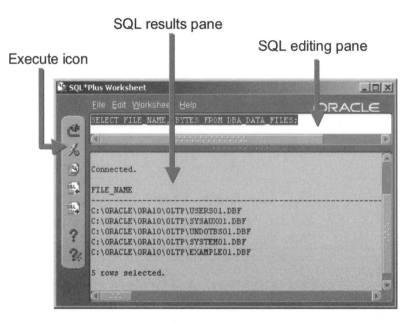

5. Click the Execute icon. The icon looks like a lightning bolt and is located on the left side of the window. The results of the query scroll down on the lower pane. Figure 1.18 shows the SQL*Plus Worksheet window at this point.

6. Modify the query by changing "FILE_NAME" to "MAX-BYTES." Notice that you can edit directly in this tool without resorting to an editor.

7. Run the changed command by clicking the Execute icon again. The results appear in the lower pane.

8. Hold your mouse over each of the icons on the left side of the window to see the other handy functions available in this tool. For example, the icon just below the Execute icon can list up to 50 previous SQL commands.

9. Exit this tool by clicking the **X** in the top window or typing EXIT and clicking the Execute icon.

The SQL*Plus Worksheet may be the most versatile of the SQL*Plus variations. You may find it easier to work with than SQL*Plus Windows or command-line versions and capable of more features than the Web version found in the next section.

Note: SQL*Plus Worksheet is the tool this book uses to guide you through learning SQL and SQL*Plus commands. Feel free to use the other tools if you prefer, although screenshots, when they are used, will display SQL*Plus Worksheet window in most cases.

1.6.4 iSQL*Plus

The Web server, called Oracle HTTP Server, can be installed with Oracle Database 10*g*. The HTTP Server is a miniature application server set up to run the Web-based tools and programming aids that come with Oracle Database 10*g*.

To start up the HTTP Server on UNIX, type this command at a command prompt:

```
$ORACLE_HOME/Apache/Apache/bin/apachectl start
```

In most cases, if you are using Windows, the Oracle HTTP Server is already running when you boot up your computer. If you need to start it, however, you can do so by selecting Start/Programs/Oracle – Orahome10/ Oracle HTTP Server/Start HTTP Server powered by Apache from the Task bar. Alternatively, you can start it by clicking Start/Services/Control Panel and opening the Services window (go to Administrative Controls first, if you are running Windows 2000). Then start the Oracle HTTP Server service.

Note: If there are problems, see the troubleshooting section in Chapter 8.

Follow these steps to look around with the iSQL*Plus tool:

1.   Open your browser.

2.   Type in this address in the Location box of your browser and press Enter. You must replace **mymachine** with the actual network name of your computer and **mydomain** with the actual domain name your computer is in (if none, leave this out). The default port number is 7778, so try that first.

```
http://<mymachine>.<mydomain>:7778/isqlplus
```

Figure 1.19
*iSQL*Plus Gives
Direct Access to the
Database.*

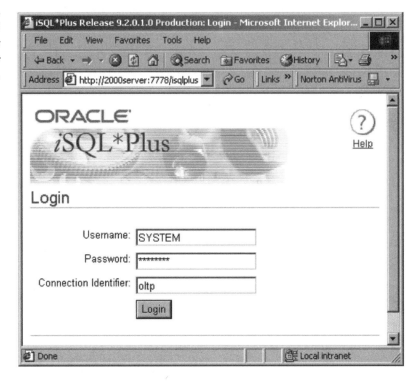

iSQL*Plus presents a login screen, as seen in Figure 1.19. If you do not see this screen, read the section on troubleshooting in Chapter 8.

3.   Type SYSTEM in the Username box, the current password for SYSTEM in the Password box, and your network name in the Connection Identifier box. Figure 1.19 shows the boxes filled in. As usual, the password is displayed as a string of asterisks for privacy. Click the Login button to go to the main screen.

4.   The main screen for iSQL*Plus appears. Type the following query into the box labeled "Enter statements," and then scroll down and click the Execute button.

```
SELECT VIEW_NAME, TEXT FROM USER_VIEWS;
```

The SQL command is executed, and the results appear at the bottom of the screen. Scroll down to view the results, as shown in Figure 1.20.

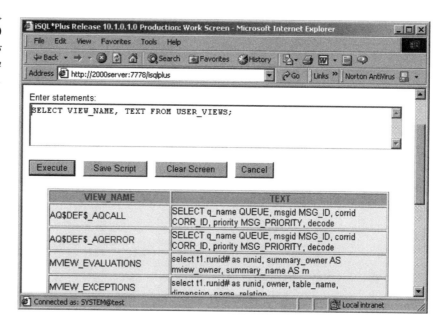

Figure 1.20
Query Results Shown as an HTML Table.

5.   Scroll back to the top of the screen. Here are some control buttons to explore, as you see in Figure 1.21. The History button is similar to the SQL History icon in SQL*Plus Worksheet. It lists previous SQL commands and loads them back into the Work Screen. The Preferences button displays a selection of settings especially for the browser window, such as the width of the output area and whether to place the results in the same browser window (the default) or in a new browser window. In addition, the Preferences screen sets SQL*Plus environmental variables (common to all versions of SQL*Plus), such as LINESIZE, ECHO, and HEADINGS. Learn more about these settings in Chapter 8.

6.   Click on the Help icon in the top right corner of the window. This brings up a directory of links to commands especially for iSQL*Plus (in the first column), and links to SQL*Plus commands that are used for all the versions of SQL*Plus in the second and third columns. Use this if you are not sure how to do SQL*Plus tasks such as setting the number of lines per page on a report, automatically displaying (or suppressing) the SQL command before running the command, and so on.

7.   Exit this window by clicking the X in the top right corner. The main iSQL*Plus window is still open.

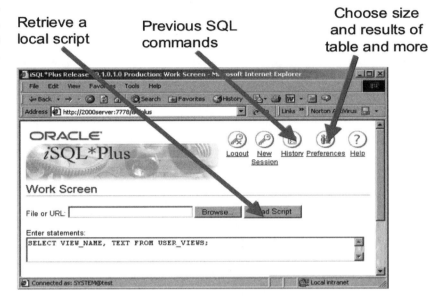

Figure 1.21
*iSQL*Plus Is a*
Rich Environment.

Retrieve a
local script

Previous SQL
commands

Choose size
and results of
table and more

8. Exit the iSQL*Plus browser by clicking Logout link, and then clicking the X in the top right corner when you see the iSQL*Plus login screen.

Note: See Chapter 8 if you cannot reach the iSQL*Plus login screen.

1.7   The MUSIC Schema

The sample data described here will be used as a basis to write your own SQL commands as you follow along with step-by-step exercises in every chapter.

Figure 1.22 shows the database design structure of the tables, including their primary keys (the columns that define a unique record) and their columns.

This schema supports a fictional music studio. The music studio keeps track of the musicians who use the studio and the time they spend in the studio recording songs. Here is a short description of each table:

Figure 1.22
The Music Studio Schema.

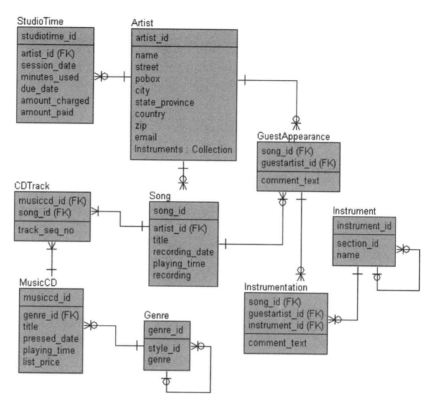

- **ARTIST.** A musician who has either recorded a song or participated in recording another musician's song. Each artist record has the name, address, and e-mail of the musician. Every artist has a unique identification number (ARTIST_ID) assigned when the record was entered into the database table. In addition, a special column called INSTRUMENTS contains a list of musical instruments the musician plays. This special column is a collection (a list of many values held in a single column).

- **SONG.** The ARTIST_ID column identifies the owner of each song in the table. Each song has a title, recording date, and playing time. The RECORDING column contains the final recorded song in an audio format, ready to play.

- **MUSICCD and CDTRACK.** A music CD has two tables for all the information. First, the MUSICCD table holds the CD title, date it was pressed, and the total playing time of the CD. Second, the CDTRACK table contains all the songs for each CD and the order in which that song appears on the CD. This arrangement of tables allows one song to be included on more than one CD. For example, The Beatles' song "Let It Be" is on the *White Album* CD and on *The Beatles' Greatest Hits* CD.

- **GENRE**. Music CDs can be categorized into genres or types of music. Genres are hierarchical in nature, where one genre can be a subset of another genre.

- **STUDIOTIME**. When a musician (artist) comes into the studio to record a song, the studio charges the artist for time spent in the studio. This table contains information needed for billing the artist. An artist may have many studio sessions, and each session is a row in the STUDIOTIME table.

- **GUESTAPPEARANCE**. A musician seldom records a song alone. Even though the musician owns the song, he or she often asks other musicians to collaborate on the recording. This table keeps track of which musician (called the guest artist) played on what other musician's songs.

- **INSTRUMENTATION**. When a guest artist plays on a song, he or she plays one or more instruments. This table keeps track of which instrument each guest artist played on each song. For example, Jim played drums and sang backup vocals (the voice is considered an "instrument" in these tables) on Amy's song. Later Amy played guitar on Jim's song.

- **INSTRUMENT**. The instrument table assigns an identifying number to each instrument. The number is used in the INSTRUMENTATION table. So, instruments are actually stored in two different ways in the schema: (1) as a collection in the ARTIST table and (2) as individual rows in the INSTRUMENT table. This is done to illustrate the variety of methods you can use when designing a database system.

1.7.1 The MUSIC Schema Sales Data Warehouse

The OLTP schema in Figure 1.22 is expanded in Figure 1.23 to create a data warehouse[5] structure for CD sales. In general, data warehouse tables can be broken into dimension and fact tables. Fact tables contain facts such as sales record history, and dimensions describe the facts such as the countries in which sales took place. Roughly, dimensions are equivalent to OLTP static tables such as a table of customers. Facts are roughly equivalent to OLTP transactional tables such as sales transactions. A data ware-

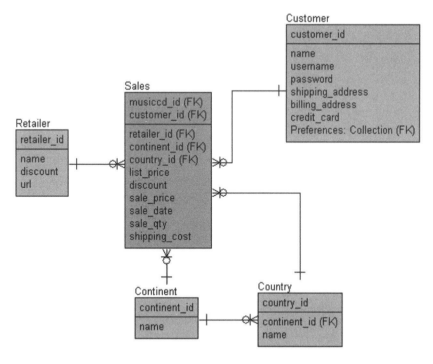

Figure 1.23
The Music Studio Schema Sales Data Warehouse.

house data model should in its ideal form be in the structure of a star (star schema) or in a less ideal form of a degraded star schema (snowflake). In Figure 1.23 the SALES table is the fact table, and all other tables are dimensions of those sales entries. The schema represented by the entity relationship diagram is in fact a snowflake schema because of the relationship between the CONTINENT and COUNTRY tables. This relationship is not strictly necessary, but it was useful during the process of writing this book.

- **Dimension Tables**. RETAILER, CONTINENT, and COUNTRY are all purely dimensional entities of SALES.

- **Partial Dimension Tables**. The CUSTOMER table could be construed as being a partial fact table describing SALES table entries, apart from the fact that there is a link to the GENRE table in the OLTP structure. Links are shown in Figure 1.24.

- **Fact Tables**. The SALES table is a fact table because it contains facts about sales or, more simply put, sales transaction records. All dimensions describe SALES such as what country a sale occurred in.

Figure 1.24
OLTP to Data
Warehouse Links.

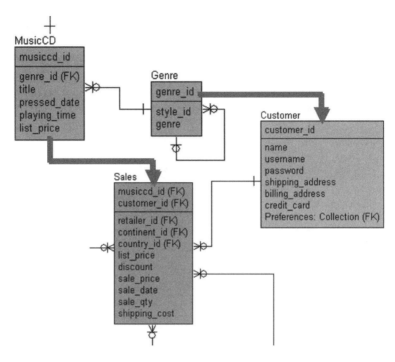

There are links between the two sets of OLTP and data warehouse tables, as highlighted in Figure 1.24.

All scripts used to create tables and their data are provided in Appendix A.

The next chapter will briefly list new features available for SQL in both Oracle Database 10*g* and Oracle Database 9*i*.

1.8   Endnotes

1.   www.oracledbaexpert.com/oracle/secure/Normalization.doc

2.   Oracle Performance Tuning for 9i and 10g (ISBN: 1-555-58305-9)

3.   My version of the Normalization is a highly simplified version. I have twisted Normal Forms deliberately.

4.   http://www.oracledbaexpert.com/oracle/secure/Denormalization.doc

5.   http://www.oracledbaexpert.com/oracle/secure/TheVeryBasicsOfDataWarehouseDesign.doc

2

New Features of Oracle SQL

In this chapter:

- What are the new features of Oracle SQL in Oracle Database 10*g*?
- What were the new features of Oracle SQL in Oracle Database 9*i*?
- What PL/SQL improvements are there?
- How is XML development better supported?
- What's new in Oracle SQL utilities?

This chapter takes a bird's-eye view of Oracle SQL changes in both Oracle Database 10*g* and Oracle Database 9*i*. Without further ado, let's get started with Oracle Database 10*g*.

2.1 New Features in Oracle Database 10*g*

Oracle Database 10*g* contains the following SQL and PL/SQL features.

2.1.1 Oracle SQL Improvements in Oracle Database 10*g*

- Oracle documentation states that case sensitivity is no longer required for filtering and sorting in SQL statements. Proving this point is a tuning exercise and does not belong in this book.
- The CONNECT BY clause now allows ancestor-descendant pairs as opposed to only parent-child pairs. In other words, pairs can be matched and returned where those pairs are not directly related within a hierarchy but related from the top to the bottom of a hierarchy (see Chapter 13).

- Object improvements include VARRAY resizing and splitting of nested table type columns into different tablespaces (see Chapter 16).

- A new row timestamp pseudocolumn called ORA_ROWSCN contains a commit point timestamp or system change number (SCN). For updates only, the SCN for a row must be retrieved to ensure that no row change occurred between a row SELECT and subsequent UPDATE.

- The following new datatypes have been added (see Chapter 16):

  - BINARY_FLOAT and BINARY_DOUBLE allow 32-bit single precision and 64-bit double precision floating-point numbers.
  - SDO_GEORASTER and SI_STILLIMAGE store raster and digital images, respectively (including object characteristics), for object-relational multimedia storage.

- A multitude of DDL commands have been altered and enhanced. Most DDL command changes are relevant to database administration and not Oracle SQL.

- Several SELECT statement and DML command syntax changes have been introduced:

  - MERGE allows insertions, updates, or both. Previously, the MERGE command always performed both insertions and updates. Additionally, MERGE can also delete rows from the target table (see Chapter 15).
  - SELECT can be executed as a flashback or versions query, retrieving data at a point in time in the past, based on an SCN or timestamp (see Chapter 13).
  - Grouped outer joins allow groupings on data where subset parts may not exist.

Note: ⓾ Grouped outer joins are omitted from this book because syntax documentation was not available at the time of writing.

- The SPREADSHEET clause extends the SELECT statement, allowing multiple dimensional array query result output. Calculations between resulting rows can be performed much like cross-tabbing or interdimensional data warehouse reporting (see Chapter 11).

Note: (10*g*) The SPREADSHEET clause has been renamed to the MODEL clause.

- Oracle Database 10*g* has recycle bin technology (see Chapter 18):
  - Recovering a table from the recycle bin requires use of the FLASHBACK TABLE command.
  - The PURGE command is used to permanently destroy objects dropped into the recycle bin. Space is not released for dropped objects until they are purged.
- New built-in functions are as follows:
  - COLLECT creates a nested table from the row set result of a single column in a table (see Chapter 16).
  - Nested tables have new collection functions (see Chapter 16):
    - CARDINALITY returns the number of elements in a collection for each row.
    - POWERMULTISET returns all set elements in a collection.
    - POWERMULTISET_BY_CARDINALITY combines the previous two functions by returning all set elements with a specified number of entries, for each collection in each row. One could find every row in a table where that collection has a specified number of entries.
    - SET converts a nested table (collection) for each row to a set. A set contains unique values only such that duplicates are removed within each collection in each row.
  - SPREADSHEET clause functions are used to facilitate cross calculations between different rows. Functions include the following (see Chapter 11):
    - CURRENTV returns a dimensional value or current value.
    - PRESENTNNV returns one expression if a value exists, otherwise another.
    - PRESENTV is as for PRESENTNNV except allowing null values.
    - PREVIOUS returns a value at the beginning of each iteration or loop.
  - New binary floating-point number functions include the following (see Chapter 9):
    - TO_BINARY_DOUBLE and TO_BINARY_FLOAT allow for conversions.

- ■ NANVL returns a replacement value if the initial value is not a number.
- ■ REMAINDER is a remainder or modulus function specifically for binary floating-point numbers.
- Regular expression functions are REGEXP_INSTR, REGEXPR_REPLACE, and REGEXPR_SUBSTR. These functions essentially expand the search-and-replace capabilities of INSTR, REPLACE, and SUBSTR to full pattern-matching regular expression capabilities. For more information, refer to the section titled "Expressions" (on page 44) in this chapter and see Chapter 14.

Note: The essential difference between simple pattern matching and regular expression matching is that simple pattern matching searches for patterns. Regular expression matching searches for patterns allowing for replacement and return of specific values found within a pattern.

- New statistical aggregation functions are covered in detail in Chapter 11. Statistical analysis can be extremely useful in data warehouse and reporting environments. There is now extensive capability in Oracle SQL for OLAP-type inter-row and cross-row analysis, which was previously only available in expensive software packages and add-ons such as Formula1.
  - ■ CORR_{S | K} calculate Pearson's correlation coefficient, measuring the strength of a linear relationship between two variables. Plotting two variables on a graph results in a lot of dots plotted from two axes. Pearson's correlation coefficient can tell you how good the straight line is.
  - ■ MEDIAN returns a median, middle, or interpolated value. Quite literally, a median is the middle sequenced value in a set of values. If a distribution is discontinuous and skewed or just all over the place, the median will not be anywhere near a mean or average of a set of values. A median is not always terribly useful.
  - ■ Other statistical functions begin with "STATS." The syntax appears like this:

```
STATS_{BINOMIAL_TEST | CROSSTAB | F_TEST | KS_TEST |
MODE | MW_TEST | ONE_WAY_ANOVA | STATS_T_TEST_* |
STATS_WSR_TEST}
```

These functions provide various statistical goodies.

- The ORA_HASH function returns a hash value for an expression.
- New and enhanced operators are as follows:
  - Collections (nested tables and VARRAY objects) can now be compared using equality (=) and inequality (<> | !=) operators.
  - CONNECT_BY_ROOT helps extend hierarchical queries from parent-child connections only, on to root and below connections (see Chapter 13).
  - Multiset operators MULTISET {EXCEPT | INTERSECT | UNION} combine results of two collections. EXCEPT is similar to the outer part of an outer join, including all elements in one collection and not another. INTERSECT is the intersection of two collections (the unique list of common values). UNION combines all elements in both collections (see Chapters 7 and 16).
- New pseudocolumns are as follows (see Chapter 7):
  - Hierarchical pseudocolumns CONNECT_BY_{ISLEAF | ISCYCLE} give an indication of contained child elements in a hierarchy.
  - Version query pseudocolumns provide versioning information for flashback version queries.
- New conditional operators are as follows (see Chapter 7):
  - Floating-point conditions IS [NOT] {NAN | INFINITE} allow undefined and infinite checks against floating-point number expressions.
  - IS [NOT] A SET implies that a collection is a set because it contains unique values only.
  - IS ANY qualifies SPREADSHEET clause dimensional values.
  - IS [NOT] EMPTY checks for an empty collection, a nested table containing no elements whatsoever, essentially a collection not as yet instantiated.
  - IS PRESENT ensures that a cell exists before the execution of a SPREADSHEET clause.
  - [NOT] MEMBER OF *collection* attempts to validate membership within a collection.
  - REGEXP_LIKE utilizes regular expressions as opposed to simple pattern matching.
  - SUBMULTISET indicates if one or more collection items are a subset of another collection. See Chapters 7 and 16 for details on collections such as nested tables and VARRAY objects.

- Expressions and the new EVALUATE operator permit what would previously have been multiple-line SQL statements to be placed into a single line of SQL or PL/SQL code. The term used by Oracle documentation is "describing user's interest in data" (see Chapter 14).

    - The Oracle Expression Filter uses an Expression datatype and the EVALUATE operator. The EVALUATE operator allows concise conditional expression evaluation.
    - Portable operating system interface (POSIX) standard regular expression capabilities allow search-and-replace functionality with changes to the LIKE operator, REPLACE, and INSTR functions. This search-and-replace capability is equivalent to search-and-replace power in Unix scripting languages or something like the SED editor or when using Perl.

2.1.2   PL/SQL Improvements in Oracle Database 10g

An intense examination of the details of PL/SQL is not required in an SQL reference-type book, so some of the items listed here are not covered in this book. However, a basic introduction to PL/SQL programming is covered in Chapter 24.

- Everything possible in Oracle SQL with respect to SQL coding can now be coded and executed from within PL/SQL. PL/SQL is now fully syntactically equivalent with Oracle SQL. In other words, all Oracle SQL commands can be coded into PL/SQL scripts.

- The PL/SQL compiler is better optimized including bulk binding and native compilation. Native compilation stores PL/SQL units in BLOB objects as a compiled binary form. Previously, PL/SQL was interpreted PL/SQL code. Interpretation implies compilation or conversion to binary at run-time; in the case of PL/SQL, coded commands were read and parsed for every execution. Binary compilation simply executes binary code at run-time and is therefore potentially much quicker to execute.

- Using binary datatypes can help number-crunching performance.

Note: Number crunching or heavily computational code should not really be constructed using a language such as PL/SQL. Java or even C is better suited, and most commonly at the application level.

- Extensive collection set operation capability encapsulates collection testing and verification coding into single commands. See the previous section on Oracle SQL improvements in Oracle Database 10*g*.

- The PLSQL_WARNINGS database configuration parameter or the DBMS_WARNINGS package can be used to enable or disable PL/SQL compilation warnings.

- PL/SQL quoting of strings within strings no longer requires the use of multiple sets of single quotation marks. A string delimiter character can now be specified.

- The collection iteration FORALL statement is improved.

- SCN_TO_TIMESTAMP and TIMESTAMP_TO_SCN functions can help with setting up flashback queries.

- The packages UTL_COMPRESS and UTL_MAIL are new. The UTL_COMPRESS package allows data compression. The UTL_MAIL package simplifies e-mail from within PL/SQL, where underlying protocol detail is not required.

2.1.2.1 Java Improvements in Oracle Database 10g

The Oracle Database kernel JVM is improved in Oracle Database 10*g* for compliance with the latest version of Java, driver enhancements, connection caching, and passing of parameters by name for PL/SQL, among various other improvements. A discussion of the Oracle kernel JVM is a topic in itself that is beyond the scope of this book.

2.1.3 XML Improvements in Oracle Database 10g

New operators can be used to convert between XML and SQL, allowing creation of highly complex XML object document structures, and storage of those XML documents. See the later section on Oracle SQL improvements in Oracle Database 9*i* for a synopsis of XML functionality. Using XML in Oracle SQL is covered in detail in Chapter 17.

2.1.4 Some Utility Improvements in Oracle Database 10g

- SQL*Plus:
  - The SPOOL [CREATE | REPLACE | APPEND] options enhance the SPOOL command in SQL*Plus.

- SET SQLPROMPT can be set to values such as a schema and the name of a database server.
- The login script in the $ORACLE_HOME/sqlplus/admin directory GLOGIN.SQL is now executed for every database connection, not only on opening the SQL*Plus utility.
- Contents of the recycle bin can be viewed.
- DBMS_OUTPUT functionality is more easily provided.

- iSQL*Plus now allows prompts for input values.

Now let's look at changes made to various database objects, those directly related to Oracle SQL, not database administration.

2.1.5   Database Object Improvements in Oracle 10g

- Tables can be purged such that they are dropped without being stored in the recycle bin. Thus the DROP TABLE command now has a PURGE clause, and a new command called the PURGE command has been introduced (see Chapter 18).

- The FLASHBACK TABLE command can be used to restore a previous version of a table back to an SCN or timestamp, perhaps even recover a mistakenly dropped table (see Chapter 18).

- These next two changes are interesting but more applicable to general database administration than to Oracle SQL specifically:

  - Multiple temporary tablespaces using tablespace groups can now be set for a user (schema) within the CREATE USER command syntax.
  - Nested table and VARRAY types can now be changed.

Now let's go backward in time and make a quick synopsis of Oracle SQL and PL/SQL features introduced in Oracle Database 9i, perhaps putting some of the changes for Oracle Database 10g into perspective.

2.2   New Features in Oracle Database 9i

Oracle Database 9i (Release 1 or Release 2) contained the following new features for SQL and PL/SQL.

2.2.1   **Oracle SQL Improvements in Oracle Database 9i**

- A new data warehousing command called MERGE.

- New features for data warehousing such as CUBE and ROLLUP GROUP BY extensions and the RANK function. These features are for use in summary and subtotal reports generated with SQL commands.

- Columns and constraints can be renamed.

- A query of data at a point in time in the past (called a Flashback query) is enhanced for use within an SQL command rather than requiring an environmental session change.

- A new datatype called TIMESTAMP supports timezone-sensitive dates and times.

- Nearly full support of SQL*Plus features in iSQL*Plus so you can create Web-based reports.

- Support for the ANSI standard JOIN command among other new ANSI standards.

- XML and partitioning enhancements when creating tables and views.

- XML functional capability enhancements allowing various new types of operations on XML datatypes:
  - XML conditions:
    - EQUALS_PATH tries to find something in an XML path.
    - UNDER_PATH finds something within an XML path.
    - DEPTH and PATH are ancillary functions of EQUALS_PATH and UNDER_PATH conditions. DEPTH is the number of levels within a path and PATH is a relative path specifier.

Note: An ancillary function is a subordinate part of whatever uses it. For example, the DEPTH function can only be used with EQUALS_PATH and is thus ancillary to the EQUALS_PATH function.

  - XML functions:
    - DEPTH and PATH (see previous explanation).
    - Working with XML document objects:
      - EXTRACTVALUE returns a scalar value from an XML document object node.

- UPDATEXML returns an XML document object including a change.
- Generating XML from Oracle SQL code:
  - XMLAGG aggregates or merges multiple XML pieces from an SQL row set.
  - XMLCONCAT concatenates XML values from an SQL row set into XML elements.
  - XMLCOLATTVAL collates XML values into XML structural elements from row sets.
  - XMLELEMENT creates an XML element from an SQL row set.
  - XMLFOREST creates an XML hierarchical structure from an SQL row set with an object for each row, and a name-value pair (element) for each column value within that row.
- Returning data from XML documents:
  - XMLSEQUENCE returns an array of elements at a specific level or path (row identifier) within an XML document.
  - XMLTRANSFORM simply applies an XSL style sheet to an XML document object.

Note: XML capabilities with Oracle SQL are covered in Chapter 17.

- Expression capabilities have been added to include CASE statements, cursor expressions using CURSOR (subquery) syntax, and scalar subqueries returning an expression.
- Numerous new functions and enhancements to existing functions.
- Privilege and DDL command enhancements, most of which fall outside the scope of this book.

2.2.2　New PL/SQL Features in Oracle Database 9i

As already stated, an intense examination of the details of PL/SQL is not required in an SQL reference book. Items in this list may or may not be covered in this book in later chapters:

- A number of object-handling enhancements, a little beyond the scope of this book.
- Most SQL syntax is supported in PL/SQL.

- CASE statement expression, as already mentioned.

- Performance is improved by native PL/SQL code compilation as opposed to direct interpretation.

- Temporary tables and cursors are no longer required to pass structured expressions between functions. Now a query can be executed against a returned set of rows.

- Bulk SQL operations can be executed using the EXECUTE IMMEDIATE command.

Note: Some Oracle Database 10g items listed in this chapter are not covered in other chapters of this book. Some things are too obscure. Any omissions are deliberate. Details can be found in Oracle documentation.

The next chapter introduces the basics of Oracle Database physical architecture. A general understanding of underlying architecture is essential to a thorough understanding of Oracle SQL.

3

Oracle Database Architecture

In this chapter:

- What are the basic architectural concepts of Oracle Database?

- What is the Oracle instance?

- What is the physical structure of an Oracle database?

- How do you start up and shut down a database?

- Enhancing the basic physical architecture of an Oracle database.

    Let's begin with some very basic concepts.

3.1   The Basic Concepts

Oracle Database 10*g* is a relational database management system (RDBMS), which means that it is a set of software programs that handles the storage of information, the security for access to the information, and the connections between various portions of the information.

Once you have installed the RDBMS software, you can create an Oracle instance and a database. Figure 3.1 shows all three of these elements installed on one computer, which is the typical way to install and run the software.

The database is made up of datafiles stored on the hard disks of the computer. This is where all of your information will be stored. To add information into the database, you must start up an Oracle instance. Once started, your computer will be running a set of background processes, which manage and manipulate the datafiles, among other things. You also have a memory area called the System Global Area (SGA) that is reserved for Oracle's use. Oracle stores as much information as possible in its memory to speed up the processing time of whatever operation you do, from retrieving data in a special sorted format (which you will learn how to do in

Figure 3.1
A Typical Oracle Database 10g Database Server.

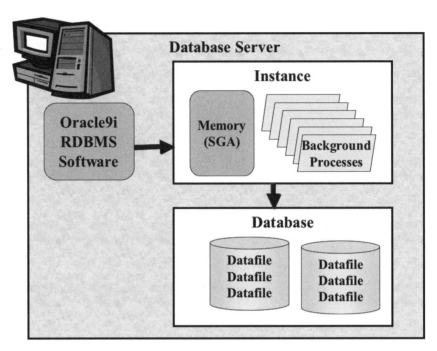

later chapters) to loading data from an online application. The computer that contains all of these elements is called the *database server*.

Note: When you install Oracle Database on a Windows 2000, NT, or XP Pro system, the installation creates the Oracle instance and a database for you and sets up the software so that the Oracle instance starts up every time you start up your computer. On UNIX and Linux platforms, it is possible to automate Oracle instance and database startup, which is not always done by the Oracle Installer. See your installation guide.

What goes into those datafiles? In a relational database of any kind, the basic storage unit within the database is called a *table*. Just like a spreadsheet, a table has rows and columns. Columns define what categories of information the table can store, and each row contains values for each of the categories for one record or item in the table.

A database is different from a spreadsheet in these ways:

■ *A database stores more data.* One Oracle Database 10*g* database can store thousands of tables with millions of rows in each table.

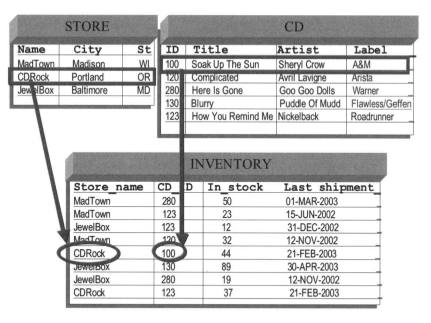

Figure 3.2
Related Tables
Interconnect and
Save Space.

- *A database can interconnect tables.* Relationships between tables can be defined in the database to enforce integrity rules called *constraints* (rules that make sure connections between tables are valid). Figure 3.2 shows three tables that are related to one another. An integrity rule for these tables would make sure that every CD in the INVENTORY table, for example, is connected to a CD in the CD table.

- *A database saves space by relating data rather than repeating data.* For example, in Figure 3.2, the title, label, and artist are listed in the CD table. The CD_ID in the fifth row of the INVENTORY table is 100. By looking back at the CD table row for ID 100, you know that the CDRock store has 44 copies of "Soak Up The Sun" by Sheryl Crow on the A&M record label.

All tables have columns, and all columns have a name and a datatype. The column's name must be unique within the table and must comply with Oracle's naming standards.

- In a nutshell, Oracle's naming standards are as follows:
    - The name should be 1 to 30 characters long.
    - The name is interpreted as uppercase (unless enclosed in double quotes).

- The name must begin with a letter and must use only letters, numbers, or these three symbols: $, #, _ (unless enclosed in double quotes).

If enclosed in double quotes, a column name is case sensitive and can begin with any character and include any letter, number, or symbol, including a space character. For instance, if a column is created as double quote enclosed and containing lowercase letters, then when selecting that named column from a table, double quotes must be used. This first example shown will cause an error (ORA-00904: invalid column name):

```
SELECT Column_xyz FROM MYTABLE;
```

You must add the double quotes like this to avoid an error:

```
SELECT "Column_xyz" FROM MYTABLE;
```

Let's look at another example to make this point clearer and create a table containing three different columns. The table is described using the DESC command in Figure 3.3. The column called A appears as A, b appears as B, "abc" is lowercase abc, and "a b c" is a b c.

```
CREATE TABLE TMP (A NUMBER, b NUMBER, "abc" NUMBER, "a b c"
NUMBER);
```

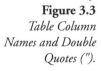

Figure 3.3
Table Column Names and Double Quotes (").

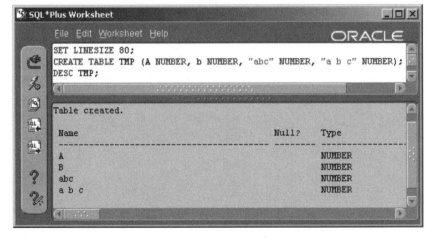

Selecting all of the columns would have to have any non-uppercase column names, including any with space characters, retrieved using double quotes ("). In the following two SELECT statements, the first will cause an error and the second will not:

```
SELECT A,B, abc, a b c FROM TMP;
SELECT A, B, "abc", "a b c" FROM TMP;
```

Figure 3.4 shows some typical column names. In addition to a name, the column has a datatype, which tells Oracle Database 10*g* the type of data that will be stored in the column once a row is added to the table. Oracle Database 10*g* has many datatypes, which are described in detail in Chapter 16. Here are some examples of the more common datatypes:

- **NUMBER.** Numbers of all kinds fit in here, from dollars to scientific notations.

- **DATE.** Calendar dates. Dates are stored as a Julian date. A Julian date is a number in seconds from an internally specified date such as January 1, 1970. You can subsequently access both date and time or any parts thereof from this type of column depending on the format applied.

- **VARCHAR2.** Character data. You specify a maximum length; however, any trailing spaces are omitted from the data to save space.

- **BLOB.** This type of column can store one value up to four gigabytes in size. BLOBs are usually reserved for multimedia applications such as storing a video or audio file.

Figure 3.4 shows the structure of the table called INVENTORY that was displayed in Figure 3.2. As you can see, the table has a name, an owner. Each column has a name and datatype.

Now you know the basic terminology for tables, rows, columns, and databases. As you know, security is always an issue when it comes to information. You may be familiar with some basic ways to protect your data: for example, adding a password to your login so only you are allowed to use your computer, or placing your files on a removable disk that you keep with you rather than storing inside the hard drive. When using a database, how do you keep track of who is allowed to do what?

Figure 3.4
*Table Definitions
Include Table and
Column
Specifications.*

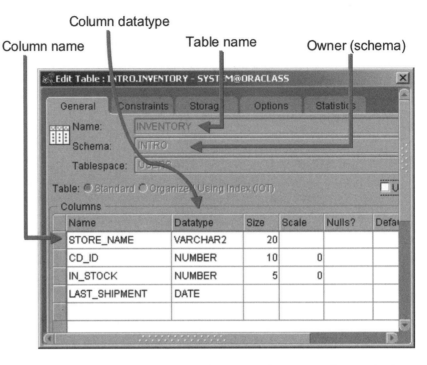

Many users, sometimes thousands, might share a single Oracle database. A user is any person who can log into the database instance. There are several ways to authenticate a user logging into the database (see Chapter 23); the typical method is to assign each person a unique user name and a password.

When so many individuals access the same database, the easiest way to keep track of them is to group them together by duties or roles. Oracle provides the capability to assign privileges to a role and then assign the role to one or more users.

For example, one user might be the database administrator (DBA). That user has the authority to start and stop the database instance, add new users, change passwords, assign other users various privileges, and so on. Another user may need to create tables, while a third user might need only to log in and view or modify data in someone else's tables. Oracle Database provides predefined roles for these typical groups of users:

- **CONNECT:** This role gives users the right to log into the database.

- **RESOURCE:** This role authorizes users to create tables (and other structures, such as indexes) in the database.

Chapter 23 shows how to create roles of your own.

> **Note:** (10g) Future releases of Oracle may not include these roles. You can create your own roles to serve these or any other purpose you need.

When a user creates a table, that user is the table's owner. A schema is the collection of all the tables owned by one user. For example, you log in as the user STANLEY and you create a table called TREASURE_CHEST and a table called JEWELRY. These two tables are in the STANLEY schema.

Chapter 18 describes how to create your own tables. For now, however, you have some already existing tables with rows of data inside. Your job is to learn how to retrieve that data using the programming language called SQL.

Now let's dig a little more seriously into the physical architecture of Oracle Database. In its most simplistic form, an Oracle Database installation consists of buffers, processes, files, network communication, and configuration, as shown in Figure 3.5.

Figure 3.5
*An Oracle
Database
Installation.*

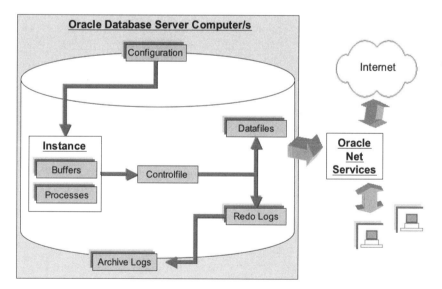

3.2   The Oracle Instance

The Oracle instance is the part of an Oracle installation executing in memory when the database is mounted, running, and available for use. That mounted and running database consists of memory structures or buffers and several processes.

- Memory structures are shown in Figure 3.6.
  - Much of the memory structure or buffers is known collectively as the Shared Global Area (SGA). The SGA contains database buffer caches, the shared pool, and the redo log buffer.
  - Somewhat more loosely connected are the large pool, the java pool, and connection session memory or program global area (PGA).
- Processes:
  - Nonbackground or foreground processes are shown in Figure 3.7 and include network connectivity and client connection service processing. These processes include listeners, agents, shared and dedicated server processes, plus dispatcher processes. Although the listener and agent processes are not part of an Oracle instance, they execute on the database server.

Figure 3.6
*Oracle Instance
Memory Buffers.*

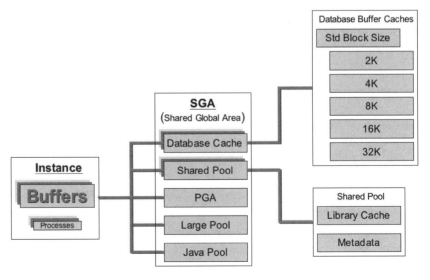

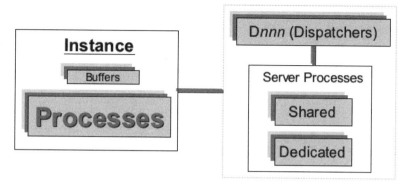

Figure 3.7
Oracle Instance Foreground Processes.

- Background processes, as shown in Figure 3.8, provide processing within the Oracle Database and communication with foreground processing.

The next part to examine briefly is the basics of the underlying physical and logical structure of an Oracle database.

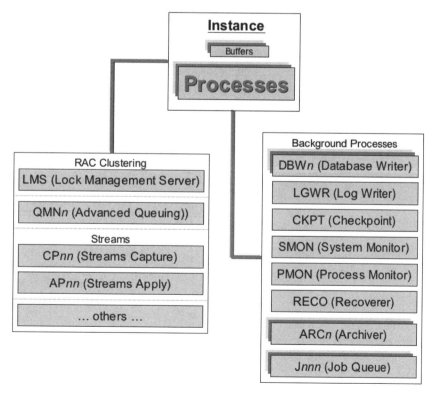

Figure 3.8
Oracle Instance Background Processes.

3.3   Oracle Database Physical Architecture

Let's break the physical and logical layers into sections:

- Where and how is data stored? In datafiles, tablespaces, and objects.

- What about recoverability? Controlfiles, logging, and archiving are used.

- How are changes undone? Rollback or undo spaces allow undoing of changes.

- How are large sorts handled? Specially formatted files are used for fast on-disk sorting.

Each of these areas is discussed in the following sections.

3.3.1   Datafiles, Tablespaces, and Objects

Figure 3.9 shows the internal physical structure of an Oracle database, showing the way in which data is stored. *Tablespaces* are logical structural overlays containing one or more datafiles. A *schema* (owner or Oracle user) is also a logical overlay structure. A schema can be spread across multiple tablespaces and contains segments or database objects such as rollback segments, temporary segments or tables, and indexes. *Segments* are physical or logical subdivisions within schemas and can be accessed across different

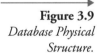

Figure 3.9
Database Physical Structure.

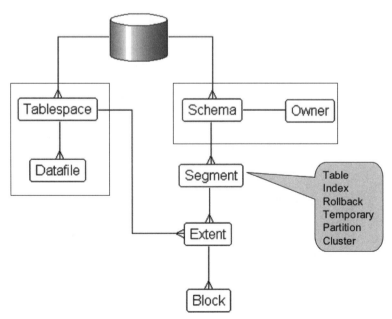

schemas. Segments are physically broken up into extents. An *extent* is a number of blocks added to a segment (datafile) when an object requires more space.

Figure 3.10 shows the different types of segments, synonymous from this perspective with a tablespace. In other words, in terms of functionality, a rollback segment accomplishes the same objective as a rollback tablespace, where rollback segments are created within rollback tablespaces.

Note: (10g) Rollback segments are generally referred to as undo or automated undo segments in Oracle Database 10g. Manual rollback is deprecated.

The SYSTEM tablespace contains Oracle system metadata, or the data about the data. Metadata contains table structures including column names, lengths, and datatypes, among many other things. The SYSAUX tablespace is new to Oracle Database 10g, containing various tool and utility objects such as for Recovery Manager (RMAN). Generally, data (DATA) and index (INDEX) tablespaces are split as shown in Figure 3.10 because tables and indexes are usually scanned at the same time. The UNDO tablespace contains data for undoing of transactions already executed plus providing flashback capability. The TEMP tablespace is specially formatted for fast on-disk sorting when memory capacity is exceeded for a sort. Temporary sort space is used for other functions as well, such as consistent exports. Partition tablespaces are both logically and physically split into chunks, where separate chunks can be accessed individually or as multiple groups executed in parallel.

The Controlfile, redo, and archive logs shown in Figure 3.10 are described in the next section.

3.3.2   Controlfiles, Logging, and Archiving

Looking once again at Figure 3.10, there are arrows pointing from the Controlfile to the redo logs and the archive logs. Redo logs and archive logs contain records of past database changes; recoverability is provided by Controlfile pointers to the redo logs and archive logs. When recovery is attempted, changes are read from log files and applied to restored datafiles. The Controlfile also contains pointers to datafiles. If datafile pointers in the datafiles are behind the Controlfile pointers for the datafiles, then the datafiles can be recovered using log file entries. When datafiles are up to date, pointers in the Controlfile, to the datafiles, and values in datafiles will be

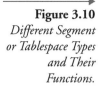

Figure 3.10
*Different Segment
or Tablespace Types
and Their
Functions.*

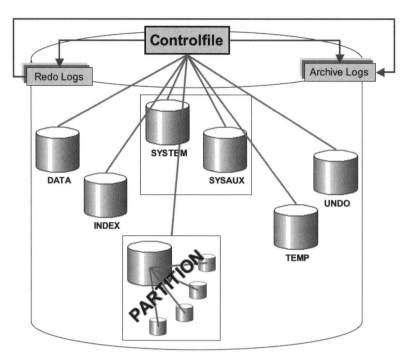

the same. Thus the lines in Figure 3.10 represent those pointer links between Controlfile, log files, and datafiles.

3.3.3   **Rollback and Undo**

It is important to Oracle SQL, both DML and DDL, to understand what exactly happens when database changes are executed. Several issues need to be covered briefly:

- Transactional control.

- Differences in the logging entries of DML and DDL.

- Differences between the COMMIT and ROLLBACK commands.

- The sequence of events when data is changed.

A transaction is a grouped (a BEGIN ... END block) set of one or more commands executed one after the other (sequentially). Dependencies may or may not exist between commands. A transaction starts at the beginning of a user session with the first executed command, or immediately after a previous transaction completes. A transaction is completed when a COM-MIT or ROLLBACK command is executed, permanently storing changes or undoing them, respectively. All DDL commands execute a COMMIT command inherently. A disconnection from a session also executes an auto-mated COMMIT command. This is an example transaction.

```
BEGIN
    INSERT INTO Artist(artist_id, name)
      VALUES(100,'A new artist');
    UPDATE Artist SET name='Delete this row'
    WHERE artist_id=100;
    DELETE FROM Artist WHERE artist_id=100;
    COMMIT;
END;
/
```

The COMMIT, ROLLBACK, SAVEPOINT, and SET TRANSAC-TION commands are used to control transactions. COMMIT stores changes, ROLLBACK removes changes, and SAVEPOINT allows partial rollback of some of the commands in a transaction. The SET TRANSAC-TION command allows specific settings to be global for an entire transac-tion. Transactional control is discussed more in Chapter 15.

DML means Data Manipulation Language and DDL means Data Defi-nition Language. The only important thing to remember about DML and DDL commands with respect to transactional control is that DDL com-mands are always automatically committed (cannot be undone). This means that DDL commands automatically end the current transaction, and nothing from that transaction may be undone once the transaction has been completed. DML commands can be committed or rolled back.

Comparing COMMIT and ROLLBACK commands is significant because committing is always faster than rolling back. Why? Well, it should be because one would hope that most applications execute far more com-mits than rollbacks. In short, COMMIT is built to be faster than ROLL-BACK because it is a much more likely event.

- What happens when a change is made to data in a table?

  - Redo log entries are written, storing log entries for data that is about to be changed.

- The database is changed, modifying the current value of data in tables.
- Rollback entries are created, storing a list of rollback entries to be applied in case a transaction is rolled back.

- What happens when a COMMIT command is executed?

  - Rollback entries are deleted. Changes are already made. Nothing else is required.

- What happens when a ROLLBACK command is executed?

  - Rollback entries are written to the redo logs, namely "undo" redo log entries.
  - Rollback is applied to the database undoing previously made changes.
  - Rollback entries are deleted.

Note: Redo log entries are always written before any database changes to ensure recoverability.

What happens when data is changed? Different DML commands have different types of redo log entries made for them. These different log entries are logical when one thinks about what needs to be stored in order to re-create a change, if need be in recovery.

- INSERT will log the ROWID (pointer) plus the data content of the entire row.

- UPDATE only needs to log the ROWID and individual column changes.

- DELETE simply logs the ROWID.

It is not essential to know these facts, but the information is interesting anyway in helping to understand how it all works.

Note: Precise syntax for COMMIT, ROLLBACK, SET TRANSACTION, and SAVEPOINT commands are covered in Chapter 15.

3.3.4 Temporary Sort Space

A temporary tablespace is an overflow for sorting onto disk when in-memory sort space limits for an executing sort have been exceeded. Sorting is sometimes for large sorts in SQL statements, where sort space required exceeds allocated session memory sorting limitations. Obviously, sorting on disk is much slower than sorting in memory. However, resources may require it. Additionally, temporary sort space is often used as a temporary physical space for some Oracle utilities.

3.4   Database Startup and Shutdown

One of the most simple and fundamental things is starting up and shutting down an Oracle database. You will not be doing much SQL code scripting if you do not know how to start up your database. Let's begin with the database STARTUP command. Defaults are highlighted.

```
STARTUP [ [ NOMOUNT ] | [ MOUNT ]
| [ OPEN [ READ WRITE | READ ONLY | RECOVER ] ]
[ FORCE ] [ RESTRICT ]
[ PFILE = <configuration parameter file> ];
```

Type the command STARTUP, and the database will start up opened in read/write, unrestricted mode. Thus STARTUP OPEN executes the NOMOUNT, MOUNT, and OPEN steps. NOMOUNT, MOUNT, and OPEN are the three steps to starting up an Oracle database:

- STARTUP NOMOUNT simply starts up all of the background processes and allocates space in virtual memory for all of the buffers.

- MOUNT mode is used for some low-level maintenance operations. MOUNT mode opens only the Controlfile, allowing access to physical datafiles through Controlfile pointers.

- NOMOUNT mode is included in mounted mode, before mounting the Controlfile.

After executing a STARTUP MOUNT operation, the ALTER DATABASE OPEN command can be executed to open the database. ALTER DATABASE MOUNT similarly applies to STARTUP NOMOUNT.

Other options are FORCE, forcing a SHUTDOWN ABORT (see later) followed by a STARTUP OPEN command. Be frugal using abort because it can ruin your database. RESTRICT starts up the database in restricted mode, allowing DBA access only. The RECOVER option places a database into recovery.

The PFILE parameter allows starting of the database with a specified database configuration parameter file. Leaving the PFILE option out starts up the database with whatever parameter file was used previously: a PFILE text parameter file or an SPFILE binary parameter file.

Looking at the SHUTDOWN command, the following syntax applies. Once again the default is highlighted.

```
SHUTDOWN [ NORMAL | TRANSACTIONAL | IMMEDIATE | ABORT ];
```

The NORMAL option waits for users to disconnect, does not allow new connections, forcibly rolls back currently running transactions, and then shuts down the database. A normal shutdown is the most prudent method of rapidly shutting down an Oracle database and should always be used if possible. The TRANSACTIONAL option automatically completes all transactions, subsequently disconnecting all connected users and shutting down the database. The IMMEDIATE option disconnects all users and shuts down the database without committing or rolling back currently executing transactions. Recovery may be required on database startup. The ABORT option is abusive brute force and should never be used. Aborting an Oracle database simply terminates all processes. The database will require recovery on startup. The ABORT option can potentially corrupt an Oracle database.

Note: Cleanup processing required by SHUTDOWN NORMAL is just as fast as recovery processing caused to the following startup by SHUTDOWN ABORT. You will not save any time using SHUTDOWN ABORT. Aborting a database causes similar recovery processing on startup. Additionally, SHUTDOWN ABORT can corrupt your Oracle database.

Now let's see how Oracle Database can be enhanced and expanded upon using various optional add-on pieces. Additional options are used to achieve and increase certain aspects for an Oracle installation. Buzzwords in this arena are scalability, high availability, distribution, easy management, plus backup and recovery enhancements, among numerous other options.

3.5   Enhancing the Physical Architecture

Architecturally expanding options for Oracle Database we will briefly introduce are as follows:

- Oracle Managed Files (OMF).

- Oracle Partitioning.

- Various forms of Replication.

- Standby/fail-over databases.

- Clustering technology.

3.5.1   Oracle Managed Files

Oracle Managed Files (OMF) will automatically create and drop datafiles, redo logs, archives, and Controlfiles in the operating system. No administrator intervention is required in the operating system. The big problem with OMF is serious performance impact. The DB_CREATE_FILE_DEST configuration parameter is used to specify placement of datafiles, redo logs, and Controlfiles. Specifying the DB_CREATE_ONLINE_LOG_DEST_*n* parameters overrides the DB_CREATE_FILE_DEST setting by managing placement of Controlfiles and redo logs. If more than one (one to five) DB_CREATE_ONLINE_LOG_DEST_*n* destinations are specified, then both redo logs are duplexed and Controlfiles are multiplexed. Duplexing and multiplexing being essentially the same thing in this situation.

3.5.2   Partitioning

Oracle Partitioning allows the splitting of large tables into separate physical spaces. As a result, different physical spaces or partitions can be operated on individually or in groups, running in parallel. Performance gains using Oracle Partitioning can be substantial.

Partitions can be of various different types:

- Range partitions split a table based on distinct ranges of values such as quarters in a year.

- List partitions split a table based on specific lists of values such as state names in the United States. For example, a partition containing data representing the Northeast United States could contain states such as NY, NJ, and PA for New York, New Jersey, and Pennsylvania, respectively. A partition for the West Coast could contain rows from states such as CA (California) and OR (Oregon).

- Hash partitions divide up partition values evenly based on hash values calculated on a column value or values in each row of a table.

- Composite partitions are partitions containing other subset partitions or subpartitions. There are two types of composite partitions:

  - A range partition containing hash subpartitions or a *range-hash partition*.
  - A range partition containing list subpartitions or a *range-list partition*.

Other than the huge impact of parallel processing of multiple partitions concurrently, or of pruning out of unwanted partitions, various tricks can be performed with partitions. Various types of operations can be performed on partitions individually, affecting only small physical parts of very large tables. Individual partitions can be:

- Added to a group of partitions, dropped from a set of partitions, or truncated as a single partition within a set of partitions. Thus we can change a small part of a very large table. Efficient!

- Split into new multiple partitions or merged together.

- Renamed, moved, or exchanged (swap one partition for another).

3.5.3 Replication

Traditionally, replication is intended to link databases distributed over large geographic areas where data is not only shared but specific chunks of data are exclusive to specific sites. In general, replication occurs in two forms as either master-to-slave replication or master-to-master replication, as shown in Figure 3.11.

Master-to-slave replication implies that data travels in only one direction, and master-to-master replication has data traveling in both directions, between two databases. There can be multiple databases in a set of replicated databases. More specifically, using Oracle Replication software, in a master-to-slave database environment, the slave database consists of a database comprised solely of materialized views. Effectively, master-to-slave replication does not exist for the Oracle Replication option.

Figure 3.11
*Master-to-Slave
versus Master-to-
Master Replication.*

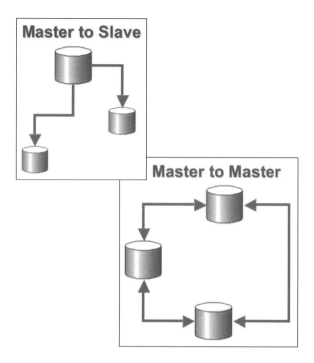

Figure 3.11
*Master-to-Slave
versus Master-to-
Master Replication.*

One of the most significant problems with the Oracle Replication option is that it is often used inappropriately for backup and fail-over databases. Oracle Replication has a level of complexity not suited to fail-over and backup management.

Another method of replication for Oracle Database involves using Oracle Streams and Oracle Advanced Queuing. A stream or pipe is established between two databases, where a master database would have a capture queue and a slave database an application queue. Oracle Streams Replication or Transparent Replication can include both master-to-master and master-to-slave replication.

3.5.4 **Standby Databases**

Standby database architecture is shown in Figure 3.12. Standby or fail-over databases can exist in two forms: a physical standby or a logical standby. A logical standby is far more comprehensive and far more flexible. Physical standby is simple but much easier to implement and maintain than logical standby.

Both physical and logical standby databases can be configured for maximum safety or maximum performance. Redo log entries for maximum

Figure 3.12
*Oracle Standby/
Fail-over Database
Architecture.*

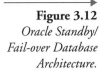

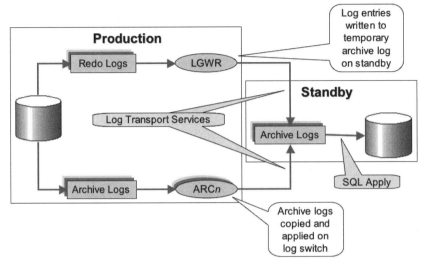

safety can be transferred to a standby as they are created using the Log Writer (LGWR), filling a precreated archive log file on the standby database. On the other hand, maximum performance can be achieved at the expense of safety, thus potentially presenting possible data loss using the Archiver (ARC*n*) to transfer log entries from primary to standby. In this case, redo log entries are transferred when a primary database log switch occurs, copying each archive log file to a standby database as it is created. Using the Archiver, redo log entries are not copied as they are created but only after primary database archiving.

Physical standby has disadvantages. A physical standby can only be accessed externally in read-only mode, and it must duplicate the source (primary) database exactly. A logical standby database is maintained in read-write mode, a completely open and accessible database. Also, a logical standby can have a subset of source database objects and can even contain objects in addition to the primary database. Once again, logical standby is much more flexible than physical standby.

3.5.5   Clustering and Oracle RAC

Clustering was previously called Oracle Parallel Server and is now called Oracle Real Application Clusters (RAC). Oracle RAC allows for sharing of a single large data source's data across more than one Oracle instance, running on more than a single database server. Thus multiple database servers share the same data, allowing for high availability, enormous scalability, and flexibility.

So far, this book has examined the underlying logical and physical structure of Oracle Database plus new features available in both Oracle Database 10*g* and Oracle Database 9*i*. Now it's time to begin looking into Oracle SQL itself. The next chapter begins this process by examining the SELECT statement.

4

The SELECT Statement

In this chapter:

- How do you write a basic query using SELECT statements?
- What types of SELECT statements are possible?
- What else is interesting about SELECT statements?

In this chapter, we dive right into the syntax and use of the SELECT statement to query the database. We also briefly discuss different types of queries, finally examining specific aspects of queries such as using DISTINCT and the DUAL table. So let's begin with the basics of the SELECT statement and some simple examples just to get into the swing of things.

4.1   The Basic SELECT Statement

SELECT is the beginning of the SQL command for querying (retrieving) data from a database table, view, or object. Objects are similar to tables, but they have a more complex structure.

4.1.1   Uses of the SELECT Statement

The SELECT statement is a specialized way to ask a question about the data in a database. Thus a SELECT statement is also called a query because it quite literally "queries" or asks questions of a database. There are several uses for the SELECT statement that give you great flexibility in the database:

- **Simple query**. A SELECT statement can be used alone to retrieve data from a table or a group of related tables. You can retrieve all columns or specify some columns. You can retrieve all rows or specify which rows you want.

- **Complex query**. A SELECT statement can be embedded within another SELECT statement. This lets you write a query within a query. The possibilities are endless. Later chapters cover the details.

- **Create a view or table**. A SELECT statement can be used to create a view or a new table. A view is a stored query that is executed whenever another SELECT statement retrieves data from the view by using the view in a query. Views are very useful to enforce security by limiting the columns or rows that particular users are allowed to see.

- **Insert, update, or delete data**. A SELECT statement can be used within the INSERT, UPDATE, or DELETE statements to add greater flexibility to these commands. Chapter 15 examines commands for manipulating data.

Note: There are numerous other more detailed types of queries using the SELECT statement to be described briefly later in this chapter and in detail in later chapters.

4.1.2   Syntax Conventions

In this section, and throughout the rest of the book, you will see SQL and SQL*Plus commands listed first with their syntax and then with many examples, some of which you could type yourself to help you better understand the commands.

The *syntax* of a command defines the set of rules governing the correct form of a command. Some parts are required and never change, others are optional, and others vary with each different statement. Figure 4.1 shows the syntax of the basic SELECT statement with descriptions of the various parts.

Here is the basic syntax of the SELECT statement in a textual form (Backus-Naur Form), as shown in Figure 4.1. See Chapter 1 for details of Backus-Naur syntax formatting.

```
SELECT { [alias.]column | expression | [alias.]* [ , … ] }
FROM [schema.]table [alias];
```

Figure 4.1
The Syntax of the SELECT Statement.

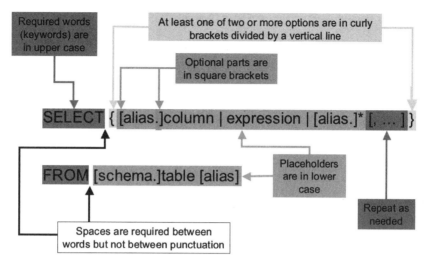

Curly braces mean you must choose from one of the choices between them. So, you can either write a list of column names, or write an expression, or use *. An asterisk (*) represents all column names within a query when used in the SELECT statement.

Square brackets mean you can include the items within the square brackets or leave them out entirely. In the SELECT command, you can list just one column or many columns, or even simply an asterisk (*) if you choose.

The lowercase words are always replaced with actual names of tables, columns, schemas, and so on. The words in the syntax give you a hint on what should be used. This structure is just the bare bones of the SELECT command. Other chapters cover all of the many variations and options available for the SELECT command.

The complete syntax definition of the SELECT command in Oracle's SQL documentation takes up five pages. The description of all the variables in the command takes up another 25 pages. In this book, you will build gradually on your knowledge, chapter by chapter, until you have enough knowledge of the SELECT command to write complex queries easily.

Note: Details of Backus-Naur syntax conventions can be found in Chapter 1. This book almost always follows a slight variation on that theme, described in Chapter 1. Any variations are generally specific to particular chapters and noted at the beginning of those chapters.

Let's look at a few examples.

4.1.3 Some Simple Example SELECT Statements

The first example retrieves rows from an Oracle metadata view:

```
SELECT VIEW_NAME, TEXT FROM USER_VIEWS;
```

This statement has a list of two columns (VIEW_NAME and TEXT), and the view queried is named USER_VIEWS. Tables and views are interchangeable in the SELECT command. No schema name is used because the view in this case belongs to the user who is running the query. As a general rule, any time you query a table or view that belongs to the user you log in as, no schema name is required. Likewise, when you query a table or view that is in another user's schema, you must use the schema name. For example, if you log in as JOE and you want to query a table name CARS owned by SAM, you would have to add the schema name CARS.

```
SELECT * FROM SAM.CARS;
```

Note: The semicolon is technically not considered part of the SQL statement's syntax. The semicolon marks the end of the statement and submission. A forward slash on a blank line following the SQL statement serves the same purpose. Submission means submission to the SQL engine, in other words "execute it!"

Now let's do some simple SELECT statement examples using the MUSIC schema.

Note: Diagrams and scripts for the MUSIC schema are in Chapter 1 and Appendix A.

Let's begin with a query listing all the data in the MUSICCD table:

```
SELECT * FROM MUSICCD;
```

Figure 4.2 shows the result. Notice the blank spaces in certain columns. This stands for a null value in the data. For example, the PLAYING_TIME column for the first row (Soak Up the Sun) is NULL.

Figure 4.2
SQL*Plus Report Layout.

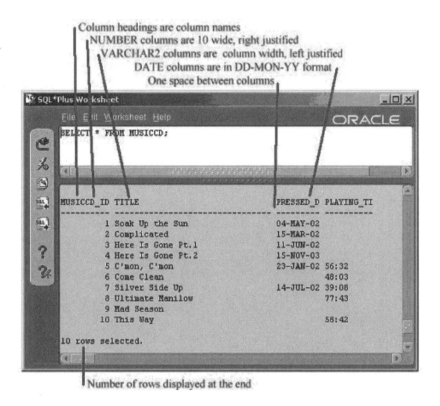

To select specific columns, the asterisk could be changed to something like PRESSED_DATE, TITLE, MUSICCD_ID, listing columns in the sequence specified.

```
SELECT PRESSED_DATE, TITLE, MUSICCD_ID FROM MUSICCD;
```

The next query contains a calculation between two columns. You can add, subtract, multiply, divide, and use parentheses to affect the calculation order of factors in expressions. When you combine columns, include calculations, or other operations, an expression is created. Expressions can be used in a SELECT statement anywhere you use a column.

```
SELECT ARTIST_ID, SESSION_DATE, AMOUNT_CHARGED-AMOUNT_PAID
FROM STUDIOTIME;
```

Observe that the column heading of the third column is AMOUNT_CHARGED - AMOUNT_PAID. This is long, and if you

Figure 4.3
*Column Aliases
Can Help Make
Queries More
Readable.*

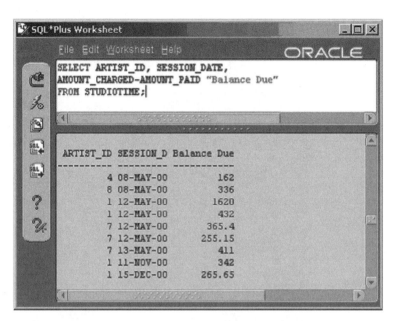

were handing a report off to someone else, you might want a more descriptive heading. To change the heading, add a column alias to the SELECT statement. A column alias redefines a column's heading in a SELECT statement. In this example, we change the second line by adding the alias "Balance Due."

```
AMOUNT_CHARGED-AMOUNT_PAID "Balance Due"
```

Using double quotes preserves the upper and lowercase appearance of the heading. Without double quotes, your alias will always appear in uppercase letters in the report. Additionally, in this case because the words "Balance" and "Due" are separated by a space, "Due" will be interpreted as a column name, causing an error. Figure 4.3 shows the output.

Now add aliases to all three columns and change the SELECT statement again:

```
SELECT ARTIST_ID Artist, SESSION_DATE "In Studio"
, AMOUNT_CHARGED-AMOUNT_PAID "Balance Due"
FROM STUDIOTIME;
```

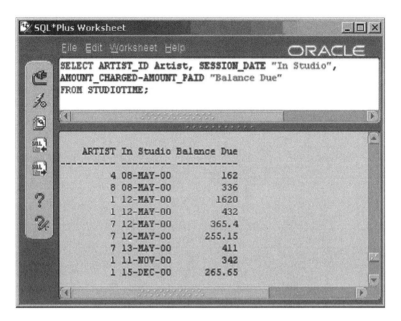

Figure 4.4
*Three Column
Aliases, with and
without Double
Quotes.*

Figure 4.4 shows the result. Headings have changed. Because the ARTIST_ID alias Artist is not in double quotes, the heading is displayed as uppercase even though it was typed in mixed case.

Now add an alias to the table name. Although this action does not affect your report, it will be useful in the future when you create more complex queries. A table alias is a shortcut name that is used as a substitute for the table name in the SELECT statement. The table alias is best being short and simple, but it does not have to be.

Note: I was once hired for a contract because I used single characters and not table names for table aliases. Why? Using table names to reference columns can make quite a mess of SQL statements. Using single-character aliases makes for much more readable, ultimately debuggable and tunable SQL code.

The table alias should be added to all of the table's columns (not column aliases) in the SELECT statement. This is a good habit to adopt because you will be able to create more readable SQL when using table aliases. Many of the examples in this book use table aliases. In this case, the letter **S** is used for the table alias:

```
SELECT S.ARTIST_ID Artist, S.SESSION_DATE "In Studio"
, S.AMOUNT_CHARGED - S.AMOUNT_PAID "Balance Due"
FROM STUDIOTIME S;
```

You could even add a schema name and a table alias to the table name in a SELECT command. For example, you are logged on as FRED and wish to query the LONGBOAT table in ANGELA's schema:

```
SELECT BOAT.BOAT_NAME, BOAT.DATE_CHRISTENED
FROM ANGELA.LONGBOAT BOAT;
```

Here are a few more tips on writing good queries:

- Use parentheses in either the SELECT or the WHERE clause to control the order of evaluation of expressions. Expressions within parentheses are evaluated first. For example:

  ```
  SELECT (TOTAL_MORTGAGE-(MONTHLY_PMT * MONTHS_PAID))/36
  ```

  Evaluates differently to:

  ```
  SELECT (TOTAL_MORTGAGE-(MONTHLY_PMT * MONTHS_PAID)/36)
  ```

- Upper and lowercase make no difference so long as they are not in quotation marks. For example, these three statements are identical as far as Oracle Database 10*g* is concerned:

  ```
  SELECT Name, Street, City from artist;
  Select name, street, city from ARTIST;
  SelEct nAmE, strEet, CITy From aRTist;
  ```

- When enclosed in quotation marks (single or double), then upper and lowercase are considered different. For example, these two statements are different:

  ```
  SELECT * from artist where name like ('%C%');
  SELECT * from artist where name like ('%c%');
  ```

- Oracle Database 10*g* ignores line breaks and spacing in SQL commands. For example, the following two SELECT statements are identical when submitted in SQL*Plus, even though spacing and line breaks make them look completely different from each other.

  ```
  SELECT  Name
  , Street
  ```

```
, City
FROM artist;
SELECT Name ,        Street ,          City
       FROM    artist ;
```

That's enough simple examples for now. Subsequent chapters examine a multitude of variations and adaptations for SELECT statements. Next we examine the different types of SELECT statements you can use.

4.2 Types of SELECT Queries

Different types of SELECT statement queries are as follows:

- Simple queries simply retrieve rows, as we have already seen earlier in this chapter.

- Filtered queries return a subset of rows using the WHERE clause to filter out unwanted rows.

- Sorted queries use the ORDER BY clause to return rows in a specified order based on column values returned.

- Grouping or aggregated queries create groupings or summaries of larger row sets.

- Join queries merge rows from more than one table, usually based on matching column values between tables.

- Subqueries are queries executed within other queries: a SELECT statement executed within another calling SELECT statement.

- Queries for table and view creation generate new tables and views from the results of a SELECT statement.

- Hierarchical queries build tree-like hierarchical output row structures from hierarchical data.

- Set operators and composite queries use special operators to concatenate results of different queries together.

- Flashback or versions queries allow access to data at a previous point in time.

- Parallel queries execute SQL statements in parallel, preferably using multiple CPU platforms and Oracle Partitioning.

Let's look at some of the query types briefly, starting with the simple query.

Figure 4.5
A Simple Query.

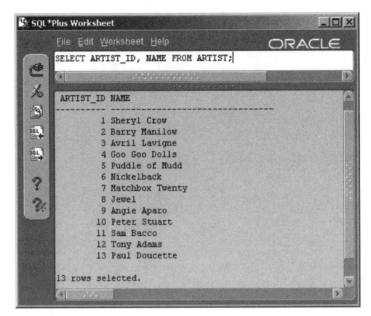

4.2.1   Simple Query

Once again, here is a simple query. The result is shown in Figure 4.5.

```
SELECT ARTIST_ID, NAME FROM ARTIST;
```

4.2.2   Filtered Query

How can we filter the results retrieved with a query? Filtering eliminates rows from a query and is done with the WHERE clause. Figure 4.6 shows all rows with artists containing the vowel "a" in their names.

```
SELECT ARTIST_ID, NAME FROM ARTIST WHERE NAME LIKE '%a%';
```

Note: The percentage character (%) is used as a wild card character representing zero or more characters. Oracle SQL wild card characters used with the LIKE clause are explained in Chapter 5 under the heading "WHERE Clause Expression Conditions."

Figure 4.6
A filtered query.

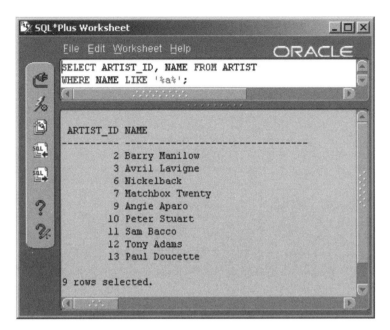

4.2.3 Sorted Query

Now let's sort. Figure 4.5 shows artists listed by their ARTIST_ID. The order in Figure 4.5 is not because of a unique key but because that is the order in which rows were inserted. Without an ORDER BY clause, the sorted order of a query depends on columns selected and other criteria such as the WHERE clause. Using the ORDER BY clause, Figure 4.7 shows artists re-sorted in the order of their names (the NAME column values). Now, the numbers in the ARTIST_ID column appear out of order.

```
SELECT ARTIST_ID, NAME FROM ARTIST ORDER BY NAME;
```

4.2.4 Grouping or Aggregated Query

Now let's do a grouping. The COUNT function in this example causes an aggregate or group on the COUNTRY column. The results are displayed in Figure 4.8 summary rows: one for each unique value found in the COUNTRY column.

```
SELECT COUNT(COUNTRY), COUNTRY FROM ARTIST GROUP BY COUNTRY;
```

Figure 4.7
A Sorted Query.

4.2.5 Join Query

The next query creates a join between the ARTIST and SONG tables. A join does not simply retrieve all rows from multiple tables but can match columns across tables. The result is shown in Figure 4.9, where 93 rows retrieved by the join is equal to the total number of songs in the SONGS table. The natural join joins the two tables on a column name or column

Figure 4.8
*A Grouping or
Aggregated Query.*

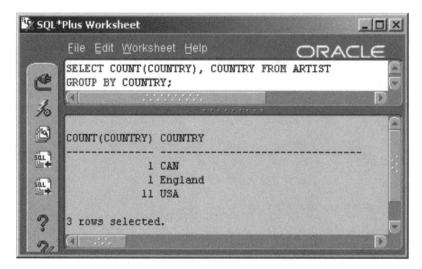

Figure 4.9
A Join Query.

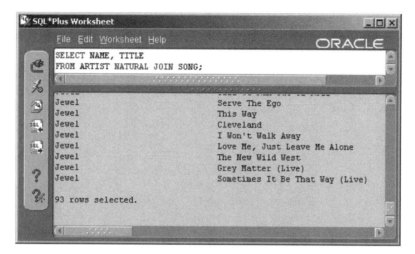

name sequence present in both tables. In this case, the natural join connected the two tables by matching values in the ARTIST_ID column found in both tables.

SELECT NAME, TITLE FROM ARTIST **NATURAL JOIN** SONG;

4.2.6 Subquery

The query containing the subquery shown in Figure 4.10 returns the same rows as the join query shown in Figure 4.9 but with only the title of the song. A subquery cannot be used to display values in the results set unless using a FROM clause embedded subquery, also known as an inline view.

```
SELECT TITLE FROM SONG WHERE ARTIST_ID IN
(SELECT ARTIST_ID FROM ARTIST);
```

4.2.7 Table or View Creation Query

We can create a new table using the join query from Figure 4.9. Selecting the data from the new view would produce the same result as the query in Figure 4.9:

```
CREATE VIEW SONGS AS
SELECT NAME, TITLE FROM ARTIST NATURAL JOIN SONG;
```

Figure 4.10
Using a Subquery.

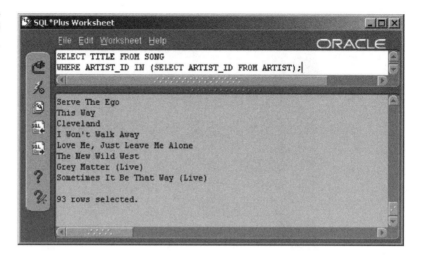

4.2.8 Hierarchical Query

Typically, hierarchical queries are used to retrieve data hierarchies placed into a single table. A common modern-day use for hierarchies is data that is obviously hierarchical in nature. Hierarchical data has parent rows containing closely related sibling rows, such as a family tree. In our case we can use the INSTRUMENT table in our MUSIC schema. Figure 4.11 shows a small section of this hierarchy.

This query will read a small section of the hierarchy including and contained within the Guitar node as shown in Figure 4.11. The result is shown in Figure 4.12.

```
SELECT LEVEL, SECTION_ID, NAME
FROM INSTRUMENT
START WITH NAME = 'Guitar'
CONNECT BY PRIOR INSTRUMENT_ID = SECTION_ID;
```

Figure 4.11
*The MUSIC
Schema
Instruments
Hierarchy.*

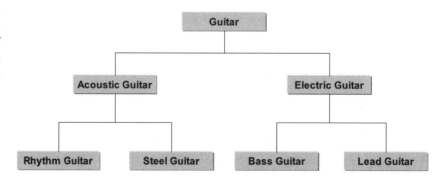

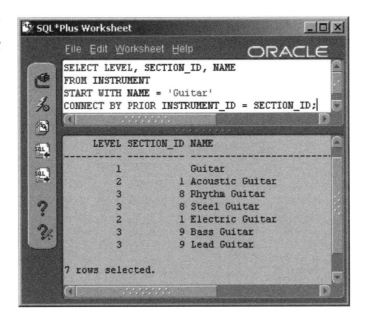

Figure 4.12
A Hierarchical Query.

We can improve on the query result from Figure 4.12 by altering it accordingly, showing the result in Figure 4.13.

```
SELECT LEVEL
, (SELECT NAME FROM INSTRUMENT
    WHERE INSTRUMENT_ID = I.SECTION_ID) "Section"
, I.NAME AS Instrument
```

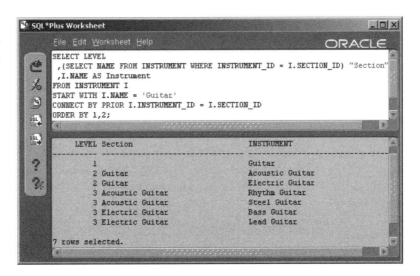

Figure 4.13
A Meaningful Hierarchical Query.

```
FROM INSTRUMENT I
START WITH I.NAME = 'Guitar'
CONNECT BY PRIOR I.INSTRUMENT_ID = I.SECTION_ID
ORDER BY 1,2;
```

4.2.9   Composite Queries

Composite queries use what are called set operators (UNION [ALL], INTERSECT, MINUS) to concatenate (add together) the results of multiple queries. Composite queries are not the same as joins. The following query would simply concatenate the results of the two queries as a UNION. The result would include all rows from both queries together in the result regardless of any relationship between the two tables.

```
SELECT NAME, ARTIST_ID FROM ARTIST
UNION
SELECT TITLE, SONG_ID FROM SONG;
```

Now that we have examined query types, let's look at some special aspects of queries.

4.3   Other Aspects of the SELECT Statement

Various other aspects of SELECT statements are important to remember:

- The DUAL table is a dummy or temporary table used to execute non-SQL-type commands with the SQL command interpreter.

- Using functions allows use of a large amount of built-in (provided) functionality or even custom-written functions.

- Arithmetic is allowed in SQL using standard arithmetic operators.

- The DISTINCT function allows retrieval of unique values from a row set containing duplicate values.

- Null values represent nothing. A space character and the value 0 are not the same as NULL. A null value is never an unknown value but is simply a value that has never been set.

- Pseudocolumns are special columns in Oracle Database that are covered in later chapters.

- Top-N queries allow restricting the number of rows to be returned from a row set by using the ROWNUM pseudocolumn in the WHERE clause.

- Parallel queries are special queries designed to run faster in parallel and are best executed on dual-CPU platforms, particularly with Oracle Partitioning.

4.3.1 The DUAL Table

All DML statements create implicit cursors. Cursors are memory chunks allocated for results of SQL statements. SELECT statements require a source for an implicit cursor to operate on. Some types of SELECT statements do not retrieve from any specific table. The DUAL table is a repository for an expression result applied to a single value, acting as a temporary repository for expression results, selected from the DUAL table.

The DUAL table can only be queried, never updated. The DUAL table is owned by SYS but can be queried by any user. DUAL is useful when you want to retrieve a constant or define a variable.

```
SELECT * FROM DUAL;
```

As you can see in Figure 4.14, the DUAL table contains a single column, a single row, and the value X in that single column. The column's

Figure 4.14
The DUAL Table Is Available for Special Use.

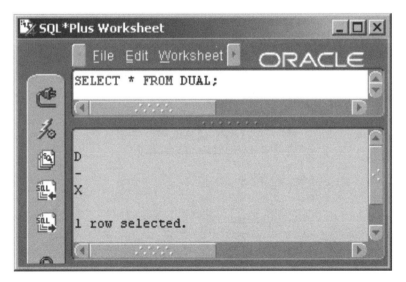

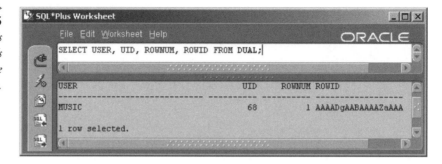

Figure 4.15
*None of This
Information Is
Found in the
DUAL Table.*

name is DUMMY, and it is a VARCHAR2(1) datatype. This does not seem like it helps much. However, the DUAL table can be used to view constant values, such as the USER and SYSDATE values. Because it returns one row, you only see these values once rather than many times (once for each row returned).

We could modify the previous query as follows. The result is shown in Figure 4.15.

```
SELECT USER, UID, ROWNUM, ROWID FROM DUAL;
```

Some other interesting examples are as follows, where the first joins the results from the DUAL table to a MUSIC schema table and the second outputs a string:

```
SELECT d.*, a.* FROM DUAL d, ARTIST a;
SELECT 'Hello World!' FROM DUAL;
```

The DUAL table is primarily used to retrieve values in a SELECT statement, where a value is retrieved such as in the following examples:

```
SELECT SYSDATE FROM DUAL;
SELECT USER FROM DUAL;
```

4.3.2 Using Functions

Functions can be placed in most parts of DML and SELECT statements. Using functions will nearly always affect performance adversely. This is especially true for custom-written functions. Even so, functions can provide enormous flexibility. Functions can be divided into the following listed groups. There will be much more on using functions in later chapters, primarily in Chapter 9 and Chapter 11.

- Single-row functions operate on one row at a time.

- Datatype conversion functions convert values such as numbers to strings.

- Group functions apply specific functionality to grouping and summary queries.

- Object reference functions reference data across objects.

- User-defined functions are custom-written functions for specific tasks not available in the functions that the Oracle Database provides.

An example function would be the use of the SUBSTR and INSTR function in the following example, retrieving the first word of each artist's name.

```
SELECT SUBSTR(NAME,1,INSTR(NAME,' ')) FROM ARTIST;
```

4.3.3   **Arithmetic Operations**

Let's use SYSDATE to calculate the time between a date stored in the database and today's date. The following query determines the number of days between the due date and today. Figure 4.16 shows the result.

```
SELECT AMOUNT_CHARGED - AMOUNT_PAID BALANCE, DUE_DATE
, SYSDATE, SYSDATE - DUE_DATE DAYS_LATE
FROM STUDIOTIME
WHERE AMOUNT_CHARGED > AMOUNT_PAID;
```

In Figure 4.16, there are two subtraction expressions in the SELECT clause:

- Subtracting two numbers (the AMOUNT_CHARGED and the AMOUNT_PAID).

- Subtracting two dates (the SYSDATE and the DUE_DATE). When you subtract dates, Oracle Database 10*g* will calculate the number of days between the two dates. Dates are stored internally as Julian dates and automatically converted with the default data display. A Julian date is a number in seconds from a specified date, such as January 1,

Figure 4.16
Date Arithmetic Made Easy.

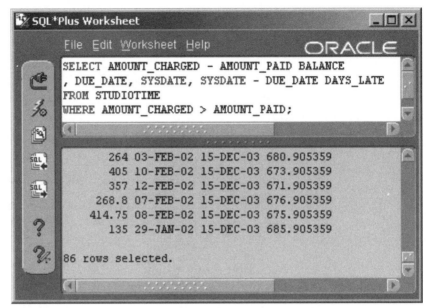

1970. The fractions you see in the results are the fraction of a day between the times in each date. Oracle Database 10*g* DATE datatypes contain both a date and a time.

4.3.4　Using DISTINCT

DISTINCT will retrieve the first value of each group in multiple groups containing duplicates. DISTINCT can operate on a single or multiple columns. General syntax for DISTINCT is as follows.

```
SELECT DISTINCT column [, column ... ] ...
SELECT DISTINCT (column [, column ... ]) ...
SELECT [ DISTINCT | ALL ] expression ...
```

Let's look at some examples using DISTINCT. Figure 4.17 shows the output for the first of the three example syntax options using DISTINCT.

```
SELECT DISTINCT COUNTRY FROM ARTIST;
```

The following query would find all unique combinations of the two columns STATE_PROVINCE and COUNTRY:

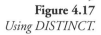

Figure 4.17
Using DISTINCT.

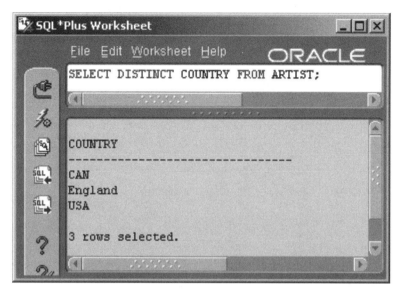

```
SELECT DISTINCT STATE_PROVINCE, COUNTRY FROM ARTIST;
```

The parentheses require a single concatenated string. Other functions could be used within the parentheses, so long as a single string or value is produced.

```
SELECT DISTINCT (STATE_PROVINCE||COUNTRY) FROM ARTIST;
```

SELECT ALL as opposed to SELECT DISTINCT is the default for the SELECT statement and is therefore seldom used. SELECT ALL simply lists all values, repeating or not, as opposed to only unique values.

4.3.5 **Null Values**

Some facts about null values are important to remember:

- NULL represents nothing, not a space, not a zero (0), or even an unknown value.
- A space character or a 0 value are not NULL.
- Null values are not included in binary tree (BTree) indexes.

- Most functions return null values when passed a null value.

- NULL can be tested for using the IS [NOT] NULL conditional operator.

- An expression containing a null value always returns a null value.

- The NVL (value, replace) function replaces null values in expressions, avoiding SQL errors. The SET NULL environment variable does the same thing in SQL*Plus.

- Null values sort as the highest value by default.

4.3.6   Using Pseudocolumns

One or two simple examples will suffice with respect to the SELECT statement. For example, the following query finds the ROWID (logical row pointer) and ROWNUM (returned row number in current query) for each row in the query. The result is shown in Figure 4.18.

```
SELECT ROWNUM, NAME, ROWID FROM ARTIST;
```

Figure 4.18
Using Pseudocolumns.

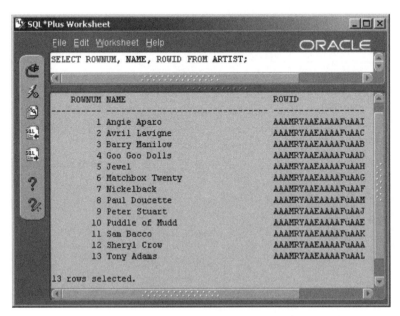

That is the basics of the SELECT statement, plus a few other small bits and pieces. Subsequent chapters will cover many of the details introduced in this chapter. This book is intended as a reference manual, building complexity piece by piece. The next chapter looks at filtering what is returned from a query.

5

Filtering Rows

In this chapter:

- How do you filter rows out of a query?

- What are conditional comparisons?

- What are logical operators?

This chapter extends the syntax of the SELECT statement by examining WHERE clause filtering, conditional comparisons, and logical operators. *Filtering* is a process of retrieving a subset of the rows retrieved by the SELECT statement.

5.1   WHERE Clause Syntax

We saw two of the primary parts (or clauses) of an SQL query in the previous chapter, namely the SELECT clause and the FROM clause. This chapter adds the WHERE clause. Here is a quick description of each clause:

- **SELECT.** List all the columns you want to see in your report here. Separate them with commas. Use an asterisk (*) instead of a list of columns to automatically show all columns in the queried table.

- **FROM.** Put the table name here. Use an alias for easier referencing in the SELECT and WHERE clauses.

- **WHERE (optional).** Adds conditions that filter out rows. Use various comparison conditions and logical operators between each filter. A query without a WHERE clause returns all rows.

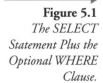

Figure 5.1
The SELECT Statement Plus the Optional WHERE Clause.

> Comparisons are symbols such as: = , > , >=, and operators such as: LIKE, IN, BETWEEN

SELECT { [schema.][table.]{ * | column } | [alias.]column | expression | [alias.]* [, ...] }

FROM [schema.]table [alias]

[WHERE

    [[schema.]table.|alias.] { column | expression }

    comparison condition [[schema.]table.|alias.] { column | expression }

    [{ AND | OR } [NOT] ...]

    ]

> Add pairs of columns with comparisons as needed

> Logical operators are used to join multiple conditions

Figure 5.1 shows the basic syntax of the SELECT statement including the WHERE clause. Examining the syntax diagram in Figure 5.1, we could do any of the following:

```
SELECT * FROM ARTIST WHERE ARTIST_ID = 1;
SELECT A.* FROM ARTIST A WHERE A.ARTIST_ID = 1;
SELECT * FROM MUSIC.ARTIST WHERE MUSIC.ARTIST.ARTIST_ID = 1;
SELECT A.* FROM MUSIC.ARTIST A WHERE A.ARTIST_ID = 1;
SELECT MUSIC.ARTIST.* FROM MUSIC.ARTIST
WHERE MUSIC.ARTIST.ARTIST_ID = 1;
SELECT ARTIST.* FROM MUSIC.ARTIST
WHERE MUSIC.ARTIST.ARTIST_ID = 1;
```

5.1.1   Some Simple WHERE Clause Examples

Here is a query with a very simple WHERE clause restricting by date:

```
SELECT S.TITLE, S.RECORDING_DATE
FROM SONG S
WHERE S.RECORDING_DATE > '01-JUL-2001';
```

The query asks for a report of songs (listing the titles and recording dates) that were recorded before July 1, 2001. Figure 5.2 shows the query and the results. Notice in the WHERE clause, we used a column on the left

Figure 5.2

Songs Are Listed Only if Matching WHERE Clause Conditions.

side of the comparison and a literal value on the right side. We can use literals, expressions (such as adding two number columns), or another column on either side of the condition.

Note: For the sake of performance, it is always best to use functions not on a side of the WHERE clause including a table or view column name.[1]

Figure 5.3 shows a diagram of how the WHERE clause works to filter out rows in the table. As you see in Figure 5.3, rows that meet the requirements are chosen, and those that fail the test are rejected.

The next example uses literals and expressions in the SELECT clause plus columns not listed in the SELECT clause inside the WHERE clause (columns not retrieved and displayed). In this query, the SELECT clause contains two literals (in single quotes) and two columns. Once again the column in the WHERE clause is not listed in the SELECT clause. Additionally, column headings are redundant and are disabled. Numerous other things could be done to make this query more easily readable. The result is shown in Figure 5.4.

```
SET HEADING OFF;
SELECT 'Song Name: ', S.TITLE
, 'Play time (M:SS): ', S.PLAYING_TIME
FROM SONG S
WHERE S.RECORDING_DATE > '01-JUL-2001';
```

More often than not, you will find that you need more than one filter or condition to obtain the information you seek in a query. The previous query can be augmented as such. The LIKE comparison operator compares

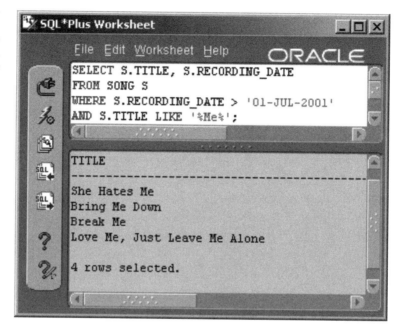

Figure 5.5
*A Second Filter
Reduces the Result
from 39 Rows to 4
Rows.*

the text in the TITLE column of each row with the text on the right side of the operator. The percentage signs (%) are wild cards. A wild card character matches any character or string of characters. So, any title containing "Me" anywhere within the song title will pass this test and be returned. The result is shown in Figure 5.5.

```
SELECT S.TITLE, S.RECORDING_DATE
FROM SONG S
WHERE S.RECORDING_DATE > '01-JUL-2001'
AND S.TITLE LIKE '%Me%';
```

That's enough examples for now. Let's look at how we can build WHERE clause comparisons between left and right sides of expressions. Followed by that we will examine joining together multiple compared sets using logical operators.

5.2   WHERE Clause Expression Conditions

Available in Oracle SQL are a number of what could be called *conditional comparisons*:

- Equi (=), anti (!=, <>), and range (<, >, =<, >=) comparison conditions are used between two expressions. A table column name is an expression.

```
expression [ = | != | > | < | >= | <= ] expression
```

For example:

```
SELECT * FROM ARTIST WHERE ARTIST_ID = 1;
SELECT * FROM ARTIST WHERE ARTIST_ID <> 1;
SELECT * FROM ARTIST WHERE ARTIST_ID <= 5;
```

A subquery is also an expression, so the following applies. This comparison condition allows a single-row subquery only. A single-row subquery returns a single row only. See Chapter 12 for details on subqueries.

```
(subquery) [ = | != | > | < | >= | <= ] (subquery)
```

- LIKE pattern-matches between strings, those strings being expressions. LIKE also requires single-row subqueries if used with a subquery.

```
expression LIKE expression
```

For example:

```
SELECT * FROM ARTIST WHERE NAME LIKE '%a%';
```

The percentage sign (%) and the underscore/underbar (_) characters are pattern-matching wild card characters. A wild card character can match any character. More specifically, the percentage sign (%) is used as a pattern-matching character representing zero or more characters in a subset of a string. The underscore/underbar character (_) is used to represent one and only one character. The previous query will find all artists with a letter "a" anywhere in their names. The next example will only find artists with a letter "a" in the second position of their names.

```
SELECT * FROM ARTIST WHERE NAME LIKE '_a%';
```

- IN set membership evaluates an expression as being within a set of elements. Because IN implies set membership, IN allows multiple-row returning subqueries.

```
expression [ NOT ] IN (expression)
```

IN is often used to check membership of one element in a list of elements. This example checks against a list of literal items:

```
SELECT NAME FROM ARTIST
WHERE COUNTRY IN ('USA', 'Canada');
```

This example uses a subquery to create the list for IN membership to check against:

```
SELECT NAME FROM ARTIST WHERE ARTIST_ID IN
(SELECT GUESTARTIST_ID FROM GUESTAPPEARANCE);
```

- EXISTS checks for membership as IN does with a few differences: (1) EXISTS only allows an expression on the left; (2) EXISTS is sometimes faster; and (3) probably most significantly, EXISTS allows a correlation and index matching between a calling query and a subquery. Like the IN condition, EXISTS implies set membership and allows multiple-row returning subqueries.

```
[ NOT ] EXISTS (expression)
```

Note: IN does allow passing of correlated values into subqueries but EXISTS is the more efficient option.[1]

In this example, the artist's name is retrieved whenever the artist is found in the GUESTAPPEARANCE table:

```
SELECT NAME FROM ARTIST WHERE EXISTS
(SELECT GUESTARTIST_ID FROM GUESTAPPEARANCE);
```

This example modifies the previous one such that a correlated value is passed from the calling query into the subquery. This effectively creates a link or correlation between calling query and subquery.

```
SELECT A.NAME FROM ARTIST A WHERE EXISTS
    (SELECT GUESTARTIST_ID FROM GUESTAPPEARANCE
  WHERE GUESTARTIST_ID  = A.ARTIST_ID);
```

Note: Queries using subqueries are sometimes called semi-joins when performing the same or a similar function as a join.

- BETWEEN validates an expression being between (inclusive of) two values, such that the first value should be less than the second. BETWEEN allows only single-row returning subqueries.

```
expression BETWEEN expression AND expression
```

```
SELECT NAME FROM ARTIST
WHERE ARTIST_ID BETWEEN 1 AND 10;
```

The next example would produce no result because there is nothing between 1 and 10 when starting the count at 10.

```
SELECT NAME FROM ARTIST
WHERE ARTIST_ID BETWEEN 10 AND 1;
```

Correct this by rewriting the statement as follows:

```
SELECT NAME FROM ARTIST
WHERE ARTIST_ID BETWEEN 1 AND 10;
```

- ANY, SOME, and ALL check set membership and allow subqueries that return multiple rows. ANY checks for membership of any element, and SOME looks for some elements. ANY and SOME are identical. ALL only returns a result if all elements in both expressions match; the two sets must be equal in size and content.

```
expression [ = | != | > | < | >= | <= ]
[ ANY | SOME | ALL ] expression
```

```
SELECT NAME FROM ARTIST WHERE ARTIST_ID = ANY
(SELECT GUESTARTIST_ID FROM GUESTAPPEARANCE);
```

Those are the conditional comparisons available in Oracle SQL. Now let's look at what I like to call logical operators.

5.3   Logical Operators in the WHERE Clause

Logical operators in Oracle SQL are AND, OR, and NOT. They work to concatenate multiple conditional expressions together. Precedence rules apply in that expressions are evaluated from left to right, unless overridden by parenthesised (bracketed) sections. NOT has higher precedence than AND, followed by OR. In the following example, the two TITLE column checks are bracketed and are thus evaluated first, followed by the RECORDING_DATE using AND. The result is shown in Figure 5.6.

```
SELECT TITLE, RECORDING_DATE FROM SONG
WHERE RECORDING_DATE > '01-JUL-2001'
AND (TITLE LIKE '%Me%' OR TITLE LIKE '%You%');
```

Removing the brackets in the following code snippet, as shown in Figure 5.7, can produce a spurious or meaningless result.

```
SELECT TITLE, RECORDING_DATE FROM SONG
WHERE RECORDING_DATE > '01-JUL-2001'
AND TITLE LIKE '%Me%' OR TITLE LIKE '%You%';
```

Next we look at Top-N queries.

5.4   Top-N Queries

Database tables grow as more and more data is added to them. One of the challenges of the DBA or application programmer is to be able to quickly assess the contents of large tables. This sometimes requires a query on thousands, even millions of rows. The Top-N query feature introduced in Oracle Database 9*i* provides the capability to retrieve small sections of a large table without having to write an application or use expensive third-party tools to dig into voluminous or copious amounts of data.

Figure 5.6
*The Bracketed
Expression Is
Evaluated First.*

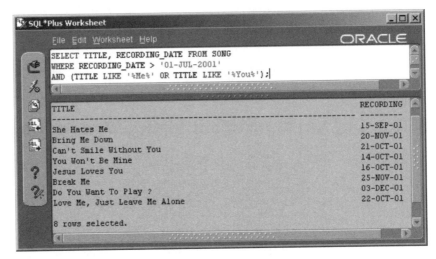

A Top-N query uses an Inline view and the ROWNUM pseudocolumn to retrieve data from a large table in a specified order. An Inline view is a type of subquery (see Chapter 12).

The following query looks at the recording date and title of songs in the SONG table. The query uses an Inline view in place of a table in the FROM clause.

```
SELECT RECORDING_DATE, TITLE
FROM (SELECT RECORDING_DATE, TITLE
   FROM SONG
   WHERE RECORDING_DATE <= '24-JAN-01'
   ORDER BY RECORDING_DATE);
```

Let's imagine that this table actually contains millions of rows and you only want to see the first 10 rows that were recorded the earliest. The rows will be sorted by date within the Inline view. By using the ROWNUM pseudocolumn in the main query, you can quickly retrieve only the first few rows of the table. Change the query to add the ROWNUM pseudocolumn in the WHERE clause. The complete query should look as follows with the change highlighted:

```
SELECT RECORDING_DATE, TITLE
FROM (SELECT RECORDING_DATE, TITLE
   FROM SONG
   WHERE RECORDING_DATE <= '24-JAN-01'
```

Figure 5.7
AND Has Higher Precedence than OR.

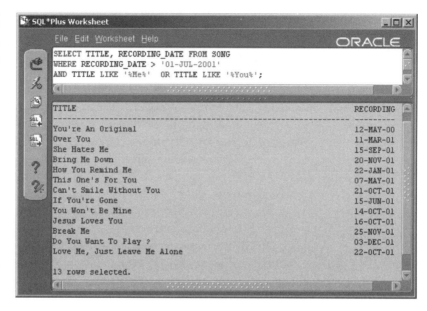

```
SQL*Plus Worksheet                                           _ |□| X |
  File  Edit  Worksheet  Help                          ORACLE
  SELECT TITLE, RECORDING_DATE FROM SONG
  WHERE RECORDING_DATE > '01-JUL-2001'
  AND TITLE LIKE '%Me%'  OR TITLE LIKE '%You%';

  TITLE                                          RECORDING
  -----------------------------------------      ---------
  You're An Original                             12-MAY-00
  Over You                                        11-MAR-01
  She Hates Me                                    15-SEP-01
  Bring Me Down                                   20-NOV-01
  How You Remind Me                               22-JAN-01
  This One's For You                              07-MAY-01
  Can't Smile Without You                         21-OCT-01
  If You're Gone                                  15-JUN-01
  You Won't Be Mine                               14-OCT-01
  Jesus Loves You                                 16-OCT-01
  Break Me                                        25-NOV-01
  Do You Want To Play ?                           03-DEC-01
  Love Me, Just Leave Me Alone                    22-OCT-01

  13 rows selected.
```

```
ORDER BY RECORDING_DATE)
WHERE ROWNUM <= 10;
```

Thus the query retrieves the Top-N or first *n* (first 10) rows of the query in the Inline view. Use Top-N queries, for instance, in a large data warehouse database where you simply want a sample of the data.

The only additional issue worth mentioning is that a Top-N query only retrieves the first *n* rows and cannot be used to retrieve the last *n* rows. Therefore, changing the WHERE clause to the following query would run successfully, but no rows would be returned.

```
WHERE ROWNUM > 10;
```

That more or less covers the basics of WHERE clause filtering of SELECT statement results. There are a few other points to remember about using WHERE clauses:

■ The WHERE clause is evaluated before the result of a row set being returned. In other words, the WHERE clause is applied to and affects physical input/output (I/O) disk reads. The WHERE clause can therefore affect SELECT statement performance drastically because it can help determine how much data the SELECT statement retrieves physically from disk.

- In general terms, indexes are physically shortened, presorted versions of table rows. A WHERE clause can allow the use of specific indexes both for reading data and for applying inherent index sorts (presorted). Therefore, WHERE clause expression orders can be extremely important to performance, particularly when matching indexes or, more specifically, attempting to utilize and take advantage of physical data ordering already available in an index. In Oracle Database 9*i*, Oracle Database 10*g*, and beyond, the Optimizer is intelligent to the point that WHERE clause expression sequences can even ignore case sensitivity to a certain extent. However, strict adherence to SQL coding standards is still advisable. Simply put, structuring WHERE clauses in the right manner can make SQL code enormously less complex and potentially much more efficient.

That is enough about the WHERE clause for now. The next chapter deals with sorting query results and the ORDER BY clause.

5.5   Endnotes

1.   Oracle Performance Tuning for 9*i* and 10*g* (ISBN: 1-55558-305-9)

6

Sorting Rows

In this chapter:

- How are rows in queries sorted both manually and automatically?
- How are null values affected when sorting rows?
- What are the types of sorting methods for the ORDER BY clause?

This chapter extends the syntax of the SELECT statement by examining ORDER BY clause sorting and the various detailed aspects of SELECT statement ORDER BY clauses.

6.1 ORDER BY Clause Syntax

Previous chapters have examined the SELECT, FROM, and WHERE clauses. This chapter adds the ORDER BY clause to the SELECT statement. Here is a quick description of each clause:

- **SELECT.** List all the columns you want to see in your report here. Separate them with commas. Use an asterisk (*) instead of a list of columns to automatically show all columns in the queried table.
- **FROM.** Put the table name here. Use an alias for easier referencing in the other clauses.
- **WHERE (optional).** Add conditions that filter out rows from your report here. Use various comparison conditions and logical operators between each filter. A query without a WHERE clause returns all rows.

- **ORDER BY (optional)**. Add sorting parameters, allowing rows to be rearranged in a specified order.

Sorting query results helps make your report more readable and useful. For example, it is very useful to list people in alphabetical order by last name. The ORDER BY clause of the SELECT statement provides sorting capability.

You can sort by any column or expression you use in your SELECT clause. In addition, you can sort by any column in the table (or any expression based on any column) you are querying, even if the column is not selected. You can sort by up to 255 columns or expressions in one SELECT statement.

The ORDER BY clause appears after the WHERE clause. Figure 6.1 shows the syntax with comments explaining the parts.

Note: The ORDER BY clause is an optional clause, as is the WHERE clause. You can have an ORDER BY clause without a WHERE clause and vice versa.

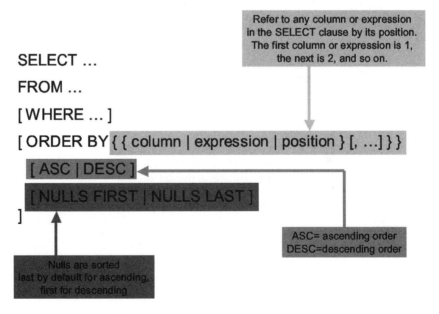

Figure 6.1
The SELECT Statement Optional ORDER BY Clause.

6.1.1   Some Simple ORDER BY Clause Examples

Here's an example query with no ORDER BY clause:

```
SELECT A.NAME "Artist", S.DUE_DATE
, SYSDATE — S.DUE_DATE DAYS_LATE
, S.AMOUNT_CHARGED — S.AMOUNT_PAID BALANCE
FROM ARTIST A NATURAL JOIN STUDIOTIME S
WHERE S.AMOUNT_CHARGED > S.AMOUNT_PAID;
```

If you want to sort the results by DUE_DATE, you could simply add this ORDER BY clause:

```
ORDER BY S.DUE_DATE;
```

Note: The column in the ORDER BY clause is referenced by its table alias, "S".

The default order is ascending. Figure 6.2 shows the query and results in ascending order by DUE_DATE.

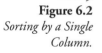

Figure 6.2
Sorting by a Single Column.

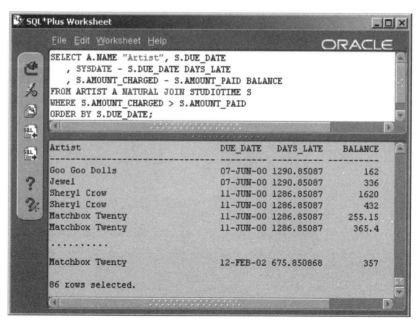

Now add the BALANCE column to the ORDER BY list. This time, you want to first sort by DUE_DATE and then by BALANCE within DUE_DATE. BALANCE can be sorted in descending order. This way, the top of your report shows you which artists owe you the most money for the longest amount of time. The ORDER BY clause can be changed as shown:

```
ORDER BY DUE_DATE, BALANCE DESC;
```

Note: The column alias is not included in this code snippet. An alias is optional in the ANSI standard natural join. Joins are covered in Chapter 10.

Figure 6.3 shows the query and results in descending order of BALANCE within ascending order by DUE_DATE.

That covers the basics of sorting in ascending order, descending order, and using one or more columns. Now let's look at some slightly more complex aspects of sorting. We begin with looking at the behavior of null values when sorting.

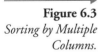

Figure 6.3
Sorting by Multiple Columns.

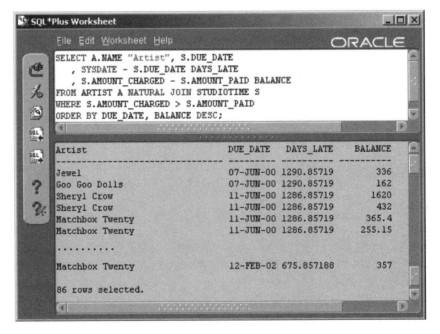

6.2   Sorting and Null Values

Null values, by definition, have an unknown value, so they cannot be logically placed in any order. To handle null values, Oracle Database 10*g* has established the following default sorting rules for null values:

- If the column containing null values is being sorted in ascending order, the rows with null values are listed at the end.
- If the column containing null values is being sorted in descending order, the rows with null values are listed at the beginning.

You can reverse either of these rules by using the NULLS FIRST or NULLS LAST keywords in your ORDER BY clause. Let's show how null values and sorting interact. This query retrieves songs with titles that start with A, B, or C and sorts by the playing time.

```
SELECT RECORDING_DATE, PLAYING_TIME, TITLE
FROM SONG
WHERE TITLE BETWEEN 'A' and 'C'
ORDER BY PLAYING_TIME;
```

Figure 6.4 shows the result. Notice that the rows with null values in PLAYING_TIME appear last in the list, using the default ascending (ASC) order.

Now we can add the NULLS FIRST parameter to the ORDER BY clause and run the query again.

```
ORDER BY PLAYING_TIME NULLS FIRST;
```

Figure 6.5 shows the result. Notice that the rows with null values in PLAYING_TIME now appear first in the list.

Remember that when you add comparisons in the WHERE clause, null values do not match unless you specifically handle them. For example, the next variation adds a WHERE clause to the query that looks for songs with playing times of less than four minutes.

Figure 6.4
*Null Values Are
Output Last when
Using Ascending
Sort Order.*

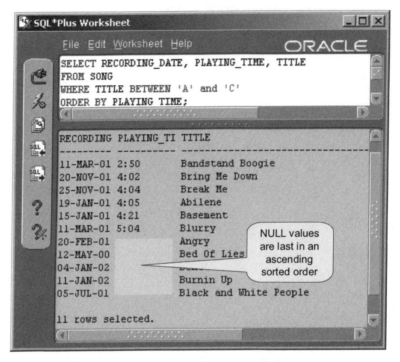

Figure 6.5
*Null Values Move
to the Top of the
List when Using
NULLS FIRST.*

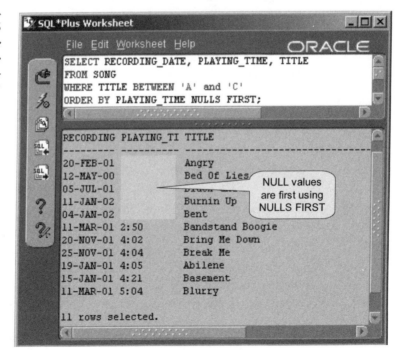

Figure 6.6
*Null Values Are
Never Greater or
Less Than Any
Value.*

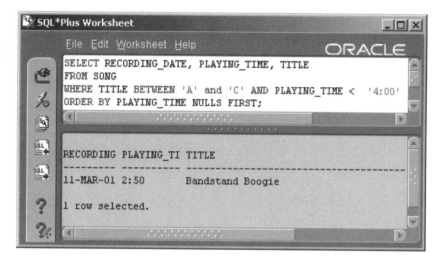

```
SELECT RECORDING_DATE, PLAYING_TIME, TITLE
FROM SONG
WHERE TITLE BETWEEN 'A' and 'C'
AND PLAYING_TIME <  '4:00'
ORDER BY PLAYING_TIME NULLS FIRST;
```

Figure 6.6 shows the result of the previous query. All of the rows containing a null value in the PLAYING_TIME column were eliminated because a null value cannot be compared successfully to a non-null value.

There are two ways to handle null values in the WHERE clause:

- Use the IS NULL comparison operator to retrieve null value rows.
- Use the NVL function to convert null values before comparing them.

Let's try them both. First, we add another comparison to the WHERE clause to handle null values:

```
WHERE TITLE BETWEEN 'A' and 'C'
AND (PLAYING_TIME  < '4:00' OR PLAYING_TIME IS NULL)
```

Figure 6.7 shows the result such that one row has a playing time less than four minutes, and five rows have null values in the PLAYING_TIME column.

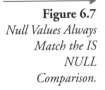
Figure 6.7
*Null Values Always
Match the IS
NULL
Comparison.*

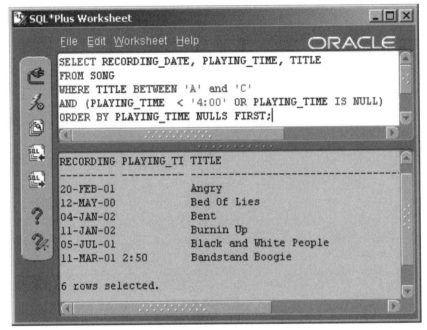

Second, we can add an NVL function to convert any row with null values in the PLAYING_TIME column to some value before comparing it. Let's make a null value equal to zero playing time. Change the WHERE clause as shown. The resulting query will have the same result as that in Figure 6.7 where null values are converted to a literal before the comparison.

```
WHERE TITLE BETWEEN 'A' and 'C'
AND NVL(PLAYING_TIME,'0:00') < '4:00'
```

One point to note about using the NVL function is that you must use an expression (an expression can be a literal value) that matches the datatype of the original column. For example, the code snippet below is invalid because the literal cannot be translated into a date. There is no such date with a value UNKNOWN.

```
NVL(RECORDING_DATE,'UNKNOWN')
```

Now let's look at some different types of sorting methods, in addition to sorting by single or multiple column names.

6.3   Sorting Methods

Other than sorting by single or multiple column names, the ORDER BY clause can be used to sort in two other ways:

- Sorting by position sorts by the position of a column or expression within the SELECT statement columns list.

- Sorting by expression allows the ORDER BY clause to contain an expression such as a calculation.

6.3.1   Sorting by Position

The following query sorts in order of the second column, the third column, and the first column. What's that in English? PLAYING_TIME by TITLE by RECORDING_DATE or RECORDING_DATE sorted within TITLE, sorted within PLAYING_TIME.

Note: Optional modifiers such as NULLS FIRST and DESC apply individually to each sorted column in the ORDER BY clause.

Figure 6.8 shows the result.

```
SELECT RECORDING_DATE, PLAYING_TIME, TITLE
FROM SONG
WHERE TITLE LIKE '%a%'
AND TITLE LIKE '%e%'
AND TITLE LIKE '%i%'
ORDER BY 2 NULLS FIRST, 3 DESC, 1;
```

There are several points to take note of in Figure 6.8, including the three annotations:

- The PLAYING_TIME column (position 2) has NULLS FIRST and thus null values are listed at the top.
- The TITLE column (position 3) is sorted within the PLAYING_TIME column (position 2) in descending (DESC) order.

Figure 6.8
*Sorting Using
SELECT List
Column Position
Numbers.*

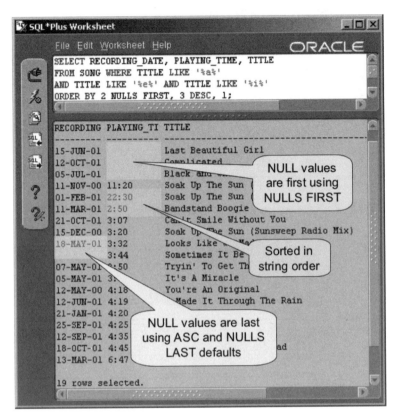

This is evident for the first three null-valued PLAYING_TIME column rows where titles appear in reverse alphabetical order.

- The PLAYING_TIME column has a side issue where PLAYING_TIME is sorted as a string. The fifth and sixth rows are sorted in the wrong order numerically. We will get to this shortly when using expressions in the ORDER BY clause.

- The RECORDING_DATE column (position 3) is last in the sorted order using the default ASC and NULLS LAST options (no modifiers). This is not apparent in the output of Figure 6.8 because there are no duplicate values in the RECORDING_DATE column for this particular output row set.

- As already noted, each modifier such as NULLS FIRST and DESC applies to each individual sorted column in the ORDER BY clause, not to all ORDER BY columns as a whole.

Now let's examine using expressions in the ORDER BY clause.

6.3.2 **Sorting by Expression**

Now let's make the query shown in Figure 6.8 a little more complex, utilizing an expression in the ORDER BY clause for the same query. In Figure 6.8, the PLAYING_TIME column (position 2) was sorted as a string. A more sensible result would require an expression converting that string to a number. Expressions can include built-in SQL functions or even user-defined functions. This is the query used in Figure 6.8.

Note: Using expressions in the ORDER BY clause can hurt performance.[1]

```
SELECT RECORDING_DATE, PLAYING_TIME, TITLE
FROM SONG
WHERE TITLE LIKE '%a%'
AND TITLE LIKE '%e%'
AND TITLE LIKE '%i%'
ORDER BY 2 NULLS FIRST, 3 DESC, 1;
```

This is the change for the ORDER BY clause of the query sorting the PLAYING_TIME column numerically, using a straightforward expression:

```
ORDER BY
TO_NUMBER(SUBSTR(PLAYING_TIME,1
,INSTR(PLAYING_TIME,':')-1))
   + TO_NUMBER(SUBSTR(PLAYING_TIME
,INSTR(PLAYING_TIME,':')+1))/60
NULLS FIRST, 3 DESC, 1;
```

Straightforward, I said. That is just nasty! That example does not really look straightforward, now does it? Let's make this a little easier, or perhaps just a little better organized, utilizing a user-defined function (see Chapter 24).

```
CREATE OR REPLACE FUNCTION GETTIME (pTIME IN VARCHAR2)
  RETURN NUMBER IS
    vSPLIT INTEGER DEFAULT 0;
    vHOURS INTEGER DEFAULT 0;
    vSECONDS INTEGER DEFAULT 0;
```

```
BEGIN
   vSPLIT := INSTR(pTIME,':');
   vHOURS := TO_NUMBER(SUBSTR(pTIME,1,vSPLIT-1));
   vSECONDS := TO_NUMBER(SUBSTR(pTIME,vSPLIT+1));
   RETURN vHOURS+(vSECONDS/60);
EXCEPTION WHEN OTHERS THEN
   RETURN 0;
END;
/
```

And now we can replace the ORDER BY clause with the function as an expression, making for a much easier to read ORDER BY clause. The result is shown in Figure 6.9.

```
ORDER BY GETTIME(PLAYING_TIME) NULLS FIRST, 3 DESC, 1;
```

Figure 6.9
Using an Expression in the ORDER BY Clause.

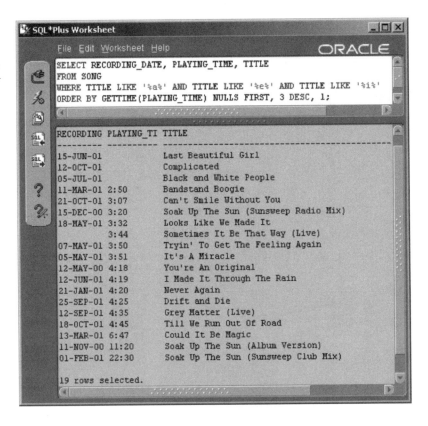

Obviously, a position number cannot be applied to the expression unless the expression is placed into the SELECT list.

Note: Copying the expression from the ORDER BY into the SELECT columns list could possibly help performance.

We can change the query something like that shown following. The expression GETTIME(PLAYING_TIME) has been added to the query, and the ORDER BY clause has been changed to accommodate it. The result in Figure 6.10 shows the same sorted order on the PLAYING_TIME column value as shown in Figure 6.9.

```
SELECT RECORDING_DATE, PLAYING_TIME, GETTIME(PLAYING_TIME)
, TITLE
FROM SONG
WHERE TITLE LIKE '%a%'
AND TITLE LIKE '%e%'
AND TITLE LIKE '%i%'
ORDER BY 3 NULLS FIRST, 4 DESC, 1;
```

Figure 6.10
ORDER BY Clause Expressions Cannot Use Positions.

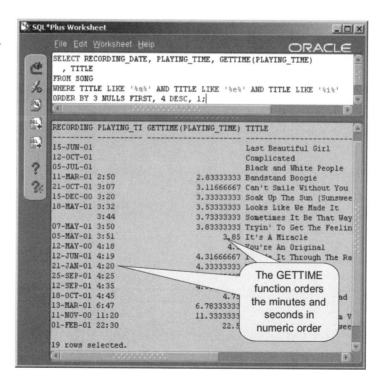

You have now added most of the fundamental features to the SELECT statement, namely the SELECT, FROM, WHERE, and ORDER BY clauses. Later chapters expand on a multitude of other features and mechanisms. The next chapter digresses somewhat and covers operators, conditions, and pseudocolumns.

6.4   Endnotes

1.   Oracle Performance Tuning for 9*i* and 10*g* (ISBN: 1-55558-305-9)

7

Operators, Conditions, and Pseudocolumns

In this chapter:

- What is precedence?

- What is an operator and what is available?

- What is a condition and what is available?

- What are pseudocolumns and what is available?

Note: Backus-Naur Form syntax angle brackets are used syntactically in this chapter to represent substitution of all types. For example, <expression> = <expression>.

Operators, conditions, and pseudocolumns are used and often explained throughout this book. This chapter may duplicate parts of other chapters with the intention of including all specific details in a single chapter. Additionally, some of the content of this chapter is common to many software products. Need it be repeated? Yes, because this title is intended for use as an SQL reference book.

Note: This chapter may reclassify the categories of operators, conditions, and pseudocolumns both with respect to Oracle documentation and other chapters in this book.

Let's begin with the simplest of things, precedence.

7.1   **Precedence**

One factor important with regards to both operators and conditions is that of precedence. Precedence implies that one operator is executed before another. Enclosing part of an expression in brackets (parentheses in mathematical jargon) forces that part of the expression to be executed first, starting with the lowest nested or parenthesized level. Let's look at arithmetic operator precedence to explain this concept.

In this first example expression, the multiplication will execute before the addition because multiplication has higher precedence than (is executed before) addition, even though reading from left to right, addition appears before multiplication.

```
x + y × z
```

Now let's fix the precedence problem and force addition to execute first by using parentheses.

```
( x + y ) × z
```

Similarly applying nesting of precedence in the next example, the subtraction will be executed first, followed by the addition and finally the multiplication, regardless of the precedence of the different operators.

```
( x + ( y - p )) × z
```

That is precedence. Simple, right? Now let's go onto operators.

7.2   **Operators**

Operators can be divided into several groups, as shown following:

- Arithmetic operators allow things like 1 + 1 or 5 * 3, where + and * are the arithmetic operators.

- Logical operators allow merging of multiple expressions.

- The concatenation operator is the || goodie allowing concatenation of strings.

- Hierarchical query operators are specialized for use in hierarchical queries.

- Set operators literally do things with sets of rows.

- Multiset operators are set operators exclusively for use with nested table objects.

- User-defined operators allow creation of your own operators.

7.2.1 **Arithmetic Operators**

An arithmetic operator allows for simple arithmetic calculations in the form shown:

```
<expression> <operator> <expression>
```

■ * and / execute multiplication and division, respectively, both having the same precedence and both having higher precedence than addition and subtraction.

■ + and – execute addition and subtraction, respectively, both having the same precedence.

This example shows use of an arithmetic operator in a SELECT statement producing the "Owed" column. The result is shown in Figure 7.1

```
SELECT ARTIST_ID, SESSION_DATE, AMOUNT_CHARGED, AMOUNT_PAID
, AMOUNT_CHARGED - AMOUNT_PAID "Owed"
FROM STUDIOTIME;
```

Figure 7.1
Arithmetic
Operators.

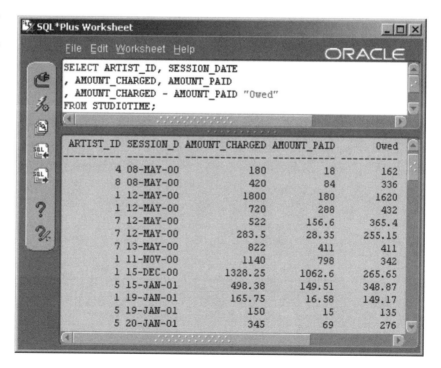

7.2.2 **Logical Operators**

Logical operators are NOT, AND, and OR, in that order of precedence. NOT implies that an expression must be false for a TRUE result; AND implies that two expressions must be true for a TRUE result; and OR implies that either of two expressions must be true for a TRUE result. There are more examples in Chapter 5.

- <expression> AND <expression> such that both expressions yield TRUE. This example finds artists whose names contain the vowel "a" and who live in the USA. Both conditions must be true for a row to be returned. The result is shown in Figure 7.2.

```
SELECT NAME, COUNTRY FROM ARTIST
WHERE COUNTRY = 'USA' AND NAME LIKE '%a%';
```

Figure 7.2
The AND Logical Operator.

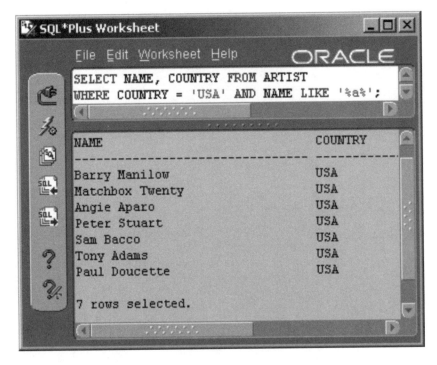

Figure 7.3
*The OR Logical
Operator.*

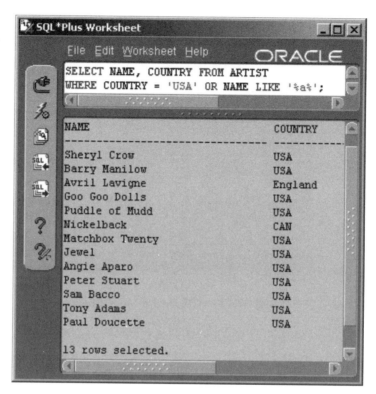

- <expression> OR <expression> such that either expression yields TRUE. This example is the same as the last except that either expression can be true. The result in Figure 7.3 shows any artists either in the USA or with the vowel "a" in their names.

```
SELECT NAME, COUNTRY FROM ARTIST
WHERE COUNTRY = 'USA' OR NAME LIKE '%a%';
```

- <expression> { AND | OR } NOT <expression> yields TRUE if both expressions (AND), or either (OR), yield TRUE. Figure 7.4 shows artists in the USA as long as the vowel "a" is not in their names.

```
SELECT NAME, COUNTRY FROM ARTIST
WHERE COUNTRY = 'USA' AND NOT NAME LIKE '%a%';
```

Figure 7.4
*The NOT Logical
Operator.*

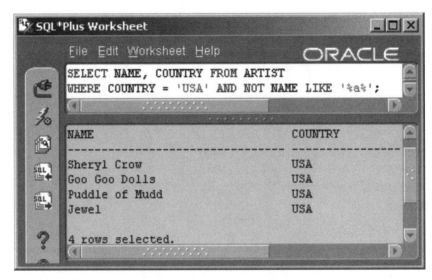

7.2.3 The Concatenation Operator

The concatenation operator (||) allows concatenation of strings. The example following concatenates two strings from two separate tables in an SQL join (see Chapter 10). The result is shown in Figure 7.5.

```
SELECT NAME||' WROTE '||TITLE
FROM ARTIST NATURAL JOIN SONG
WHERE TITLE LIKE '%A%';
```

7.2.4 Hierarchical Query Operators

There are two hierarchical query operators, which are discusssed in more detail with examples in Chapter 13.

- PRIOR is used with the CONNECT BY condition evaluating the subsequent expression for each parent row of each current row, using a current row column to hook into a parent row column.

- (10g) CONNECT_BY_ROOT performs a similar function to that of CONNECT BY PRIOR except using the root row of the hierarchy as opposed to the parent row.

Figure 7.5
*The Concatenation
(||) Operator.*

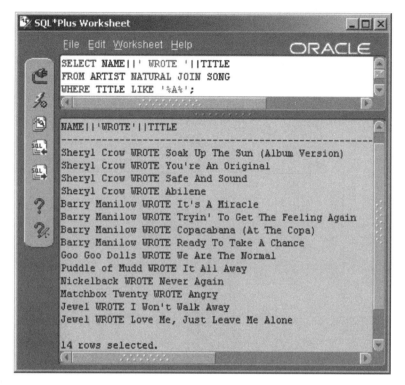

7.2.5 Set Operators

The various set operators effectively allow the merging of results of two separate queries in the form of <query> operator <query> (more detail and examples in Chapter 13).

- UNION [ALL] retrieves all rows in both queries. The ALL modifier includes all duplicates; otherwise only unique rows are retrieved.

- INTERSECT returns the intersection of two queries, namely rows common to both queries.

- MINUS returns all unique rows in the first query but not in the second query.

7.2.6 (10g) Multiset Operators

Where set operators do things with query results of two queries, multiset operators perform a similar function between two nested tables. Requirements are that the two nested tables must be of the same type, and thus returning the same nested table type as well. All options default to ALL but can return only DISTINCT values as well.

- MULTISET EXCEPT returns exceptions in the first nested table and not in the second, returning a nested table containing elements in the first and not the second nested table.

```
<nested table> MULTISET EXCEPT [ DISTINCT | ALL ]
<nested table>
```

For example, the following procedure will output elements in nested table P1 but not in nested table P2, namely the string "one":

```
DECLARE
    TYPE PCOLL IS TABLE OF VARCHAR2(32);
    P1 PCOLL := PCOLL('one','two','three');
    P2 PCOLL := PCOLL('two','three','four');
    P3 PCOLL;
BEGIN
    P3 := P1 MULTISET EXCEPT P2;
    FOR i IN P3.FIRST..P3.LAST LOOP
        DBMS_OUTPUT.PUT_LINE(P3(i));
    END LOOP;
END;
/
```

- MULTISET INTERSECT returns the intersection of two nested tables or, in other words, elements common to both.

```
<nested table> MULTISET INTERSECT [ DISTINCT | ALL ]
<nested table>
```

- MULTISET UNION returns all elements in both.

```
<nested table> MULTISET UNION [ DISTINCT | ALL ]
<nested table>
```

Note: Nested tables are covered in Chapter 16.

7.2.7 User-Defined Operators

User-defined operators can be created using the DDL CREATE OPERA-TOR command.

The next thing to look at is conditions.

7.3 Conditions

A *condition* is a condition or state of the result of an expression. Because a state is implied, a condition will return a Boolean result of TRUE or FALSE, indicating something being on or off. Conditions can be divided into the following listed groups:

- *Comparison* compares expressions as shown (see Chapter 5):

    ```
    <expression> condition <expression>
    ```

    Set membership using IN and EXISTS is a type of comparison in that it verifies membership of an expression in a set of values. Once again, examples are in Chapter 5.

    ```
    <expression> member (<expression>, …, <expression>)
    ```

- (10g) The *floating-point condition* allows checking for a number as being defined or undefined. The syntax is as follows such that NAN represents Not A Number and INFINITE is undefined.

    ```
    <expression> IS [ NOT ] { INFINITE | NAN }
    ```

- A NULL can be tested for using the NULL conditional comparison.

    ```
    <expression> IS [ NOT ] NULL
    ```

    In the example shown following, three different counts are made counting songs with playing times not yet entered into the database and not entered as zero or a space character. The sum of the row counts returned by the second and third queries is identical to the first query's row count. The result is shown in Figure 7.6.

    ```
    SELECT COUNT(*) FROM SONG;
    SELECT COUNT(*) FROM SONG WHERE PLAYING_TIME IS NULL;
    ```

Figure 7.6
*The IS NULL
Comparison
Condition.*

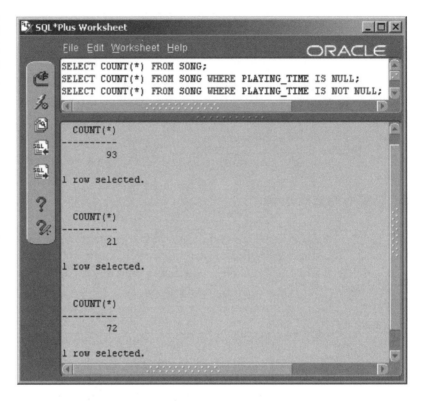

```
SELECT COUNT(*) FROM SONG
WHERE PLAYING_TIME IS NOT NULL;
```

■ XML conditions are EQUALS_PATH and UNDER_PATH.
  EQUALS_PATH searches the entire path from the root node of an
  XML object and UNDER_PATH a relative path. A relative path
  begins at a specified node in an XML structure.

```
EQUALS_PATH (<column>, <path>) = <expression>
UNDER_PATH (<column> [, levels], <path>)
= <expression>
```

  See Chapter 17 for more detail on using XML in Oracle SQL.

■ Object collection conditions are as follows (see Chapter 16 for more
  detail on nested tables):

- ⑩*g* IS A SET implies that a collection is a set because it contains unique values only.

  ```
  <nested table> IS [NOT] A SET
  ```

- ⑩*g* IS EMPTY checks for an empty collection, a nested table containing no elements whatsoever, essentially a collection not as yet instantiated.

  ```
  <nested table> IS [NOT] EMPTY
  ```

- ⑩*g* MEMBER OF attempts to validate membership within a collection.

  ```
  <expression> [NOT] MEMBER OF <nested table>
  ```

- ⑩*g* SUBMULTISET indicates if one or more collection items are a subset of another collection.

  ```
  <nested table> [NOT] SUBMULTISET [OF]

  <nested table>
  ```

- IS OF TYPE checks object datatypes.

  ```
  <expression> IS [NOT] OF [TYPE].
  ```

- ⑩*g* Equality and inequality. Nested tables and VARRAY collections can be compared using equality (=) and inequality operators (!=, <>).

- ⑩*g* REGEXP_LIKE utilizes regular expressions as opposed to simple pattern matching (see Chapter 14).

  ```
  <regular expression> REGEXP_LIKE (<source>

  , <pattern>, <match>)
  ```

- ⑩*g* The SPREADSHEET clause extends the SELECT statement allowing for calculations between cells and rows (see Chapter 11).

  - IS ANY qualifies SPREADSHEET clause dimensional values.

    ```
    <dimension> IS ANY
    ```

  - IS PRESENT ensures that a cell exists before the execution of a SPREADSHEET clause.

    ```
    <cell> IS PRESENT
    ```

7.4   **Pseudocolumns**

Pseudocolumns are virtual columns or expression calculators, the expression being a constant or another expression. To use a pseudocolumn, you simply name it in the SQL statement. You can select a pseudocolumn or use it in an expression or WHERE clause. You cannot insert, update, or delete the value in a pseudocolumn.

Note: Contrary to popular belief, values such as SYSDATE, SYSTIMES-TAMP, USER, and UID are not pseudocolumns but built-in functions.

Table 7.1 lists available pseudocolumns.

Table 7.1   *Pseudocolumns in Oracle Database.*

Classification	Pseudocolumn	Purpose
	`ROWID`	A relative pointer to a row in the database based on logical and physical database objects. A concatenated set of numbers and letters comprising relative address pointers to a tablespace, a datafile block within a tablespace, a row within a block, and a tablespace datafile number. May also contain a different format if the row is located outside the database.
	`ROWNUM`	The sequence number of each row retrieved in a query. Note that ROWNUM is evaluated after a WHERE clause (before the ORDER BY clause). The first row is 1, and so on.
Sequences	`<sequence>.CURRVAL`	Retrieves the current value of a sequence and must be defined for the session first with NEXTVAL. See Chapter 22.
Sequences	`<sequence>.NEXTVAL`	Retrieves the next value of a sequence. Used to increment a sequence. See Chapter 22.
Hierarchical	`LEVEL`	Used only in hierarchical queries (using the CONNECT BY clause). This returns the level (1, 2, etc.) of the row. See Chapter 13.
Hierarchical	(10*g*) `CONNECT_BY_{IS[LEAF|CYCLE]}`	These pseudocolumns determine if hierarchical data can be expanded upon. Does an element have ancestor and/or child entries? More on this in Chapter 13.

Table 7.1 *Pseudocolumns in Oracle Database. (continued)*

XML	XMLDATA	Special holder for XML data to allow modifications of storage parameters. XML will be covered in detail in Chapter 17.
Flashback	(10g) VERSIONS_{…}	There are six different flashback version query pseudocolumns. See Chapter 13.
	OBJECT_ID	Column object identifier.
	OBJECT_VALUE	System-generated column names.

That more or less covers any referential information on operators, conditions, and pseudocolumns. The next chapter covers more detail using SQL*Plus, particularly with respect to formatting. Further SQL*Plus output formatting detail is essential to proper use and understanding of Oracle SQL.

8

*Using SQL*Plus*

In this chapter:

- What are environmental settings for SQL*Plus formatting?

- How are variables used in SQL*Plus?

- How are scripts used in SQL*Plus?

- How are reports formatted in SQL*Plus?

- How is iSQL*Plus used for reporting?

This chapter shows you how to use the environmental settings, variables, and special SQL*Plus commands to generate acceptable output and reports. Examples in this book use both SQL*Plus Worksheet and SQL*Plus. SQL*Plus Worksheet is more of an end-user tool. A final part of this chapter shows some brief example use of iSQL*Plus.

Let's start by looking at some environmental settings.

8.1   Environmental Settings

An environmental variable is set for the duration of a session using the SET command or as a default.

Note: Defaults can be set for SQL*Plus in the GLOGIN.SQL configuration file in the $ORACLE_HOME/sqlplus/admin directory.

The SET command changes the value of an environmental variable, and the SHOW command displays its value. Detailed information on available environmental variables is available in Oracle documentation.

SQL*Plus has a group of settings that define various aspects of your working environment. These settings, as a group, are called *environmental settings*. For example, the default setting for the width of the screen output is 1,024 characters when using SQL*Plus Worksheet.

There are well in excess of 70 different environmental variables you can set. Most environmental variables are SQL*Plus variables you adjust for your Oracle Database 10*g* session and can only be used with SQL*Plus tools (i.e., SQL*Plus, SQL*Plus Worksheet, and iSQL*Plus).

Look at the entire list by running the following statement in SQL*Plus Worksheet:

```
SHOW ALL
```

Figure 8.1 shows part of the results.

Figure 8.1

Environmental Variables, Settings, and Some Explanations.

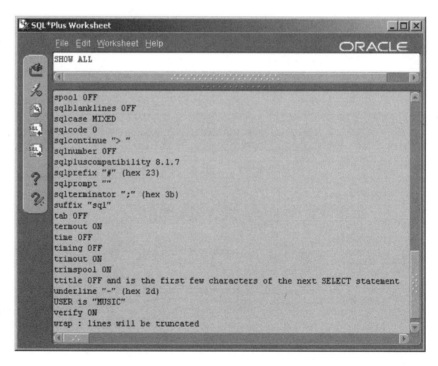

If you want to view only a single variable, use the SHOW command with that variable's name as in SHOW { variable name }. For example, to see the setting for PAGESIZE, type the following:

```
SHOW PAGES[IZE]
```

The page size can also be found using the abbreviation for PAGESIZE, PAGES. Here is a list of some of the commonly used settings with their standard abbreviations (if any). Some of these environmental variables have already been used in previous chapters, such as LINESIZE and HEADING.

Note: Environmental settings usually have shortened versions for faster access, some being as small as three characters.

- **AUTO[COMMIT]**. By default, AUTOCOMMIT is set to OFF. Setting this variable to ON will commit all DML changes automatically. If you ever plan to undo DML changes with a ROLLBACK command, do not tamper with this setting.

- **ARRAY[SIZE]**. Sets the number of rows SQL*Plus retrieves as a block from the database. The default is 15 and the valid range is 1 to 5,000. Retrieving many rows at once can improve performance, but Oracle advises that values higher than 100 do not help.

- **CMDS[EP]**. Sets the character that marks the end of a command (command separator) when you allow multiple commands on one line. The default is OFF, meaning you cannot have multiple commands on one line. You can set it to ON, which allows multiple commands on one line and sets the command separator to ";". You can also set it to a different character. For example, to set the command separator to "~" and then use multiple commands on one line, execute these commands in SQL*Plus Worksheet:

```
SET CMDSEP ~
COL NAME HEADING "Artist" ~ COL CITY HEADING "Location"
SELECT NAME, CITY FROM ARTIST;
SET CMDSEP OFF
```

- **COLSEP**. Sets the character used between columns in a report. The default is a blank space.

- **ECHO**. Tells SQL*Plus to either list the command before executing it (ON) or to not list the command in the output (OFF). The default is OFF. This command only affects commands that are run using the START command, which you use to run a script stored in a file.

- **ESC[APE]**. An escape character allows a command-level character to be used without executing its inherent command. ESCAPE ON sets the default, a backslash (\\).

- **FEED[BACK]**. Determines whether to display feedback (ON), suppress feedback (OFF), or display feedback only when the number of rows returned is greater than whatever number you set. The default is ON. The feedback is that informational line displayed in SQL*Plus, such as "1 row returned" or "1 row inserted." Suppressing feedback is useful when producing carefully formatted reports.

- **HEAD[ING]**. Set to OFF for no column headings. Set to ON (the default) to display column headings.

- **LINE[SIZE]**. The number of characters on one line before SQL*Plus starts a new line. The default in SQL*Plus is 80, and the default in SQL*Plus Worksheet is 1,024. Set it to any number from 1 to a maximum number that varies for different operating systems. Executing the following commands would show different line size truncations. Truncating chops off or removes characters from the output. Figure 8.2 shows the width of the line limited to 10 characters only, truncating large parts of artist names. This example is not particularly useful and quite possibly humongously silly. However, the point about page width is made. I usually set my default to 132 (see WRAP as well). The result is shown in Figure 8.2.

```
SET LINESIZE 10
SELECT NAME, CITY FROM ARTIST;
```

- **LONG**. Set the default number of bytes retrieved and displayed for a column with the LONG, CLOB, NCLOB, or XML type datatype. The default is 80. The maximum is 2 gigabytes; this could produce lots of nasty on-screen output, so you might want to be prepared to kill your session if using as such.

Note: XML documents are stored as CLOB objects. To view XML documents in a readable format, use SET LONG 2000 (see Chapter 17).

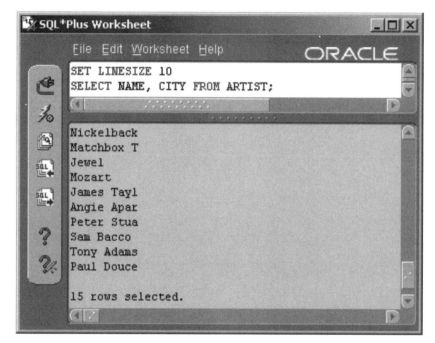

Figure 8.2
*Setting the Width,
Length, or Size of a
Line.*

- **MARK[UP] HTML**. Vaguely, this option can be used to generate HTML script from SQL*Plus output.

- **NEWP[AGE]**. Sets the number of blank lines to print before printing the title (if any) and headings on a new page. If setting NEWPAGE to NONE, SQL*Plus lists the report output as if it were on a single very long page. This variable is not used in iSQL*Plus.

- **NULL**. Sets the string displayed when a null value is returned in a report. The default is a blank space. The example in Figure 8.3 replaces null values in the POBOX column with a replacement string.

```
SET NULL '---NONE---'
SELECT ARTIST_ID, POBOX FROM ARTIST;
```

Null value replacements can even be generated into a table, as in the following example. The new table will be produced exactly as the query is specified, replacing null values with the string value. This environment setting can sometimes be used to replace time-consuming functionality such as using DECODE and NVL functions.

Figure 8.3
*Replacing Null
Values Using SET
NULL.*

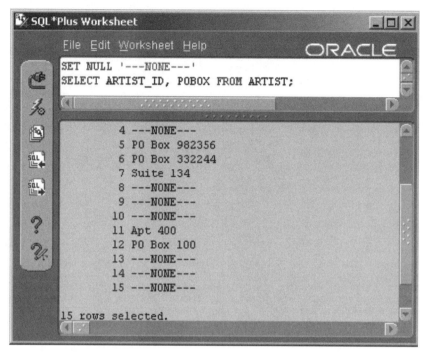

```
SET NULL '---NONE---'
CREATE TABLE TMP AS
SELECT ARTIST_ID, POBOX FROM ARTIST;
```

- **NUMF[ORMAT] { format }**. Apply a format to all output numbers. For instance, SET NUMFORMAT '999,999,999,990.00' displays all numbers with two decimal places, even if they are integers.

- **NUMW[IDTH]**. Reset the default of 10 for display width of numbers.

- **PAGES[IZE]**. Sets the number of lines per report page. This is most important when you are printing out a report. The LINESIZE and PAGESIZE must be set correctly to match the printable area of the page. The default in SQL*Plus is 24 and in SQL*Plus Worksheet is 1,024. Execute SET PAGES 0 to suppress formatting, including headings, titles and form feeding.

- **PAU[SE]**. This command only works in SQL*Plus and performs the same type of function as the PAUSE or MORE command in various operating systems. SET PAUSE ON will wait for the user to press

Enter before issuing a page break and displaying the next screen of data.

- **RECSEP.** Can be set to WRAPPED to output a record separator when a line wraps. Set to OFF to disable and EACH to include a record separator for every line.

- **RECSEPCHAR.** This option allows resetting of the record separator. Using the code following, Figure 8.4 changes the record separator and separates each record with a line containing asterisks (*):

```
SET RECSEPCHAR '*'
SET RECSEP EACH
SELECT * FROM ARTIST;
```

- **SERVEROUT[PUT].** Turns on or off the ability to display messages on your screen. Use SET SERVEROUTPUT OFF when executing scripts generating code into a spooled file; messages are suppressed.

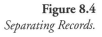

Figure 8.4
Separating Records.

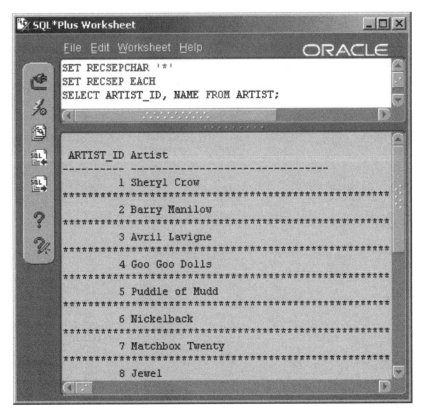

When running PL/SQL code, SET SERVEROUTPUT ON will display buffered messages built within PL/SQL blocks using the DBMS_OUTPUT.PUT procedures. These messages are useful for debugging PL/SQL code but will only be displayed on completion of a code block, not within the block. Additionally, the buffer has a limited size of 2,000 characters. Increase buffer size to 1,000,000 characters using the DBMS_OUTPUT.ENABLE procedure. Thus the following code snippet applies to large output quantities within a PL/SQL block. The DBMS_OUTPUT.DISABLE procedure sets the buffer back to 2,000 characters to reclaim memory space.

```
SET SERVEROUTPUT ON;
EXEC DBMS_OUTPUT.ENABLE(1000000);
DECLARE
 J INTEGER DEFAULT 1000;
BEGIN
 FOR I IN 1..J LOOP
  DBMS_OUTPUT.PUT_LINE(TO_CHAR(I)||' of '||TO_CHAR(J));
 END LOOP;
END;
/
EXEC DBMS_OUTPUT.DISABLE;
SET SERVEROUTPUT OFF;
```

Figure 8.5 shows the result of the previous script with the buffer (DBMS_OUTPUT.DISABLE) set to its default of 2,000 characters.

■ **SQLP[ROMPT]**. This option changes the SQL prompt. Use the command SET SQLPROMPT ' ' to remove the prompt altogether. Use SET SQLPPROMPT 'SQL> ' to return to the default. The example as shown following sets an interesting prompt, resulting in the prompt shown in Figure 8.6. Setting ESCAPE allows output of the period character. See ESCAPE.

```
COLUMN INSTANCE NEW_VALUE _INSTANCE
COLUMN USERNAME NEW_VALUE _USERNAME
SELECT INSTANCE_NAME INSTANCE FROM V$INSTANCE;
SELECT USER USERNAME FROM DUAL;
SET ESCAPE ON
SET SQLPROMPT '&_INSTANCE\.&_USERNAME> '
SET ESCAPE OFF
```

Figure 8.5
*Execute
DBMS_OUTPU
T.ENABLE(1000
000) To Avoid
Buffer Overflow.*

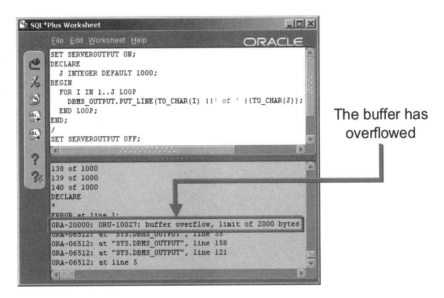

Figure 8.5
*Execute
DBMS_OUTPU
T.ENABLE(1000
000) To Avoid
Buffer Overflow.*

Note: SET SQLPROMPT does not apply to SQL*Plus Worksheet because SQL*Plus Worksheet has no command-line prompt.

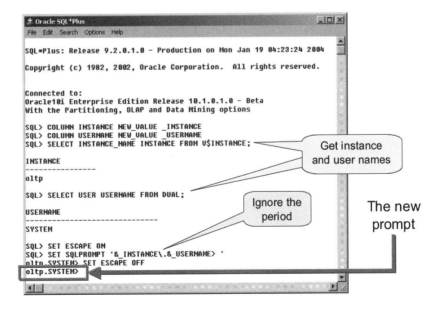

Figure 8.6
*Changing the
SQL*Plus Prompt.*

- **TERM[OUT]**. Turns on or off the screen display. Useful when you want to spool output to a file rather than seeing the output on the screen. Not supported in SQL*Plus Worksheet or in iSQL*Plus.

- **TIMI[NG]**. Turns on or off the display of elapsed time after each executed SQL command.

- **WRAP**. Word or line wrapping implies that text overflowing the available page width (LINESIZE) is wrapped onto the next line. WRAP OFF will truncate text greater than LINESIZE.

Let's look at some more examples using different environmental settings to slowly build into something useful. The first query, as shown in Figure 8.7, joins the MUSICCD, CDTRACK, SONG, and ARTIST tables to display the CD title, artist name, and song title of all songs on all CDs.

```
SELECT M.TITLE, A.NAME, S.TITLE
FROM MUSICCD M JOIN CDTRACK T ON (M.MUSICCD_ID=T.MUSICCD_ID)
JOIN SONG S ON (T.SONG_ID=S.SONG_ID)
JOIN ARTIST A ON (S.ARTIST_ID=A.ARTIST_ID)
ORDER BY 1,2,3;
```

Change some settings to see a different effect. We can simply edit the query in the top pane of SQL*Plus Worksheet, adding the SET COLSEP =

Figure 8.7
The Default Environmental Settings (No Changes).

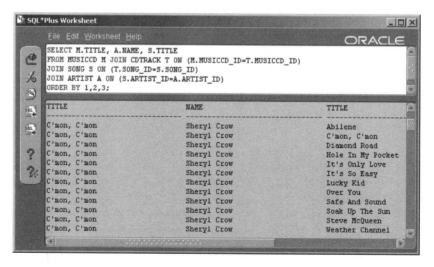

Figure 8.8
*The Equals Sign Is
Now the Column
Separator.*

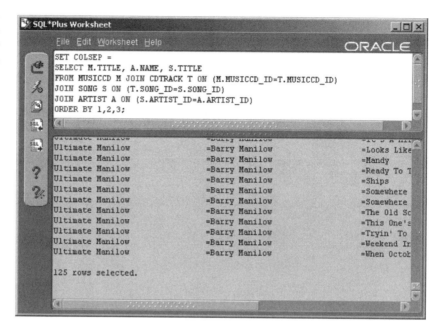

command on a line above the query, changing the column separator to an equals sign.

```
SET COLSEP =
```

Figure 8.8 shows the result. Notice that the SET command appears just above the query in the top pane of the worksheet. The column separator (=) appears between the column headings and between each column in each row of data in the report.

We could add SET FEEDBACK OFF such that the text "… rows selected." does not appear at the end of the returned rows. Additionally, we can change the page size to repeat headings more often. If printed, there would be a page feed at the end of each page and headings at the start of each printed page. Figure 8.9 shows the result.

```
SET FEEDBACK OFF PAGESIZE 20;
```

There is just one more thing: Generally, I use SQL*Plus for administration. I find the default wrapping and page width settings of ON and 80, respectively, extremely irritating. On every client machine I use, assuming I am not stepping on anyone else's toes, I add the line SET WRAP OFF

Figure 8.9
Shorter Page Size
Affects the Page
Break or Page
Eject.

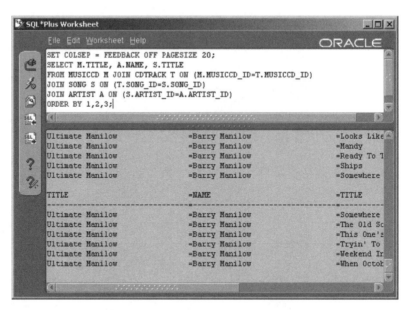

LINESIZE 132; to the end of the SQL*Plus configuration file called GLO-GIN.SQL in the $ORACLE_HOME/sqlplus/admin directory. Rarely do I need to use other settings. If so, I change these values manually, usually for specific queries.

That's enough about environmental variables. Let's now look at using scripts and variables.

8.2   Using Scripts and Variables

SQL*Plus supports a simple method of defining and prompting for variables using ampersand characters (&). Any string beginning with & or && is a variable! In programming, the act of replacing a variable with a value is known as *variable substitution*. A named variable is a bucket or placeholder for a value, where the variable is used to reference or access its contained value.

The & tells SQL*Plus to prompt for a value every time it encounters the variable. The && tells SQL*Plus to use the same value of the variable it already prompted for.

Note: Use SQL*Plus instead of SQL*Plus Worksheet when using variables because you will be able to respond to prompts from SQL*Plus more easily. It is possible, but not usually practical, to use variables with SQL*Plus Worksheet. iSQL*Plus does not support variables yet.

Let's say you want to revise the query we have been using so that it displays only the artists and songs for one CD at a time. You must revise the query's WHERE clause. First, change the query so that it retrieves only the songs for the CD with MUSICCD_ID = 1. An editing session can be initiated from within SQL*Plus using the EDIT command.

```
EDIT
```

In the background, SQL*Plus writes a file named AFIEDT.BUF and then opens the file with the editor. The exact editor used depends on platform and configuration. For Windows, it is usually Notepad and for UNIX quite often VI. Add a WHERE clause to the query.

```
SELECT M.TITLE, A.NAME, S.TITLE
FROM MUSICCD M JOIN CDTRACK T ON (M.MUSICCD_ID=T.MUSICCD_ID)
JOIN SONG S ON (T.SONG_ID=S.SONG_ID)
JOIN ARTIST A ON (S.ARTIST_ID=A.ARTIST_ID)
WHERE M.MUSICCD_ID = 1
ORDER BY 1,2,3
/
```

The file can then be saved and the editor exited. Execution immediately returns to SQL*Plus with the modified query loaded into the workspace, as shown in Figure 8.10.

Let's say that you want to be able to tell SQL*Plus which CD to report each time you run this query. Add a variable in the WHERE clause to accomplish this task.

You can place the query in your editor again by typing ED (the shortcut for the command EDIT). Then, change the WHERE clause so that instead

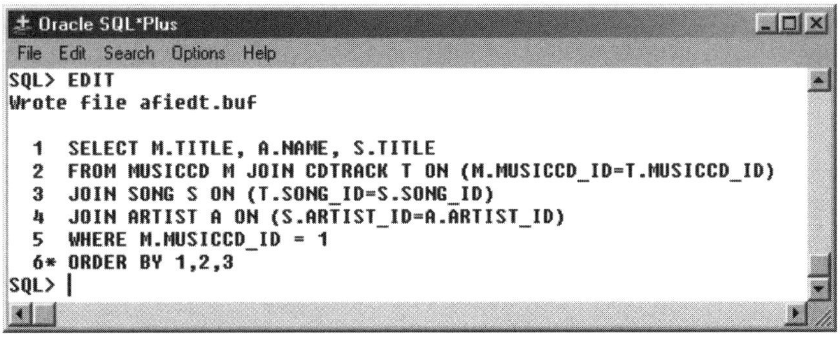

Figure 8.10

*An Edited Script Is Passed Back to SQL*Plus.*

```
± Oracle SQL*Plus                                          _ □ ×
File  Edit  Search  Options  Help
SQL> EDIT
Wrote file afiedt.buf

  1   SELECT M.TITLE, A.NAME, S.TITLE
  2   FROM MUSICCD M JOIN CDTRACK T ON (M.MUSICCD_ID=T.MUSICCD_ID)
  3   JOIN SONG S ON (T.SONG_ID=S.SONG_ID)
  4   JOIN ARTIST A ON (S.ARTIST_ID=A.ARTIST_ID)
  5   WHERE M.MUSICCD_ID = 1
  6*  ORDER BY 1,2,3
SQL> |
```

of specifying the number 1, you replace it with a variable called CDNUM. Variables are identified by a preceding ampersand, & or && symbol, so you must add that as well. The final query should look as follows:

```
SELECT M.TITLE, A.NAME, S.TITLE
FROM MUSICCD M JOIN CDTRACK T ON (M.MUSICCD_ID=T.MUSICCD_ID)
JOIN SONG S ON (T.SONG_ID=S.SONG_ID)
JOIN ARTIST A ON (S.ARTIST_ID=A.ARTIST_ID)
WHERE M.MUSICCD_ID = &CDNUM
ORDER BY 1,2,3
/
```

Once again, exiting the editor returns the query to SQL*Plus. A forward slash will execute the query. SQL*Plus prompts you to enter a value for the variable. Figure 8.11 shows how this looks.

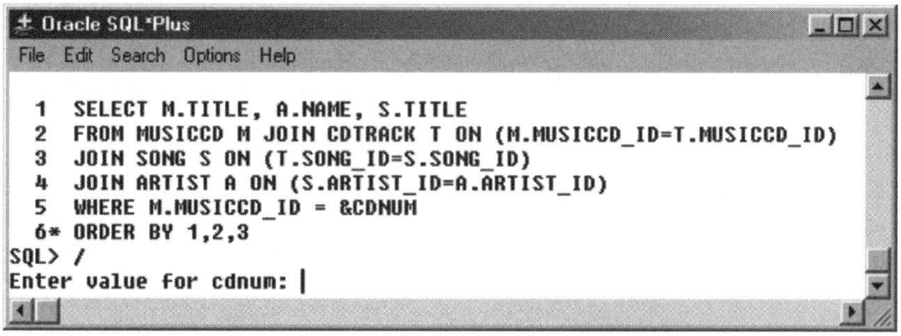

Figure 8.11
*SQL*Plus Can*
Prompt for
Variable Values.

Typing the number 1 and pressing Enter forces SQL*Plus to replace the variable with a number 1 and execute the query. Figure 8.12 shows the result.

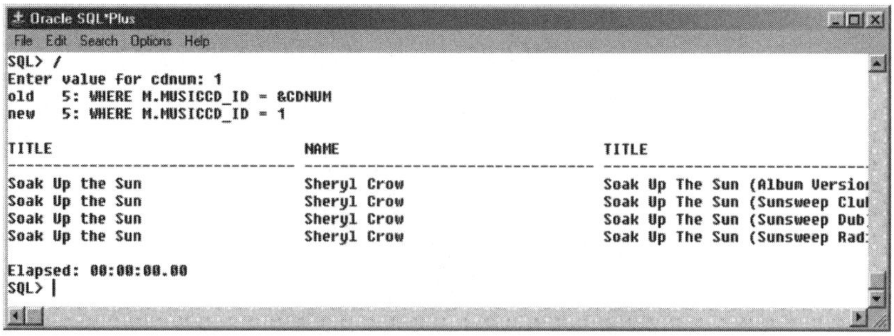

Figure 8.12
*SQL*Plus Variable*
Substitution.

You can also use the DEFINE command to set the value of the variable before executing the query. It follows that the value of the CDNUM variable can be predefined as a value, negating the need for a user prompt.

```
DEFINE CDNUM=2
/
```

And remove a defined variable from your session using the UNDEFINE command.

```
UNDEFINE CDNUM
```

Use the SAVE command to write the SQL buffer contents to a file so you can edit and run it whenever you want. This also allows you to add SQL*Plus commands to the file, which do not get saved when working only with the SQL buffer file.

```
SAVE CDREPORT
```

The file is named CDREPORT.SQL. The .SQL extension is a default. If you specify the extension (suffix) in the SAVE command file name, the default .SQL is overridden with the specified extension. Now that the query is inside a file, you can edit the file with the following command:

```
EDIT CDREPORT
```

The editor is instantiated as before, but the file you are editing is now the CDREPORT.SQL file, rather than the SQL buffer's default file. You could add the following line of code to the beginning of the file. The ACCEPT command is another method of defining a variable that is used in a query. The PROMPT variation can be added as an option to define the text SQL*Plus displays when prompting you to enter a value for the variable.

```
ACCEPT CDNUM PROMPT 'What CD number do you want to see? '
```

Save the file and exit the editor to return to SQL*Plus. Notice that the buffer was not re-displayed this time. To run the file you just edited, you should use the START command because the SQL*Plus script is now in a file other than the SQL buffer file. A SQL*Plus script is a file containing a combination of SQL commands, such as queries, and SQL*Plus commands such as SET and ACCEPT.

The next command instructs SQL*Plus to retrieve and execute the SQL*Plus script in the file CDREPORT.SQL.

```
START CDREPORT
```

Another way to run a script is to use the @ or RUN commands. For example, you could type each of these two lines, entering the number 3 when prompted for the CD number, trying each variation.

```
@CDREPORT
RUN CDREPORT
```

All three of the commands: START, @, and RUN have the same effect.

A fourth way of executing a script is to use @@. This tells SQL*Plus to run the script and, in addition, to look for any scripts called within this script in the same directory. This is very useful when you are creating a series of scripts that call one another. With this method you only need to tell SQL*Plus where the first script is located and it can find all the others, assuming you located them in the same directory. For example, imagine you have three scripts named A.SQL, B.SQL, and C.SQL in the C:\TEMP directory /tmp on UNIX. The script A.SQL has an SQL*Plus command to run the B.SQL and B.SQL calls C.SQL. You could start the primary script by typing this command. The other two scripts will be found because they are stored in the same directory.

```
@@C:\TEMP\A
```

The double @@ command simply tells SQL*Plus to use the current directory to search for contained scripts as in the following:

```
SET SERVEROUTPUT ON;
EXEC DBMS_OUTPUT.PUT_LINE('Executing A.SQL');
@@B.SQL;
EXEC DBMS_OUTPUT.PUT_LINE ('Completed A.SQL');
SET SERVEROUTPUT OFF;
```

The same effect can be obtained by hard-coding the path name into the script using only a single @ character command as shown following. Obviously, calling B.SQL with a single @ command character would require the B.SQL and C.SQL calls to be executed with full path names. The A.SQL script looks as follows:

```
SET SERVEROUTPUT ON;
EXEC DBMS_OUTPUT.PUT_LINE('Executing A.SQL');
@C:\TEMP\B.SQL;
EXEC DBMS_OUTPUT.PUT_LINE ('Completed A.SQL');
SET SERVEROUTPUT OFF;
```

The script B.SQL looks as follows:

```
EXEC DBMS_OUTPUT.PUT_LINE('Executing B.SQL');
@@C.SQL;
EXEC DBMS_OUTPUT.PUT_LINE ('Completed B.SQL');
```

The script C.SQL looks as follows:

```
EXEC DBMS_OUTPUT.PUT_LINE('Executing C.SQL');
EXEC DBMS_OUTPUT.PUT_LINE ('Completed C.SQL');
```

Look at the execution of the three aforementioned scripts as shown in Figure 8.13.

Creating and using scripting in SQL*Plus is easy. There are a few simple commands to remember. Now let's go onto formatting of specific queries or reports, as opposed to using environmental variables to change global settings.

8.3 Formatting Query Output in SQL*Plus

Scripting with simple queries and variables is just the beginning of the reporting process. In this section, you learn how to customize reports by adding environmental settings to the script, changing column headings, adding page headings, and creating reports with outlined structures. Let's start with column settings.

Figure 8.13
*Executing Scripts
within Scripts.*

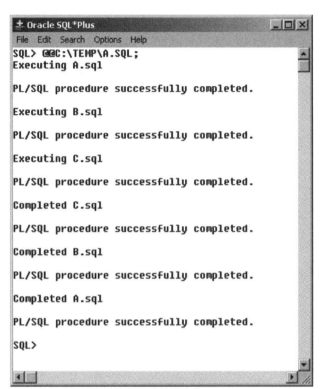

8.3.1 Column Formatting and Headings

The syntax of the COLUMN command, which is used to adjust the width and the heading of a column, is shown in Figure 8.14.

The CDREPORT script used previously in this chapter can be beautified for readability using COLUMN command settings. The columns seem a little spread out, so let's change the format of the columns. I have added some column commands to the query by editing the CDREPORT file (EDIT CDREPORT) previously created, as shown in the following script. Changes are highlighted.

```
DEFINE CDNUM=9
COLUMN CDTITLE FORMAT A15 WRAP
COLUMN NAME FORMAT A12 TRUNCATE HEADING "Artist Name"
COLUMN SONGTITLE HEADING "Song|Title" FORMAT A20 WORD_WRAP
SELECT M.TITLE CDTITLE, A.NAME, S.TITLE SONGTITLE
FROM MUSICCD M JOIN CDTRACK T ON (M.MUSICCD_ID=T.MUSICCD_ID)
JOIN SONG S ON (T.SONG_ID=S.SONG_ID)
```

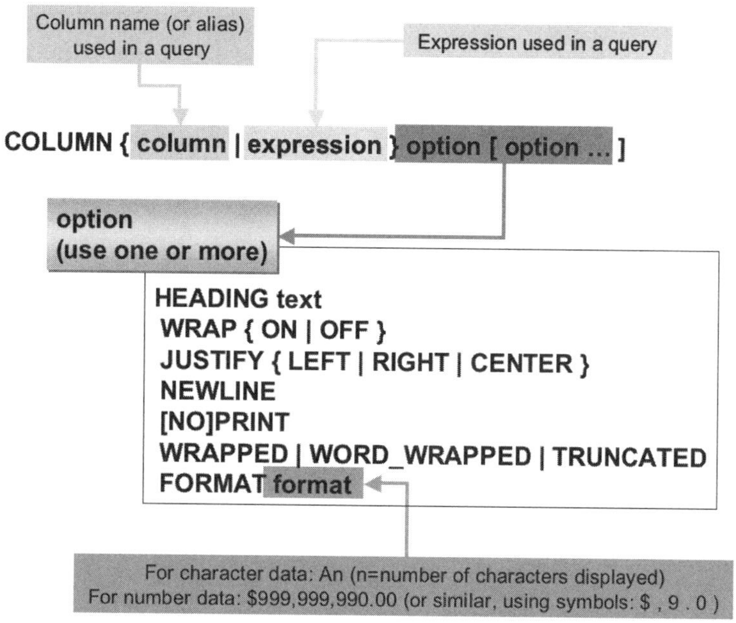

Figure 8.14
*The COLUMN
Command Is
Exclusive to
SQL*Plus.*

```
JOIN ARTIST A ON (S.ARTIST_ID=A.ARTIST_ID)
WHERE M.MUSICCD_ID = &CDNUM
ORDER BY 1,2,3
/
UNDEFINE CDNUM
```

The query is executed again with column formatting as shown in Figure 8.15. Notice that the artist's name is truncated and that some of the song titles are on two lines. These were caused by the COLUMN commands, before adjusting with wrapping such that the artist's name is not truncated.

In Figure 8.15, a title is wrapped onto more than one line. There is also a blank line after that song. The WORD_WRAP option as opposed to the WRAP option wraps entire words to the subsequent line. Removing the blank line after the wrapped song title requires removal of the RECSEP setting.

```
SET RECSEP OFF
```

Here is another query and COLUMN command. This query has a number in it. Additionally, in this query the artist name will be formatted the same way that it was for the CDREPORT script! This is because our

Figure 8.15
*Using the
COLUMN
Command.*

new query has a column with the same name, which happens to be "NAME," that is used in the previous COLUMN command. To turn off the column formatting for the NAME column, use the COLUMN NAME OFF command as shown.

```
COLUMN NAME OFF
SELECT A.NAME, S.MINUTES_USED, S.AMOUNT_CHARGED,
S.AMOUNT_PAID
FROM ARTIST A, STUDIOTIME S
WHERE A.ARTIST_ID = S.ARTIST_ID
ORDER BY 1
/
```

In fact, you can turn off all of COLUMN command formatting by typing the CLEAR COLUMN command.

```
CLEAR COLUMN
```

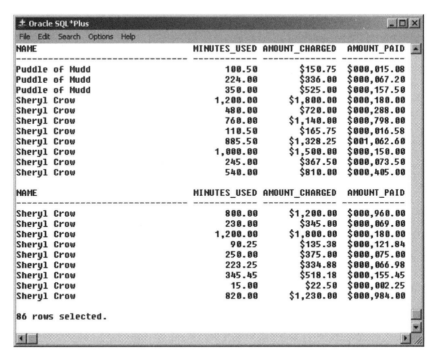

Figure 8.16
Three Number Column Format Variations.

Now we can add formatting to the three number columns by typing these lines and executing again:

```
COLUMN MINUTES_USED FORMAT 99,999.99
COLUMN AMOUNT_CHARGED FORMAT $999,990.00
COLUMN AMOUNT_PAID FORMAT $000,000.00
/
```

Figure 8.16 shows the result. A zero in a column format is a placeholder, padding with zeros when the value is not as large as the format. The nine collapses or trims the number, moving the $ sign, for example, to the right so it is next to the number. The comma is only used when needed if you have nines around it and will always be displayed if you have zeros around it. See the SQL*Plus COLUMN command syntax in Oracle's documentation for a complete list of all the available formatting symbols for numbers. Also see Chapter 9 for some detail on datatype conversion function formatting patterns.

A few notes about the COLUMN command:

- The COLUMN command uses the alias of the column in the query, not the column prefixed with the schema. For example, in the CDREPORT.SQL script file, use CDTITLE in the COLUMN command, not M.TITLE.
- The vertical bar (|) indicates a line break in the heading. See the COLUMN command for the SONGTITLE column.
- WORD_WRAP makes column data break between words, whereas WRAP always breaks at the exact width defined in the FORMAT.
- The COLUMN command should be on a single line. To make SQL*Plus read a second line, add a dash or hyphen (-) to the end of the first line, indicating that the second line is a continuation of the first line. See the COLUMN command for the SONGTITLE column.
- A COLUMN command is in effect for your entire session or until you issue another COLUMN command on the same column or expression.
- The COLUMN command can be used to format character and number data but not dates. Format dates using the TO_CHAR function in the query.

Let's take a look at formatting of dates.

8.3.1.1 Formatting Dates

Here is a query containing a date column:

```
COLUMN TITLE FORMAT A30 WRAP
SELECT S.TITLE, S.RECORDING_DATE FROM SONG S
WHERE S.RECORDING_DATE > '01-JUL-2001';
```

Dates cannot be formatted with the COLUMN FORMAT command, except to limit the width of the column. Let's add general formatting for all dates by adjusting the default date format for the current session.

```
ALTER SESSION SET NLS_DATE_FORMAT = 'Day, Month DD, YYYY';
```

Figure 8.17
Formatting Dates Globally for a Session.

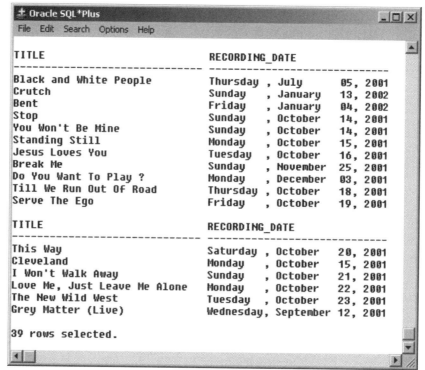

Also, because all date formatting is changed globally, we have to alter the previous query to comply with the required date formatting. Otherwise, the query will produce an error.

```
COLUMN TITLE FORMAT A30 WRAP
SELECT S.TITLE, S.RECORDING_DATE FROM SONG S
WHERE S.RECORDING_DATE > 'Sunday, July 01, 2001';
```

The result of the query is shown in Figure 8.17.

Making global changes like that is a little drastic and can be dangerous because other things can be altered, usually where you least expect it, very likely causing headaches and problems. The better way to format a date is by using the TO_CHAR function. However, using functions in queries can cause performance problems. Restore the default date format by typing and executing this command.

```
ALTER SESSION SET NLS_DATE_FORMAT = 'DD-MON-YY';
```

What we could have done in the first place would have been as follows. The result would be identical to that in Figure 8.17.

```
COLUMN TITLE FORMAT A30 WRAP
SELECT S.TITLE, TO_CHAR(S.RECORDING_DATE
, 'Day, Month DD, YYYY')
FROM SONG S
WHERE S.RECORDING_DATE > '01-JUL-2001';
```

That covers formatting of columns and headings in SQL*Plus using the COLUMN command. The next section looks into lines, pages, and breaks using the TTITLE, BREAK ON, and COMPUTE commands.

8.3.2 Lines, Pages, and Breaks

You have already seen how to adjust line width and page length using the SET command. This section introduces page headings and summary breaks. To add a page heading, use the TTITLE command, whose syntax is shown in Figure 8.18. You can use the same syntax for BTITLE, which places footers at the end of each page.

Figure 8.18
TTITLE and BTITLE Set Page Headers and Footers.

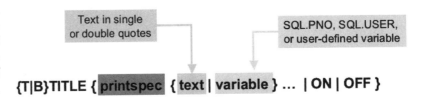

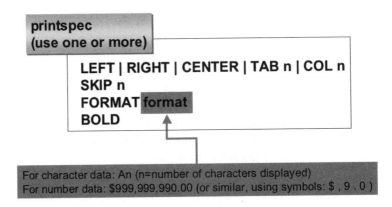

Once again, we could edit the CDREPORT script (EDIT CDREPORT) to add a title, adding highlighted lines.

```
DEFINE CDNUM=9
COLUMN CDTITLE FORMAT A15 WRAP
COLUMN NAME FORMAT A12 TRUNCATE HEADING "Artist Name"
COLUMN SONGTITLE HEADING "Song|Title" FORMAT A20 WORD_WRAP
SET LINESIZE 60
TTITLE LEFT 'Music CD # '  CDNUM -
CENTER 'User: ' SQL.USER RIGHT 'Page:' SQL.PNO SKIP 2
SELECT M.TITLE CDTITLE, A.NAME, S.TITLE SONGTITLE
FROM MUSICCD M JOIN CDTRACK T ON (M.MUSICCD_ID=T.MUSICCD_ID)
JOIN SONG S ON (T.SONG_ID=S.SONG_ID)
JOIN ARTIST A ON (S.ARTIST_ID=A.ARTIST_ID)
WHERE M.MUSICCD_ID = &CDNUM
ORDER BY 1,2,3
/
UNDEFINE CDNUM
```

Figure 8.19
The Report Now Has a Title.

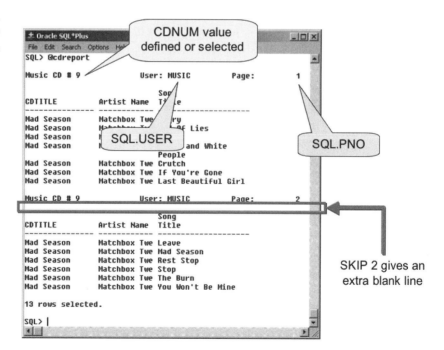

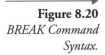

Figure 8.20
BREAK Command
Syntax.

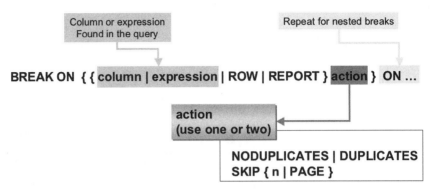

We use a dash or hyphen (-) to continue the TTITLE command to a second line. The CDNUM variable is defined in the script and therefore can be used in the title. Do not include the ampersand (&) when naming a variable in the title. LINESIZE was changed to 60, so the title can be seen more easily. The result of executing this script is shown in Figure 8.19.

The final component of an SQL*Plus report is adding a break within the report to cause an outlining effect, also called a master detail style report. You probably have noticed that the CD Title in our report is output for every line even though it is the same. This does look somewhat clumsy. You can easily suppress the repeated title by adding the BREAK command. This means that a repeating element is only printed once. The syntax of the BREAK command is shown in Figure 8.20.

The BREAK command, like the TTITLE command and other SQL*Plus commands, is used for your session until you log off or execute another BREAK command. The following lines could be added to the beginning of the CDREPORT file:

```
SET PAGESIZE 40
BREAK ON CDTITLE NODUPLICATES SKIP 2 ON NAME NODUPLICATES
```

The second line tells SQL*Plus to only display the CDTITLE at the top of a page or when it changes, to skip 2 lines when it encounters a new CDTITLE, and to only display the artist's name (the NAME column) at the top of each page or when it changes. On the first line, changing the PAGESIZE to 40 lines makes it easier to see the report's breaks.

Also change the WHERE clause so that you are returning all CDs less than or equal to the number you enter. This will show you how the BREAK works on the CD titles.

```
WHERE M.MUSICCD_ID <= &CDNUM
```

You would have to remove the CDNUM variable definition (including output in the header) from the CDREPORT.SQL script and enable an ACCEPT command for the variable once again. Add the following line:

```
ACCEPT CDNUM PROMPT 'What CD number do you want to see? '
```

Remove the following lines:

```
DEFINE CDNUM=9
UNDEFINE CDNUM
```

Change the following line from:

```
TTITLE LEFT 'Music CD # ' CDNUM —
```

to:

```
TTITLE LEFT 'Music CD'.
```

The query in Figure 8.21 now displays part of the result of all CDs from 1 to 9.

There is another cool trick to add to this report in the form of summary data (subtotals) added at the break points. Summary information is added by using the COMPUTE command. This command can only be used in conjunction with the BREAK command. The two work together to create a report with breaks and summaries for each break. The syntax of the COMPUTE command is shown in Figure 8.22.

Like the BREAK command, you should keep the COMPUTE command on a single line or add a dash or hyphen (-) to continue the command to another line.

Using our CDREPORT.SQL example again, let's add a count of the number of songs on each CD to the break point between CDs. This line can be added at the beginning of the CDREPORT.SQL script.

```
COMPUTE COUNT OF SONGTITLE ON CDTITLE
```

Figure 8.21
*The Report Shows
Multiple CDs.*

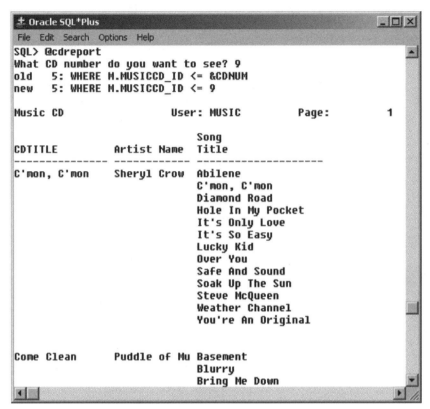

Figure 8.22
*COMPUTE Will
Only Function
Properly in
Conjunction with
the BREAK
Command.*

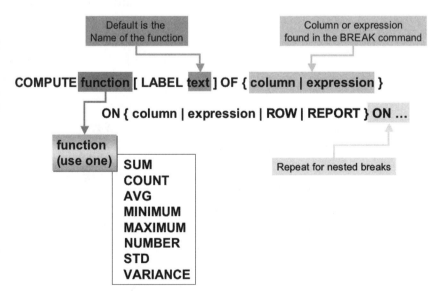

Figure 8.23
The Report Displays a Count of Songs per CD.

```
Oracle SQL*Plus                                       _ □ ×
File  Edit  Search  Options  Help
SQL> @cdreport
What CD number do you want to see? 9
old    5: WHERE M.MUSICCD_ID <= &CDNUM
new    5: WHERE M.MUSICCD_ID <= 9

Music CD                     User: MUSIC        Page:       1

                                    Song
CDTITLE           Artist Name  Title
---------------   ------------  --------------------
C'mon, C'mon      Sheryl Crow  Abilene
                               C'mon, C'mon
                               Diamond Road
                               Hole In My Pocket
                               It's Only Love
                               It's So Easy
                               Lucky Kid
                               Over You
                               Safe And Sound
                               Soak Up The Sun
                               Steve McQueen
                               Weather Channel
                               You're An Original
***************  ************  --------------------
count                          13

Come Clean        Puddle of Mu Basement
```

Figure 8.23 shows part of the results. Because we did not specify a label, the word "count" is displayed in the first column, and the count is listed in the column that was counted (SONGTITLE).

You have seen how to generate a report with summaries, breaks, customized headings, and variables. Now let's examine the report-generating possibilities in another SQL*Plus tool, iSQL*Plus.

8.4   Using iSQL*Plus

As you know, iSQL*Plus is the Web-based version of SQL*Plus. It gives you a way to write queries and other SQL commands via the Internet or across a network, in a Web browser. An Oracle installation comes with a miniature Web server, called HTTP Server, and is configured automatically by Oracle Installer.

The HTTP Server that is provided as part of Oracle is usually automatically started when you start up your computer. If not, you can start it up yourself. In Windows, on the task bar, click **Start/Programs/Oracle – OraHome10/Oracle HTTP Server/Start HTTP Server powered by**

Apache. A window appears with status information. Minimize the window by clicking the minus sign in the top right corner of the window. Do not close the window; closing the window stops the HTTP Server. On UNIX, type **apache -k start** in a command-line shell.

Start up your Web browser and type the address for the iSQL*Plus service on the HTTP Server. On Windows and UNIX, the Web address is usually as follows. Replace the hostname with the name of your database server.

```
http://<hostname>:7778/isqlplus
```

Note: If there is no response from the browser, see the later section in this chapter on "Troubleshooting iSQL*Plus." on page 171.

Login requires username, password, and connection identifier, as shown in Figure 8.24.

Figure 8.24
*Log into iSQL*Plus as with SQL*Plus.*

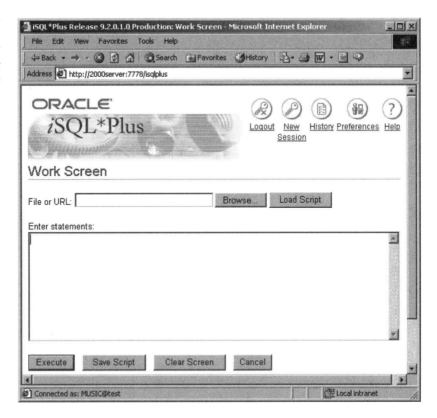

Figure 8.25
*iSQL*Plus Has*
Features That
*Mimic SQL*Plus*
Functionality.

After clicking the Login button, the primary interface for iSQL*Plus will appear in the browser, as shown in Figure 8.25.

iSQL*Plus output looks like an HTML table. Here is a simple query example, which can be placed into the Enter Statements block in the iSQL*Plus interface window, as shown in Figure 8.25.

```
SELECT SONG_ID, RECORDING_DATE, PLAYING_TIME, TITLE
FROM SONG
ORDER BY 1
/
```

Clicking the Execute button runs the query. iSQL*Plus processes the query and returns the results in an HTML format in the browser. Scroll down to the lower part of the screen to see the results, as shown in Figure 8.26.

Figure 8.26
*Output in
iSQL*Plus Is
Different from
SQL*Plus.*

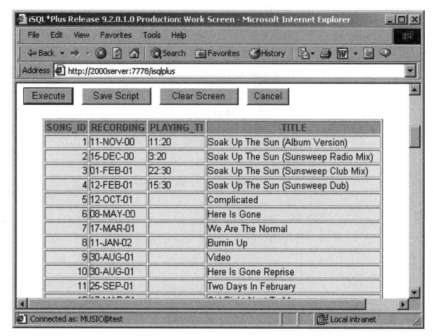

The most apparent difference between SQL*Plus and iSQL*Plus is appearance. Columns are formatted in an HTML table layout, not just as plain text. The page breaks are simply displayed as a repetition of the column headings. Scroll to the end of the report, and you will see the record count displayed after the end of the table of report records.

8.4.1 Embedding Scripts in HTML

A cool feature is the ability to create an HTML document that calls iSQL*Plus and runs a predefined report. You have already created a report in a file named CDREPORT.SQL previously in this chapter. You can embed this report into your own customized HTML document. This can be run by anyone who can access your HTTP Server.

The HTTP Server runs iSQL*Plus by accessing the iSQL*Plus Server process that is automatically configured within it. The iSQL*Plus Server is running whenever your HTTP Server is running. The architecture that should be used for iSQL*Plus is called a three-tier architecture and is commonly used with Web-based applications. The client tier is your Web browser; the middle tier is the HTTP Server; and the database tier is the Oracle Database 10*g* Server. Each of the three tiers can be located on separate computers, which makes this type of architecture portable, scalable, and capable of connecting across the Internet with ease.

Here is an example of the HTML code to call our CDREPORT.SQL script. You must change the hostname, port number, and database name to suit your installation. The parts you must change are highlighted.

```
<HTML>
<HEAD><TITLE>CD Dynamic Report</TITLE></HEAD>
<BODY>
<H1>CD Dynamic Report</H1>
<H2>CDs with specified CD ID Numbers.</H2>
<FORM METHOD=get ACTION="http://hostname:7778/isqlplus">
<INPUT TYPE="hidden" NAME="userid" VALUE="music/music@SID">
<INPUT TYPE="hidden" NAME="script"
VALUE="http://hostname:7778/CDREPORT.SQL">
Enter the highest CD ID Number to report:
<INPUT TYPE="number" NAME="CDNUM" SIZE="4">
<INPUT TYPE="submit" VALUE="Run Report">
</FORM></BODY></HTML>
```

This HTML file, along with the script CDREPORT.SQL, should be placed into the HTTP Server's document directory on the server. The default document directory location is $ORACLE_HOME/Apache/Apache/htdocs. Before copying the two files, remove the following line from the CDREPORT.SQL file because iSQL*Plus does not allow the ACCEPT command:

```
ACCEPT CDNUM PROMPT 'What CD number do you want to see? '
```

After copying the two files to the document directory on the HTTP server machine, go to the browser on the client machine and enter the URL for the HTML page, changing the hostname and the port number as needed.

```
http://<hostname>:7778/cdreport.html
```

Figure 8.27 shows the result.

Typing an appropriate number into the box and clicking the Run Report button produces a result as shown in Figure 8.28. The script is exe-

Figure 8.27
*Your Customized
Report Running
Web Page.*

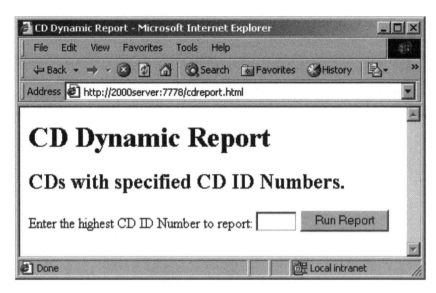

cuted within the browser HTML page, both of which are stored on the
server running the HTTP server process.

Figure 8.28
*The CDREPORT
Script Was Run
and Displayed.*

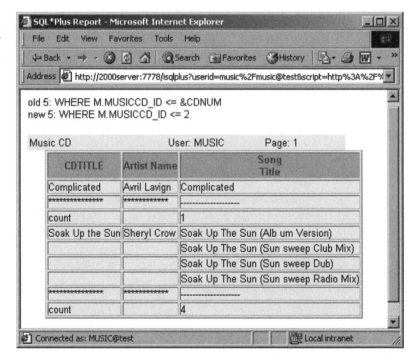

This example placed the username, password, and Oracle database network name (SID) in the source code. This is not necessarily a good idea in a commercial environment from a security perspective. Anyone can view the source code of an HTML document and retrieve information. It would be better to modify the HTML in your document so that the user is required to enter a username and password. Additionally, secure socket layers (SSL) can be used to encrypt data traveling between a Web browser and the server.

8.4.2 iSQL*Plus versus SQL*Plus

The main features of iSQL*Plus are similar to the features of SQL*Plus or SQL*Plus Worksheet:

- Enter SQL commands in a box and click the Execute button to display the results. Results can be displayed below the box or in a new browser window.

- Adjust environment settings by clicking the Preferences button, using a series of radio buttons and boxes to modify settings such as HEADING, RECSEP, and so on.

- Use variables just like SQL*Plus, except you cannot use the ACCEPT or PROMPT commands to prompt for values. iSQL*Plus displays its own prompt.

Note: (10*g*) iSQL*Plus allows prompts for input values.

- Review and retrieve previous SQL commands by clicking the History button, much like SQL*Plus Worksheet.

8.4.3 Troubleshooting iSQL*Plus

If there are problems running iSQL*Plus, configuration settings and other things can be checked on the server.

- Check that the port number is the default 7778 value in the file HTTPD.CONF in the $ORACLE_HOME/Apache/Apache/conf directory.

- The port number should also be in the SETUPINFO.TXT file in the directory $ORACLE_HOME/Apache/Apache. This file should contain entries such as the following:

```
http://<hostname>:7778
http://<hostname>:4443
```

Note: Replace hostname as appropriate.

- The file called ORACLE_APACHE.CONF in the $ORACLE_HOME/Apache/Apache/conf directory must include the file ISQLPLUS.CONF in the ORACLE_HOME/sqlplus/admin directory. The include command should be of the following form. Be sure there are no comments (#) in unexpected places.

```
include "$ORACLE_HOME/sqlplus/admin/isqlplus.conf"
```

- Try stopping and restarting the HTTP Server, especially if you have made any changes to any configuration files. A bug in Oracle 9.2 for Windows 2000 caused errors when starting and stopping the HTTP Server using both the Windows service and the Apache command on the Start menu. A solution to this issue is to set the service to Manual and always start and stop Apache and the HTTP Server with the following commands executed in a DOS shell (the command line):

```
C:\oracle\ora92\Apache\Apache\apache -k start
C:\oracle\ora92\Apache\Apache\apache - k shutdown
```

8.4.4   Customizing iSQL*Plus Display

Numerous preferences can be changed from the iSQL*Plus interface on the client machine. Additionally, on the server there is an HTML cascading style sheet.[1] This style sheet can be altered to change output appearance. The HTML cascading style sheet is called IPLUS.CSS and is located in the $ORACLE_HOME/sqlplus/admin/iplus directory on the server. Changing the style sheet allows customization of colors and fonts used by iSQL*Plus when it formats output for queries. Using the same simple query used pre-

Figure 8.29
*Changing the
iSQL*Plus Style
Sheet on the Server.*

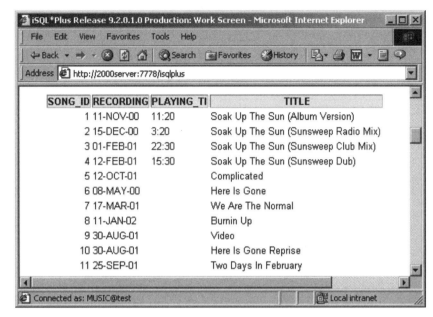

viously in Figure 8.26, Figure 8.29 has an altered appearance as a result of changes to the style sheet file on the server.

In Figure 8.29, all text color is removed, all background colors apart from that in the headings is removed, and all borders are removed from everything but headings. The style sheet has numerous elements. I changed the following two elements:

- The TH or HTML table heading tag or element is changed where highlighted.

```
TH {
    font : bold 10pt Arial, Helvetica, sans-serif;
    color : black;
    background : #f0f0f0;
    padding : 0px 0px 0px 0px;
}
```

- The combination TABLE, TR, TD element is also changed where highlighted.

```
TABLE, TR, TD {
    font : 10pt Arial, Helvetica, sans-serif;
```

```
    color : Black;
    background : white;
    border : 1
    padding : 0px 0px 0px 0px;
    margin : 0px 0px 0px 0px;
}
```

This is a quick introduction to iSQL*Plus that should help you get started with your own experimentation. Remember to review the help screens provided inside iSQL*Plus for more examples of code and quick reference to SQL syntax.

This chapter has covered more detail on SQL*Plus and related tools, in addition to the introductory information provided in Chapter 1. The next chapter moves back into Oracle SQL and looks at functions, namely single-row functions.

8.5   Endnotes

1.   www.oracledbaexpert.com/menu/DHTML.html

9

Single-Row Functions

In this chapter:

- What types of built-in functions are available?
- What are single-row functions?
- What are the categories of single-row functions?
- How do functions work with queries?
- What are the options when formatting strings, numbers, and dates?
- What are data conversion functions?
- How are functions combined?

This chapter uses the queries you have worked with in previous chapters and expands the way you can use columns by introducing functions. You will examine the types of functions used for different data types. Finally, you will experiment with combining functions together for more flexibility.

A function is a built-in PL/SQL program that always returns a single value. You can use the predefined functions (such as the ones discussed in this chapter) or you can create your own (see Chapter 24). A function always returns a single value, as opposed to a procedure, which is a similar type of program but is able to return more than one value. You can call a function within a query or other SQL command. You have already seen a few functions in previous chapters (e.g., NVL and SYSDATE). Before we examine single-row functions in detail, let's look at Oracle-provided built-in functions in general. Grouping functions are covered in Chapter 11, regular expression functions in Chapter 14, object reference functions in Chapter 16, and XML functions in Chapter 17.

9.1   Types of Functions

Oracle divides all functions into the following categories:

- **Single-Row Functions**. Functions that operate on a single row at a time. This chapter examines this type of function. For example, the UPPER() function converts characters to uppercase.

- **Grouping Functions**. Chapter 11 covers grouping functions in detail.

  - **Aggregate Functions**. Functions that operate on a group of rows at one time and return a single row. For example, the COUNT() function counts the number of rows in a table.

  - **Analytical Functions**. Functions that operate on groups of rows and return one or more summary rows. For example, the STD-DEV() OVER() function returns the standard deviation rows based on values in one or more columns.

- **Object Reference Functions**. Functions that manipulate the value in columns with the REF datatype in object tables. For example, the DEREF() function returns the value of an attribute in the referenced object table (see Chapter 16).

- **User-Defined Functions**. Functions that are built by you and perform whatever data manipulations you program them to do. Examples of user-defined functions are given throughout this book, with syntactical details in Chapter 24.

This chapter covers many of the dozens of single-row functions available for your use in queries.

9.2   Single-Row Functions

Single-row functions add a great deal of power to queries. Use functions in the SELECT clause to modify the appearance of dates, for example. Add functions to the WHERE clause to help determine which rows to include in query results. Place functions in the ORDER BY clause to fine-tune sorting.

> **Note:** Placing functions in WHERE and ORDER BY clauses can be detrimental to performance.[1]

There are so many single-row functions that there is not room to cover them all in this chapter. However, you will gain experience with the commonly used functions. Other more obscure functions are detailed in Oracle documentation. Single-row functions can be subdivided into the following categories:

- **Character or String Functions**. Functions that require a character value or string as input (see Figure 9.1).

- **Number Functions**. Functions that require a number as input. Most of these return a number. For example, the SIGN function returns -1 if the number is negative, 0 if it is zero, and 1 if it is positive (see Figure 9.2).

    - (10*g*) **Binary Floating-Point Number Functions**. These functions are new to Oracle Database 10*g* and could possibly be viewed as a subset of number functions, except that they operate specifically on binary floating-point numbers (see Figure 9.2).

- **Datetime Functions**. Functions that require a date value as input (see Figure 9.3).

- **Conversion Functions**. Functions that convert one datatype to another. For example, the TO_CHAR function can convert a date or number to a character value (see Figure 9.4).

- **Miscellaneous Functions**. Functions that perform unusual tasks. For example, the DECODE function acts like an IF-THEN-ELSE construct or CASE statement (see Figure 9.5).

Figures 9.1 through 9.5 show all the different types of single-row functions. Functions highlighted and marked with an asterisk (*****INITCAP**) in each figure are discussed in this chapter. Additionally, many functions are referred to in other chapters.

See Chapter 14

Figure 9.1
Single-Row String Functions.

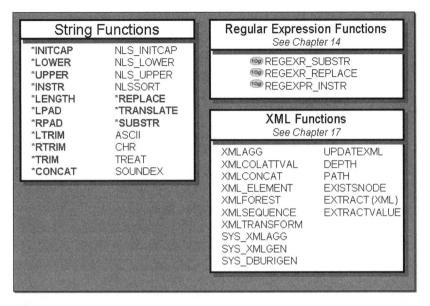

Figure 9.2
Single-Row Number Functions.

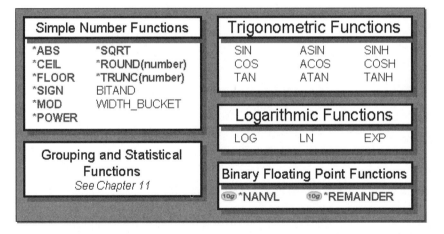

Figure 9.3
Single-Row Datetime Functions.

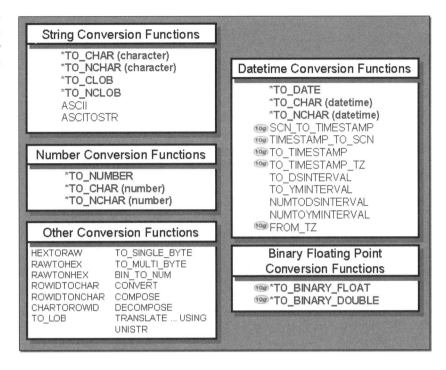

Figure 9.4
*Single-Row
Conversion
Functions.*

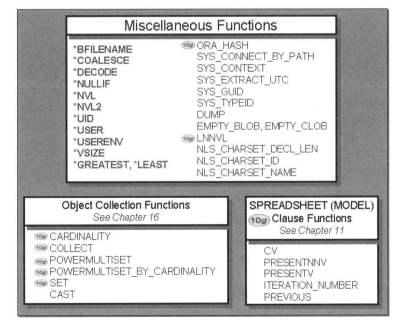

Figure 9.5
*Single-Row
Miscellaneous
Functions.*

The next sections define all of the functions highlighted in Figures 9.1 and 9.2, divided by their categories. Functions detailed in this chapter are generally the more useful functions. As already stated, the remaining functions tend to be obscure and seldom used. In fact, some functions included in this chapter are obscure. Let's begin with string functions.

9.2.1 String Functions

The string functions manipulate alphanumeric data. In this section, after each function is defined, an example shows how the function is used and what it returns.

- **CONCAT(expression, expression).** Concatenation of strings is the adding together of two strings. This function performs the same task as the string concatenation operator ∥ (see Chapter 7).

  ```
  CONCAT('Oracle',' Database 10g') = 'Oracle Database 10g'
  'Oracle'||' Database '||'10g' = 'Oracle Database 10g'
  'My name is '||FIRST_NAME = 'My name is Jim'
  ```

- **LOWER(expression)**, **UPPER(expression)**, and **INITCAP(expression)**. LOWER converts to lowercase, UPPER to uppercase, and INITCAP to mixed case (first letter of each word in uppercase).

  ```
  INITCAP('oracle certified professional')
  = 'Oracle Certified Professional'
  ```

- **INSTR(expression, substring [, position [, occurrence]]).** Returns the position of a substring within a string (the first character in the string is at position 1). The position and occurrence parameters are optional. The position parameter determines a start point to search from, and occurrence indicates which duplicate, if any, of the substring should be matched. In the following example, the second occurrence of the string 10g begins at position 19:

  ```
  INSTR('oracle 10g oracle 10g oracle 10g','10g',1,2) = 19
  ```

- **LENGTH(expression).** The length in characters of a string.

  ```
  LENGTH('oracle certified professional') = 29
  LENGTH(LAST_NAME) = length of the data in the column
  ```

- **LPAD(expression, n [, expression])** and **RPAD(expression, n [, expression]).** Left or right pad a string from the left or the right (start or end of the string) with the specified characters in the second string, up to a string length of *n* characters.

```
LPAD('oracle',10,'X') = 'XXXXoracle'
RPAD('oracle',10,'X') = 'oracleXXXX'
```

Note: Padding a string is sometimes referred to as filling a string.

- **TRIM([[LEADING|TRAILING|BOTH] character FROM] expression), LTRIM(expression, string-set),** and **RTRIM(expression, string-set).** LTRIM and RTRIM will remove from the left and the right of the string, respectively, any characters contained within the string set, until a character not in the string set is found. The LTRIM and RTRIM functions are less useful than the TRIM function. TRIM will remove characters from the string from the left, the right, or both. In its simplest form, TRIM can be used to remove leading and trailing spaces from a string.

  ```
  TRIM('   oracle   ') = 'oracle'
  ```

  Remember that spaces embedded between other characters do not get removed, until a character not in the string set is found. As a result, for the next example there is no change.

  ```
  TRIM(' o r a c l e ') = 'o r a c l e'
  TRIM( LEADING '-' FROM '---608-444-3029') = '608-444-3029'
  ```

- **REPLACE(expression, search [, replace])** and **TRANSLATE(expression, search [, replace]).** REPLACE will replace every occurrence of the search string with the replacement string. Where the REPLACE function matches any search string within the string, TRANSLATE will match each character between the search and replace strings by the position of characters in both the search and replace strings. Phew! In simple terms, REPLACE replaces groups of characters and TRANSLATE translates individual characters.

  ```
  REPLACE(' o r a c l e',' ','') = 'oracle'
  REPLACE('My dog has fleas.','as','odd')
     = 'My dog hodd fleodd.'
  ```

  In the first TRANSLATE function example following, nothing is changed because the space in the search string has no corresponding value in the replace string.

  ```
  TRANSLATE(' o r a c l e ','oracle ','12345X')
     = '12345X'
  TRANSLATE('My dog has fleas.','agf','AGF')
     = 'My doG hAs FleAs.'
  ```

- **SUBSTR(expression, [-]position[, length])**. The SUBSTR function returns a portion of a string. If the length parameter is omitted, then all characters after the value of position are returned. If the position parameter is positive, then the substring value is extracted from the left of the string; otherwise, if the parameter is negative, the value is extracted from the right (end) of the string.

```
SUBSTR('oracle certified professional', 8,9)
   = 'certified'
SUBSTR('oracle certified professional',-12,12)
   = 'professional'
```

Here is a quick example using some of the string functions mentioned previously. Figure 9.6 shows the results. The query shows the complete value of the NAME column, followed by the length of the value, a section of the name, and finally, the position of the second occurrence of the letter "a" in the name. Notice that the INSTR function returns zero if it cannot find a match.

```
SELECT NAME, LENGTH(NAME) "Length"
, SUBSTR(NAME,5,5) "Letters 5 thru 9"
, INSTR(NAME,'a',1,2) "Second a"
FROM ARTIST;
```

Now let's proceed to number functions.

9.2.2 Number Functions

Number functions require numbers, not strings, as input. They nearly always return a numeric value.

- **ABS(n)**. Finds an absolute value of a number. An absolute value function returns the positive or unsigned value of a negative or positive number.

```
ABS(-125) = 125
ABS(125) = 125
```

- **CEIL(n)** and **FLOOR(n)**. Ceiling and floor are similar to rounding and truncating functions. Ceiling returns the next integer greater than n. Floor returns the next integer less than n.

```
CEIL(1.1) = 2
```

Figure 9.6
Some String Functions.

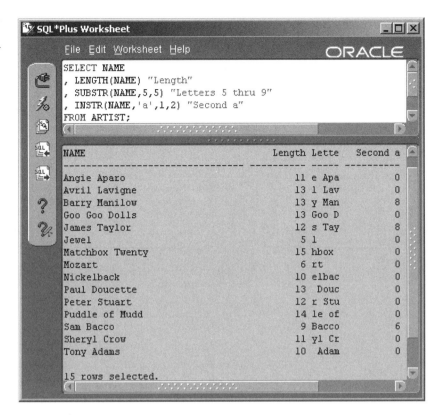

```
SQL*Plus Worksheet                                    _□×
File  Edit  Worksheet  Help                    ORACLE

SELECT NAME
, LENGTH(NAME) "Length"
, SUBSTR(NAME,5,5) "Letters 5 thru 9"
, INSTR(NAME,'a',1,2) "Second a"
FROM ARTIST;

NAME                         Length Lette   Second a
--------------------------- ------ ----- ----------
Angie Aparo                      11 e Apa          0
Avril Lavigne                    13 l Lav          0
Barry Manilow                    13 y Man          8
Goo Goo Dolls                    13 Goo D          0
James Taylor                     12 s Tay          8
Jewel                             5 l               0
Matchbox Twenty                  15 hbox           0
Mozart                            6 rt              0
Nickelback                       10 elbac          0
Paul Doucette                    13  Douc          0
Peter Stuart                     12 r Stu          0
Puddle of Mudd                   14 le of          0
Sam Bacco                         9 Bacco          6
Sheryl Crow                      11 yl Cr          0
Tony Adams                       10  Adam          0

15 rows selected.
```

```
FLOOR(1.9) = 1
```

- **MOD(m, n).** MOD is the modulus or remainder function, which returns the remainder of the first value divided by the second value (*m* divided by *n*). The first value is returned if the second value is zero.

```
MOD(5,2) = 1
MOD(4,0) = 4
MOD(9,3) = 0
MOD(23,4) = 3
```

- **POWER(m, n).** The exponential function raises *m* to the power of *n* (the *nth* power).

```
POWER(2,3) = 8 (2³ = 2 * 2 * 2 = 4 * 2 = 8)
```

- **ROUND(n [, places]).** ROUND is a proper mathematical rounding function as opposed to the CEIL and FLOOR functions. For the ROUND function, a decimal 5 and over will be rounded up and below 5 will be rounded down. The third example following is rounded to two decimal places and the fourth to three decimal places.

```
ROUND(1.4) = 1
ROUND(1.5) = 2
ROUND(1.42356,2) = 1.42
ROUND(1.42356,3) = 1.424
ROUND(18755.24,-2) = 18800
```

- **SIGN(n)**. Returns −1 if negative, 0 if 0, and 1 if positive.

```
SIGN(-5032) = -1
SIGN(0) = 0
SIGN(5000) = 1
```

- **SQRT(n)**. Calculates the square root of a number.

```
SQRT(4) = 2 (2 * 2 = 4)
```

- **TRUNC(n [, places])**. TRUNC is a truncate function. A truncate function always rounds down by removing trailing numerals from a number, effectively rounding down regardless of the .5 cutoff value. TRUNC can also truncate both sides of the decimal point.

```
TRUNC(147.65,1) = 147.6
TRUNC(147.65,-2) = 100
```

- **Other Mathematical Functions**. The following functions perform obscure mathematical or trigonometric calculations. These types of functions are rarely used other than in financial or numerically related applications. Some of these functions are listed here. There are many other Oracle built-in functions to do all sorts of weird and wonderful things (see Oracle documentation).

  - *SIN(n), COS(n), and TAN(n).* Sine, cosine, and tangent.
  - *ASIN(n), ACOS(n), and ACOS(n).* Arcsine, arccosine, and arctangent (the inverse of sine, cosine, and tangent).
  - *SINH(n), COSH(n), and TANH(n).* Hyperbolic sine, cosine, and tangent.
  - *EXP(n), LN(n), and LOG(n).* e raised to the *nth* power, the natural logarithm, and the logarithm.

Here is a query using some of the number functions mentioned. The query uses the STUDIOTIME table and applies various functions to the AMOUNT_CHARGED column values. The result is shown in Figure 9.7.

```
SELECT ST.ARTIST_ID, ST.AMOUNT_CHARGED "Amount"
 , ROUND(ST.AMOUNT_CHARGED,1) "Rounded to one decimal"
```

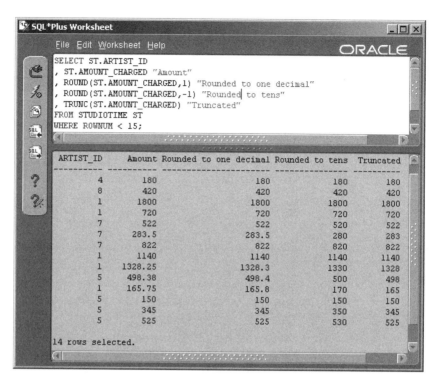

Figure 9.7
Number Functions Return Results Based on the Column Value.

```
, ROUND(ST.AMOUNT_CHARGED,-1) "Rounded to tens"
, TRUNC(ST.AMOUNT_CHARGED) "Truncated"
FROM STUDIOTIME ST
WHERE ROWNUM < 15;
```

9.2.2.1 (10*g*) Binary Floating-Point Number Functions

As already mentioned, these functions are new to Oracle Database 10*g* and could possibly be viewed as a subset of number functions, except that they operate specifically on binary floating-point numbers. This section is partially repeated from Chapter 2.

- **TO_BINARY_DOUBLE(expression, format)** and **TO_BINARY_ FLOAT(expression, format)** allow for conversions. Essentially, these functions are conversion functions, but they are listed here because they deal with binary floating-point numbers.

- **NANVL(value, replace)**. NANVL returns a replacement value if the initial value is not a number.

- **REMAINDER(n, m)**. This function is a remainder or modulus function specifically for binary floating-point numbers.

The next section covers date functions.

9.2.3 Date Functions

- **ADD_MONTHS(date, months)**, **NEXT_DAY(date, weekday)**, **LAST_DAY(date)**, and **MONTHS_BETWEEN(date, date)**. ADD_MONTHS will add or subtract a number of months to a date where differences in the number of days in months default to the last day in the resulting month. NEXT_DAY finds the first day from the date specified for the day of the week in the string contained in the second parameter. LAST_DAY finds the last day in the month. MONTHS_BETWEEN will return the number of months between two dates.

```
ADD_MONTHS('27-AUG-02',4) = 27-DEC-02
NEXT_DAY('27-AUG-02','MONDAY') = 02-SEP-02
LAST_DAY('27-AUG-02') = 31-AUG-02
MONTHS_BETWEEN('27-AUG-02','01-JAN-02')
   = 7.83870968 months
```

Note: In the examples listed, note how dates are listed as strings and a TO_DATE conversion function is not required. This is because DD-MON-YY is the default date format and there is an implicit string-to-date datatype conversion. The default date format can be altered. Datatypes are covered in Chapter 16.

- **SYSDATE, CURRENT_DATE, CURRENT_TIMESTAMP(precision), LOCALTIMESTAMP(precision)**, and **SYSTIMESTAMP**. SYSDATE and CURRENT_DATE find the system date setting on the database server where CURRENT_DATE is timezone sensitive. The other functions all provide different variations on timestamps.

```
SQL> SELECT SYSDATE FROM DUAL;
SYSDATE

--------------
23-JAN-04
SQL> SELECT SYSTIMESTAMP FROM DUAL;
SYSTIMESTAMP

-----------------------
23-JAN-04 01.03.20.661000 AM -05:00
```

Table 9.1 *Some of the ROUND and TRUNC Function Date Formatting*

Format Characters	Rounding and Truncating
CC	The first year in a century.
YYYY, YEAR, YY	The nearest year, rounds up on July 1st.
Q	The nearest quarter, rounds up on the 16th of month two.
MONTH, MON, MM	The nearest month, rounds up on the 16th.
WW	The same day of the week as the first day of the year.
W	The same day of the week as the first day of the month.
DDD, DD	The day.
DAY, D	The first day of the week.
HH, HH12, HH24	The hour (HH24 is a 24-hour clock).
MI	The minute.

- **ROUND(date [, format]) and TRUNC(date [, format])**. These two functions round up or truncate dates according to the format specification. See Table 9.1 with date formatting rules for the ROUND and TRUNC functions.

  Some examples of date ROUND and TRUNC functions are as follows. Let's say that our current date is 26-AUG-02.

  ```
  ROUND(SYSDATE,'YEAR') = 01-JAN-03
  TRUNC(SYSDATE,'YEAR') = 01-JAN-02

  ROUND(SYSDATE,'MONTH') = 01-SEP-02
  TRUNC(SYSDATE,'MONTH') = 01-AUG-02

  ROUND(SYSDATE,'WW') = 27-AUG-02
  TRUNC(SYSDATE,'WW') = 20-AUG-02
  ```

- **EXTRACT (format, date)**. The EXTRACT date function is probably one of the most useful and largely unknown date functions. Format settings are simple, specific, and can be YEAR, MONTH, DAY, HOUR, MINUTE, SECOND, or various TIMEZONE options.

Two examples in the following two queries have their results shown in Figure 9.8.

```
SELECT EXTRACT(YEAR FROM DATE '2004-02-09') AS YEAR
   , EXTRACT(MONTH FROM DATE '2004-02-09') AS MONTH
   , EXTRACT(DAY FROM DATE '2004-02-09') AS DAY
FROM DUAL;

SELECT EXTRACT(YEAR FROM SYSDATE) AS YEAR
   , EXTRACT(MONTH FROM SYSDATE) AS MONTH
   , EXTRACT(DAY FROM SYSDATE) AS DAY
FROM DUAL;
```

Looking at some general date function examples, the next query uses several date functions. The final expression uses the SYSDATE function and subtracts two dates. The results are in days, so to help compare the MONTHS_BETWEEN function and the next column, that following col-

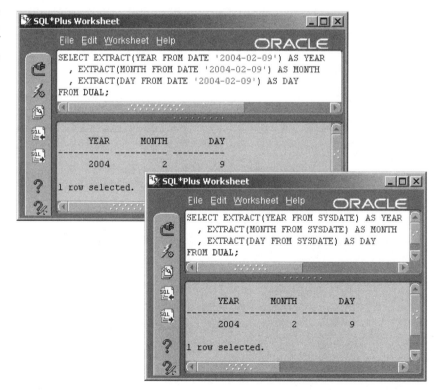

Figure 9.8
The EXTRACT Function Retrieves Parts of Dates.

umn is divided by the average number of days per month (30.44). The two values Months-1 and Months-2 are very close but not identical. This is a rather odd example, but Figure 9.9 shows the result.

```
SELECT SESSION_DATE
  , ADD_MONTHS(SESSION_DATE,3) "Plus 3 Months"
  , ROUND(SESSION_DATE,'Month') "Round off"
  , MONTHS_BETWEEN(SYSDATE,DUE_DATE) "Months-1"
  , (SYSDATE-DUE_DATE)/30.44 "Months-2"
FROM STUDIOTIME
WHERE ROWNUM < 15;
```

The next section examines datatype conversion functions.

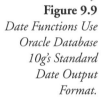

Figure 9.9
Date Functions Use Oracle Database 10g's Standard Date Output Format.

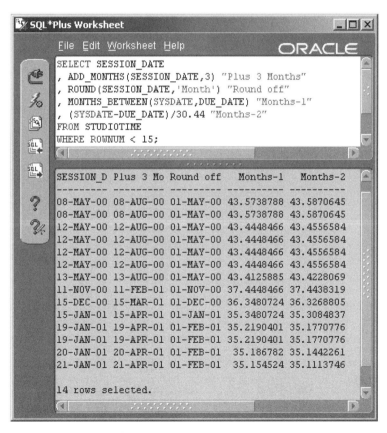

9.2.4   **Datatype Conversion Functions**

Before we get to examples and combining of functions, where we often use conversion functions, we will describe the most useful datatype conversion functions. Conversion functions are important in two ways:

1.   The obvious is that they allow conversions between different datatypes.

2.   The more important and less obvious is that conversion functions allow the combination of different datatypes into expressions to produce a single datatype result.

The conversion functions we are most interested in are as listed here.

- Date conversion functions:

  - **TO_DATE(date[, format])**. Converts a string representation of a date to a date.
  - **TO_CHAR(date [, format])**. Converts a date to a string.

- Number conversion functions:

  - **TO_CHAR(number [, format])**. Converts a number to a string.
  - **TO_NUMBER(string [, format])**. Converts a string to a number.

- Other conversion functions:

  - **TO_CLOB(string)**. Converts a simple string to a CLOB or binary text object. Converting from a CLOB object to a string is transparent. Transparent is a computerese jargon term meaning automatic. No conversion function is required.
  - **TO_N{CHAR|DATE|NUMBER|CLOB}(expression [, format])**. This function can be used to convert an expression, string, date, or number from the database character set to the national character set. For example, TO_NCHAR converts an incoming value to a national character set value.

Now we need to examine conversion function format options. Conversion formats are applied as a datatype conversion takes place.

9.2.4.1   **Number Conversion Function Formats**

TO_CHAR(number[, format]) is used to convert from a number to a string, and TO_NUMBER(string [, format]) is used to convert from a string to a number. As with the ROUND and TRUNC functions, there are numerous applicable formatting rules.

Table 9.2 *Some of the Number Formatting Models*

Number Format Models	What Is It?
9,999,999	Delimit thousands with commas (1000000 shows 1,000,000).
99.99	Number of decimal places (95.3359 shows 95.34).
$9999	Display a leading $ sign (1000 shows $1000).
09999, 99990	Leading and trailing zeros (05633 shows 05633).
99999	Format to a specified number of numerals (05633 shows 5633).
B9999.99	Integer shown as blanks (0.99 shows .99).
C999	Leading ISO currency symbol (839 shows USD839).
9.9EEEE	Scientific notation (2000000 shows 2.0E+06).
9999MI	Negative value has a trailing minus sign and positive a trailing blank (-500 shows 500-).
9999PR	Negative value in <999> and positive with a leading and trailing blank (-500 shows <500>).
S9999, 9999S	S replaces negative value with a minus sign or positive sign depending on value (-500 shows −500 and 500 shows +500).
RN, rn	Roman numerals in upper or lowercase (2002 shows MMII).

A number format implies a display format imposed on a number when that number is converted to a string using the TO_CHAR function. The conversion is required in order to format the number into an easily readable form. Some of the available number conversion format modifiers are shown in Table 9.2.

9.2.4.2 Date Conversion Function Formats

The TO_DATE(date[, format]) and TO_CHAR(date [, format]) functions are used to convert between strings and dates. Converting a date to a string requires that the string is a string representation of a date. As with the ROUND, TRUNC, and number conversion functions, there are numerous applicable formatting rules. Table 9.3 shows some of the date conversion format modifiers.

Table 9.3   *Some of the Date Formatting Models*

Date Format Models	What Is It?
- / , . ;	Permitted punctuation with date string representation.
YEAR	The year (2002 shows TWO THOUSAND TWO).
YYYY	4-digit year.
YYY, YY & Y	Last *n* digits of the year.
Q	Quarter of year, 1 to 4.
MM	Month, 01 to 12.
MONTH & MON	Month name and abbreviated month name.
WW	Week of year, 1 to 53.
W	Week of month, 1 to 5.
D	Week day, 1 to 7.
DAY & DY	Day name and abbreviated day name.
DD	Day of month, 1 to 31.
DDD	Day of year, 1 to 366.
HH & HH12	Hour of day, 1 to 12.
HH24	24-hour clock, 0 to 23.
MI	Minutes, 0 to 59.
SS	Seconds, 0 to 59.
AM & PM	AM or PM.
AD & BC	BC or AD.
J	Julian day or number of days since 01/01/4712 BC.
RM	Roman month, I to XII.

Here are some examples using datatype conversion functions. Figure 9.10 shows part of the results. The TO_CHAR function for dates allows you to format the date in a huge variety of ways.

```
SELECT TO_CHAR(RECORDING_DATE,'Day, Month dd, YYYY')
"Spell the day"
  , TO_CHAR(RECORDING_DATE,'MM/DD/YY') "American style"
```

Figure 9.10
*Three Variations
on the Date
Format with
TO_CHAR.*

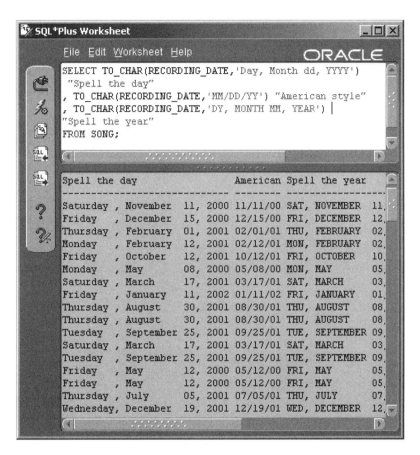

, TO_CHAR(RECORDING_DATE,'DY, MONTH MM, YEAR')
"Spell the year"
FROM SONG;

The next query shows the TO_CHAR function for numbers. Figure 9.11 shows part of the result.

```
SELECT ARTIST_ID, AMOUNT_CHARGED
,TO_CHAR(AMOUNT_CHARGED,'$9,999,990.00') FORMAT1
,TO_CHAR(AMOUNT_CHARGED,'0999990.9999') FORMAT2
FROM STUDIOTIME;
```

Figure 9.11
Numbers Converted to Characters Helps Format Results.

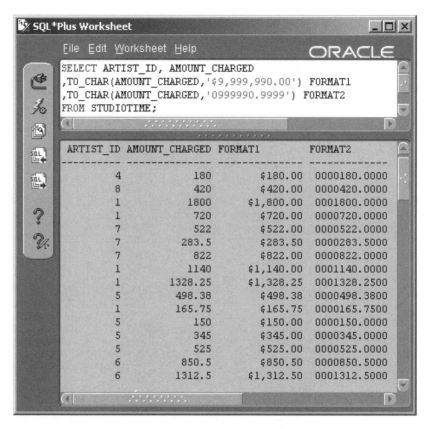

The next section covers miscellaneous functions. These functions are miscellaneous essentially because they cannot be classified as being part of any of the previous sections.

9.2.5 Miscellaneous Functions

- **COALESCE(expression)**. The COALESCE function retrieves the first non-null-valued expression in a list of expressions.

```
COALESCE(NULL,NULL,'33','testing') = 33
```

- **DECODE(expression, search, replace[, default])**. This function is similar to an IF-THEN-ELSE construct or CASE statement in programming. There is also an inline CASE statement available in Oracle SQL (see Chapter 14).

```
DECODE('Harry'
    ,'Harry','It is Harry!'
    ,'Joe','It is Joe!'
```

```
      ,'Not Harry or Joe.') = 'It is Harry!'
DECODE('Joe'
   ,'Harry','It is Harry!'
   ,'Joe','It is Joe!'
   ,'Not Harry or Joe.') = 'It is Joe!'
DECODE('Mary'
   ,'Harry','It is Harry!'
   ,'Joe','It is Joe!'
   ,'Not Harry or Joe.') = 'Not Harry or Joe.'
```

- **GREATEST(expression[, expression ...])** and **LEAST(expression [, expression ...])**. These two functions return the greatest and least values, respectively, of a list of expressions.

```
GREATEST('Amy', 'Joe', 'ant', 'Giant') = 'ant'
LEAST(7,12, 2, 15) = 2
```

- **NULLIF(expression, expression)**. Returns a null value when both expressions are equal. If they are not equal, the first expression is returned.

```
NULLIF('blue','green') = 'blue'
NULLIF('green','green') = NULL
```

- **NVL(expression, replace)** and **NVL2(expression, replace, replace)**. NVL exchanges a null-valued result with a replacement value. If the expression is not NULL, the expression is returned unchanged. NVL2, on the other hand, will return the first replacement expression if not NULL and the second replacement expression if NULL.

```
NVL('Bird','NULL was found') = 'Bird'
NVL('','NULL was found') = 'NULL was found'
NVL2('This is not NULL','Not NULL','NULL') = 'Not NULL'
NVL2('','Not NULL','NULL') = 'NULL'
```

- **USER and UID**. These two functions return the Oracle username (schema name) and unique user ID for the currently logged-in user, respectively. These values can also be found in the USER_USERS view and have no parameters. The first example requires that the current session be logged in as the MUSIC user. The UID or user ID value is very likely to be different for every session.

```
USER = MUSIC
UID = 101
```

- **USERENV(parameter)**. Returns user session environmental settings based on the input parameter value. This function is retained in Oracle Database 10*g* for backward compatibility. Parameter values are numerous. Some of them are CLIENT_INFO, ENTRYID, ISDBA, LANG, LANGUAGE, SESSIONID, and TERMINAL. The SESSIONID is likely to be different for every session.

```
USERENV('SESSIONID') = 1520
```

■ **VSIZE(expression)**. The number of bytes in an expression.

```
VSIZE('Oracle Certified Professional') = 29
VSIZE(100.234) = 5
```

Note: Regular expression functions are covered in Chapter 14. XML functions are covered in Chapter 17. BFILENAME is covered in Chapter 16.

Let's take a quick peek at the DECODE function. The next query uses the home state of the artist in a whimsical DECODE statement, replacing the name of the state with various phrases. For example, the state code "OR" is replaced by the phrase "Tree hugger." The default value is always listed last after the search-and-replace value pairs. In this example, the default is the phrase "Whatever!" Figure 9.12 shows the result.

```
SELECT STATE_PROVINCE
, DECODE(STATE_PROVINCE,'CA','Surfer',
                        'NH','Snow bunny',
                        'OR', 'Tree hugger',
                        'FL', 'Retired',
                        'Whatever!')
FROM ARTIST;
```

Now let's look at combining various functions.

9.3   Combining Functions

So far in this chapter, we have looked at a lot of single-row function definitions. Now let's get to more practical uses for these functions by combining various functions into single expressions. Remember, single-row functions return a single value when passed various parameters and always work with the values on one row of data at a time.

Let's use a combination of SUBSTR and INSTR to retrieve the first name of the artist. We know that there will always be a space between the first name and the last name. So we use the INSTR function to determine the location of the space and then use SUBSTR to return the characters

Figure 9.12
*The DECODE
Function Is Useful
for Short Lists of
Values.*

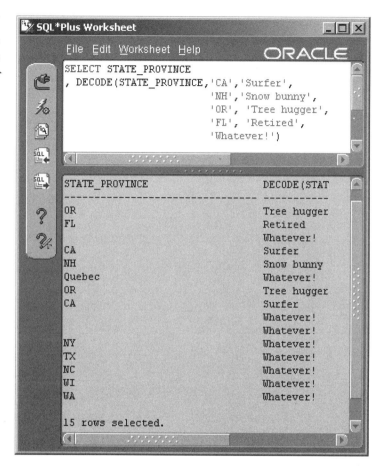

from the beginning of the NAME column, up to the space character. The first two columns in the query are included to show the values being worked with, helping understand what the combination of the two functions returns Figure 9.13 shows the result.

```
SELECT NAME, INSTR(NAME,' ')
, SUBSTR(NAME,1,INSTR(NAME,' ')) FIRSTNAME
FROM ARTIST;
```

Now let's find the last name, once again using the INSTR and SUBSTR functions. The result is shown in Figure 9.14.

```
COLUMN LASTNAME FORMAT A20
```

Figure 9.13

*Extract the First
Name from a
Column
Containing First
and Last Names.*

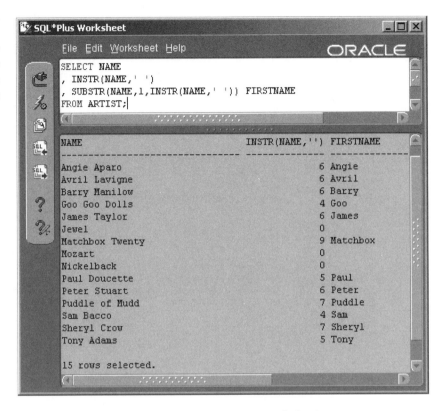

```
SELECT NAME, LENGTH(NAME), INSTR(NAME,' ')+1
, SUBSTR(NAME,(INSTR(NAME,' ')+1)) LASTNAME
FROM ARTIST;
```

This next example uses several functions. The PLAYING_TIME column contains the minutes and seconds of playing time for a song in the format m:ss (minutes:seconds). This query is built gradually in sections. First, find the colon and separate minutes from seconds using the INSTR and SUBSTR functions. Extract the minutes:

```
SUBSTR(PLAYING_TIME,1,INSTR(PLAYING_TIME,':')-1)
```

Extract the seconds:

```
SUBSTR(PLAYING_TIME,INSTR(PLAYING_TIME,':')+1)
```

Figure 9.14
*Start at the
Character
Following the
Blank Space to Get
the Last Name.*

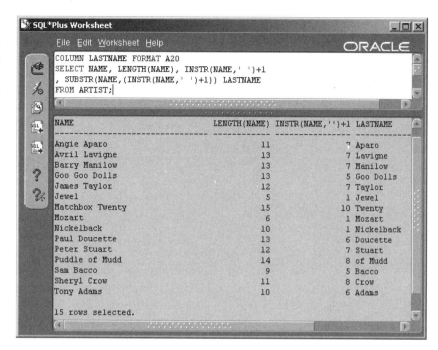

```
COLUMN LASTNAME FORMAT A20
SELECT NAME, LENGTH(NAME), INSTR(NAME,' ')+1
, SUBSTR(NAME,(INSTR(NAME,' ')+1)) LASTNAME
FROM ARTIST;
```

```
NAME                                    LENGTH(NAME) INSTR(NAME,'')+1 LASTNAME
--------------------------------------- ------------ ---------------- --------
Angie Aparo                                       11                7 Aparo
Avril Lavigne                                     13                7 Lavigne
Barry Manilow                                     13                7 Manilow
Goo Goo Dolls                                     13                5 Goo Dolls
James Taylor                                      12                7 Taylor
Jewel                                              5                1 Jewel
Matchbox Twenty                                   15               10 Twenty
Mozart                                             6                1 Mozart
Nickelback                                        10                1 Nickelback
Paul Doucette                                     13                6 Doucette
Peter Stuart                                      12                7 Stuart
Puddle of Mudd                                    14                8 of Mudd
Sam Bacco                                          9                5 Bacco
Sheryl Crow                                       11                8 Crow
Tony Adams                                        10                6 Adams

15 rows selected.
```

In the next extract, when the minutes are NULL, the word "Unknown" is substituted for the null value using the NVL function. Additionally, the words "Minutes and " are concatenated onto the minutes.

```
NVL(SUBSTR(PLAYING_TIME,1,INSTR(PLAYING_TIME,':')-1)
,'Unknown')||' Minutes and '
```

Next, seconds are extracted using SUBSTR and INSTR again. Then, add the NVL function to substitute the word "Unknown" if the results are NULL. In this case, there are trailing blanks, because the column is CHAR datatype (rather than VARCHAR2, which excludes trailing blanks). So, add the RTRIM function to remove the trailing blanks.

```
RTRIM(NVL(SUBSTR(PLAYING_TIME,INSTR(PLAYING_TIME,':')+1)
      ,'Unknown'))||' Seconds.'
```

Finally, concatenate the minutes to the seconds and additionally concatenate " Seconds." to the end of the whole thing. The first two columns are displayed as reference points so you can see how the functions have worked on the original values in the PLAYING_TIME column. The following query is the resulting script, and Figure 9.15 shows part of the result.

```
SELECT PLAYING_TIME, INSTR(PLAYING_TIME,':') DIVIDER
, NVL(
    SUBSTR(PLAYING_TIME,1,INSTR(PLAYING_TIME,':')-1)
    ,'Unknown')||' Minutes and '
||RTRIM(NVL(
    SUBSTR(PLAYING_TIME,INSTR(PLAYING_TIME,':')+1)
    ,'Unknown')
    )||' Seconds.'  PLAYING_TIME
FROM SONG;
```

Now let's examine an example with the TRUNC and DECODE functions. This query shows how to use DECODE to categorize the rows in the STUDIOTIME table into ranges of values. First, the query uses the

Figure 9.15
Multiple Layers of Functions Can Get Complex to Follow but Yield Useful Results.

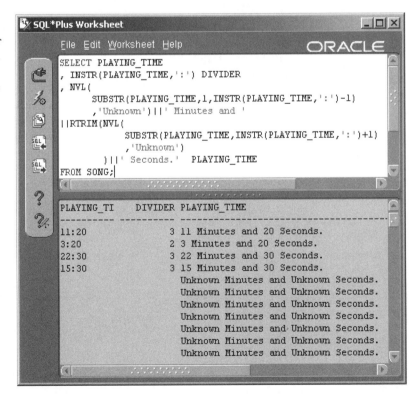

TO_DATE function to choose only those rows that fall in the year 2002 using a WHERE clause.

```
WHERE TO_CHAR(SESSION_DATE,'YYYY') = '2002'
```

To sift a range of values using DECODE, you need a finite list of numbers. The AMOUNT_CHARGED is converted into the next highest 100, providing values such as 100, 500, 1200, and so on.

```
TRUNC(AMOUNT_CHARGED,-2)+100
```

The following list can be used in the DECODE function. We want the DECODE function to sort values into the following categories:

- If the AMOUNT_CHARGED is less than $400, this is a "Low Risk" amount.
- If the AMOUNT_CHARGED is at least $400 but less than $700, this is a "Medium Risk" amount.
- Otherwise, this is a "High Risk" amount.

Here is the complete query, including the DECODE function. The results are sorted by the AMOUNT_CHARGED and shown in Figure 9.16.

```
SELECT AMOUNT_CHARGED
,TRUNC(AMOUNT_CHARGED,-2)+100 NEXT_HIGHEST_HUNDRED
, DECODE (ROUND(AMOUNT_CHARGED,-2)+100,
          100, 'Low Risk',
          200, 'Low Risk',
          300, 'Low Risk',
          400, 'Low Risk',
          500, 'Med Risk',
          600, 'Med Risk',
          700, 'Med Risk',
        'High Risk') RISK_FACTOR
FROM STUDIOTIME
WHERE TO_CHAR(SESSION_DATE,'YYYY') = '2002'
ORDER BY 1;
```

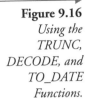

Figure 9.16
Using the
TRUNC,
DECODE, and
TO_DATE
Functions.

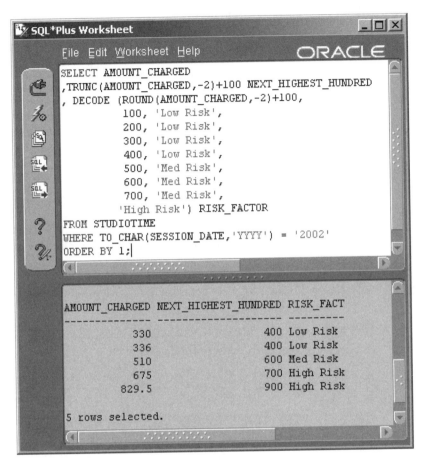

Note how amounts in Figure 9.16 are truncated and then $100 is added to the amount. This expression is then used as the search parameter in the DECODE function.

Note: Using functions in the WHERE clause will hurt performance unless function-based indexes are used. However, be aware of overindexing with function-based indexes. Creating too many indexes can hurt performance as well. The best option is not to use functions in the WHERE clause, other than with literal values, if possible.

Once again, further details on Oracle SQL single-row functions can be found in Oracle documentation both online and in Oracle software documentation. Specific reference details of all functions can be found in the SQL Reference Manual section under the Oracle documentation list of books.

This chapter is intended to provide a good start on using single-row functions. You have probably already thought of some good applications for these functional tools. The next chapter describes joining tables into single-result sets, which gives you even more power to manipulate data using increasingly powerful and versatile queries.

9.4   Endnotes

1.   Oracle Performance Tuning for $9i$ and $10g$ (ISBN: 1-55558-305-9)

10

Joining Tables

In this chapter:

- What is a join?
- What is Oracle's proprietary format for joins?
- What is the ANSI join format?
- What types of joins can be performed?
- How can joins be implemented?

A join is retrieval of data from more than one table. This chapter shows you how to merge rows from multiple tables into a single query. Merging of rows is known as a *join*. This chapter experiments with example SELECT statements containing many different types of joins.

In previous chapters you have explored the SELECT, FROM, WHERE, and ORDER BY clauses. Both the American National Standards Institute (ANSI) format JOIN clause and the Oracle proprietary format for joining tables are used in all examples where possible. The JOIN clause is the ANSI equivalent of the Oracle proprietary join syntax. We examine both formats for the following reasons:

- The Oracle proprietary format has not as yet been deprecated in favor of the ANSI JOIN clause; therefore, it is important that even new DBAs be familiar with its use. As a side issue, Oracle Certification exams may test both formats.

- Both formats are useful for explaining how joins behave and how to select the most appropriate format. In addition, one type of join, the full outer join, cannot be done in Oracle's proprietary format. Thus the ANSI format must be used at least to describe full outer joins.

Let's begin by looking at the two different join formats in detail.

10.1 Join Formats

As already stated, the two join formats available are the Oracle proprietary format and the ANSI standard join format.

10.1.1 Oracle's Proprietary Format

Oracle's proprietary join format may eventually be superseded by the ANSI format JOIN clause syntax. At present, this is not the case. In the Oracle proprietary format, join syntax is part of the WHERE clause. Outer joins are handled by using an outer join operator denoted by a plus sign enclosed in parentheses, (+). The outer join operator is placed after a column name reference in the WHERE clause on all columns belonging to the table on the outer side of the join, the side deficient in information or rows. Figure 10.1 shows the basic syntax of the SELECT statement, including the WHERE clause and Oracle proprietary format join syntax using the (+) operator.

10.1.2 ANSI Format

The ANSI format JOIN clause has been included in Oracle as optional when joining tables. Figure 10.2 shows the syntax of the ANSI JOIN clause. The following points should be noted:

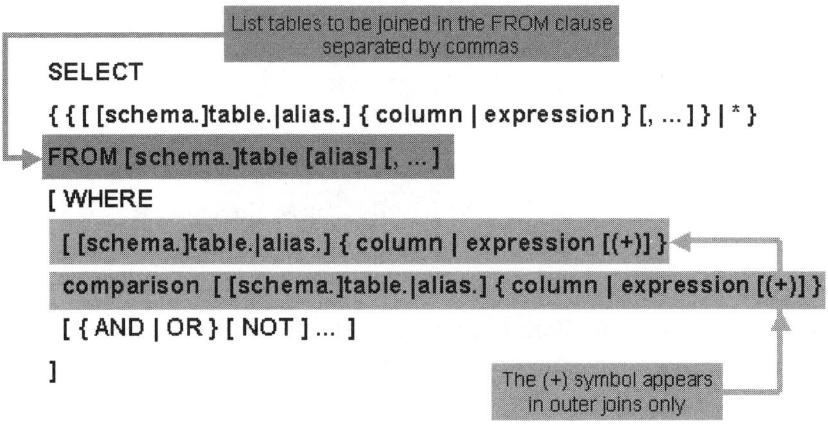

Figure 10.1
Oracle's Proprietary Join Syntax Using the (+) Operator.

List tables to be joined in the FROM clause separated by commas

```
SELECT
  { { [ [schema.]table.|alias.] { column | expression } [, ... ] } | * }
FROM [schema.]table [alias] [, ... ]
[ WHERE
    [ [schema.]table.|alias.] { column | expression [(+)] }
    comparison  [ [schema.]table.|alias.] { column | expression [(+)] }
    [ { AND | OR } [ NOT ] ... ]
]
```

The (+) symbol appears in outer joins only

Figure 10.2
ANSI Join Syntax.

```
SELECT
{ { [ [schema.]table.|alias.] { column | expression } [, ... ] } | * }
FROM table-reference
[
    CROSS JOIN table-reference
  | NATURAL [ join-type ] JOIN table-reference
  | {
      [ join-type ] JOIN table-reference
      {
          ON (column = column [ { AND | OR } [ NOT ] ... ] column = column ... )
        | USING (column [, column ... ])
      }
    }
]
[ WHERE ... ]
[ ORDER BY ... ]
}

table-reference = [schema.]table [alias]

join-type = INNER | [ LEFT | RIGHT | FULL ] OUTER
```

- More than two tables in a join forces specification of columns using the USING or ON clauses, or both.

- For the ANSI format, tables are joined from left to right. Thus join conditions can only reference columns in the current join or from previous joins to the left. For the Oracle format, tables are joined from left to right and top to bottom, allowing reference to any join condition in the WHERE clause from anywhere in the WHERE clause.

Note: When tuning using the Optimizer and the EXPLAIN PLAN command, in the deeper layers of Oracle tuning tools, these facts are not always strictly true. For the purposes of this Oracle SQL book, these facts will suffice.[1]

Now let's look at different types of joins you are able to build in Oracle.

10.2   Types of Joins

Let's look at the available types of joins and what exactly they do:

- **Cross-join or Cartesian product.** Merges all data selected from both tables into a single result set.

- **Inner join.** Combines rows from both tables using matching column names and column values. The result set includes only rows that match.

- **Outer join.** Selects rows from both tables as with an inner join but including rows from one or both tables that do not have matching rows in the other table. Missing values are replaced with null values.

  - **Left outer join.** All rows from the left table plus all matching rows from the right table. Column values from the right table are replaced with null values when the matching right-side row does not exist in the left-side table.
  - **Right outer join.** All rows from the table on the right plus matching rows from the left table, the opposite of the left outer join.
  - **Full outer join.** All rows from both tables, with null values replacing missing values.

- **Self-join.** This joins a table to itself.

- **Equi-joins, anti-joins, and range joins.** An equi-join combines table data based on equality (=), an anti-join matches data based on inequality (!=, <> or NOT), and a range join compares data using a range of values (<, > or BETWEEN).

- **Mutable and complex joins.** A mutable join is a join of more than two tables. A complex join is a mutable join with added filtering.

This is a lot of technical jargon. Let's explain what joins are using simple mathematical set theory. Relational database theory is based on set theory. Do you remember learning set theory at school? A direct correlation can be made between simple set theory and relational database joins.

Figure 10.3 shows two completely unrelated sets, Set A and Set B. That is, the two sets are not related to one another in any way. You can see that

Figure 10.3
Two Unrelated Sets.

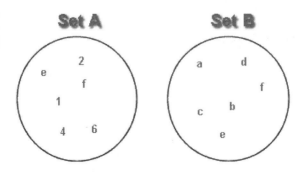

Figure 10.4
A Natural Join or
Intersection.

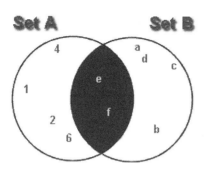

some of the elements of each set appear in both sets. With respect to a relational database, until we create some kind of relationship between the two sets, they are still unrelated.

In Figure 10.4, we can see the same two sets but now showing the intersection of those two sets. The intersection of Sets A and B would be the equivalent of an inner join. An inner join contains only those elements found in both sets.

Figure 10.5 shows all elements in Set A that are also in Set B (the intersection) plus all those elements in Set A that are not in Set B. This the equivalent of a left outer join. As you can see, the picture contains the left set outside the intersection area, plus only the parts of the right set that match elements in the left set. "Why not just use Set A?" you ask. The answer will be very clear when you begin using actual tables. Imagine these examples as containing only one column each of two tables. Once matched, you can find the values of all the other columns. For example, if Set A is a table of cats and Set B is a table of dogs, you could use a left outer join to list all the names of dogs (Set A) along with all the names of cats with the same color fur as each dog (intersection, matching on fur color, of Set B). You could not get this kind of list from Set A alone.

Figure 10.5
A Left Outer Join.

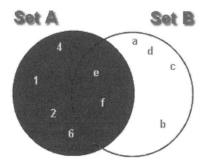

Figure 10.6
*A Right Outer
Join.*

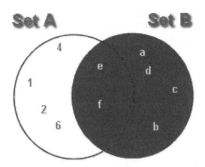

Figure 10.6 shows all elements in both sets including all elements in Set B that are not in Set A. This is the equivalent of a right outer join. Visually, it is easy to see why the diagram in Figure 10.6 is called a right outer join.

Finally, in Figure 10.7, all elements in both sets are included. This is the equivalent of a full outer join.

Figure 10.7
A Full Outer Join.

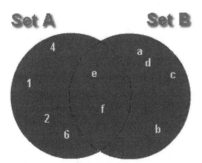

So now we know what types of joins can be performed to join tables or row sets together. Now let's examine different join types in detail and by example.

10.3 Examining Different Types of Joins

Let's examine each type of join in turn using specific examples.

10.3.1 Cross-Join or Cartesian Product

A cross-join merges all data from all tables into a single result set regardless of matching column names or their values. The select statement in Figure 10.8 is a cross-join creating a Cartesian product between the two tables. Additionally, the SONG and MUSICCD tables are only indirectly related through the many-to-many join resolution represented by the CDTRACK

Figure 10.8
A Cross-Join Between the SONG and MUSICCD Tables.

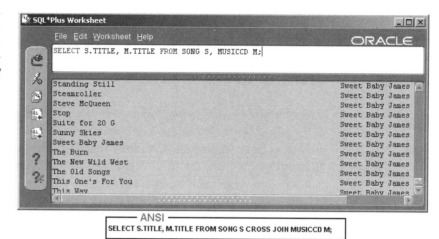

```
ANSI
SELECT S.TITLE, M.TITLE FROM SONG S CROSS JOIN MUSICCD M;
```

table. The Cartesian product retrieves all music CDs with every song regardless of whether a CD contains the song or not. The SONG table has 118 rows and the MUSICCD table has 13 rows. The resulting row count is 1,534 rows. This is because 118 Songs multiplied by 13 CDs gives us 1,534 combinations. Figure 10.8 shows the result of the following query:

```
SELECT S.TITLE, M.TITLE FROM SONG S, MUSICCD M;
```

Row counts selected can be verified with the following queries. The third query contains a subquery (see Chapter 12) and counts the number of rows returned by the cross-join.

```
SELECT COUNT(*) FROM SONG;
SELECT COUNT(*) FROM MUSICCD;
SELECT COUNT(*) FROM
(SELECT S.TITLE, M.TITLE FROM SONG S, MUSICCD M);
```

- MUSICCD has 13 rows.

- SONG has 118 rows.

- The cross-join has 1,534 (13 * 118) rows.

This particular cross-join is typical. Most cross-joins are created in error. The MUSICCD and SONG tables should have been related to one another with the MUSICCD_ID column through the CDTRACK table.

Because the relationship was omitted from the query, Oracle assumes that each row in the first table is related to every row in the second table: a Cartesian Product or multiplication of both tables.

10.3.2 Natural or Inner Join

The objective of joins is to allow the retrieval of rows from separate tables, using an existing relationship. Thus, when selecting data from two tables, it is best to link the rows in the tables together based on common values. When selecting from the SONG and ARTIST tables, without linking the songs to their respective artists, a meaningless result is returned. The entity relationship diagram in Chapter 1 shows the SONG and ARTIST tables linked by a common column called ARTIST_ID. Figure 10.9 shows the result of the following query:

```
SELECT A.NAME, S.TITLE FROM ARTIST A, SONG S
WHERE A.ARTIST_ID = S.ARTIST_ID;
```

The result in Figure 10.9 shows a result of 118 rows. This is the correct value because the SONG table has a total of 118 rows and the ARTIST table has 15 rows. There is a one-to-many relationship between the ARTIST and SONG tables. The maximum number of selectable rows using an inner join between these two tables is the number of rows on the many side of the relationship.

Figure 10.9
A Natural Join Between the ARTIST and SONG Tables.

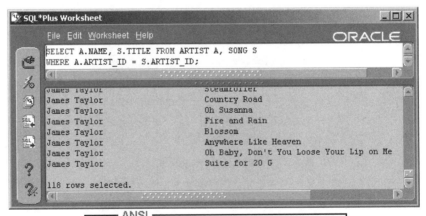

The ANSI format would allow a natural join by matching the ARTIST_ID column names on the ARTIST and SONG tables. Use caution with the ANSI format of the natural join. The NATURAL JOIN clause matches all columns with identical column names in the two tables. If columns have identical names but are not actually appropriate for joining, such as the COMMENT_TEXT columns in the GUESTAPPEAR-ANCE and INSTRUMENTATION tables, the ANSI format would match the tables incorrectly. Similarly, if there are no matching column names, the ANSI NATURAL JOIN format results in a Cartesian product. Because of the potential problems with a natural join, we have to be able to define the columns to be used in a join. This leads us to the ANSI join format USING and ON clauses.

10.3.2.1 The USING clause

The USING clause can be added to the ANSI join format where columns with identical names should be omitted from the join. The Oracle proprietary join format does not have the USING clause because you always name the columns to be joined in the WHERE clause. The result of the following query is shown in Figure 10.10:

```
SELECT SONG_ID, GUESTARTIST_ID, INSTRUMENT_ID
FROM GUESTAPPEARANCE NATURAL JOIN INSTRUMENTATION;
```

Figure 10.10
A Natural Join without the USING Clause.

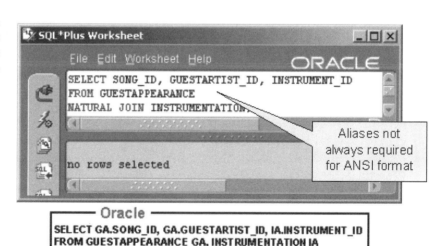

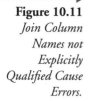

Figure 10.11
*Join Column
Names not
Explicitly
Qualified Cause
Errors.*

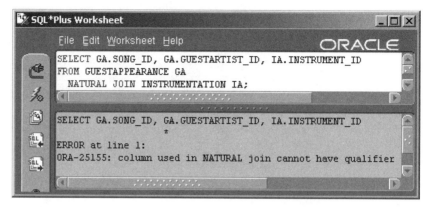

The query in Figure 10.10 returned a message indicating that no rows were selected. This is because the NATURAL JOIN clause will attempt to match the two tables on all column names common to both tables. Examine the Oracle format equivalent in Figure 10.10. Note how the COMMENT_TEXT columns are included in the WHERE clause. The Oracle format equivalent in this case is an exact interpretation of the ANSI format for the purposes of clear explanation.

Note: Aliases are not always required for the ANSI format example.

The result of the next query is shown in Figure 10.11:

```
SELECT GA.SONG_ID, GA.GUESTARTIST_ID, IA.INSTRUMENT_ID
FROM GUESTAPPEARANCE GA NATURAL JOIN INSTRUMENTATION IA;
```

The error is returned in Figure 10.11 because Oracle attempts the join using the SONG_ID, GUESTARTIST_ID, and COMMENT_TEXT columns; these three column names are common to both tables. The addition of the alias to the column names in the previous query effectively changes the names of the columns. Thus GA.SONG_ID is not the same as IA.SONG_ID or SONG_ID.

Getting back to the original query: The ANSI format requires some refinement to remove the unwanted COMMENT_TEXT column from the join. This is done with the USING clause. The result is shown in Figure 10.12. Note the absence of the NATURAL keyword. This join is no longer a purely naturally occurring join because column names are specified.

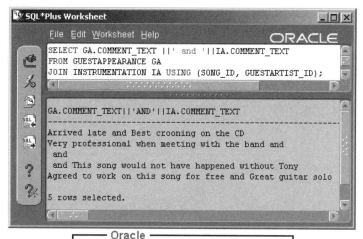

Figure 10.12
*The JOIN Clause
and the USING
Clause.*

```
SELECT GA.COMMENT_TEXT ||' and '||IA.COMMENT_TEXT
FROM GUESTAPPEARANCE GA JOIN INSTRUMENTATION IA
USING (SONG_ID, GUESTARTIST_ID);
```

Note: ||' and '|| concatenates the fields as trimmed strings. This is an alternative to preformatting of columns using the COLUMN clause. See Chapter 8 for more information on formatting.

The previous example in Figure 10.12 demonstrates how to exclude unwanted columns from a join. The USING clause was used to prevent joining on the COMMENT_TEXT column between the INSTRUMENTATION and GUESTAPPEARANCE tables. In some cases, the opposite is required. The ON clause is used to join tables on column names where the column names required in the join are not the same names in separate tables. This therefore leads us to an analysis of the ANSI format ON clause.

10.3.2.2   The ON clause

The result of the following query is shown in Figure 10.13:

```
SELECT A.NAME, GA.COMMENT_TEXT FROM GUESTAPPEARANCE GA
NATURAL JOIN ARTIST A;
```

Figure 10.13
*The JOIN Clause
without the ON
Clause.*

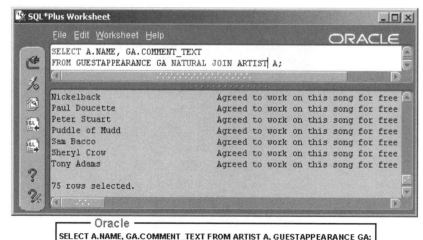

The ARTIST table has 15 rows and the GUESTAPPEARANCE table has 5 rows. When you execute the join, you get 75 rows: 15 multiplied by 5 equals 75 rows. This is another unwanted Cartesian product. The two tables are not being joined correctly because there is no common column name for the JOIN clause to utilize. There is a column in both tables having related values, but the column name is different in each table. In the ARTIST table it is called ARTIST_ID, and in the GUESTAPPEARANCE table it is called GUESTARTIST_ID.

Another row count can now be verified.

```
SELECT COUNT(*) FROM GUESTAPPEARANCE;
```

- ARTIST has 15 rows.

- GUESTAPPEARANCE has 5 rows.

This Cartesian product in Figure 10.13 caused by lack of common column names can be resolved by utilizing the ON clause. The result of the next query is shown in Figure 10.14:

```
SELECT A.NAME, GA.COMMENT_TEXT FROM GUESTAPPEARANCE GA
JOIN ARTIST A ON (GA.GUESTARTIST_ID = A.ARTIST_ID);
```

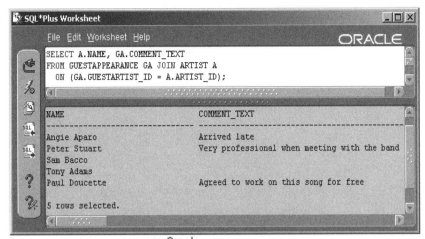

Figure 10.14
The JOIN Clause with the ON Clause.

10.3.3   Outer Join

An outer join selects rows from both tables including rows from one or both tables without matching rows in the other table. To show how outer joins work, we will use the ARTIST, SONG, and GUESTAPPEARANCE tables. The GUESTAPPEARANCE table contains some artists and some songs.

Examine the MUSIC schema entity relationship diagram in Chapter 1 again. An outer join is only useful if at least one side of the relationship can be zero. In the diagram, the symbols ⤙ or ⤚ indicate that zero rows only on the left side of the symbol may be related to the table on the right side of the symbol. The many-to-many relationship between the ARTIST and SONG tables through the GUESTAPPEARANCE table effectively makes the relationship between the ARTIST and SONG tables a zero, one- or many-to-zero, or one-to-many relationship. In other words, one artist may have been a guest appearance artist on no songs, or on one song, or on many songs. And a single song may have no guest appearances, or one guest appearance, or many guest appearances. Thus by joining these three tables, we can demonstrate the use of left, right, and full outer joins.

Before we execute join queries, we need to know which artist and song rows are present on the GUESTAPPEARANCE table. The result in Figure 10.15 shows artists who do not appear as guests on any particular song.

```
SELECT NAME FROM ARTIST WHERE ARTIST_ID NOT IN
(SELECT GUESTARTIST_ID FROM GUESTAPPEARANCE);
```

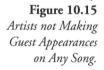

Figure 10.15
*Artists not Making
Guest Appearances
on Any Song.*

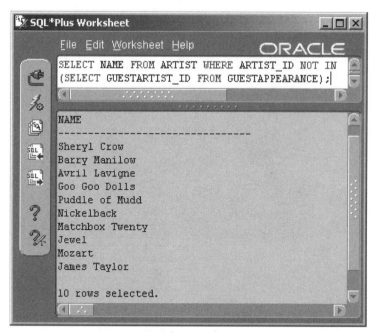

The result of the next query is shown in Figure 10.16, showing all songs without guest appearances and including the word "Me" in the song title. There is no longer a need to verify the health of join statements with row counts. Filtering and sorting can now be implemented using the WHERE and ORDER BY clauses, respectively. See Chapter 5 for filtering and Chapter 6 for sorting.

```
SELECT TITLE FROM SONG WHERE SONG_ID NOT IN
(SELECT SONG_ID FROM GUESTAPPEARANCE)
AND (TITLE LIKE '%Me%' OR TITLE LIKE '%Me');
```

When creating outer joins, the examples used here contain three tables in order to retrieve both artist names and song titles in the same query. Any join made up of more than two tables is called a mutable join. Mutable joins are explained at the end of this chapter. One format version of each type of outer join will be used, along with each Oracle proprietary or ANSI standard example, in order to explain both join formats with more clarity.

10.3.3.1 Left Outer Join

A left outer join will return all rows from the table on the left of the join plus any matching rows from the table on the right. Rows from the table on

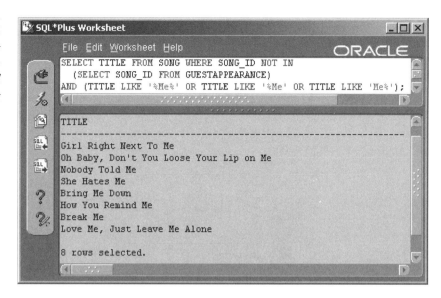

Figure 10.16
All Songs without Guest Appearances Including the Word "Me" in the Song Title.

the left with no matching rows in the table on the right will contain null values for the columns from the table on the right side.

Three queries are used to explain left outer joins, each becoming progressively more complex. The result of the first query is shown in Figure 10.17 with a left outer join of the ARTIST and GUESTAPPEARANCE tables. SONG_ID and GUESTARTIST_ID columns contain null values for ARTIST rows that do not exist as guest appearances.

```
SELECT A.NAME, GA.SONG_ID, A.ARTIST_ID, GA.GUESTARTIST_ID
FROM ARTIST A, GUESTAPPEARANCE GA
WHERE A.ARTIST_ID = GA.GUESTARTIST_ID(+);
```

Note: The rule of thumb for the (+) operator is it appears on the side of the join "deficient in information." In plain English: The table "deficient in information" is the table that cannot match every single row in the other table. A null valued "row" is added to the deficient table, using the plus sign, taking the place of the missing rows in the resulting join query. Put the (+) symbol on the "deficient" table's column found in the WHERE clause. Remember, without the (+) symbol, only rows that match in BOTH tables are selected.

Figure 10.17
*Oracle Format Left
Outer Join of
ARTIST and
GUESTAPPEARA
NCE Tables.*

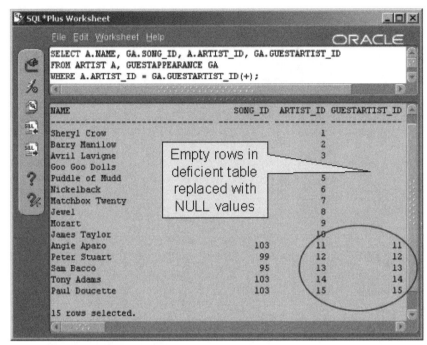

Refer back to Figure 10.15 to validate artists who do not have guest appearances on any songs. You will see that these artists (starting with Sheryl Crow and ending with James Taylor) appear in Figure 10.17 with a blank space in the SONG_ID and GUESTARTIST_ID. The query could not match any row in the GUESTAPPEARANCE table with these artists in the ARTIST table. Oracle Database 10*g* automatically returns a null value as a placeholder in the results for the unmatched rows.

Look at the last five rows in Figure 10.17. These are the artists who do make guest appearances. Notice that the ARTIST_ID column and the GUESTARTIST_ID column contain the same number in every row. This makes sense because the query equates the values in the two columns. These rows are finding themselves in the ARTIST table. Any row in the GUE-STAPPEARANCE table must match a row in the ARTIST table.

The second left outer join query, shown following, is the ANSI version of the first left outer join query. The result is shown in Figure 10.18. One difference between the Oracle format join in Figure 10.17 and the ANSI format join in Figure 10.18 is the sorted order of null values.

```
SELECT A.NAME, GA.SONG_ID, A.ARTIST_ID, GA.GUESTARTIST_ID
FROM ARTIST A LEFT OUTER JOIN GUESTAPPEARANCE GA
ON (A.ARTIST_ID = GA.GUESTARTIST_ID);
```

Figure 10.18
*ANSI Format Left
Outer Join of the
ARTIST and
GUESTAPPEARA
NCE Tables.*

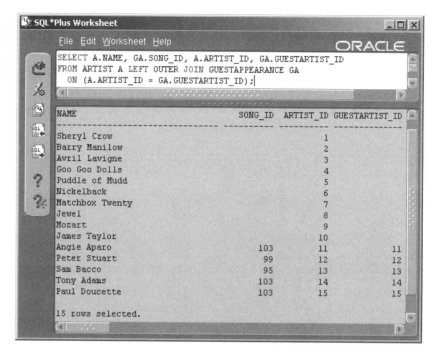

The third and last left outer join query is a more complex variation of the first two using the ANSI format and the DECODE function.

Note: The DECODE function is an embedded case statement (see Chapter 9).

The following query lists all of the artists in the ARTIST table. It returns one of two phrases, depending on whether the artist makes a guest appearance on a song or not. If not, the phrase " is an Artist." follows the artist's name. If otherwise, the phrase " made a guest appearance on ..." follows the artist's name, including the appropriate song title. The result as shown in Figure 10.19 is a left outer join between all three ARTIST, GUESTAPPEARANCE, and SONG tables.

```
SELECT A.NAME||
    DECODE (S.TITLE, NULL,' is an Artist.'
        ,' made a guest appearance on '||S.TITLE||'.'
    ) as "What they did"
FROM ARTIST A LEFT OUTER JOIN GUESTAPPEARANCE GA
ON (A.ARTIST_ID = GA.GUESTARTIST_ID)
    LEFT OUTER JOIN SONG S ON (S.SONG_ID = GA.SONG_ID)
ORDER BY A.NAME, S.TITLE;
```

Figure 10.19
*Left Outer Join
Between ARTIST,
GUESTAPPEAR
ANCE, and
SONG Tables.*

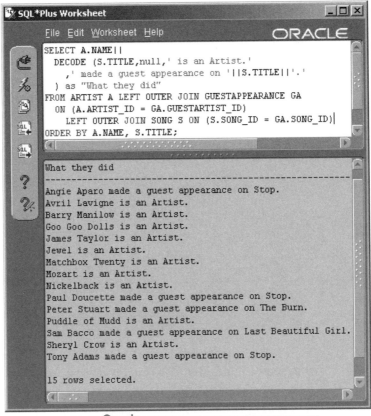

```
Oracle
SELECT A.NAME||
        DECODE (S.TITLE,null,' is an Artist.'
                ,' made a guest appearance on '||S.TITLE||'.'
        ) as "What they did"
FROM ARTIST A, GUESTAPPEARANCE GA, SONG S
WHERE A.ARTIST_ID = GA.GUESTARTIST_ID(+)
AND GA.SONG_ID = S.SONG_ID(+)
ORDER BY A.NAME, S.TITLE;
```

Notice in the Oracle-formatted query in Figure 10.19 that the two left outer joins are identified by the (+) symbol next to the appropriate columns in the WHERE clause.

Here is another variation that returns the same result. In the following query, the Oracle format uses an embedded subquery statement (see Chapter 12) rather than a WHERE clause addition using the SONG and GUESTAPPEARANCE tables. SQL is very versatile. There are many options available in SQL.

```
SELECT A.NAME||
DECODE(NVL(
(SELECT TITLE FROM SONG WHERE SONG_ID = GA.SONG_ID)
, NULL), NULL,' is an Artist.'
  ,' made a guest appearance on '
  ||NVL((SELECT TITLE FROM SONG
WHERE SONG_ID = GA.SONG_ID),NULL)||'.'
) AS "What they did"
FROM ARTIST A, GUESTAPPEARANCE GA
WHERE A.ARTIST_ID = GA.GUESTARTIST_ID(+)
ORDER BY A.NAME, GA.SONG_ID;
```

10.3.3.2   Right Outer Join

A right outer join is the converse of a left outer join. A right outer join returns all rows from the table on the right of the join plus any matching rows from the table on the left. Rows from the table on the right with no matching rows in the table on the left will contain null values for the columns from the table on the left side.

Following is an example of an ANSI-formatted right outer join statement. The equivalent Oracle form with an outer join on three tables does not exist unless a subquery is used (see Chapter 12). It is not possible to execute an outer join between more than two tables in a single query using the Oracle format; an error will result (ORA-01417: a table may be outer joined to at most one other table).

The result of the following query is shown in Figure 10.20. The query in Figure 10.20 is an ANSI format right outer join between all three ARTIST, GUESTAPPEARANCE, and SONG tables.

```
SELECT A.NAME "Artist", S.TITLE "Song"
FROM GUESTAPPEARANCE GA RIGHT OUTER JOIN SONG S
ON (GA.SONG_ID = S.SONG_ID)
RIGHT OUTER JOIN ARTIST A
ON (GA.GUESTARTIST_ID = A.ARTIST_ID)
ORDER BY S.TITLE, A.NAME;
```

The query first performs a right outer join between the GUESTAP-PEARANCE and SONG tables. Because the SONG table is on the right, all songs are retrieved. Next, this result set is right outer joined to the ARTIST table using the GUESTARTIST_ID. Because not all songs have a guest appearance, those songs have null values in the GUESTARTIST_ID and

Figure 10.20

A Right Outer Join Between ARTIST, GUESTARTIST, and SONG Tables.

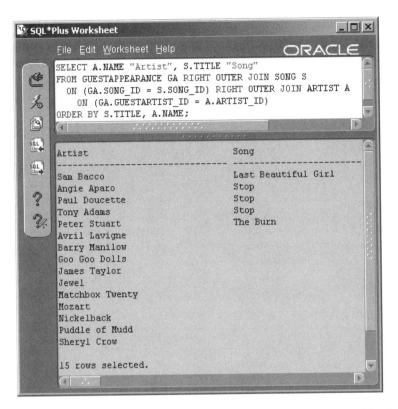

therefore are not able to match with a row in the ARTIST table. Because the ARTIST table is now on the right, the final result returns all artists and only the songs having a guest appearance.

The song "Stop" is listed three times because three artists played as guests on "Stop": Angie Aparo, Paul Doucette, and Tony Adams.

10.3.3.3 Full Outer Join

A full outer join will return all rows in both tables, filling in missing values with null values when a row is not present on the other side of the join.

Note: There is no Oracle format equivalent for a full outer join.

The next query is an ANSI standard format, full outer join between the ARTIST, GUESTAPPEARANCE, and SONG tables. The result is shown in Figure 10.21.

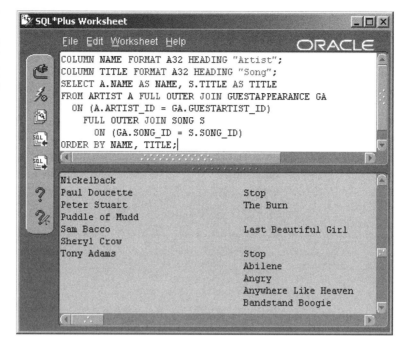

```
COLUMN NAME FORMAT A32 HEADING "Artist"
COLUMN TITLE FORMAT A32 HEADING "Song"
SELECT A.NAME AS NAME, S.TITLE AS TITLE
FROM ARTIST A FULL OUTER JOIN GUESTAPPEARANCE GA
ON (A.ARTIST_ID = GA.GUESTARTIST_ID)
FULL OUTER JOIN SONG S ON (GA.SONG_ID = S.SONG_ID)
ORDER BY NAME, TITLE;
```

The query lists all artists and all songs, matching songs and artists together if the artist makes a guest appearance on the related song. If an artist does not make a guest appearance, the song title is NULL (outer join between artists and guest appearances). If a song has no guest appearances, the artist name is NULL (outer join between songs and guest appearances).

Figure 10.21 shows only part of the results, illustrating how either the title or the name can be NULL. There are 130 rows returned in the query.

10.3.4 Self-Join

A self-join joins a table to itself. Table aliases must be used to distinguish between two different copies of the same table. A table such as this would be a candidate for further Normalization or is a result of a Denormalization performance improvement. Some examples of situations in which self-joins might be useful would be grouping self-joins or hierarchical (fishhook) self-joins.

Note: A fishhook is a table with a one-to-many relationship to its own primary key. Thus the primary key would be both primary key and a unique foreign key.

10.3.4.1 Grouping Self-Join

A grouping self-join implies that some rows have a one-to-many relationship with other rows in the same table. There is a "Best of" compilation CD by Sheryl Crow in the MUSIC schema containing songs on other CDs.

The self-join query following lists SONG_ID values appearing on more than one CD. Note that the line in the WHERE clause containing the inequality operator will prevent any song from being listed twice. The result is shown in Figure 10.22.

```
SELECT B.MUSICCD_ID, B.TRACK_SEQ_NO, A.SONG_ID
FROM CDTRACK A JOIN CDTRACK B ON (A.SONG_ID = B.SONG_ID)
WHERE B.MUSICCD_ID <> A.MUSICCD_ID
ORDER BY MUSICCD_ID, TRACK_SEQ_NO, SONG_ID;
```

This self-join searches for tracks (songs) that are found on more than one CD. Picture in your mind's eye two copies of the CDTRACK table side by side. Each row in the left table (Table A) is matched with one row (itself) or more than one row (same song on another CD) in the right table (Table B). Eliminate the rows where you have matched a track to itself by comparing the MUSICCD_ID in the two rows. If the SONG_ID values are the same but the MUSICCD_ID values are different, the song is selected in the query. The SONG_ID value 1 in Figure 10.22 appears on two CDs: #1 and #11.

The next query contains all tracks by Sheryl Crow; the inequality operator is now missing. The result is shown in Figure 10.23.

```
SET PAGES 80 LINESIZE 132
COLUMN CD FORMAT A24 HEADING "CD"
COLUMN TRACK FORMAT 990 HEADING "Track"
```

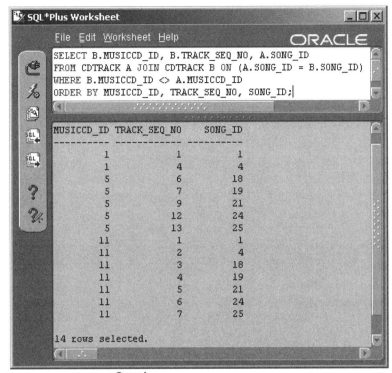

Figure 10.22
*A Barebones Self-
Join on the
CDTRACK Table.*

```
COLUMN SONG FORMAT A36 HEADING "Song"
SELECT CD.TITLE AS CD, T.TRACK_SEQ_NO AS TRACK
, S.TITLE AS SONG
FROM SONG S, CDTRACK T, MUSICCD CD, ARTIST A
WHERE A.NAME = 'Sheryl Crow'
AND A.ARTIST_ID = S.ARTIST_ID
AND S.SONG_ID = T.SONG_ID
AND T.MUSICCD_ID = CD.MUSICCD_ID
ORDER BY CD, SONG;
```

Including the CD and song titles in Figure 10.23 makes it easier to see how the query works. The CD called "The Best of Sheryl Crow" has six songs. Two of the songs are from the "Soak Up the Sun" CD and four of the songs are from the "C'mon, C'mon" CD.

Figure 10.23
*Descriptive Form
of the Self-Join in
Figure 10.22.*

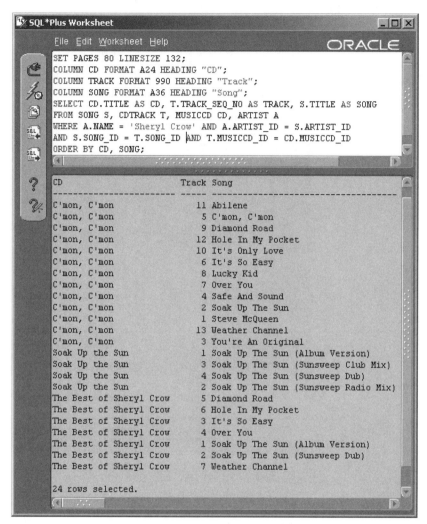

10.3.4.2   Hierarchical (Fishhook) Self-Join

A hierarchical or fishhook self-join is a tree-like structure where parent rows have child rows, which can in turn be parent rows of other child rows. A common use for this type of join is to represent family tree data. The MUSIC schema used in this book has two tables containing hierarchical structures: the INSTRUMENT and GENRE tables. Only the INSTRUMENT table contains hierarchical data, in addition to just structure.

```
SELECT PARENT.NAME "Parent", CHILD.NAME "Child"
FROM INSTRUMENT PARENT JOIN INSTRUMENT CHILD
```

```
ON (PARENT.INSTRUMENT_ID = CHILD.SECTION_ID)
ORDER BY PARENT.NAME, CHILD.NAME;
```

Figure 10.24 contains the result of the query. Notice how the Alto Horn, Baritone Horn, and Clarinet are part of Woodwind instruments. Additionally, Woodwind instruments are part of Wind instruments. That is a three-layer hierarchical representation.

Note: See Chapter 13 for details on hierarchical queries.

Figure 10.24
A Hierarchical Data Fishhook Self-Join.

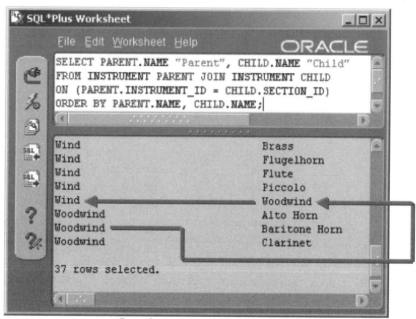

10.3.5 Equi-Joins, Anti-Joins, and Range Joins

Equi-, anti-, and range joins are not join types in themselves but more operators applied within joins. A brief theoretical explanation is warranted because of potential effects on performance.[1]

- **Equi-Join**. This join simply uses an equals sign = between two columns in a join. An equi-join is the fastest join type because it can find an exact match (a single row). An equi-join is best used on unique indexes such as primary keys.

- **Anti-Join**. This type of join uses the "not equal to" symbols: <> or !=. An anti-join can also use "NOT (a=b)" syntax to reverse an equi-join. Anti-joins should be avoided if possible because they will read all rows in a table. If you are trying to read a single row from one million rows, a lot of time will be wasted finding a row not matching a condition.

- **Range Join**. In this case, a range scan is required using the <, >, or BETWEEN operators.

- **The [NOT] IN clause**. The IN clause allows value checking against a list of items and is sometimes known as a semi-join. A semi-join is not really a join but more like a half-join. The IN list can be a list of literal values or a subquery. Beware of a subquery returning a large number of rows (see Chapter 12). The optional NOT clause implies an anti-join. The IN clause is best used with a fixed number of predefined literal values.

- **The [NOT] EXISTS clause**. See Chapter 12. EXISTS is similar to IN except it can be more efficient. Again, because the NOT modifier reverses the logic and creates an anti-join, avoid using NOT EXISTS if possible.

10.3.6 Mutable and Complex Joins

Some mutable joins have already appeared in the section discussing outer joins, but more detail is warranted at this point. A *mutable join* is a join of more than two tables. The word *mutable* means "subject to change." Perhaps the person originally applying the term *mutable* to these types of joins was implying that these types of joins should be changed. Multiple-table mutable joins affect performance, usually adversely.

A complex join is by definition a two-table or mutable join containing extra filtering using Boolean logic AND, OR, IN, and EXISTS clause filtering. Mutable joins are extremely common in modern-day object applications written in languages such as Java. Object applications and relational databases require a complex mapping process between the two different object and relational approaches. The reality is that object and relational methodologies usually overlap. The result is mutable joins. At some point mutable joins become complex joins. Complex joins can have 10 or even more tables. Complex joins are usually indicative of other problems such as a lack of Denormalization or use of a purely top-down design.

Following is a simple example of a multiple-table join using four tables. Start by finding row counts. The only extra row count we have to find at this stage is for the CDTRACK table.

```
SELECT COUNT(*) FROM CDTRACK;
```

- MUSICCD has 13 rows.

- CDTRACK has 125 rows.

- ARTIST has 15 rows.

- SONG has 118 rows.

- SONG_GUESTARTIST has 5 rows.

Let's begin with an Oracle format query, the result of which is shown in Figure 10.25. This query returns 125 rows, equivalent to the largest table, validating this query as not being a Cartesian product.

```
COLUMN CD FORMAT A24 HEADING "CD"
COLUMN TRACK FORMAT 90 HEADING "Track"
COLUMN SONG FORMAT A40 HEADING "Song"
COLUMN NAME FORMAT A32 HEADING "Artist"
SELECT M.TITLE AS CD, C.TRACK_SEQ_NO AS TRACK
, S.TITLE AS SONG, A.NAME AS ARTIST
FROM ARTIST A, SONG S, CDTRACK C, MUSICCD M
WHERE A.ARTIST_ID = S.ARTIST_ID
AND S.SONG_ID = C.SONG_ID
AND C.MUSICCD_ID = M.MUSICCD_ID
ORDER BY 1,2,3,4;
```

Figure 10.25
A Mutable Join of Four Tables.

Looking at Figure 10.25, it is obvious that some kind of formatting eliminating all the repetition of the CD title and artist name would be desirable.

The next three examples shown as follows are different versions of the ANSI format for the join query of four tables in Figure 10.25. All of the next three examples (except the first, which returns an error) give you the same results as shown in Figure 10.25.

Note: The important thing to remember about ANSI mutable joins is that tables are joined from left to right with join conditions able to reference columns relating to the current join and those already executed from the left. The converse applies to subqueries where conditions are passed down into subqueries and not up to the calling query (see Chapter 12).

- **First Example**. Attempt to join four tables without specifying any details of how the join is to be done.

  ```
  SELECT M.TITLE CD, C.TRACK_SEQ_NO, S.TITLE, A.NAME
  ```

```
FROM ARTIST A JOIN SONG S JOIN CDTRACK C
   JOIN MUSICCD M
ORDER BY 1, 2, 3, 4;
```

The previous query will return the error message ORA-00905: missing keyword.

- **Second Example**. Add the USING clause to each JOIN clause. This query will succeed and return 125 rows (one for each song in each CD).

```
SELECT M.TITLE CD, C.TRACK_SEQ_NO, S.TITLE, A.NAME
FROM ARTIST A JOIN SONG S USING (ARTIST_ID)
   JOIN CDTRACK C USING (SONG_ID)
   JOIN MUSICCD M USING (MUSICCD_ID)
ORDER BY 1, 2, 3, 4;
```

- **Third Example**. Here, the USING clause is replaced by the ON clause. The result of this query is identical to the second (previous) example where 125 rows will be returned.

```
SELECT M.TITLE, C.TRACK_SEQ_NO, S.TITLE, A.NAME
FROM ARTIST A JOIN SONG S ON (A.ARTIST_ID = S.ARTIST_ID)
 JOIN CDTRACK C ON (S.SONG_ID = C.SONG_ID)
   JOIN MUSICCD M ON (C.MUSICCD_ID =M.MUSICCD_ID)
ORDER BY 1, 2, 3, 4;
```

This chapter has exposed you to a wide variety of methods and syntax types for joining tables. Joins can get much more complicated than those contained within this chapter. However, some highly complex mutable joins can be simplified with the use of subqueries. Chapter 12 examines subqueries.

The next chapter shows you how to summarize data using aggregate functions with the GROUP BY clause.

10.4 Endnotes

1.   Oracle Performance Tuning for *9i* and *10g* (ISBN: 1-55558-305-9)

Grouping and Summarizing Data

In this chapter:

- How do we group and sort with the GROUP BY clause?

- What are group functions?

- What are aggregate and analytic functions?

- What does the HAVING clause do?

- What do the ROLLUP, CUBE, and GROUPING SETS clauses do?

- What is the SPREADSHEET[1] clause?

This chapter shows you how to aggregate and summarize rows in queries based on specific columns and expressions, using the GROUP BY clause in conjunction with various types of functions. Functions can be placed into various sections of a SELECT statement, including the WHERE clause (see Chapter 5), the ORDER BY clause (see Chapter 6), the GROUP BY clause (plus extensions), the HAVING clause, and finally the SPREADSHEET clause. In this chapter, we start by examining the syntax of the GROUP BY clause and its various additions, proceed onto grouping functions, and finish with the SPREADSHEET clause. The SPREADSHEET clause is new to Oracle Database 10*g*.

11.1 GROUP BY Clause Syntax

In previous chapters you have explored the SELECT, FROM, WHERE, and ORDER BY clauses, plus methods of joining tables using both an Oracle proprietary join syntax and the ANSI JOIN clause syntax. This chapter introduces summarizing of query results into groups using the GROUP BY clause. Rows can be grouped using Oracle built-in functions or custom-written functions.

The GROUP BY clause can be separated into a number of parts, as shown in Figure 11.1, and as follows:

- **GROUP BY**. Group rows based on column value, returning a single summary row for each group.

- **HAVING**. Filter to remove selected groups from the result, much like the WHERE clause is used to filter rows retrieved by the SELECT statement.

- **ROLLUP AND CUBE**. Further group the summary rows created by the GROUP BY clause to produce groups of groups or super aggregates.

- **GROUPING SETS**. Add filtering and the capability for multiple super aggregates using the ROLLUP and CUBE clauses.

- **SPREADSHEET**. The SPREADSHEET clause allows representation and manipulation of data into a spreadsheet-type format. The SPREADSHEET clause literally allows the construction of a spreadsheet from within SQL. The SPREADSHEET clause will be explained later on in this chapter.

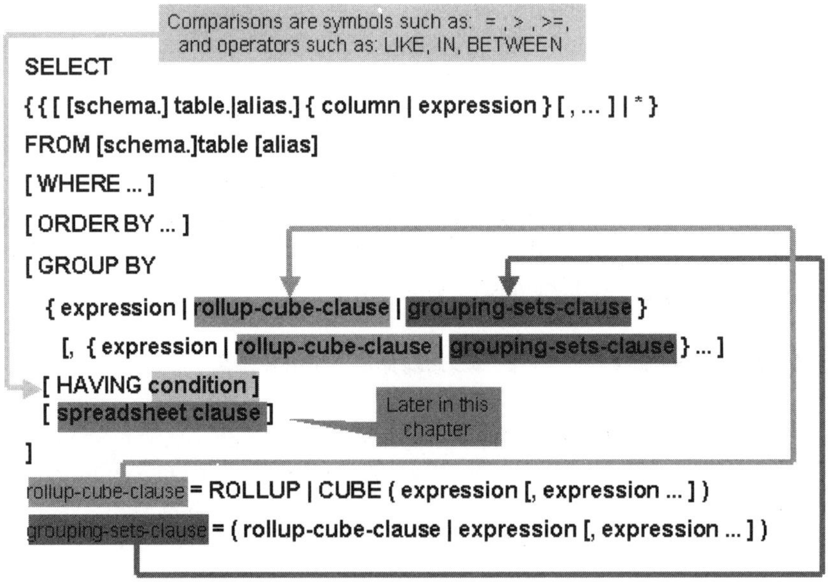

Figure 11.1
The Syntax of the
GROUP BY
Clause.

Comparisons are symbols such as: = , > , >=, and operators such as: LIKE, IN, BETWEEN

```
SELECT
{ { [ [schema.] table.|alias.] { column | expression } [ , ... ] | * }
FROM [schema.]table [alias]
[ WHERE ... ]
[ ORDER BY ... ]
[ GROUP BY
    { expression | rollup-cube-clause | grouping-sets-clause }
      [, { expression | rollup-cube-clause | grouping-sets-clause } ... ]
[ HAVING condition ]
[ spreadsheet clause ]
]
rollup-cube-clause = ROLLUP | CUBE ( expression [, expression ... ] )
grouping-sets-clause = ( rollup-cube-clause | expression [, expression ... ] )
```

Later in this chapter

11.2 Types of Group Functions

Group functions are different from single-row functions in that group functions work on data in sets, or groups of rows, rather than on data in a single row. For example, you can use a group function to add up all payments made in one month. You can combine single-row and group functions to further refine the results of the GROUP BY clause.

There are many group functions available to use with the GROUP BY clause. Functions operating on groups of rows fall into the following categories:

- **Aggregate Functions**. Functions that summarize data into a single value, such as the MAX function, returning the highest value among the group of rows.

    - **Statistical Functions**. These functions are essentially aggregation functions in that they perform explicit calculations on specified groups of rows. However, statistical functions are appropriate to both aggregation and analytics.

- **Analytic Functions**. Functions that summarize data into multiple values based on a sliding window of rows using an analytic clause. These structures are used most frequently in data warehousing to analyze historical trends in data. For example, the statistical STD-DEV function can be used as an analytic function that returns standard deviations over groups of rows.

- **SPREADSHEET Clause Functions**. SPREADSHEET clause functions enhance the SPREADSHEET clause. These functions are covered later in this chapter in the section on the SPREADSHEET clause.

Let's begin with aggregate functions.

11.2.1 Aggregate Functions

An aggregate function applies an operation to a group of rows returning a single value. A simple example of an aggregate function is in the use of the SUM function as shown following. See the result in Figure 11.2.

```
SELECT SUM(AMOUNT_CHARGED), SUM(AMOUNT_PAID) FROM STUDIOTIME;
```

Figure 11.2
Using an Oracle Built-in SQL Aggregate Function.

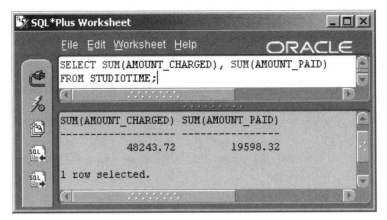

What are the available aggregate functions and how are they used? Let's go through the definitions. Functions have been divided into different sections.

11.2.1.1 Simple Summary Functions

- **AVG(expression)**. The average.

- **COUNT(*|expression)**. The number of rows in a query.

- **MIN(expression)**. The minimum.

- **MAX(expression)**. The maximum.

- **SUM(expression)**. The sum.

An **expression** can be anything: a column name, a single-row function on a column name, or simple calculations such as two columns added together. Anything you might place in the SELECT clause can be used as an expression within a group function.

11.2.1.2 Statistical Function Calculators

- **STDDEV(expression)**. The standard deviation is the average difference from the mean. The mean is similar to the average.

- **VARIANCE(expression)**. The variance is the square of the standard deviation and thus the average squared difference from the mean, or the average deviation from the mean.

- **STDDEV_POP(expression)**. The population standard deviation.

- **STDDEV_SAMP(expression)**. The sample standard deviation.

- **VAR_POP(expression)**. The population variance, excluding null values.

- **VAR_SAMP(expression)**. The sample variance, excluding null values.

- **COVAR_POP(expression, expression)**. The population covariance of two expressions. The covariance is the average product of differences from two group means.

- **COVAR_SAMP(expression, expression)**. The sample covariance of two expressions.

- **CORR(expression, expression)**. The coefficient of correlation of two expressions. A correlation coefficient assesses the quality of a least-squares fitting to the data. The least-squares procedure finds the best-fitting curve to a given set of values.

- **REGR_[SLOPE | INTERCEPT | COUNT | R2 | AVGX| AVGY | SXX | SYY | SXY](expression, expression)**. Linear regression functions fit a least-squares regression line to two expressions. Linear regression is used to make predictions about a single value. Simple linear regression involves discovering the equation for a straight line that most nearly fits the given data. The discovered linear equation is then used to predict values for the data. A linear regression curve is a straight line through a set of plotted points. The straight line should get as close as possible to all points at once.

- (10g) **CORR_{S | K}**. This function calculates Pearson's correlation coefficient, measuring the strength of a linear relationship between two variables. Plotting two variables on a graph results in a lot of dots plotted from two axes. Pearson's correlation coefficient can tell you how good the straight line is.

- (10g) **MEDIAN**. A median is a middle or interpolated value. A median is the value literally in the middle of a set of values. If a distribution is discontinuous and skewed or just all over the place, then the median will not be anywhere near a mean or average of a set of values. A median is not always terribly useful.

- (10g) **STATS_{BINOMIAL_TEST | CROSSTAB | F_TEST | KS_TEST | MODE | MW_TEST | ONE_WAY_ANOVA | STATS_T_TEST_* | STATS_WSR_TEST}**. These functions provide various statistical goodies. Explaining what all of these very particular statistics functions do is a little bit more of statistics than Oracle SQL for this book.

11.2.1.3 Statistical Distribution Functions

- **CUME_DIST(expression [, expression ...]) WITHIN GROUP (ORDER BY expression [, expression])**. The cumulative distribution of an expression within a group of values. A cumulative frequency distribution is a plot of the number of observations falling within or below an interval, a histogram. The cumulative distribution function is the probability that a variable takes a value less than or equal to a given value.

- **PERCENTILE_{ CONT | DISC }(expression) WITHIN GROUP (ORDER BY expression)**. The percent point function or the inverse distribution function for a **CONT**inuous or a **DISC**rete distribution. Because the percent point function is an inverse distribution function, we start with the probability and compute the corresponding value for the cumulative distribution.

11.2.1.4 Ranking Functions

- **RANK(expression [, expression ...]) WITHIN GROUP (ORDER BY expression [, expression])**. The rank of a value in a group of values.

- **PERCENT_RANK(expression [, expression ...]) WITHIN GROUP (ORDER BY [, expression ...])**. A cumulative distribution ranking function. See **CUME_DIST** above.

- **DENSE_RANK(expression [, expression ...]) WITHIN GROUP (ORDER BY expression [, expression ...])**. The rank of a row within an ordered group of rows.

- **FIRST | LAST (expression [, expression ...]) WITHIN GROUP (ORDER BY expression [, expression ...])**. The first and last ranking row in a sorted group of rows.

11.2.1.5 Grouping Functions

Grouping functions are used with analysis enhancements to define the sliding window of data used for analysis.

- **GROUP_ID()**. Filters duplicate groupings from a query.

- **GROUPING(expression)**. Distinguishes between superset aggregate rows and aggregate grouped rows.

- **GROUPING_ID(expression [, expression ...]).** Finds a GROUP BY level for a particular row.

11.2.2 Enhancing Grouping Functions for Analysis

Analysis is used to calculate cumulative, moving, centered, and reporting summary aggregate values often used in data warehouse environments. Unlike aggregate functions, analytic functions return multiple rows for each group. Each group of rows is called a *window* and is effectively a variable group, consisting of a range of rows. The number of rows in a window can be based on a specified row count or an interval such as a period of time. Apart from the ORDER BY clause, analytic functions are always executed at the end of a query statement.

The following functions allow analysis and thus analytics using tools such as the windowing clause:

- COUNT, SUM, AVG, MIN, and MAX.

- FIRST_VALUE and LAST_VALUE.

- STDDEV, VARIANCE, and CORR.

- STDDEV_POP, VAR_POP, and COVAR_POP.

- STDDEV_SAMP, VAR_SAMP, and COVAR_SAMP.

Let's examine syntax and demonstrate what Oracle means by analytics. We will use a SUM function. In short, the SUM function adds things up, and everyone knows what that means. We could use something like a STDDEV or VARIANCE function, but not everyone knows what those are. For some, who cares? In Chapter 1, we built some data warehouse–type fact and dimension tables. The SALES table is a fact table because it contains facts about sales (a history of sales transactions). Thus the SALES table is appropriate for some analysis of this nature.

Using the SUM function, let's examine total sales as shown in Figure 11.3.

```
COLUMN SALES FORMAT $999,990.00
SELECT SUM(SALE_PRICE) AS SALES FROM SALES;
```

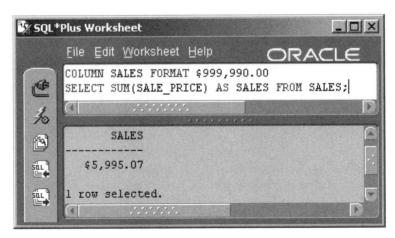

Once again using the SUM function, let's examine total sales by country and restrict to two continents, namely North America and Europe, as shown in Figure 11.4.

```
COLUMN COUNTRY FORMAT A16
SELECT CY.NAME AS COUNTRY, SUM(S.SALE_PRICE) AS SALES
FROM CONTINENT CT, COUNTRY CY, SALES S
WHERE CT.NAME IN ('North America', 'Europe')
AND CT.CONTINENT_ID = S.CONTINENT_ID
AND CY.COUNTRY_ID = S.COUNTRY_ID
GROUP BY CY.NAME;
```

11.2.2.1 The OVER Clause

Now we get to the analytic part. The OVER clause in the following query forces a cumulative sum on the SALES grouped result column, resulting in a total sales number for each continent plus a cumulative sales number for all rows returned so far, for every row returned. The result is shown in Figure 11.5. Neat, huh?

```
COLUMN CUMULATIVE FORMAT $999,990.00
SELECT COUNTRY, SALES
    , SUM(SALES) OVER (ORDER BY COUNTRY) AS CUMULATIVE
FROM (
SELECT CY.NAME AS COUNTRY, SUM(S.SALE_PRICE) AS SALES
    FROM CONTINENT CT, COUNTRY CY, SALES S
    WHERE CT.NAME IN ('North America', 'Europe')
    AND CT.CONTINENT_ID = S.CONTINENT_ID
```

Figure 11.4
*Grouping and
Filtering a SUM
Function.*

```
COLUMN COUNTRY FORMAT A16
SELECT CY.NAME AS COUNTRY, SUM(S.SALE_PRICE) AS SALES
FROM CONTINENT CT, COUNTRY CY, SALES S
WHERE CT.NAME IN ('North America', 'Europe')
AND CT.CONTINENT_ID = S.CONTINENT_ID
AND CY.COUNTRY_ID = S.COUNTRY_ID
GROUP BY CY.NAME;


COUNTRY                 SALES
----------------   ------------
Canada                $146.74
France                $123.06
Germany                $76.56
Mexico                 $95.70
Netherlands           $133.98
Spain                 $202.07
Sweden                $227.81
United Kingdom        $202.17
United States         $207.39

9 rows selected.
```

```
AND CY.COUNTRY_ID = S.COUNTRY_ID
GROUP BY CY.NAME);
```

There is a lot more to the OVER clause than the query in Figure 11.5. Figure 11.6 shows the syntax for the OVER clause as demonstrated by the previous example shown in Figure 11.5.

- **PARTITION BY**. This clause can be used to break the query into groups.

- **ORDER BY**. This clause we have already seen.

- **Windowing Clause**. The windowing clause syntax allows placement of a window or subset picture onto a set of data, applying analysis to that data window subset only.

In fact, looking at the syntax diagram in Figure 11.6, the mind boggles at what can be done with the OVER clause.

Figure 11.5
*A Cumulative
Aggregation Using
the OVER Clause.*

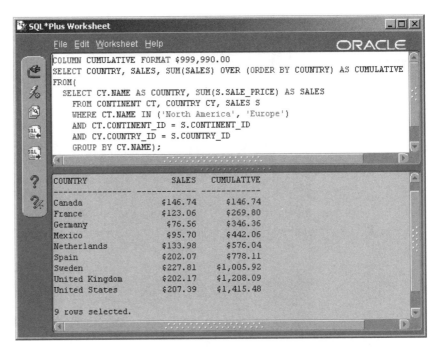

Figure 11.6
*OVER Clause
Syntax.*

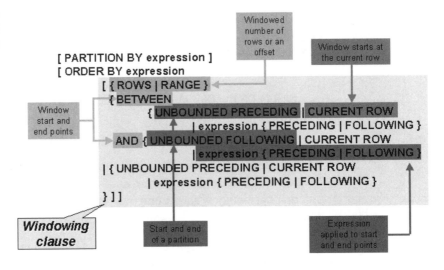

11.3 Special Grouping Function Behavior

Two factors that should be briefly discussed are the way that group functions behave with null values and the use of DISTINCT. Let's begin with null values.

11.3.1 Group Functions and Null Values

Most functions, except for COUNT(*) and GROUPING, when passed a null value, will return a NULL result. COUNT(*) will always return one row. Any other function returns a null value if no rows are found. The NVL function can be used to replace a NULL with a value as shown in the query following. The result is shown in Figure 11.7.

```
SELECT A.NAME, NVL(ST.MINUTES_USED,0) FROM ARTIST A
NATURAL LEFT OUTER JOIN STUDIOTIME ST;
```

By converting NULLs into zeros, you can then use the rows with zeros in the group function. For example, calculating the average time per artist will yield a different result if you use zero for artists without studio time (by using the NVL function), rather than calculating the average time per artist where NULL rows are thrown out before the average is done.

Figure 11.7
Group Functions and Null Values.

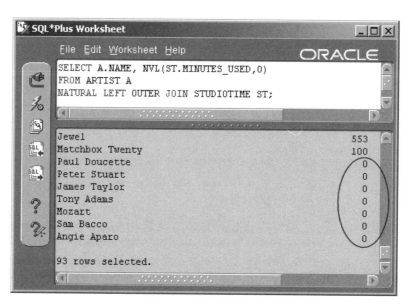

11.3.2 Selecting DISTINCT or ALL in Group Functions

Most single-expression grouping functions accept the DISTINCT or ALL (the default) clauses. DISTINCT or ALL is executed on the expression after the resolution of that expression. All of the functions listed as follows allow selecting of DISTINCT or ALL values. DISTINCT or ALL clauses are applied to the expression argument of each function, in the case of an SQL statement, each row.

- AVG ([DISTINCT | ALL] expression).
- COUNT ({ * | [DISTINCT | ALL] expression }).
- MAX ([DISTINCT | ALL] expression).
- MIN ([DISTINCT | ALL] expression).
- SUM ([DISTINCT | ALL] expression).
- STDDEV ([DISTINCT | ALL] expression).
- VARIANCE ([DISTINCT | ALL] expression).

The following query specifies ALL within the COUNT function. The GROUP BY clause is discussed later in this chapter. See the result in Figure 11.8.

```
SELECT A.ARTIST_ID, A.NAME "Artist"
, COUNT(ALL ST.ARTIST_ID) "Studio Visits"
FROM ARTIST A, STUDIOTIME ST
WHERE A.ARTIST_ID = ST.ARTIST_ID(+)
GROUP BY A.ARTIST_ID, A.NAME
ORDER BY COUNT(ALL ST.ARTIST_ID) DESC;
```

Note three points about the query in Figure 11.8:

- The ALL default has been explicitly specified in COUNT(ALL ST.ARTIST_ID).
- The COUNT function will always return one row (see Group Functions and Null Values previously in this chapter). The COUNT function never returns a null value. If the column being counted has null values, COUNT returns a zero.

Figure 11.8
*Number of Studio
Visits for All
Artists.*

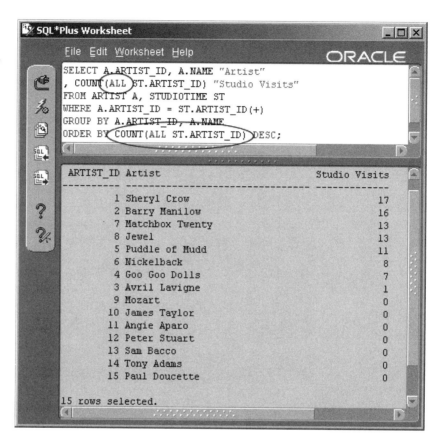

- The ORDER BY clause is sorting using the result of the COUNT function.

- Now we execute the same query by applying the DISTINCT clause modifier to the COUNT function as shown in the next query, to see the difference.

```
SELECT A.ARTIST_ID, A.NAME "Artist"
, COUNT(DISTINCT ST.ARTIST_ID) "Studio Visits"
FROM ARTIST A, STUDIOTIME ST
WHERE A.ARTIST_ID = ST.ARTIST_ID(+)
GROUP BY A.ARTIST_ID, A.NAME
ORDER BY COUNT(DISTINCT ST.ARTIST_ID) DESC;
```

Figure 11.9
*Multiple Rows
with the Same
ARTIST_ID Are
Counted Once.*

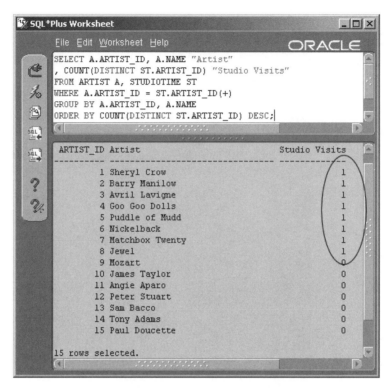

Figure 11.9 shows the result. Notice that because the COUNT function is counting DISTINCT values of the ARTIST_ID, it returns 1 for artists with one or more visits.

To show how this feature can be useful, add the DECODE function to the query to list artists as having either worked in the studio or not worked in the studio, based on the value of the COUNT function. The following query does this. See the result in Figure 11.10.

```
COLUMN ID FORMAT 90 HEADING "ID";
COLUMN ARTIST FORMAT A32 HEADING "Artist";
COLUMN VISITS FORMAT A32 HEADING "Atleast 1 Visit ?"
SELECT A.ARTIST_ID AS ID, A.NAME AS ARTIST
, DECODE(COUNT(DISTINCT
(ST.ARTIST_ID)),1,'Yes','No') AS VISITS
FROM ARTIST A, STUDIOTIME ST
WHERE A.ARTIST_ID = ST.ARTIST_ID(+)
GROUP BY A.ARTIST_ID, A.NAME;
```

Figure 11.10
*Artists Who Have
Spent Time in the
Studio.*

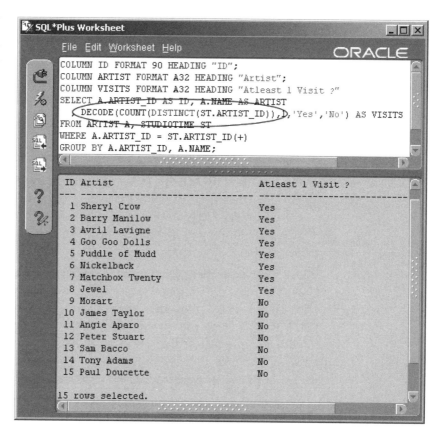

```
COLUMN ID FORMAT 90 HEADING "ID";
COLUMN ARTIST FORMAT A32 HEADING "Artist";
COLUMN VISITS FORMAT A32 HEADING "Atleast 1 Visit ?"
SELECT A.ARTIST_ID AS ID, A.NAME AS ARTIST
       DECODE(COUNT(DISTINCT(ST.ARTIST_ID)),0,'Yes','No') AS VISITS
FROM ARTIST A, STUDIOTIME ST
WHERE A.ARTIST_ID = ST.ARTIST_ID(+)
GROUP BY A.ARTIST_ID, A.NAME;
```

```
ID Artist                              Atleast 1 Visit ?
--- -----------------------------      -------------------------
 1 Sheryl Crow                         Yes
 2 Barry Manilow                       Yes
 3 Avril Lavigne                       Yes
 4 Goo Goo Dolls                       Yes
 5 Puddle of Mudd                      Yes
 6 Nickelback                          Yes
 7 Matchbox Twenty                     Yes
 8 Jewel                               Yes
 9 Mozart                              No
10 James Taylor                        No
11 Angie Aparo                         No
12 Peter Stuart                        No
13 Sam Bacco                           No
14 Tony Adams                          No
15 Paul Doucette                       No

15 rows selected.
```

Note in Figure 11.10 how functions can call other functions where, for instance, the DECODE function calls the COUNT function.

11.4   Using the GROUP BY Clause

We have seen a lot of use of the GROUP BY clause so far in this chapter. Let's now attempt to explain what the GROUP BY clause is and what it does. In its simplest form, the GROUP BY clause can be used to summarize rows into a group or groups of rows based on a grouping function placed into the SELECT clause. The HAVING clause can then be used to filter out unwanted groups much like the WHERE clause (see Chapter 5) applied to a SELECT statement. The ROLLUP and CUBE clauses are used to produce groups of groups or super aggregates, and the GROUPING SETS clause can make grouping more efficient by removing rows before aggregation.

There are a few standard rules to remember about the GROUP BY clause:

- The GROUP BY clause column list must include all columns in the SELECT statement not affected by any aggregate functions.

- The expression for the SELECT statement must include at least one grouping function such as COUNT().

- The GROUP BY clause cannot use the column positional specification like the ORDER BY clause because the result set columns do not exist when the GROUP BY clause is executed and do exist when the ORDER BY clause is executed. The GROUP BY clause summarizes rows for output, and the ORDER BY clause sorts the result set of a query.

Note: The GROUP BY clause is executed during query execution, and the ORDER BY clause runs after retrieval and grouping of all rows. The ORDER BY clause will always add performance overhead to a query. Implicit or inherent sorting can often be executed in the WHERE and GROUP BY clauses.

11.4.1   Grouping Rows

The example in Figure 11.2 showed how to apply an aggregate function to all rows in a table, by summing up all amounts on the STUDIOTIME table. Now we can take this a step further by breaking down the query in Figure 11.2 into subset groups as in the next query. The result is shown in Figure 11.11.

```
SELECT ARTIST_ID, SUM(AMOUNT_CHARGED), SUM(AMOUNT_PAID)
FROM STUDIOTIME
GROUP BY ARTIST_ID;
```

Now let's take the same query a little further, modify and beautify it. The result is shown in Figure 11.12.

```
COLUMN ARTIST FORMAT A20 HEADING "Artist"
COLUMN OUTSTANDING FORMAT $999990.00 -
```

Figure 11.11
Grouping on a Single Table Query.

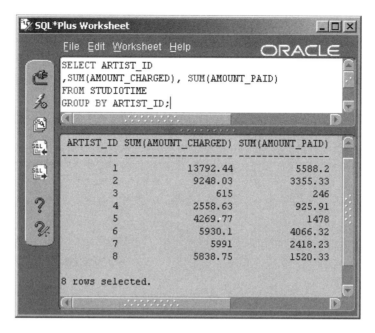

Figure 11.12
Grouping on a Two-Table Join Query.

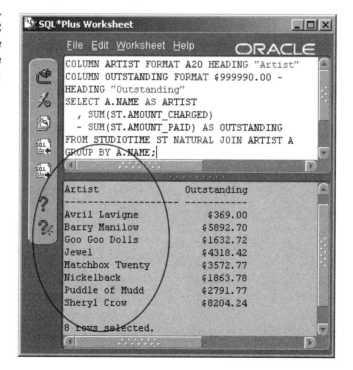

```
HEADING "Outstanding"
SELECT A.NAME AS ARTIST
, SUM(ST.AMOUNT_CHARGED) - SUM(ST.AMOUNT_PAID) AS OUTSTANDING
FROM STUDIOTIME ST NATURAL JOIN ARTIST A
GROUP BY A.NAME;
```

Sorting with the GROUP BY Clause

Did you notice how rows were sorted by the name of the artist in Figure 11.12? The GROUP BY clause will sort by the elements listed in the GROUP BY clause. Let's change that sort order by changing the GROUP BY clause. The result of the following query is shown in Figure 11.13.

```
COLUMN ARTIST FORMAT A24 HEADING "Artist"
COLUMN EMAIL FORMAT A24 HEADING "Email Address"
COLUMN OUTSTANDING FORMAT $999990.00 —
HEADING "Outstanding";
SELECT A.NAME AS ARTIST, A.EMAIL AS EMAIL
, SUM(ST.AMOUNT_CHARGED) - SUM(ST.AMOUNT_PAID) AS OUTSTANDING
FROM STUDIOTIME ST NATURAL JOIN ARTIST A
GROUP BY A.EMAIL, A.NAME;
```

Figure 11.13
Changing the Sort Order Using the GROUP BY Clause.

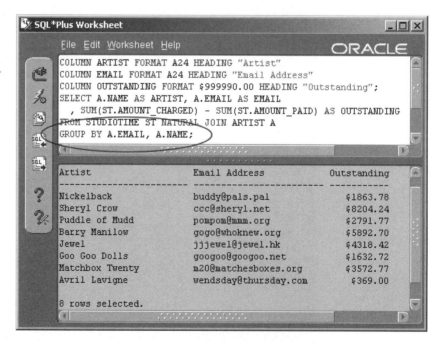

Notice that the GROUP BY clause in Figure 11.13 now contains both the EMAIL and NAME columns from the ARTIST table. The clause GROUP BY A.EMAIL, A.NAME will force the query to sort primarily by the e-mail addresses of the artists, not their names as in Figure 11.12.

Note: The GROUP BY clause column list in Figure 11.13 includes all columns listed in the SELECT statement (ARTIST.NAME and ARTIST.EMAIL) not affected by any aggregate functions.

11.4.2   Filtering Grouped Results with the Having Clause

The HAVING clause is used as an extension to the GROUP BY clause to remove selected groups from the result, much like the WHERE clause is used to filter rows retrieved by the SELECT clause (the WHERE clause filters rows at the source of data retrieval). The HAVING clause filters the result of the GROUP BY clause. The GROUP BY clause executes on all data retrieved after the WHERE clause has filtered the initial selection.

Note: Filtering using the WHERE clause will nearly always outperform the HAVING clause. Never replace a WHERE clause with a HAVING clause as in the query in Figure 11.14.

The result of the following query is shown in Figure 11.14.

```
COLUMN ARTIST FORMAT A24 HEADING "Artist"
COLUMN EMAIL FORMAT A24 HEADING "Email Address"
COLUMN OUTSTANDING FORMAT $999990.00 -
HEADING "Outstanding"
SELECT A.NAME AS ARTIST, A.EMAIL AS EMAIL
, SUM(ST.AMOUNT_CHARGED) - SUM(ST.AMOUNT_PAID) AS OUTSTANDING
FROM STUDIOTIME ST NATURAL JOIN ARTIST A
GROUP BY A.NAME, A.EMAIL
HAVING (A.NAME BETWEEN 'A%' AND 'P%');
```

For best performance, use the WHERE clause to filter out rows before grouping whenever possible. For example, the query shown in Figure 11.14 could be revised to use the WHERE clause instead of the HAVING clause

Figure 11.14
Restricting Groups
with the HAVING
Clause.

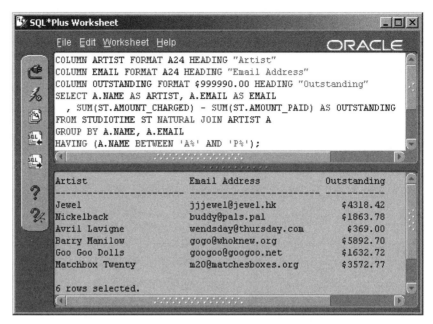

Figure 11.14
Restricting Groups with the HAVING Clause.

as shown in the following query. The result of the next query will be identical to that of Figure 11.14.

```
SELECT A.NAME AS ARTIST, A.EMAIL AS EMAIL
, SUM(ST.AMOUNT_CHARGED) - SUM(ST.AMOUNT_PAID) AS OUTSTANDING
FROM STUDIOTIME ST NATURAL JOIN ARTIST A
WHERE (A.NAME BETWEEN 'A%' AND 'P%')
GROUP BY A.NAME, A.EMAIL;
```

So what is the best time to use the HAVING clause? When you want to eliminate certain groups of rows based on the results of an aggregate function. For example, continuing with the previous situation, let's say that you want to see only the artists who have an outstanding balance greater than $4,000. Change the query by adding the last line as follows. Execute the query. Note that in this case as well, the WHERE clause would probably still be a better choice with respect to performance. Figure 11.15 shows the result.

```
SELECT A.NAME AS ARTIST, A.EMAIL AS EMAIL
, SUM(ST.AMOUNT_CHARGED) - SUM(ST.AMOUNT_PAID) AS OUTSTANDING
FROM STUDIOTIME ST NATURAL JOIN ARTIST A
```

Figure 11.15
Using the HAVING Clause with Aggregate Functions.

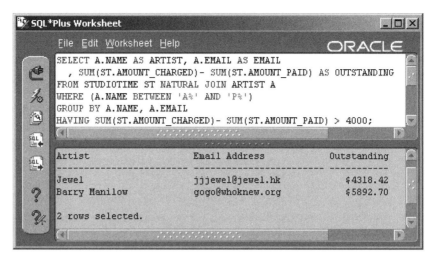

```
WHERE (A.NAME BETWEEN 'A%' AND 'P%')
GROUP BY A.NAME, A.EMAIL
HAVING SUM(ST.AMOUNT_CHARGED) - SUM(ST.AMOUNT_PAID) > 4000;
```

You can even use HAVING with aggregate functions not listed in the SELECT clause. For example, change the HAVING clause in the query so that you are listing only artists with more than five visits. The following query achieves this task, with its result shown in Figure 11.16.

```
SELECT A.NAME AS ARTIST, A.EMAIL AS EMAIL
, SUM(ST.AMOUNT_CHARGED) - SUM(ST.AMOUNT_PAID) AS OUTSTANDING
FROM STUDIOTIME ST NATURAL JOIN ARTIST A
WHERE (A.NAME BETWEEN 'A%' AND 'P%')
GROUP BY A.NAME, A.EMAIL
HAVING COUNT(*) > 5;
```

That is the basics of the HAVING clause. Now let's go a little deeper and examine the ROLLUP, CUBE, and GROUPING SETS clauses.

11.4.3 Extending the GROUP BY Clause Further

A ROLLUP or CUBE clause can be used as a much more efficient substitute for numerous SELECT statements merged together, for instance, with a UNION ALL clause. The ROLLUP clause is best suited to hierarchical data, and the CUBE clause is best for multidimensional data.

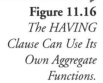

Figure 11.16
*The HAVING
Clause Can Use Its
Own Aggregate
Functions.*

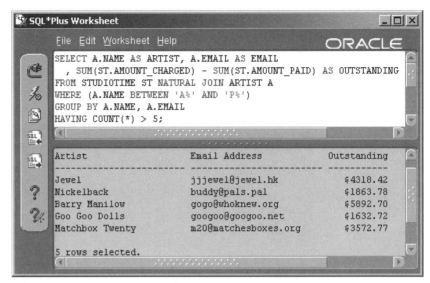

11.4.3.1 The ROLLUP Clause

Rollup is an extension to the GROUP BY clause and is used to create super aggregates or groupings of groupings. The ROLLUP clause is commonly used to create subtotals plus a grand total, on multiple levels for all columns listed in the GROUP BY clause. Totals are based on the order of columns listed in the GROUP BY clause, moving through the GROUP BY clause from the right to the left. Rollup can be very useful for creation of summary tables or materialized views. The result of the next query is shown in Figure 11.17.

Note: The user-defined function GETTIME is described in Chapter 24 (PL/SQL). GETTIME is required for the next query.

```
CREATE OR REPLACE FUNCTION GETTIME(pTIME IN VARCHAR2)
RETURN NUMBER IS
vLEN INTEGER DEFAULT 0;
vSPLIT INTEGER DEFAULT 0;
vHOURS INTEGER DEFAULT 0;
vSECONDS INTEGER DEFAULT 0;
BEGIN
vSPLIT := INSTR(pTIME,':');
vLEN := LENGTH(pTIME);
vHOURS := TO_NUMBER(SUBSTR(pTIME,1,vSPLIT-1));
```

```
vSECONDS := TO_NUMBER(SUBSTR(pTIME,vSPLIT+1,vLEN-vSPLIT));
RETURN vHOURS+(vSECONDS/60);
EXCEPTION WHEN OTHERS THEN
RETURN 0;
END;
/
```

Here is the query:

```
COLUMN CD FORMAT A24 HEADING "CD";
COLUMN SONG FORMAT A40 HEADING "Song";
COLUMN TIME FORMAT 99990.00 HEADING "Time(mins)";
SELECT M.TITLE AS CD, S.TITLE AS SONG,
SUM(GETTIME(S.PLAYING_TIME)) AS TIME
FROM MUSICCD M JOIN CDTRACK T USING (MUSICCD_ID)
JOIN SONG S USING (SONG_ID)
WHERE S.PLAYING_TIME IS NOT NULL AND M.TITLE LIKE 'Th%'
GROUP BY ROLLUP (M.TITLE, S.TITLE);
```

The query in Figure 11.17 shows rollup grouping on the title of a CD and the title of its song. Because a song is at the lowest level of grouping detail, no subtotal is shown for each song. Do you see the subtotals for both CDs plus the grand total at the end?

Note: The function GETTIME() is custom written and can be found in Chapter 24. GETTIME() is necessary to convert a string value of minutes and seconds to a real (floating-point) number value. The use of the GETTIME() function shows that custom functions can be used in GROUP BY clauses.

11.4.3.2   The CUBE Clause

Unlike the ROLLUP clause, which can be used to produce subtotals and grand totals for subset groups, the CUBE clause can be used to produce all combinations for a GROUP BY expression. The CUBE clause can be used to create three-dimensional cross-tabulation reports. The result of the following query is shown in Figure 11.18.

```
COLUMN COUNTRY FORMAT A10 HEADING "Country";
COLUMN STATE FORMAT A10 HEADING "State";
```

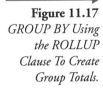

Figure 11.17
GROUP BY Using
the ROLLUP
Clause To Create
Group Totals.

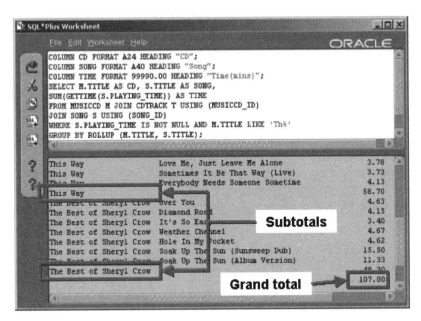

```
COLUMN TIME FORMAT 99990.00 HEADING "Time(mins)";
SELECT A.COUNTRY AS COUNTRY, A.STATE_PROVINCE AS STATE
, SUM(ST.MINUTES_USED) AS STUDIOTIME
FROM ARTIST A JOIN STUDIOTIME ST USING (ARTIST_ID)
WHERE A.STATE_PROVINCE IS NOT NULL
GROUP BY CUBE (A.STATE_PROVINCE, A.COUNTRY);
```

Note how the query in Figure 11.18 contains subtotals for each state and subtotals for each country, in addition to the grand total.

Note: ROLLUP and CUBE clauses can be implemented on all columns in the GROUP BY clause (GROUP BY ROLLUP | CUBE (column [, column ...]}) or partially using (GROUP BY column [, column ...]} ROLLUP | CUBE (column [, column ...]).

11.4.3.3   The **GROUPING SETS** Clause

The GROUPING SETS clause extends the GROUP BY clause by allowing specification of multiple groups and removal of unwanted aggregations produced by ROLLUP or CUBE clauses. The result of the following query is shown in Figure 11.19.

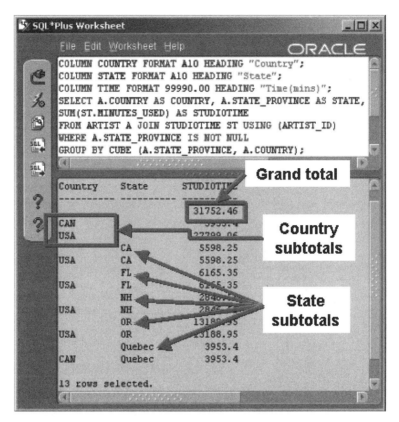

```
COLUMN COUNTRY FORMAT A10 HEADING "Country";
COLUMN STATE FORMAT A10 HEADING "State";
COLUMN TIME FORMAT 99990.00 HEADING "Time(mins)";
SELECT A.COUNTRY AS COUNTRY, A.STATE_PROVINCE AS STATE
, SUM(ST.MINUTES_USED) AS STUDIOTIME
FROM ARTIST A JOIN STUDIOTIME ST USING (ARTIST_ID)
WHERE A.STATE_PROVINCE IS NOT NULL
GROUP BY GROUPING SETS(
    (A.STATE_PROVINCE, A.COUNTRY),
    (A.STATE_PROVINCE),
    (A.COUNTRY));
```

Note in Figure 11.19 that the GROUPING SETS clause creates subtotals for all three of states within countries, states, and finally countries. There is much more to ROLLUP, CUBE, and GROUPING SETS, but we will pass on further detail.

Figure 11.19
GROUP BY and
the GROUPING
SETS Clause.

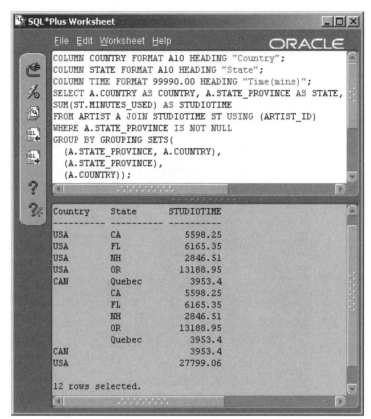

The next great leap is the SPREADSHEET clause, and a giant leap it most certainly is! The SPREADSHEET clause is introduced in Oracle Database 10*g*.

11.5 (10*g*) The SPREADSHEET (MODEL) Clause

The SPREADSHEET clause[1] can be used to create spreadsheet-style output and can be extremely complex. The SPREADSHEET clause extends the SELECT statement, allowing multidimensional array query output. Calculations between resulting rows can be performed much like cross-tabbing or interdimensional data warehouse reporting. The result is a spreadsheet or model. Let's look briefly at syntax.

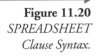

Figure 11.20
SPREADSHEET Clause Syntax.

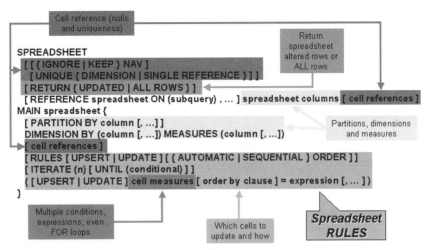

11.5.1 SPREADSHEET (MODEL) Clause Syntax

Refer to Oracle documentation for more specific details, particularly with respect to cell measures. Figure 11.20 shows a brief picture of SPREADSHEET clause syntax. That's brief?

The PARTITION BY clause effectively creates multiple arrays. The DIMENSION BY clause is a subset of partitions in that it creates identifying columns for each row within each of multiple partitions. The MEASURE clause defines the cells in the rows (dimensions) within each array (partitions). Some examples will explain more shortly. Now let's look at some SPREADSHEET clause-specific functions.

11.5.2 SPREADSHEET (MODEL) Clause Functions

The SPREADSHEET clause is new to Oracle Database 10g. There are several SPREADSHEET clause-specific functions also introduced in Oracle Database 10g. These new functions apply to interrow calculations and only as part of SPREADSHEET clause rules.

- **CURRENTV[2](dimension)**. Returns a dimensional value or current value.

- **PRESENTNNV(cell, expression, expression)**. Returns one expression if a value exists, otherwise another.

- **PRESENTV(cell, expression, expression)**. As for PRESENTNNV, but allowing null values.

- **PREVIOUS(cell)**. Returns a value at the beginning of each iteration or loop.

- **ITERATION_NUMBER**. Returns a completed loop iteration sequence number; the subscript of a loop.

11.5.3 Using the SPREADSHEET (MODEL) Clause

So how do we demonstrate use of the SPREADSHEET clause in a simplistic manner? Good question. Looks nasty, doesn't it? Well, it is! However, without a tool such as the SPREADSHEET clause, this would be much more complicated. Let's once again use our data warehouse SALES fact table. Here's a simple query, creating a view (best in a data warehouse as a materialized view) on the SALES table, with various dimensions thrown in. The query summarizes sales, breaking them down into continent, country, and year, including sales quantities and revenues.

```
CREATE VIEW SALESSUM AS
SELECT CT.NAME AS CONTINENT, CY.NAME AS COUNTRY
, TO_NUMBER(TO_CHAR(S.SALE_DATE, 'YYYY')) AS YEAR
, COUNT(S.SALE_QTY) AS SALES
, SUM(S.SALE_PRICE) AS REVENUE
FROM CONTINENT CT, COUNTRY CY, SALES S
WHERE CT.CONTINENT_ID = S.CONTINENT_ID
AND CY.COUNTRY_ID = S.COUNTRY_ID
GROUP BY CT.NAME, CY.NAME, TO_CHAR(S.SALE_DATE, 'YYYY');
```

Now let's take a quick peek at the data in the view, limiting to North America only, as shown in Figure 11.21.

```
COLUMN CONTINENT FORMAT A16
COLUMN COUNTRY FORMAT A16
COLUMN YEAR FORMAT 9999
COLUMN SALES FORMAT 990
COLUMN REVENUE FORMAT $999,999.00
SELECT * FROM SALESSUM WHERE CONTINENT IN ('North America');
```

Now let's use the 2003 and 2004 figures to project estimates into 2005, as shown in Figure 11.22. The following script is the query. Note the calculation of the 2005 quarterly projection as being the following (((2004 −

Figure 11.21
*Some Summarized
Data.*

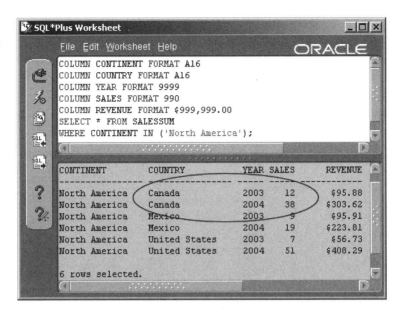

2003) / 2004) + 1) * 2004. Thus the numbers for Canada plugged into the equation would be (((38 − 12) / 38) + 1)38 = 1.68 + 38 = 64 (an increase in sales quantities of about 168%).

```
SELECT COUNTRY, YEAR, Q FROM SALESSUM S
WHERE CONTINENT IN ('North America')
SPREADSHEET
    PARTITION BY (COUNTRY)
    DIMENSION BY (YEAR)
    MEASURES (S.SALES Q)
    RULES(Q[2005]=(((Q[2004]-Q[2003])/Q[2004])+1)*Q[2004])
ORDER BY COUNTRY, YEAR;
```

Thus in Figure 11.21, we have rows for 2003 and 2004, Canada shows sales quantities of 12 for 2003 and 38 for 2004. Therefore, the projected sales quantity for Canada for 2005 is 64 items, as already described.

Let's look at a slightly more detailed example. The following query analyzes both quarterly sales and quarterly revenues, selecting two continents and partitioning by both continent and country. A partial result is shown in Figure 11.23. Continents are sorted in descending order to show the break between North America and Europe.

Figure 11.22
*A SPREADSHEET
Clause Projection.*

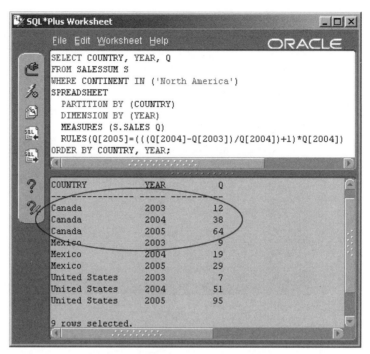

Figure 11.23
*A more detailed
SPREADSHEET
clause projection.*

Figure 11.24
For Loops in the SPREADSHEET Clause.

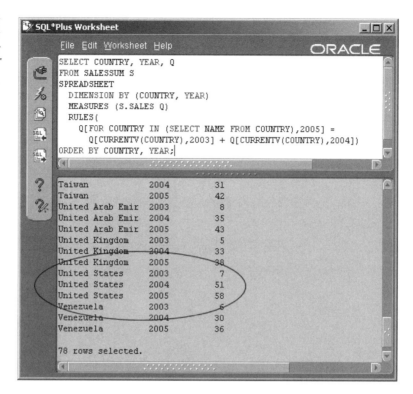

```
COLUMN QS FORMAT 9990 HEADING "Sales"
COLUMN QR FORMAT $9,990.99 HEADING "Revenue"
SELECT CONTINENT, COUNTRY, YEAR, QS, QR FROM SALESSUM S
WHERE CONTINENT IN ('Europe', 'North America')
SPREADSHEET
    PARTITION BY (CONTINENT, COUNTRY)
    DIMENSION BY (YEAR)
    MEASURES (S.SALES QS, S.REVENUE QR)
    RULES
    (
        QS[2005]=(((QS[2004]-QS[2003])/QS[2004])+1)*QS[2004]
        ,QR[2005]=(((QR[2004]-QR[2003])/QR[2004])+1)*QR[2004]
    )
ORDER BY CONTINENT DESC, COUNTRY, YEAR;
```

Using the SPREADSHEET clause, one can even use *for* loops to scroll through sets of rows and create multidimensional cross-tabulations of all cells in a query. The example in Figure 11.24 shows 2003 and 2004 figures summed into 2005, for all countries. Unlike Figures 11.22 and 11.23, the example in Figure 11.24 is a sum rather than a projection based on the incremental percentage increase between two previous years. The SPREAD-SHEET clause is extremely versatile and can become highly complex. Once again, the SPREADSHEET clause resolves some perplexing and highly complex coding problems.

In the next chapter you will learn all about subqueries. Subqueries are, in some respects, the most powerful aspect of SQL, particularly with respect to tuning and managing complexity.

11.6 Endnotes

1. The SPREADSHEET clause has been renamed to the MODEL clause.

2. The CURRENTV function is renamed to CV.

12

Subqueries

In this chapter:

- What is a subquery?

- What are the types of subqueries?

- Where can subqueries be used?

- Why do we need subqueries?

Subqueries are probably one of the more complex aspects of SQL. Subqueries are often used to resolve complexity by breaking down large queries into many smaller queries, which interact with each other. In some situations, subqueries can also be used to improve SQL statement performance. Let's begin by looking at types of subqueries.

12.1 Types of Subqueries

I like to think of subqueries such that there are two methods of categorizing subqueries. The first method of categorization is that a subquery can be scalar, correlated, nested, or an inline view. We will get to some of these types of subqueries later on. I am going to define subquery types based on the second method of categorization, including some of the first. I find the second method clearer. Following is my second method of categorization. Note that the different types of subqueries as defined here can be combinations of several types. At the end of this chapter you should understand why.

A subquery is an SQL statement called from another query or another subquery. Subqueries can return various result sets and can be defined based on what they return.

- **Single Row / Single Column**. This type of subquery can be used to find a single value (e.g., the ARTIST_ID of a particular song).

- **Multiple Rows / One Column Each**. This type of subquery returns a list of values (e.g., the SONG_IDs of all songs by a specific artist).

- **Multiple Columns / Single or Multiple Rows**. This is the most complex variation. For example, a subquery with multiple columns as a single row could return the STATE and COUNTRY of one artist from the ARTIST table. An example of a subquery with multiple columns and multiple rows could return a list of the STATE and COUNTRY for all artists.

Note: A single-row query or subquery returning a single value can also be referred to as a scalar query or subquery, scalar meaning returning a single scalar or literal value, often TRUE, FALSE, or NULL.

A subquery can be of a regular or correlated format, correlated implying a connection between calling and called queries (subqueries):

- **Regular Subquery**. A self-contained query implying that there is no direct relationship between the calling query and the called query.

- **Correlated Subquery**. The word *correlation* is used to describe a relationship between the calling query and the subquery. The rule to remember with correlated subqueries is that a correlating column must be passed down into the subquery from the calling query, not the other way around. Thus a correlated subquery is always dependent on the calling query.

Subqueries can also be defined as nested or as inline views:

- **Nested Subquery**. Subqueries can call other subqueries and so on ad infinitum. In other words, subqueries can be nested within subqueries, within subqueries.

- **Inline View**. An inline view is a subquery embedded in the FROM clause of a calling SELECT statement, which by the way is also a subquery. Values can be passed from the inline view to the calling query, or subquery.

That covers different subquery types and the combinations thereof. Now let's examine where subqueries can be used.

12.2   Where Can Subqueries Be Used?

Subqueries can be used almost anywhere in an SQL statement, in any SQL command where an expression can be placed. Following are listed SQL statement clauses in which a subquery can be placed:

- SELECT clause.

- WHERE clause.

- ORDER BY clause.

- FROM clause (Inline view).

- VALUES clause of an INSERT statement.

- UPDATE statement SET clause = (subquery).

- CASE statement expression.

- Function parameter.

- The SPREADSHEET clause.

The next step is to look again at comparison conditions as described in Chapters 5 and 7, except now exclusively as applied to subqueries.

12.3   Comparison Conditions and Subqueries

Many comparison conditions are applicable to subqueries. A subquery syntax diagram is shown in Figure 12.1. The type of results allowed from a subquery depends on the comparison operator that you use. In Figure 12.1, the highlighted operators require single-row subqueries. This includes the equality and inequality operators (=, <=, >=, >, <, and !=), plus the LIKE and BETWEEN operators. Other operators allow multiple rows to be returned from the subquery. Multiple rows are allowed for the IN, NOT IN, EXISTS, NOT EXISTS, plus equality operators combined with ANY, SOME, or ALL.

We now know about different types of subqueries, where subqueries can be used, and some basic comparison condition syntax for using subqueries.

Figure 12.1
*Subquery
Comparison
Condition Syntax.*

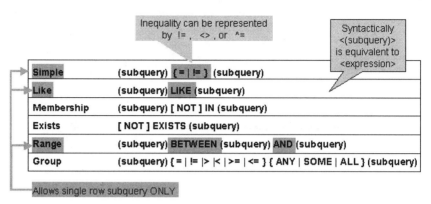

A subquery itself is generally syntactically equivalent to a SELECT statement. Chapters 4, 5, 6, and 11 apply to subqueries in this respect.

So far in this chapter, we have seen a lot of information. The easiest way to explain subqueries is simply to demonstrate.

12.4   Demonstrating Subqueries

This section demonstrates use of the different types of subqueries:

- Single-row subqueries.

- Multiple-row subqueries.

- Multiple-column subqueries.

- Regular versus correlated subqueries.

- Nested subqueries.

- Inline views or FROM clause embedded subqueries.

- Subqueries can be used in numerous SQL code commands and their subset clauses.

12.4.1   Single-Row Subqueries

A single-row subquery is exactly as its name implies: a subquery that returns a single row. If more than one row is returned, an error will result (ORA-01427: single-row subquery returns more than one row). Simple (equality), LIKE, and Range (BETWEEN) comparison conditions are restricted to single-row subquery results. See the syntax diagram in Figure 12.1.

Here is an easy way of understanding the concept of the single-row subquery. You can ask if "Apple Pie" equals "Apple Pie," but you cannot ask if "Apple Pie" is equal to both "Apple Pie" and "Pumpkin Pie" because you get two different answers at once. Apple pie is equal to apple pie but not equal to pumpkin pie. The same applies to testing for a number, say 10, being BETWEEN five other numbers because it does not make sense. For example, 10 BETWEEN 5 AND (20, 4, 30) cannot be evaluated because it is both true and false. The same applies to the LIKE clause because a single LIKE comparison condition can only be used to match a single pattern, not many patterns.

Following is an example of a single-row subquery. The ROWNUM pseudocolumn is used to restrict the subquery to a single row no matter how many rows it returns. See the result in Figure 12.2.

```
SELECT SONG_ID, GUESTARTIST_ID, INSTRUMENT_ID
FROM INSTRUMENTATION WHERE INSTRUMENT_ID =
(SELECT INSTRUMENT_ID FROM INSTRUMENT
WHERE NAME = 'Acoustic Guitar');
```

In the next example, the query in Figure 12.2 is altered to ensure that multiple rows are returned from the subquery. Removing the WHERE clause filter from the query in Figure 12.2 results in an error, as shown in Figure 12.3. The subquery in Figure 12.3 returns all rows in the INSTRUMENT table.

Figure 12.2
A Single-Row Subquery.

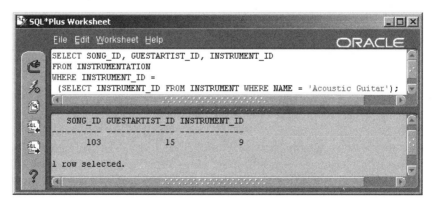

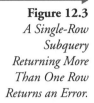

Figure 12.3
A Single-Row Subquery Returning More Than One Row Returns an Error.

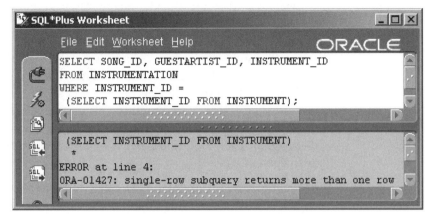

12.4.2   Multiple-Row Subqueries

A multiple-row subquery returns multiple rows. The IN, EXISTS, and Group (ANY, ALL, SOME) comparison conditions allow multiple-row subquery results. See the syntax diagram in Figure 12.1.

- A multiple-row subquery can provide the set of values needed for the IN comparison condition.

- The EXISTS comparison condition usually uses indexes to match values in the subquery to values in the calling query. Regardless of correlated indexed columns between calling and subquery, EXISTS will stop execution of the subquery when the appropriate value is found. IN will build all values in the set for the subquery before passing its result back to the calling query. Using EXISTS rather than IN often results in better performance of the query. EXISTS may not perform better than IN when the set produced by the subquery is a limited set of literal values or a very small number of rows.

- ANY, ALL, and SOME imply any value, all values, and some values, respectively. Because these subquery comparison conditions test against a set of values, a multiple-row query can in reality return zero, one, or many rows.

Note: It is important to note that a multiple-row subquery can return zero rows because the Membership, Exists, and Group comparison conditions return a set of values. That set of values can be an empty set. An empty set is a valid set.

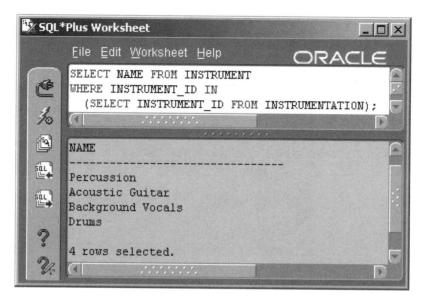

Figure 12.4
*The IN
Comparison
Condition.*

Following are some multiple-row subquery examples, perhaps allowing for a better understanding of multiple-row subquery comparison conditions.

This query returns the names of all instruments in the INSTRUMENT table that are used by artists doing guest appearances. The subquery is a regular (noncorrelated) multiple-row subquery using the IN comparison condition. The result is shown in Figure 12.4.

```
SELECT NAME FROM INSTRUMENT
WHERE INSTRUMENT_ID IN
(SELECT INSTRUMENT_ID FROM INSTRUMENTATION);
```

This query returns the name of instruments played when ARTIST_ID of 1 made a guest appearance. Because ARTIST_ID 1 made no guest appearances on any songs, no rows are returned by the subquery. This shows that a subquery returning a NULL set of rows is valid. The subquery is a regular, multiple-row subquery using the IN comparison condition. The result is shown in Figure 12.5.

```
SELECT NAME FROM INSTRUMENT WHERE INSTRUMENT_ID IN
(SELECT INSTRUMENT_ID FROM INSTRUMENTATION
WHERE GUESTARTIST_ID = 1);
```

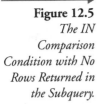

Figure 12.5
*The IN
Comparison
Condition with No
Rows Returned in
the Subquery.*

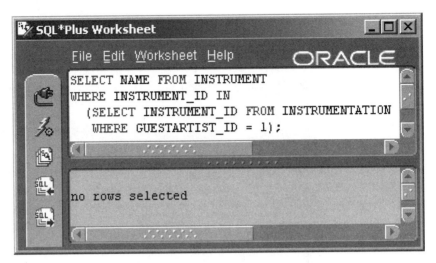

This query lists artists who never made guest appearances on any songs. The subquery is a correlated multiple-row subquery and uses the NOT EXISTS comparison condition. The result is shown in Figure 12.6.

```
SELECT NAME FROM ARTIST A WHERE NOT EXISTS
(SELECT GA.GUESTARTIST_ID
     FROM GUESTAPPEARANCE GA
     WHERE GA.GUESTARTIST_ID = A.ARTIST_ID);
```

This query returns the names of artists who recorded songs before May 1, 2001. The subquery is a regular multiple-row subquery using the ANY comparison condition. If you want to list the recording date in your query results, you must use a join or a FROM clause subquery. The result is shown in Figure 12.7.

```
SELECT NAME FROM ARTIST A WHERE A.ARTIST_ID = ANY
(SELECT S.ARTIST_ID FROM SONG S
  WHERE S.RECORDING_DATE < '01-MAY-2001');
```

This query returns the titles of CDs that have songs with a guest appearance. The subquery is a regular multiple-row subquery using the SOME comparison condition (SOME is identical to ANY). The result is shown in Figure 12.8.

Figure 12.6
NOT EXISTS with a Correlated Subquery.

```
SELECT DISTINCT M.TITLE FROM MUSICCD M
JOIN CDTRACK CT ON (M.MUSICCD_ID = CT.MUSICCD_ID)
WHERE CT.SONG_ID = SOME
(SELECT SONG_ID FROM GUESTAPPEARANCE GA);
```

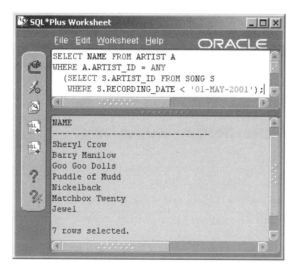

Figure 12.7
= ANY with a Subquery.

Figure 12.8
= SOME with a Subquery.

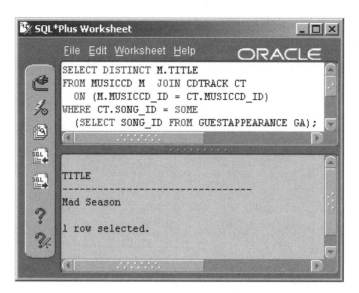

This example returns the names of artists who have not been in the studio after January 1, 2000. The subquery is a correlated multiple-row subquery using the ALL comparison condition.

Note: Note: If you want to list the session date in your query results, you must use a join or a FROM clause subquery (inline view) instead of a subquery in the WHERE clause.

The result is shown in Figure 12.9.

```
SELECT A.NAME FROM ARTIST A WHERE '01-JAN-2000' > ALL
(SELECT ST.SESSION_DATE FROM STUDIOTIME ST
  WHERE ST.ARTIST_ID = A.ARTIST_ID);
```

12.4.3   Multiple-Column Subqueries

A multiple-column subquery can return a single or multiple rows. It simply returns more than one column for each row. Typically, a multiple-column subquery is used to validate a set of columns against another set of columns in a WHERE clause or as a tuned FROM clause row filter (inline view), as shown in the two examples following.

The first example following uses the IN set membership comparison to find a row set of two columns from the ARTIST table where the name of the

Figure 12.9
> *ALL with a*
Subquery.

artist contains a lowercase letter "u". See the result in Figure 12.10. Notice that the subquery SELECT clause contains two columns. Notice also that the calling query WHERE clause filter has a list, in parentheses, of two columns that are to be compared to the two columns returned by the subquery.

```
SELECT A.ARTIST_ID, A.NAME, S.TITLE FROM ARTIST A, SONG S
WHERE (A.ARTIST_ID, A.NAME) IN
(SELECT ARTIST_ID, NAME FROM ARTIST
 WHERE NAME LIKE '%u%') AND A.ARTIST_ID = S.ARTIST_ID;
```

The next and second example of a multiple-column subquery will produce the same result as shown in Figure 12.10. In Figure 12.11, an element of the FROM clause contains the same subquery as in the first example in Figure 12.10.

Note: This example is better than the previous one for a very large ARTIST table because the filter is executed before the join of the ARTIST rows with the SONG rows. The query will perform better because the join occurs on a smaller number of rows.[1]

Figure 12.10
*The WHERE
Clause Contains a
Multiple-Column
Subquery.*

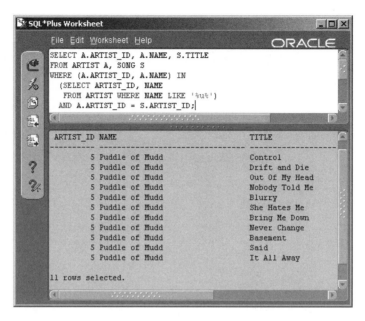

```
SELECT A.ARTIST_ID, A.NAME, S.TITLE FROM SONG S,
(SELECT ARTIST_ID, NAME
 FROM ARTIST WHERE NAME LIKE '%u%') A
WHERE A.ARTIST_ID = S.ARTIST_ID;
```

Figure 12.11
*The FROM Clause
Contains a
Multiple-Column
Subquery.*

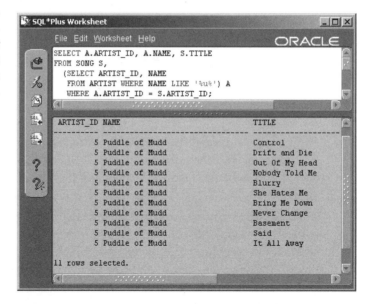

12.4.4 **Regular versus Correlated Subqueries**

This section discusses the pros and cons of using regular or correlated subqueries.

A correlated subquery allows the correlation or matching of a column between a calling query and a subquery. The calling query can pass an aliased column name into the subquery, not the other way around. Queries are parsed from left to right and from top to bottom. The SQL parser will not understand what to do with an attempt to pass a column alias from bottom to top and will produce a syntax (SQL parse) error. A subquery is parsed and executed before its calling query or subquery. For example, the following query has a SELECT clause that references a column from a correlated subquery found in the WHERE clause. The following query passes the ARTIST_ID column value from the calling query into the subquery, matching each ARTIST table row with related STUDIOTIME table rows.

```
SELECT A.NAME FROM ARTIST A
WHERE '01-JAN-2000' > ALL
(SELECT ST.SESSION_DATE FROM STUDIOTIME ST
  WHERE ST.ARTIST_ID = A.ARTIST_ID);
```

The most common use for correlated subqueries is using the EXISTS comparison condition as in the script shown following. The ARTIST_ID column value is passed from the calling query into the subquery. A correla-

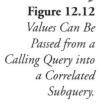

Figure 12.12
Values Can Be Passed from a Calling Query into a Correlated Subquery.

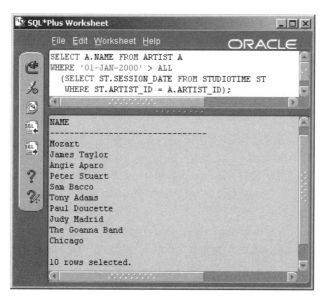

tion or match is drawn between the ARTIST.ARTIST_ID and GUESTAP-PEARANCE.GUESTARTIST_ID column values. This query is a variation on a similar query shown previously in this chapter in Figure 12.6. The query in Figure 12.6 is slightly different in that it uses NOT EXISTS as opposed to EXISTS.

```
SELECT NAME FROM ARTIST A WHERE EXISTS
(SELECT GA.GUESTARTIST_ID
     FROM GUESTAPPEARANCE GA
     WHERE GA.GUESTARTIST_ID = A.ARTIST_ID);
```

Regular subqueries maintain no relationship or correlation between the calling query and the subquery. A regular subquery will execute before the calling query such that the calling query will operate on the result set produced by the subquery. You cannot reference any columns within the subquery from the calling query. For example, this query has a regular subquery, a variation on the query in Figure 12.12 except excluding the correlated columns, passed from the calling query into the subquery.

```
SELECT S.RECORDING_DATE FROM SONG S
WHERE S.RECORDING_DATE > ALL
(SELECT ST.SESSION_DATE FROM STUDIOTIME ST);
```

Regardless of when Oracle parses the subquery, the calling query cannot contain references to any columns that belong to the subquery. The only exception to this rule is when the subquery is in the FROM clause. In that case, the subquery columns are available to the calling query and can be used in the SELECT and WHERE clauses of the calling query.

12.4.5 Nested Subqueries

A nested subquery is a subquery nested or buried within another subquery. For example, the following query has a nested subquery executed against the CDTRACK table, called from the subquery executed against the MUS-ICCD table. The result is shown in Figure 12.13.

```
SELECT GENRE FROM GENRE WHERE GENRE_ID IN
    (SELECT GENRE_ID FROM MUSICCD WHERE MUSICCD_ID IN
        (SELECT MUSICCD_ID FROM CDTRACK));
```

Figure 12.13
A Multilayer Nested Subquery.

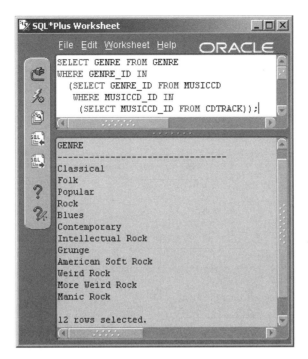

```
SELECT GENRE FROM GENRE
WHERE GENRE_ID IN
   (SELECT GENRE_ID FROM MUSICCD
     WHERE MUSICCD_ID IN
       (SELECT MUSICCD_ID FROM CDTRACK));
```

```
GENRE
---------------------------------
Classical
Folk
Popular
Rock
Blues
Contemporary
Intellectual Rock
Grunge
American Soft Rock
Weird Rock
More Weird Rock
Manic Rock

12 rows selected.
```

12.4.6 Inline Views

Demonstrating an inline view is simple. Let's modify the example used in Figure 12.13. In the example in Figure 12.13, only columns from the GENRE table can be retrieved. In most cases, column values cannot be passed from subquery to calling query, except for subqueries placed in the FROM clause. This type of query is commonly known as an Inline View. Let's alter the query in Figure 12.13 and retrieve a column value from each of the subqueries. The result of this following query is shown in Figure 12.14.

```
SELECT G.GENRE_ID, M.TITLE, M.TRACK_SEQ_NO
FROM GENRE G
, (SELECT MCD.GENRE_ID, MCD.TITLE, CD.TRACK_SEQ_NO
   FROM MUSICCD MCD
     , (SELECT MUSICCD_ID, TRACK_SEQ_NO FROM CDTRACK) CD
WHERE CD.MUSICCD_ID = MCD.MUSICCD_ID) M
WHERE M.GENRE_ID = G.GENRE_ID;
```

Figure 12.14
*A Multilayer
Nested Inline View
(FROM Clause
Subquery).*

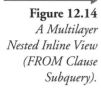

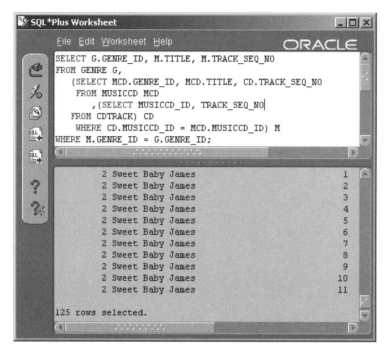

The query in Figure 12.14 has many more rows than the query in Figure 12.13 because Figure 12.14 retrieves the join between the three tables and Figure 12.13 represents on DISTINCT genres from the GENRE table.

12.4.7 **Other Uses for Subqueries**

We have already seen that subqueries can be used in many places, syntactically speaking, as listed previously in this chapter.

Note: In Oracle Database 8*i*, use of subqueries was limited. In Oracle Database 9*i* and Oracle Database 10*g*, restrictions are almost completely lifted.

Two significant uses of subqueries not covered in this chapter so far are DML command subqueries, as in the INSERT and UPDATE statements. Placing subqueries in the VALUES clause of an INSERT statement and in UPDATE statements can be useful. Be aware of performance impact when using subqueries in ORDER BY clauses, CASE statement expressions, the SPREADSHEET clause, and as function parameters. Here is an example of an INSERT statement with a subquery that returns the ARTIST_ID of

Sheryl Crow for inserting into the SONG row. This statement would add a new song by Sheryl Crow.

```
INSERT INTO SONG(SONG_ID,ARTIST_ID, TITLE)
VALUES(SONG_ID_SEQ.NEXTVAL
, (SELECT ARTIST_ID FROM ARTIST WHERE NAME='Sheryl Crow')
,'Where are you?');
```

The next command will update the song just inserted with a playing time. The statement makes the PLAYING_TIME for "Where are you?" equal to the PLAYING_TIME of the song named "Safe and Sound."

```
UPDATE SONG SET PLAYING_TIME =
(SELECT PLAYING_TIME FROM SONG
 WHERE TITLE = 'Safe And Sound')
WHERE TITLE = 'Where are you?';
```

Figure 12.15 shows the resulting inserted and subsequently updated row for Sheryl Crow.

That completes this chapter on subqueries. The next chapter looks at the more unusual or less used query types, including composites, hierarchical queries, flashback versions, and parallel queries.

Figure 12.15
Subqueries in INSERT and UPDATE Statements.

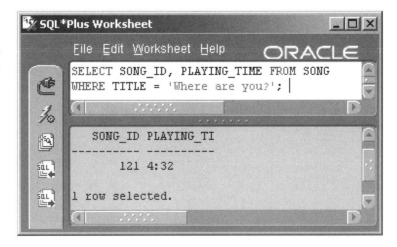

12.5 Endnotes

1. Oracle Performance Tuning for 9*i* and 10*g* (ISBN: 1-55558-305-9)

13

Unusual Query Types

In this chapter:

- What is a composite query and what are set operators?

- What is a hierarchical query?

- What are versions queries and what is flashback?

- What are parallel queries?

Unusual query types are detailed in this chapter because they may be rarely used. On the other hand, certain types of queries do not really belong in previous chapters because they are either so obscure or just too complicated, until now. We begin with composite queries.

13.1 Composite Queries

So what is a composite query? A composite query is simply a composite or concatenation of two queries. Special set operators are used to concatenate the results of two separate queries. There are certain restrictions, such as: both SELECT column sets in the two queries, must have the same number of columns, and datatypes must be compatible, dependent on SELECT column list position. So what are the available set operators?

13.1.1 Set Operators

As already stated, set operators are used to combine two separate queries into a single result set.

- **UNION ALL**. Retrieves all rows from both queries including duplicates. Duplicate rows are rows returned by both queries.

- **UNION**. Same as for UNION ALL, but duplicate rows are only returned once. In other words, duplicate rows are removed.

- **INTERSECT**. Returns distinct rows from both queries. An intersection is a little like an inner join.

- **MINUS**. Returns one query less the other, a little like the outer part of a left outer join where only distinct rows in the first query are returned.

13.1.2 Using Composite Queries

In order to demonstrate a sensible use of composite queries, let's create a view, removing all styles from genres in the GENRES view. Styles in the GENRE table are numbered as GENRE_ID 1, 2, and 3; the GENRES view will include only these rows.

```
CREATE VIEW GENRES AS
SELECT GENRE_ID AS ID, GENRE
FROM GENRE WHERE STYLE_ID IS NOT NULL;
```

The following query concatenates the GENRE table and GENRES view. We are trying to retrieve duplicated rows. The resulting row count includes all rows in the GENRE table and the GENRES view. The resulting duplicated rows can be clearly seen in Figure 13.1. The ORDER BY clause is used to show duplications (see Chapter 6).

```
SELECT GENRE_ID, GENRE FROM GENRE
UNION ALL
SELECT * FROM GENRES
ORDER BY 1;
```

Now let's change the query in Figure 13.1 and remove the duplications as in the following query using the UNION set operator instead of the UNION ALL operator. The result is shown in Figure 13.2.

```
SELECT GENRE_ID, GENRE FROM GENRE
UNION
SELECT * FROM GENRES
ORDER BY 1;
```

Figure 13.1
*Duplicating Rows
with UNION
ALL.*

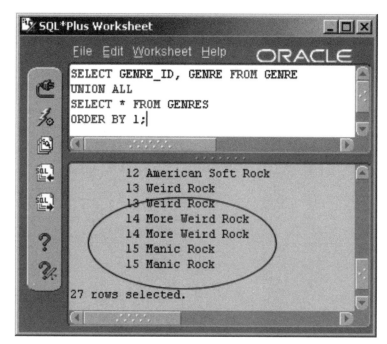

The INTERSECT operator returns an intersection or natural join type result between two queries. In the following example, all nonstyle entries are returned from the GENRE table. The result is shown in Figure 13.3.

```
SELECT GENRE_ID, GENRE FROM GENRE
INTERSECT
SELECT * FROM GENRES;
```

In the next example, the MINUS operator is used to remove all genres from the GENRE table using the GENRES view, returning only GENRE style rows 1, 2, and 3. The result is shown in Figure 13.4.

```
SELECT GENRE_ID, GENRE FROM GENRE
MINUS
SELECT * FROM GENRES;
```

Figure 13.2
*Removing
Duplicates with
UNION.*

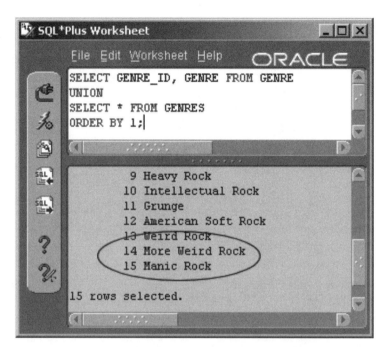

Figure 13.3
*INTERSECT
Returns Rows
Common to Both
Queries.*

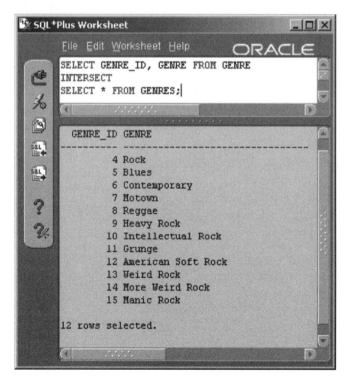

Figure 13.4
MINUS Returns Rows in the First Query Only.

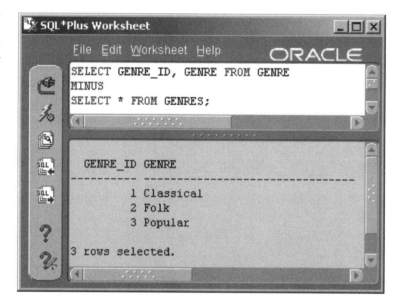

That covers composite queries using set operators. Now let's look at hierarchical queries.

13.2 Hierarchical Queries

A hierarchical query allows display of hierarchical data in a single table. The MUSIC schema described in Chapter 1 contains two tables with a hierarchical structure, namely the INSTRUMENT and GENRE tables. However, the INSTRUMENT table contains hierarchical data, while the GENRE table does not. The GENRE table contains a single-level hierarchy and the INSTRUMENT table contains multiple levels. Before we look at any examples, there are various hierarchical operators and pseudocolumns we should examine (see Chapter 7).

Note: (10*g*) The CONNECT BY clause now allows ancestor-descendant pairs as opposed to only parent-child pairs. In other words, pairs can be matched and returned where those pairs are not directly related within a hierarchy but related from the top to the bottom of a hierarchy.

13.2.1   Hierarchical Query Operators

- **PRIOR.** Used with the CONNECT BY condition evaluating the subsequent expression for each parent row of each current row, using a current row column to hook into a parent row column.

- (10*g*) **CONNECT_BY_ROOT.** Performs a similar function to that of CONNECT BY PRIOR except using the root row of the hierarchy as opposed to the parent row.

13.2.2   Hierarchical Query Pseudocolumns

- **LEVEL.** Used only in hierarchical queries (using the CONNECT BY clause). This returns the level (1, 2, etc.) of the row.

- (10*g*) **CONNECT_BY_ISLEAF and CONNECT BY_ISCYCLE.** These pseudocolumns determine if hierarchical data can be expanded upon. Does an element have ancestor and/or child entries?

Now let's demonstrate use of hierarchical queries.

13.2.3   Using Hierarchical Queries

In this first example, PRIOR is used with the CONNECT BY condition evaluating the subsequent expression for each parent row of each current row, using a current row column to hook into a parent row column. Figure 13.5 shows the result. The START WITH modifier simply begins at a specific point within the hierarchy.

```
SELECT INSTRUMENT_ID, NAME, SECTION_ID, LEVEL
FROM INSTRUMENT
START WITH INSTRUMENT_ID = 10
CONNECT BY PRIOR INSTRUMENT_ID = SECTION_ID
ORDER BY 4, 2;
```

Notice in Figure 13.5 that the LEVEL column is included in the query. All the brass instruments are in the brass section. The row Brass is therefore level 1 and the other rows, the brass instruments section, are all level 2.

The following second example shows (10*g*) CONNECT_BY_ROOT performing a similar function to that of CONNECT BY PRIOR except using the root row of the hierarchy as opposed to the parent row. The previous query is changed, as shown with the result in Figure 13.6.

```
SELECT CONNECT_BY_ROOT NAME "Section"
```

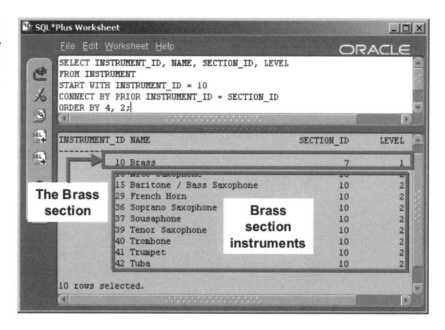

Figure 13.5
*A Hierarchical
Query on
Hierarchical Data.*

```
, NAME "Instrument", LEVEL
FROM INSTRUMENT
START WITH INSTRUMENT_ID = 10
CONNECT BY PRIOR INSTRUMENT_ID = SECTION_ID
ORDER BY 1, 2;
```

The third and fourth examples, shown next, demonstrate the use of the new ⑩*g* CONNECT_BY_ISCYCLE and ⑩*g* CONNECT_BY_ISLEAF pseudocolumns. CONNECT_BY_ISCYCLE will return 1 if a row has a child where that child row is also an ancestor of the row. Thus in the third example shown following the result is 0 and no further rows are shown, because none are both children and ancestors at the same time. The result is shown in Figure 13.7.

```
SELECT CONNECT_BY_ISCYCLE "IsCycle"
, INSTRUMENT_ID, NAME, SECTION_ID, LEVEL
FROM INSTRUMENT
START WITH INSTRUMENT_ID = 10
CONNECT BY NOCYCLE INSTRUMENT_ID = SECTION_ID
ORDER BY 4, 2;
```

Figure 13.6
The
CONNECT
_ BY_ROOT
Operator.

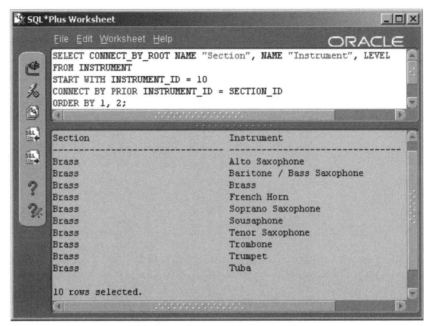

The CONNECT_BY_ISLEAF pseudocolumn returns a 1 when part of the CONNECT BY row set, indicating expansion possibilities. Thus for the fourth example, in the following query (the result in Figure 13.8), both instrument number 10 and its child instruments are shown. However, only instrument 10 has leaves; the other instruments are child rows, and they have no further children.

```
SELECT CONNECT_BY_ISLEAF "IsLeaf"
, INSTRUMENT_ID, NAME, SECTION_ID, LEVEL
FROM INSTRUMENT
START WITH INSTRUMENT_ID = 10
CONNECT BY PRIOR INSTRUMENT_ID = SECTION_ID
ORDER BY 4, 2;
```

Next we look at flashback and versions queries.

13.3 Flashback and Versions Queries

A flashback query literally allows flashing back to the state that data was in at a previous point in time. Oracle Database 9*i* allowed AS OF flashback queries back to a point in time using a timestamp or SCN. Oracle Database

Figure 13.7
The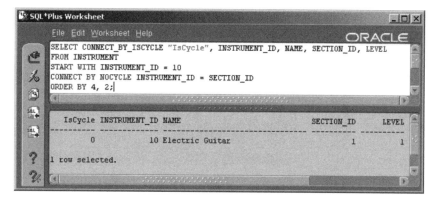
(10g) CONNECT
_BY_ ISCYCLE
Pseudocolumn.

Figure 13.8
The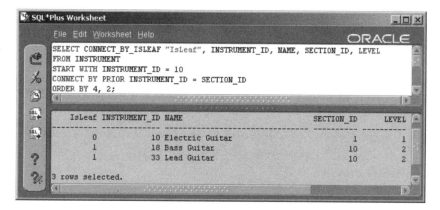
(10g) CONNECT
_BY_ ISLEAF
Pseudocolumn.

10g additionally allows what are called *flashback versions queries*. A flashback versions query can be used to return more than one version of a single row both before and after a change.

Note: Flashback queries require automated undo. Manual rollbacks, now desupported, will not support flashback queries.

13.3.1 Flashback Query Syntax

Figure 13.9 shows the syntax for flashback queries.

Note: The DBMS_FLASHBACK package can be used to create flashback queries at the session level.

Figure 13.9
Flashback AS OF
and
(10g) *VERSIONS*
Query Syntax.

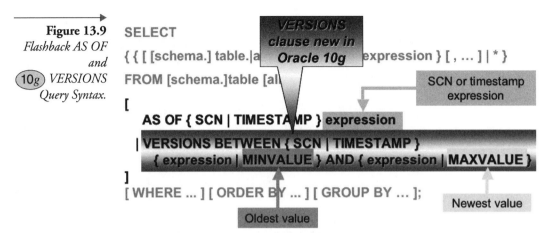

```
SELECT
{ { [ [schema.] table.|a        expression } [ , ... ] | * }
FROM [schema.]table [al
[
    AS OF { SCN | TIMESTAMP } expression
    | VERSIONS BETWEEN { SCN | TIMESTAMP }
        { expression | MINVALUE } AND { expression | MAXVALUE }
]
[ WHERE ... ] [ ORDER BY ... ] [ GROUP BY ... ];
```

VERSIONS clause new in Oracle 10g

SCN or timestamp expression

Newest value

Oldest value

13.3.2 (10g) Versions Query Pseudocolumns

Several versions query pseudocolumns allow retrieval of identifying information about different versions of the same row in a flashback query:

- **ORA_ROWSCN**. Returns a row SCN.

- **VERSIONS_{START|END}TIME**. First and last version timestamp.

- **VERSIONS_{START|END}SCN**. First and last version SCN.

- **VERSIONS_XID**. Transaction identifier.

- **VERSIONS_OPERATION**. Returns (I)nsert, (U)pdate, or (D)elete.

Now let's look at some simple examples of flashback queries.

13.3.3 Using Flashback Queries

First I add a new row to the CONTINENT table.

```
INSERT INTO CONTINENT VALUES(CONTINENT_ID_SEQ.NEXTVAL
, 'South East Asia');
```

Now I use an AS OF flashback query to look at all continents before inserting South East Asia. Figure 13.10 shows that the row did not exist yesterday.

```
SELECT * FROM CONTINENT
AS OF TIMESTAMP(SYSTIMESTAMP - INTERVAL '1' DAY);
```

Figure 13.10
An AS OF Flashback Query.

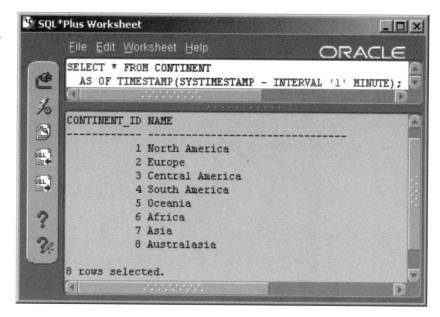

Now let's update an existing row, not the one we previously inserted, so that we can execute a flashback versions query.

```
UPDATE CONTINENT SET NAME = 'Australia and New Zealand'
WHERE NAME = 'Australasia';
```

Now we execute a flashback versions query. Figure 13.11 shows two versions of rows for Australasia plus Australia and New Zealand.

```
SELECT * FROM CONTINENT
VERSIONS BETWEEN TIMESTAMP MINVALUE AND MAXVALUE;
```

The following script, as shown in Figure 13.12, simply adds in all of the versions flashback query pseudocolumns.

```
COLUMN ID FORMAT 990
COLUMN CONTINENT A16
COLUMN STIME FORMAT A5
COLUMN ETIME FORMAT A5
COLUMN DML FORMAT A6
SELECT CONTINENT_ID "ID", NAME "CONTINENT"
```

Figure 13.11
*A Flashback
Versions Query.*

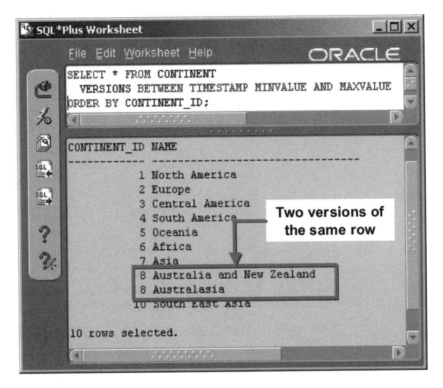

```
, TO_CHAR(VERSIONS_STARTTIME, 'HH24:MI:SS') "STime"
, TO_CHAR(VERSIONS_ENDTIME, 'HH24:MI:SS') "ETime"
, VERSIONS_STARTSCN "SSCN"
, VERSIONS_ENDSCN "ESCN"
, VERSIONS_OPERATION
, DECODE(VERSIONS_OPERATION,'I','Insert','U'
,'Update','D','Delete','Error') "DML"
FROM CONTINENT VERSIONS BETWEEN TIMESTAMP
    MINVALUE AND MAXVALUE
ORDER BY CONTINENT_ID;
```

(10g) Oracle Database 10*g* now allows both FLASHBACK DATABASE and FLASHBACK TABLE operations, as in the following syntax:

```
FLASHBACK [ STANDBY ] DATABASE [ database ]
    TO { SCN | TIMESTAMP } expression;

FLASHBACK TABLE { [ schema.]table , ... }
    TO { SCN | TIMESTAMP } expression
```

Figure 13.12
A Flashback Versions Query Including Pseudocolumns.

```
COLUMN ID FORMAT 990
COLUMN CONTINENT FORMAT A16
COLUMN STIME FORMAT A5
COLUMN ETIME FORMAT A5
COLUMN DML FORMAT A1
COLUMN COMMAND FORMAT A6
SELECT CONTINENT_ID "ID", NAME "CONTINENT"
    ,TO_CHAR(VERSIONS_STARTTIME, 'HH24:MI:SS') "STime"
    ,TO_CHAR(VERSIONS_ENDTIME, 'HH24:MI:SS') "ETime"
    ,VERSIONS_STARTSCN "SSCN", VERSIONS_ENDSCN "ESCN"
    ,VERSIONS_OPERATION "DML"
    ,DECODE(VERSIONS_OPERATION,'I','Insert'
        ,'U','Update','D','Delete','Error') "Command"
FROM CONTINENT VERSIONS BETWEEN TIMESTAMP MINVALUE AND MAXVALUE
ORDER BY CONTINENT_ID;
```

```
  ID CONTINENT        STime ETime       SSCN      ESCN D Comman
----  ---------------  ----- -----  ----------  ---------- - ------
   1 North America    23:58            4365261            I Insert
   2 Europe           23:58            4365261            I Insert
   3 Central America  23:58            4365261            I Insert
   4 South America    23:58            4365261            I Insert
   5 Oceania          23:58            4365261            I Insert
   6 Africa           23:58            4365261            I Insert
   7 Asia             23:58            4365261            I Insert
   8 Australia and Ne 01:04            4412060            U Update
   8 Australasia      23:58 01:04      4365261   4412060 I Insert
  10 South East Asia  01:04            4412060            I Insert

10 rows selected.
```

```
[ { ENABLE | DISABLE } TRIGGERS ];
```

FLASHBACK DATABASE and FLASHBACK TABLE allow restore of either the entire database or a single table back to—and in the case of a table, even forward to—a different SCN.

The next step is to examine parallel queries.

13.4 Parallel Queries

In an ideal world, parallel queries are useful on multiple CPU platforms when Oracle Partitioning is being used with separate disks or RAID arrays. Generally, parallel queries are only an advantage for very large tables or in very large databases such as data warehouses. Using parallel queries on small, highly active concurrent OLTP databases can sometimes cause rather than solve performance problems. The following types of SQL can be executed in parallel[1]:

- Any query with at least a single table scan using SELECT, INSERT, UPDATE, and DELETE commands.

- The CREATE INDEX and ALTER INDEX REBUILD commands.

- The CREATE TABLE command when generating a table from a SELECT command.

- Any query on partitions with local indexes, where a local index is an index created on each separate partition.

There are two ways to execute queries against tables in parallel. The first involves the PARALLEL hint and the second involves the CREATE TABLE or ALTER TABLE commands including the parallel clause. For instance, the PARALLEL hint can be used as follows to execute two parallel processes, executing the query:

```
SELECT /*+ PARALLEL(SALES, 2) */ * FROM SALES;
```

The CREATE TABLE and ALTER TABLE commands can be used with the following syntax:

```
{ CREATE | ALTER } TABLE … [ NOPARALLEL | PARALLEL [n] ];
```

Thus the SALES table could be altered to have a degree of parallelism of 2 with the following command:

```
ALTER TABLE SALES PARALLEL 2;
```

Note: No parallel query examples are given in this book, because parallel queries tend to execute with improved performance only when using Oracle Partitioning. Further detail and examples on Oracle Partitioning and parallel queries can be found in my other book, Oracle Performance Tuning for 9*i* and 10*g* (ISBN 1-55558-305-9).

That completes this chapter on composite, hierarchical, flashback, and parallel queries. The next chapter examines Oracle Expressions, new to Oracle Database 10*g*.

13.5 Endnotes

1.   Oracle Performance Tuning for 9*i* and 10*g* (ISBN: 1-55558-305-9)

Expressions

In this chapter:

- How can expressions be classified?
- What are regular expressions?
- What is the Oracle Expression Filter?

There are three distinct parts to this chapter. The first part covers details of expressions in Oracle, which are covered more or less throughout this book. This chapter attempts to simply break things into logical parts. The second part of this chapter deals with regular expressions catering for text pattern matching and searching. The third part briefly covers the Oracle Expression Filter.

A fundamental but often difficult to answer question is this: What is an expression? There is a simple explanation. Anything resulting in a value is an expression. An expression can consist of a single scalar value or a highly complex formula. Here are some example expressions:

1 is an expression.

x + y is an expression.

mc^2 is an expression.

The subquery (highlighted) in the following query is a list of expressions:

```
SELECT * FROM COUNTRY WHERE CONTINENT_ID IN
(SELECT CONTINENT_ID FROM CONTINENT);
```

Brackets, or, as mathematically termed, parentheses, are used to change the sequence of evaluation within expressions, effectively creating expressions within expressions. The sequence of evaluation is called *precedence*. See Chapter 7 for details on precedence. Let's try to classify expressions.

14.1 Types of Expressions

Most of expression classification is simple common sense, and so often by both DBA and programmer alike, is taken for granted.

- **Basic**. In Oracle SQL, a basic expression is really only a string, a value, a column, or perhaps a sequence reference within a SELECT statement list. For example, 'My name is Joe.'

- **Compounding**. A compound expression is multiple expressions put together with operators. For example, 10 + 20 or $P(1 + r)^n$, a formula for compound interest calculations.

- **Lists**. A list of expressions such as (1, 2, x + y, (SELECT * FROM COUNTRY), 'My name is Joe').

- **Functions**. Any built-in or user-defined function comprises a functional expression. For example, the function POWER(2, 3) will return 8.

- **Dates, Times, and Intervals**. Uses various functions and formats to return a Datetime. Intervals return times between dates.

- **Scalar Subqueries**. A scalar subquery returns a single value, regardless of the number of rows (see Chapter 12).

- **CURSOR**. A SELECT statement can contain a CURSOR expression of the form as shown:

```
SELECT CY.NAME, CURSOR
(SELECT NAME FROM CONTINENT
  WHERE CONTINENT_ID = CY.CONTINENT_ID)
FROM COUNTRY CY;
```

- **CASE Statements**. A CASE statement can be used as an inline expression within an SQL query, similar to an IF-THEN-ELSE programming construct. The syntax for an inline CASE statement is as

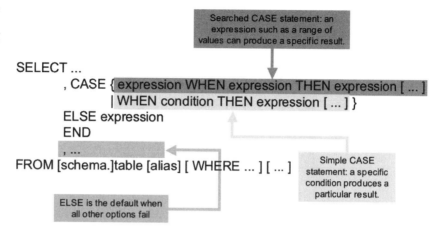

Figure 14.1
SQL Inline CASE Statement Syntax.

shown in Figure 14.1. See Chapter 24 for the PL/SQL version of the CASE statement.

Chapter 9 contained a DECODE example based on the states in which artists live, duplicated here for convenience:

```
SELECT STATE_PROVINCE
, DECODE(STATE_PROVINCE,'CA','Surfer',
                'NH','Snow bunny',
                   'OR', 'Tree hugger',
                   'FL', 'Retired',
                      'Whatever!')
FROM ARTIST;
```

Now let's convert the Chapter 9 DECODE example to use an inline CASE statement rather than the DECODE function. The following example contains a simple CASE statement format, which will produce the same result as the DECODE example in Chapter 9, Figure 9.12:

```
SELECT STATE_PROVINCE
  , CASE STATE_PROVINCE
    WHEN 'CA' THEN 'Surfer'
    WHEN 'NH' THEN 'Snow bunny'
    WHEN 'OR' THEN 'Tree hugger'
    WHEN 'FL' THEN 'Retired'
    ELSE 'Whatever!' END
FROM ARTIST;
```

Figure 14.2
*An SQL Inline
Searched CASE
Statement
Example.*

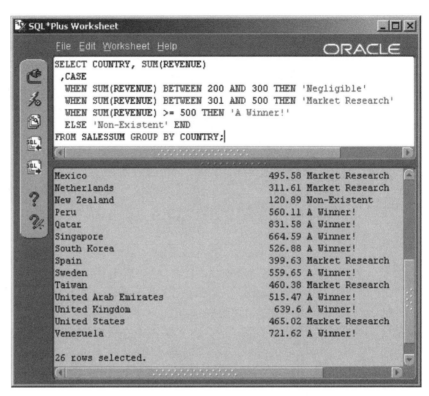

Here is a second example of an inline CASE statement expression using a searched CASE statement format. The result is shown in Figure 14.2.

```
SELECT COUNTRY, SUM(REVENUE)
 ,CASE
  WHEN SUM(REVENUE) BETWEEN 200 AND 300 THEN 'Negligible'
  WHEN SUM(REVENUE) BETWEEN 301 AND 500 THEN 'Market Research'
  WHEN SUM(REVENUE) >= 500 THEN 'A Winner!'
  ELSE 'Non-Existent' END
FROM SALESSUM GROUP BY COUNTRY;
```

■ **Objects**. Objects are accessed as TABLE.TYPE.ATTRIBUTE. In other words, a table containing a type definition (collection or structure) will have type column names accessed by the table, the type name, and followed by the name of the attribute (column) defined within the type. Object datatypes are covered in Chapter 16.

- **Modeling**. Model expressions are part of the SPREADSHEET clause (see Chapter 11).

Note: The SPREADSHEET clause is renamed as the MODEL clause.

- **Object Type Constructors**. Expression to instantiate an object from a type.

There are other expression types, but they are either trivial or represented fully in other chapters in this book. What we are really interested in for this chapter are regular expressions and the Oracle Expression Filter. Let's start with regular expressions.

14.2 ⑩ Regular Expressions

Oracle regular expressions conform to and enhance POSIX[1] standards, much like regular expression support in a programming language such as Perl. There are two parts to using regular expressions in Oracle SQL. The first part is the functions that execute regular expression matching, and the second part is the matching patterns. I am reversing the accepted approach and examining the functions first. It makes more sense to me to understand what all of these wonderful patterns are used for before presenting a large set of meaningless characters.

14.2.1 Regular Expression Functions

Regular expression functions can be used anywhere a function is used, both built-in and user-defined. Duplicated parameters in the following list are not explained more than once.

- **REGEXP_INSTR (source, pattern [, position [, occurrence [, return [, parameter]]]])**. Finds the position of a string within a string.
  - **Position**. Represents the position in a string to begin searching. Defaulted at position 1.
  - **Occurrence**. Implies that if a pattern exists more than once, then a position after the first can be found. The default is 1. If a search passes all occurrences or if there are none, then 0 is returned.

- **Return.** 0 (the default) returns the position of the target pattern, and 1 returns the position after the target pattern.
- **Parameter.** This value can be set to three different values: c = case sensitive, i = case insensitive, m = more than one line in the source.

- **REGEXP_SUBSTR (source, pattern [, position [, occurrence [, parameter]]]).** Extracts a string from a string.

- **REGEXP_REPLACE (source, pattern [, replace [, position [, occurrence [, parameter]]]]).** Replaces a string within a string.

Regular expression functions are much like their relative Oracle built-in string functions. See Chapter 9 for Oracle built-in string functions.

14.2.2 Regular Expression Patterns

Regular expression patterns are POSIX standard with some additions by Oracle. It is not necessary to detail expression pattern-matching characters because they can be found in Oracle documentation and online. The basics are as shown in Table 14.1.

Table 14.1   *Basic Regular Expression Pattern-Matching Characters.*

Character	What Is It?
*	Zero or more.
.	Any character (not null).
?	Zero or one.
+	One or more.
|	OR
^	Start of line.
$	End of line.
[...]	List of elements allowing match of any expression contained within.
(...)	Expression parentheses.
{ i }, { i, }, and { i, j }	i matches exactly, at least i matches, and at least i matches but <= j.

14.2.3 Using Regular Expressions

The following example uses REGEXP_INSTR to find the position of all song titles containing a capital letter A. The result is shown in Figure 14.3.

```
COLUMN TITLE FORMAT A32
SELECT TITLE, VAL FROM(SELECT TITLE
,REGEXP_INSTR(title, 'A(/*)') AS VAL FROM SONG
) WHERE VAL > 0;
```

The following SQL code statement would find the same result as that in Figure 14.3.

```
SELECT TITLE FROM SONG WHERE TITLE LIKE '%A%';
```

Where the INSTR (REGEXP_INSTR) function retrieves the position of a string, the SUBSTR (REGEXP_SUBSTR) function retrieves a portion of a string. The following script will retrieve the second occurrence of every song title where the string is enclosed by spaces. Therefore, a string

Figure 14.3
REGEXP_INSTR and Finding the Position of All Song Titles Containing the Letter A.

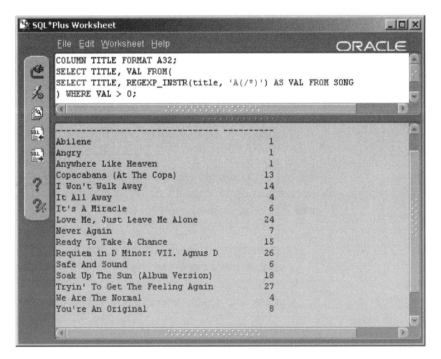

Figure 14.4
*REGEXP_SUBSTR
and Finding Song
Titles with Three
or More Words.*

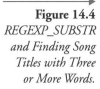

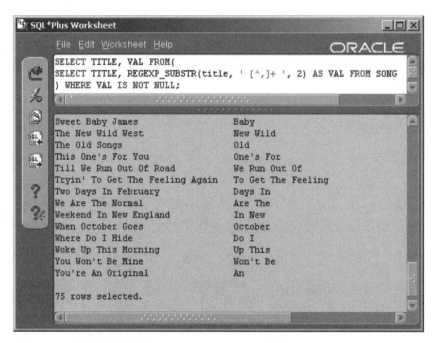

with three words returns the middle word; a string with four words returns the middle two words; and strings with either one or two words are not returned at all. In other words, the first and last words are removed as long as there are three words or more to the song title. The result is shown in Figure 14.4.

```
SELECT TITLE, VAL FROM(SELECT TITLE
, REGEXP_SUBSTR(title, ' [^,]+ ', 2) AS VAL FROM SONG
) WHERE VAL IS NOT NULL;
```

The next example uses the REGEXP_REPLACE function to replace all occurrences of the capital letter A in song titles with a string of three asterisks. The result is shown in Figure 14.5.

```
SELECT TITLE, VAL FROM(SELECT TITLE
, REGEXP_REPLACE(title, 'A(/*)', '***\1') AS VAL
FROM SONG
) WHERE VAL LIKE '%***%';
```

Figure 14.5
*REGEXP_REPLA
CE and Changing
Song Titles.*

That is the rudimentary basics of regular expressions. It is strongly suggested that if you want to use regular expression functions and syntax, that you do more research first. The point is made that Oracle SQL now has regular expression capability. Now let's look at the Oracle Expression Filter.

14.3 (10g) Oracle Expression Filter

Oracle Expression Filter in its simplest form allows application of generically formed WHERE clauses stored in a table. The easiest way to explain this concept is to demonstrate it functioning. Let's start off by creating a view against the MUSIC data warehouse schema SALES table, plus some of the dimension tables. Three important attributes are highlighted; why will soon be explained.

```
CREATE OR REPLACE VIEW SALESDATA AS(
    SELECT S.SALES_ID AS SALE, G.GENRE AS GENRE
        , CT.NAME AS CONTINENT, CY.NAME AS COUNTRY
        , S.SALE_PRICE, S.SALE_QTY
        , TO_NUMBER(TO_CHAR(S.SALE_DATE, 'MM')) AS MONTH
        ,TO_NUMBER(TO_CHAR(S.SALE_DATE, 'YYYY')) AS YEAR
    FROM SALES S JOIN MUSICCD M ON(S.MUSICCD_ID = M.MUSICCD_ID)
```

```
    JOIN GENRE G ON(M.GENRE_ID = G.GENRE_ID)
    JOIN CONTINENT CT ON(CT.CONTINENT_ID = S.CONTINENT_ID)
    JOIN COUNTRY CY ON(CY.COUNTRY_ID = S.COUNTRY_ID));
```

So now there is a view on a part of the sales data with various other attributes included. Typically, in a data warehouse, this view might be created as a materialized view. Now we need to create a few goodies for the expression filters to function. We have to create what is called an *attribute set*, essentially an Oracle TYPE object (class or structure). The following anonymous PL/SQL procedure (see Chapter 24) uses an Oracle-provided package called DBMS_EXPFIL. An attribute set or type called HitCD is created, and three attributes are added: Continent, Country, and Genre.

```
BEGIN
 DBMS_EXPFIL.CREATE_ATTRIBUTE_SET(ATTR_SET=>'HitCD');
 DBMS_EXPFIL.ADD_ELEMENTARY_ATTRIBUTE(ATTR_SET=>'HitCD'
  , ATTR_NAME=>'Continent', ATTR_TYPE=>'VARCHAR2(32)');
 DBMS_EXPFIL.ADD_ELEMENTARY_ATTRIBUTE(ATTR_SET=>'HitCD'
  , ATTR_NAME=>'Country', ATTR_TYPE=>'VARCHAR2(32)');
 DBMS_EXPFIL.ADD_ELEMENTARY_ATTRIBUTE(ATTR_SET=>'HitCD'
  , ATTR_NAME=>'Genre', ATTR_TYPE=>'VARCHAR2(32)');
END;
/
```

Now we create a table to contain the filters (WHERE clauses) and assign the attribute set to that new table and filter column using another anonymous PL/SQL procedure.

```
CREATE TABLE SALESANALYSIS(Filter VARCHAR2(4000));
BEGIN
DBMS_EXPFIL.ASSIGN_ATTRIBUTE_SET(ATTR_SET=>'HitCD'
, EXPR_TAB=>'SALESANALYSIS', EXPR_COL=>'FILTER');
END;
/
```

Now we create the filter rows in the SALESANALYSIS table. The first filter is highlighted.

```
INSERT INTO SALESANALYSIS VALUES('CONTINENT=''North America''
AND COUNTRY = ''United States'' and GENRE=''American Soft
Rock''');
INSERT INTO SALESANALYSIS VALUES('CONTINENT=''North America''
AND COUNTRY = ''Mexico'' and GENRE=''American Soft Rock''');
INSERT INTO SALESANALYSIS VALUES('CONTINENT=''Europe'' AND
COUNTRY = ''United Kingdom'' and GENRE=''American Soft
Rock''');
INSERT INTO SALESANALYSIS VALUES('CONTINENT=''South America''
AND COUNTRY = ''Argentina'' and GENRE=''American Soft
Rock''');
COMMIT;
```

Now let's look at a summary of all American Soft Rock rows in the SALESDATA view. All expression filters are created as American Soft Rock. It is important for subsequent queries to understand the full extent of the data. In short, we need to see these rows first. The result is shown in Figure 14.6.

```
COLUMN CONTINENT FORMAT A16
COLUMN COUNTRY FORMAT A16
SELECT SD.CONTINENT, SD.COUNTRY, COUNT(*) FROM SALESDATA SD
WHERE SD.GENRE = 'American Soft Rock'
GROUP BY SD.CONTINENT, SD.COUNTRY;
```

Figure 14.6
Sales Data Summarized by Continent and Country.

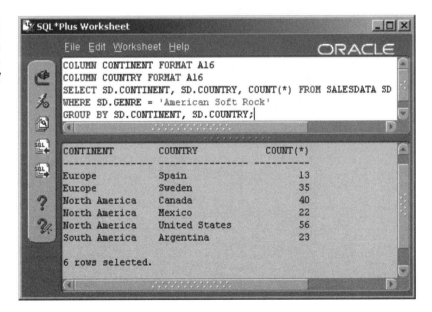

So Figure 14.6 shows us what data we have, with a restriction. Now let's run a very simple query, grouping by country and applying all the expression filters stored in the SALESANALYSIS table. The EVALUATE operator applies expression filters. The result is shown in Figure 14.7.

```
SELECT DISTINCT SD.CONTINENT, COUNT(*)
FROM SALESANALYSIS SA, SALESDATA SD
WHERE EVALUATE(SA.FILTER
  , HitCD.getVarchar(SD.CONTINENT, SD.COUNTRY, SD.GENRE))=1
GROUP BY SD.CONTINENT, SD.COUNTRY;
```

Examining the SALESANALYSIS table filter entries and Figure 14.6, it should be obvious that all expression filters have been applied in Figure 14.7. Only the United States, Mexico, and Argentina have SALESDATA view rows for American Soft Rock; the United Kingdom does not. This is shown with greater clarity by going a small step further and grouping by both continent and country. The script following will suffice. The result is shown in Figure 14.8.

```
SELECT SD.CONTINENT, SD.COUNTRY, COUNT(*)
FROM SALESANALYSIS SA, SALESDATA SD
WHERE EVALUATE(SA.FILTER
  , HitCD.getVarchar(SD.CONTINENT,SD.COUNTRY, SD.GENRE))=1
GROUP BY SD.CONTINENT, SD.COUNTRY;
```

Figure 14.7
Apply the Expression Filters in the SALESANALYSIS Table.

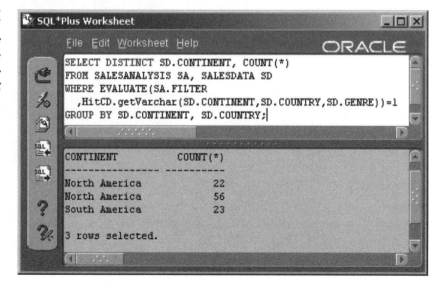

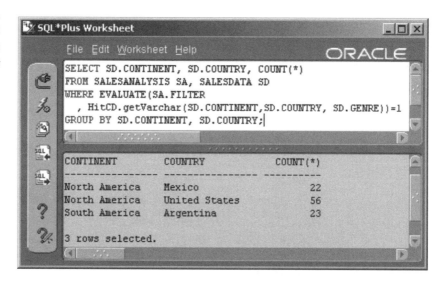

Figure 14.8
*More Detail in
Addition to That
in Figure 14.7.*

Now let's look at a more complex example, using all of the relevant SALESDATA view columns, once again using the SALESANALYSIS table expression filters. The result is shown in Figure 14.9.

```
COLUMN YEAR FORMAT 9990
COLUMN MONTH FORMAT 99990
COLUMN SALES FORMAT 99990
COLUMN REVENUE FORMAT $990.00
SELECT SD.YEAR, SD.MONTH, SD.CONTINENT, SD.COUNTRY
, SUM(SD.SALE_QTY) AS SALES
, SUM(SD.SALE_PRICE) AS REVENUE
FROM SALESANALYSIS SA, SALESDATA SD
WHERE EVALUATE(SA.FILTER
    ,HitCD.getVarchar(SD.CONTINENT,SD.COUNTRY,SD.GENRE))=1
AND SD.MONTH = 10
GROUP BY SD.YEAR, SD.MONTH, SD.CONTINENT, SD.COUNTRY;
```

That wraps up expressions. We have examined general expression types, regular expressions, and Oracle Expression Filter, the latter two of which are new to Oracle Database 10*g*.

Note: Because regular expressions and Oracle Expression Filter are new to Oracle Database 10*g*, coverage thereof is deliberately scant in this chapter.

Figure 14.9
Listing the
SALESDATA
Using Expression
Filters.

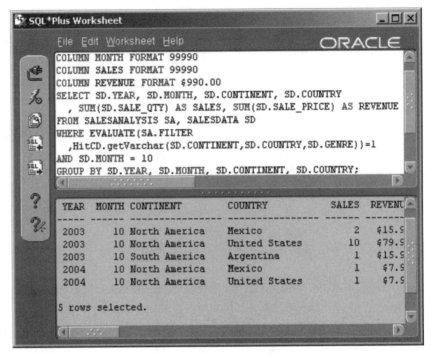

The next chapter looks into using the Data Manipulation Language (DML), changing data in Oracle.

14.4   Endnotes

1.   www.opengroup.org/onlinepubs/007904975/toc.htm

Data Manipulation Language (DML)

In this chapter:

- What are DML and transaction control?

- How do you use the INSERT command?

- How do you update existing rows?

- How do you delete one or more rows?

- How do you merge two tables together?

This chapter demonstrates the Data Manipulation Language (DML), showing the syntax and plenty of examples. DML commands are used in SQL to add, modify, and remove rows of data in database tables. Transaction control using ROLLBACK and COMMIT commands, among others, plus the MERGE command, are also covered in this chapter.

In previous chapters we have explored a wide variety of methods and variations of data retrieval. Now, it is time to learn how to make up your own data!

15.1   What Is DML?

Data Manipulation Language (DML) is the blanket term for any command that modifies data in an Oracle database.

The four types of commands that fall under the DML umbrella are as follows:

- **INSERT.** Add a new row.

- **UPDATE.** Modify the data in one or more columns of an existing row.

- **DELETE.** Eliminate a row.

- **MERGE.** Insert all the rows in one table into another table that already has existing rows. If the key of the incoming row matches an existing row, update the existing row instead of inserting a new row.

Note: MERGE was a new feature of Oracle Database 9*i*. The MERGE command is improved in Oracle Database 10*g*.

Note: Data Definition Language (DDL) commands are SQL commands that modify the structure of the database (the database metadata) by adding, removing, or changing tables, views, or other objects (see Chapters 18 to 23).

Here are some pointers that are common for all DML commands:

- DML commands are usually executed against a single table at a time. The only exceptions to this rule are rare multiple-table inserts, a variation of the INSERT command and the MERGE command. Multiple-table inserts are typically used for repetitive data warehouse Denormalization or logical archiving of table rows into separate historical tables or partitions.

- You must have permission to use DML commands on tables that you do not own (see Chapter 23). For this chapter, assume you always own the tables you are working on, so you automatically have the privileges needed.

- Oracle Database enforces constraints defined for the table (such as unique primary key values) whenever you use DML commands on a table. Constraints are rules that the database keeps track of for each table you create. Chapter 20 covers constraints in detail.

- One constraint that you will see very often is the NOT NULL constraint, placed on a column. This means that no row in the table can have a null value in any column with a NOT NULL constraint. The DESCRIBE command tells you whether the column has a NOT NULL constraint or not. If it says NOT NULL, the column cannot contain any null values. Otherwise, it can contain null values.

- You can undo your DML commands with the ROLLBACK command. There are some conditions for this operation, which are discussed in the next section.

So before going into the precise details of DML commands and changing database data, we need to examine what is called *transaction control*. Transaction control literally allows the control of transactions.

15.2 Transaction Control

So what is a transaction? A *transaction* is a set of one or more SQL commands that change data. A transaction begins when you execute an SQL command, changing something in the database. As you make further changes to table data, you execute additional SQL commands. All of these commands can be considered part of a single transaction for two reasons: (1) because changes may depend on each other, and (2) because as long as a COMMIT or ROLLBACK command is not executed, those changes are not set in stone and can be undone.

It is possible to query tables and view changes before saving them. During your transaction, all the changes you make to tables are actually made to the database. The precise details of how to use the rollback and undo functions can be found in Chapter 3 under the section titled "Rollback and Undo" (Oracle Database Architecture).

In simple terms, when you change something in a table, before committing the changes, Oracle writes changes to both the table and what is called a rollback or undo file. When you save your changes using the COMMIT command, Oracle will simply remove the undo record, because the changes have already been made to your table. If you were to use the ROLLBACK command instead of the COMMIT command and undo your changes, Oracle will apply the undo record to the already changed table. Think about this carefully. The execution of a COMMIT command is always faster than the execution of a ROLLBACK command because the COMMIT command is doing less work, and less work is better performance.

A transaction ends and will execute a COMMIT or a ROLLBACK command when you do any one of these things:

1. Save your changes to the database with the COMMIT command.

2. Undo your changes with the ROLLBACK command.

3.   Execute any DDL command, table (object level), and control level (ALTER DATABASE).

4.   Exit SQL*Plus.

5.   Lose your database connection because of system failure.

6.   Execute any DML command in an SQL*Plus session where the environment has been changed to commit automatically. The SET AUTOCOMMIT ON command causes this behavior. The default is set to OFF.

An interesting feature of transaction control is called *read consistency*. While you are making changes to a table, another user, in a separate session, might query the same table. Your changes do not appear in the query results of the other user. The other user sees the table as it was before you started your transaction. Read consistency is provided by a combination of table data and undo records. Read consistency helps concurrent users share the database. The term *concurrent users* implies concurrency, things happening at the same time.

15.2.1 Locks

Older databases would sometimes lock out any queries on a table while you made changes to it. The lock was then released when your transaction ended. With the advent of read consistency, other users are allowed to query the table you are changing, and they will not even know you are working on that table. If two users try to update the same row or rows of a table, Oracle Database 10*g* makes the second user wait until the first user completes his or her work. This greatly reduces the chances of two users interfering with each other's work. Two users can update the same table, so long as they are not updating the same rows at the same time.

When you update a row in a table, your transaction obtains a *row-level lock*. This lock prevents others from updating the row you have updated until you end the transaction.

Another type of lock, called a *table-level lock*, reserves the entire table for your changes so no other user can make changes to any row in the table. Table-level locks have several degrees of exclusivity, ranging from very strict (exclusive lock) to very unrestricted (row-share lock). Usually, allowing Oracle Database 10*g* to handle locking works the best. However, in special cases, you can use the LOCK TABLE command to impose a specific lock mode on a table. The syntax for the LOCK TABLE command is

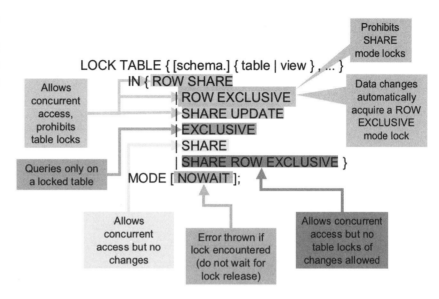

Figure 15.1
LOCK TABLE
Command Syntax
(Rare Situations
Only).

shown in Figure 15.1. Annotations in Figure 15.1 adequately describe the various options available for the LOCK TABLE command. Nothing more needs to be said.

Now let's look at explicit transaction control using the SET TRANSACTION command.

15.2.2 The SET TRANSACTION Command

You can use an optional command called SET TRANSACTION to modify default behavior for a particular transaction. For example, you can cause

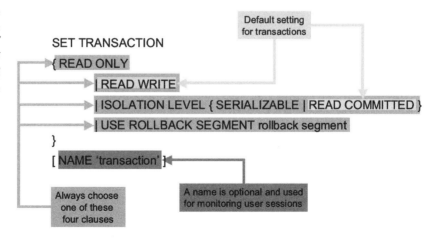

Figure 15.2
Use SET
TRANSACTION
(Special
Circumstances
Only).

Figure 15.3
A Transaction Is Set.

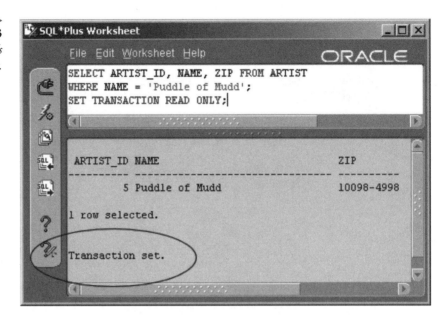

your DML command to fail rather than wait if another user is updating the same row you try to update. Another common use is assigning large transactions to very large rollback segments. Figure 15.2 shows the syntax of the SET TRANSACTION command

Let's query an ARTIST row and start a read-only transaction using the following commands. SQL*Plus Worksheet displays "Transaction set." in the lower pane. The result is shown in Figure 15.3.

```
SELECT ARTIST_ID, NAME, ZIP FROM ARTIST
WHERE NAME = 'Puddle of Mudd';
SET TRANSACTION READ ONLY;
```

Now let's try to change the zip code using the following script.

```
UPDATE ARTIST SET ZIP='10099'
WHERE NAME = 'Puddle of Mudd';
```

Figure 15.4 shows an error message. No changes can be made to the database inside a read-only transaction. In addition, a read-only transaction does not see changes to the database made by other users after the transaction starts. This might be useful when you are generating a set of reports that summarize data and must be consistent from beginning to end. For

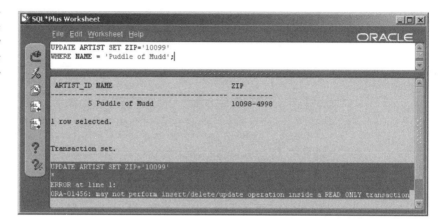

Figure 15.4
*Read-Only
Transactions
Prevent Database
Changes.*

example, you run a summary of sales from the beginning of the year up to today and then (in the same transaction) run a detail report of sales activity. If users are updating the SALES table between your first and second reports, the two reports will not match. Use a read-only transaction to preserve the state of the database when you begin the first report.

Note: Setting read-only transactions can cause serious concurrency issues for other users. Applications will not be able to respond properly when other users preserve data for exclusive use. This type of activity is inadvisable because it could upset end users (your clients).

The default transaction setting is READ WRITE, which allows changes and sees other users' changes immediately after being committed. The current transaction can be completed using the COMMIT or ROLLBACK commands.

Other options are transaction isolation levels, which can be set to SERIALIZABLE or READ COMMITTED. The default mode is ISOLATION LEVEL READ COMMITTED, where SQL will wait until any locks on data it wants to modify are released. Using the SET TRANSACTION ISOLATION LEVEL SERIALIZABLE command, SQL commands handle locking differently. If a problem is encountered, the SERIALIZABLE option will cause a transaction to fail immediately without waiting. This can be useful in a batch job that runs overnight, where it is preferable to stop the entire batch job as opposed to risking the overnight job spilling over into daytime hours.

Note: Once again, be aware of conflict with concurrent applications and potentially upsetting clients.

15.2.3   **The SAVEPOINT Command**

Another transaction-related command you may want to use is the SAVE-POINT command. The syntax is simply as follows, where the label implies a point within a transaction to undo changes back to:

```
SAVEPOINT label;
```

SAVEPOINT is useful when you are making many changes to the database and you want the ability to undo only part of the changes made. For example, you have inserted some testing rows into a table specifically to test an UPDATE command. You want to be able to undo the UPDATE command while keeping the inserted rows. This way, you can repeat the UPDATE command.

Demonstrating using the SAVEPOINT command, we can do the following: Begin by updating a zip code and creating a target label (SAVE-POINT). Then make a different change to the same row already updated and query to see row changes. The result of the following script is shown in Figure 15.5.

```
UPDATE ARTIST SET ZIP='10099'
WHERE NAME = 'Puddle of Mudd';
SAVEPOINT AFTERUPDATE;
UPDATE ARTIST SET NAME='Mud Puddle'
WHERE NAME = 'Puddle of Mudd';
SELECT ARTIST_ID, NAME, ZIP FROM ARTIST
WHERE NAME = 'Mud Puddle';
```

In the next script, we undo (rollback) the name change, done after the SAVEPOINT label, and query again. We see that the name change no longer exists, but the zip code is still changed. In other words, the first update is stored and the second is removed. The result of the following script is shown in Figure 15.6.

Figure 15.5

Two Updates to the Same Row with a SAVEPOINT Label Between the Updates.

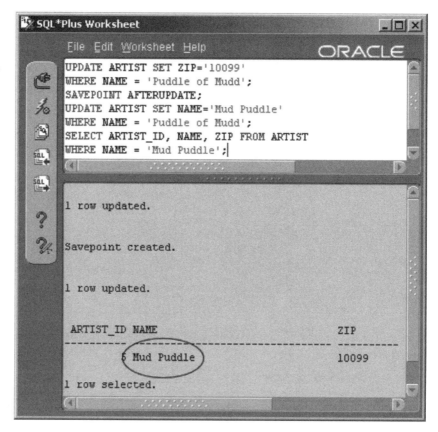

```
UPDATE ARTIST SET ZIP='10099'
WHERE NAME = 'Puddle of Mudd';
SAVEPOINT AFTERUPDATE;
UPDATE ARTIST SET NAME='Mud Puddle'
WHERE NAME = 'Puddle of Mudd';
SELECT ARTIST_ID, NAME, ZIP FROM ARTIST
WHERE NAME = 'Mud Puddle';
```

```
1 row updated.

Savepoint created.

1 row updated.

ARTIST_ID NAME                                    ZIP
--------- -------------------------------------- ----------
        5 Mud Puddle                              10099

1 row selected.
```

```
ROLLBACK TO SAVEPOINT AFTERUPDATE;
SELECT ARTIST_ID, NAME, ZIP FROM ARTIST
WHERE NAME = 'Mud Puddle';
SELECT ARTIST_ID, NAME, ZIP FROM ARTIST
WHERE NAME = 'Puddle of Mudd';
```

Finally, we can undo the remaining change from the first UPDATE command and end the transaction using a ROLLBACK command.

The rest of this chapter deals with making changes to the database using DML commands to add, change, and remove data. We begin with the INSERT command.

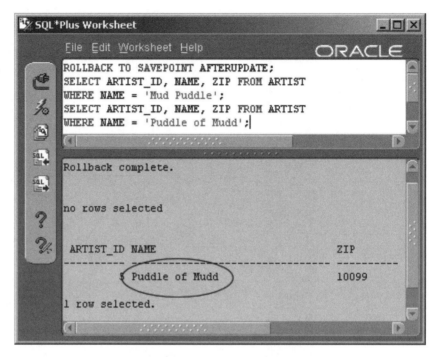

Figure 15.6
*Undo Changes
Back to a
SAVEPOINT
Label.*

15.3 Adding Data (INSERT)

Adding new rows into a table is done with the INSERT command. The INSERT command can be used to add to a single table or multiple tables. The syntax of the single-table INSERT command is shown in Figure 15.7.

You can insert one row into a table using expressions, individual subqueries for each column, or a single subquery for all columns. For a single subquery filling all columns, use a subquery that retrieves multiple rows instead of a list of literal values. We cover the multiple-table INSERT command shortly. The RETURNING portion of the INSERT, UPDATE, and DELETE statements is essentially PL/SQL (see Chapter 24) but is covered here as well for the sake of completeness.

Note: Any literal value such as "hello" or the number 50,000 is an expression. See Chapter 14 for more information on expressions.

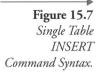

Figure 15.7
Single Table
INSERT
Command Syntax.

INSERT INTO [schema.]table [(column [, column ...])]   Use only when needed
{
    {
        VALUES ({ expression | DEFAULT | (subquery) }
               [, { expression | DEFAULT | (subquery) } ...])
        [RETURNING expression [, expression] INTO variable [, variable]]
        | subquery
    }
    | multiple table insert
}

multiple table insert: later in this section

Returns any list of expressions into pre-declared variables. Using the RETURNING clause allows expressions not to have to be recalculated for following SQL statements.

One or more variables can be returned. More than one row returns an array.

15.3.1 **Inserting One Row**

Let's start with an easy example, adding a single row to the INSTRU-MENT table.

```
INSERT INTO INSTRUMENT
    VALUES (INSTRUMENT_ID_SEQ.NEXTVAL
    ,(SELECT INSTRUMENT_ID FROM INSTRUMENT
      WHERE NAME = 'String')
    , 'Harp');
```

You do not need to list what value goes into which column if you list the values in the same order as columns appear in the table, and all table columns are filled. In this case, there are only three columns to worry about.

The first column uses a sequence that generates a number that is used as the unique identifier for the instrument. See Chapter 22 for details on sequences. The NEXTVAL function always returns the next available value from a sequence. The second column finds the strings section in the INSTRUMENTS table, the same table. The third column adds a new instrument name.

Here is an example in which you list the columns in a different order than they appear in the table, additionally omitting columns.

```
INSERT INTO MUSICCD (MUSICCD_ID, TITLE, PLAYING_TIME)
VALUES (MUSICCD_ID_SEQ.NEXTVAL, 'SPIDER-MAN','60:35');
```

When you omit columns, Oracle Database 10*g* sets missing columns to null values except when a default value is defined for a column. In that case, Oracle fills the column with the default value. If you omit any non-nullable columns, which do not have a default value setting, then an error will result.

15.3.2　Inserting with a Subquery

You can also insert a group of rows all at once using a subquery instead of a list of values. Each row returned by the subquery becomes a row inserted into the table. In this example, we create a table and insert rows using a subquery.

```
CREATE TABLE TESTMUSICCD(
   TITLE               VARCHAR2(32)
,  ARTIST_NAME         VARCHAR2(32) NOT NULL
,  PRESSED_DATE        DATE
,  ARTIST_COUNTRY      VARCHAR2(32));
```

Now we use an INSERT statement to query the ARTIST and MUSICCD tables and load the resulting rows into the new table.

```
INSERT INTO TESTMUSICCD
SELECT DISTINCT M.TITLE, A.NAME, M.PRESSED_DATE
, A.COUNTRY
FROM ARTIST A , SONG S, CDTRACK T, MUSICCD M
WHERE A.ARTIST_ID = S.ARTIST_ID
AND S.SONG_ID = T.SONG_ID
AND T.MUSICCD_ID = M.MUSICCD_ID;
```

This INSERT command creates 13 rows at once. Figure 15.8 shows the new rows using the following simple query:

```
SELECT * FROM TESTMUSICCD;
```

The rows in the table have not yet been saved to the database. We could save them by executing a COMMIT command. And now that you have some data in a new table, you can experiment with updates and deletes. However, first let's examine multiple-table inserts.

Figure 15.8
*The New Rows
Were Derived from
a Subquery Join on
Four Tables.*

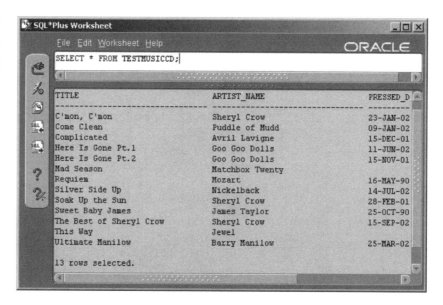

15.3.3 The Multiple-Table INSERT Command

Figure 15.9 describes the syntax for the multiple-table form of the INSERT command.

Now let's look at an example, once again using the data warehouse SALES table as a basis. The following query shows a breakdown for the SALES table by retailer. Next, we use the SALES table to create three separate empty tables. Following that we insert rows into all of the three separate tables at once. The rows will originate from the SALES table, using a single multiple-table INSERT command, inserting into the three tables based on the retailer data in each row. The initial query is shown in Figure 15.10, showing the breakdown of the SALES table based on retailers (RETAILER_ID).

```
SELECT (SELECT NAME FROM RETAILER
WHERE RETAILER_ID = S.RETAILER_ID) "Retailer"
, COUNT(S.RETAILER_ID) "Sales"
FROM SALES S GROUP BY S.RETAILER_ID;
```

Now we can create three empty tables from the SALES table. The WHERE clause using the ROWNUM < 1 condition is a simple method of copying the structure of the SALES table without copying any rows. See Top-N queries in Chapter 5.

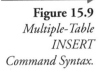

Figure 15.9
*Multiple-Table
INSERT
Command Syntax.*

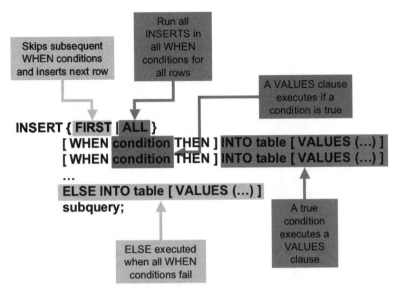

```
CREATE TABLE AMAZON AS SELECT * FROM SALES WHERE ROWNUM < 1;
CREATE TABLE BANDN AS SELECT * FROM SALES WHERE ROWNUM < 1;
CREATE TABLE CDSHOP AS SELECT * FROM SALES WHERE ROWNUM < 1;
```

Figure 15.10
*SALES Table
Entries Are
Distributed Among
Three Different
Retailers.*

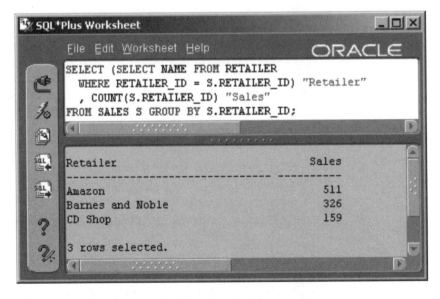

The following script is the multiple-table INSERT command, filling all three tables with the appropriate rows in the three new tables. In this case, an ELSE clause is not required, and the FIRST option can be used.

```
INSERT FIRST
WHEN RETAILER_ID = (SELECT RETAILER_ID FROM RETAILER
WHERE NAME = 'Amazon') THEN INTO AMAZON
WHEN RETAILER_ID = (SELECT RETAILER_ID FROM RETAILER
WHERE NAME = 'Barnes and Noble') THEN INTO BANDN
WHEN RETAILER_ID = (SELECT RETAILER_ID FROM RETAILER
WHERE NAME = 'CD Shop') THEN INTO CDSHOP
SELECT * FROM SALES;
```

Figure 15.11 shows resulting table counts after the execution of the multiple-table INSERT command, distributing sales entries to the three separate retailer tables. The correct row counts can be verified by comparing row counts between those shown in Figures 15.10 and 15.11.

That covers the INSERT command and adding data. Let's look at other DML commands, starting with the UPDATE command used to change existing data.

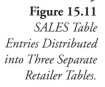

Figure 15.11
SALES Table Entries Distributed into Three Separate Retailer Tables.

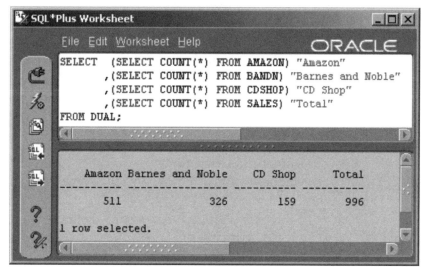

15.4   Changing Data (UPDATE)

The syntax for the UPDATE command is as shown in Figure 15.12.

You can update all rows in the table by omitting the WHERE clause. List any or all column settings in the updated table after the SET keyword. Any subquery must be a single-row subquery. A subquery can be a correlated or regular subquery. Several UPDATE commands will be demonstrated in the next sections.

Figure 15.12
UPDATE
Command Syntax.

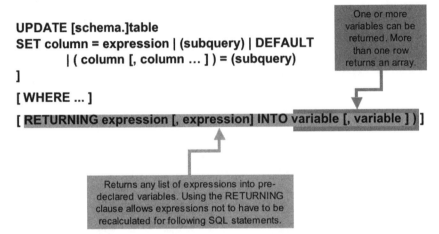

UPDATE [schema.]table
SET column = expression | (subquery) | DEFAULT
** | (column [, column ...]) = (subquery)**
]
[WHERE ...]
[RETURNING expression [, expression] INTO variable [, variable])]

One or more variables can be returned. More than one row returns an array.

Returns any list of expressions into pre-declared variables. Using the RETURNING clause allows expressions not to have to be recalculated for following SQL statements.

Use the NULL keyword to set a column to a null value. Use the DEFAULT keyword to set a column to its default value (as defined in the table).

15.4.1   Updating One Row

You find out that Jewel now lives in Brazil, so you update the row containing Jewel's data. Note that we are using the TESTMUSICCD table created in the previous section on the INSERT command.

```
UPDATE TESTMUSICCD SET ARTIST_COUNTRY='Brazil'
WHERE ARTIST_NAME = 'Jewel';
```

SQL*Plus Worksheet will reply, "1 row updated." The same syntax can be used to update more than one row.

15.4.2 **Updating Many Rows**

There are three rows with the name and country of Sheryl Crow because there are three of her CDs in the table we created. Update all three at once, changing her country to Canada.

```
UPDATE TESTMUSICCD SET ARTIST_COUNTRY='Canada'
WHERE ARTIST_NAME = 'Sheryl Crow';
```

SQL*Plus Worksheet will reply, "3 rows updated."

Another method of updating data is to use subqueries. For example, let's say you want to update ARTIST_COUNTRY column values in TESTMUSICCD with data from the ARTIST table. You can use a correlated subquery to match the artist's name between the ARTIST and TESTMUSICCD tables to find the country. The following query removes the changes to countries of residence for both Jewel and Sheryl Crow.

```
UPDATE TESTMUSICCD T SET ARTIST_COUNTRY=
(SELECT COUNTRY FROM ARTIST A
  WHERE A.NAME = T.ARTIST_NAME);
```

SQL*Plus Worksheet will reply, "13 rows updated."

Note: Updated rows must comply with any constraints defined for a table. If one row does not comply, all rows updated by the statement are automatically rolled back.

You can also update more than one column, whether you are updating one row or many rows. For example, change the title and the country with one update command. In the next example, we change the ARTIST_NAME column of each TESTMUSICCD table row to uppercase using a function, and change the PRESSED_DATE using a correlated subquery that finds the most recent RECORDING_DATE from the songs on the CD (TESTMUSICCD table). You also use a WHERE clause in the UPDATE command so that you only update Sheryl Crow's three rows.

```
UPDATE TESTMUSICCD T
SET ARTIST_NAME=UPPER(ARTIST_NAME),
    PRESSED_DATE = (SELECT MAX(RECORDING_DATE)
```

```
        FROM SONG S, CDTRACK C, MUSICCD M
WHERE M.TITLE = T.TITLE
AND M.MUSICCD_ID = C.MUSICCD_ID
AND C.SONG_ID = S.SONG_ID)
WHERE ARTIST_NAME = 'Sheryl Crow';
```

SQL*Plus Worksheet will reply, "3 rows updated."

Let's illustrates several points about the UPDATE command:

- The data in the current row is available for use, so you can update a value using itself or other values in the current row. This refers to the correlating column alias called T.TITLE shown in the previous query, passed from the calling query to the subquery.

- The WHERE clause (in the UPDATE command) can reference columns that are updated, using the value before the update.

- You can use a mixture of literals, subqueries, and functions in the same UPDATE command.

Figure 15.13
Sheryl Crow Is Now Uppercase as a Result of an UPDATE Command.

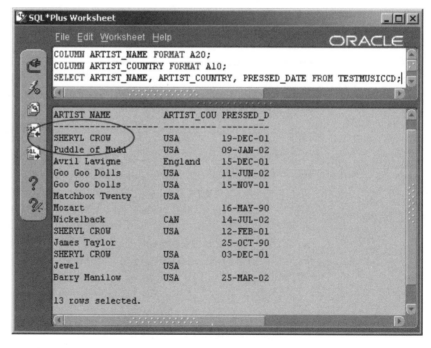

Figure 15.13 shows the result of all changes made using the UPDATE command, using the following query against the TESTMUSICCD table.

```
COLUMN ARTIST_NAME FORMAT A20;
COLUMN ARTIST_COUNTRY FORMAT A10;
SELECT ARTIST_NAME, ARTIST_COUNTRY, PRESSED_DATE FROM
TESTMUSICCD;
```

The rows updated in the table have not yet been saved to the database. They could be saved using the COMMIT command.

Removing rows using the DELETE command is easier than inserting and updating rows.

15.5   Deleting Data (DELETE)

The syntax for the DELETE command is as shown in Figure 15.14.

As with the UPDATE command, use the WHERE clause to delete selected rows from a table, and omit the WHERE clause to delete all the rows in a table.

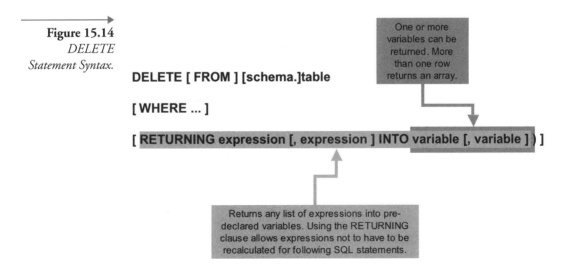

Figure 15.14
DELETE
Statement Syntax.

15.5.1 Deleting One Row

Using the WHERE clause, you can specify one row when deleting. In the TESTMUSICCD table, delete the row for the "C'mon, C'mon" CD by typing this DELETE command:

```
DELETE FROM TESTMUSICCD
WHERE TITLE = 'C''mon, C''mon';
```

SQL*Plus Worksheet will reply: "1 row deleted."

Notice the use of quotation marks in the title. The title has two single quotes in it where the data actually has a single quote. This is called a string escape sequence. Because Oracle Database 10*g* uses single quote marks to delimit literal values, you must indicate that the single quote in the middle is not a delimiter by typing two single quote marks together. Remember that two single quotes are not the same as one double quotation mark.

15.5.2 Deleting Many Rows

Just like the UPDATE command, simply revising the WHERE clause to select more rows enables you to delete multiple rows in one command. For example, deleting all CDs by the Goo Goo Dolls can be accomplished using the following command:

```
DELETE FROM TESTMUSICCD
WHERE ARTIST_NAME = 'Goo Goo Dolls';
```

SQL*Plus Worksheet will reply: "2 rows deleted."

The following query will show that rows for the Goo Goo Dolls and for the CD named "C'mon, C'mon" are no longer in the table. Figure 15.15 shows the result.

```
SELECT * FROM TESTMUSICCD;
```

If a table is the parent of another table, such as the MUSICCD table, which is the parent to the CDTRACK table, you cannot delete a row in the MUSICCD table that has related child rows (CD tracks) in the CDTRACK table. You should remove the child rows first and the parent row last.

Figure 15.15
*Three Rows Were
Deleted by Two
DELETE
Commands.*

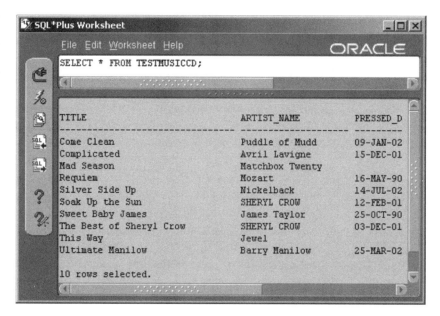

```
SELECT * FROM TESTMUSICCD;

TITLE                          ARTIST_NAME           PRESSED_D
------------------------------ --------------------- ---------
Come Clean                     Puddle of Mudd        09-JAN-02
Complicated                    Avril Lavigne         15-DEC-01
Mad Season                     Matchbox Twenty
Requiem                        Mozart                16-MAY-90
Silver Side Up                 Nickelback            14-JUL-02
Soak Up the Sun                SHERYL CROW           12-FEB-01
Sweet Baby James               James Taylor          25-OCT-90
The Best of Sheryl Crow        SHERYL CROW           03-DEC-01
This Way                       Jewel
Ultimate Manilow               Barry Manilow         25-MAR-02

10 rows selected.
```

Note: This is not always strictly true if CASCADE DELETE is used with constraints. See Chapter 1 for details on Referential Integrity and Chapter 20 for information on constraints.

15.5.3 Deleting All Rows

You can delete all the rows in a table by leaving out the WHERE clause. The following command will delete all rows in the TESTMUSICCD table:

```
DELETE FROM TESTMUSICCD;
```

SQL*Plus Worksheet will reply, "8 rows deleted."

You could also finally remove the temporarily created table TESTMUS-ICCD by dropping it.

```
DROP TABLE TESTMUSICCD;
```

The final section in this chapter discusses the MERGE command, a new feature of Oracle Database 9*i* and much improved in Oracle Database 10g.

The MERGE command enables a combination insert and update to a table using a single DML command.

15.6 (10g) Merging New and Old Data (MERGE)

There are some enhancements to the MERGE command between Oracle Database 9*i* and Oracle Database 10*g*. The purpose of the MERGE command is to allow you to build on an already existing table's rows. For example, you have a central database that tracks contact information for clients. Your salespeople have handheld palmtop units that they use to record contact information for new and existing clients. The palmtop's client table has only half the data for existing customers, because that is all the salespeople need in the field. When salespeople return to the central office, they plug in their palmtops and dump the data about all their clients. The central computer must determine whether the client is new or already existing in the central database client table. Then, if it is new, a row is inserted. If it already exists, the existing row is updated, preserving the data in columns that are not provided in the palmtop record.

In the past, a merging or migration process would have required an application program, perhaps even custom coding and scripting. Now, you can use the MERGE command to handle these issues. Figure 15.16 shows

Figure 15.16
Merge Looks Complex but Has Familiar Components.

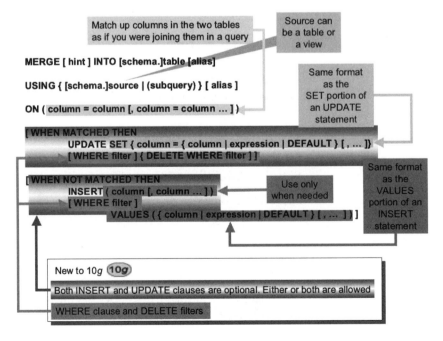

the syntax of the MERGE command, including updates for Oracle Database 10*g*.

As you can see, there are two tables used in a MERGE command: (1) the target table, which receives the inserts and updates, and (2) the source table, which is used to determine whether to insert or update the target table. Usually, the source table provides the data to be inserted or updated in the target table, but you can also provide literal values, expressions, and so on.

15.6.1   How To Use MERGE

Use the MERGE command when you need to handle ongoing inserts and updates into a table. For an easy example of the MERGE command, first create a new table that is an exact copy of the STUDIOTIME table, but contains only nine of the rows. This simulates a situation where a copy of the STUDIOTIME table was created at the end of the year 2000.

```
CREATE TABLE HISTORY_STUDIOTIME AS
SELECT * FROM STUDIOTIME
WHERE SESSION_DATE <= '31-DEC-00';
```

Now, let's imagine that it is the end of the year 2002 and you want to add all the remaining rows into the HISTORY_STUDIOTIME table. In addition, because payments were made on sessions from the year 2000, imagine that some of the rows that already exist in the history table need to be updated with some of the data from the current table. The MERGE command would look as in the following script:

```
MERGE INTO HISTORY_STUDIOTIME HS
USING STUDIOTIME S ON (S.STUDIOTIME_ID = HS.STUDIOTIME_ID)
WHEN MATCHED THEN UPDATE
SET DUE_DATE = S.DUE_DATE,
    AMOUNT_PAID = S.AMOUNT_PAID,
    AMOUNT_CHARGED = S.AMOUNT_CHARGED
WHEN NOT MATCHED THEN INSERT VALUES
(S.STUDIOTIME_ID, S.ARTIST_ID, S.SESSION_DATE,
    S.MINUTES_USED, S.DUE_DATE,
    S.AMOUNT_CHARGED, S.AMOUNT_PAID);
```

SQL*Plus Worksheet will reply, "86 rows merged."

Looking closely at the previous statement, observe these points:

- The target table (the one receiving rows) is the HISTORY_STUDIOTIME table.

- The source table (the one sending rows) is the STUDIOTIME table.

- The two tables are matched on the value of the STUDIOTIME_ID.

- When both tables contain a row with matching STUDIOTIME_ID, three columns in the HISTORY_STUDIOTIME table are updated with values from columns in the STUDIOTIME table.

- When only the STUDIOTIME table has a row, and there is no matching row in the HISTORY_STUDIOTIME table, a row is inserted into the HISTORY_STUDIOTIME table using values in the STUDIOTIME table's row.

The MERGE command can be very useful in situations that otherwise would require separate INSERT and UPDATE commands.

Note: Rows in the target table that do not match those in the source table are not affected by a MERGE command.

This chapter has covered the Data Manipulation Language (DML), comprising commands to change data in tables in an Oracle database. We have covered the INSERT, UPDATE, DELETE, and MERGE commands.

The next chapter examines datatypes in detail.

16

Datatypes and Collections

In this chapter:

- What are datatypes?

- What are simple datatypes?

- What are complex datatypes?

- What is a user-defined datatype?

- What are object datatypes?

- What types of object collection functionality exist?

- What are special Oracle datatypes?

This chapter examines simple, complex, and object datatypes. Additionally, this chapter includes user-defined datatypes plus details of special object datatype functions. Object functions are included in this chapter because they are specific to object datatypes. Object functions do not belong with single-row functions in Chapter 9 or with grouping functions in Chapter 11.

Like Chapter 7, this chapter contains some information found in other chapters, but it also contains new information. It is necessary to place this information in a single chapter in order to put everything in one place.

Let's begin with what could be termed simple datatypes.

16.1 Simple Datatypes

I like to classify simple datatypes as those containing single scalar values, such as strings, numbers, and dates. Table 16.1 shows a summary of Oracle simple datatypes.

Table 16.1 *Oracle Simple Datatypes.*

Datatype	Parameters	Example
`VARCHAR2(n)`	n = 1 to 4,000	VARCHAR2(25)
	Text string with variable length up to 4,000 bytes. If the column data's length is shorter than *n*, Oracle adjusts the length of the column to the size of the data. Trailing blanks are truncated. Use VARCHAR2 in favor of CHAR to avoid wasting space. VARCHAR is still a valid datatype but is replaced in favor of VARCHAR2.	
`CHAR(n)`	n = 1 to 2000	CHAR(14)
	Same as VARCHAR2 except it holds up to 2,000 bytes and is a static (fixed-length) text string, regardless of the length of the data. Trailing blanks are preserved. Shorter data is padded to right with blanks. CHAR is the same as CHAR(1). Use CHAR rather than VARCHAR2 for short strings of a semi-fixed length or precisely known number of characters.	
`NVARCHAR2(n)`	n = 1 to 4,000	NVARCHAR2(65)
	Same as VARCHAR2, except that it stores characters for any language (national character set) supported by Oracle.	
`NCHAR(n)`	n = 1 to 2,000	NCHAR(30)
	Same as CHAR, except that the characters stored depend on a national character set (e.g., Chinese characters).	
`NUMBER(p,s)`	p = 1 to 38, s = -84 to 127	NUMBER(10,2)
	Precision (*p*) is the total number of digits, and the scale (*s*) is the number of digits to the right of the decimal. Oracle rounds data you insert if it has too many decimal places.	
`INTEGER`	38-byte number	Creates the same datatype as NUMBER(38).
`SMALLINT`	38-byte number	Creates the same datatype as NUMBER(38).
`FLOAT(p)`	p = 1 to 126	FLOAT(20)
	A floating-point or real number.	
`DATE`	None	DATE

Table 16.1 *Oracle Simple Datatypes. (continued)*

	Valid dates range from January 1, 4712 B.C. to December 31, 9999 A.D. Oracle stores DATE datatype values internally as 7-byte numbers including the time in hours, minutes, and seconds. If no time is specified when inserting a date, the time is set to midnight.	
`TIMESTAMP(p)`	p = fractions of a second	TIMESTAMP(3)
	Same range as a DATE datatype, except this contains fractions of a second. For example, TIMESTAMP(4) has precision to 1/1000th of a second.	
`TIMESTAMP(p)` `WITH TIME ZONE`	p = fractions of a second	TIMESTAMP(4) WITH TIME ZONE
	Same as TIMESTAMP except the value includes the time zone of the user that inserts or updates the value.	

`TIMESTAMP(p)`
`WITH LOCAL TIME`
`ZONE`
	p = fractions of a second	TIMESTAMP(4) WITH LOCAL TIME ZONE

	Same as TIMESTAMP except the value converts the date to the time zone of the database, and displays the time in the local time zone for the viewer.	
`ROWID`	None	ROWID
	Internal Oracle datatype that stores the physical locator string or logical pointer for a row of data.	
`UROWID`	None	
	Universal ROWID. Hexadecimal string containing ROWID values for an index-organized table, object table, or non-Oracle entity. Can be up to 4,000 bytes.	
(10*g*) `BINARY_FLOAT`	None	BINARY_FLOAT
	32-bit binary precision floating-point number including values for infinity and NaN. NaN means "not a number."	
(10*g*) `BINARY_DOUBLE`	None	BINARY_DOUBLE
	64-bit binary precision floating-point number including values for infinity and NaN. NaN means "not a number."	

16.2   Complex and Object Datatypes

From my perspective, a complex datatype is any datatype not containing a single scalar value. Thus a complex datatype can be a binary object, a reference (a pointer, not a ROWID), or a structural definition. At this stage, complex and object datatypes are broken into multiple separate sections, starting with straightforward binary object storage datatypes.

16.2.1   Binary Object Datatypes

Binary object datatypes are shown in Table 16.2. This table includes some now-desupported binary object datatypes for the sake of consistency. BLOB datatypes can be used to store multimedia objects such as images, video, and sound files (see BFILE pointers in the next section on reference datatypes). CLOB objects can be used to store string data values that are too large for VARCHAR2 datatypes.

Table 16.2   *Oracle Complex Binary Object Datatypes.*

Datatype	Parameters	Example
BLOB	None	BLOB
	Stores unstructured data in binary format, up to 4 GB.	
CLOB	None	CLOB
	Character data up to 4 GB. Used for high-volume text data.	
NCLOB	None	NCLOB
	Stores large (up to 4 GB) data in unicode or a national character set.	
LONG	None	LONG *(Desupported)*
	Maximum size is 2 GB. Used for text data. You should use BLOB instead of LONG when creating new tables.	
RAW(n)	n = 1 to 2,000	RAW(500) *(Desupported)*
	Raw binary data of variable length, up to 2,000 characters. Use CLOB instead.	
LONG RAW	None	LONG RAW *(Desupported)*
	Raw binary data of variable length. The maximum length is 2 GB. Use BLOB instead.	

Note: The BLOB, CLOB, and NCLOB datatypes are only available in Oracle 8 and up. The LONG, RAW, and LONG RAW datatypes will eventually be removed in a future release in favor of the LOB datatypes. LOB stands for "large object" or "binary large object."

16.2.2 Reference Pointer Datatypes

A reference pointer datatype is used to point to a point in space. Nothing Einsteinian is implied; the space exists only somewhere in an Oracle database. The reference pointer datatype can be used to gain access to the value referenced by the reference pointer. Reference pointer datatypes are shown in Table 16.3.

Table 16.3 *Oracle Reference Pointer Datatypes.*

Datatype	Parameters	Example
BFILE	None	BFILE
	Stores pointers to an external file, such as an audio track. Oracle provides predefined functions for reading, storing, and writing a BFILE column. Requires a directory object in order to function.	
REF	REF schema.objname	REF MUSIC.INSTRUMENT_OBJ
	Reference object identifier. Used for object tables to define a referential or object-parent to another object table, similar to a foreign key.	

Note: BFILE or BFILENAME pointers became available in Oracle 8 and should be used in favor of any LONG or RAW datatypes.

A BFILE pointer is commonly used to store static multimedia objects. Generally, unless multimedia objects are annotated or continually altered, they can be considered static. A BFILE pointer only stores a reference to an object such as an image. The image is stored external to the database on disk. From a database perspective, storing multimedia outside the database is the most efficient method available for both storage and subsequent access.

16.2.2.1   **Using the REF Datatype**

The MUSIC schema ARTIST table contains an address, split into separate columns. Let's begin by creating a TYPE structure to contain an address. To illustrate the REF datatype, we create two object tables: ADDRESSES containing artist addresses and ARTIST2 containing the artist names and a reference to the ADDRESSES table.

```
CREATE OR REPLACE TYPE TADDRESS AS OBJECT(
   STREET VARCHAR2(32), POBOX CHAR(20), CITY VARCHAR2(32)
, STATE_PROVINCE VARCHAR2(32), COUNTRY VARCHAR2(32)
, ZIP CHAR(10), EMAIL VARCHAR2(32));
/
```

Now we create a table based on the TADDRESS type structure we just created:

```
CREATE TABLE ADDRESSES OF TADDRESS;
```

Now we create a new table for artists from the original ARTIST table using the type we just created:

```
CREATE TABLE ARTIST2 AS
SELECT ARTIST_ID, NAME, INSTRUMENTS FROM ARTIST;
```

Now add the new addresses substructure to the new artists table:

```
ALTER TABLE ARTIST2 ADD (ADDRESS REF TADDRESS SCOPE IS
ADDRESSES);
```

Fill up the ADDRESSES table:

```
INSERT INTO ADDRESSES
SELECT STREET, POBOX, CITY, STATE_PROVINCE
, COUNTRY, ZIP, EMAIL FROM ARTIST;
```

Now update the REF column in the new artists table with the reference pointer to each relative address in the ADDRESSES table, establishing the REF pointer link between the ARTIST2 table and the ADDRESSES table:

Figure 16.1
REF Stored the
Pointer Value
between Tables.

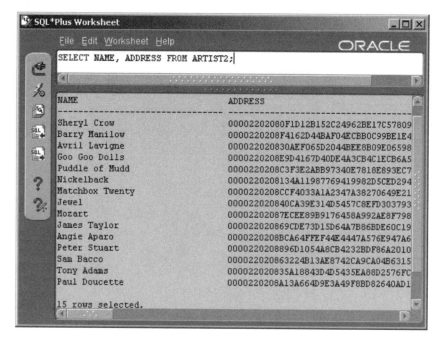

```
UPDATE ARTIST2 A2 SET A2.ADDRESS = (
    SELECT REF(AD) FROM ADDRESSES AD JOIN ARTIST A
    ON(AD.STREET = A.STREET)
WHERE A.ARTIST_ID = A2.ARTIST_ID);
```

The following script finds the REF pointer for each address in the new artists table, between the ARTIST2 and ADDRESSES tables. The result is shown in Figure 16.1.

```
SELECT NAME, ADDRESS FROM ARTIST2;
```

Now we could use the DEREF function to dereference or access the value in the ADDRESSES table for each row in the ARTISTS2 table. The result is shown in Figure 16.2.

Other less-used REF pointer functions are MAKE_REF, VALUE, and REFTOHEX.

16.2.2.2 Using the BFILE Datatype

As already stated, a BFILE datatype is used as a pointer to a binary object, such as multimedia, stored externally to a database. The MUSIC schema

Figure 16.2
*The DEREF
Function Finds a
Pointer Value.*

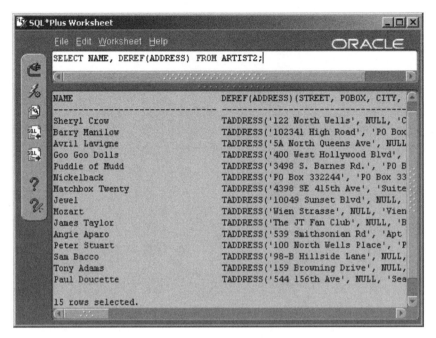

Figure 16.2
*The DEREF
Function Finds a
Pointer Value.*

has a RECORDING column in the SONG table. Obviously, this table contains no data because that would infringe on copyright regulations. In the MUSIC schema, the SONG.RECORDING column is a BLOB datatype. Like in the previous section, for the sake of example we will cre-

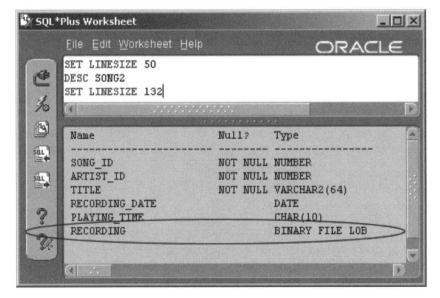

Figure 16.3
*A BFILE Datatype
in the SONG2
Table.*

ate a copy of the SONG table called SONG2. This way we can re-create the RECORDING column as a BFILE pointer. Figure 16.3 shows the structure of the new SONG2 table, where the BFILE datatype is shown as a BINARY FILE LOB.

```
CREATE TABLE SONG2 AS SELECT SONG_ID, ARTIST_ID, TITLE
, RECORDING_DATE, PLAYING_TIME
FROM SONG;
ALTER TABLE SONG2 ADD (RECORDING BFILE);
```

A BFILE datatype uses the BFILENAME function for instantiation. The syntax is as follows:

BFILENAME ('directory', 'filename'). The directory is an Oracle DIRECTORY object, essentially being an alias type full path name pointer to a directory on a server.

```
CREATE DIRECTORY MULTIMEDIA
AS 'c:\oracle\ora10\oltp\multimedia';
```

Note: The CREATE ANY DIRECTORY system privilege may be required.

```
UPDATE SONG2 SET RECORDING =
BFILENAME('MULTIMEDIA', 'recording.wav')
WHERE SONG_ID = 1;
```

The next section examines user-defined datatypes.

16.2.3 User-Defined Datatypes

Creating an object type with the CREATE TYPE command, such as a VARRAY or nested table type, creates a user-defined datatype. Oracle sometimes refers to user-defined datatypes as user types. All these user-defined datatypes are available for use in column definitions, just like the standard Oracle Database 10*g* datatypes. You will see how this works when you reach Chapter 18 and begin creating your own tables. There will be much more on VARRAY and nested table collection datatypes later in this chapter.

The following commands describe the ARTIST table's definition and a collection object contained therein. The first DESC command shows the ARTIST table, and the second DESC command displays the structure of the INSTRUMENTSCOLLECTION type. The INSTRUMENTSCOL-

Figure 16.4
Users Can Create Their Own Datatypes, also Called Object, Array, or Table Types.

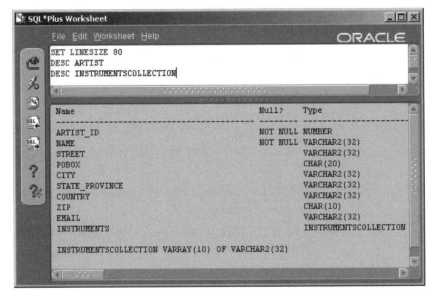

```
SET LINESIZE 80
DESC ARTIST
DESC INSTRUMENTSCOLLECTION

Name                               Null?    Type
-------------------------------    -------- --------------------
ARTIST_ID                          NOT NULL NUMBER
NAME                               NOT NULL VARCHAR2(32)
STREET                                      VARCHAR2(32)
POBOX                                       CHAR(20)
CITY                                        VARCHAR2(32)
STATE_PROVINCE                              VARCHAR2(32)
COUNTRY                                     VARCHAR2(32)
ZIP                                         CHAR(10)
EMAIL                                       VARCHAR2(32)
INSTRUMENTS                                 INSTRUMENTSCOLLECTION

INSTRUMENTSCOLLECTION VARRAY(10) OF VARCHAR2(32)
```

LECTION type was created as a user-defined datatype using the CREATE TYPE command. The results are shown in Figure 16.4.

```
SET LINESIZE 100
DESC ARTIST
DESC INSTRUMENTSCOLLECTION
```

The INSTRUMENTSCOLLECTION datatype is a VARRAY or fixed-length array that can hold up to 10 values with the datatype of VARCHAR2(32).

Now that we have looked at simple user-definable datatypes, let's look in more detail at object collection datatypes.

16.2.4   Object Collection Datatypes

An object collection is a referenced set of elements contained within an array. These arrays can be fixed length, dynamic, or indexed dynamic. A dynamic array is an array where the number of array iterations is undetermined. Therefore, a dynamic array is essentially a pointer. Object collection datatypes are shown in Table 16.4.

Let's look at some examples, beginning with the simplest to use, VARRAY collections.

Table 16.4 *Oracle Object Collection Datatypes.*

Datatype	Parameters	Example
VARRAY	(subscript)	Object(subscript)
	Fixed-length array or reserved chunk of memory for a fixed number of array elements. (10*g*) VARRAY collections can be resized and used in temporary tables.	
Nested Table	TABLE(…)	TABLE (SELECT …)
	Dynamic array or pointer to a variable number of array elements. (10*g*) Nested table columns can be divided into separate tablespaces.	
Associative Array	Only available in PL/SQL. PL/SQL is covered in Chapter 24.	
	Indexed dynamic array. Faster access than a nested table using an index.	

16.2.4.1 Using VARRAY Collections

The ARTIST table contains a VARRAY collection object called INSTRU-MENTSCOLLECTION. We have already been introduced to the INSTRUMENTSCOLLECTION datatype in this chapter. The following script snippets are a small section of the MUSIC schema creation script (see Appendix A). The first thing we do is create a type for the collection of instruments. The INSTRUMENTSCOLLECTION type has a fixed number of 10 elements for each ARTIST table entry.

```
CREATE OR REPLACE TYPE INSTRUMENTSCOLLECTION
AS VARRAY(10) OF VARCHAR2(32);
/
```

Next we create the ARTIST table including the INSTRUMENTSCOL-LECTION type. Because the INSTRUMENTSCOLLECTION is effectively a new datatype (user-defined type), it simply becomes the datatype definition for the INSTRUMENTS column.

```
CREATE TABLE ARTIST(
     ARTIST_ID NUMBER NOT NULL
, NAME VARCHAR2(32) NOT NULL, STREET VARCHAR2(32)
, POBOX CHAR(20), CITY VARCHAR2(32)
  , STATE_PROVINCE VARCHAR2(32), COUNTRY VARCHAR2(32)
```

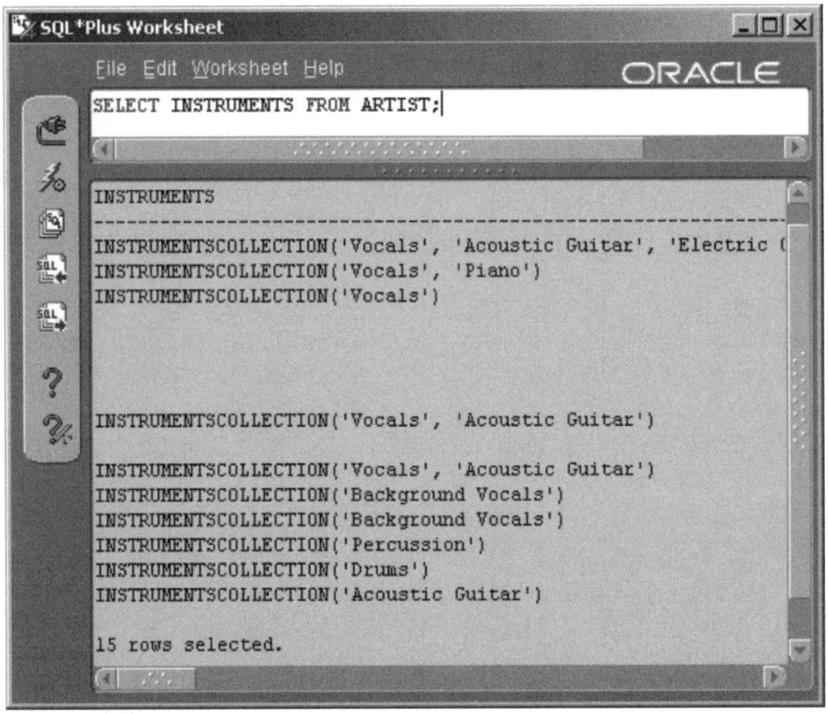

Figure 16.5
*The MUSIC
Schema ARTIST
Table
INSTRUMENTS
COLLECTION
Datatype.*

```
, ZIP CHAR(10), EMAIL VARCHAR2(32)
, INSTRUMENTS INSTRUMENTSCOLLECTION
, CONSTRAINT XPKARTIST PRIMARY KEY (ARTIST_ID));
CREATE UNIQUE INDEX XUK_ARTIST_NAME ON ARTIST (NAME);
```

Accessing the collection from the ARTIST table is shown following. The result is shown in Figure 16.5. PL/SQL can be used to access individual VARRAY elements. See Chapter 24 for details on PL/SQL.

```
SELECT INSTRUMENTS FROM ARTIST;
```

16.2.4.2   Using Nested Table Collections

A nested table is effectively created as a table within another table. You will notice in this section frequent use of the keyword TABLE. The TABLE keyword is used to access the table within the table, the former being the nested table object collection or dynamic array.

For the purposes of example, we create yet another copy of the ARTIST table, except this time we use a nested table collection as opposed to a

VARRAY collection for the INSTRUMENTSCOLLECTION datatype column. First, we make a copy of the ARTIST table, excluding the INSTRUMENTS column:

```
CREATE TABLE ARTIST3 AS SELECT ARTIST_ID, NAME, STREET
, POBOX, CITY, STATE_PROVINCE, COUNTRY, ZIP
, EMAIL FROM ARTIST;
```

Now we create a new type to contain the instruments collection:

```
CREATE OR REPLACE TYPE NEWCOLLECTION AS TABLE OF
VARCHAR2(32);
/
```

Now we add the nested table collection, NEWCOLLECTION, to the ARTIST3 copy table:

```
ALTER TABLE ARTIST3 ADD(INSTRUMENTS NEWCOLLECTION)
NESTED TABLE INSTRUMENTS STORE AS INSTRUMENTSTABLE;
```

Now we can add the instruments collection from the original ARTIST table into the new ARTIST3 table:

```
UPDATE ARTIST3 SET INSTRUMENTS =
NEWCOLLECTION('Vocals','Acoustic Guitar','Electric Guitar')
WHERE ARTIST_ID = 1;
UPDATE ARTIST3 SET INSTRUMENTS =
NEWCOLLECTION('Piano','Vocals') WHERE ARTIST_ID = 2;
UPDATE ARTIST3 SET INSTRUMENTS = NEWCOLLECTION('Vocals')
WHERE ARTIST_ID = 3;
UPDATE ARTIST3 SET INSTRUMENTS =
NEWCOLLECTION('Vocals','Acoustic Guitar') WHERE ARTIST_ID =
8;
UPDATE ARTIST3 SET INSTRUMENTS =
NEWCOLLECTION('Vocals','Acoustic Guitar') WHERE ARTIST_ID =
10;
UPDATE ARTIST3 SET INSTRUMENTS = NEWCOLLECTION('Background
Vocals') WHERE ARTIST_ID = 11;
UPDATE ARTIST3 SET INSTRUMENTS = NEWCOLLECTION('Background
Vocals') WHERE ARTIST_ID = 12;
```

Figure 16.6
Retrieving the Contents of a Nested Table Collection Object.

```
SELECT INSTRUMENTS FROM ARTIST3 WHERE ARTIST_ID = 1;
SELECT * FROM TABLE(
   SELECT INSTRUMENTS FROM ARTIST3 WHERE ARTIST_ID = 1);

INSTRUMENTS

NEWCOLLECTION('Vocals', 'Acoustic Guitar', 'Electric Guitar')

1 row selected.


COLUMN_VALUE
--------------------------------
Vocals
Acoustic Guitar
Electric Guitar

3 rows selected.
```

```
UPDATE ARTIST3 SET INSTRUMENTS = NEWCOLLECTION('Percussion')
WHERE ARTIST_ID = 13;
UPDATE ARTIST3 SET INSTRUMENTS = NEWCOLLECTION('Drums') WHERE
ARTIST_ID = 14;
UPDATE ARTIST3 SET INSTRUMENTS = NEWCOLLECTION('Acoustic
Guitar') WHERE ARTIST_ID = 15;
```

This is how items are retrieved from a nested table collection. Figure 16.6 shows the result.

```
SELECT INSTRUMENTS FROM ARTIST3 WHERE ARTIST_ID = 1;
SELECT * FROM TABLE(SELECT INSTRUMENTS FROM ARTIST3 WHERE
ARTIST_ID = 1);
```

16.2.5   **Object Collection Functions**

In the previous two sections entitled "Using VARRAY Collections" and "Using Nested Table Collections," you may have noticed some rather odd scripting, or at least convoluted and overly complicated scripting. There are object collection functions that can make things easier, particularly when dealing with VARRAY and nested table objects at the same time. These object collection functions are the following:

- **CAST ({ collection | MULTISET (subquery) } AS type)**. Changes one datatype into another datatype or changes one type into another type. The CAST function, in object-oriented design parlance, is a typecasting function. A typecasting function casts one datatype into another or changes one type to another. The following example simply typecasts or converts from a numeric to a string value. Obviously, converting from a string to a number would require numerals. Therefore, the first query will work and the second will not.

```
SELECT CAST(ARTIST_ID AS VARCHAR2(38)) FROM ARTIST); --valid
SELECT CAST('abc' AS NUMBER) FORM DUAL; --invalid
```

The CAST function, the MULTISET operator, and a subquery can be used to create a nested table from a relational table. MULTISET operators are explained in Chapter 7.

```
CREATE OR REPLACE TYPE tINSTRUMENT AS OBJECT(
   INSTRUMENT_ID NUMBER
, SECTION_ID NUMBER, NAME VARCHAR2(32));
/
CREATE OR REPLACE TYPE tINSTRUMENTS AS TABLE OF tINSTRUMENT;
/
SELECT CAST(MULTISET(SELECT * FROM INSTRUMENT) AS
tINSTRUMENTS) FROM DUAL;
```

- **(10g) COLLECT (columnar expression)**. Returns a nested table from the row set result of a column expression in a table. The following queries are valid:

```
SELECT COLLECT(NAME) FROM INSTRUMENT;
SELECT COLLECT(TO_CHAR(SECTION_ID)||','||NAME)
FROM INSTRUMENT;
```

The following query is not valid because a columnar expression is required:

```
SELECT COLLECT(*) FROM INSTRUMENT;
```

- (10*g*) **SET (nested table).** Returns a set of the unique values in a nested table.

```
SELECT SET(INSTRUMENTS) FROM ARTIST3;
```

- (10*g*) **CARDINALITY (nested table).** Returns the number of elements in a nested table.

```
SELECT CARDINALITY(INSTRUMENTS) FROM ARTIST3;
```

- (10*g*) **POWERMULTISET (nested table).** Returns all set elements in a collection.

- (10*g*) **POWERMULTISET_BY_CARDINALITY (nested table, cardinality).** This function combines the POWERMULTISET and CARDINALITY functions by returning all set elements with a specified number of entries for each collection in each row. One could find every row in a table where that collection has a specified number of entries.

16.2.6 Metadata Views

This section simply describes metadata views applicable to complex and object datatypes. Chapter 19 describes the basis and detail of Oracle Database metadata views.

- **USER_TYPES.** Structure of user-defined types.

- **USER_TYPE_ATTRS.** A subset of USER_TYPES except showing type attributes.

- **USER_TYPE_METHODS.** Once again, a subset of USER_TYPES except showing methods. A method is a chunk of executable code attached to and executable by an instance of a type, much like a class method in an object structure.

- **USER_NESTED_TABLES** and **USER_NESTED_TABLE_COLS.** These views describe the structure of nested tables.

- **USER_VARRAYS.** This view describes the structure of VARRAYs.

We have already seen plenty of collection examples in this chapter, so no additional examples are shown here. Now let's look briefly at some other, perhaps extremely complex or unusual, datatypes.

16.3 Special Datatypes

Special datatypes used in Oracle are shown in Table 16.5. These special datatypes are often specific to a particular environment or application type.

Table 16.5 *Special Oracle Datatypes.*

Datatype	Description
XML	XML documents can be stored, retrieved, and manipulated as XML documents (see Chapter 17).
Spatial	Special spatially oriented datatypes allowing for multiple dimensions such as for graphic (geographic) information systems (maps), architectural and construction design, and various other types of geometric modeling data.
Media	Special multimedia datatypes of which there are numerous different datatypes.
Any	Unknown or generic datatypes.

This chapter has covered various different datatypes plus some object collection datatype functionality not appropriate to be covered elsewhere in this book. The next chapter delves into the details of using XML with Oracle.

XML in Oracle

In this chapter:

- What is XML?

- What is XSL?

- What are the different XML generation methods for Oracle SQL?

- How do we create XML objects from database tables?

- How can XML document objects stored in the database be viewed and altered?

As in many modern databases, there is immense capability in Oracle SQL for utilizing the power of XML. This chapter only covers XML as directly related to Oracle SQL. In other words, we examine how XML documents can be created, accessed, and manipulated directly from within Oracle SQL. To begin with, let's briefly summarize exactly what XML is. To accomplish this, we have to start at the root of browser scripting languages, HTML. So what is XML?

17.1 What Is XML?

Hypertext Markup Language (HTML) is limited to a predefined set of tags. Those tags allow the creation of documents that are generally executable in a Web browser.[1] This is a very simple HTML document:

```
<HTML>
<HEAD>
<P>This is the document header.</P>
</HEAD>
```

```
<BODY>
<H1>Headings Layer 1</H1>
<P>This is section 1.</P>
<H2>Headings Layer 2</H2>
<P>This is section 1.1.</P>
</BODY>
</HTML>
```

An extension of HTML is DHTML[2] or Dynamic HTML. Dynamic HTML extends HTML using a combination of technologies. This combination of technologies exists in the document object model plus client- and server-based scripting languages such as JavaScript, Active Server Pages (ASP), and Java Servlets (JSP), among many others. DHTML allows creation of Web pages with much more flexibility than HTML.

The flexibility of DHTML leads us to the definition of the eXtensible Markup Language (XML). XML essentially allows for a context-sensitive interface. What is this in English? It allows Web pages to vary based on who is reading them and the specific needs of the person browsing a Web page. Thus XML can be used as a Web page scripting language, sensitive to unique requirements of individual people.

Ultimately, XML[3] is not limited to a predefined set of tags as in HTML. XML allows for creation of customized tags, on the fly, based on data content, and more specifically based on the content of a database. The content of a database is flexible in terms of what information is stored in that database. Therefore, the advantages of using XML are flexibility for data and Web page integration, open standards, enhanced scalability, and compression in Web page delivery. Additionally, the order of tags within an XML document is not that important to XML, apart from the fact that all elements must be contained within other elements, except for the root node, of course. eXtensible Style Sheets (XSL) extend XML, perhaps in a similar way to that in which DHTML extends HTML. XSL allows for consistent patterns or pictures to be applied to data with consistent patterns, namely rows from a query. Once again, what is all that in English? It is best to demonstrate.

The following script shows a simple XML document, listing things about various cities. Figure 17.1 shows the same code but from the perspective of what this document looks like in a Web browser.

```
<?xml version="1.0"?>
<world>
```

```
<countries>
 <country>
  <name>Canada</name>
  <states>
   <state>
    <name>Quebec</name>
    <cities>
     <city>
      <name>Montreal</name>
      <type>French</type>
     </city>
    </cities>
   </state>
        ...
</world>
```

Figure 17.1
A Simple XML Document in a Web Browser.

17.1.1   What Is XSL?

XSL extends XML by applying repetitive transformations for repeating groups. What does that mean? A relational database table can be used to produce multiple XML elements, repeating groups or rows (each row in a table has the same structure of columns). Thus XSL can be used to apply a common style or appearance to each of those rows. XSL basically applies a template to each row and makes it look nice. Once again, let's demonstrate. The following XSL script in Figure 17.2 shows a style sheet applicable to the example in Figure 17.1. The result of combining the XML page data and the style sheet is shown in Figure 17.3.

Figure 17.2
An XSL Document.

```
<?xml version="1.0"?>

<HTML xmlns:xsl="http://www.w3.org/TR/WD-xsl">
<BODY STYLE="font-family:Arial, helvetica, sans-serif; font-size:12pt; background-color:#EEEEEE">

<H2>Cities</H2>

<UL>
  <xsl:for-each select="world/countries/country">
    <LI><FONT COLOR="red"><xsl:value-of select="name"/></FONT></LI>
    <UL>
      <xsl:for-each select="states/state">
        <LI><FONT COLOR="blue"><xsl:value-of select="name"/></FONT></LI>
        <UL>
          <xsl:for-each select="cities/city">
            <LI><FONT COLOR="green"><xsl:value-of select="name"/></FONT> is <xsl:value-of select="type"/></LI>
          </xsl:for-each>
        </UL>
      </xsl:for-each>
    </UL>
  </xsl:for-each>
</UL>

</BODY>
</HTML>
```

So now we very briefly know what HTML, DHTML, XML, and XSL all are. Now let's look into XML as applied to Oracle SQL.

17.2   Using XML in Oracle

In its most basic form, XML in Oracle SQL consists of the XMLType datatype and several functions. The XMLType stores the text of XML documents and allows access to the XML document object model. The document object model allows access to all of the elements in an XML document programmatically.

The objective of this chapter is to briefly introduce using XML in Oracle SQL. So in order to keep it simple, let's look at it this way: What would

Figure 17.3
*Applying a Style
Sheet to an XML
Document.*

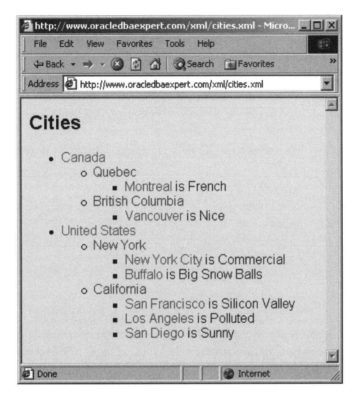

we want to do with XML documents in Oracle SQL, without digging up too much detail?

- Create XML documents.

- Store and retrieve XML documents.

- Add to, make changes in, and destroy XML documents.

17.2.1 Creating XML Documents

The obvious first step is to look at the XMLType datatype.

17.2.1.1 The XMLType Datatype

The XMLType datatype is a special datatype for storing XML documents. An XMLType can be stored in a specially built table, in a column in a table, or in something like a CLOB object. Note that even for a table or a column, the default storage mode for an XMLType datatype is a CLOB object. So, for example, we could create a table as being of XMLType datatype.

```
CREATE TABLE XMLDOCUMENT OF XMLTYPE;
```

We could also create a table containing an XMLType datatype column.

```
CREATE TABLE XML (ID NUMBER NOT NULL, XML XMLTYPE
, CONSTRAINT XPK_XML PRIMARY KEY (ID));
```

We can also use XMLType datatypes in PL/SQL (see Chapter 24).

```
DECLARE
    XML XMLTYPE;
BEGIN
    NULL;
END;
/
```

That is all we need to know about the XMLType datatype with respect to Oracle SQL. The XMLType datatype is merely a storage medium and has little to do with actually "doing things" to XML structures, with Oracle SQL commands. We want to know the "what" and not the "how." In other words, what can we do with XML documents in Oracle SQL, not how are they stored. The "how" part is another book all by itself.

17.2.1.2 Generating XML from Tables

The following are various methods of generating XML code from tables in an Oracle database:

- **SQL/XML Standard**. Various SQL/XML functions and attributes adhere to the SQL Standard for XML standardized by INCITS[4] (International Committee for Information Technology Standards). Basic functions create elements (tags), assign attributes to elements (attributes within individual tags), and various other functions.

- **DBMS_XMLGEN**. This package is complex and creates an XML document based on an entire query.

- **SYS_XMLGEN**. This function creates an XML document for each row read.

- **XSU**. The Java XML SQL utility.

- **Various Other Methods**. Beyond the scope of this book.

Because the SQL/XML functions are the accepted standard, we shall examine these functions in detail.

17.2.1.2.1   The SQL/XML Standard

As already stated, SQL/XML adheres to SQL/XML INCITS standards. The following functions are available to Oracle SQL:

- **XMLELEMENT ([NAME] identifier [, attributes] [, expression [, ...]])**. Creates XML tag elements such as <Name> ... </Name>.

- **XMLATTRIBUTES (expression [AS alias] [, ...])**. Assigns attribute values into tags such as <Artist Name= "...">...</Artist>.

- **XMLCONCAT (XMLType object)**. This function concatenates multiple XML element tags.

- **XMLAGG (XMLType object [ORDER BY ...])**. This function creates a single column or expression from multiple rows by aggregating them into a single row and XML tag. For example:

```
<Artist><Name>Angie Aparo</Name><Name>Avril Lavigne</Name>
... </Artist>
```

- **XMLSEQUENCE (XMLType object)**. Returns an array of XML-Type objects.

- **XMLCOLATTVAL (expression [AS alias] [, ...])**. This particular function might seem a little odd at first with respect to applicability to XML. However, it attempts to standardize for relational structure. Every subset unit is given the tag "column," and the original name of the tag becomes an attribute of the column tag. For example, <Name> Sheryl Crow</Name> becomes <column name = "NAME">Sheryl Crow</column>.

- **XMLFOREST (expression [AS alias] [, ...])**. Functions the same way as multiple XMLELEMENT executions, where each element is created as a tag, containing their respective values.

- **XMLTRANSFORM (XMLType object, XMLType object)**. Executes a transformation for repeating groups in an XML document,

Figure 17.4
XML Element Tags.

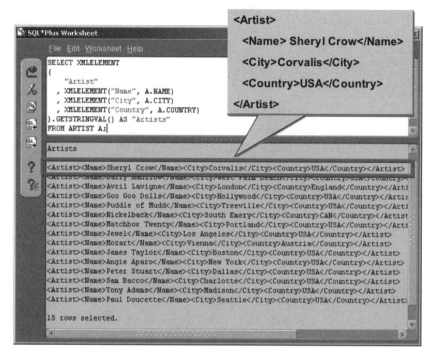

applying an eXtensible Style Sheet (XSL) to each repeating group item in the XML document.

Let's explain various functions by example, that being the easiest method to communicate details. The first example shown by the following script and in Figure 17.4 simply creates XML element tags for three columns in the ARTIST table:

```
SELECT XMLELEMENT( "Artist"
, XMLELEMENT("Name", A.NAME)
, XMLELEMENT("City", A.CITY)
, XMLELEMENT("Country", A.COUNTRY)).GETSTRINGVAL()
FROM ARTIST A;
```

The next example shown following and in Figure 17.5 shows a mixture of elements and tag attributes for the same columns shown in Figure 17.4:

```
SELECT XMLELEMENT(
  "Artist", XMLATTRIBUTES(A.NAME AS "Name")
```

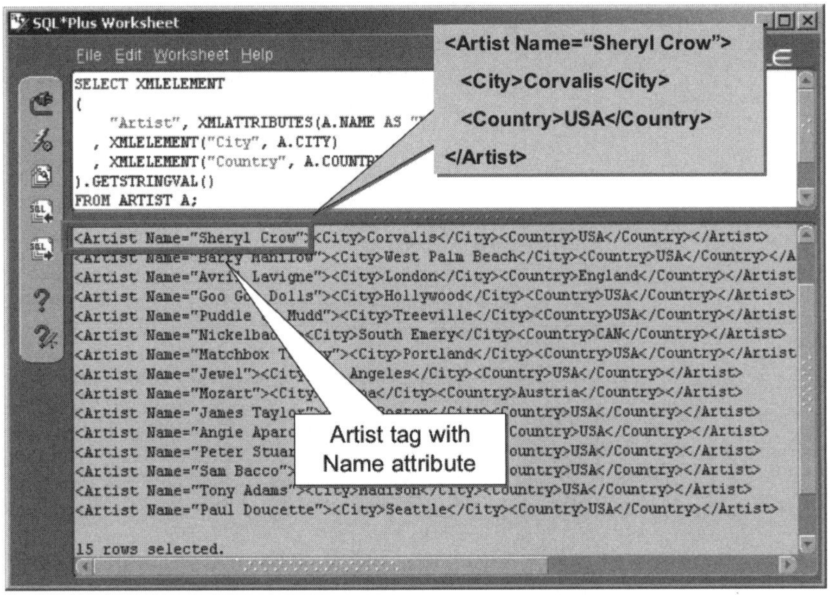

Figure 17.5
XML Element Tags with Tag Attributes.

```
, XMLELEMENT("City", A.CITY)
, XMLELEMENT("Country", A.COUNTRY)).GETSTRINGVAL()
FROM ARTIST A;
```

Multiple child tags occurring in more than one parent tag can be aggregated into a single parent tag. In the following script, all artist names are placed within a single Artist tag, as shown in Figure 17.6.

```
SELECT XMLELEMENT("Artist"
, XMLAGG(XMLELEMENT("Name", A.NAME))).GETSTRINGVAL()
FROM ARTIST A;
```

The only downside to the XMLAGG function is that only a single column can be aggregated. Thus the next example will cause an error because more than one XML tag is created.

```
SELECT XMLELEMENT( "Artist"
, XMLAGG(XMLELEMENT("Name", A.NAME)
, XMLELEMENT("City", A.CITY))).GETSTRINGVAL()
FROM ARTIST A;
```

Figure 17.6

Aggregating into a Single Parent Tag.

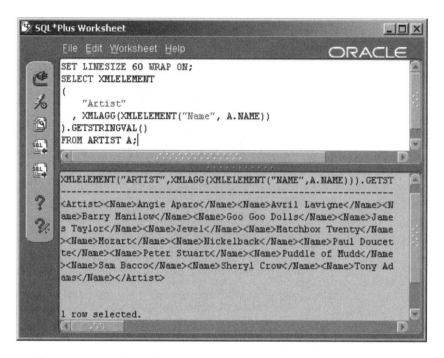

The next example will not cause an error because the two columns are concatenated into a single element tag. However, in this case the result probably is not particularly useful because two distinctly different types of data are returned as single items.

```
SELECT XMLELEMENT( "Artist"
, XMLAGG(XMLELEMENT("Artist", A.NAME||' '||A.CITY))
).GETSTRINGVAL() FROM ARTIST A;
```

The result of the next script is shown in Figure 17.7 and uses the XML-COLATTVAL function. Figure 17.7 provides explanation.

The next example uses the XMLFOREST function to effectively create multiple XML element tags at once. The result is shown in Figure 17.8 and is identical to the result shown in Figure 17.4.

```
SELECT XMLELEMENT("Artist"
, XMLFOREST(A.NAME AS "Name", A.CITY AS "City"
, A.COUNTRY AS "Country")).GETSTRINGVAL()
FROM ARTIST A;
```

Figure 17.7
Changing Tag Names Using XMLCOLATTVAL.

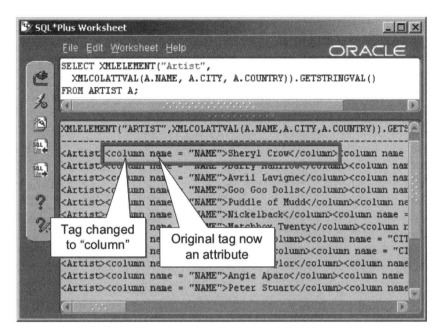

Figure 17.8
Creating Multiple Tags at Once Using XMLFOREST.

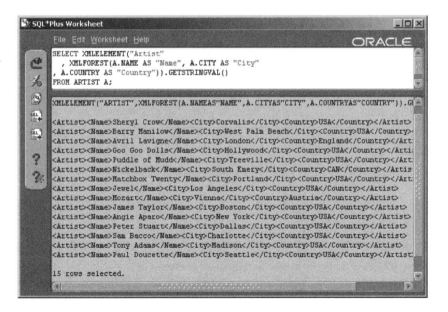

Figure 17.9
A Complex Join of Five Tables.

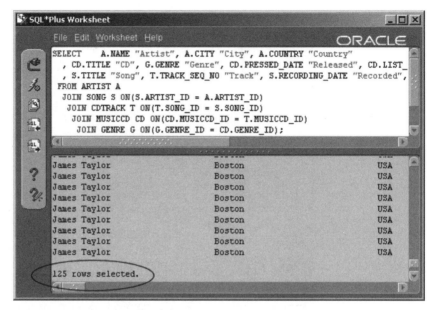

```
SELECT    A.NAME "Artist", A.CITY "City", A.COUNTRY "Country"
, CD.TITLE "CD", G.GENRE "Genre", CD.PRESSED_DATE "Released", CD.LIST_
, S.TITLE "Song", T.TRACK_SEQ_NO "Track", S.RECORDING_DATE "Recorded",
FROM ARTIST A
  JOIN SONG S ON(S.ARTIST_ID = A.ARTIST_ID)
   JOIN CDTRACK T ON(T.SONG_ID = S.SONG_ID)
    JOIN MUSICCD CD ON(CD.MUSICCD_ID = T.MUSICCD_ID)
     JOIN GENRE G ON(G.GENRE_ID = CD.GENRE_ID);
```

James Taylor	Boston	USA
James Taylor	Boston	USA
James Taylor	Boston	USA
James Taylor	Boston	USA
James Taylor	Boston	USA
James Taylor	Boston	USA
James Taylor	Boston	USA
James Taylor	Boston	USA

125 rows selected.

Now let's look at a much more complex application example. We start out with a mutable join of five tables, as shown in the following query and the result in Figure 17.9.

```
SELECT A.NAME "Artist", A.CITY "City", A.COUNTRY "Country"
     , CD.TITLE "CD", G.GENRE "Genre"
, CD.PRESSED_DATE "Released", CD.LIST_PRICE "Price"
     , S.TITLE "Song", T.TRACK_SEQ_NO "Track"
, S.RECORDING_DATE "Recorded", S.PLAYING_TIME "Length"
 FROM ARTIST A
   JOIN SONG S ON(S.ARTIST_ID = A.ARTIST_ID)
    JOIN CDTRACK T ON(T.SONG_ID = S.SONG_ID)
     JOIN MUSICCD CD ON(CD.MUSICCD_ID = T.MUSICCD_ID)
      JOIN GENRE G ON(G.GENRE_ID = CD.GENRE_ID);
```

Now let's push that complex join query into an XML generation format, as shown in the following script. The result is shown in Figure 17.10. Note how the number of rows in Figure 17.10 are the same as in Figure 17.9.

```
SELECT XMLELEMENT("Artist", XMLATTRIBUTES(A.NAME "Name")
     , XMLFOREST(A.CITY "City", A.COUNTRY "Country")
      , XMLELEMENT("CD", XMLATTRIBUTES(CD.TITLE "Title"
```

```
, G.GENRE "Genre")
        , XMLFOREST(CD.PRESSED_DATE "Released"
, CD.LIST_PRICE "Price")
        , XMLELEMENT("Song", XMLATTRIBUTES(S.TITLE "Title"
, T.TRACK_SEQ_NO "Track")
        , XMLFOREST(S.RECORDING_DATE "Recorded"
, TRIM(S.PLAYING_TIME) "Length")
))).GETSTRINGVAL()
FROM ARTIST A
  JOIN SONG S ON(S.ARTIST_ID = A.ARTIST_ID)
    JOIN CDTRACK T ON(T.SONG_ID = S.SONG_ID)
      JOIN MUSICCD CD ON(CD.MUSICCD_ID = T.MUSICCD_ID)
        JOIN GENRE G ON(G.GENRE_ID = CD.GENRE_ID);
```

Now we need to look at the detail of the XML produced in Figure 17.10. Exchanging the GETSTRINGVAL() function with the EXTRACT('/*') function and the command SET LONG <lots> (the default is 80) will create a beautified picture of XML. We will get to that

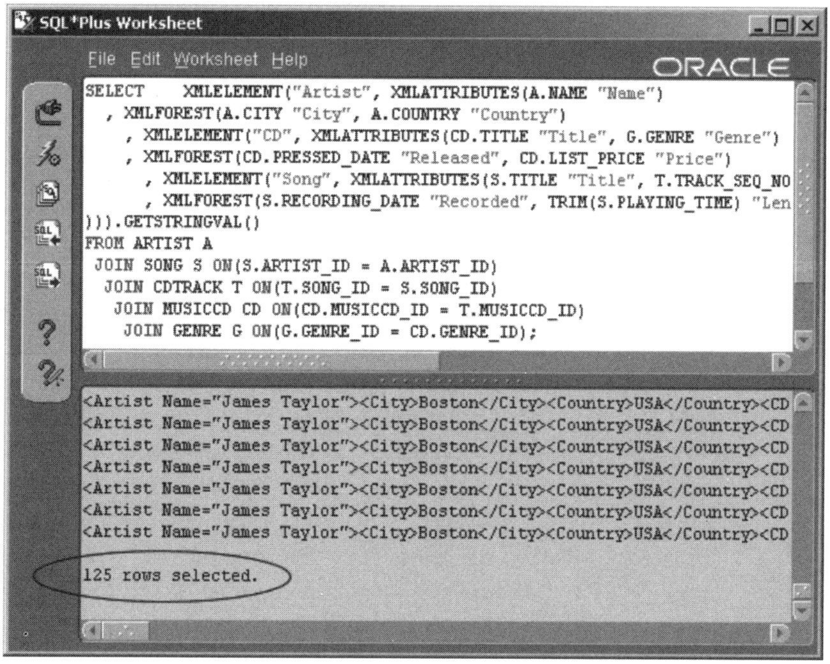

Figure 17.10
The Complex Join in Figure 17.9 in XML.

Figure 17.11
Duplicating Parent Tags.

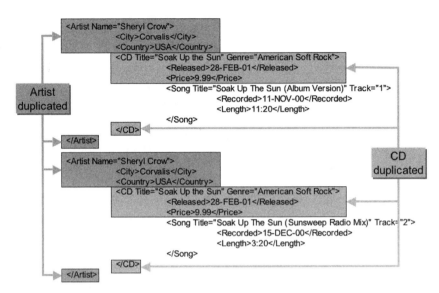

later in this chapter. For now all I have done is copy the first two rows in Figure 17.10 and pasted and annotated them into Figure 17.11.

Most relational database interpretation of XML is direct and dumps rows into two dimensions, as results would appear in row form, such as in this join.

Note: Two-dimensional data is useful for platform-independent transfer between multiple databases. However, there are other, faster methods for achieving this task with Oracle Database.

The beauty of XML is its potential object hierarchical nature, effectively allowing removal of duplicated data. Figure 17.11 clearly shows that duplication is present in abundance. What can we do about this? We can use a function called XMLAGG to aggregate data. In its simplest form, XMLAGG is limited, because it appears to be capable of descending only into a single level of a hierarchy. XMLCONCAT does not help either in this respect because of conflict between the aggregation functions and the GROUP BY clause. The result of the following query as shown in Figure 17.12 is much better than that of Figure 17.11, but it is still not correct, as can be seen by appropriate annotations in Figure 17.12, because artists remain duplicated.

```
SELECT XMLELEMENT("Artist", XMLATTRIBUTES(A.NAME "Name")
```

```
        , XMLFOREST(A.CITY "City", A.COUNTRY "Country")
          , XMLELEMENT("CD", XMLATTRIBUTES(CD.TITLE "Title"
, G.GENRE "Genre")
        , XMLFOREST(CD.PRESSED_DATE "Released"
, CD.LIST_PRICE "Price")
          , XMLAGG(XMLELEMENT("Song"
, XMLATTRIBUTES(S.TITLE "Title"
, T.TRACK_SEQ_NO "Track")
          , XMLFOREST(S.RECORDING_DATE "Recorded"
, TRIM(S.PLAYING_TIME) "Length"))
))).GETSTRINGVAL()
FROM ARTIST A
 JOIN SONG S ON(S.ARTIST_ID = A.ARTIST_ID)
  JOIN CDTRACK T ON(T.SONG_ID = S.SONG_ID)
   JOIN MUSICCD CD ON(CD.MUSICCD_ID = T.MUSICCD_ID)
    JOIN GENRE G ON(G.GENRE_ID = CD.GENRE_ID)
GROUP BY A.NAME, A.CITY, A.COUNTRY, CD.TITLE, G.GENRE
, CD.PRESSED_DATE, CD.LIST_PRICE;
```

Figure 17.12
XMLAGG Removes Lowest-Level Duplication Layer.

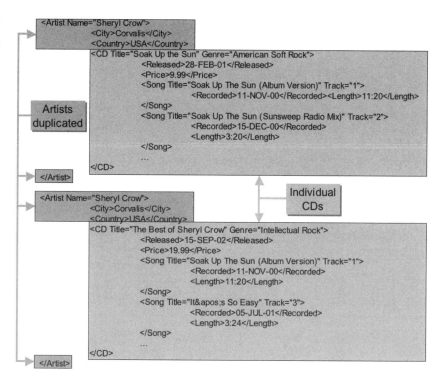

The point to make about Figure 17.12 is that all duplication cannot be removed; thus the duplicated artist tags cannot be removed. The reason why is as follows: Even if an XMLAGG function could contain another embedded XMLAGG function, the GROUP BY clause cannot have more than a single layer. There are alternative methods of solving this multilayered duplication issue. Obviously, other XML generation methods can be used. Additionally, a CAST(MULTISET(... into a nested table for each subset may help. Other obvious answers are a FROM clause inline view embedded subquery and using PL/SQL, which may be the best option. Another point to make is that if programming languages have to be resorted to at the second layer of a hierarchy, then something like PL/SQL may be the better option than SQL/XML. In PL/SQL or another programming language, the complex query we have been using would be a simple multilayered nested cursor procedure, dumping values using the DBMS_OUTPUT procedure. Therefore, I will not pursue this topic any further using SQL/XML. See Chapter 24 for details on PL/SQL.

The SYS_XMLGEN function in the next section shows multilayered capabilities using CAST(MULTISET(... functionality and user-defined types. I still think PL/SQL might be easier to code.

17.2.1.2.2   The SYS_XMLGEN Function

The **SYS_XMLGEN** function creates an XML document for each row read. Unfortunately, this function does not appear to work properly in my current release of Oracle Database 10g, but this is more or less how it is supposed to work. In general, it passes subset row arrays into subset type arrays (nested tables).

```
CREATE OR REPLACE TYPE tSONG AS OBJECT(
TITLE VARCHAR2(64), RECORDING_DATE DATE
, PLAYING_TIME CHAR(10));
/
CREATE OR REPLACE TYPE tSONG_LIST AS TABLE OF tSONG;
/
CREATE OR REPLACE TYPE tARTIST AS OBJECT(
    NAME VARCHAR2(32), CITY VARCHAR2(32)
  , COUNTRY VARCHAR2(32), SONG_LIST tSONG_LIST);
/
SELECT SYS_XMLGEN(tARTIST(A.NAME, A.CITY, A.COUNTRY,
CAST(MULTISET(SELECT tSONG(S.TITLE
, S.RECORDING_DATE, S.PLAYING_TIME)
```

```
        FROM SONG S
        WHERE S.ARTIST_ID = A.ARTIST_ID)
        AS tSONG_LIST))).GETCLOBVAL()
    AS ARTISTXML FROM ARTIST A;
```

Now let's look at how XML documents can be changed in an Oracle database.

17.2.2 XML and the Database

In this section we examine XML and Oracle Database in three ways: (1) creating new XML documents in the database; (2) retrieving XML documents stored in the database, both in whole and in part; and (3) changing XML documents stored in the database.

17.2.2.1 New XML Documents

This command creates a table to store XML documents. This same table creation command has already been shown earlier in this chapter but is repeated here for convenience.

```
CREATE TABLE XML (ID NUMBER NOT NULL, XML XMLType
, CONSTRAINT XPK_XML PRIMARY KEY (ID));
```

There are various methods of adding XML data to a database. In short, an XML document string can be added as a CLOB object, typecast as XMLType datatype from a string, or added using XMLELEMENT and similar SQL/XML functions. The XMLELEMENT function produces an XMLType datatype. In this case, the query shown following is described by the XML document shown in Figure 17.12. This INSERT command will create an XMLType data object in the XML table just created.

```
INSERT INTO XML(ID,XML)
  SELECT CD.MUSICCD_ID, XMLELEMENT("Artist"
    , XMLATTRIBUTES(A.NAME "Name")
    , XMLFOREST(A.CITY "City", A.COUNTRY "Country")
    , XMLELEMENT("CD", XMLATTRIBUTES(CD.TITLE "Title"
    , G.GENRE "Genre")
    , XMLFOREST(CD.PRESSED_DATE "Released"
    , CD.LIST_PRICE "Price")
    , XMLAGG(XMLELEMENT("Song", XMLATTRIBUTES(S.TITLE "Title"
```

```
        , T.TRACK_SEQ_NO "Track")
      , XMLFOREST(S.RECORDING_DATE "Recorded"
      , TRIM(S.PLAYING_TIME) "Length")))))
FROM ARTIST A
  JOIN SONG S ON(S.ARTIST_ID = A.ARTIST_ID)
    JOIN CDTRACK T ON(T.SONG_ID = S.SONG_ID)
      JOIN MUSICCD CD ON(CD.MUSICCD_ID = T.MUSICCD_ID)
        JOIN GENRE G ON(G.GENRE_ID = CD.GENRE_ID)
GROUP BY CD.MUSICCD_ID, A.NAME, A.CITY, A.COUNTRY, CD.TITLE
        , G.GENRE, CD.PRESSED_DATE, CD.LIST_PRICE;
```

That was easy! Now let's find out how to retrieve XML data.

17.2.2.2　Retrieving from XML Documents

XMLType datatype column values can be retrieved using SQL SELECT commands, XML extraction functions, and special Oracle text operators.

When extracting CLOB values, the SET LONG <lots> command is required in SQL*Plus in order to show enough of the string value in the CLOB object. SET LONG 80 is the default and restricts width to 80 characters, which is not much when it comes to XML. Here are four simple examples for showing entire XML value contents. The first two examples will return the entire XML value in a single row on a single line. The third and fourth examples will beautify the result, as shown in Figure 17.13. The fourth example specifically must have SET LONG <lots> applied, otherwise only one row will be returned.

```
SET LONG 2000;
SELECT X.XML.GETSTRINGVAL() AS Artist FROM XML X WHERE ID = 4;
SELECT X.XML.GETCLOBVAL() AS Artist FROM XML X WHERE ID = 4;
SELECT X.XML.EXTRACT('/*') AS Artist FROM XML X WHERE ID = 4;
SELECT XML FROM XML WHERE ID = 4;
```

Now let's examine how to extract individual pieces from within an XML document. XML document subset parts are searched for and retrieved using pattern-matching methods and various functions. Pattern-matching methods are similar to regular expressions (see Chapter 14). An XML document is effectively parsed for specific strings or tags and then the parts within the matched patterns are returned. Various standard pattern-matching characters are used for XML subset searches:

Figure 17.13
*Beautifying
XMLType Datatype
Output.*

- **/**. Specifies a root node either as the root of an entire XML tree or a subtree, and used as a multiple-path specification separation character. Thus Artist/CD/Song/Length finds all CDs with a Length tag.

- **//**. Finds all child elements from a specified root. Therefore, /Artist//Length finds once again all CDs with a Length tag.

- **[…]**. Used to build predicates within expressions such as /Artist[City="Vienna" or City="Boston"], which finds all artists resident in Vienna and Boston.

- **@**. The @ sign is used in XML to access tag attributes. /Artist/@Name will find the name Mozart in the tag <Artist Name="Mozart">.

Before we show some examples, there are several functions we need to cover in addition to pattern-matching characters already described.

- **EXISTSNODE (XMLType object, search path, expression).** Searches for the expression in a path (search path) within an XML document XMLType object. This function will return 1 if a node exists.

- **EXTRACT (XMLType object, search path, expression).** As already seen, the EXISTSNODE function verifies the presence of a string. The EXTRACT function returns the tag and its contents.

- **EXTRACTVALUE (XMLType object, search path, expression).** This function finds the same strings or patterns as the EXTRACT function except it returns scalar values, as opposed to tags. Therefore, where the EXTRACT function returns <City>Los Angeles</City>, the EXTRACTVALUE function returns the value between the City tags, namely Los Angeles.

Now let's demonstrate by example. The first example finds the CD identifier where that CD has at least one Length value (SONG.PLAYING_TIME) in its structure:

```
SELECT ID FROM XML WHERE EXISTSNODE(XML
, 'Artist/CD/Song/Length') = 1;
```

This query will verify the previous query by looking at the data in the tables. Figure 17.14 shows both of these queries put together.

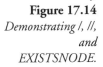

Figure 17.14
Demonstrating /, //, and EXISTSNODE.

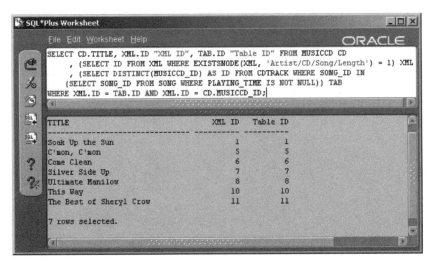

Figure 17.15
Demonstrating EXTRACT and EXTRACTVALUE.

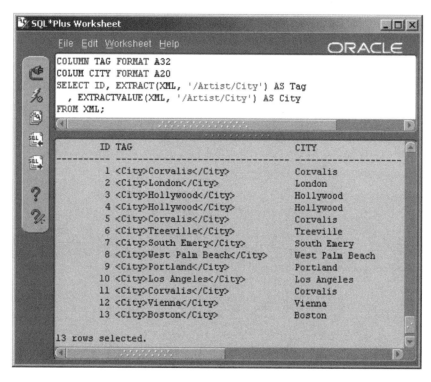

```
SELECT DISTINCT(MUSICCD_ID) FROM CDTRACK WHERE SONG_ID IN
    (SELECT SONG_ID FROM SONG
WHERE PLAYING_TIME IS NOT NULL);
```

The next example extracts every City tag and the value within every City tag for all entries in the XML document. The result is shown in Figure 17.15.

```
COLUMN TAG FORMAT A32
COLUM CITY FORMAT A20
SELECT ID, EXTRACT(XML, '/Artist/City') AS Tag
, EXTRACTVALUE(XML, '/Artist/City') AS City
FROM XML;
```

The next two examples use EXTRACT to retrieve, EXISTSNODE to validate and predicate pattern matching to find multiple elements. Results are shown in Figures 17.16 and 17.17.

Figure 17.16
*Demonstrating
EXTRACT,
EXISTSNODE,
and a Single-Value
Pattern Match.*

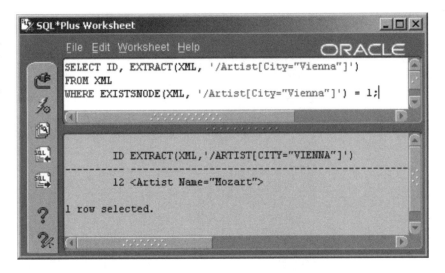

```
SELECT ID, EXTRACT(XML, '/Artist[City="Vienna"]') FROM XML
WHERE EXISTSNODE(XML, '/Artist[City="Vienna"]') = 1;
SELECT ID, EXTRACT(XML, '/Artist[City="Vienna" or
City="Boston"]')
FROM XML WHERE EXISTSNODE(XML, '/Artist[City="Vienna"
or City="Boston"]') = 1;
```

Figure 17.17
*Demonstrating
EXTRACT,
EXISTSNODE,
and a Multiple-
Value Pattern
Match.*

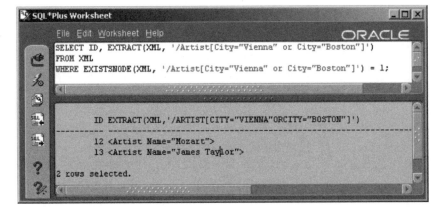

That covers data retrieval for XML documents in Oracle SQL.

17.2.2.3   Changing and Removing XML Document Content

An XML document is stored internally as a CLOB or large binary text
object. As a result, updating the contents of an XML document in an

XMLType datatype simply replaces the entire document. The easiest method of changing XML document content is using the UPDATEXML function.

- **UPDATEXML(XMLType object, search path, expression [, search path, expression], 'replace string')**. The UPDATEXML function can be used to change pattern-matched parts of XML documents.

There are some important things to remember about the UPDA-TEXML function:

- UPDATEXML can be used to update single tags, tag attributes, and even entire subtrees.

- Deleting XML document content is essentially the same as updating. If a value is to be removed, simply find it and set it to NULL using UPDATEXML.

- Remember that the UPDATEXML function can only find and update what already exists in the XML structure. If some values are null valued when initially creating an XML document from relational tables, those values will not exist in the XML document at all, not even as tags. The only method of using UPDATEXML in this situation is to edit an entire parent tag.

Let's change Mozart's name and city as shown in Figures 17.15, 17.16, and 17.17. The result is shown in Figure 17.18.

```
SET LONG 2000 WRAP ON LINESIZE 5000;
UPDATE XML SET XML =
UPDATEXML(XML, '/Artist/City/text()', 'Wien')
WHERE ID = 12;
UPDATE XML SET XML =
UPDATEXML(XML, '/Artist/@Name', 'Wolfgang Amadeus Mozart')
WHERE ID = 12;
SELECT X.XML.EXTRACT('/*') FROM XML X WHERE X.ID = 12;
```

Figure 17.18
*Using
UPDATEXML to
Change XML
Documents.*

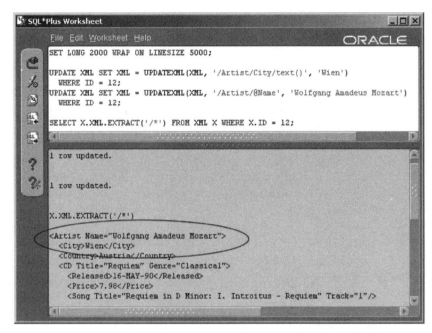

Now let's remove Mozart's single CD from the XML document altogether, as shown in the following script and in Figure 17.19.

```
SET LONG 2000 WRAP ON LINESIZE 5000;
UPDATE XML SET XML = UPDATEXML(XML, '/Artist//CD', NULL)
WHERE ID = 12;
SELECT X.XML.EXTRACT('/*') FROM XML X WHERE X.ID = 12;
```

To add Mozart's CD back into the XML document, we can either recreate from the source tables or update the entire node with the original XML subtree.

17.3   Metadata Views

This section describes metadata views applicable to XML tables. Chapter 19 examines the basis and detail of Oracle Database metadata views.

■ **USER_XML_TABLES** and **USER_XML_TAB_COLS**. The structure of XML tables from the perspective of both tables and columns.

Figure 17.19
*UPDATEXML
Can Delete an
Entire Subtree.*

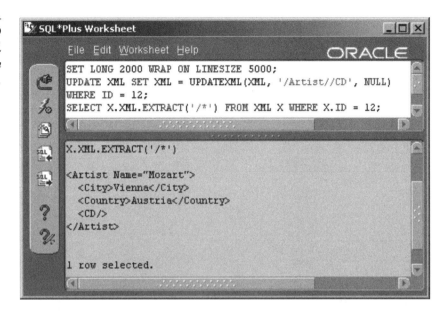

- **USER_XML_VIEWS and USER_XML_VIEW_COLS**. The structure of XML views and their columns structures.

- **USER_XML_SCHEMAS**. Registered XML schemas.

This chapter has attempted to introduce the use of XML directly from within Oracle SQL. XML is vastly more complex and detailed than presented in this chapter, both with respect to XML itself and to that of Oracle software. This chapter is merely included to present the usefulness of XML with respect to both Oracle Database and relational databases in general. The next chapter will begin coverage of Data Definition Language (DDL) commands by looking at tables.

17.4 Endnotes

1. www.oracledbaexpert.com/menu/HTML.html

2. www.oracledbaexpert.com/menu/DHTML.html

3. www.oracledbaexpert.com/menu/xml.html

4. www.incits.org

18

Tables

In this chapter:

- What is a table?

- How do we create a table?

- How do we change and destroy tables?

- How are comments added to tables?

- What is the recycle bin?

This chapter shows you how to do all sorts of stuff with tables. Creating and changing of tables includes defining and creating structure within tables and making changes to those structures. Subsequent chapters cover views and constraints. This chapter concentrates solely on tables.

18.1   What Is a Table?

Tables are used as structural definitions of data. The structure of a table defines what kind of data can be stored in the table. Rows of repeating data items are stored in tables in an Oracle schema. A schema is the Oracle user that owns the tables. A user and a schema are the same thing as far as Oracle Database is concerned. An Oracle relational database can contain many Oracle schemas. A schema in Oracle is the equivalent of a single database in other relational databases such as Sybase or Ingres.

18.1.1   Types of Tables

Oracle Database 10*g* supports many different types of tables. The easiest method of explanation is to list the different available table types as follows:

- **Relational Table**. The basic structure and core of a relational database, holding user data.

- **Object Table**. A table using an object type for its column definition, or it can contain instances of strictly typed objects, such as type structures, collections, or binary objects.

- **Temporary Table**. Temporary tables are available to all sessions, but a separate data set is temporarily available for each session using a temporary table.

- **Index-Organized Table**. Index-Organized tables are often called IOTs. A simple relational table, described previously, holds table data in one physical object and index data in another physical object. For an IOT, all columns in the table, not just the indexed columns, are stored as a BTree index, based on the primary key. The data rows are organized in the order of the index. This can improve performance in some situations.

- **Cluster**. Used to store multiple indexes of frequently joined tables into a single, physical object. A cluster is similar to an IOT where more data than usual is stored with indexes, increasing data access performance. Performance especially improves when the joined tables are most commonly accessed together, such as in a view or join query. A cluster is much more of an index than an IOT is and therefore is covered in detail in Chapter 21.

- **External Table**. A read-only table storing data external to the database, such as in a text file.

- **XMLType Table**. A table with an Oracle internally managed XML datatype structure, either as the table or in a column of a table. XML is covered in Chapter 17.

- **Partitioned Table**. Tables can be subdivided into partitions and subpartitions. Partitions are an effective performance-tuning approach for dividing large tables on a range, list value, or hashing algorithm basis. Partitioned tables are useful in data warehouse environments or very large databases where parallel processing and rapid datafile movement can be utilized.

18.1.2   Methods of Creating Tables

Tables can be created in one of three ways:

- **Scripted**. The CREATE TABLE command can be used to list each column's attributes.

- **CREATE TABLE ... AS subquery**. The CREATE TABLE command can be executed as a creation from a subquery.

- **Tools**. There are numerous tools available, which can be used to create tables both in a graphical user interface (GUI) or as generated, modifiable scripting.

18.1.2.1   Scripted Method

Examine the script shown following. This example is a part of the script used to create the ARTIST table for the MUSIC schema (see Appendix A).

```
CREATE OR REPLACE TYPE
INSTRUMENTSCOLLECTION AS VARRAY(10) OF VARCHAR2(32);
/
CREATE TABLE ARTIST(
  ARTIST_ID               NUMBER NOT NULL
    , NAME                VARCHAR2(32) NOT NULL
    , STREET              VARCHAR2(32)
    , POBOX               CHAR(20)
    , CITY                VARCHAR2(32)
    , STATE_PROVINCE      VARCHAR2(32)
    , COUNTRY             VARCHAR2(32)
    , ZIP                 CHAR(10)
    , EMAIL               VARCHAR2(32)
    , INSTRUMENTS         INSTRUMENTSCOLLECTION
    , CONSTRAINT          XPKARTIST PRIMARY KEY (ARTIST_ID)
);
CREATE UNIQUE INDEX XUK_ARTIST_NAME ON ARTIST (NAME);
```

Each column has a name, a datatype, a size (if needed for the datatype), and a position in the table. There are several points to note about the ARTIST table creation script:

- The ARTIST table is by definition an object table and not a relational table. Why? A very simple reason. The ARTIST table contains an object as one of its object types. The INSTRUMENTS column is an object collection column of the user-defined structural type INSTRUMENTSCOLLECTION.

- The XPKARTIST column is a primary key constraint. Constraints are covered in Chapter 20. This particular constraint is a primary key placed onto the ARTIST_ID column. Being a primary key column, the ARTIST_ID can never be the same for more than a single row in the ARTIST table.

- The final command in the script shown previously is an index creation command. Indexes are covered in Chapter 21. The only important point to note about this index at this point is that the NAME column, like the primary key ARTIST_ID column, must be unique. This index simply enforces that uniqueness of names.

18.1.2.2   CREATE TABLE ... AS Subquery

The subquery table creation method creates a copy of an existing table or tables using a subquery. In the next example shown, we create a new table as a join between five of the MUSIC schema tables. The output shows guest appearances and then drops the table at the end because we do not want to keep it. The result is shown in Figure 18.1.

```
CREATE TABLE EXTRAS AS
    SELECT S.TITLE AS SONG, A.NAME AS ARTIST
, I.NAME AS INSTRUMENT
    FROM GUESTAPPEARANCE GA, ARTIST A, SONG S
, INSTRUMENTATION IA, INSTRUMENT I
    WHERE GA.GUESTARTIST_ID = A.ARTIST_ID
    AND GA.GUESTARTIST_ID = S.SONG_ID
    AND IA.SONG_ID = GA.SONG_ID
    AND IA.GUESTARTIST_ID = GA.GUESTARTIST_ID
    AND I.INSTRUMENT_ID = IA.INSTRUMENT_ID;
SELECT ARTIST||' played '||INSTRUMENT||' on '
||SONG AS "Who Played What?" FROM EXTRAS;
DROP TABLE EXTRAS;
```

18.1.2.3   Tools

Other methods of creating tables include use of tools such as Oracle Enterprise Manager, which provides a GUI for database object creation, including table creation. Additionally, data modeling tools such as ERwin can be utilized to generate scripts, which create entire application table sets. Figure 18.2 shows the table creation tool in Oracle Enterprise Manager.

Figure 18.1
Demonstrating
CREATE TABLE
... AS Subquery.

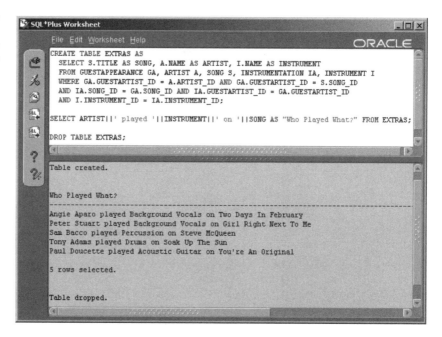

So far we have looked at different types of tables and various methods for creating those different table types. Now we examine syntax for the CREATE TABLE command, which is used for, you guessed it, creating tables.

18.2 CREATE TABLE Syntax

The syntax of the CREATE TABLE command is highly complex at first glance in Oracle documentation. However, the focus of this book is on Oracle SQL and not database administration. Database administration functionality for the CREATE TABLE command includes any physical storage parameters such as tablespace locations and most types of physical properties. Therefore, we get to leave a lot of the syntax out because we are only dealing with Oracle SQL. This makes it a lot easier, but unfortunately not easy enough. So syntax for the CREATE TABLE command has to be divided into sections. Let's begin with a very simple form of the syntax, perhaps it could be called a pseudo-like syntax, for creating tables, as shown in Figure 18.3.

What we do from this point onward is to pass through each table type in turn, examining syntax and describing by example.

Figure 18.2
*Creating a Table
Using Oracle
Enterprise
Manager.*

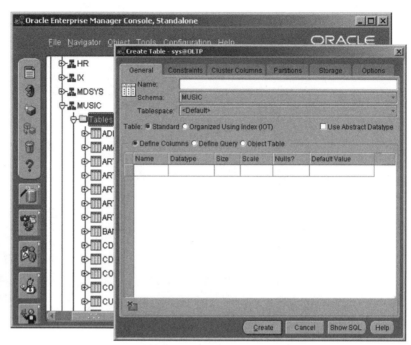

18.3   Creating Different Table Types

An easy way of simplifying CREATE TABLE syntax is to divide it up into
the different table types, as already briefly described in this chapter. XML-
Type tables will be ignored in this section because they are extremely simple
and covered in Chapter 17.

Note: It is important to remember that different table types do not always
fit precisely within the classifications assigned to them here. For example,
an IOT or a temporary table can be relational or object tables and vice
versa. The table types are simply divided neatly to facilitate ease of compre-
hension for the reader.

18.3.1   Creating Relational Tables

A relational table is termed *relational* because of the way in which tables are
linked together. We get to that shortly and in more detail in Chapter 20
when discussing constraints. The syntax for creating a simple relational

Figure 18.3
*A CREATE
TABLE Pseudo-
like Syntax.*

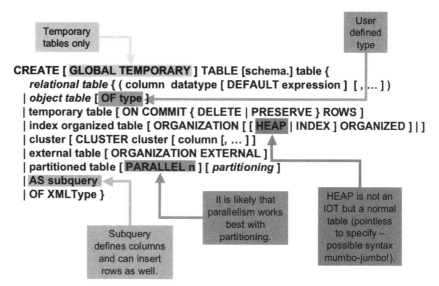

table is shown in Figure 18.4. Inline and out-of-line constraints are covered in detail in Chapter 20.

We have already looked at the ARTIST table in this chapter. Let's look at the data warehouse section SALES table. The SALES table has more columns than the ARTIST table and many more different datatypes for its columns. Once again, all primary and foreign keys are constraints and are covered in Chapter 20. Additionally, NOT NULL is a constraint prohibiting a column from being empty within a row. Other than those points, the only thing to note is that DEFAULT clauses have been added to allow for column values with nothing added to them. Various numeric columns will be set to zero if a row is added to the SALES where those defaulted columns are not specified. In these cases, null values will be replaced with default values specified. Note that the DEFAULT clauses are not included in the MUSIC schema table creation scripts. The DEFAULT clause is rarely used.

```
CREATE TABLE SALES (
        SALES_ID          NUMBER NOT NULL
      , MUSICCD_ID        NUMBER NOT NULL
      , CUSTOMER_ID       NUMBER NOT NULL
      , RETAILER_ID       NUMBER
      , CONTINENT_ID      NUMBER
      , COUNTRY_ID        NUMBER
      , LIST_PRICE        FLOAT DEFAULT 0
      , DISCOUNT          FLOAT DEFAULT 0
```

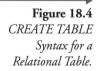

Figure 18.4
CREATE TABLE Syntax for a Relational Table.

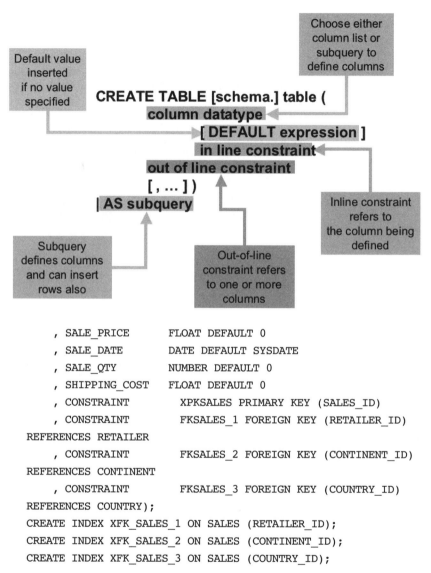

```
        , SALE_PRICE        FLOAT DEFAULT 0
        , SALE_DATE         DATE DEFAULT SYSDATE
        , SALE_QTY          NUMBER DEFAULT 0
        , SHIPPING_COST     FLOAT DEFAULT 0
        , CONSTRAINT          XPKSALES PRIMARY KEY (SALES_ID)
        , CONSTRAINT          FKSALES_1 FOREIGN KEY (RETAILER_ID)
REFERENCES RETAILER
        , CONSTRAINT          FKSALES_2 FOREIGN KEY (CONTINENT_ID)
REFERENCES CONTINENT
        , CONSTRAINT          FKSALES_3 FOREIGN KEY (COUNTRY_ID)
REFERENCES COUNTRY);
CREATE INDEX XFK_SALES_1 ON SALES (RETAILER_ID);
CREATE INDEX XFK_SALES_2 ON SALES (CONTINENT_ID);
CREATE INDEX XFK_SALES_3 ON SALES (COUNTRY_ID);
```

18.3.2   Creating Object Tables

Creating an object table has a slightly different syntax from that of a relational table. Figure 18.5 shows the CREATE TABLE command syntax, highlighting aspects particular to object tables.

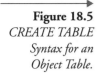

Figure 18.5
*CREATE TABLE
Syntax for an
Object Table.*

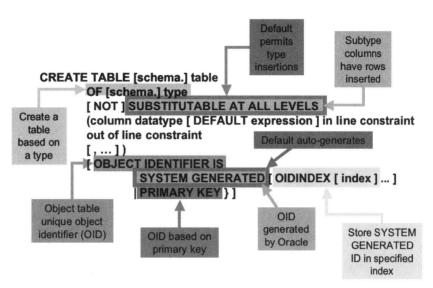

Let's run through some simple examples. We can create a table similar to an existing table as an object table. First, let's create a new type duplicating the structure of the MUSIC schema INSTRUMENT table.

```
CREATE OR REPLACE TYPE INSTRUMENTTYPE AS OBJECT(
   INSTRUMENT_ID NUMBER
, SECTION_ID NUMBER
, NAME VARCHAR2(32));
/
```

Second, create a table using the new type.

```
CREATE TABLE INSTRUMENTS OF INSTRUMENTTYPE;
```

Let's try something else. First, drop the INSTRUMENT table and then re-create it, but this time using a specified index for a system-generated object identifier (OID), which is presumed to be unique throughout an entire database. The index is shown in Figure 18.6. The query used examines all of a current user's indexes and is included in Appendix B.

```
DROP TABLE INSTRUMENTS;
CREATE TABLE INSTRUMENTS OF INSTRUMENTTYPE
OBJECT IDENTIFIER IS SYSTEM GENERATED
OIDINDEX OIDX_INSTRUMENTS;
```

Figure 18.6
*A System-
Generated OID
Index
(OIDX_INSTRU
MENTS).*

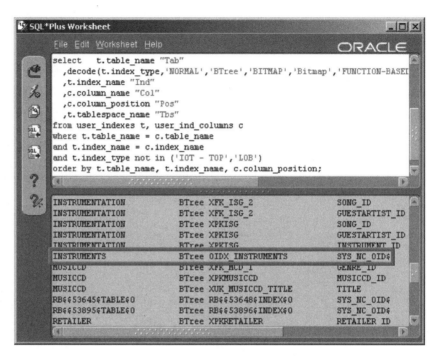

Now let's create multiple layers of types and make subtypes noninsert-able. We must drop tables and types in the proper order. We will also clean up at the end of the script.

```
DROP TABLE INSTRUMENTS;
DROP TYPE INSTRUMENTTYPE;
CREATE OR REPLACE TYPE INSTRUMENTTYPE AS OBJECT(
     INSTRUMENT_ID NUMBER
   , NAME VARCHAR2(32));
/
CREATE OR REPLACE TYPE SECTIONTYPE AS OBJECT(
     SECTION_ID NUMBER);
/
CREATE TABLE SECTIONS OF SECTIONTYPE
     NOT SUBSTITUTABLE AT ALL LEVELS
(SECTION_ID PRIMARY KEY)
OBJECT IDENTIFIER IS PRIMARY KEY;
DROP TYPE INSTRUMENTTYPE;
DROP TABLE SECTIONS;
DROP TYPE SECTIONTYPE;
```

What do all of these object table examples prove? Not much! Personally, I prefer to avoid using too much pure object-like structure in a relational database because object and relational structure are completely different in nature. I prefer to save the object-things for applications or even an object database.

18.3.3   Creating Temporary Tables

Figure 18.7 shows a syntax diagram containing syntax details for creating temporary tables.

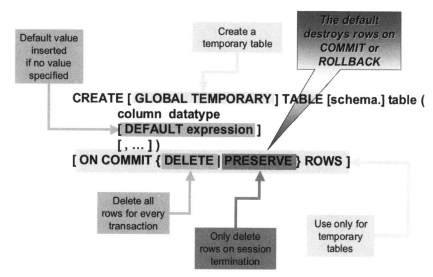

Figure 18.7
CREATE TABLE
Syntax for a
Temporary Table.

A global temporary table is used to store data temporarily for a specific session. The GLOBAL keyword dictates that the structure of the table is available to all sessions but not the rows. Rows created in a temporary table can be made available, with the ON COMMIT PRESERVE ROWS modifier, for the life of the session that created rows in that temporary table. ON COMMIT DELETE ROWS is the default and will remove all session-specific rows from the table on execution of a COMMIT command.

Note: When two sessions create rows in the same temporary table, each session is able to use only the rows it created. The other session's rows are not available.

In the following examples, we execute from two sessions and show how temporary tables function in a session-specific manner. These examples use two sessions by opening up a second SQL*Plus Worksheet instance, which is necessary to show how temporary tables function.

In the first SQL*Plus Worksheet, the following script is executed. (If you already have a table called TEMP, drop that table first by typing the command DROP TABLE TEMP;.) See the result of the script in Figure 18.8.

```
CREATE GLOBAL TEMPORARY TABLE temp (col1 number)
ON COMMIT PRESERVE ROWS;
INSERT INTO TEMP(col1) VALUES(1);
INSERT INTO TEMP(col1) VALUES(2);
INSERT INTO TEMP(col1) VALUES(3);
COMMIT;
SELECT * FROM TEMP;
```

We have created a temporary table named TEMP with one column called COL1. By using the ON COMMIT PRESERVE ROWS clause when creating the table, we tell the database that we want rows inserted or updated to remain in place after issuing a COMMIT command. The default setting for temporary tables is ON COMMIT DELETE ROWS, which deletes all of a session's rows whenever a COMMIT command is executed. Next we inserted three rows into the table with column values of 1, 2, and 3. Then the transaction was completed using the COMMIT command. Finally the TEMP table was queried displaying the three rows inserted, as shown in Figure 18.8.

In the second SQL*Plus Worksheet instance, we execute the second script as shown following . See the result in Figure 18.9.

```
INSERT INTO TEMP(col1) VALUES(1);
INSERT INTO TEMP(col1) VALUES(4);
INSERT INTO TEMP(col1) VALUES(5);
INSERT INTO TEMP(col1) VALUES(6);
COMMIT;
SELECT * FROM TEMP;
```

We do not create another temporary table in the second session. Instead, we use the temporary table created in the first session. Because we are

Figure 18.8

Create a Temporary Table and Add Some Rows in the First Session.

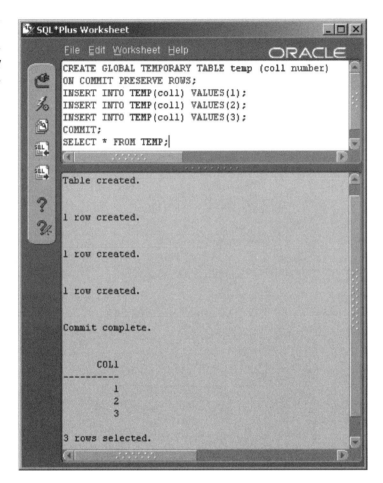

logged in as MUSIC in both sessions, both sessions share the same schema and can use the TEMP table.

We then insert four rows into the TEMP table in the second session with values 1, 4, 5, and 6 in the column, and then commit the transaction and query the TEMP table once again. The result is shown in Figure 18.9.

Here are some important points demonstrated in this example:

- Rows added in either of the two sessions are not visible to the other session; only the structure of the table is visible to both sessions.

- The row value 1 in the first session and the second session are not the same rows, even though their values are the same.

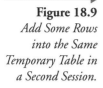

Figure 18.9
Add Some Rows into the Same Temporary Table in a Second Session.

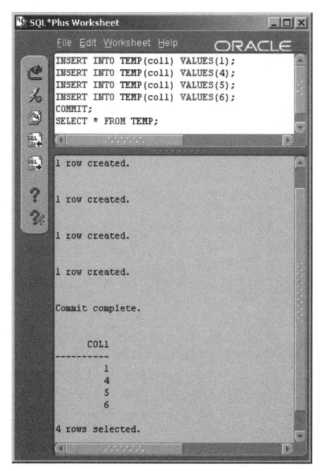

- When selecting rows in the first session, the select statement retrieves only rows created in the first session. Conversely, when selecting rows in the second session, the select statement retrieves only rows created in the second session.

The temporary table must be removed using the following sequence of steps. These steps are needed because one session cannot drop a temporary table that another session is using.

1. **In the second session**. TRUNCATE TABLE TEMP;

2. **In the first session**. TRUNCATE TABLE TEMP;

3. **In either session**. DROP TABLE TEMP;

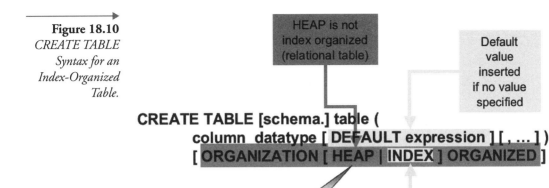

Figure 18.10
*CREATE TABLE
Syntax for an
Index-Organized
Table.*

18.3.4   Creating Index-Organized Tables (IOTs)

An index-organized table (IOT) simply organizes data in the table in the order of the primary key index, in a BTree structure. In other words, the entire table becomes a sorted BTree index. That sorted table can subsequently be accessed as an index in index-sorted order. The obvious performance benefit is primary key sorted order scanning. The downside is that an IOT is more likely to be a better performer when reading rather than changing data, although the word out there is that IOTs can perform very well in even OLTP databases.[1]

Figure 18.10 shows a syntax diagram containing syntax details relevant to creating IOTs.

As an example, we create an IOT version of the MUSIC schema SALES table called SALESIOT.

```
CREATE TABLE SALESIOT(
        SALES_ID          NUMBER NOT NULL
      , MUSICCD_ID        NUMBER NOT NULL
      , CUSTOMER_ID       NUMBER NOT NULL
      , RETAILER_ID       NUMBER
      , CONTINENT_ID      NUMBER
      , COUNTRY_ID        NUMBER
      , LIST_PRICE        FLOAT
      , DISCOUNT          FLOAT
      , SALE_PRICE        FLOAT
      , SALE_DATE         DATE
```

```
        , SALE_QTY        NUMBER
        , SHIPPING_COST   FLOAT
        , CONSTRAINT      XPKSALESIOT PRIMARY KEY (SALES_ID))
ORGANIZATION INDEX;
INSERT INTO SALESIOT SELECT * FROM SALES;
```

An IOT is a single table, organized in the order of a BTree index. In other words, the data space columns are added into the index structure leaf blocks of a binary tree. An IOT is effectively a BTree table where the entire table is the index. The same block space is occupied by both data and index values.

18.3.5   Creating External Tables

An external table is read-only data stored externally to or outside the logical structure of an Oracle database, at the operating system level. Figure 18.11 shows a syntax diagram containing syntax details relevant to creating external tables.

Let's create an external version of the data warehouse SALES table. The first thing we have to do is create a directory object.

```
CREATE OR REPLACE DIRECTORY DATA AS 'c:\oracle\ora10\oltp\
data';
```

Figure 18.11
CREATE TABLE
Syntax for External
Tables.

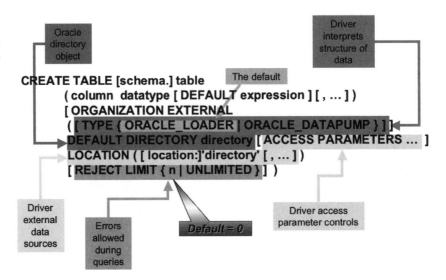

Now we can create an externally organized table. All constraints have been removed, including the NOT NULL and primary key constraint. External tables do not appear to allow these constraints. See Chapter 20 for details on constraints. The default directory is the DATA directory on the database server machine.

```
CREATE TABLE SALESEXT(
      SALES_ID          NUMBER
    , MUSICCD_ID        NUMBER
    , CUSTOMER_ID       NUMBER
    , RETAILER_ID       NUMBER
    , CONTINENT_ID      NUMBER
    , COUNTRY_ID        NUMBER
    , LIST_PRICE        FLOAT
    , DISCOUNT          FLOAT
    , SALE_PRICE        FLOAT
    , SALE_DATE         DATE
    , SALE_QTY          NUMBER
    , SHIPPING_COST     FLOAT)
ORGANIZATION EXTERNAL
(
    DEFAULT DIRECTORY data
    LOCATION ('salesext.txt')
)
REJECT LIMIT UNLIMITED;
```

To put data into the SALESEXT table, do the following in SQL*Plus:

```
SET COLSEP, REPSEP OFF LINESIZE 5000 PAGESIZE 5000 HEAD OFF;
SPOOL C:\TMP\SALESEXT.TXT;
SELECT * FROM SALES;
SPOOL OFF;
```

Then parse-replace all space characters in a text editor to make the text file look like this:

```
1,12,1,3,7,24,7.98,0,7.98,03-NOV-03,1,0
2,11,2,3,7,22,19.99,0,19.99,03-NOV-03,1,0
3,8,3,2,7,17,19.99,.05,18.99,03-NOV-03,1,0
...
996,3,5,1,2,6,14.99,.2,11.99,17-DEC-03,1,0
```

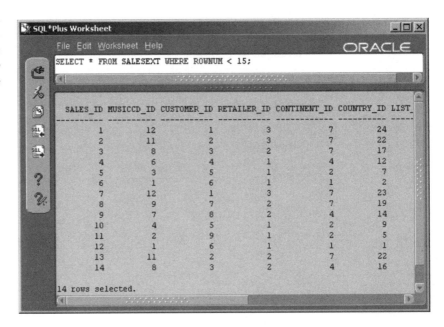

Figure 18.12
*Reading an
Externally
Organized Table's
Data.*

Then copy the SALESEXT.TXT file to your database server into the directory defined by the DATA directory object already created. At that point, you can read rows directly from the SALESEXT table using SQL*Plus, which in turn reads from the SALESEXT.TXT file in the operating system on the database server machine. The following query demonstrates this process, with the result shown in Figure 18.12.

```
SELECT * FROM SALESEXT WHERE ROWNUM < 15;
```

We could expand on the SALESEXT table definition to include the ACCESS PARAMETERS clause. The SALESEXT table must be dropped first because it has already been created. Dropping the external table definition in the database does not affect the SALESEXT.TXT file on the server or the DATA directory object.

```
DROP TABLE SALESEXT;
CREATE TABLE SALESEXT(
        SALES_ID          INTEGER
    , MUSICCD_ID        INTEGER
    , CUSTOMER_ID       NUMBER
    , RETAILER_ID       NUMBER
    , CONTINENT_ID      NUMBER
```

```
                    , COUNTRY_ID        NUMBER
                    , LIST_PRICE        FLOAT
                    , DISCOUNT          FLOAT
                    , SALE_PRICE        FLOAT
                    , SALE_DATE         DATE
                    , SALE_QTY          NUMBER
                    , SHIPPING_COST     FLOAT)
        ORGANIZATION EXTERNAL
        (
            DEFAULT DIRECTORY data
            ACCESS PARAMETERS
            (
                FIELDS TERMINATED BY ","
                (
                        SALES_ID            INTEGER EXTERNAL(5)
                      , MUSICCD_ID          INTEGER EXTERNAL(5)
                      , CUSTOMER_ID         INTEGER EXTERNAL(5)
                      , RETAILER_ID         INTEGER EXTERNAL(5)
                      , CONTINENT_ID        INTEGER EXTERNAL(5)
                      , COUNTRY_ID          INTEGER EXTERNAL(5)
                      , LIST_PRICE          FLOAT EXTERNAL
                      , DISCOUNT            FLOAT EXTERNAL
                      , SALE_PRICE          FLOAT EXTERNAL
                      , SALE_DATE           DATE "DD-MON-YY"
                      , SALE_QTY            INTEGER EXTERNAL(5)
                      , SHIPPING_COST       FLOAT EXTERNAL
                )
            )
            LOCATION ('salesext.txt')
        )
        REJECT LIMIT UNLIMITED;
```

Note: Access parameter field definitions require INTEGER datatypes to be declared as an EXTERNAL(n) datatype, not EXTERNAL as for SQL*Loader. There are no strings in the SALES table, but all strings would have to be represented as CHAR(n) fixed-length strings, n representing a maximum length.

Executing another query would give the same result as that shown in Figure 18.12.

18.3.6 **Creating Partitioned Tables**

Partitioned tables are part and parcel of an add-on option called Oracle Partitioning. Oracle Partitioning working in concert with parallel processing and separate disk spindles or RAID arrays can provide fairly substantial performance improvements. Oracle Partitioning and parallelism is an immense subject all by itself.[2] Additionally, numerous interesting tricks can be done when using Oracle Partitioning. All we want to do in this section is demonstrate using partitions from the Oracle SQL perspective, namely syntax and some examples.

18.3.6.1 **What Are the Types of Partitions?**

There are five different types of partitions as follows:

- **Range**. Divides up rows based on ranges of values.

- **Values List**. Divides up rows based on sets of literal values.

- **Hash**. Uses a hashing algorithm to divide rows, resulting in the most consistently sized partitions.

- **Composite Partitions**. Contains subpartitions within each separate partition:

  - **Range-Hash**. A range partition containing hash subpartitions within each range partition.
  - **Range-List**. A range partition containing list value subpartitions within each range partition.

18.3.6.1.1 **Partition Indexing**

Partitions can have indexes. How are indexes built for partitions? There are two types of partitioning indexes:

- **Local Index**. These indexes have the same structure as their relative table partitions. Local indexes are preferred because of their more automated maintenance. A local partition index applies to each partition.

- **Global Index**. These indexes are created on partitioned tables but are not the same structure as the partitioning key. A global index applies to all partitions in a partitioned table.

Note: (10g) There is a new type of global partition index called a hash partitioned global index. A hash algorithm allows for an even spread of index values.

18.3.6.2   **CREATE TABLE Partition Syntax**

The syntax diagrams listed in this section on Oracle Partitioning do not contain all available table creation partitioning syntax. There is simply too much detail to include in this book. Examples will suffice to get you started syntactically. Refer to Oracle documentation for more information.

Note: CREATE TABLE partition syntax is shown in Figures 18.13 to 18.17. These syntax diagrams are cumulative with respect to annotations. In other words, annotations present in Figure 18.13 may still apply to Figure 18.17 but may not be present in Figure 18.17 for the sake of avoiding diagrams being just too cluttered.

18.3.6.2.1   **CREATE TABLE Range Partition Syntax**

The following script creates a very simple range partition using a subquery from the SALES table:

```
CREATE TABLE SALESRANGE PARTITION BY RANGE(SALE_DATE)(
  PARTITION S2001 VALUES LESS THAN
(TO_DATE('2002-01-01','YYYY-MM-DD'))
, PARTITION S2002 VALUES LESS THAN
(TO_DATE('2003-01-01','YYYY-MM-DD'))
, PARTITION S2003 VALUES LESS THAN(MAXVALUE))
AS SELECT * FROM SALES;
```

We could also create a partition index where indexing is local to each partition, but this is a little advanced for this book.

```
CREATE INDEX LK_SALESRANGE_1 ON SALESRANGE
(SALE_DATE, CONTINENT_ID, COUNTRY_ID) LOCAL;
```

18.3.6.2.2   **CREATE TABLE List Partition Syntax**

The following script creates a simple list partition using a subquery from the SALES table:

Figure 18.13
*CREATE TABLE
Syntax for Range
Partitions.*

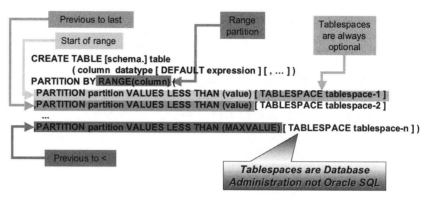

```
CREATE TABLE SALESLIST PARTITION BY LIST (CONTINENT_ID)(
    PARTITION EuropeAndAmerica VALUES (1,2,3,4)
   ,PARTITION EverywhereElse VALUES (5,6,7,8,9,10))
AS SELECT * FROM SALES;
```

Figure 18.14 displays the CREATE TABLE list partition index.

Figure 18.14
*CREATE TABLE
Syntax for List
Partitions.*

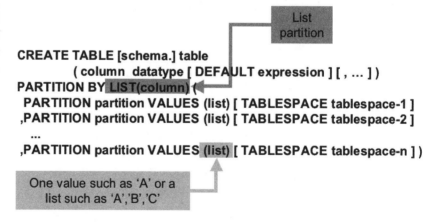

18.3.6.2.3   CREATE TABLE Hash Partition Syntax

Once again, another simple example except this time using a hash partition created as a subquery from the SALES table. (See Figure 18.15 for a diagram of the syntax.)

```
CREATE TABLE SALESHASH
PARTITION BY HASH (SALES_ID) PARTITIONS 10
```

```
AS SELECT * FROM SALES;
```

Figure 18.15
*CREATE TABLE
Syntax for Hash
Partitions.*

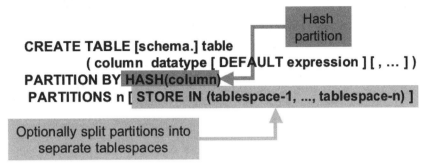

18.3.6.2.4   CREATE TABLE Range-Hash Partition Syntax

This time we have a simple example but of a range-hash partition or a set of hash subpartitions contained within each range partition, created as a subquery from the SALES table. (See Figure 18.16 for a diagram of the syntax.)

```
CREATE TABLE SALESRANGEHASH
PARTITION BY RANGE(SALE_DATE)
SUBPARTITION BY HASH(CONTINENT_ID)
(PARTITION S2001 VALUES LESS THAN
   (TO_DATE('2002-01-01','YYYY-MM-DD'))
 , PARTITION S2002 VALUES LESS THAN
        (TO_DATE('2003-01-01','YYYY-MM-DD'))
 , PARTITION S2003 VALUES LESS THAN(MAXVALUE))
AS SELECT * FROM SALES;
```

18.3.6.2.5   CREATE TABLE Range-List Partition Syntax

Finally, the following is an example of a range-list partition or a set of list subpartitions contained within each range partition, as with all the others, created as a subquery from the SALES table. (See Figure 18.17 for a diagram of the syntax.)

```
CREATE TABLE SALESRANGELIST
PARTITION BY RANGE(SALE_DATE) SUBPARTITION BY
LIST(CONTINENT_ID) (
   PARTITION S2001 VALUES LESS THAN (TO_DATE('2002-01-
01','YYYY-MM-DD'))
      (SUBPARTITION S2001EuropeAndAmerica VALUES (1,2,3,4)
```

```
CREATE TABLE [schema.] table
        ( column  datatype [ DEFAULT expression ] [ , ... ])
PARTITION BY RANGE(column1)
SUBPARTITION BY HASH(column2)
   SUBPARTITIONS n STORE IN (tablespace-1, ..., tablespace-n) (
   PARTITION partition VALUES LESS THAN (value) [ TABLESPACE tablespace-1 ]
  ,PARTITION partition VALUES LESS THAN (value) [ TABLESPACE tablespace-2 ]
   ...
  ,PARTITION partition VALUES LESS THAN (MAXVALUE) [ TABLESPACE tablespace-n ] ) )
```

```
    ,   SUBPARTITION S2001EverywhereElse VALUES (5,6,7,8,9,10))
    , PARTITION S2002 VALUES LESS THAN (TO_DATE('2003-01-
01','YYYY-MM-DD'))
       (SUBPARTITION S2002EuropeAndAmerica VALUES (1,2,3,4)
    ,   SUBPARTITION S2002EverywhereElse VALUES (5,6,7,8,9,10))
    , PARTITION S2003 VALUES LESS THAN(MAXVALUE)
       (SUBPARTITION S2003EuropeAndAmerica VALUES (1,2,3,4)
    ,   SUBPARTITION S2003EverywhereElse VALUES (5,6,7,8,9,10)))
AS SELECT * FROM SALES;
```

That more or less covers everything about creating tables using the
CREATE TABLE command. Now let's look at changing tables using the
ALTER TABLE command.

```
CREATE TABLE [schema.] table
        ( column  datatype [ DEFAULT expression ] [ , ... ])
PARTITION BY RANGE(column1)
SUBPARTITION BY LIST(column2) (
 PARTITION partition VALUES LESS THAN (value) [ TABLESPACE tablespace-1 ]
   SUBPARTITION subpartition-1-1 VALUES(list) [ TABLESPACE tablespace-1-1 ]
    ...
  ,SUBPARTITION subpartition-1-2 VALUES(list) [ TABLESPACE tablespace-1-2 ]
  ,SUBPARTITION subpartition-1-n VALUES(list) [ TABLESPACE tablespace-1-n ]
 ,PARTITION partition VALUES LESS THAN (value) [ TABLESPACE tablespace-2 ]
   SUBPARTITION subpartition-2-1 VALUES(list) [ TABLESPACE tablespace-1-1 ]
    ...
  ,SUBPARTITION subpartition-2-2 VALUES(list) [ TABLESPACE tablespace-1-2 ]
  ,SUBPARTITION subpartition-2-n VALUES(list) [ TABLESPACE tablespace-1-n ]
    ...
 ,PARTITION partition VALUES LESS THAN (MAXVALUE) [ TABLESPACE tablespace-n ]
   SUBPARTITION subpartition-n-1 VALUES(list) [ TABLESPACE tablespace-1-1 ]
    ...
  ,SUBPARTITION subpartition-n-2 VALUES(list) [ TABLESPACE tablespace-1-2 ]
  ,SUBPARTITION subpartition-n-n VALUES(list) [ TABLESPACE tablespace-1-n ])
```

18.4 Changing Table Structure

As a designer, you will discover that there are many reasons why the structure of a table must be changed after it is initially designed and created. For example, a table storing information on credit applications may contain a column that is no longer used because the application form has been changed. Occasionally, the datatype of a column was incorrectly specified in the original design or the column's name was misspelled.

Many attributes and properties of tables can be changed. We focus on these types of changes:

- **Table Changes**. The name of a table can be changed and a table can be moved. Moving a table is a database administration task because it is commonly used to relocate tables between different tablespaces.

- **Adding or Changing Columns**. A column's datatype, length, or name can be changed. You can change a column from nullable to not nullable as well.

- **Removing Columns**. Removing a column from a table can remove both or either of the column or its data from existing rows.

- **Rebuilding Tables**. An Oracle-supplied package in Oracle Database 9*i* allowed changes that previously required a great deal of effort. Changes such as reordering the columns in a table, adding columns between existing columns, and changing the primary key of a table can be done with this package.

Figure 18.18 is a general syntax diagram for the ALTER TABLE statement. Altering of constraints is covered in Chapter 20. Looking at the complexity of the syntax diagram in Figure 18.18 should tell you why the syntax is broken into small pieces for the CREATE TABLE command. In my mind, too much complexity at once simply creates confusion, so it's easier to break things into smaller, more manageable pieces.

Note: Constraints are covered in Chapter 20.

Figure 18.18
ALTER TABLE syntax.

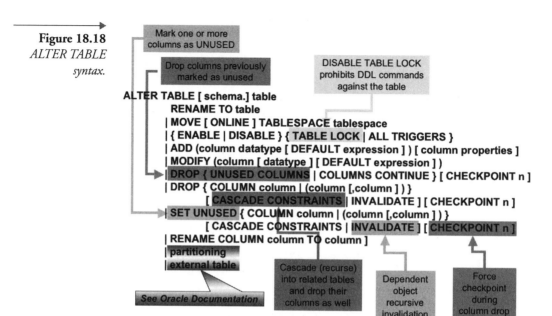

18.4.1 Adding, Modifying, and Removing Columns

First we create a new table using a subquery on some of the MUSIC schema tables. The following script creates a table named RELEASESIN2001. The table has five columns: CD, ARTIST, COUNTRY, SONG, and RELEASED.

```
CREATE TABLE RELEASESIN2001 (CD,ARTIST,COUNTRY,SONG,RELEASED)
AS SELECT CD.TITLE AS "CD", A.NAME AS "ARTIST"
, A.COUNTRY AS "COUNTRY", S.TITLE AS "SONG"
, CD.PRESSED_DATE AS RELEASED
FROM MUSICCD CD, CDTRACK T, ARTIST A, SONG S
WHERE CD.PRESSED_DATE BETWEEN '01-JAN-01' AND '31-DEC-01'
AND T.MUSICCD_ID = CD.MUSICCD_ID
AND S.SONG_ID = T.SONG_ID
AND A.ARTIST_ID = S.ARTIST_ID;
```

Now we need to examine the table we have just created. See the result in Figure 18.19.

```
SET LINESIZE 100
DESC RELEASESIN2001
```

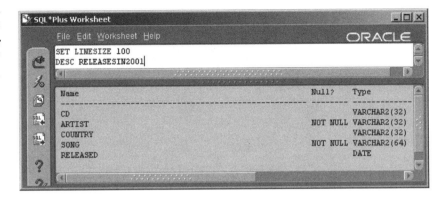

Figure 18.19
*Describing the
RELEASESIN2001
Table.*

Let's add a column to the RELEASESIN2001 table. This column will contain only the month part of the release date of the CD. See the result in Figure 18.20.

```
ALTER TABLE RELEASESIN2001
ADD(RELEASE_MONTH CHAR(10) NOT NULL);
```

The previous ALTER TABLE command produced an error. The RELEASE_MONTH column is non-nullable. When you create a new column in a table that already has rows, the column is created with null values in all existing rows. We tried to create a column that does not allow null values (because of the NOT NULL constraint, see Chapter 20). Because there are rows in the table, the ALTER TABLE statement in Figure 18.20 attempts to add a non-nullable column to a table while placing null values into that column for all existing rows; this causes the error.

There is, of course, another way to accomplish the task of adding a non-nullable column to a table. You first add the column, allowing null values. Then you populate the column with values. And finally, you change the column to NOT NULL.

We can accomplish all three steps using the following script:

```
ALTER TABLE RELEASESIN2001 ADD(RELEASE_MONTH CHAR(10));
UPDATE RELEASESIN2001 SET RELEASE_MONTH =
INITCAP(TO_CHAR(RELEASED,'MONTH'));
ALTER TABLE RELEASESIN2001
MODIFY(RELEASE_MONTH CHAR(10) NOT NULL);
```

Figure 18.20
*Cannot Add a
Non-nullable
Column to a
Nonempty Table.*

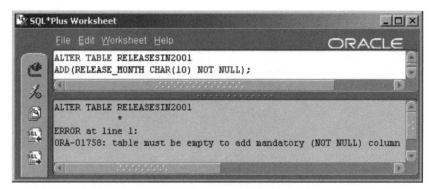

Note: The CHAR(10) datatype was used for the new RELEASE_MONTH column because the length of the value to be placed in this column is known, the longest value being "September." Using a VARCHAR2(10) datatype would be misleading. VARCHAR2 datatypes are intended for storing variable-length strings of up to 4,000 characters.

Look at the results, shown in Figure 18.21, by executing these commands. The SELECT DISTINCT statement simply retrieves a month of release for each individual CD.

```
SET WRAP OFF HEADING OFF;
DESC RELEASESIN2001;
SELECT DISTINCT CD||' was released in '
||RELEASE_MONTH "Month of Release"
FROM RELEASESIN2001;
```

We added a column to the RELEASESIN2001 table, and then we put some data into it and finally modified the column to be non-nullable. To remove the column added, type the ALTER TABLE command shown as follows. You can execute the DESC RELEASESIN2001; command again to make sure that the column RELEASE_MONTH has been dropped.

```
ALTER TABLE RELEASESIN2001 DROP (RELEASE_MONTH);
```

Take another look at the ALTER TABLE syntax diagram in Figure 18.18. Here are some points regarding column changes:

Figure 18.21
Add a Non-nullable Column to a Nonempty Table.

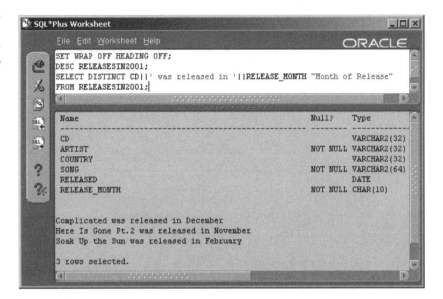

- Columns can be renamed within a table.

- Columns can be set as unused. Setting a column to unused marks the column and its data as being inaccessible from SQL. The data is not removed. This option is effective for extremely large tables. Removing a column from a table requires extensive physical restructuring and can be very time consuming.

- Unused columns can be dropped. At some stage, unused columns could occupy excessive physical space. The original motivation for setting the column unused rather than simply dropping it could be outweighed by a need for space. In addition, you can render columns inaccessible right away and then perform the time-consuming task of removing columns overnight or over the weekend when your users will not be disturbed.

Note: On a modern global scale, OLTP database downtime might be a rarity.

Opting to set columns as unused, as opposed to dropping them, avoids data restructuring. What is restructuring of data? Every row occupies physical space on a disk. This physical space equates to a row length for each row. This row length can be fixed or variable for each table, depending on column datatypes. Therefore, variable row lengths are assumed. Restructuring of data as a result of column length changes or column additions in tables requires that data will have to be moved. The performance implications of restructuring can be enormous.

18.4.2 Rebuilding a Table

It is possible to rebuild a table online using a package introduced in Oracle Database 9*i* called DBMS_REDEFINITION. Rebuilding a table online implies that the table and its rows can still be accessed during the rebuild of the table. In Oracle Database 8*i*, rebuilding a table would have required the following steps:

1. Restrict access to the first table.

2. Copy the first table and its rows into a second table using a CREATE TABLE AS subquery statement.

3. Make changes to the second table.

4. Drop the first table.

5. Re-create the first table from the altered second table or remove rows from the first table and insert from the second table.

6. Re-create all constraints, indexes, and object privileges that were dropped automatically when the first table was dropped.

7. Drop the second temporary table.

From Oracle Database 9*i*, you can now redefine tables online, as already stated, by executing procedures in the DBMS_REDEFINITION package as shown in the following steps:

1. Check to see if you can redefine the table:

    ```
    EXECUTE DBMS_REDEFINITION.CAN_REDEF_TABLE
    ('MUSIC','<original table>');
    ```

    This step must succeed in order to use the package. Certain table structures, such as tables containing object types, are not yet supported by the package.

2. Create a copy of the table with the new structure. Use any of the three methods (i.e., script, subquery, or tools) to create the table exactly as you want it to appear after the restructuring. This step creates an interim table.

3. Place the contents of the old table into the interim table:

```
EXECUTE DBMS_REDEFINITION.START_REDEF_TABLE
('MUSIC','<original table>','<interim table>',NULL);
```

4. Add constraints you want to the interim table, such as foreign keys, using the ALTER TABLE command. These will be carried over to the new, restructured table.

5. Remove the original table, rename the interim table, and clean up other intermediate structures used behind the scenes:

```
EXECUTE DBMS_REDEFINITION.FINISH_REDEF_TABLE
('MUSIC','<original table>','<interim table>');
```

Note: DBMS_REDEFINITION works for purely relational tables only, not object tables or relational tables containing object columns. Additionally, DBMS_REDEFINITION requires special privileges.

Explicit details and examples are not given for the DBMS_REDEFINITION package, because it is not precisely Oracle SQL and perhaps a little beyond the scope of this book.

18.4.3 Renaming a Table

Take another quick peek at the ALTER TABLE syntax diagram in Figure 18.18. Can you see the RENAME TABLE section? Let's rename the table called RELEASESIN2001 that we created in the previous section.

```
ALTER TABLE RELEASESIN2001 RENAME TO NEW_RELEASES_FOR_2001;
```

Using the following commands, you can see that the table RELEASESIN2001 no longer exists and has been renamed to NEW_RELEASES_FOR_2001. See the result in Figure 18.22. The first DESC command produced an error.

```
DESC RELEASEIN2001
DESC NEW_RELEASES_FOR_2001
```

That covers changing table structure. Next we examine dropping and truncating tables.

Figure 18.22
The Table
RELEASESIN2001
Renamed to
NEW_RELEASES
_IN_2001.

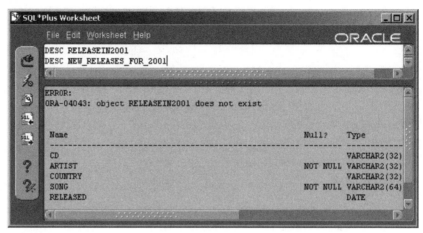

18.5   Dropping a Table

Dropping a table is a very simple command, as shown in the DROP table command that follows. Figure 18.23 shows syntax for the DROP TABLE command.

```
DROP TABLE NEW_RELEASES_FOR_2001;
```

When you drop a table, the following items are automatically dropped along with the table:

- Indexes on the table.

- Constraints on the table, including any primary key and foreign key constraints.

- Object privileges granted on the table (Chapter 23 contains information about object privileges and security in general.)

When you drop a table, these items are not dropped, but are marked invalid and must be corrected later:

- Views containing the table.

- Foreign keys in other tables referencing the dropped table.

- Synonyms referencing the table (see Chapter 22).

- All PL/SQL named procedures, functions, and triggers that reference the dropped table (see Chapter 24).

Figure 18.23
DROP TABLE
Command Syntax.

Sometimes DBAs will need to clear a table completely. Using the TRUNCATE command can be a better option than dropping and re-creating the same table. Dropping and re-creating a table implies using the DROP TABLE and CREATE TABLE commands. Using the TRUNCATE command will prevent you from having to re-create all indexes and constraints on the table.

18.5.1 Truncating Instead of Dropping Tables

Sometimes you need to remove all the rows in a table without disturbing the table's structure. For example, you may have a table that is loaded with rows from an external file of billing data at the beginning of each month's billing cycle. The rows from last month's billing cycle must be removed before inserting this month's data.

There are three ways to remove all the rows in a table: DELETE, TRUNCATE, or DROP TABLE plus CREATE TABLE. The TRUNCATE command has the same effect as deleting all the rows in a table except that it preserves table structure, unlike the DROP TABLE command. For large tables, the DELETE command is too slow. Figure 18.24 shows the syntax of the TRUNCATE command.

So let's compare between the TRUNCATE and DELETE commands when completely clearing a table's rows. There are several differences between using the TRUNCATE command or the DELETE command to remove all rows in a table. These differences make the TRUNCATE command much faster but also irreversible.

- TRUNCATE does not produce rollback entries. This means that you cannot undo from a TRUNCATE command using the ROLLBACK command. A DELETE command can be undone using rollback.

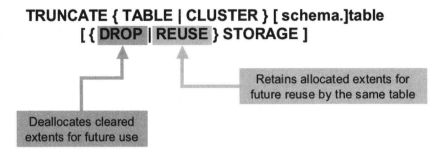

Figure 18.24
TRUNCATE
Command Syntax.

- You cannot use a WHERE clause filter with a TRUNCATE command like you can with a DELETE command. Thus TRUNCATE will always delete all rows from a table.

You can use the TRUNCATE command to remove all rows from the table NEW_RELEASES_FOR_2001 as shown following:

```
TRUNCATE TABLE NEW_RELEASES_FOR_2001;
```

Note: TRUNCATE is a DDL command. All DDL commands commit changes automatically, instantly upon completion. TRUNCATE is not reversible!

Now let's examine adding comments to tables.

18.6 Adding Comments to Tables

Comments can also be called remarks. As their name implies, comments are informational text added to either a script or a schema object. Comments can be included in both SQL and PL/SQL scripts and can be attached to schema objects.

18.6.1 Adding Comments to Schema Objects

See the syntax diagram in Figure 18.25 for details on adding comments to database schema objects, such as tables and table columns.

Let's add some brief comments to some of the tables in the MUSIC schema.

Figure 18.25
Adding Comments to Database Schema Objects.

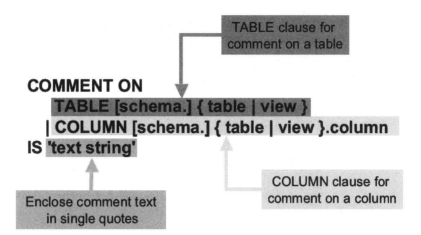

```
COMMENT ON TABLE ARTIST IS 'Artists';
COMMENT ON TABLE CDTRACK IS 'Tracks';
COMMENT ON TABLE INSTRUMENTATION
IS 'Guest Instruments Played';
COMMENT ON TABLE INSTRUMENT IS 'Musical Instruments';
COMMENT ON TABLE MUSICCD IS 'Audio Compact Disks';
COMMENT ON TABLE SONG IS 'Songs';
COMMENT ON TABLE GUESTAPPEARANCE IS 'Guest Artists';
COMMENT ON TABLE STUDIOTIME IS 'Studio Recording Time';
```

Comments added to tables can be viewed by querying the USER_TAB_COMMENTS metadata view. These commands will show the comments added. Figure 18.26 shows the results.

```
COLUMN TABLE_NAME FORMAT A32 HEADING "Table";
COLUMN COMMENTS FORMAT A32 HEADING "Comments";
SELECT TABLE_NAME, COMMENTS FROM USER_TAB_COMMENTS
WHERE COMMENTS IS NOT NULL;
```

Now we add some comments to the columns in a single table. Let's use the ARTIST table.

```
COMMENT ON COLUMN ARTIST.ARTIST_ID
IS 'Artist unique identifier (internally generated)';
COMMENT ON COLUMN ARTIST.NAME IS 'The Artist';
COMMENT ON COLUMN ARTIST.STREET IS 'Street address';
```

Figure 18.26
*Adding Comments
to all of the
MUSIC Schema
Tables.*

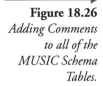

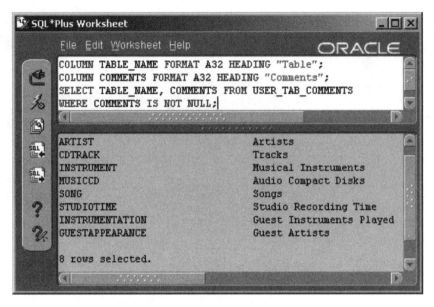

```
COMMENT ON COLUMN ARTIST.POBOX IS 'Post office box number';
COMMENT ON COLUMN ARTIST.CITY IS 'City';
COMMENT ON COLUMN ARTIST.STATE_PROVINCE IS 'State';
COMMENT ON COLUMN ARTIST.COUNTRY IS 'Country';
COMMENT ON COLUMN ARTIST.ZIP IS 'Zip code';
COMMENT ON COLUMN ARTIST.EMAIL IS 'Electronic mail address';
COMMENT ON COLUMN ARTIST.INSTRUMENTS
IS 'Artist instruments collection';
```

Column comments can be viewed through the USER_COL_COMMENTS metadata dictionary view. The following query shows the comments added to some ARTIST table columns. See the result in Figure 18.27.

```
COLUMN TABLE_NAME FORMAT A16 HEADING "Table";
COLUMN COLUMN_NAME FORMAT A16 HEADING "Column";
COLUMN COMMENTS FORMAT A48 HEADING "Comments";
SELECT TABLE_NAME, COLUMN_NAME, COMMENTS
FROM USER_COL_COMMENTS WHERE TABLE_NAME='ARTIST';
```

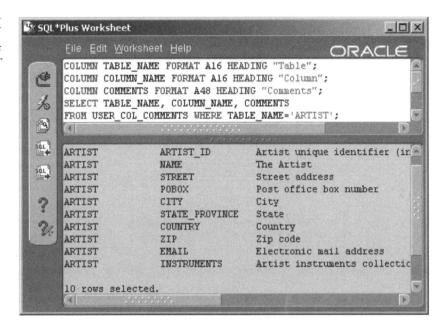

Figure 18.27
*Adding Comments
to the ARTIST
Table.*

To remove a comment, you simply change the comment to a null-valued string. Remove the comment from the CDTRACK table by typing and executing the following command:

```
COMMENT ON TABLE CDTRACK IS '';
```

18.6.2 Scripting and SQL Code Comments

There are several methods for adding comments to a script, an SQL command, or a PL/SQL command. A script is a list of multiple SQL or PL/SQL commands and is usually stored in a file:

- **Multiple-Line Comments**. Create multiple-line comments by enclosing a commented area between /* and */ character strings. This is useful for longer documentation, such as listing the creator of a script, the date it was created, its purpose, and so on.

- **Inline Comments**. Precede inline comments with two consecutive hyphen marks (--). This method marks everything found after the double hyphens on the same line as a comment. You can comment an entire line by placing the hyphens at the beginning of the line. You can also add a comment to the end of a line of code by placing the hyphens after all executable code.

- **Single-Line Comments**. Precede a line with the REM or REMARK keyword to mark that line as a comment.

The following query demonstrates all three types of comments. See the result in Figure 18.28.

```
REM     This query looks for Artists with
REM     a letter "a" in their names.
SELECT
/* Ignore this line
and this line
and this line too
*/
NAME
--this is the FROM clause
FROM ARTIST
WHERE NAME LIKE '%a%' --and this is the WHERE clause
;
```

In a color graphic, the comments would be highlighted in red within SQL*Plus Worksheet. This makes them much easier to see. I have highlighted commented sections by boxing them, as shown in Figure 18.28.

The penultimate section in this chapter on tables will examine the recycle bin, which is newly introduced in Oracle Database 10*g*.

18.7 ⑩ **The Recycle Bin**

Oracle Database 10*g* introduces a recycle bin. This feature is certainly useful from the perspective of database administration, but it could cause problems with space and perhaps performance if the recycle bin is not regularly monitored and cleared. There are several changes to various DDL commands associated with the recycle bin as listed below. The syntax diagram in Figure 18.29 shows generally applicable recycle bin syntax.

- The DROP TABLE command now requires a PURGE option if an object is not to be retained in the recycle bin.

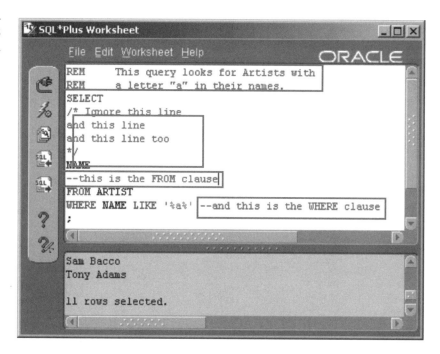

Figure 18.28
*Commenting SQL
Code.*

- The new PURGE command is required to allow clearing the recycle bin.

- The Oracle Database 10*g* SQL Reference Manual states that the FLASHBACK TABLE command is used to recover a table from the recycle bin.

This chapter concludes with a short section on database metadata as directly applicable to this chapter.

18.8 **Metadata Views**

This section lists metadata views allowing access into the structural details of tables. Chapter 19 describes the basis and detail of Oracle Database metadata views.

- **USER_TABLES**. Table structural definitions.

- **USER_TAB_COLS** and **USER_TAB_COLUMNS**. Table column definitions where USER_TAB_COLS includes hidden columns.

Figure 18.29
*Syntax for the
Recycle Bin.*

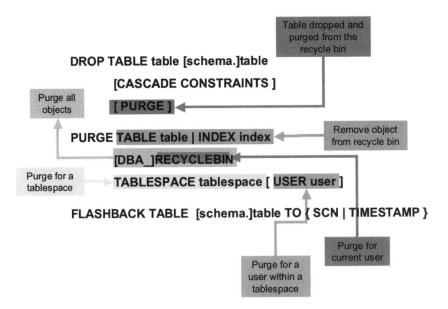

- **USER_TAB_COMMENTS** and **USER_COL_COMMENTS**. Comments on table columns.

- **USER_UNUSED_COL_TABS**. This view shows columns in tables marked as SET UNUSED and not physically dropped from tables.

- (10*g*) **DBA_RECYCLEBIN** and **USER_RECYCLEBIN**. These two metadata views represent all recycle bins for all users and the specific connected user recycle bin. The RECYCLEBIN view is often referred to and is simply a synonym for the USER_RECYCLEBIN view. See Chapter 22 for details on synonyms.

- **USER_OBJECT_TABLES**. Object type table structures.

- **USER_TAB_PARTITIONS** and **USER_TAB_SUBPARTITIONS**. Table partition and subpartition structures.

- **USER_PART_TABLES**. Table partitioning details of tables at the partition rather than the table level, as is the case for the USER_TAB_PARTITIONS and USER_TAB_SUBPARTITIONS views.

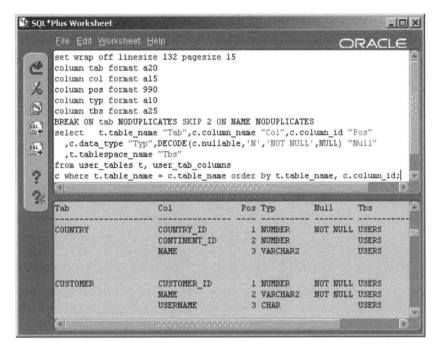

Figure 18.30
Querying
USER_TABLES
and
USER_TAB_COL
UMNS.

The script executed in Figure 18.30 matches all tables and table columns for the currently logged-in user. This gives an example of the power of metadata views. The script is included in Appendix B.

That covers all we want to cover about tables at present. Chapter 20 covers constraints and partially returns to the subject of tables. The next chapter looks at views.

18.9 Endnotes

1. Oracle Performance Tuning for 9*i* and 10*g* (ISBN: 1-55558-305-9)

19

Views

In this chapter:

- What is a view?
- What types of views are available?
- How do we use views?
- What are metadata views?

There are various examples of views in other chapters. This chapter describes views in detail. A view is an overlay onto one or more other data sources. A data source can be a table, view, or multiples thereof.

19.1 What Is a View?

Imagine that you are working in an insurance company, where part of your job duties are to help users who have trouble writing queries for reports. The users have had basic training in writing SQL queries, but they often get stuck when they must join many tables or use subqueries. If you could set up the join or subquery ahead of time, then the users would have no trouble adding to it to refine their report requirements. This is one of the best reasons to create a view.

Note: This approach can, however, be bad for performance because the entire query in the view will always be executed, whatever filtering is placed on a query against a view.[1]

A *view* is a query that is stored in the database and executed to create a virtual table. A view is given a name, is owned by a schema, and is executed whenever a query or other SQL command uses the view. The tables referenced in the view's query are called *base tables*.

Views do not contain any data of their own, and therefore do not require storage. Views belong to a schema, and you can grant privileges such as SELECT, INSERT, UPDATE, and DELETE on views, even if the user does not have any privileges on the base table(s) used in the view.

Views are most often used for security purposes and as an aid to querying the database; however, some views can be used to insert, update, and delete data in the underlying table.

19.2   Types and Uses of Views

Here are some of the more common reasons for creating a view:

- **Security**. Create a view with a limited subset of the rows and/or columns in a table or tables and give the user permission to use the view, but not the base tables.

- **Simplicity**. Create a view that combines tables that have complex relationships so users writing queries do not need to understand the relationships.

- **Complex Joins**. Sometimes queries cannot be done without great difficulty unless you create a view in something like a temporary table first. For example, you can create a view with a GROUP BY clause that summarizes data. You can join that summary data with other tables only by using a view.

- **Materialized Views**. This is not a view as such because the data in the view is physically stored in the materialized view, thus the term *materialized*. Materialized views are a little too specialized for this book.

Regardless of why a view is created, it falls into one of three basic categories or types of views:

- **Simple View**. A simple view contains a query on a single table. For example, a view that lists the names, addresses, and zip codes of all artists in the USA is a simple view because only the ARTIST table is queried in the view. Simple views can be used to narrow the focus or visible data window of a specific user from the entire table to a subset of the rows or a subset of the columns. The best explanation for this type of view is security where, for instance, different customers sharing the same database can only view their own data. With a few restrictions (examined later in this chapter), you can update the table on which the view is built by updating the view. You can also insert and delete rows in the base table through the view.

- **Constraint View.** A constraint view can be used to insert a new row into the underlying table as long as the row would be returned by the query, or the row exists for the view. For example, if the view only looks at ARTIST rows in the USA, you could not insert an ARTIST row where the artist is in France. The same rule applies to rows that are updated via the constraint view. Most constraint views are based on simple views, although certain complex views can also be used as constraint views. Constraint views are most often used as an easy way to enforce business rules in applications without the application developer doing any extra coding.

Note: This approach applies views to ease of application coding rather than security. Views are possibly more applicable in client-server environments. Scalability issues may arise for large, very busy OLTP databases.

- **Complex View.** A complex view contains a query on more than one table. This type of view allows you to wrap complexities inside the view's query so they are hidden from the user or application developer. Complex views are most often used for simplifying end-user reporting by providing a table-like structure for users to query. For example, you could create a view that displays the CD title, artist name, and song title (which are found in three different tables). Complex views usually cannot be used to insert, update, or delete rows from the underlying tables.

19.3 CREATE VIEW Syntax

Figure 19.1 shows the syntax of the CREATE VIEW statement. The same syntax applies to all types of views.

The next three sections look at how to create each of the three types of views: simple, constraint, and complex.

Figure 19.1
*CREATE VIEW
Syntax Is Fairly
Simple.*

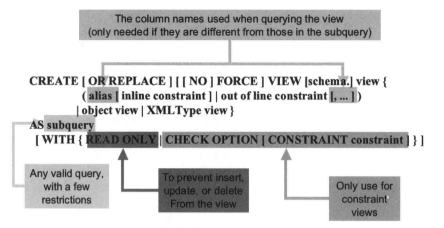

19.3.1   Creating Simple Views

A simple view is the easiest type of view to create.

```
CREATE VIEW USARTISTS AS
SELECT ARTIST_ID, NAME, CITY, STATE_PROVINCE, ZIP
FROM ARTIST WHERE COUNTRY = 'USA';
```

The view we have just created can be queried as if it were a table. When you execute a query on a view, the entire query contained within the view definition is executed to retrieve the columns and rows of the subquery, Then your query is applied to the view and the final results are displayed. Query the view by executing these format commands and query. Figure 19.2 shows the result.

```
COLUMN NAME FORMAT A20
COLUMN CITY FORMAT A15
COLUMN STATE_PROVINCE FORMAT A10
SELECT * FROM USARTISTS;
```

You can use a view in a join as if it were another table. For example, you can list all U.S. artist names and their song titles with this query:

```
SELECT NAME, TITLE FROM USARTISTS NATURAL JOIN SONG
ORDER BY 1,2;
```

Figure 19.2
Querying a View Is Just Like Querying a Table.

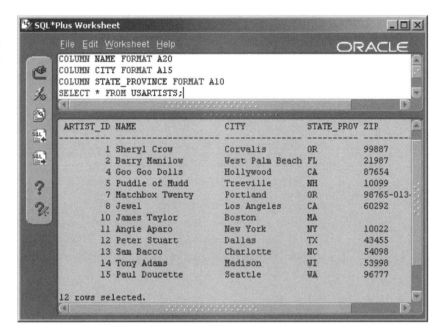

Now let's take the simple view and add a constraint clause. The result will be a constraint view.

19.3.2 Creating Constraint Views

A simple view usually allows you to update data in the underlying table through the view. You will examine this capability later in this chapter. There is a problem that sometimes crops up when using views to insert or update data: You can create a record that does not fit the view's query and therefore does not appear in the view. For example, imagine that you use the USARTISTS view to update the country from USA to Canada for one of the artists. You want to check the results, but querying the view no longer displays the record. It is as if the record disappeared after you updated it. Obviously, the record is in the table and simply is not displayed in the view. However, this fact may not be obvious to other users who are not familiar with the query that is used by the view.

To prevent users from updating or inserting records not fitting within the view, you create a constraint view. Another good reason to use a constraint view is that it provides a form of security. Views are frequently used to limit a user's access to certain rows and columns within the base table. The user should not be able to update rows not appearing in the view, but without the constraint clause, this could happen and could be a violation of your business rules.

Create a constraint view that looks like the simple view, except it includes the WITH CHECK OPTION clause, by running the following command:

```
CREATE VIEW CONSTRAINT_USARTISTS AS
SELECT ARTIST_ID, NAME, CITY, STATE_PROVINCE, ZIP, COUNTRY
FROM ARTIST WHERE COUNTRY = 'USA'
WITH CHECK OPTION CONSTRAINT AMERICANARTIST;
```

You can leave out the "CONSTRAINT AMERICANARTIST" portion of the constraint clause. If you omit it, Oracle Database 10*g* will assign a system-generated name for the constraint. Next we insert a row for a Mexican artist:

```
INSERT INTO CONSTRAINT_USARTISTS VALUES
(ARTIST_ID_SEQ.NEXTVAL, 'Chrystal Perez',
'Mexico City', NULL, NULL, 'Mexico');
```

Figure 19.3 shows the result. The error message tells you that the row to be inserted has failed to comply with the WHERE clause of the view.

You would get the same error if you tried to update one of the rows in the view with a country other than USA.

Now, let's look at some more interesting things you can do using complex views.

19.3.3   Creating Complex Views

Complex views have more than one base table. Complex views include a wide variety of queries. Two common ones are views with joins and views with inline subqueries.

19.3.3.1   Views with Joins

Let's dive right in by creating a complex view that displays artist guest appearances and the instrument they played.

```
CREATE VIEW INSTRUMENTS(ARTIST_NAME, INSTRUMENT) AS
```

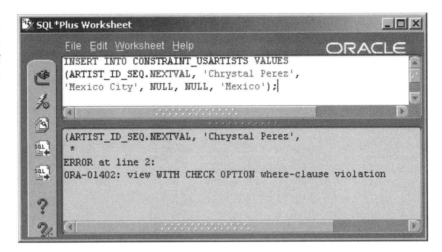

```
SELECT A.NAME, I.NAME
FROM ARTIST A JOIN INSTRUMENTATION IA
ON (IA.GUESTARTIST_ID = A.ARTIST_ID)
  JOIN INSTRUMENT I ON (IA.INSTRUMENT_ID = I.INSTRUMENT_ID);
```

Now let's look at the rows returned from the view issuing the following query.

```
SELECT * FROM INSTRUMENTS;
```

The view joins three tables and displays two columns of information. Notice the list of columns just after the view name. This is needed for the view because the two columns in the SELECT clause happen to have the same name. By listing different names for each of the two columns, the view can be created.

Here is a view that summarizes an artist's billing for studio time.

```
CREATE VIEW ARTIST_MONTHLY_STATEMENT AS
SELECT ARTIST_ID, NAME
, TO_CHAR(DUE_DATE,'MON/YY') BILLING_MONTH
, SUM(AMOUNT_CHARGED) DUE, SUM(AMOUNT_PAID) PAID
, SUM(AMOUNT_CHARGED) - SUM(AMOUNT_PAID) BALANCE
FROM ARTIST NATURAL JOIN STUDIOTIME
GROUP BY ARTIST_ID, NAME, TO_CHAR(DUE_DATE,'MON/YY');
```

This view shows how you can use grouping and functions in a view. In addition, notice that column aliases are used as a way to give the columns more appropriate names rather than using a column list in front of the query. Expressions, such as the columns with functions or group functions on them, must be given a valid name when the view is created.

Imagine that you need to know which artists have balances over $500 for any month after 2000. The following query simplifies the work required by selecting from a view:

```
SELECT NAME, BALANCE, BILLING_MONTH
FROM ARTIST_MONTHLY_STATEMENT
WHERE BALANCE > 500
AND TO_DATE(BILLING_MONTH, 'MON/YY') > '31-DEC-2000'
ORDER BY BALANCE DESC;
```

Figure 19.4 shows the result of this query. The BILLING_MONTH column is converted to a date in the WHERE clause. This is needed because it was converted to a character field in the view. If you did not convert it to a date, it would be compared as a character field (alphabetically) when evaluating the WHERE clause.

19.3.3.2   Inline Subquery Views

Another example of a complex view is one that contains a subquery. Subqueries can be used in the SELECT, FROM, and WHERE clauses of a query. A view based on a query with a subquery in any of these SQL command clause locations is valid.

```
CREATE VIEW CD_SONGS AS
SELECT M.MUSICCD_ID, M.TITLE, T.TRACK_SEQ_NO,
(SELECT TITLE FROM SONG S
  WHERE T.SONG_ID = S.SONG_ID) SONG_TITLE
FROM MUSICCD M JOIN CDTRACK T
ON (M.MUSICCD_ID = T.MUSICCD_ID);
```

The following script queries the view. Figure 19.5 shows the result.

```
COLUMN TITLE FORMAT A25
COLUMN SONG_TITLE FORMAT A40
SELECT TITLE, TRACK_SEQ_NO, SONG_TITLE FROM CD_SONGS
```

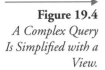

Figure 19.4

A Complex Query Is Simplified with a View.

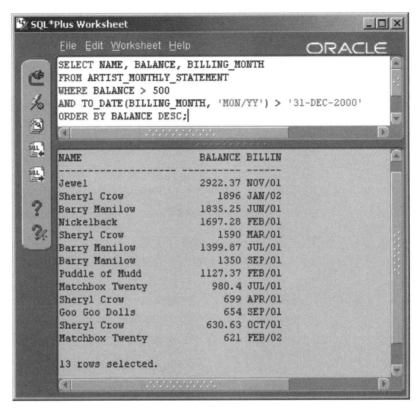

```
SELECT NAME, BALANCE, BILLING_MONTH
FROM ARTIST_MONTHLY_STATEMENT
WHERE BALANCE > 500
AND TO_DATE(BILLING_MONTH, 'MON/YY') > '31-DEC-2000'
ORDER BY BALANCE DESC;
```

```
NAME                    BALANCE BILLIN
-------------------- ----------- ------
Jewel                    2922.37 NOV/01
Sheryl Crow                 1896 JAN/02
Barry Manilow            1835.25 JUN/01
Nickelback               1697.28 FEB/01
Sheryl Crow                 1590 MAR/01
Barry Manilow            1399.87 JUL/01
Barry Manilow               1350 SEP/01
Puddle of Mudd           1127.37 FEB/01
Matchbox Twenty            980.4 JUL/01
Sheryl Crow                  699 APR/01
Goo Goo Dolls                654 SEP/01
Sheryl Crow               630.63 OCT/01
Matchbox Twenty              621 FEB/02

13 rows selected.
```

```
WHERE TITLE='Soak Up the Sun' ORDER BY 1,2;
```

19.4 Changing and Dropping Views

Syntax for changing and dropping views is as shown in Figure 19.6. Note that nearly all syntax for the ALTER VIEW command applies to constraints. Constraints are covered in Chapter 20.

What happens if you drop a table that is used in a view? The view becomes marked invalid and must be repaired.

Sometimes you may have a new requirement from users that calls for a change in a view. Views are much easier to change than tables because they are generally nothing more than a stored query. Revise the stored query, and you have revised the view!

To change a view, you revise the query and use the OR REPLACE option in the CREATE VIEW command, as in CREATE OR REPLACE VIEW. This assumes, of course, that constraint changes are not required.

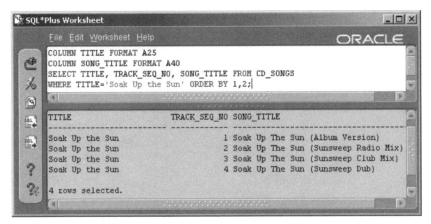

The next view combines the SONG, CDTRACK, and MUSICCD tables to show the title of the CD along with details about each song on the CD.

```
CREATE VIEW CD_DETAILS AS
SELECT CD.TITLE CDTITLE, CD.PRESSED_DATE
, CT.TRACK_SEQ_NO ,S.TITLE SONGTITLE, A.NAME
, S.PLAYING_TIME
FROM MUSICCD CD, CDTRACK CT, SONG S, ARTIST A
WHERE CD.MUSICCD_ID = CT.MUSICCD_ID
AND CT.SONG_ID = S.SONG_ID
AND S.ARTIST_ID = A.ARTIST_ID
ORDER BY 1, 3;
```

This view has column aliases for the two TITLE columns (one in the MUSICCD table and the other in the SONG table); it has an ORDER BY clause; and it uses Oracle's proprietary syntax for the join.

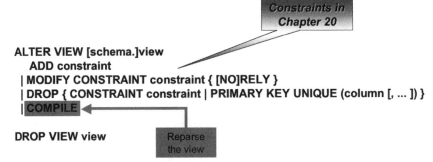

Imagine that the users who wanted this view for reporting asked you to add the playing time of the CD into the view. Revise the view by making changes requested to the original CREATE VIEW command and using CREATE OR REPLACE instead of CREATE. The following script highlights changes:

```
CREATE OR REPLACE VIEW CD_DETAILS AS
SELECT CD.TITLE CDTITLE, CD.PRESSED_DATE
, CD.PLAYING_TIME CD_TIME, CT.TRACK_SEQ_NO
, S.TITLE SONGTITLE, A.NAME, S.PLAYING_TIME
FROM MUSICCD CD, CDTRACK CT, SONG S, ARTIST A
WHERE CD.MUSICCD_ID = CT.MUSICCD_ID
AND CT.SONG_ID = S.SONG_ID
AND S.ARTIST_ID = A.ARTIST_ID
ORDER BY 1, 3;
```

Note: You can create a brand-new view using CREATE OR REPLACE VIEW instead of CREATE VIEW.

To drop a view, simply use the DROP VIEW command. The CD_DETAILS view can be dropped executing the following command:

```
DROP VIEW CD_DETAILS;
```

Dropping a view does not affect the base table or tables referenced by the view.

19.5 Working with Views

Most views are used to query the base tables on which they are built. Some views are used to insert, update, and delete data in the base tables. The next sections show you how to query views and how to make changes to data using views. Following this section, we deal with Oracle Database metadata data dictionary views.

19.5.1 Querying a View

A query on a view looks just like a query on a table. Behind the scenes, however, the Oracle Database 10g Optimizer merges the query that defines

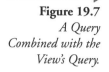

Figure 19.7
A Query Combined with the View's Query.

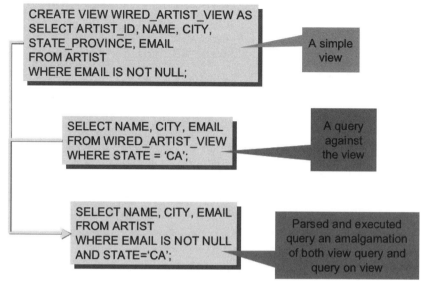

the view with the query that uses the view, into a single query. This query is parsed and stored in the shared SQL memory. Then the query is executed and the data retrieved. Figure 19.7 illustrates this activity.

Let's try some examples. Create the following view joining three tables to list a song and the artist, including any artists making guest appearances.

```
CREATE VIEW ALLSONGS AS
SELECT S.TITLE, A1.NAME ARTIST, GA.GUESTARTIST_ID
FROM SONG S JOIN ARTIST A1
ON (S.ARTIST_ID = A1.ARTIST_ID)
LEFT OUTER JOIN GUESTAPPEARANCE GA
ON (S.SONG_ID = GA.SONG_ID);
```

We would like to see the name of the artist making a guest appearance. The following query joins the view with the ARTIST table, which would become a very complex query without the view. The complexity is simply passed on to Oracle Database, potentially hurting performance in larger, busier environments. Figure 19.8 shows part of the result.

```
SELECT V.ARTIST, V.TITLE, A.NAME GUEST
FROM ALLSONGS V LEFT OUTER JOIN ARTIST A
ON (V.GUESTARTIST_ID = A.ARTIST_ID)
ORDER BY ARTIST;
```

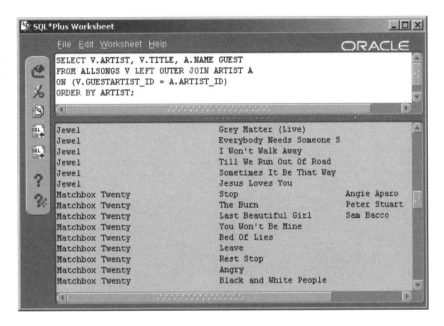

Figure 19.8
*Joining Four Tables
Is Easy When Three
Are Joined in a
View.*

19.5.2   Views and DML Commands

Although views have no data of their own, it is possible in certain cases to use views to modify data in the base table that is queried by the view. This can be very useful for tables for which the user does not have permission to access the base table but has access to a view.

Oracle Database has rules that it tests against any view to determine whether it is inherently updatable. An inherently updatable view is one in which some or all of the view's columns pass the test and can be used to update the base table. Some of the rules for simple views include the following:

- The view must not be created with the WITH READ ONLY clause.

- The view cannot contain GROUP BY, group functions, ORDER BY, or DISTINCT.

- The view cannot contain a subquery in the SELECT clause.

- The view must include the primary key and all NOT NULL columns, unless there are provisions (such as default values or a trigger) that plug values into the NOT NULL columns.

The data dictionary table USER_UPDATABLE_COLUMNS lists each view and its columns, specifying whether the column can be referenced when updating, inserting, or deleting through the view. Execute this query to see which views are updatable, including their respective changeable columns. The query is shown in Figure 19.9, including the page size altered to show the CONSTRAINT_USARTISTS view and headings in the same image.

```
COLUMN COLUMN_NAME FORMAT A20
SELECT TABLE_NAME, COLUMN_NAME, UPDATABLE, INSERTABLE
, DELETABLE
FROM USER_UPDATABLE_COLUMNS U
WHERE EXISTS (SELECT VIEW_NAME FROM USER_VIEWS V
              WHERE U.TABLE_NAME = V.VIEW_NAME)
ORDER BY 1, 2;
```

Note: The complete syntax of the INSERT, UPDATE, and DELETE commands can be found in Chapter 15. The same syntax applies to both views and tables.

Figure 19.9
The CONSTRAINT_ USARTISTS View Can Be Updated, Inserted into, and Deleted from.

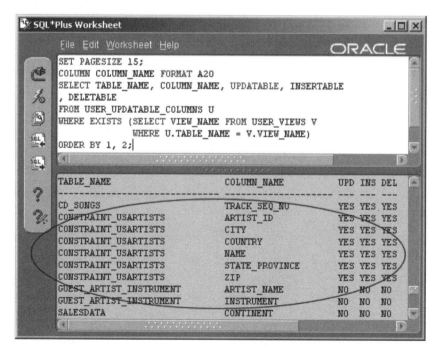

Now let's continue and perform some inserts, updates, and deletes using the views USARTISTS and CONSTRAINT_USARTISTS created earlier in the chapter. Let's say you have a new artist who will be using your studio to record her latest song. The following command will insert a row into the ARTIST table using the CONSTRAINT_USARTISTS view:

```
INSERT INTO CONSTRAINT_USARTISTS VALUES
(ARTIST_ID_SEQ.NEXTVAL, 'Judy Madrid', 'Madison'
, 'WI','53887', 'USA');
```

When inserting or updating rows using a constraint view, like the CONSTRAINT_USARTISTS view, the new or modified row must still fit within the view. In this case, because the WHERE clause of the view is WHERE COUNTRY='USA', that means the row's COUNTRY column must be USA.

Here is another important point about inserting data with a view: You can only insert values into the columns listed in the view. All other columns will be NULL or assigned a default value. In this example, the following columns will be NULL in the newly inserted row: STREET, POBOX, EMAIL, and INSTRUMENTS.

Now try updating the row just inserted using the USARTISTS view:

```
UPDATE USARTISTS SET ZIP = '53200'
WHERE NAME = 'Judy Madrid';
```

Finally, delete the row using the CONSTRAINT_USARTISTS view:

```
DELETE FROM CONSTRAINT_USARTISTS
WHERE NAME = 'Judy Madrid';
```

Views that have columns made up of functions or other expressions can still be used to modify the base table. This view can illustrate that point:

```
CREATE OR REPLACE VIEW SONG_VIEW AS
SELECT SONG_ID, ARTIST_ID, TITLE, RECORDING_DATE
, SUBSTR(PLAYING_TIME,1,1) MINUTES
, SUBSTR(PLAYING_TIME,3) SECONDS
FROM SONG;
```

The last two columns break up the PLAYING_TIME column into minutes and seconds. If you try to insert a new row using those last two columns, an error will be returned (ORA-01733: virtual column not allowed here). Nonetheless, you can still use the other columns to insert a row as in the following script:

```
INSERT INTO SONG_VIEW (SONG_ID, ARTIST_ID, TITLE
, RECORDING_DATE)
VALUES (SONG_ID_SEQ.NEXTVAL,
(SELECT ARTIST_ID FROM ARTIST WHERE NAME='Jewel')
, 'Happy Birthday','15-JUL-02');
```

Notice that a list of columns was included in the INSERT command to specify which of the view's columns to use in the insert.

Many simple views are capable of being used to modify data in the base table. Sometimes, this is not the intent of the view. To ensure that the view is never used for updating, you can create it with the WITH READ ONLY clause as in the following example:

```
CREATE OR REPLACE VIEW OLDMUSIC_VIEW AS
SELECT MUSICCD_ID, TITLE CDNAME
,  PRESSED_DATE, PLAYING_TIME
FROM MUSICCD
WHERE PRESSED_DATE < '01-JUL-01'
WITH READ ONLY;
```

Simple views and simple constraint views are really not too much different from inserting into the base table itself, simply having more limitations.

19.5.2.1　DML and Views with Joins

Modifying data through a view that joins two tables is tricky. In addition to all the rules that Oracle Database 10*g* imposes on simple views, there are still more rules for views with joins. The most important ones to know are as follows:

- All the rules for simple views.

- The primary key column(s) must be included for one of the tables.

■ If there is no primary key, all the columns of a unique index on one of the tables must be included.

The next view is an example of an updatable join view:

```
CREATE OR REPLACE VIEW STUDIOARTISTS AS
SELECT S.STUDIOTIME_ID, A.NAME, S.ARTIST_ID
, S.SESSION_DATE, MINUTES_USED, AMOUNT_CHARGED
FROM STUDIOTIME S JOIN ARTIST A
ON (A.ARTIST_ID = S.ARTIST_ID);
```

The columns from the STUDIOTIME table are updatable. The following command will insert a new row:

```
INSERT INTO STUDIOARTISTS (STUDIOTIME_ID, ARTIST_ID
, SESSION_DATE, MINUTES_USED)
VALUES (STUDIOTIME_ID_SEQ.NEXTVAL
, (SELECT ARTIST_ID FROM ARTIST
   WHERE NAME = 'Barry Manilow'), '15-MAY-02', 180);
```

The view can be updated with a script such as this one:

```
UPDATE STUDIOARTISTS SET AMOUNT_CHARGED =
MINUTES_USED*6
WHERE AMOUNT_CHARGED IS NULL;
```

And finally, delete using the view:

```
DELETE FROM STUDIOARTISTS WHERE MINUTES_USED=180;
```

19.6   Metadata Views

■ **USER_VIEWS**. Describes view and view column details.

■ **USER_UPDATABLE_COLUMN**. Joins view columns, which can be updated or can have underlying table column values changed using DML commands.

19.7 Data Dictionary Views (Metadata)

Metadata views applicable for specific chapters are presented at the end of those chapters. This section describes what the metadata views are. Oracle Database contains a set of predefined views that contain information about tables, views, users, storage, and more.

There are two sets of metadata views. More distinctly, there are metadata views and performance views. The metadata views look at database dictionary data or data about the data. The data about the data are the tables and their columns, indexes, clusters, and so on. The meaning of the word *metadata* is data describing data. A database's metadata is all the objects created in a database to contain your actual data about your business and applications.

In general, metadata views are named as ALL_name, DBA_name, and USER_name. ALL_ implies all users, DBA_ implies only accessible by a DBA user, and USER_ implies the current user. Performance views are generally named as V$name. V$ views store and track all types of performance statistics and data in the database. Performance views relate to tuning an Oracle Database[2] and are largely out of the scope for this book on Oracle SQL.

All of the metadata views overlay and access the metadata from system tables stored either in the SYS, SYSTEM, or SYSAUX schemas. The database system tables are complex and can sometimes have cryptic names and even more cryptic column names.

As a DBA or programmer, you need some of this information. How do you find the names of users or tables in the database, for example? Oracle Database provides a set of views that are easily accessible, with readable view names and column names. These views are called, collectively, the *data dictionary views*.

So metadata or data dictionary views can be roughly divided into four groups, based on the prefix of the name of the view:

- **DBA_name.** These require special privileges to view. They generally give information covering the entire database system. For example, DBA_TABLES lists all tables created by any user in the database. DBA_name views require DBA privileges to access.

- **USER_name.** These are accessible by any user. They give information about the user and objects owned by the user, the currently connected user. For example, USER_TABLES lists all tables created by the current user. USER_name views access information available to and about the currently logged-in user; in our case, the user is the same as our schema, MUSIC.

- **ALL_name.** These are accessible by any user and show information about any object that the current user either owns or has privileges to use. For example, ALL_TABLES lists all tables created by the user plus those created by other users where the user has received permission to access the table.

- **Other Views.** These have names that do not follow the naming patterns above. Some are for the DBA and others are for all users. Some of these views are holdovers from previous releases of the database and will gradually be removed in future releases. These views can also cover obscure optional Oracle add-on packages or be newly developed and not yet completely incorporated.

Let's look at some queries. One of the most important metadata and performance view queries is a query that lists all of the metadata and performance views:

```
SELECT TABLE_NAME FROM DICTIONARY ORDER BY TABLE_NAME;
```

If I wanted to show all metadata views for the current logged-in user, I could use a query such as this one:

```
SELECT TABLE_NAME FROM DICTIONARY
WHERE TABLE_NAME LIKE 'USER_%' ORDER BY TABLE_NAME;
```

Now let's look at some specific examples. The following query lists all of the tables owned by the currently connected user.

```
SELECT TABLE_NAME FROM USER_TABLES;
```

Next we can find out how many other tables the currently logged-in user has permission to see. Note that this query uses the ALL_TABLES view to find all accessible tables, not just tables owned by the current user.

```
SELECT OWNER, TABLE_NAME FROM ALL_TABLES
WHERE OWNER <> USER;
```

Figure 19.10

The USER Pseudocolumn Was Used to Eliminate Tables You Own from the Query Results.

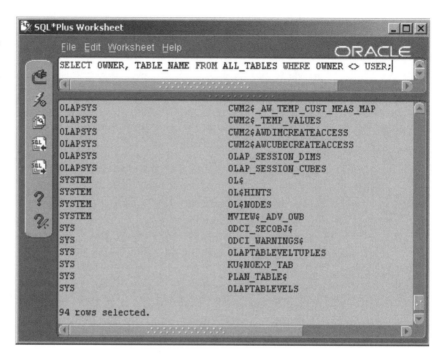

Figure 19.10 shows the result. Most of the owners you see here are users created by Oracle Database 10*g* for special functions during the installation of the database. Similarly, we could use both the USER_VIEWS and ALL_VIEWS metadata views to find information on views as opposed to tables.

Another interesting metadata view is the USER_OBJECTS view. Figure 19.11 shows the result of the following query:

```
COL OBJECT_NAME FORMAT A16 HEADING "Object"
COL OBJECT_TYPE FORMAT A24 HEADING "Type"
SELECT OBJECT_NAME, OBJECT_TYPE, STATUS
FROM USER_OBJECTS ORDER BY 1,2;
```

In the current release of Oracle Database 10*g*, the query SELECT COUNT(*) FROM DICTIONARY yields a count of 600 data dictionary metadata and performance views. As you work with Oracle Database, you will learn more about at least some of these views.

This chapter has described views, changing views, and using views to make changes to a database. Additionally, the meaning and structure of

Figure 19.11
*The
USER_OBJECTS
Metadata View.*

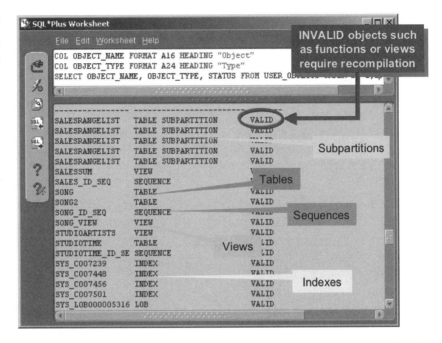

Oracle Database metadata data dictionary views was also discussed. The next chapter examines constraints, which can be placed on both tables and views.

19.8 Endnotes

1.   Oracle Performance Tuning for 9*i* and 10*g* (ISBN: 1-55558-305-9)

2.   Oracle Performance Tuning for 9*i* and 10*g* (ISBN: 1-55558-305-9)

20

Constraints

In this chapter:

- What is Referential Integrity?
- What are constraints and how are they used to implement Referential Integrity?
- How are constraints placed into tables?
- What else can constraints do?

This chapter shows you how to define constraints on tables. Constraints perform validation on data both within and between tables and, to a lesser degree, with views.

Primary and foreign key constraints are probably the most significant of constraints. These constraints can be used to enforce the validity (integrity) of relationships (references) between rows in tables (entities). A primary key reference is placed on a unique identifying column in a superset entity. A foreign key is placed on a subset table, which contains a copy of the primary key value from the superset entity. Oracle uses primary and foreign key constraints to validate values between superset and subset tables. Referential Integrity can be enforced using constraints or triggers, or can be coded at the application level. My personal recommendation is to use constraints.

Note: A superset contains a subset. The superset contains a primary key and the subset contains a foreign key. A foreign key can have many iterations of a primary key.

So let's move on to looking at constraints in detail.

20.1   What Are Constraints?

A *constraint*, as the word implies, constrains or applies a rule to an object or a part of an object. In Oracle Database 10*g*, constraints are used to restrict values in tables or make validation checks on one or more columns in a table, or check values between columns in different tables.

20.1.1   Types and Uses of Constraints

There are two levels of constraints you can place on relational tables:

- **Inline Constraint**. A constraint that applies to an individual column in a table.

- **Out-of-Line Constraint**. A constraint that applies to a table as a whole or to multiple columns in a table.

The six types of constraints are listed as follows. Some of these are always inline constraints, whereas others can be either inline or out-of-line, depending on how they are defined.

- **NOT NULL**. This constraint is always an inline constraint and will produce an error if no value is placed into this column when you insert or update a row in the table.

- **Unique**. Enforces uniqueness on a column value and can be inline or out of line. When you create a unique constraint, Oracle Database 10*g* will create an internal unique index if no index is available to enforce the constraint. Whenever you insert a row or update a row, the value in the column belonging to a unique constraint is verified as being different from any other value in the column for every other row in the table. You can define a unique constraint that checks more than one column. In this case, the value of both columns combined must be unique.

Note: A unique column does not have to be declared as NOT NULL, but it should be. Null values in a column are considered identical by the unique constraint, so allowing unique constraints to be nullable is probably poor design practice.

- **Check**. Applies a condition to a column value where that value must evaluate to TRUE and can be inline or out-of-line. A condition is of the form **expression condition expression**, such as **columnA = 5**. See Chapter 7 for details on comparison conditions and how to construct conditions.

- **Primary Key**. A primary key defines the column or set of columns that uniquely identify each row in a table. The primary key can be referenced by and validated against foreign keys in other tables (or in a different column or set of columns in the same table). It can be defined either inline (if it uses one column) or out-of-line (if it uses one or more columns). Because a primary key uniquely identifies a superset entity relationship, it must be unique. Therefore, a primary key automatically contains a unique constraint. Additionally, a primary key cannot be a null value because null values are not included in indexes. Indexes are covered in Chapter 21. Remember, a primary key inherently has both a unique constraint and a NOT NULL constraint.

- **Foreign Key**. A foreign key defines the relationship between the parent (superset) table and the child (subset) table. The foreign key resides in the child table. A foreign key must reference the primary key (or a unique key) of the referenced table. A foreign key constraint requires that the column value in the foreign key must be identical to a primary key value in the referenced table. Like the primary and unique key constraints, a foreign key can use one column or a set of columns. A foreign key constraint must be defined out-of-line if it contains more than a single column and can be either inline or out-of-line if it uses a single column.

- **REF**. A REF constraint is a reference between an object and an object type.

20.2 Managing Constraints

A constraint can be applied to an individual column in a table or, in some cases, to a table as a whole. Constraints can even be used in views. An individual column constraint is known as an inline constraint because it only applies to that specific column. A table-level constraint is known as an out-of-line constraint because it applies to the table as a whole.

So how do we create and maintain constraints? Constraints can be applied and used in the CREATE TABLE, CREATE VIEW, ALTER

Figure 20.1
CREATE TABLE
with Constraints
Syntax.

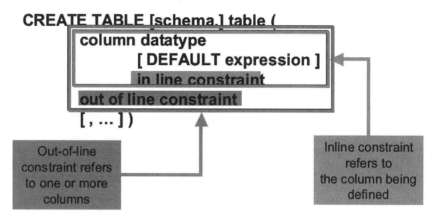

TABLE, and ALTER VIEW commands. CREATE TABLE and CREATE VIEW commands obviously only allow constraint creation. The ALTER TABLE and ALTER VIEW commands allow creation of constraints on existing tables and views, plus modification of existing constraints. Let's examine the syntax of each command in detail. This chapter is intended to focus on constraints only and thus syntax for the aforementioned commands is in addition to that in Chapters 18 and 19.

20.2.1　CREATE TABLE Syntax

Let's begin with inline and out-of-line constraints. As you can see clearly in Figure 20.1, an inline constraint is attached to a column, whereas an out-of-line constraint can be pictured as being a column in itself.

Getting a little more complicated, Figure 20.2 shows the details of CREATE TABLE syntax for inline constraints, out-of-line constraints, and constraint states.

Note: Constraint states are covered in detail later in this chapter under the section on the ALTER TABLE command.

Let's look at some examples. Constraints can be added to tables when tables are created using the CREATE TABLE statement. Let's experiment with different types of constraints.

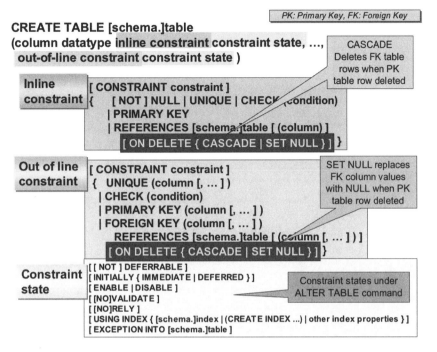

Figure 20.2
CREATE TABLE with Detailed Constraints Syntax.

20.2.1.1 Primary Key and Unique Constraints

A unique constraint forces a column value to be unique within all rows of a table. A primary key is forced to be a unique value and can reference foreign key column values in subset tables.

Let's start by creating a table similar to the ARTIST table in the MUSIC schema, using inline constraints.

```
CREATE TABLE ARTISTS(
   ARTIST_ID NUMBER PRIMARY KEY
, NAME VARCHAR2(32) NOT NULL UNIQUE);
```

Notice how the NAME column has the NOT NULL constraint whereas the primary key column, ARTIST_ID, does not. The primary key column has an inherent NOT NULL constraint. The primary key constraint has no name and is defined inline (for one specific column). The unique constraint on the NAME column is also defined inline and has no name. When no name is specified for the constraint, Oracle Database 10*g* will assign a name of its own.

The main difference between the primary key constraint and a unique constraint is that a primary key can be linked to foreign keys in subset tables where the foreign key value is the same as the primary key. Additionally, a unique constraint allows null values. Most of the time, it makes sense to add NOT NULL to the unique column because this ensures that all values in the column will be added to the constraint's index. Indexes make queries on the column run faster. Occasionally, a unique column can be left nullable (by omitting the NOT NULL constraint). For example, a table may carry a unique column containing the old inventory number for a store item. All items have been assigned a new inventory number, which is stored in the primary key. New items have a new inventory number (in the primary key column) but have null values in the old inventory number column.

20.2.1.2 Foreign Key Constraints

Now let's create a table similar to the SONG table in the MUSIC schema. This new table will have a foreign key. The foreign key references the ARTIST_ID column in the ARTISTS table. The ARTISTS table was created in the previous section as a copy of the original ARTIST table.

```
CREATE TABLE SONGS(
    SONG_ID NUMBER PRIMARY KEY
, ARTIST_ID NUMBER NOT NULL
REFERENCES ARTISTS (ARTIST_ID)
, TITLE VARCHAR2(64) NOT NULL UNIQUE);
```

In the new SONGS table, we have used only inline constraints and have allowed Oracle Database 10*g* to name the constraints. The constraints created are as follows:

- A primary key constraint on the SONG_ID column, indicating that every song must have a unique value as its SONG_ID.

- A foreign key constraint and a NOT NULL constraint on the ARTIST_ID column, indicating that an ARTIST_ID value in this table must have a matching value found in the ARTISTS.ARTIST_ID column.

- A unique constraint and a NOT NULL constraint on the TITLE column, indicating that every song must have a title and the title must be unique compared to all other songs in the table.

The foreign key constraint must name the table referenced by the foreign key. Optionally, it can name the primary key or unique key column referenced as well. A foreign key constraint created inline is not allowed to have a name you define. Out-of-line foreign key constraints can be named.

Notice how this foreign key column is declared as NOT NULL. It is possible to declare a foreign key column as being nullable, but this requirement is rare in reality unless your data model uses one-to-many or zero-entity relationships. This type of relationship is common in multidimensional, multiple-inheritance object structures and sometimes in data warehouse fact tables (e.g., MUSIC schema SALES table). As far as objects are concerned, Oracle Database is a relational database, not an object database. The ARTIST_ID foreign key column will automate validation between the ARTIST_ID columns in both of the new ARTISTS and SONGS tables.

20.2.1.2.1 Out-of-Line Primary and Foreign Keys

We have used inline, column-level constraints in the previous two table creation scripts for the ARTISTS and SONGS tables. We could have used out-of-line or table-level constraints for all but the NOT NULL constraints in these tables. Table-level constraints are applied to the table as a whole after all columns have been created. For the ARTISTS and SONGS tables, it is not necessary to use table-level constraints.

Situations where table-level constraints are required can involve constraints created on multiple columns. The CDTRACK table in the MUSIC schema is a perfect example. Let's create a copy of the CDTRACK table called CDTRACKS.

```
CREATE TABLE CDTRACKS(
  MUSICCD_ID NUMBER NOT NULL
, SONG_ID NUMBER NOT NULL
, TRACK_SEQ_NO NUMBER NOT NULL
, CONSTRAINT PKCDTRACKS
PRIMARY KEY (MUSICCD_ID,SONG_ID)
, CONSTRAINT FKCDTRACKS_SONG
FOREIGN KEY (SONG_ID) REFERENCES SONGS
, CONSTRAINT FKCDTRACK_CD
FOREIGN KEY (MUSICCD_ID) REFERENCES MUSICCD);
```

Out-of-line constraints are defined immediately after the column definitions. You can place them before the column definitions as well, although locating them after the column definitions is the most commonly used method. All of these out-of-line constraints have names.

Note how the primary key constraint (named PKCDTRACKS) names two columns: MUSICCD_ID and SONG_ID. A primary key with multiple columns is sometimes called a *composite primary key*.

The two foreign keys have also been created at table level for the sake of consistency, even though they are both single-column keys.

Note: The same column can be named in a primary key and a foreign key.

Now let's try something interesting going through a sequence of steps. Drop and re-create the CDTRACKS table as in the following script. We are adding a new column, called TRACK_ID, which will become the primary key later. Note how all the columns are now declared as nullable because all NOT NULL constraints have been removed. Also, both the primary and foreign keys have been removed.

```
DROP TABLE CDTRACKS;
CREATE TABLE CDTRACKS(TRACK_ID NUMBER, MUSICCD_ID NUMBER
, SONG_ID NUMBER, TRACK_SEQ_NO NUMBER);
```

The resulting table's description using the DESC command is shown in Figure 20.3. All of the columns in the CDTRACKS table are allowed to contain null values.

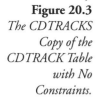

Figure 20.3
The CDTRACKS Copy of the CDTRACK Table with No Constraints.

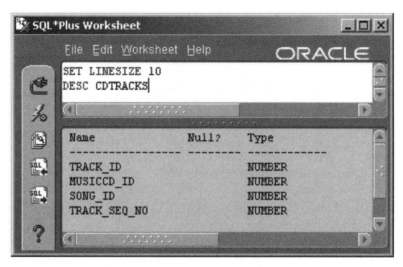

Now let's put the table-level primary and foreign key constraints back into the creation of the CDTRACKS table without the NOT NULL constraints and see what happens to the nullability of the columns. This time, we will name the TRACK_ID column as the primary key and keep the foreign key constraints the same as before.

These commands drop the table and create it with primary and foreign keys. There are no NOT NULL constraints added.

```
DROP TABLE CDTRACKS;
CREATE TABLE CDTRACKS(TRACK_ID NUMBER, MUSICCD_ID NUMBER
, SONG_ID NUMBER, TRACK_SEQ_NO NUMBER
, CONSTRAINT PKCDTRACKS PRIMARY KEY (TRACK_ID)
, CONSTRAINT FKCDTRACKS_SONG
FOREIGN KEY (SONG_ID) REFERENCES SONGS
, CONSTRAINT FKCDTRACK_CD
FOREIGN KEY (MUSICCD_ID) REFERENCES MUSICCD);
```

Now let's view the CDTRACKS table again using the DESC command as shown in Figure 20.4.

Notice in Figure 20.4 how the primary key column has been forced to have the NOT NULL constraint, even though the NOT NULL constraint was not specified for the column when creating the CDTRACKS table. The foreign key columns still remain nullable.

Figure 20.4
A NOT NULL Constraint Is Automatically Added to the Primary Key Column.

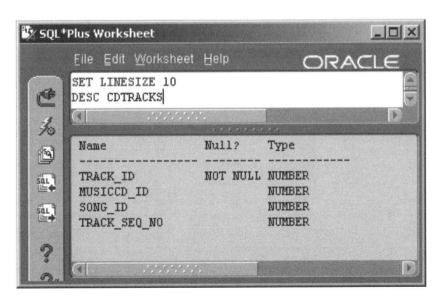

- Primary key constraints cannot be NULL and will force the addition of a NOT NULL constraint.

- Foreign key constraints can be nullable. A foreign key constraint should only be nullable where a row in the foreign key table does not have to have a parent row in a primary key table. This somewhat negates the use of Referential Integrity in the first place. However, data warehouse fact tables and object structures sometimes do this sort of thing. I do not recommend allowing foreign key columns to be nullable.

20.2.1.3   Check Constraints

A check constraint applies a condition to an expression of a row, such as checking a column value. If the result is not TRUE and evaluated as a null value, then an error results and the SQL statement involving the row fails. Typically, a check constraint can be used for validation of a column in a row or a check across multiple columns in the same row.

A check constraint can be inline or out-of-line. An inline check constraint must apply as a check on an individual column, whereas an out-of-line check constraint could apply to a single column or multiple columns. Let's go ahead and create a copy of the ARTISTS table again and demonstrate some check constraints. We want to start by dropping the ARTISTS table copy of the ARTIST table first. Because the ARTISTS table is linked to the SONGS table by a referential relationship using primary and foreign keys, and the SONGS table is in turn linked to the CDTRACKS table, simply dropping the ARTISTS table will produce an error. Thus we have to drop all three tables in the correct sequence, from the bottom of the referential hierarchy, upward.

```
DROP TABLE CDTRACKS;
DROP TABLE SONGS;
DROP TABLE ARTISTS;
```

Note: We could have used the DROP TABLE ... CASCADE CONSTRAINTS statement to drop only the ARTISTS table and all related constraints in other tables. This would result in only the ARTISTS table being dropped. We would still have to drop the other tables. Avoiding the CASCADE option is cleaner and perhaps a little more logically safe because it does not use brute force!

Now we can create the ARTISTS table again, but this time we add a few more columns and some check constraints into the script.

```
CREATE TABLE ARTISTS(
   ARTIST_ID NUMBER PRIMARY KEY
 , NAME VARCHAR2(32) NOT NULL, CITY VARCHAR2(32)
 , STATE_PROVINCE VARCHAR2(32) CONSTRAINT STATE CHECK
   (LENGTH(STATE_PROVINCE) >= 2 OR STATE_PROVINCE IS NULL)
 , COUNTRY VARCHAR2(32) CONSTRAINT COUNTRY CHECK
   (COUNTRY IN('USA','Canada','England','Australia'))
 , MEDIA_ROYALTIES FLOAT, RECORD_SALES_ROYALTIES FLOAT
 , PERFORMANCE_PROFITS FLOAT
 , CONSTRAINT ROYALTIES CHECK (MEDIA_ROYALTIES
   + RECORD_SALES_ROYALTIES + PERFORMANCE_PROFITS > 0));
```

The constraints created in the ARTISTS table are as follows:

- An inline primary key constraint on the ARTIST_ID column.

- An inline NOT NULL constraint on the NAME column.

- An inline CHECK constraint named STATE that checks the length of the STATE_PROVINCE column. If the length of the value is greater than or equal to 2, or if the value is NULL, the value passes the test.

- An inline CHECK constraint named COUNTRY that looks for certain values. If the value in the COUNTRY column is in the list of four countries provided, the value passes; otherwise it fails.

- An out-of-line CHECK constraint named ROYALTIES that looks at an expression. If the sum of MEDIA_ROYALTIES, RECORD_SALES_ROYALTIES, and PERFORMANCE_PROFITS is greater than zero, the row passes the test; otherwise it fails.

Now we want to show the use of the CHECK constraints added to the newly created ARTISTS table. Two of the following five INSERT commands will add a row. The other three will produce an error. See the output in Figure 20.5. Invalid values (if any) in each of the INSERT commands are highlighted.

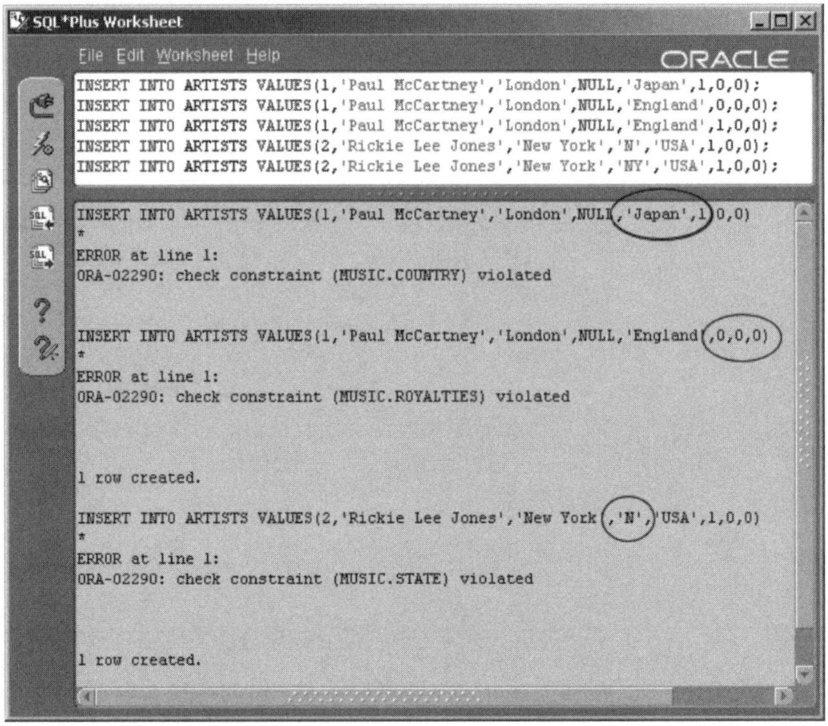

Figure 20.5
Using CHECK Constraints.

```
INSERT INTO ARTISTS VALUES
(1,'Paul McCartney','London',NULL,'Japan',1,0,0);
INSERT INTO ARTISTS VALUES
(1,'Paul McCartney','London',NULL,'England',0,0,0);
INSERT INTO ARTISTS VALUES
(1,'Paul McCartney','London',NULL,'England',1,0,0);
INSERT INTO ARTISTS VALUES
(2,'Rickie Lee Jones','New York','N','USA',1,0,0);
INSERT INTO ARTISTS VALUES
(2,'Rickie Lee Jones','New York','NY','USA',1,0,0);
```

In Figure 20.5, for the first INSERT command, Japan is not an allowed country. For the second INSERT command, at least one of the three monetary amounts must be greater than zero to make their sum greater than zero. In the fourth INSERT command, the state is incorrectly typed as a single character and thus violates both the two-character length limit and the NULL check constraint.

Figure 20.6
*REF Constraints
Syntax.*

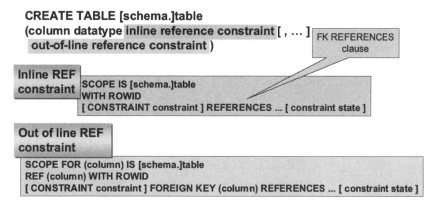

20.2.1.4   REF Constraints

A REF constraint is used to control a relationship determined by a REF datatype column and the table being referenced (see Chapter 16 for details on REF datatypes). REF constraint syntax is shown in Figure 20.6.

A REF constraint consists of either a scope definition, a ROWID pointer, or a Referential Integrity validation between REF column datatype primary and foreign key definitions. Let's examine these three options in turn:

- **SCOPE IS**. Scope defines a single table where a referenced row can be found. Why? A REF datatype is for all intents and purposes an object pointer. An object pointer can point to any data item in a database, thus it can point to other tables. SCOPE IS simply limits searching to a single table.

- **WITH ROWID**. This option stores a ROWID pointer value with a REF datatype value. It should make for faster access but less efficient use of storage space.

- **REFERENCES**. This option simply allows a foreign key REF datatype column to be referentially validated against a primary key superset table using the REF datatype column and a special object identifier column in the parent table.

Having worked with both object application SDKs and object databases in the past, I shudder at the thought of creating object structures in a relational database. This is a personal preference. My reasoning for this preference is as follows: PL/SQL should never be used for number crunching.

Java is a better option. Database modeling is an even deeper layer than PL/SQL for a relational database. Therefore, building object structures in a relational database is somewhat counterintuitive because object applications and particularly object databases thrive on complex structures. Relational databases can collapse in a pile of rubble in complex environments but thrive on simplicity. How many of us have seen ERDs (Entity Relationship Diagrams) covering the entire wall of an office? In a relational database, complexity usually leads to more complexity, and so on, ad infinitum.

20.2.2 CREATE VIEW Syntax

Constraint syntax for the CREATE VIEW command is shown in Figure 20.7. The way in which constraints are handled for the CREATE VIEW command is the same as for the CREATE TABLE command. As a result, no examples in addition to those in Chapter 19 are required in this chapter. See Chapter 19 for details.

20.3 Adding, Modifying, and Dropping Constraints

20.3.1 ALTER TABLE Syntax

Let's begin with the ALTER TABLE command syntax including only constraint details. The syntax diagram is shown in Figure 20.8. Examining Figure 20.8, we can see that constraints can be renamed, modified, added new, or dropped using the ALTER TABLE syntax.

Figure 20.7
CREATE VIEW
Constraints Syntax.

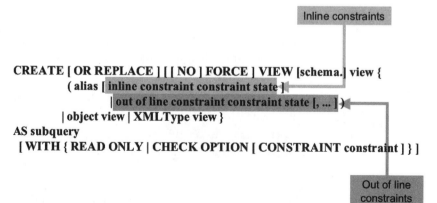

Figure 20.8
ALTER TABLE
Constraints Syntax.

ADD Out of
line only

ALTER TABLE [schema.]table
   RENAME CONSTRAINT name TO name
| MODIFY {
        CONSTRAINT constraint | PRIMARY KEY | UNIQUE (column [, ...]) }
        constraint state
| ADD out of line constraint constraint state
| DROP {
       CONSTRAINT name [CASCADE]
      | PRIMARY KEY [CASCADE] [{ KEEP | DROP } INDEX]
      | UNIQUE (column [, ...] [CASCADE] [{ KEEP | DROP } INDEX] }

PK: Primary Key, FK: Foreign Key

Drop dependent integrity constraints such as FKs

PK/Unique indexes can be retained

Out of line and out of line REF constraint

See CREATE TABLE syntax in Figures 20.1, 20.2 and 20.6

Constraint state

[[NOT] DEFERRABLE]
[INITIALLY { IMMEDIATE | DEFERRED }]
[ENABLE | DISABLE]
[[NO]VALIDATE]
[[NO]RELY]
[USING INDEX { [schema.]index | (CREATE INDEX ...) | other index properties }]
[EXCEPTION INTO [schema.]table]

Constraint states change constraint behavior

20.3.2 ALTER VIEW Syntax

As with the CREATE TABLE and CREATE VIEW commands, constraint syntax for the ALTER VIEW command is similar to that of the ALTER TABLE command. ALTER VIEW command syntax is shown in Figure 20.9. Once again, please see Chapter 19 for details on working with constraints and views.

Figure 20.9
ALTER VIEW
Constraints Syntax.

ALTER VIEW [schema.]view {
     ADD out of line constraint
     | MODIFY CONSTRAINT constraint [NO]RELY
     | DROP { CONSTRAINT constraint | PRIMARY KEY | UNIQUE
        (column [, ...])

20.3.3 Working with Constraints and ALTER TABLE

Now let's explain using constraints by using some ALTER TABLE command examples.

Once you have created a table, you can add new constraints, modify, and drop existing constraints using the ALTER TABLE command.

Note: Constraints can only be added, modified, or dropped at the table level (out-of-line constraints). The exception to this rule is the NOT NULL constraint where the column is modified. For example, to add a NOT NULL constraint to the NAME column, the command is: ALTER TABLE ARTISTS MODIFY (NAME VARCHAR2(32) NOT NULL).

Once again, let's use the three tables: ARTISTS, SONGS, and CDTRACKS. First, drop the ARTISTS table again so that we can start with a clean slate.

```
DROP TABLE ARTISTS;
```

Now let's go ahead and create the ARTISTS and SONGS tables without any constraints.

```
CREATE TABLE ARTISTS(ARTIST_ID NUMBER, NAME VARCHAR2(32));
CREATE TABLE SONGS(SONG_ID NUMBER, ARTIST_ID NUMBER
, TITLE VARCHAR2(64));
```

20.3.3.1   Adding a Constraint to an Existing Table

Now we need to add the constraints for the ARTISTS and SONGS tables. Add a primary key constraint to the ARTISTS table on the ARTIST_ID column:

```
ALTER TABLE ARTISTS ADD CONSTRAINT PK_ARTISTS
PRIMARY KEY(ARTIST_ID);
```

Add a unique constraint to the ARTISTS table on the NAME column:

```
ALTER TABLE ARTISTS ADD CONSTRAINT UK_ARTISTS UNIQUE(NAME);
```

Add a primary key constraint to the SONGS table on the SONG_ID column:

```
ALTER TABLE SONGS ADD CONSTRAINT PK_SONGS
PRIMARY KEY(SONG_ID);
```

Add a foreign key constraint to the SONGS table on the ARTIST_ID column, referencing the ARTISTS table:

```
ALTER TABLE SONGS ADD CONSTRAINT FK_ARTISTS
FOREIGN KEY(ARTIST_ID) REFERENCES ARTISTS;
```

Add a unique constraint to the SONGS table on the TITLE column. This constraint will be given a system-generated name because the CONSTRAINT keyword is omitted.

```
ALTER TABLE SONGS ADD UNIQUE(TITLE);
```

20.3.3.2   Modifying Constraints on Existing Tables

Let's modify the ARTISTS and SONGS tables to make sure that names and titles are non-nullable.

```
ALTER TABLE ARTISTS MODIFY (NAME VARCHAR2(32) NOT NULL);
ALTER TABLE SONGS MODIFY (TITLE VARCHAR2(64) NOT NULL);
```

Note: When changing constraints other than the NULL constraint, only the state of a constraint can be modified.

This leads us to constraint states.

20.3.3.3   Constraint States

The state of a constraint determines how a constraint is handled. Each of the constraint settings following applies to an individual constraint placed onto a table. Most but not all constraint states can be set using all of the CREATE TABLE, CREATE VIEW, ALTER TABLE, and ALTER VIEW commands. Several constraint states are very specific.

- **ENABLE | DISABLE**. Switch constraint checking on (ENABLE) or off (DISABLE), for a specific constraint. ENABLE is obviously the default state.
  - **[NO]VALIDATE**. This state applies when a constraint is enabled. VALIDATE column values in a table for both existing and newly inserted rows. NOVALIDATE validates only new rows, avoiding validation of already existing rows. Validation depends on the constraint being enabled (ENABLE). VALIDATE is the default state.

- **[NOT] DEFERRABLE**. Validation of the constraint can be done at the end of a transaction instead of immediately when the row is inserted, updated, or deleted. The default state is NOT DEFERRABLE or immediately. Changing the DEFERRABLE constraint state requires table re-creation.

  - **INITIALLY { IMMEDIATE | DEFERRED }**. This state functions with deferrable constraints only. IMMEDIATE initiates a check at the end of every SQL command and DEFERRED at the completion of every transaction. It is only relevant when the constraint is also DEFERRABLE. The default state is INITIALLY IMMEDIATE.

- **RELY**. Applicable to data marts and materialized views in data warehousing. When RELY is selected, a NOVALIDATE (nonvalidated) constraint state specifies a constraint as being valid for query rewrites, thus materialized views. It is only usable in the ALTER TABLE command.

- **USING INDEX clause**. Allows index specification for primary and unique key constraints. Indexing is covered in Chapter 21.

- **EXCEPTIONS clause**. Stores ROWID values for all rows violating any current constraint states into an exceptions table providing a record of errors.

Let's try disabling a constraint in the SONGS table. Disable the foreign key constraint on the ARTIST_ID column.

```
ALTER TABLE SONGS MODIFY CONSTRAINT FK_ARTISTS DISABLE;
```

Note: Constraint states can be implemented using both table and view DDL commands.

20.3.4 **Renaming a Constraint**

Constraints can be renamed without modification to the table, avoiding any time-consuming data restructuring or table modifications. In the previous section on adding constraints to an existing table, we created a unique constraint named UK_ARTISTS on the ARTISTS table that is a unique constraint on the NAME column.

The term "UK_" implies "unique key." Technically, this constraint is actually better termed as an alternate key rather than a unique key, because the table already has a unique identifier in the form of a primary key created on the ARTIST_ID column. So we could change the name of the constraint from UK_ARTISTS to AK_ARTISTS using the ALTER TABLE command shown as follows:

```
ALTER TABLE ARTISTS RENAME CONSTRAINT UK_ARTISTS
TO AK_ARTISTS;
```

20.3.5 Dropping Constraints

As we can see in Figure 20.8, constraints can be dropped with the ALTER TABLE command.

Currently, we should still have the SONGS and ARTISTS tables in the MUSIC schema. Let's go ahead and drop all of the constraints on those two tables. We will start with the unique (alternate) keys on the SONGS.TITLE and the ARTISTS.NAME columns. Note the two different methods of dropping the unique constraints. The first does not use the constraint name. This is useful when the constraint was created without a specific name. The actual constraint name was system-generated and is something like SYS_C004463 and can be found by querying the USER_CONSTRAINTS data dictionary view (more on this later).

```
ALTER TABLE SONGS DROP UNIQUE(TITLE);
ALTER TABLE ARTISTS DROP CONSTRAINT AK_ARTISTS;
```

Now let's drop Referential Integrity constraints between the ARTISTS and SONGS tables. We have to drop the foreign key on the SONGS table before we drop the primary key on the ARTISTS table. If we try to drop the primary key on the ARTISTS table first, we will get an error because the foreign key on the SONGS table depends on the primary key on the ARTISTS table. Again, notice that the first and third commands use only the type of constraint, not the name.

```
ALTER TABLE SONGS DROP PRIMARY KEY;
ALTER TABLE SONGS DROP CONSTRAINT FK_ARTISTS;
ALTER TABLE ARTISTS DROP PRIMARY KEY;
```

You can also specify the KEEP or DROP INDEX options when dropping primary and foreign key constraints. The KEEP INDEX option retains index files for the constraints while still removing the constraints from the tables. The default behavior is to drop the index when the primary key is dropped.

20.3.5.1 Dropping Constraints with CASCADE

Both tables and constraints can be dropped with the CASCADE clause. With respect to Referential Integrity, the term CASCADE implies that when one constraint is dropped, any dependent constraints will be dropped as well. Cascading generally applies a domino effect of dropping any foreign key constraints, referentially related to the constraint of the table being dropped. For example, dropping the primary key on the ARTISTS table with the CASCADE clause also drops the ARTIST_ID foreign key constraint on the SONGS table. The result is that the ARTIST_ID column and its data still exist in the SONGS table, but the foreign key constraint is gone.

We can demonstrate this using the ARTISTS and SONGS tables. First, we drop and re-create the ARTISTS and SONGS table to start with a fresh copy of the tables.

```
DROP TABLE SONGS;
DROP TABLE ARTISTS;
CREATE TABLE ARTISTS(ARTIST_ID NUMBER PRIMARY KEY
, NAME VARCHAR2(32) NOT NULL UNIQUE);
CREATE TABLE SONGS(SONG_ID NUMBER PRIMARY KEY
, ARTIST_ID NUMBER NOT NULL
REFERENCES ARTISTS (ARTIST_ID)
, TITLE VARCHAR2(64) NOT NULL UNIQUE);
```

The following query shows resulting constraint details as shown in Figure 20.10.

```
SELECT TABLE_NAME "Table"
,DECODE(CONSTRAINT_TYPE,'P','Primary'
,'R','Foreign','') "Key"
FROM USER_CONSTRAINTS
WHERE TABLE_NAME IN ('ARTISTS','SONGS')
AND CONSTRAINT_TYPE IN ('P','R');
```

Figure 20.10
Primary and Foreign Key Constraints on ARTISTS and SONGS Tables.

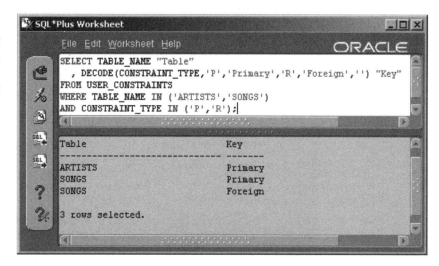

In Figure 20.10, the USER_CONSTRAINTS query shows the primary and foreign key constraints on the ARTISTS and SONGS tables created above. Now go ahead and drop the ARTISTS table primary key with the CASCADE option.

```
ALTER TABLE ARTISTS DROP PRIMARY KEY CASCADE;
```

Now we will use the USER_CONSTRAINTS query in Figure 20.10 once again to verify that the primary key has been removed from the ARTISTS table and the related foreign key has been removed from the

Figure 20.11
Primary Key Drop with Constraints Cascade on the ARTISTS Table.

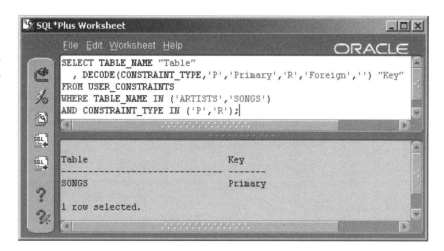

Figure 20.12
*Querying
USER_CONSTR
AINTS and
USER_CONS_
COLUMNS.*

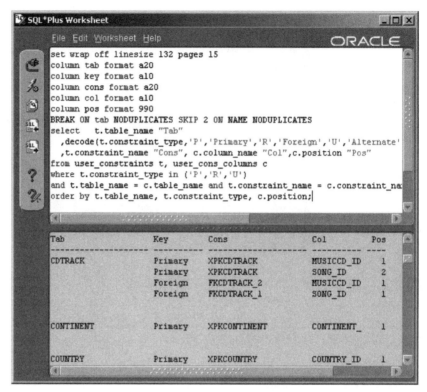

```
set wrap off linesize 132 pages 15
column tab format a20
column key format a10
column cons format a20
column col format a10
column pos format 990
BREAK ON tab NODUPLICATES SKIP 2 ON NAME NODUPLICATES
select    t.table_name "Tab"
  ,decode(t.constraint_type,'P','Primary','R','Foreign','U','Alternate'
  ,t.constraint_name "Cons", c.column_name "Col",c.position "Pos"
from user_constraints t, user_cons_columns c
where t.constraint_type in ('P','R','U')
and t.table_name = c.table_name and t.constraint_name = c.constraint_na
order by t.table_name, t.constraint_type, c.position;
```

Tab	Key	Cons	Col	Pos
CDTRACK	Primary	XPKCDTRACK	MUSICCD_ID	1
	Primary	XPKCDTRACK	SONG_ID	2
	Foreign	FKCDTRACK_2	MUSICCD_ID	1
	Foreign	FKCDTRACK_1	SONG_ID	1
CONTINENT	Primary	XPKCONTINENT	CONTINENT_	1
COUNTRY	Primary	XPKCOUNTRY	COUNTRY_ID	1

SONGS table. As shown in Figure 20.11, only the primary key on the SONGS table remains.

Cascading of constraints can also be applied in the DROP TABLE statement where all dependent constraints in the current and referentially dependent tables are dropped in order to allow the dropped table to be successfully removed. For instance, the DROP TABLE statement that follows would drop the ARTISTS table plus the foreign key constraint on the SONGS.ARTIST_ID column and any other related subset foreign key constraints. This can be verified using the same USER_CONSTRAINTS query as used in the previous example. (You would have to once again drop and create the ARTISTS and SONGS tables, including their respective primary and foreign keys.)

```
DROP TABLE ARTISTS CASCADE CONSTRAINTS;
```

20.4 **Metadata Views**

This section simply describes metadata views applicable to constraints. Chapter 19 describes the basis and detail of Oracle Database metadata views.

- **USER_CONSTRAINTS**. Structure of constraints, such as who owns it, its type, the table it is attached to, and states, among other details.

- **USER_CONS_COLUMNS**. Describes all columns in constraints.

The script executed in Figure 20.12 matches constraints and constraint columns for the currently logged-in user. The script is included in Appendix B.

This chapter has dealt with constraints, their states, and adding, modifying, and destroying them. The next chapter looks at indexes.

21

Indexes and Clusters

In this chapter:

- What is an index and what is the purpose of an index?
- What types of indexes are there, and how do they work?
- What are the special attributes of indexes?
- What is a cluster?

Recent chapters have discussed various database objects such as tables, views, and constraints. This fourth chapter on database objects covers indexing and clustering. Understanding database objects is essential to a proper understanding of Oracle SQL, particularly with respect to building efficient SQL code; tuning is another subject.[1] It is important to understand different database objects, indexes and clusters included.

21.1 Indexes

Let's start by briefly discussing what exactly an index is, followed by some salient facts about indexing.

21.1.1 What Is an Index?

An index is a database object, similar to a table, that is used to increase read access performance. A reference book, for instance, having an index, allows rapid access to a particular subject area on a specific page within that book. Database indexes serve the same purpose, allowing a process in the database quick access directly to a row in the table.

An index contains copies of specific columns in a table where those columns make up a very small part of the table row length. The result is an index. An index object is physically much smaller than the table and is therefore faster to search through because less I/O is required. Additionally, special forms of indexes can be created where scanning of the entire index is seldom required, making data retrieval using indexes even faster as a result.

Note: A table is located in what is often called the data space and an index in the index space.

Attached to each row in an index is an address pointer (ROWID) to the physical location of a row in a table on disk. Reading an index will retrieve one or more table ROWID pointers. The ROWID is then used to find the table row precisely. Figure 21.1 shows a conceptual view of a table with an index on the NAME column. The index stores the indexed column (NAME) and the ROWID of the corresponding row. The index's rows are stored in sorted order by NAME. The table's data is not stored in any sorted order. Usually, rows are stored into tables sequentially as they are inserted, regardless of the value of the NAME or any other column. In other words, a table is not ordered, whereas an index is ordered.

Figure 21.1
Each Index Entry
Points to a Row of
Data in the Table.

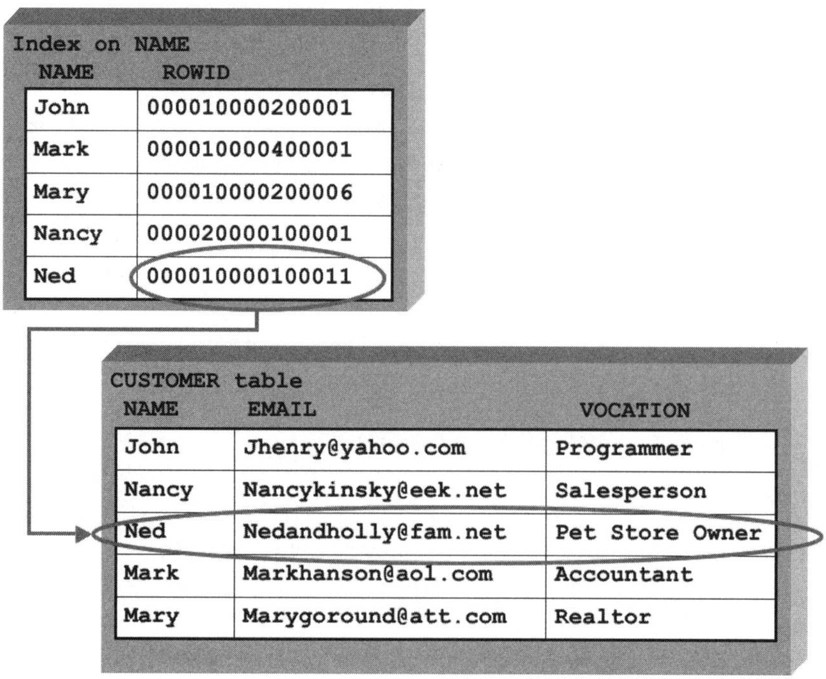

Continuing with the example in Figure 21.1, here is a query on the CUSTOMER table:

```
SELECT VOCATION FROM CUSTOMER WHERE NAME = 'Ned';
```

Because the WHERE clause contains the indexed column (NAME), the Optimizer should opt to use the index. Oracle Database 10*g* searches the index for the value "Ned", and then uses the ROWID as an address pointer to read the exact row in the table. The value of the VOCATION column is retrieved ("Pet Store Owner") and returned as the result of the query.

A large table search on a smaller index uses the pointer (ROWID) found in the index to pinpoint the row physical location in the table. This is very much faster than physically scanning the entire table.

When a large table is not searched with an index, then a full table scan is executed. A full table scan executed on a large table, retrieving a small number of rows (perhaps even retrieving a single row), is an extremely inefficient process.

Note: Although the intent of adding an index to a table is to improve performance, it is sometimes more efficient to allow a full table scan when querying small tables. The Optimizer will often assess a full table scan on small tables as being more efficient than reading both index and data spaces, especially when a table is physically small enough to occupy a single data block.

Many factors are important to consider when creating and using indexes. This shows you that simply adding an index may not necessarily improve performance but usually does:

- Too many indexes per table can improve read access and degrade the efficiency of data changes.

- Too many table columns in an index can make the Optimizer consider the index less efficient than reading the entire table.

- Integers, such as a social security number, are more efficient to index than items such as dates or variable data like a book title.

- Different types of indexes have specific applications. The default index type is a BTree index, the most commonly used index type.

BTree indexes are often the only index type used in anything but a data warehouse.

- The Optimizer looks at the SQL code in the WHERE, ORDER BY, and GROUP BY clauses when deciding whether to use an index. The WHERE clause is usually the most important area to tune for index use because the WHERE clause potentially filters out much unwanted information before and during disk I/O activity. The ORDER BY clause, on the other hand, operates on the results of a query, after disk I/O has been completed. Disk I/O is often the most expensive phase of data retrieval from a database.

- Do not always create indexes. Small tables can often be read faster without indexes using full table scans.

- Do not index for the sake of indexing.

- Do not overindex.

- Do not always include all columns in a composite index. A composite index is a multiple-column index. The recommended maximum number of columns in a composite index is three columns. Including more columns could make the index so large as to be no faster than scanning the whole table.

Next we discover what types of indexes there are, plus how and where those different types of indexes can be used.

21.1.2 **Types of Indexes**

Oracle Database 10*g* supports many different types of indexes. You should be aware of all these index types and their most appropriate or common applications. As already stated, the most commonly used indexed structure is a BTree index.

- **BTree Index**. BTree stands for binary tree. This form of index stores dividing point data at the top and middle layers (root and branch nodes) and stores the actual values of the indexed column(s) in the bottom layer (leaf nodes) of the index structure. The branch nodes contain pointers to the lower-level branch or leaf node. Leaf nodes contain index column values plus a ROWID pointer to the table row. Oracle Database 10*g* will attempt to balance the branch and leaf nodes so that each branch contains approximately the same number of branch and leaf nodes. Figure 21.2 shows a conceptual view of a BTree index. When Oracle Database 10*g* searches a BTree index, it travels from the top node, through the branches, to the leaf node in three or four quick steps. Why three or four quick steps? From top node to leaf nodes implies what is called a *depth-first search*. Oracle Database BTree indexes are generally built such that there are between 0 and 2 branch levels with a single leaf node level. In other words, a depth-first search on a single row will read between one and three blocks, no matter how many rows are in the index. BTree indexes are efficient even when the number of rows indexed is in the millions, if used correctly.

- **Bitmap Index**. A bitmap contains binary representations for each row. A 0 bitmap value implies that a row does not have a specified value, and a bitmap value of 1 denotes a row having the value. Bitmaps are very likely susceptible to overflow over long periods of use in OLTP systems and are probably best used for read-only data such as in data warehouses. They are best suited to indexing columns that have a small number of distinct values, such as days of the week, gender, and similar columns. However, bitmap indexes have been known to be relatively successful in large data warehouse tables with up to thousands of distinct values.

- **Function-Based Index**. Contains the result of an expression precalculated on each row in a table and stored as the expression result in a BTree index structure. This type of index makes queries with an indexed expression in the WHERE clause much faster. Often, functions in the WHERE clause cause the Optimizer to ignore indexes. A function-based index provides with the Optimizer the ability to use an index in queries that otherwise would require full table scans.

- **Index-Organized Table (IOT)**. Physical clustering of index and data spaces together for a single table, in the order of the index, usually the primary key. An IOT is a table as well as an index; the table and the index are merged. This works better for tables that are static and frequently queried on the indexed columns. However, large OLTP systems do use IOTs with some success, and these IOTs are likely to be for tables with a small number of columns or short row length (see Chapter 18).

- **Cluster**. A clustered index contains values from joined tables rather than a single table. A cluster is a partial merge of index and data spaces, ordered by an index, not necessarily the primary key. A cluster is similar to an IOT except that it can be built on a join of two or

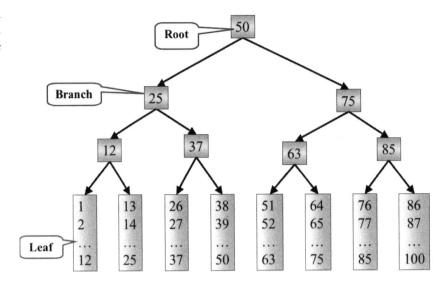

Figure 21.2
*A BTree Index on
Numbers 1 to 100.*

more tables. Clusters can be ordered using binary tree structures or hashing algorithms. A cluster is perhaps conceptually both a table and an index because clustering partially merges index and data spaces into single physical chunks (clusters).

- **Bitmap Join Index**. Creates a single bitmap used for one of the tables in a join.

- **Domain Index**. Specific to certain application types using contextual or spatial data, among other variations.

Note: It usually is best, especially for OLTP systems, to use only BTree and function-based index types. Other index types are more appropriate to data warehouse systems that have primarily static, read-only tables.

21.1.2.1 Index Attributes

In addition to the type of index, Oracle Database 10*g* supports what I like to call index attributes. Most types of indexes can use these attributes. You will practice using some of these attributes as you work through this chapter creating and modifying indexes.

- **Ascending or Descending**. Indexes can be ordered in either direction.

- **Uniqueness**. Indexes can be unique or nonunique. Primary key constraints and unique constraints use unique indexes. Other indexed columns, such as names or countries, sometimes need unique indexes and sometime need nonunique indexes.

- **Composites**. A composite index is made up of more than one column in a table.

- **Compression**. Applies to BTree indexes and not bitmap indexes where duplicated prefix values are removed. Compression speeds up data retrieval but can slow down table changes.

- **Reverse keys**. Bytes for all columns in the index are reversed without changing the column order. Reverse keys can help performance in clustered server environments (Oracle Real Application Clusters, formerly Oracle Parallel Server) by ensuring that changes to similar key values will be better physically spread. Reverse key indexing can apply to rows inserted into OLTP tables using sequence integer generators, where each number is very close to the previous number. Inserting groups of rows with similar sequence numbers can cause some contention because sequential values might be inserted into the same block at the same time.

- **Null values**. If all of the indexed columns in a row contain null values, rows are not included in an index.

- **Sorting**. The NOSORT clause tells Oracle Database 10*g* that the index being built is based on data that is already in the correct sorted order. This can save a great deal of time when creating an index, but will fail if the data is not actually in the order needed by the index. This assumes that data space is physically ordered in the desired manner, and the index will copy the physical order of the data space.

You are ready to begin creating some indexes.

21.1.3 Creating Indexes

Figure 21.3 shows a syntax diagram detailing the CREATE INDEX command.

Let's start by creating a table called RELEASESIN2001.

```
CREATE TABLE RELEASESIN2001 (CD,ARTIST,COUNTRY,SONG,RELEASED)
AS SELECT CD.TITLE AS "CD", A.NAME AS "ARTIST"
, A.COUNTRY AS "COUNTRY", S.TITLE AS "SONG"
```

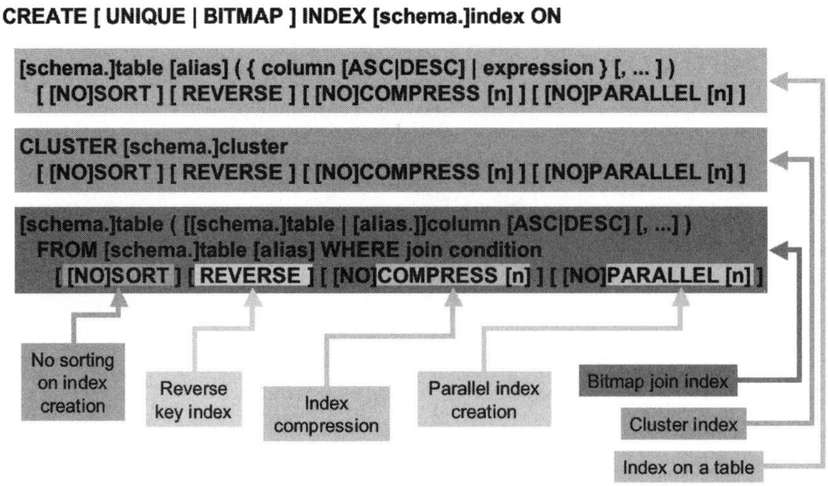

Figure 21.3
CREATE INDEX
Syntax.

```
CREATE [ UNIQUE | BITMAP ] INDEX [schema.]index ON
```

[schema.]table [alias] ({ column [ASC|DESC] | expression } [, ...])
   [[NO]SORT] [REVERSE] [[NO]COMPRESS [n]] [[NO]PARALLEL [n]]

CLUSTER [schema.]cluster
   [[NO]SORT] [REVERSE] [[NO]COMPRESS [n]] [[NO]PARALLEL [n]]

[schema.]table ([[schema.]table | [alias.]]column [ASC|DESC] [, ...])
   FROM [schema.]table [alias] WHERE join condition
      [[NO]SORT] [REVERSE] [[NO]COMPRESS [n]] [[NO]PARALLEL [n]]

No sorting on index creation
Reverse key index
Index compression
Parallel index creation
Bitmap join index
Cluster index
Index on a table

```
, CD.PRESSED_DATE AS RELEASED
FROM MUSICCD CD, CDTRACK T, ARTIST A, SONG S
WHERE CD.PRESSED_DATE BETWEEN '01-JAN-01' AND '31-DEC-01'
AND T.MUSICCD_ID = CD.MUSICCD_ID
AND S.SONG_ID = T.SONG_ID
AND A.ARTIST_ID = S.ARTIST_ID;
```

The table is created with a subquery, so data is inserted as the table is created. Look at the rows created in the new RELEASESIN2001 table you have just created. The result of the query is shown in Figure 21.4.

```
SET WRAP OFF LINESIZE 100
COLUMN CD FORMAT A16
COLUMN ARTIST FORMAT A12
COLUMN COUNTRY FORMAT A8
COLUMN SONG FORMAT A36
SELECT * FROM RELEASESIN2001;
```

Now let's create some indexes on our RELEASESIN2001 table. First, create an index on the CD column. This is a nonunique index because the CD name repeats for each song on the CD.

```
CREATE INDEX RELEASES_CD ON RELEASESIN2001 (CD);
```

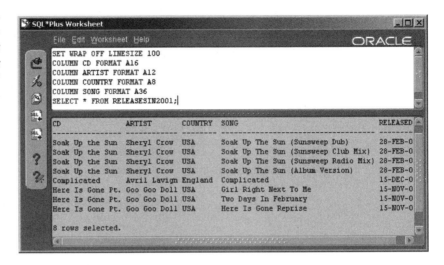

Figure 21.4
Selecting the Rows
in the
RELEASESIN2001
Table.

Next, create an index on both the CD and the SONG columns and compress the index to save space.

```
CREATE INDEX RELEASES_CD_SONG
ON RELEASESIN2001 (CD, SONG) COMPRESS;
```

The following index is a compound index on three columns. The CD column is sorted in descending order.

```
CREATE INDEX RELEASES_CD_ARTIST_SONG
ON RELEASESIN2001 (CD DESC, ARTIST, SONG);
```

This index is a unique index on the SONG table. Each song in this table is unique, allowing you to create a unique index.

```
CREATE UNIQUE INDEX RELEASES_SONG
ON RELEASESIN2001 (SONG);
```

This final index is a bitmap index on the COUNTRY column. This column has very low cardinality. Low cardinality means that there are a small number of distinct values in relation to the number of rows in the table. A bitmap index may be appropriate.

```
CREATE BITMAP INDEX RELEASES_COUNTRY
```

```
ON RELEASESIN2001 (COUNTRY);
```

Note: Be very careful using bitmap indexes in place of BTree indexes.

We have just created five indexes on the RELEASESIN2001 table.

Note: Every DML operation (INSERT, UPDATE, or DELETE) would change the table and five indexes: six updates in total! Having so many indexes on one table is not advisable with respect to performance. However, for a data warehouse table it is fine, because changes to the tables are usually done in batches periodically. You could possibly remove the indexes during updates and then re-create the indexes afterward.

Now let's get a little more specialized and create a function-based index. The following example creates a function-based index on the MUSIC schema SALES data warehouse fact table.

```
CREATE INDEX XAKFB_SALES_1
ON SALES((SALE_PRICE-SHIPPING_COST)*SALE_QTY);
```

We could then query the SALES table and probably persuade the Optimizer to access the index in the WHERE clause with a query something like the following. The result is shown in Figure 21.5.

```
SELECT CD.TITLE "CD"
, SUM(S.SALE_PRICE-S.SHIPPING_COST) "Net Price"
, SUM(S.SALE_QTY) "Qty"
, SUM((SALE_PRICE-SHIPPING_COST)*SALE_QTY) "Revenue"
FROM MUSICCD CD JOIN SALES S USING (MUSICCD_ID)
WHERE ((SALE_PRICE-SHIPPING_COST)*SALE_QTY) > 10
GROUP BY CD.TITLE;
```

There are some points to note about function-based indexes. Some specific settings are required in Oracle Database to allow use of function-based indexes.

- Cost-based optimization is required.

Figure 21.5
Using a Function Based Index.

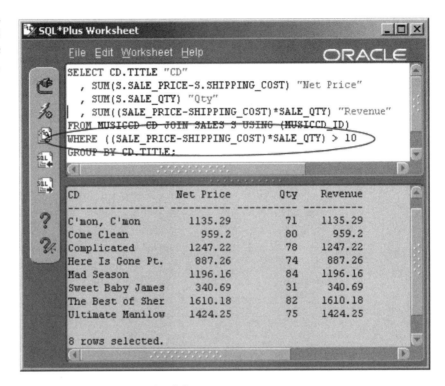

- The user must have the following:

  - The QUERY_REWRITE system privilege.
  - Execute privileges on any user-defined functions.

- Oracle Database configuration parameters must be set as follows:

  - QUERY_REWRITE_ENABLED = TRUE.
  - QUERY REWRITE_INTEGRITY = TRUSTED.

Now let's try a bitmap join index. The previous query demonstrating a function-based index joined the MUSICCD table and the SALES fact table. The MUSICCD table in this case could be considered a dimension of the SALES fact table. Thus a bitmap index would be created on the SALES table MUSICCD_ID column and joined to the MUSICCD_ID primary key column on the MUSICCD facts table.

```
CREATE BITMAP INDEX XAKBJ_SALES_2
ON SALES (S.MUSICCD_ID)
   FROM MUSICCD CD, SALES S
WHERE S.MUSICCD_ID = CD.MUSICCD_ID;
```

What this command has done is to create what is effectively a prejoined index between the SALES and MUSICCD tables. The ON clause identifies the SALES table as the fact table, including both fact and dimension tables in the FROM clause, and the WHERE clause performs the join. Voilà! A bitmap join index.

Now let's look into changing and dropping indexes.

21.1.4 Changing and Dropping Indexes

The indexes we created in the previous section were adequate, but they can be improved. Many index improvements and alterations can be made using the ALTER INDEX command, whose syntax is shown in Figure 21.6. What about those improvements to our indexes created on the RELEASESIN2001 table? Some of the indexes cannot be changed using the ALTER INDEX command. Some index changes have to be made by dropping and re-creating the index. The syntax for the DROP INDEX command is very simple and is also shown in Figure 21.6.

Let's go ahead and change some of the indexes we created in the previous section. First, compress the index you created on the CD column. The ONLINE option creates the index in temporary space, only replacing the original index when the new index has completed rebuilding. This minimizes potential disruption between building an index and DML or query activity during the index rebuild. If, for example, an index build fails

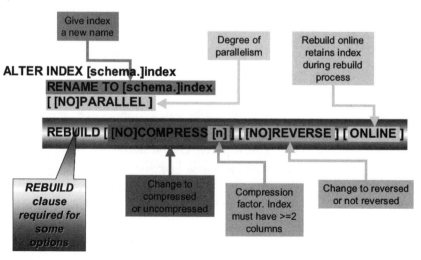

Figure 21.6
ALTER INDEX and DROP INDEX Syntax.

because of lack of space, and nobody notices, any subsequent queries using the index, as instructed to do so by the Optimizer, will simply not find table rows not rebuilt into the index.

```
ALTER INDEX RELEASES_CD REBUILD COMPRESS ONLINE;
```

In fact, to rebuild an index, with all defaults, simply execute the following command. The ONLINE option is a good idea in an active environment but not a syntactical requirement.

```
ALTER INDEX RELEASES_CD REBUILD ONLINE;
```

Next, we want to change the index on CD and SONG to a unique index. An index cannot be altered from nonunique to unique using the ALTER INDEX command. We must drop and re-create the existing index in order to change the index to a unique index. The new index is also created as a compressed index.

```
DROP INDEX RELEASES_CD_SONG;
CREATE UNIQUE INDEX RELEASES_CD_SONG
ON RELEASESIN2001 (CD, SONG) COMPRESS;
```

Incidentally, compression can be instituted using the ALTER INDEX command, so we compress the index using the ALTER INDEX command as shown in the following command:

```
ALTER INDEX RELEASES_CD REBUILD ONLINE COMPRESS;
```

Finally, rename the index on CD, ARTIST, and SONG.

```
ALTER INDEX RELEASES_CD_ARTIST_SONG RENAME TO RELEASES_3COLS;
```

21.1.5 More Indexing Refinements

Here are a few more points you should know about using indexes:

- **Primary, Foreign, and Unique Keys**. Primary and unique key constraints have indexes created automatically by Oracle Database. It is recommended to create indexes for all foreign key constraints.

- **Matching WHERE Clauses to Indexes**. If your query's WHERE clause contains only the second column in an index, Oracle Database 10*g* may not use the index for your query because you don't have the first column in the index included in the WHERE clause. Consider the columns used in the WHERE clauses whenever adding more indexes to a table.

- **Skip Scanning Indexes**. A new feature introduced in Oracle Database 9*i* called Index Skip Scanning may help the Optimizer use indexes, even for queries not having the first indexed column in the WHERE clause. In other words, Index Skip Scanning is employed by the Optimizer to search within composite indexes, without having to refer to the first column in the index, commonly called the *index prefix*.

- **Bitmap Indexes and the WHERE Clause**. Using bitmap indexes allows optimized SQL statement parsing and execution, without having to match WHERE clause order against composite index orders. In other words, multiple bitmap indexes can be used in a WHERE clause. However, bitmap indexes can only be used for equality comparisons (e.g., COUNTRY='USA'). The Optimizer will not use a bitmap index if the WHERE clause has range comparisons (e.g., COUNTRY LIKE 'U%') on the indexed columns.

Refer to the Oracle documentation for more details on how the Optimizer evaluates the WHERE clause for index usage.[2]

The next section delves briefly into using clusters.

21.2   **Clusters**

A cluster is somewhat like an IOT and somewhere between an index and a table. A cluster, a little like a bitmap join index, can also join multiple tables to get prejoined indexes.

21.2.1   **What is a Cluster?**

A cluster is literally a clustering or persistent "joining together" of data from one or more sources. These multiple sources are tables and indexes. A cluster places data and index space rows together into the same object. Obviously, clusters can be arranged such that they are very fast performers for read-only data. Any type of DML activity on a cluster will overflow. Rows read from overflow will be extremely heavy on performance. Clusters are intended for data warehouses.

A standard cluster stores index columns for multiple tables and some or all nonindexed columns. A cluster simply organizes parts of tables into a combination index and data space sorted structure. Datatypes must be consistent across tables.

21.2.2 Types of Clusters

- **Regular Cluster**. This is simply a cluster.

- **Hash Cluster**. A cluster indexed using a hashing algorithm. Hash clusters are more efficient than standard clusters and are even more appropriate for read-only type data. In older relational databases, hash indexes were often used against integer values for better data access speed. If data was changed, the hash index had to be rebuilt.

- (10*g*) **Sorted Hash Cluster**. Uses the SORT option shown in Figure 21.7, essentially breaking up data into groups of hash values. Hash values are derived from a cluster key value, forcing common rows to be stored in the same physical location. A sorted hash cluster has an additional performance benefit for queries accessing rows in the order in which the hash cluster is ordered, thus the term *sorted hash cluster*.

21.2.3 Creating Clusters

I always find it a little confusing attempting to classify a cluster as a table or an index. Because clusters have aspects of both, I find it wise to include an explanation of clusters with that of indexing, after tables have been explained. Tables are covered in Chapter 18. In simple terms, a cluster is a database object that when created has tables added to it. A cluster is not a table, even though it is created using a CREATE TABLE command. Figure 21.7 shows a syntax diagram containing syntax details relevant to creating a cluster.

Note: There is an ALTER CLUSTER command, but it only allows physical changes; thus, it is database administration and irrelevant to the Oracle SQL content of this book.

Let's look at a simple example. Note that in the following example, we have created both a cluster and a cluster index.

Figure 21.7
*CREATE TABLE
Syntax for a
Cluster.*

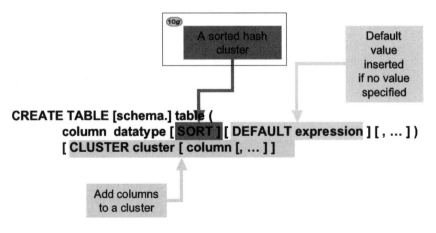

Note: The CREATE TABLE and CREATE CLUSTER system privileges are required.

```
CREATE CLUSTER SALESCLU (SALES_ID NUMBER);
CREATE INDEX XSALESCLU ON CLUSTER SALESCLU;
```

Now we add two dimension tables to the fact cluster:

```
CREATE TABLE CONTINENT_SALESCLU CLUSTER
SALESCLU(CONTINENT_ID)
AS SELECT * FROM CONTINENT;
CREATE TABLE COUNTRY_SALESCLU CLUSTER SALESCLU(COUNTRY_ID)
AS SELECT * FROM COUNTRY;
```

We could add a join to the cluster. Because the structure of the cluster is being altered, we need to drop the tables already added to the cluster and drop and re-create the cluster, because of the table content of the join. This cluster joins two dimensions, continent and country, to the SALES fact table.

```
DROP TABLE CONTINENT_SALESCLU;
DROP TABLE COUNTRY_SALESCLU;
DROP CLUSTER SALESCLU;
CREATE CLUSTER SALESCLU (CONTINENT_ID NUMBER
, COUNTRY_ID NUMBER, CUSTOMER_ID NUMBER
```

```
, SALES_ID NUMBER);
CREATE INDEX XSALESCLU ON CLUSTER SALESCLU;
CREATE TABLE JOIN_SALESCLU CLUSTER SALESCLU
(CONTINENT_ID, COUNTRY_ID, CUSTOMER_ID, SALES_ID)
AS SELECT S.CONTINENT_ID AS CONTINENT_ID
, S.COUNTRY_ID AS COUNTRY_ID
, S.CUSTOMER_ID AS CUSTOMER_ID
, S.SALES_ID AS SALES_ID
FROM CONTINENT CT, COUNTRY CY, CUSTOMER C, SALES S
WHERE CT.CONTINENT_ID = S.CONTINENT_ID
AND CY.COUNTRY_ID = S.COUNTRY_ID
AND C.CUSTOMER_ID = S.CUSTOMER_ID;
```

Note: Note how not all columns in all tables are added into the cluster from the join. A cluster is intended to physically group the most frequently accessed data and sorted orders.

That's enough about clusters as far as Oracle SQL is concerned.

21.3 Metadata Views

This section simply describes metadata views applicable to indexes and clusters. Chapter 19 describes the basis and detail of Oracle Database metadata views.

- **USER_INDEXES**. Structure of indexes.

- **USER_IND_COLUMNS**. Column structure of indexes.

- **USER_IND_EXPRESSIONS**. Contains function-based index expressions.

- **USER_JOIN_IND_COLUMNS**. Join indexes such as bitmap join indexes.

- **USER_PART_INDEXES**. Index information at the partition level.

- **USER_IND_PARTITIONS**. Partition-level indexing details.

- **USER_IND_SUBPARTITIONS**. Subpartition-level indexing details.

- **USER_CLUSTERS**. Structure of constraints such as who owns it, its type, the table it is attached to, and states, among other details.

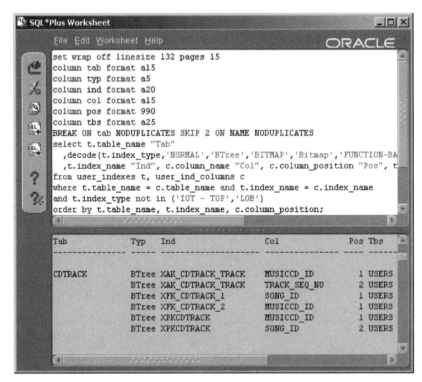

Figure 21.8
Querying
USER_INDEXES
*and USER_IND_*
COLUMNS.

- **USER_CLU_COLUMNS**. Describes all columns in constraints.

- **USER_CLUSTER_HASH_EXPRESSIONS**. Hash clustering functions.

The script executed in Figure 21.8 matches indexes and index columns for the currently logged-in user. The script is included in Appendix B.

This chapter has described both indexing and clustering. Indexes are of paramount importance to building proper Oracle SQL code and general success of applications. The next chapter covers sequences and synonyms.

21.4 **Endnotes**

1.   Oracle Performance Tuning for 9*i* and 10*g* (ISBN: 1-55558-305-9)

2.   Oracle Performance Tuning for 9*i* and 10*g* (ISBN: 1-55558-305-9)

22

Sequences and Synonyms

In this chapter:

- What is a sequence object?

- What are the uses of sequences?

- What is a synonym?

In recent chapters we have examined tables, views, constraints, indexes, and clusters. Last but not least of the database objects we shall deal with directly in this book are sequences and synonyms.

Let's begin this chapter with sequences, usually called Oracle sequence objects.

22.1 Sequences

A sequence allows for generation of unique, sequential values. Sequences are most commonly used to generate unique identifying integer values for primary and unique keys. Sequences are typically used in the types of SQL statements listed as follows:

- The VALUES clause of an INSERT statement.

- A subquery SELECT list contained within the VALUES clause of an INSERT statement.

- The SET clause of an UPDATE statement.

- A query SELECT list.

A sequence is always accessed using the CURRVAL and NEXTVAL pseudocolumns in the format as shown:

- **sequence.CURRVAL**. Returns the current value of the sequence. The sequence is not incremented by the CURRVAL pseudocolumn.

- **sequence.NEXTVAL**. Returns the value of the sequence and increases the sequence one increment. Usually, sequences increase by increments of one each time; however, you can set a sequence to a different increment if needed.

22.1.1 Creating Sequences

A sequence can be created as shown in the syntax diagram in Figure 22.1.

Creating a sequence does not require any parameters other than the sequence name. Executing the command shown as follows will create a sequence called A_SEQUENCE in the current schema with an initial value of zero and an incremental value of one. See the result of the following commands in Figure 22.2.

```
CREATE SEQUENCE A_SEQUENCE;
SELECT A_SEQUENCE.NEXTVAL FROM DUAL;
```

Figure 22.1
CREATE
SEQUENCE
Syntax.

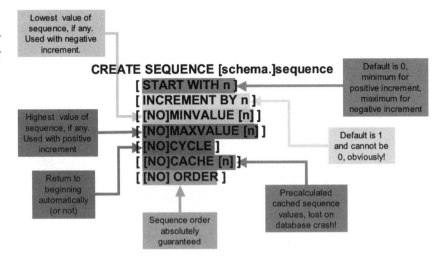

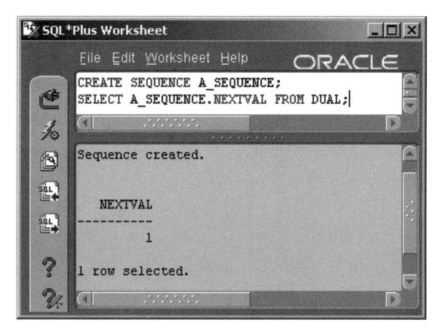

Figure 22.2
*Create a Sequence
and Select the Next
Value.*

We could, of course, create a sequence including START WITH and INCREMENT BY parameters without relying on the defaults. We can even set the INCREMENT BY value to a negative value and make the sequence count backward. Let's drop the sequence we just created and demonstrate this point. See the result of the following commands in Figure 22.3.

```
DROP SEQUENCE A_SEQUENCE;
CREATE SEQUENCE A_SEQUENCE INCREMENT BY -1;
SELECT A_SEQUENCE.NEXTVAL FROM DUAL;
SELECT A_SEQUENCE.NEXTVAL FROM DUAL;
SELECT A_SEQUENCE.NEXTVAL FROM DUAL;
```

Other parameters for sequence creation, so far not discussed but shown in the syntax diagram in Figure 22.1, are as listed. All of these parameters are switched off by default.

- **MINVALUE.** Sets a minimum value for a sequence. The default is NOMINVALUE. This is used for sequences that decrease rather than increase.

Figure 22.3
*Create a Sequence
That Counts
Backward.*

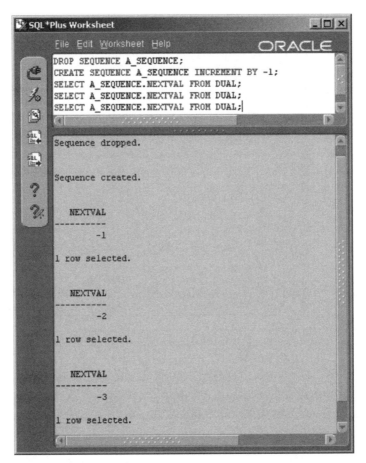

- **MAXVALUE.** Sets a maximum value for a sequence. The default is NOMAXVALUE. Be aware that a column datatype may cause an error if the number grows too large. For example, if the sequence is used to populate a column of NUMBER(5) datatype, once the sequence reaches 99999, then the next increment will cause an error.

- **CYCLE.** Causes a sequence to cycle around to its minimum when reaching its maximum for an ascending sequence, and to cycle around to its maximum when reaching its minimum for a descending sequence. The default is NOCYCLE. If you reach the maximum value on a sequence having NOCYCLE, you will get an error on the next query that tries to increment the sequence.

- **CACHE.** This option caches precalculated sequences into a buffer. If the database crashes, then those sequence values will be lost. Unless it

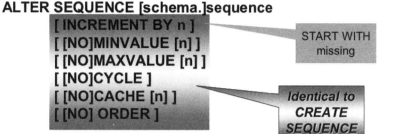

Figure 22.4
*ALTER
SEQUENCE
Syntax.*

ALTER SEQUENCE [schema.]sequence
[INCREMENT BY n]
[[NO]MINVALUE [n]]
[[NO]MAXVALUE [n]]
[[NO]CYCLE]
[[NO]CACHE [n]]
[[NO] ORDER]

START WITH
missing

Identical to
CREATE
SEQUENCE

DROP SEQUENCE [schema.]sequence

is absolutely imperative to maintain exact sequence counters, then the default of CACHE 20 is best left as it is.

- **ORDER**. Ordering simply guarantees that sequence numbers are created in precise sequential order. In other words, with the NOORDER option, sequence numbers can possibly be generated out of sequence sometimes, when there is excessive concurrent activity on the sequence.

22.1.2 Changing and Dropping Sequences

When changing a sequence, the only parameter not changeable is the START WITH parameter. It is pointless to start an already started sequence. Therefore, resetting the sequence to an initial value requires either recycling (CYCLE) or dropping and re-creating the sequence. The syntax for changing a sequence is as shown in the syntax diagram in Figure 22.4.

Let's change the sequence A_SEQUENCE we created in the previous section, currently a descending sequence, into an ascending sequence. The result of the following commands is shown in Figure 22.5.

```
ALTER SEQUENCE A_SEQUENCE INCREMENT BY 1;
SELECT A_SEQUENCE.NEXTVAL FROM DUAL;
SELECT A_SEQUENCE.NEXTVAL FROM DUAL;
```

We can drop the sequence A_SEQUENCE to clean up.

```
DROP SEQUENCE A_SEQUENCE;
```

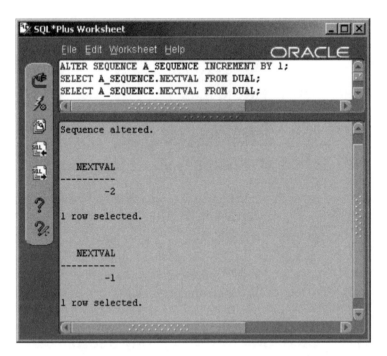

Figure 22.5
*Change a Reverse-
Counting Sequence
to a Forward-
Counting
Sequence.*

22.1.3   Using Sequences

Sequences are valuable as unique key generators because they never issue a duplicate value, even when many users are retrieving numbers from the sequence. For example, let's imagine that you have 10 operators entering customer information into your online system. Each time a new customer row is inserted, it uses a number from the CUSTOMER_SEQ for the primary key, using CUSTOMER_SEQ.NEXTVAL. Even if all 10 operators simultaneously insert a new customer, Oracle Database 10*g* will give each session a unique number. There are never any duplicates.

Another interesting feature of sequences is that they never use the same number again, even if the user cancels the transaction that retrieved the number. Continuing with the operators entering customer information, let's imagine that the tenth operator gets the customer entered and it has retrieved the number 101 from the CUSTOMER_SEQ sequence. Then the operator cancels the transaction (say, the customer changes his mind and hangs up the phone). The next operator to retrieve a sequence gets 102. When using sequences, there may be gaps in the numbers you see in the table caused by retrieving a sequence number and then not actually committing the insert. Obviously, this can have serious implications for accounting systems (e.g., where perhaps tax laws require all numbers to exist as transactions).

22.1.3.1 Using the CURRVAL and NEXTVAL Pseudocolumns

Whenever referring to a sequence within a session, use of the CURRVAL pseudocolumn must be preceded by using the NEXTVAL pseudocolumn. NEXTVAL initializes the sequence for the current session. The very first time a sequence is accessed, NEXTVAL will return its initial value; every subsequent access will return its next incremental value.

Let's use, for example, the ARTIST_ID_SEQ sequence in the MUSIC schema. This sequence is used to generate a primary key identifier value for every row in the ARTIST table. Let's try to find its current value using the following query. See the result in Figure 22.6.

```
SELECT ARTIST_ID_SEQ.CURRVAL FROM DUAL;
```

Looking at Figure 22.6, we can see that we get an error. A sequence must always be initialized for a session using the NEXTVAL pseudocolumn before the CURRVAL pseudocolumn can be used.

Now let's change the previous command and add a first use of the NEXTVAL pseudocolumn into the SQL*Plus Worksheet session before use of the CURRVAL pseudocolumn on the ARTIST_ID_SEQ sequence. The following script has its result in Figure 22.7. The actual number you see may be different if other DML commands are accessing the sequence concurrently.

```
SELECT ARTIST_ID_SEQ.NEXTVAL FROM DUAL;
SELECT ARTIST_ID_SEQ.CURRVAL FROM DUAL;
```

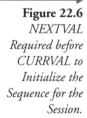

Figure 22.6
NEXTVAL Required before CURRVAL to Initialize the Sequence for the Session.

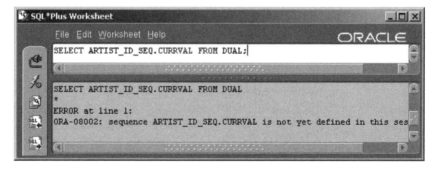

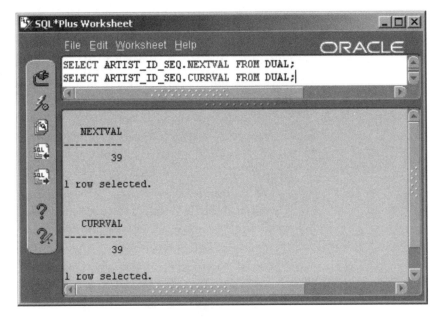

Figure 22.7
*Initializing a
Sequence for a
Session Using
NEXTVAL.*

22.1.3.2   Using Sequences in an INSERT Statement

Sequences can be used to generate primary and foreign keys in INSERT statements. There is plenty of use of sequences in Appendix A, containing the MUSIC schema generation scripts. Following is a sample of one of those scripts called the SONGANDTRACK.SQL script file. This script sample adds a single row to the CDTRACK table. The CDTRACK table has two foreign keys: MUSICCD_ID and SONG_ID.

```
INSERT INTO CDTRACK(MUSICCD_ID,SONG_ID,TRACK_SEQ_NO) VALUES(
 (SELECT MUSICCD_ID FROM MUSICCD
  WHERE TITLE='Soak Up the Sun')
, (SELECT SONG_ID FROM SONG
  WHERE TITLE='Soak Up The Sun (Album Version)')
, 1);
```

There are two subqueries in the previous script sample; each subquery populates a foreign key column with the value of a primary key in another table. The values in the primary key were originally generated from sequences. The first subquery finds the MUSICCD_ID for the CD titled "Soak up the Sun." The second subquery selects the SONG_ID for the song "Soak Up The Sun (Album Version)" by Sheryl Crow.

What about the primary keys? The sample script that follows, again taken from the SONGANDTRACK.SQL script, shows the INSERT command that created the primary key value for a row in the SONG table using a sequence number. The song is "Soak up the Sun (Album Version)" by Sheryl Crow. This unique identifier is the primary key column for the SONG table. Incidentally, the SONG table contains a foreign key to the ARTIST table in the SONG.ARTIST_ID column. The foreign key in the following script is also highlighted and is selected using a subquery from the ARTIST table:

```
INSERT INTO SONG(SONG_ID,ARTIST_ID,TITLE, PLAYING_TIME)
VALUES(SONG_ID_SEQ.NEXTVAL
  , (SELECT ARTIST_ID FROM ARTIST WHERE NAME='Sheryl Crow')
  , 'Soak Up The Sun (Album Version)','11:20');
```

22.1.3.3   Other Uses of Sequences

We have so far used sequences in SELECT statements, INSERT statements, and subqueries. Sequences can be used in UPDATE statements, in a similar fashion to that of INSERT statements, where a sequence already inserted into a primary key column can be used to retrieve a description column value based on an identifier value. For example, you have an order system where a customer can enter a new mailing address when he or she makes a new order (stored in the ORDERS table). Later, your database system updates the master CUSTOMER table with new mailing addresses from the ORDERS table.

```
UPDATE CUSTOMER  SET LATEST_ADDRESS =
(SELECT MAILING_ADDRESS FROM ORDERS
  WHERE ORDERS.CUST_ID = CUSTOMER.CUST_ID);
```

The CUST_ID column in the CUSTOMER table was originally assigned using a sequence.

Another common use for sequences is more indirect than those already mentioned. Sometimes it is useful to retrieve the NEXTVAL of a sequence and use it to insert rows in two related tables (e.g., ARTIST and SONG). When using PL/SQL code (see Chapter 24), you can place a sequence number into a variable and use it within the PL/SQL code. Here is a sample snippet of PL/SQL code, showing an INSERT command using a variable for assigning the primary key (ID) in a table:

```
INSERT INTO table (ID NUMBER) VALUES (sequence.NEXTVAL)
RETURNING ID INTO vID;
```

This brings us to the second topic of discussion for this chapter, synonyms.

22.2 Synonyms

A synonym can effectively provide an alias to any object in any schema in the database, assuming that the user has privileges to view the underlying objects. It makes an object appear as if you own it, because you do not have to use a schema prefix when querying or performing other tasks with the object. Synonyms can provide the following benefits:

- **Transparency**. A synonym masks the name of the schema owning the object. The object can even be in a remote database when you include a database link in the definition of the synonym. A database link is a direct gateway from one database to another database.

- **Simplified SQL code**. Code is simplified because schema names do not have to be included for table accesses where objects are in different schemas.

- **Easy Changes**. Moving objects to different schemas or databases in distributed environments does not require application changes because only synonyms need to be changed.

There is one potential problem with using too many synonyms: A table is a logical overlay on top of physical data on disk. A synonym is another overlay onto a table, a logical overlay overlaying a logical overlay (the table). Why can this be a problem? Let's put it into perspective using a large-scale environment. Assume that you run a database for an online bookstore. Every time a user accesses a table, the application code accesses the table through the synonym. If there are thousands of concurrent users, then both the synonym and table are accessed thousands of times per second. That makes for double the number of system queries into database metadata. Large-scale systems could have problems as a result. No amount of buffer tuning and physical organization will solve an issue such as this one. The same concept applies to views (see Chapter 19). Always be aware of potentially sacrificing database performance for the sake of ease and neatness of application coding.[1] In large OLTP and data warehouse environments, this

Figure 22.8
CREATE
SYNONYM
Syntax.

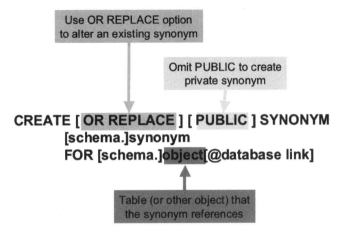

type of thing can cause serious performance problems, but not in smaller-scale client-server environments.

Synonyms can be created as publicly or privately available. All users automatically have access to public synonyms. Private synonyms are available to the schema they are created in, although access can be granted to other users. Access privileges and security are covered in Chapter 23.

22.2.1 Creating Public Synonyms

In the syntax diagram in Figure 22.8, the PUBLIC option determines if a synonym is created publicly or not.

To create a public synonym, you would have to have the system privilege CREATE PUBLIC SYNONYM. Use your SQL*Plus Worksheet session to perform these steps so the MUSIC user is able to create a public synonym. You would have to be logged in as a database administration user such as SYS or SYSTEM to execute these commands.

```
GRANT CREATE SYNONYM TO MUSIC;
GRANT CREATE PUBLIC SYNONYM TO MUSIC;
```

To create a public synonym for the ARTIST table in the MUSIC schema, available to all users, the following command would be executed:

```
CREATE PUBLIC SYNONYM CD FOR MUSICCD;
```

Once the synonym exists, you can change the table it references by using the CREATE OR REPLACE form of the CREATE SYNONYM command. For example, if you had misspelled ARTIST in the previous command, you could fix it by running the following command:

```
CREATE OR REPLACE PUBLIC SYNONYM CD FOR MUSICCD;
```

Note: The act of creating a public synonym does not actually give access to the underlying table's data. Although the synonym is available to all public users, the underlying table is not available, unless specifically granted to a user or a role. Granting privileges is covered in Chapter 23.

22.2.2 Creating Private Synonyms

To create a private synonym, simply create a synonym as before, excluding the PUBLIC keyword, as shown in the following command. Note that if you attempt to create a synonym called ARTIST, Oracle Database will return an error because you cannot create a synonym with the same name as an already existing object, the ARTIST table.

```
CREATE OR REPLACE SYNONYM MYARTISTS FOR MUSIC.ARTIST;
```

The most common use for private synonyms is to create a synonym for a table in another schema. If the table does not have a public synonym, and you use it in queries, you must include the schema name and the table name. Creating a private synonym is like creating an alias that you can use instead of the full schema and table name in your own queries. For example, you can create a private synonym for an object (in this case, for a public synonym) with a long name, as shown in the following command:

```
CREATE SYNONYM MYCOLS FOR USER_TAB_COLUMNS;
```

22.2.3 Using Synonyms

We have already created a private synonym in the MUSIC schema called MYARTISTS, a synonym for the ARTIST table. Let's prove that it works. The following commands should suffice. See the result in Figure 22.9.

```
--Select from the ARTIST table
SELECT ARTIST_ID, NAME FROM ARTIST WHERE NAME LIKE '%u%';
```

Figure 22.9
*Selecting Rows
from a Table and a
Synonym on That
Table.*

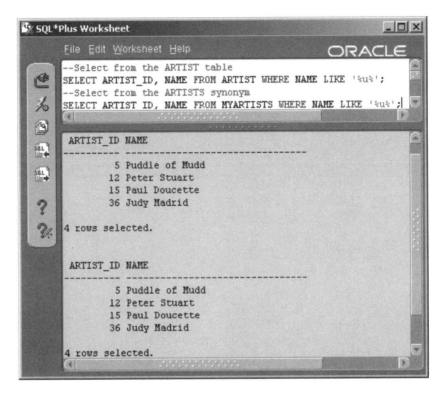

--Select from the ARTISTS synonym
SELECT ARTIST_ID, NAME FROM MYARTISTS WHERE NAME LIKE '%u%';

As you can see, both queries return exactly the same results.

22.3 Metadata Views

This section simply describes metadata views applicable to sequences and synonyms. Chapter 19 describes the basis and detail of Oracle Database metadata views.

- **USER_SEQUENCES**. Current user sequence objects.
- **USER_SYNONYMS**. Private synonym details.

This chapter has described sequences and synonyms, completing chapters on Oracle database objects commonly used directly by Oracle SQL. The next chapter discusses security, users, and privileges.

22.4 Endnotes

1. Oracle Performance Tuning for 9*i* and 10*g* (ISBN: 1-55558-305-9)

23

Security

In this chapter:

- How do you create a user?

- How do you change a user, and what can be changed?

- What are privileges?

- How are privileges classified?

- How do roles group privileges?

- When are roles and privileges used?

This chapter covers general Oracle Database 10*g* access privilege and security issues. You will find out how to share your table data with others using privileges and roles. You will also learn the DBA tasks of creating new users and giving them authority to perform various kinds of work within the database. Creating and managing users and privileges are often DBA tasks. As a result, many DBA-type options are omitted from this chapter. On the other hand, simple security and access skills are very useful for Oracle SQL programmers, especially in isolated development environments.

23.1 Users

You might have been practicing throughout reading this book on a database using the MUSIC schema. You know, of course, that you have been logging into Oracle Database as an Oracle user. The user has a name, such as MUSIC, and a password. The MUSIC user has authority to create tables in its own schema. The MUSIC user was created by another user, who has authority to create users and assign them the capabilities they need, such as the ability to create a table.

One of the most important reasons for creating more users is so you can isolate and limit the privileges of the person who logs into the database, giving that person only the privileges needed to perform his or her duties and nothing more. After all, you don't want the intern you just hired to be allowed to drop an entire schema full of tables by mistake.

Typically, the DBA creates an Oracle user for each person who needs to use the database. This user has a unique password, which should be kept secret and should be known only by the DBA and the user. This gives you the most flexibility in designing your security around the specific tasks each person carries out in the database. For example, one person enters customer orders while working on the company's toll-free phone line. Another person processes the orders and uses the database to update the customer orders with a shipping date. A third person handles customer billing and returns, updating the customer's account information as needed for payments or refunds.

Note: In the age of the Internet, Oracle usernames are generally shared among many users through the use of connection pooling, application servers, and Web servers.

How do you get started creating users? You start with a small group of users that was already created when you began using your database.

23.1.1 Users Provided by Oracle

To create a user, you must log into the database as a DBA user. The SYSTEM user, created as part of the Oracle Database 10*g* database creation process, is a DBA user. So, you can log in as SYSTEM to create more users. Oracle Database 10*g* comes with a multitude of predefined users that have specific uses. For the purposes of Oracle SQL, we are interested in the SYS and SYSTEM users only, and obviously your application usernames, such as the MUSIC schema.

- **SYS**. SYS is the internal table owner. This user owns most of the tables that are used internally for the database's functioning. This user has the greatest amount of access to all areas of the database. Be careful when logged in as SYS because you have the power to do things that can completely disable your database. For example, SYS can drop an internal table or modify data in an internal table, possibly rendering the database useless. Log in as the SYS user primarily when performing these tasks. A SYS user connection always requires the SYSDBA or SYSOPER (special system privileges) to perform the following tasks:

- Exporting and importing data.
- Shutting down and starting up the database.
- Database recovery.

- **SYSTEM**. SYSTEM is the database administrator. This user is frequently used by the DBA to perform day-to-day tasks of monitoring and administering the database. SYSTEM can do many of the same tasks as the SYS user, without the danger of accidentally damaging internal tables or bouncing the database. Log in as the SYSTEM user when performing these tasks:

  - Creating new users, changing user passwords.
  - Assigning system privileges to users or roles (you will understand what this means when you get further into this chapter).
  - Monitoring database activity and performance.
  - Adjusting database parameters (usually to improve performance).
  - Adding more space to the database.

- **Feature-Related Users**. These users are the owners of tables and other objects related to specific Oracle Database 10*g* features such as replication, spatial support, and advanced queuing. Depending on how many features were installed with your database, there may be quite a few of these users. Do not log in as any of these users unless specifically instructed to do so by Oracle Database 10*g* documentation.

Note: In the past, passwords for SYS and SYSTEM were defined as part of the database creation process and defaulted to "change_on_install" and "manager," respectively. Oracle Database 10*g* forces password definition on installation. You know what they are if you installed the database. If not, ask the person who did the installation for the passwords. If you need those passwords, they will be given to you.

23.1.2 Creating Users

The syntax for creating users is much easier than the syntax for creating a table! There are far fewer options. Figure 23.1 shows the syntax.

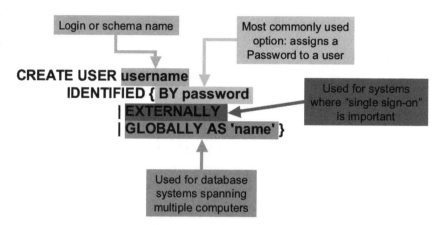

Figure 23.1
Creating a User Is Straightforward.

There are three methods available for Oracle Database 10*g* user authentication:

- **IDENTIFIED BY password**. Assigning a password to the user is the most commonly used method. This password is only good for logging onto the database and must be used every time you log on. The password is stored in the database as an encrypted string that even the DBA cannot decrypt.

- **IDENTIFIED EXTERNALLY**. This method tells Oracle Database 10*g* to ask the operating system to tell it who is logging in. This means that if you log into your Windows 2000 computer as CAROLINE, then Oracle Database 10*g* logs you in as CAROLINE. Sometimes a prefix is added to the username, just so you can tell the difference between users identified by passwords or by external names. The default prefix is OPS$, so Oracle Database 10*g* actually logs CAROLINE into the database with the username OPS$CAROLINE. Oracle Database 10*g* does not store any password information for this type of user.

- **IDENTIFIED GLOBALLY AS 'name'**. This method tells Oracle Database 10*g* to look for a global variable (stored in the network somewhere) that has your user name in it. This feature of Oracle Database 10*g* allows a user to log into a remote site and access a database at another site without having to provide an additional username and password. Oracle Database 10*g* does not store password information for this type of user.

> **Note:** In this book, you work only with users who are assigned a password.

You must be logged into the database as a user who has authority to create new users. The SYSTEM user has this capability. Let's say you have a person who wants to view the CDs that you have in the MUSIC schema. The first step in allowing the user access to the tables is to give him or her access to the database.

> **Note:** Passwords can include numbers, letters, and even characters to make them harder to crack.

Let's create a new user. First, I connect as my SYSTEM user, allowing me to create a user. Replace the password and network connection string (OLTP) with values appropriate for your database:

```
CONNECT SYSTEM/password@OLTP;
```

The following command creates a new user with the name JACKIE and her password set to J25RX:

```
CREATE USER JACKIE IDENTIFIED BY J25RX;
```

JACKIE is now an Oracle user, but she cannot actually log in until she is given the basic privilege to do so. The CREATE SESSION privilege allows a user to connect to the database. Connecting to the database creates a session.

```
GRANT CREATE SESSION TO JACKIE;
```

JACKIE would now be able to log in to the database using a CONNECT command.

```
CONNECT JACKIE/J25RX@OLTP;
```

Figure 23.2
*JACKIE Is
Logged On.*

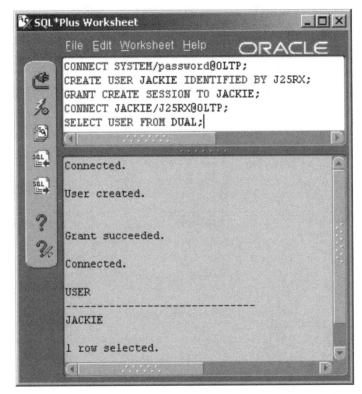

Once logged in as JACKIE, you could check your username by typing the following command. Figure 23.2 shows the result of the four commands executed previously plus the following simple query:

```
SELECT USER FROM DUAL;
```

Once a user is created and given the CREATE SESSION privilege, he or she can log on but cannot do much of anything else. One thing any user can do, however, is to change his or her password.

23.1.3   Modifying User Passwords

A user can change his or her password at any time. In addition, the SYS-TEM user (or another user with the appropriate privileges) can change any user's password. The syntax for changing a password is shown in Figure 23.3. The syntax is identical, whether you are changing your own password or another user's password.

Figure 23.3
Change the Password with the ALTER USER Command.

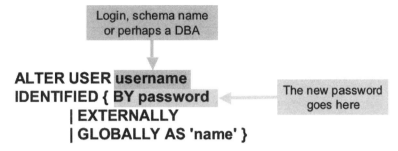

Now let's change the password for Jackie. If not already logged in as JACKIE, then the first command will do that:

```
CONNECT JACKIE/J25RX@OLTP;
```

Now let's change Jackie's password to JACKIE001:

```
ALTER USER JACKIE IDENTIFIED BY JACKIE001;
```

You could then test the change by reconnecting with the new password:

```
CONNECT JACKIE/JACKIE001@OLTP;
```

Now we could reconnect to the SYSTEM user to practice changing another user's password:

```
CONNECT SYSTEM/password@OLTP;
```

We could once again change Jackie's password by running the same command that Jackie ran. This time, change the password to JACKIE#1:

```
ALTER USER JACKIE IDENTIFIED BY JACKIE#1;
```

We could verify Jackie's new password by connecting with the new password:

```
CONNECT JACKIE/JACKIE#1@OLTP;
```

- That was easy!

Note: No one can view a password stored in the database, not even the SYS or SYSTEM users.

Let's imagine that a DBA must remove old users from the database. Some employees may have quit or retired. Others may have moved to different jobs, no longer requiring database access.

23.1.4   Dropping Users

When you remove a user, it is called dropping the user. The syntax is shown in Figure 23.4, and this is about as brief as it gets.

If a user has created tables, indexes, or other objects, you must add the CASCADE keyword to the command so that all of the user's objects are dropped first, followed by the user.

Here are a few rules about dropping users:

- You cannot drop yourself.
- You cannot drop a user who is logged on.
- You cannot drop the SYS or SYSTEM users.

The user JACKIE can be removed from the database by running the following command:

```
DROP USER JACKIE;
```

Figure 23.4
Dropping a User Must Be Done by the DBA.

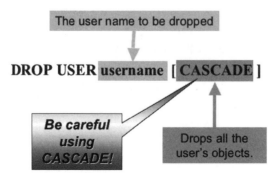

The user name to be dropped

DROP USER username [CASCADE]

Be careful using CASCADE!

Drops all the user's objects.

As you can see, adding and removing users is very easy. Giving the appropriate privileges to the appropriate users gets a bit more complex. So let's now examine privileges.

23.2 Privileges

A privilege gives a user permission to perform certain tasks or access specific objects in the database. There are two types of privileges:

- **System Privileges**. These give a user the capability to do something in the database, such as create tables or create views.
- **Object Privileges**. These give a user access to the data in an object, such as the privilege to select or update rows in a specific table.

When you assign (grant) a privilege, you can give a user the ability to assign the privilege to others. You have to be logged on with a user who has the privilege and has the right to assign that privilege as well. The SYSTEM user, being a DBA, has just about every privilege needed to assign privileges to others.

23.2.1 Granting Privileges

The syntax for granting system and object privileges is very similar. Figure 23.5 shows both system and object privileges.

Roles are discussed later in this chapter. For now, focus on the commands as they are used to grant system and object privileges to users. Some important differences to note between granting system privileges and granting object privileges are as follows:

- When granting system privileges, the WITH ADMIN OPTION can be used.
- When granting object privileges, the WITH GRANT OPTION can be used.
- Only object privileges name a specific object, such as a table, with the ON clause.

Now let's demonstrate executing granting of privileges. Once again, we begin by connecting as the SYSTEM user.

Figure 23.5
*Granting System
and Object
Privileges Uses
Similar Syntax.*

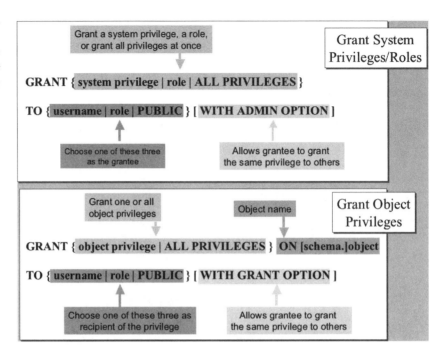

```
CONNECT SYSTEM/password@OLTP;
```

Start by creating two new users on which to experiment by running the following commands. The PRINCE user will be creating tables, so he needs additional parameters that allow him to use a tablespace for the tables.

```
CREATE USER ARIEL IDENTIFIED BY MERMAID;
CREATE USER PRINCE IDENTIFIED BY CHARMING
DEFAULT TABLESPACE USERS QUOTA 2M ON USERS;
```

Note: The DEFAULT TABLESPACE and QUOTA options are DBA things but necessary to allow creation of stuff like tables.

Grant the system privilege that allows these two users to connect to the database.

```
GRANT CREATE SESSION TO ARIEL, PRINCE;
```

You can grant a system privilege to several users at once.

Let's say that PRINCE needs to be able to create his own tables and views. Plus, you want PRINCE to be allowed to give these privileges to other users. The following command gives him the privileges needed:

```
GRANT CREATE TABLE, CREATE VIEW TO PRINCE
WITH ADMIN OPTION;
```

As you can see, it is possible to list more than one system privilege in a single GRANT command.

Now, let's say that ARIEL needs to be able to run queries and modify data in the MUSICCD table. Because ARIEL does not own the table, she must be granted object privileges. Both the DBA user and the owner of a table can grant object privileges on a table. So we can connect to the MUSIC schema and grant privileges to other users.

```
CONNECT MUSIC/MUSIC@OLTP;
```

Now run this command to give ARIEL the capabilities she needs:

```
GRANT SELECT, INSERT, UPDATE, DELETE
ON MUSIC.MUSICCD TO ARIEL;
```

You decide that the information about artists should be viewable by any user who can log onto the database. The PUBLIC user group is a special group accessible by all users. Rather than granting privileges to all users individually, use PUBLIC. Any privilege granted to PUBLIC is granted to all users, even users that are created after you issue the GRANT command. The next command gives all users the ability to query the ARTIST table:

```
GRANT SELECT ON MUSIC.ARTIST TO PUBLIC;
```

Now you could log in as ARIEL and test out what you are allowed to see in the MUSIC schema.

```
CONNECT ARIEL/MERMAID@OLTP;
```

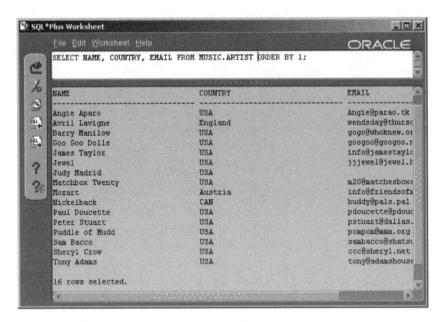

Figure 23.6
Add the Schema Name to the Table Name when Querying Tables You Do Not Own.

Test the ability of ARIEL to query the ARTIST table in the MUSIC schema by executing a query while logged in as ARIEL. The result of this query is shown in Figure 23.6.

```
SELECT NAME, COUNTRY, EMAIL FROM MUSIC.ARTIST
ORDER BY 1;
```

Now we could query the SONG table, which ARIEL has no privileges to view, still logged in as ARIEL.

```
SELECT TITLE, RECORDING_DATE FROM MUSIC.SONG
ORDER BY 1;
```

Figure 23.7 shows the result. Oracle Database 10*g* tells us the table does not exist! This may seem confusing, but it is intended to prevent hackers from trying to find tables in the database. If Oracle Database 10*g* gave the unauthorized user even a hint that he had found the name and schema of a table, but simply did not have access to it, that could give the user enough information to continue attempting to access the table. The deliberately vague message discourages snooping.

Figure 23.7
A Table That Really Exists Is Invisible to an Unauthorized User.

A different message appears when you do not have the system privilege needed to perform a task. We could create a simple table, such as the following:

```
CREATE TABLE SEASHELLS (SHELLNAME VARCHAR2(20));
```

Figure 23.8 shows the result. ARIEL has not been granted the CREATE TABLE system privilege, and therefore Oracle Database 10*g* issues an error message stating "insufficient privileges."

Figure 23.8
Cannot Create a New Table without the CREATE TABLE System Privilege.

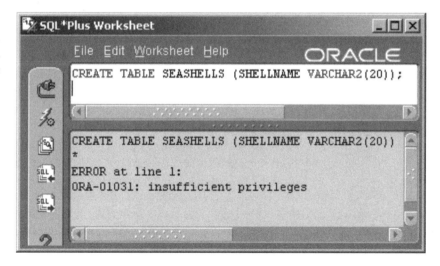

Now let's connect to PRINCE and experiment with his privileges.

```
CONNECT PRINCE/CHARMING@OLTP;
```

Let's create a small table owned by PRINCE.

```
CREATE TABLE MYHORSES (NAME VARCHAR2(30) PRIMARY KEY
, STALL NUMBER);
```

Now grant the object privilege to ARIEL, for querying this new table.

```
GRANT SELECT ON MYHORSES TO ARIEL;
```

SQL*Plus will reply with, "Grant succeeded." The owner of a table, PRINCE, can grant object privileges on that table.

Additionally, PRINCE has WITH ADMIN OPTION on the CREATE TABLE and CREATE VIEW system privileges, so he can grant them to others. The next command will allow PRINCE to grant the ability to create views to ARIEL.

```
GRANT CREATE VIEW TO ARIEL;
```

Let's take a small step back for a moment and look briefly at system and object privileges. There are a multitude of system privileges. For a complete list, see Oracle documentation. As far as Oracle SQL is concerned, you do

Table 23.1 *System Privileges*

System Privilege	Description
CREATE ANY TABLE	Create a table in any user's schema.
CREATE TABLE	Create a table in your own schema only.
CREATE USER	Create a new Oracle user.
ALTER DATABASE	Modify database settings with the ALTER DATA-BASE command.
CREATE ANY INDEX	Create an index on a table in any schema.

Table 23.1 *System Privileges (continued)*

System Privilege	Description
EXECUTE ANY PROCEDURE	Run any procedure (useful for the DBA, who may need to run Oracle-provided procedures).
CREATE ROLE	Create a role (see the next section in this chapter).
CREATE SEQUENCE	Create a sequence in your own schema.
SELECT ANY SEQUENCE	Query a sequence, using CURRVAL and NEXTVAL, in any schema.
SELECT ANY TABLE	Query any schema's tables.
CREATE PUBLIC SYNONYM	Create a public synonym.

not need to know about all available privileges. However, you should know the more common ones. Table 23.1 lists commonly used system privileges.

Object privileges are much easier to swallow because there are far fewer of them. The basic object privileges available on tables are as shown in Table 23.2.

There are slightly different object privileges for different types of objects. For example, views have nearly the same privileges as tables because they are similar in structure. Packages and procedures, on the other hand, have

Table 23.2 *Object Privileges*

Object Privilege	Description
SELECT	Allows retrieval of rows from a table.
INSERT	Allows adding of new rows to a table.
UPDATE	Allows changing of rows in a table.
DELETE	Allows deletion of rows from a table.
INDEX	Allows a user to create an index on a table using the CREATE INDEX command.
ALTER	With respect to tables, allow execution of the ALTER TABLE command and table structural changes.
REFERENCES	Allows creation of table references constraints.

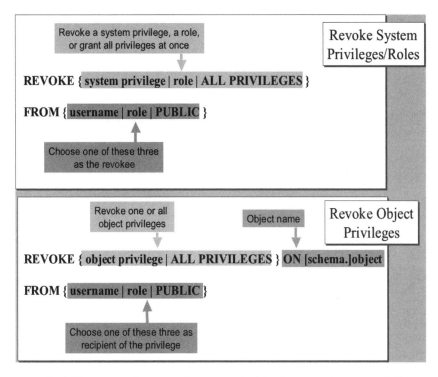

Figure 23.9
Revoking
Privileges.

entirely different privileges, such as EXECUTE, because they are a different type of database object.

What if you have granted a privilege (system or object) to PUBLIC and later decide that you would rather only grant that privilege to a small set of users? You must remove the privilege you originally granted. This brings us to the REVOKE command.

23.2.2 Revoking Privileges

You use the REVOKE command to remove both system privileges and object privileges. Like the GRANT command, the REVOKE command has two similar formats: one for revoking system privileges and one for revoking object privileges. Figure 23.9 shows the syntax for the REVOKE command.

- **Revoke System Privileges**. To revoke a system privilege, you must have been granted the same system privilege WITH ADMIN OPTION. The SYSTEM user has this privilege.

■ **Revoke Object Privileges**. To revoke an object privilege, you must either have granted the privilege originally or you must have the GRANT ANY OBJECT PRIVILEGE system privilege.

As with the GRANT command, let's go through a sequence of steps demonstrating use of the REVOKE command. Let's revoke privileges from the two users, PRINCE and ARIEL.

First, connect as PRINCE.

```
CONNECT PRINCE/CHARMING@OLTP;
```

Now we can revoke an object privilege that was granted by PRINCE. Revoke the SELECT privilege on the MYHORSES table from ARIEL. ARIEL will no longer be able to read PRINCE's MYHORSES table.

```
REVOKE SELECT ON MYHORSES FROM ARIEL;
```

Next we can connect to the SYSTEM user and revoke a system privilege granted earlier.

```
CONNECT SYSTEM/password@OLTP;
```

We have decided that PRINCE should not be allowed to create views.

```
REVOKE CREATE VIEW FROM PRINCE;
```

What happens to ARIEL's ability to create views (granted by PRINCE) when PRINCE loses his privilege to create views? System privileges remain until specifically revoked from a user, even if the granting user loses the privilege. We can verify this fact by connecting to ARIEL.

```
CONNECT ARIEL/MERMAID@OLTP;
```

Now create a view on the MUSIC.ARTIST table by running the next command. ARIEL has the ability to SELECT from that table because the object privilege was granted to PUBLIC. This verifies that even though PRINCE has been denied the ability to create views, ARIEL has not.

PRINCE originally granted the CREATE VIEW privilege to ARIEL. Revoked system privileges do not cause cascading revokes; only object privilege revokes can do that.

```
CREATE VIEW CA_ARTISTS AS
SELECT * FROM MUSIC.ARTIST WHERE STATE_PROVINCE='CA';
```

We will now examine some rules about revoking privileges. Using graphic examples, here are some key points to remember about how revoking of privileges works.

23.2.2.1 Revoked System Privileges DO NOT Cascade

When you revoke a system privilege, the revoke affects only the user you are naming and does not affect any objects or users created. For example, SYSTEM grants the CREATE USER privilege WITH ADMIN OPTION to ASSISTANT. Then ASSISTANT creates a user named INTERN and grants her the CREATE USER privilege. Now, INTERN creates another user named JOE. Figure 23.10 illustrates these events.

Figure 23.10
One New User Is Created by Each of These Users: SYSTEM, ASSISTANT, and INTERN.

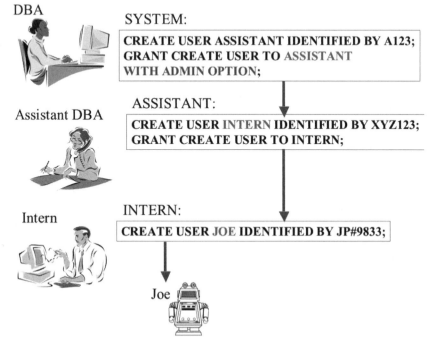

DBA

SYSTEM:
CREATE USER ASSISTANT IDENTIFIED BY A123;
GRANT CREATE USER TO ASSISTANT
WITH ADMIN OPTION;

Assistant DBA

ASSISTANT:
CREATE USER INTERN IDENTIFIED BY XYZ123;
GRANT CREATE USER TO INTERN;

Intern

INTERN:
CREATE USER JOE IDENTIFIED BY JP#9833;

Joe

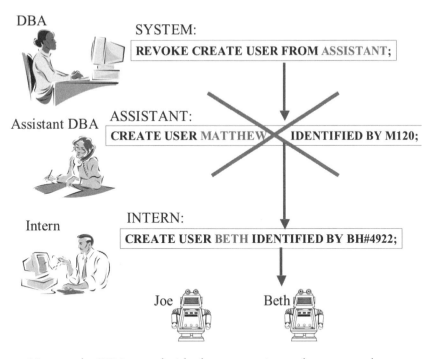

Figure 23.11
*ASSISTANT
Failed to Create
MATTHEW, but
INTERN Created
BETH.*

Now, as the DBA, you decide that your assistant does not need to create users at this point, so you revoke the CREATE USER privilege from ASSISTANT.

ASSISTANT can no longer create users; however, the users she created still exist. And, INTERN, who received the system privilege CREATE USER from ASSISTANT, retains that privilege. Figure 23.11 illustrates this idea by showing that ASSISTANT cannot create a user, while INTERN can create a user.

23.2.2.2 Revoked Object Privileges DO Cascade

Revoking an object privilege does result in a cascading set of revoked privileges. For example, imagine that SYSTEM grants SELECT on MUSIC.ARTIST to ASSISTANT using the WITH GRANT OPTION clause. Then ASSISTANT grants the same object privilege to INTERN who in turn grants the privilege (without the WITH GRANT OPTION) to JOE. Figure 23.12 shows the scenario.

After careful thought, you decide that your assistant no longer requires the SELECT privilege on the MUSIC.ARTIST table, so you revoke the privilege. The revoke actually cascades and revokes the privilege from INTERN, and then it cascades again and revokes the privilege from JOE.

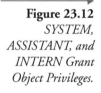

Figure 23.12
SYSTEM,
ASSISTANT, and
INTERN Grant
Object Privileges.

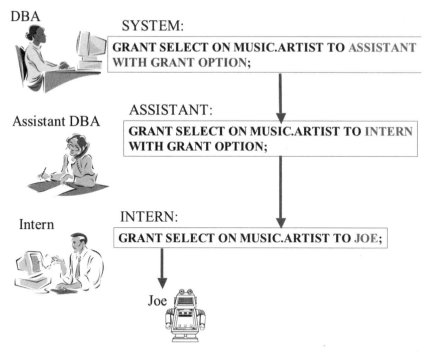

DBA

SYSTEM:

GRANT SELECT ON MUSIC.ARTIST TO ASSISTANT
WITH GRANT OPTION;

Assistant DBA

ASSISTANT:

GRANT SELECT ON MUSIC.ARTIST TO INTERN
WITH GRANT OPTION;

Intern

INTERN:

GRANT SELECT ON MUSIC.ARTIST TO JOE;

Joe

Now, only SYSTEM can successfully query the MUSIC.ARTIST table. Figure 23.13 shows how this works.

Remember that revoked system privileges do not cascade and revoked object privileges do cascade.

One of the more repetitive DBA tasks is that of granting the proper privileges to new users and maintaining privileges for all existing users. Very often, a group of users has identical privileges. The next section shows you how to take advantage of this with roles. Roles allow groupings of privileges and subsequent granting of privilege groups with a single granting or revoke of a role.

23.3 Grouping Privileges Using Roles

A role is a set or grouping of object and/or system privileges that is assigned a name. Once a role is established, you can grant the role instead of granting all of the individual privileges to a user. This capability saves a great deal of time!

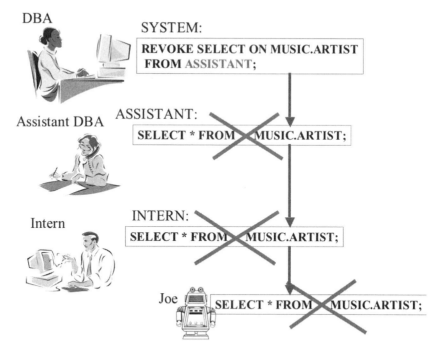

Figure 23.13
*Revoking an Object
Privilege Cascades
to Other Users to
whom the Revokee
Granted the Same
Object Privilege.*

Note: PL/SQL code blocks may not recognize database access through roles. Explicit object privileges may be required for PL/SQL. PL/SQL is covered in Chapter 24.

23.3.1 Creating and Altering Roles

Figure 23.14 shows the syntax of the CREATE ROLE and ALTER ROLE commands. Options are identical for both commands. Any user with the CREATE ROLE system privilege can create a role. The SYSTEM user, of course, has this privilege. The DBA often grants this privilege to users who own tables, so that users can create roles associated with their tables and grant those roles to other users.

A role that will contain sensitive privileges can be assigned a password. Any user who wants to use that role must provide the password (except when the role is one of the user's default roles). You will find out more about default roles later. At this stage, all we will do is lay some groundwork for later and create two roles, substitute strings where appropriate.

Figure 23.14
A New Role Does Not Contain Any Privileges at First.

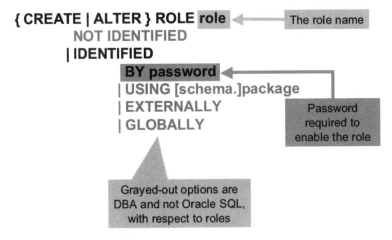

```
CONNECT SYSTEM/password@OLTP;
CREATE ROLE MINIDBA;
CREATE ROLE MUSIC_ACCESS;
```

The MINIDBA role will be a highly privileged role, thus I am using the ALTER ROLE command to restrict access using a password.

```
ALTER ROLE MINIDBA IDENTIFIED BY DBA#9876;
```

Note: The password is the only portion of a role that can be altered. You can add, change, or remove the password on a role. If you want to change the name of a role, you must drop and then re-create it with the changed name.

Once roles are created, privileges can be granted to them as if they are users. Then roles can be granted to users. Once a user has a role granted, he or she inherits all of the privileges assigned to that role.

23.3.2 Granting and Revoking Privileges on Roles

Granting privileges to a role is exactly the same (syntax-wise) as granting privileges to a user. Figures 23.5 and 23.9 show the syntax of granting and revoking privileges to and from roles. Roles can be granted to a user, a role, or PUBLIC.

Let's grant some privileges. First connect to the SYSTEM user.

```
CONNECT SYSTEM/password@OLTP;
```

Now we give the MINIDBA role three system privileges that you wish to delegate to an assistant DBA.

```
GRANT CREATE USER, CREATE SESSION, CREATE ROLE
TO MINIDBA;
```

Connect to the MUSIC user to grant some object privileges to the other role.

```
CONNECT MUSIC/MUSIC@OLTP;
```

Let's say that you are the designer for the MUSIC schema's application and you know that all users need to be able to change and query some tables and only query other tables.

```
GRANT SELECT ON ARTIST TO MUSIC_ACCESS;
GRANT SELECT ON SONG TO MUSIC_ACCESS;
GRANT SELECT ON MUSICCD TO MUSIC_ACCESS;
GRANT SELECT, INSERT, UPDATE, DELETE
ON STUDIOTIME TO MUSIC_ACCESS;
GRANT SELECT, INSERT, UPDATE, DELETE
ON GUESTAPPEARANCE TO MUSIC_ACCESS;
```

Now that roles are configured, we should now grant the roles to users. Granting a role to a user uses the same syntax as granting a system privilege. Refer to Figures 23.5 and 23.9 again. Notice that you can grant a system privilege, a role, or ALL PRIVILEGES. A role can even be granted to another role! This can be useful when you have subsets of privileges that can be logically grouped together under a single role.

So we have added privileges to both roles and now wish to grant roles to users. The MUSIC user did not create any roles and does not have the GRANT ANY ROLE system privilege. We have to connect to SYSTEM again.

```
CONNECT SYSTEM/password@OLTP;
```

Let's say that you want PRINCE to be allowed to use the MUSIC application. In addition, PRINCE will be allowed to grant the role to other users. Grant the appropriate role to PRINCE using this command:

```
GRANT MUSIC_ACCESS TO PRINCE WITH ADMIN OPTION;
```

Granting a role to a user has the same syntax as granting system privileges; therefore, you use the WITH ADMIN OPTION when you want the user to be able to grant the role to others.

We also decide that the MINIDBA role should have all privileges granted to the MUSIC_ACCESS role in addition to the system privileges already granted to it. Grant the MUSIC_ACCESS role to the MINIDBA role.

```
GRANT MUSIC_ACCESS TO MINIDBA;
```

Now, grant the MINIDBA role to ARIEL.

```
GRANT MINIDBA TO ARIEL;
```

ARIEL has all privileges from both roles.

Connect to PRINCE.

```
CONNECT PRINCE/CHARMING@OLTP;
```

PRINCE is allowed to grant the MUSIC_ACCESS role. He grants it to ARIEL.

```
GRANT MUSIC_ACCESS TO ARIEL;
```

After doing this, we realize that ARIEL already has the MUSIC_ACCESS role because it is included in the MINIDBA role. So PRINCE can revoke the redundant role.

```
REVOKE MUSIC_ACCESS FROM ARIEL;
```

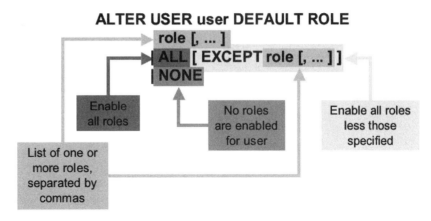

Figure 23.15
*Modify a User's
Default Roles with
ALTER USER.*

Note: Roles can be granted to other roles, establishing groups of groupings of privileges.

23.3.3   Setting User Roles

A role, once assigned to a user, can be either enabled or disabled in the user's session. By default, any role assigned to a user is enabled. The DBA can adjust which roles are enabled by default for each user when that user logs in, using the ALTER USER command. In addition, a user can enable a role using the SET ROLE command.

The ALTER USER command syntax is shown in Figure 23.15. The ALTER USER command has many other uses. Figure 23.15 shows only portions of syntax catering to user default roles.

When a user starts a session (connects to a database), roles are enabled according to settings made by the DBA using the ALTER USER command. A user can modify his or her session and change the enabled role set using the SET ROLE command. Figure 23.16 shows the syntax for the SET ROLE command.

Let's show some use of role allocation. First, reconnect to SYSTEM using this command:

```
CONNECT SYSTEM/password@OLTP;
```

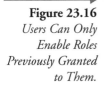

Figure 23.16
*Users Can Only
Enable Roles
Previously Granted
to Them.*

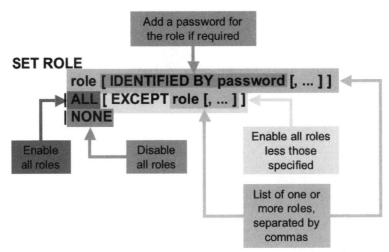

All roles assigned to a user start out enabled by default, including roles with passwords. If you want the user to be required to use the password before enabling the role, you must remove the role from the user's list of default roles. The MINIDBA role has a password and has been granted to ARIEL. Remove this role from ARIEL's default roles.

```
ALTER USER ARIEL DEFAULT ROLE ALL EXCEPT MINIDBA;
```

Now connect to ARIEL replacing the variable as usual.

```
CONNECT ARIEL/MERMAID@OLTP;
```

ARIEL cannot perform any tasks that need the system privileges found in the MINIDBA role (such as creating new users), because the role is disabled. She enables the MINIDBA role by using the SET ROLE command, including the appropriate password.

```
SET ROLE MINIDBA IDENTIFIED BY DBA#9876;
```

Note: Be careful to include all of the roles you wish to enable in your SET ROLE command.

Roles not included in the SET ROLE command become disabled. For example, let's say you have three roles enabled by default (VIEWMUSIC, UPDATEMUSIC, and DELETEMUSIC) and one role (INSERTMUSIC) disabled by default. If the command SET ROLE INSERTMUSIC is executed, you will enable the INSERTMUSIC role and disable the VIEW-MUSIC, UPDATEMUSIC, and DELETEMUSIC roles. Oracle Database 10g provides some predefined roles you can use if you wish. There are many predefined roles. Some of them are listed as follows:

- **CONNECT**. System privileges needed to log on and work as a database developer. Privileges include CREATE TABLE, CREATE VIEW, CREATE SESSION, CREATE CLUSTER, and so on. Each operating system has a slightly different group of privileges, but generally, you have all you need to do basic database work.

- **RESOURCE**. System privileges needed for other database development, such as creating types. Privileges include CREATE TYPE and CREATE PROCEDURE. Like the CONNECT role, the exact privileges vary from system to system.

- **SELECT_CATALOG_ROLE**. Allows access to data dictionary metadata and performance views, the catalog.

Use these to help you get started in administering your database. Oracle recommends, however, that you study the underlying privileges and create your own roles for most tasks. The CONNECT and RESOURCE roles may not be created automatically in future releases of Oracle.

23.3.4 Dropping Roles

This final section on roles involves removing roles. Whenever you remove a role, it is revoked from all users who currently have the role. Syntax for the DROP ROLE command is shown in Figure 23.17.

Roles are an excellent way to consolidate privileges needed for running applications.

Figure 23.17
Dropping a Role Also Revokes the Role from Users.

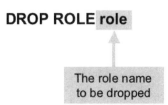

23.4 **Metadata Views**

This section simply describes metadata views applicable to users, privileges, and roles. Chapter 19 describes the basis and detail of Oracle Database metadata views.

- **USER_USERS**. Information on the logged-in user. ALL_USERS and DBA_USERS detail information for all users currently existing in the database.
- **USER_SYS_PRIVS**. Granted system privileges.
- **USER_TAB_PRIVS[_MADE|RECD]**. All object privileges (granted to and from plus owned). **MADE** and **RECD** implies granted object privileges and grantee object privileges, respectively.

Note: The term grantee implies that a user has been granted a privilege by another user.

- **USER_COL_PRIVS[_MADE|RECD]**. As for USER_TAB_PRIVS but as applied to specific columns only, not entire tables.
- **ROLE_PRIVS**. Roles granted to a user, both enabled and disabled.
- **USER_ROLE_PRIVS**. Roles granted to the connected user, both enabled and disabled.
- **SESSION_ROLES**. A connected session's enabled roles.
- **ROLE_ROLE_PRIVS**. Roles granted to other roles.
- **ROLE_TAB_PRIVS**. Object privileges granted to roles.
- **ROLE_SYS_PRIVS**. System privileges granted to roles.
- **DBA_ROLE_PRIVS**. Roles granted to users and other roles, who or which role granted it to the user or role, respectively, and whether the user has WITH ADMIN OPTION for the role.

This chapter has described security and controlling database access using users, both system and object privileges, and finally privilege groupings using roles. The next chapter, the final chapter in this book, digresses from Oracle SQL more so than this chapter, examining the very basics of Programming Language/SQL (PL/SQL).

24

Basic PL/SQL

In this chapter:

- What is PL/SQL?

- What are variables and PL/SQL datatypes?

- What are procedures, functions, triggers, and packages?

- How is data retrieved from the database using PL/SQL?

- What programming control structures exist in PL/SQL?

- What is dynamic or generic SQL?

This chapter covers basic reference material and examples on how to write programs in PL/SQL. It should be noted that the PL/SQL is a wrapper extension of Oracle SQL in that its original purpose was that of database access only. However, in recent years, PL/SQL has been expanded voluminously to become more of a programming language.

24.1   What is PL/SQL?

PL/SQL is an acronym for Programming Language/SQL. Structured Query Language (SQL) is a scripting language. A scripting language usually does not allow any dependencies between separate, following commands.

Note: This is not strictly true for all scripting languages. Even though UNIX shell scripting has many features, attempting to write complex applications using only UNIX shell scripting can lead to expensive problems.

PL/SQL extends SQL with programming controls and features such as procedures, variables, and control structures. Let's begin the meat of this chapter by asking: Why is PL/SQL classified as a programming language?

24.2 Why Is PL/SQL a Programming Language?

PL/SQL is a programming language because, unlike SQL, it allows dependencies to exist between multiple SQL commands, within the same block of code. In Oracle SQL, each SQL statement cannot pass a result on to another SQL statement or control structure, but PL/SQL can. Also, perhaps more important, a programming language block structure allows one procedure to call another, allowing for a modular, compartmentalized, or perhaps even pseudo-object hierarchical programming structure.

Therefore, PL/SQL is a programming language because it contains the ability to do the following things:

- Allows dependencies between commands within the same block of code.

- Allows for parameter passing up and down code block hierarchies. It allows for structure, namely modular.

- Contains a definition of variable scope across code block hierarchies, strict data typing, and allows use of commonly used programming control structures.

The downside of PL/SQL is that it should be primarily used as a database access programming language. PL/SQL does not perform well as a number cruncher like C or Java.

One more point to make is as follows: PL/SQL is becoming increasingly more capable as an object-like programming language, where the Oracle relational database allows for hierarchical object data structures. It tries to anyway. For what it is worth in my experienced opinion, I would avoid using Oracle Database or PL/SQL to manage objects. If you want to use object methodologies to manage complexity, put it at the application level using something like Java or use an object database.

24.2.1 Blocks and Exception Trapping

A block of code is a group of lines of SQL or PL/SQL code enclosed between BEGIN and END statements. A block of code is parsed and executed after the END statement is submitted using the front slash (/) character. The following SQL block consists of a variable declaration section followed by a BEGIN to END code block. See the result in Figure 24.1. This block of code queries the ARTIST table for the ARTIST_ID of Sheryl Crow. It stores the ARTIST_ID in a variable and then uses the variable to find the title of the first song of Sheryl Crow in the SONG table. It stores the title in another variable. Then it displays the title and completes.

```
SET SERVEROUTPUT ON;
DECLARE
    vARTIST_ID ARTIST.ARTIST_ID%TYPE;
    vTITLE SONG.TITLE%TYPE;
BEGIN
    SELECT ARTIST_ID INTO vARTIST_ID FROM ARTIST
    WHERE NAME='Sheryl Crow';
    SELECT TITLE INTO vTITLE FROM SONG
    WHERE ARTIST_ID = vARTIST_ID AND ROWNUM = 1;
    DBMS_OUTPUT.PUT_LINE(vTITLE);
EXCEPTION WHEN OTHERS THEN
    RAISE;
END;
/
SET SERVEROUTPUT OFF;
```

Note: The statement SET SERVEROUTPUT ON is essential for the proper functioning of the DBMS_OUTPUT.PUT_LINE packaged procedure. DBMS_OUTPUT is an Oracle-provided package. The PUT_LINE procedure within that package sends a line to the output. SET SERVEROUTPUT OFF switches output off.

Note: %TYPE sets a variable to the datatype of the specified TABLE.COLUMN.

Figure 24.1

*PL/SQL Block
Structure and
Exception
Trapping.*

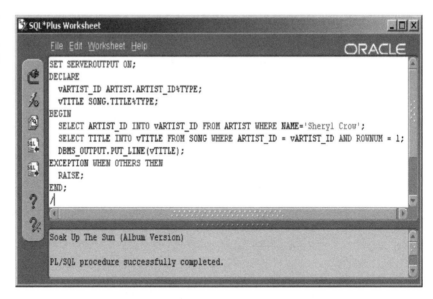

The block of code in Figure 24.1 is an anonymous PL/SQL block, which is effectively an unnamed procedure without parameters. It is executed by the front slash (/) character, is not stored, and thus cannot be executed again as a stored, named object.

The last two lines in Figure 24.1 before the block END statement comprise an error exception trap. Any errors occurring between the BEGIN statement and the EXCEPTION statement will cause control to pass to the EXCEPTION trap, which executes the RAISE statement. The RAISE statement does nothing in this procedure, passing an exception to the calling block. If no calling block exists, then an error called *unhandled exception* will be returned to the calling application. In our case, SQL*Plus Worksheet is the calling application.

24.2.2   Procedures, Functions, Triggers, and Packages

Unlike an anonymous block, stored procedures are named, compiled, and stored in the database. They can be executed repeatedly in the future by executing the procedure name. PL/SQL stored objects include procedures, functions, triggers, and packages. What are the differences between these four compiled, executable database objects? They are as follows:

- **Procedure**. Allows by value and by reference parameters with no return value.

■ **Function**. Like a procedure but allows a return value.

■ **Trigger**. No transactional termination commands allowed and executed automatically by database event occurrences. Triggers are known as event-driven procedures.

■ **Package**. Groups multiple procedures and functions together into blocked units.

24.2.2.1 Using Named Procedures

The following named procedure is a slightly more sophisticated copy of the anonymous procedure presented previously. The procedure now has a name, accepts a parameter, is stored in the database, and can be executed repeatedly by executing the procedure name as shown in the following script. The result is shown in Figure 24.2.

```
CREATE OR REPLACE PROCEDURE GETSONG (pARTIST IN VARCHAR2) AS
    vARTIST_ID ARTIST.ARTIST_ID%TYPE;
    vTITLE SONG.TITLE%TYPE;
BEGIN
    SELECT ARTIST_ID INTO vARTIST_ID FROM ARTIST
    WHERE NAME=pARTIST;
    SELECT TITLE INTO vTITLE FROM SONG
    WHERE ARTIST_ID = vARTIST_ID AND ROWNUM = 1;
    DBMS_OUTPUT.PUT_LINE(vTITLE);
EXCEPTION WHEN OTHERS THEN
    RAISE;
END;
/
SET SERVEROUTPUT ON;
EXEC GETSONG('Sheryl Crow');
EXEC GETSONG('Avril Lavigne');
SET SERVEROUTPUT OFF;
```

24.2.2.2 Using Functions

Following are two versions of a function used previously in this book. This function will split a string time value of HH:SS into its hours and seconds constituent parts and convert them to a real number.

```
CREATE OR REPLACE FUNCTION GETTIME(pTIME IN VARCHAR2)
 RETURN NUMBER IS
    --variable declaration section
```

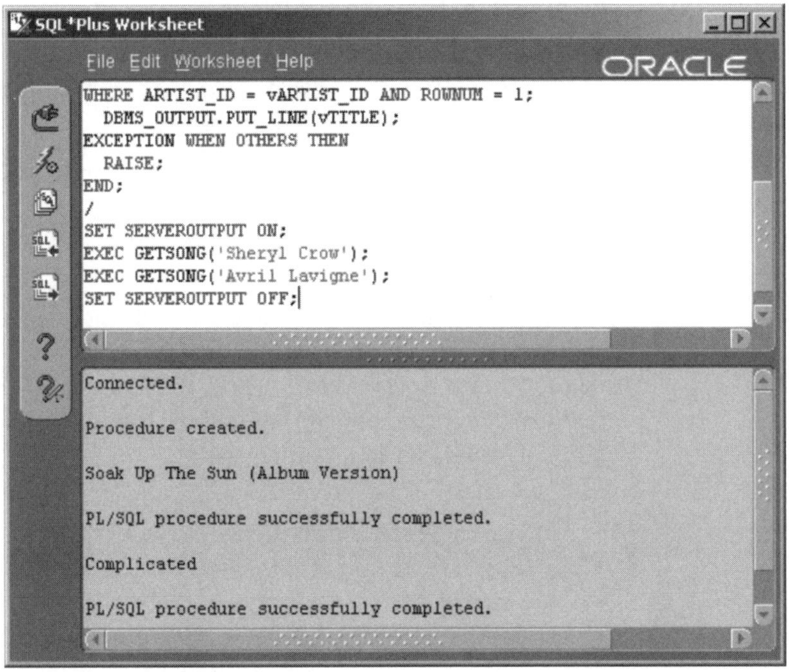
SQL*Plus Worksheet
File Edit Worksheet Help
ORACLE
WHERE ARTIST_ID = vARTIST_ID AND ROWNUM = 1;
DBMS_OUTPUT.PUT_LINE(vTITLE);
EXCEPTION WHEN OTHERS THEN
RAISE;
END;
/
SET SERVEROUTPUT ON;
EXEC GETSONG('Sheryl Crow');
EXEC GETSONG('Avril Lavigne');
SET SERVEROUTPUT OFF;
Connected.
Procedure created.
Soak Up The Sun (Album Version)
PL/SQL procedure successfully completed.
Complicated
PL/SQL procedure successfully completed.

Figure 24.2 *PL/SQL Block Structure and Exception Trapping.*

```
vLEN INTEGER DEFAULT 0;
vSPLIT INTEGER DEFAULT 0;
vHOURS INTEGER DEFAULT 0;
vSECONDS INTEGER DEFAULT 0;
BEGIN
   --execution section
   vSPLIT := INSTR(pTIME,':');
   vLEN := LENGTH(pTIME);
   vHOURS := TO_NUMBER(SUBSTR(pTIME,1,vSPLIT-1));
   vSECONDS := TO_NUMBER(SUBSTR(pTIME,
   vSPLIT+1,vLEN-vSPLIT));
   RETURN vHOURS+(vSECONDS/60);
EXCEPTION WHEN OTHERS THEN
    --exception trap section
RETURN 0;
END;
/
```

Note: Note in the previous PL/SQL code how variables are accessed as variable := value; This is PL/SQL syntax.

Here is a single-line version of the same function showing how best to write properly performing PL/SQL code:

```
CREATE OR REPLACE FUNCTION GETTIME(pTIME IN VARCHAR2)
 RETURN NUMBER IS
BEGIN
RETURN TO_NUMBER(SUBSTR(pTIME,1,INSTR(pTIME,':')-
1))+(TO_NUMBER(SUBSTR(pTIME,INSTR(pTIME,':')+1,LENGTH(pTIME)-
INSTR(pTIME,':')))/60);
EXCEPTION WHEN OTHERS THEN RETURN 0;
END;
/
```

I can execute the GETTIME function on the SONG table PLAYING_TIME column (SONG.PLAYING_TIME) using the following script. The result is shown in Figure 24.3.

```
SELECT PLAYING_TIME, GETTIME(PLAYING_TIME) FROM SONG
WHERE PLAYING_TIME IS NOT NULL;
```

Note: The GETTIME function is also known as a custom-written or user-defined function.

24.2.2.3 Using Triggers

Here are some simple example triggers. The first trigger detects insertions to the ARTIST table, the second updates, and the third deletions. Figure 24.4 shows the response from an INSERT, an UPDATE, and a DELETE command, one after the other.

```
CREATE OR REPLACE TRIGGER iARTIST
    AFTER INSERT ON ARTIST FOR EACH ROW
BEGIN
    DBMS_OUTPUT.PUT_LINE('New Artist '||:NEW.NAME||'
added.');
```

Figure 24.3
*Executing a
Named, Stored
Procedure from
within SQL.*

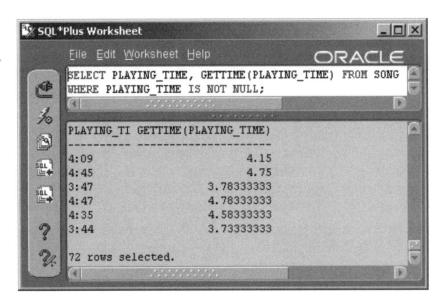

```
EXCEPTION WHEN OTHERS THEN
    DBMS_OUTPUT.PUT_LINE(SQLERRM(SQLCODE));
    RAISE;
END;
/
CREATE OR REPLACE TRIGGER uARTIST
    AFTER UPDATE OF NAME ON ARTIST FOR EACH ROW
BEGIN
    DBMS_OUTPUT.PUT_LINE('Artist changed from '
||:OLD.NAME||' to '||:NEW.NAME);
EXCEPTION WHEN OTHERS THEN
    DBMS_OUTPUT.PUT_LINE(SQLERRM(SQLCODE));
    RAISE;
END;
/
CREATE OR REPLACE TRIGGER dARTIST
    AFTER DELETE ON ARTIST FOR EACH ROW
BEGIN
    DBMS_OUTPUT.PUT_LINE('Artist '||:OLD.NAME
||' has been deleted');
EXCEPTION WHEN OTHERS THEN
    DBMS_OUTPUT.PUT_LINE(SQLERRM(SQLCODE));
    RAISE;
END;
```

Figure 24.4
*Executing Triggers
from DML
Commands.*

```
/
SET SERVEROUTPUT ON;
INSERT INTO ARTIST(ARTIST_ID,NAME)
VALUES(100,'Robert Alan Zimmerman');
UPDATE ARTIST SET NAME='Bob Dylan'
WHERE NAME='Robert Alan Zimmerman';
DELETE FROM ARTIST WHERE NAME='Bob Dylan';
SET SERVEROUTPUT OFF;
```

24.2.2.4 Using Packages

Packages can be used to group commonly stored PL/SQL units into a single chunk of code. A package must have a declaration section and a body section. The declaration simply defines named units within the package, and the package body contains the actual procedures. The following script is a simple package converting temperatures between degrees Fahrenheit (F°), degrees Celsius (C°), and degrees Kelvin (K°). Example executions of the various functions are shown in Figure 24.5.

```
CREATE OR REPLACE PACKAGE TEMPERATURE AS
    FUNCTION cTOf(c VARCHAR2 DEFAULT 0) RETURN VARCHAR2;
    FUNCTION fTOc(f VARCHAR2 DEFAULT 0) RETURN VARCHAR2;
```

```
            FUNCTION fTOK(f VARCHAR2 DEFAULT 0) RETURN VARCHAR2;
            FUNCTION KTOf(K VARCHAR2 DEFAULT 0) RETURN VARCHAR2;
            FUNCTION cTOK(c VARCHAR2 DEFAULT 0) RETURN VARCHAR2;
            FUNCTION KTOc(K VARCHAR2 DEFAULT 0) RETURN VARCHAR2;
        END;
        /
        CREATE OR REPLACE PACKAGE BODY TEMPERATURE AS
            FUNCTION cTOf(c VARCHAR2 DEFAULT 0) RETURN VARCHAR2 AS
            BEGIN
                RETURN TO_CHAR(c)||'C° = '||ROUND(32+((9/
        5)*c),0)||'F°';
            END;
            FUNCTION fTOc(f VARCHAR2 DEFAULT 0) RETURN VARCHAR2 AS
            BEGIN
                RETURN TO_CHAR(f)||'F° = '||ROUND((5/9)*(f-
        32),0)||'C°';
            END;
            FUNCTION fTOK(f VARCHAR2 DEFAULT 0) RETURN VARCHAR2 AS
            BEGIN
                RETURN TO_CHAR(f)||'F° = '||ROUND(32+((9/5)*f)-
        273.15,0)||'K°';
            END;
            FUNCTION KTOf(K VARCHAR2 DEFAULT 0) RETURN VARCHAR2 AS
            BEGIN
                RETURN TO_CHAR(K)||'K° = '||ROUND((5/9)*(K+273.15-
        32))||'F°';
            END;
            FUNCTION cTOK(c VARCHAR2 DEFAULT 0) RETURN VARCHAR2 AS
            BEGIN
                RETURN TO_CHAR(c)||'C° = '||ROUND(c-273.15,0)||'K°';
            END;
            FUNCTION KTOc(K VARCHAR2 DEFAULT 0) RETURN VARCHAR2 AS
            BEGIN
                RETURN TO_CHAR(K)||'K° = '||ROUND(K+273.15,0)||'C°';
            END;
        END;
        /
```

Now let's look into variables and datatypes for PL/SQL.

Figure 24.5
Using a Package to Group Procedures.

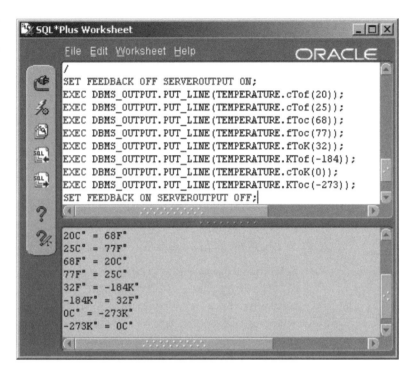

24.3 Variables and Datatypes in PL/SQL

PL/SQL contains all of the predefined datatypes included in SQL, as explained in Chapter 16, plus some additional datatypes. Some of these additional datatypes are listed as follows:

- **NUMBER Datatypes**. There are numerous NUMBER subtypes provided for ANSI standard compliance. These subtypes will all convert to NUMBER or FLOAT datatypes both for Oracle table columns and internally in PL/SQL. For example, INTEGER and SMALLINT.

- **BINARY_INTEGER**. Stores a signed integer value. There are various subtypes.

- **BOOLEAN**. Stores a TRUE, FALSE, or null value.

- **RECORD**. Composite structure similar to a VARRAY or TABLE datatype allowing the creation of a table row structure in memory. The following line uses ROWTYPE to duplicate the column structure of an ARTIST table row into the RECORD called RARTIST.

```
RARTIST ARTIST%ROWTYPE;
```

In the following code, a new record structure is built using one new field (ID), the ARTIST.NAME field, and the SONG.NAME field. A RECORD datatype is then declared as having the structure of the new type, TARTISTSONGS.

```
TYPE TARTISTSONGS IS RECORD (ID INTEGER
, ARTISTS ARTIST.NAME%TYPE
, SONGS SONG.TITLE%TYPE);
RARTISTSONGS TARTISTSONGS;
```

There are examples using RECORD datatypes later in this chapter when discussing cursors.

- **Reference Datatypes**. In addition to the REF object pointer type, PL/SQL also includes a REF cursor. A REF cursor is a by reference cursor (byref), which implies that a variable is a pointer and can be passed into as well as out of a procedure, including returning any changes made to the REF cursor within the procedure. There will be more on cursors later in this chapter.

- **Associative Arrays**. Associative arrays are currently only allowed in PL/SQL and not Oracle SQL. An associative array is a dynamic array much like a nested table object (see Chapter 16). The only difference is that an associative array is indexed and thus capable of much better performance than a nested table. The following script snippet shows how an associative array is declared in PL/SQL as opposed to VARRAYs and nested tables:

```
DECLARE
    TYPE tTable IS TABLE OF VARCHAR2(32);
    TYPE tVARRAY IS VARRAY(100) OF INTEGER;
    TYPE tITable IS TABLE OF VARCHAR2(32) INDEX BY
BINARY_INTEGER;
    vPointer tTable;
    vArray tVARRAY;
    vIndexedPointer tITable;
BEGIN
    NULL;
END;
/
```

The next thing we should deal with is retrieving data from the database from within PL/SQL.

24.4 Retrieving Data in PL/SQL

What is a cursor? A *cursor* is a temporary area in memory used to store the results of a query. Oracle Database calls the area of memory in which a cursor is temporarily placed a Work Area. In programming terms, a cursor is a pointer to an address in memory, a chunk of memory. Query and DML command results are placed into and processed in cursors during execution. In PL/SQL, cursors can be created as programming data structures. Cursors can be used for queries returning one or many rows and can be of two types: implicit and explicit cursors. An implicit cursor is declared automatically by PL/SQL, and an explicit cursor is declared by the programmer. An explicit cursor gives more control to the programmer.

24.4.1 Explicit Cursors

An explicitly declared cursor allows more programmer access to a cursor, for each row in that cursor, using the cursor OPEN, FETCH, and CLOSE commands.

What is an explicit cursor? Let's explain it in steps: the first step is to declare a cursor. This example names the cursor CARTIST. The query (SELECT * FROM ARTIST) retrieves rows of data and places them in the cursor's memory area. At the same time, we declare a RECORD type to contain each row retrieved. We use the record type called RARTIST, seen before in this chapter, to retrieve each row of data from the cursor.

```
SET SERVEROUTPUT ON;
DECLARE
    CURSOR CARTIST IS SELECT * FROM ARTIST;
    RARTIST ARTIST%ROWTYPE;
```

The second step is to open the cursor. This parses the query and loads the first portion of rows into the cursor in preparation for retrieval by the program:

```
BEGIN
    OPEN CARTIST;
```

Now we loop through the open cursor, selecting each row. There will be more about loops later in this chapter. This loop has three commands. The first one places the next row from the cursor into the RARTIST record variable. The second command causes the looping to end if the status of the cursor is NOTFOUND (meaning there are no rows left to retrieve.) The third line places a line on the screen that displays the artist name. This line is executed only if there was a row retrieved from the cursor. The three lines are repeated for every row retrieved from the cursor:

```
LOOP
    FETCH CARTIST INTO RARTIST;
    EXIT WHEN CARTIST%NOTFOUND;
    DBMS_OUTPUT.PUT_LINE(RARTIST.NAME);
END LOOP;
```

Do not forget to close your cursor! Explicit cursors should be closed as soon as they are no longer needed to improve performance, prevent locking issues, and ensure that cursor limits are not reached.

```
CLOSE CARTIST;
END;
/
SET SERVEROUTPUT OFF;
```

The execution of the pieces of the anonymous procedure looping through the explicit cursor just described is shown in Figure 24.6.

There are other variations of how explicit cursors can be coded, but we do not need to go into any further detail.

24.4.2 **Implicit Cursors**

Every SQL statement both in SQL and inside a PL/SQL block not declared explicitly as a cursor is an implicit cursor. An implicit cursor is opened and closed by SQL or PL/SQL and is used to process INSERT, UPDATE, DELETE, and SELECT statements. A special type of implicit cursor exclusive to PL/SQL is called a cursor FOR loop. A cursor FOR loop is an implicit cursor on the basis that it does not require use of the OPEN, FETCH, and CLOSE statements.

Figure 24.6
Using an Explicit Cursor.

Following are three example PL/SQL anonymous blocks: the first contains INSERT and UPDATE statements, the second a SELECT … INTO statement, and the third a cursor FOR loop.

24.4.2.1 The Internal SQL Implicit Cursor

The results of the most recently executed implicit cursor are stored in an internal Oracle cursor called SQL. Note how the first example uses SQL%NOTFOUND to decide on executing the INSERT statement. The block begins by updating all rows in the ARTIST table where the artist's name is the band called Chicago. We know that there are no artists by that name in our MUSIC database. The update does not succeed, and the implicit cursor used for the update has a status of NOTFOUND. The block checks the implicit cursor status using SQL%NOTFOUND and inserts a row into the artist table with a name of Chicago.

In Figure 24.7, you can see output at the end displaying one occurrence of "Inserted Chicago" and two occurrences of "Updated Chicago." The anonymous block is executed three times. The IF statement is used in this script, the syntax of which is explained later in this chapter.

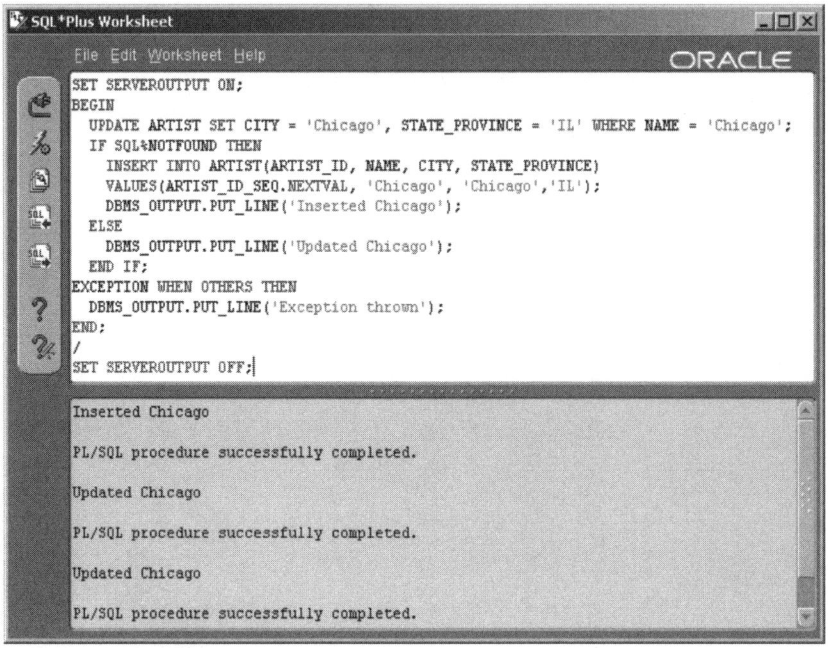

Figure 24.7
*Using Implicit
Cursors.*

```
SET SERVEROUTPUT ON;
BEGIN
    UPDATE ARTIST SET CITY = 'Chicago'
    , STATE_PROVINCE = 'IL'
    WHERE NAME = 'Chicago';
    IF SQL%NOTFOUND THEN
        INSERT INTO ARTIST(ARTIST_ID, NAME, CITY
        , STATE_PROVINCE)
        VALUES(ARTIST_ID_SEQ.NEXTVAL, 'Chicago'
        , 'Chicago','IL');
        DBMS_OUTPUT.PUT_LINE('Inserted Chicago');
    ELSE
        DBMS_OUTPUT.PUT_LINE('Updated Chicago');
    END IF;
EXCEPTION WHEN OTHERS THEN
DBMS_OUTPUT.PUT_LINE('Exception thrown');
END;
/
SET SERVEROUTPUT OFF;
```

> **Note:** Note that the UPDATE statement in the PL/SQL block does not throw an exception when the row searched for is not found, but it does set the cursor SQL to being NOTFOUND.

24.4.2.2 Single-Row SELECT Implicit Cursor

When using an implicit cursor with a query, the query must return no more than one row. If it returns multiple rows, the procedure will fail. You can use an explicit cursor or a cursor FOR loop (see the next example) for queries returning multiple rows.

For a single-row SELECT statement, the INTO clause must be used. When selecting a single row in a PL/SQL block, the value or values retrieved by the query are placed into variables declared within the PL/SQL block, as shown following in the second example. In this example, four variables are declared: one for each of the four columns in the SELECT statement. The query uses the INTO clause to place each column value into each corresponding variable. The variables are then used to construct a line that is displayed on the screen. See the result of the following code in Figure 24.8.

```
SET SERVEROUTPUT ON;
DECLARE
    VARTIST_ID ARTIST.ARTIST_ID%TYPE;
    VNAME ARTIST.NAME%TYPE;
    VCITY ARTIST.CITY%TYPE;
    VSTATE_PROVINCE ARTIST.STATE_PROVINCE%TYPE;
BEGIN
    SELECT ARTIST_ID,NAME,CITY,STATE_PROVINCE
    INTO VARTIST_ID,VNAME,VCITY,VSTATE_PROVINCE
    FROM ARTIST WHERE NAME = 'Chicago';
    DBMS_OUTPUT.PUT_LINE('OUTPUT IS : '||TO_CHAR(VARTIST_ID)
||' '||VNAME||' '||VCITY||' '||VSTATE_PROVINCE);
END;
/
SET SERVEROUTPUT OFF;
```

24.4.2.3 Cursor FOR Loop Implicit Cursor

A cursor FOR loop is often used as a substitute for an explicit cursor, thereby simplifying code. In the example shown following, note how the

Figure 24.8
The SELECT ...
INTO Statement.

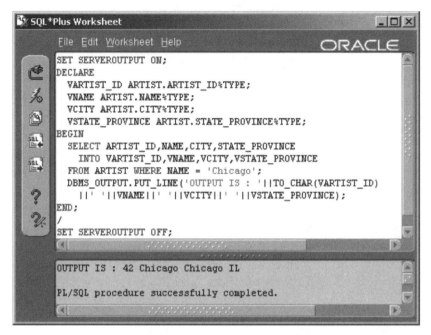

cursor declaration section creates a RECORD object called RARTIST and that no opening and closing cursor operations are required.

In this example, the cursor is declared and has a name of CARTIST. However, instead of declaring a record variable and using OPEN, FETCH, and CLOSE to retrieve rows, all that is needed is the FOR clause. The loop automatically opens the cursor and reads each row and places it into the RARTIST variable. Inside the loop, the artist's name is displayed on the screen. When no more rows are found, the loop automatically closes the cursor and ends the loop. The result of the following code is shown in Figure 24.9.

```
SET SERVEROUTPUT ON;
DECLARE
    CURSOR CARTIST IS SELECT * FROM ARTIST ORDER BY NAME;
BEGIN
    FOR RARTIST IN CARTIST LOOP
        DBMS_OUTPUT.PUT_LINE(RARTIST.NAME);
    END LOOP;
END;
/
SET SERVEROUTPUT OFF;
```

Figure 24.9
An Implicit Cursor FOR Loop.

Now let's describe some small facts about changing data from within PL/SQL blocks.

24.5 Changing Data in PL/SQL

Not only can data in tables be changed from within PL/SQL blocks, but there are some small additions making coding a little easier and more efficient. One of these additions is the RETURNING INTO clause, as shown in the combined syntax for INSERT, UPDATE, and DELETE commands in Figure 24.10.

In general. the RETURNING INTO clause can be used to return expressions used in DML statements back into variables in the calling PL/SQL block. These variables can be used by subsequent commands in the PL/SQL block. In the code snippet shown as follows, the first INSERT command effectively passes the ARTIST_ID directly to the second INSERT command. Without the RETURNING INTO clause, the ARTIST_ID value would have to be retrieved using a SELECT command between the two INSERT commands.

Figure 24.10
*Syntax for the
DML
RETURNING
INTO Clause.*

{ INSERT INTO | UPDATE | DELETE } [schema.]table

...

One or more
variables can be
returned. More
than one row
returns an array.

[RETURNING expression [, expression] INTO variable [, variable])]

Returns any list of expressions into pre-
declared variables. Using the RETURNING
clause allows expressions not to have to be
recalculated for following SQL statements.

```
DECLARE
    VARTIST_ID ARTIST.ARTIST_ID%TYPE;
BEGIN
    INSERT INTO ARTIST(ARTIST_ID,NAME)
    VALUES(ARTIST_ID_SEQ.NEXTVAL,'The Goanna Band')
        RETURNING ARTIST_ID INTO VARTIST_ID;
    INSERT INTO SONG(SONG_ID, ARTIST_ID, TITLE)
    VALUES(SONG_ID_SEQ.NEXTVAL, VARTIST_ID
    , 'The Razor''s Edge');
END;
/
```

The next section looks at dynamic SQL. Dynamic SQL is SQL or PL/
SQL code generated on the fly, usually generically from within an application or some other calling process.

24.6 Dynamic SQL

Dynamic or generic programming is a term applied to programming where
portions of the code are constructed at run-time. As a result, dynamic SQL
is flexible based on user or parameter input. Two types of dynamic SQL can
be used:

■ The EXECUTE IMMEDIATE command.

- The DBMS_SQL package. This option is out of date, and the EXE-CUTE IMMEDIATE command is now recommended.

The command EXECUTE IMMEDIATE is used to submit a string value as an Oracle SQL command to the Oracle SQL parser from inside a PL/SQL block. In this example, you are creating a stored procedure named GETROWS that you can call, passing a value to the procedure for the input parameter VTABLE. The procedure then executes a query that counts the rows in whatever table you named in the VTABLE parameter. The second and third last lines are commands that call the procedure you created. See the result in Figure 24.11.

```
SET SERVEROUTPUT ON;
CREATE OR REPLACE PROCEDURE GETROWS (VTABLE IN VARCHAR2) AS
VCOUNT INTEGER;
BEGIN
    EXECUTE IMMEDIATE 'SELECT COUNT(*) FROM '||VTABLE
    INTO VCOUNT;
    DBMS_OUTPUT.PUT_LINE('There are '||TO_CHAR(VCOUNT)
||' rows in the '||VTABLE||' table');
END;
/
EXEC GETROWS('ARTIST');
EXEC GETROWS('SONG');
SET SERVEROUTPUT OFF;
```

The next example shows the use of the EXECUTE IMMEDIATE command to execute a DDL command inside a PL/SQL block. All DDL commands executed from within a PL/SQL block should be executed using the EXECUTE IMMEDIATE command.

```
BEGIN
    EXECUTE IMMEDIATE 'ALTER INDEX XUK_ARTIST_NAME REBUILD';
END;
/
```

Note: Previous versions of Oracle used a provided package called DBMS_SQL to execute dynamic SQL code inside PL/SQL blocks. DBMS_SQL can still be used, but the recommended method is the EXE-CUTE IMMEDIATE statement.

Figure 24.11
*Using EXECUTE
IMMEDIATE to
Execute SQL DML
PL/SQL Blocks.*

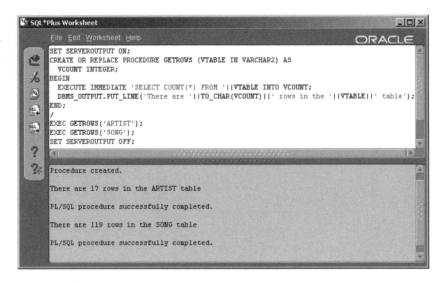

24.6.1   Building Cursors Dynamically

Cursors can also be executed dynamically. The following example uses a REF cursor. There are other methods of coding dynamic cursors in PL/SQL, but a simple example will suffice here. The result of the following code is shown in Figure 24.12.

```
SET SERVEROUTPUT ON;
CREATE OR REPLACE PROCEDURE GETROWS
  (VCOUNTRY IN ARTIST.COUNTRY%TYPE) AS
    TYPE TARTIST IS REF CURSOR;
    CARTIST TARTIST;
    RARTIST ARTIST%ROWTYPE;
BEGIN
    OPEN CARTIST FOR 'SELECT * FROM ARTIST
    WHERE COUNTRY = '''||VCOUNTRY||''''';
    LOOP
        FETCH CARTIST INTO RARTIST;
        EXIT WHEN CARTIST%NOTFOUND;
        DBMS_OUTPUT.PUT_LINE(RARTIST.NAME
||' comes from '||RARTIST.COUNTRY);
    END LOOP;
    CLOSE CARTIST;
END;
/
EXEC GETROWS('CAN');
```

Figure 24.12
Using a REF Cursor.

```
SET SERVEROUTPUT ON;
CREATE OR REPLACE PROCEDURE GETROWS (VCOUNTRY IN ARTIST.COUNTRY%TYPE) AS
  TYPE TARTIST IS REF CURSOR;
  CARTIST TARTIST;
  RARTIST ARTIST%ROWTYPE;
BEGIN
  OPEN CARTIST FOR 'SELECT * FROM ARTIST WHERE COUNTRY = '''||VCOUNTRY||'''';
  LOOP
    FETCH CARTIST INTO RARTIST;
    EXIT WHEN CARTIST%NOTFOUND;
    DBMS_OUTPUT.PUT_LINE(RARTIST.NAME||' comes from '||RARTIST.COUNTRY);
  END LOOP;
  CLOSE CARTIST;
END;
/
EXEC GETROWS('CAN');
EXEC GETROWS('England');
SET SERVEROUTPUT OFF;
```

```
Nickelback comes from CAN

PL/SQL procedure successfully completed.

Avril Lavigne comes from England

PL/SQL procedure successfully completed.
```

```
EXEC GETROWS('England');
SET SERVEROUTPUT OFF;
```

24.7 Control Structures

Any program can be coded using basic control structures. PL/SQL contains all of the necessary requirements. Basic control structures include these elements: selection, iteration, and sequence controls. Control structures allow for modular programming. This makes it easier to share code with other programmers or to divide a larger, more complex program into smaller, more easily understood components. In PL/SQL, the control structures are as follows:

- **Selection**. IF and CASE statements.

- **Iteration** or **Repetition**. Multiple types of loops, sometimes including completion conditions, such as a WHILE loop.

- **Sequence Controls**. GOTO and NULL. A GOTO statement jumps from any point in a block of code to another. The NULL command simply does nothing at all and can be used as a placeholder.

> **Note:** Avoid using GOTO statements. Purist modular programming does not allow use of GOTO statements. It is always possible to construct a piece of code properly without using GOTO statements. GOTO statements lead to spaghetti code.

24.7.1 Selection

The IF and the CASE statements allow you to execute different code depending on the value of some expression. The expression must be a Boolean expression. That is, the expression must always evaluate to true, false, or NULL, where NULL is equivalent to false.

24.7.1.1 The IF Statement

Each branch of an IF statement will be executed based on a condition. The situation where all conditions fail is covered by the default ELSE clause. Every condition can be a different Boolean expression. The syntax of the IF statement is shown in Figure 24.13.

Now let's use an IF statement to display total dollars due based on due dates for outstanding amounts of money. In this example, we define a date called TODAY. The IF statement causes an addition to a total based on the due date of each row. See the result in Figure 24.14.

Figure 24.13
IF Statement Syntax.

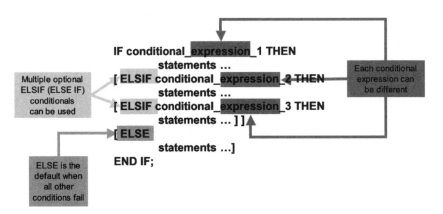

```
SET SERVEROUTPUT ON
DECLARE
TODAY DATE DEFAULT '01-JUL-2001';
```

```
CURSOR CSTUDIO IS
    SELECT A.COUNTRY,A.NAME,S.DUE_DATE
       ,NVL(S.AMOUNT_CHARGED - NVL(S.AMOUNT_PAID,0),0)
               AS   AMOUNT
       FROM ARTIST A JOIN STUDIOTIME S USING (ARTIST_ID)
       ORDER BY 1,2,3;
    AT90DAYS INTEGER DEFAULT 0;
    AT60DAYS INTEGER DEFAULT 0;
    AT30DAYS INTEGER DEFAULT 0;
    NOTDUE INTEGER DEFAULT 0;
BEGIN
/* Loop through all the rows, adding amounts to the
   4 variables. */
  FOR RSTUDIO IN CSTUDIO LOOP
     IF TODAY - RSTUDIO.DUE_DATE > 90 THEN
         AT90DAYS := AT90DAYS + RSTUDIO.AMOUNT;
     ELSIF TODAY - RSTUDIO.DUE_DATE > 60 THEN
         AT60DAYS := AT60DAYS + RSTUDIO.AMOUNT;
     ELSIF TODAY - RSTUDIO.DUE_DATE > 30 THEN
         AT30DAYS := AT30DAYS + RSTUDIO.AMOUNT;
     ELSE
             NOTDUE := NOTDUE + RSTUDIO.AMOUNT;
     END IF;
  END LOOP;
/* Print results now */
DBMS_OUTPUT.PUT_LINE('90 +  days:   '||TO_CHAR(AT90DAYS,'$999,999.99'));
DBMS_OUTPUT.PUT_LINE('60 - 89 days: '||TO_CHAR(AT60DAYS,'$999,999.99'));
DBMS_OUTPUT.PUT_LINE('30 - 59 days: '||TO_CHAR(AT30DAYS,'$999,999.99'));
DBMS_OUTPUT.PUT_LINE('< 30 days:    '||TO_CHAR(NOTDUE,'$999,999.99'));
END;
/
```

24.7.1.2   The CASE Statement

The CASE statement can be used in place of lengthy IF statements where a condition is tested against a single Boolean expression. Internally, a CASE statement is more efficient than an IF statement. There are two forms of the CASE statement in PL/SQL. Both forms of the CASE statement will yield a Boolean result (TRUE, FALSE, or NULL) for each option. The syntax of both forms of the CASE statement is shown in Figure 24.15.

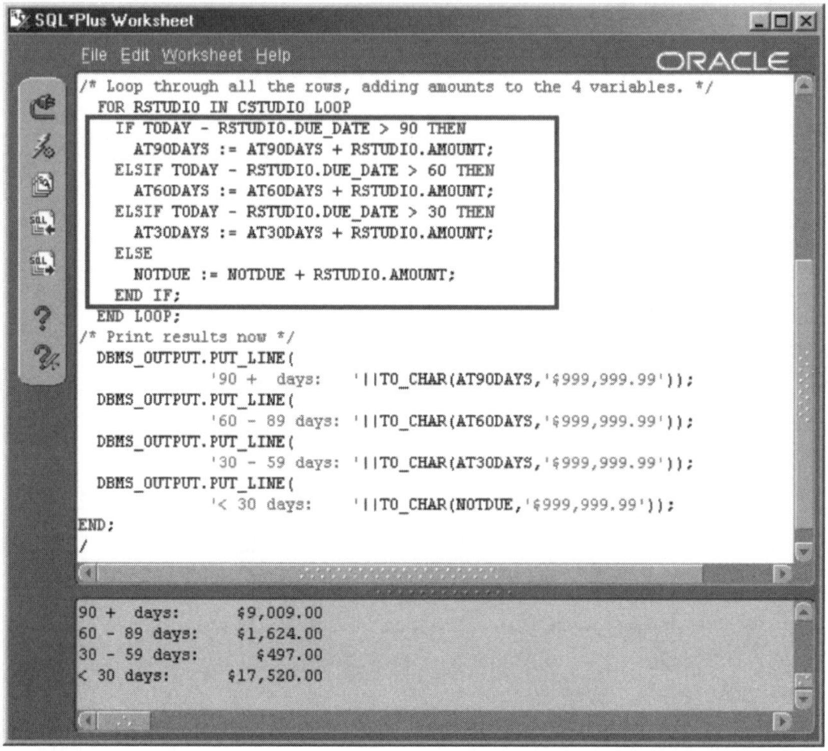

Figure 24.14
*Splitting Results
Using an IF
Statement.*

- **Search Condition**. A search condition with no selector. This form of the CASE statement is very similar to the IF statement shown in Figure 24.14.

- **Selector and Expression**. A selector with an expression result for the selector.

24.7.1.2.1   CASE Statement Search Condition

To demonstrate the use of the CASE statement, we can show a modification of the PL/SQL block we created to demonstrate use of the IF statement. This CASE statement example will use the search condition version of the CASE statement. Change the IF statement code of the previous example. See the result in Figure 24.16.

Figure 24.15
CASE statement syntax.

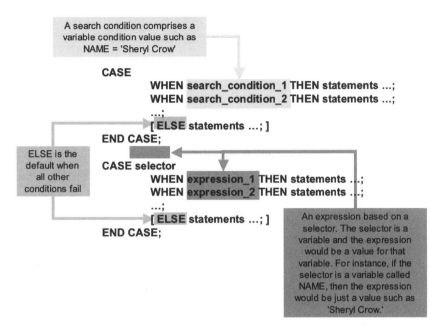

A search condition comprises a variable condition value such as NAME = 'Sheryl Crow'

CASE
      WHEN search_condition_1 THEN statements ...;
      WHEN search_condition_2 THEN statements ...;
      ...;
      [ELSE statements ...;]
END CASE;

ELSE is the default when all other conditions fail

CASE selector
      WHEN expression_1 THEN statements ...;
      WHEN expression_2 THEN statements ...;
      ...;
      [ELSE statements ...;]
END CASE;

An expression based on a selector. The selector is a variable and the expression would be a value for that variable. For instance, if the selector is a variable called NAME, then the expression would be just a value such as 'Sheryl Crow.'

Figure 24.16
Splitting Results Using a Nonselector-type CASE Statement.

```
/* Loop through all the rows, adding amounts to the 4 variables. */
  FOR RSTUDIO IN CSTUDIO LOOP
    CASE
    WHEN TODAY - RSTUDIO.DUE_DATE > 90 THEN
       AT90DAYS := AT90DAYS + RSTUDIO.AMOUNT;
    WHEN TODAY - RSTUDIO.DUE_DATE > 60 THEN
       AT60DAYS := AT60DAYS + RSTUDIO.AMOUNT;
    WHEN TODAY - RSTUDIO.DUE_DATE > 30 THEN
       AT30DAYS := AT30DAYS + RSTUDIO.AMOUNT;
    ELSE
       NOTDUE := NOTDUE + RSTUDIO.AMOUNT;
    END CASE;
  END LOOP;
/* Print results now */
  DBMS_OUTPUT.PUT_LINE(
             '90 + days:    '||TO_CHAR(AT90DAYS,'$999,999.99'));
  DBMS_OUTPUT.PUT_LINE(
             '60 - 89 days: '||TO_CHAR(AT60DAYS,'$999,999.99'));
  DBMS_OUTPUT.PUT_LINE(
             '30 - 59 days: '||TO_CHAR(AT30DAYS,'$999,999.99'));
  DBMS_OUTPUT.PUT_LINE(
             '< 30 days:    '||TO_CHAR(NOTDUE,'$999,999.99'));
END;
/
```

```
90 + days:     $9,009.00
60 - 89 days:  $1,624.00
30 - 59 days:  $497.00
< 30 days:     $17,520.00
```

```
SET SERVEROUTPUT ON
DECLARE
TODAY DATE DEFAULT '01-JUL-2001';
CURSOR CSTUDIO IS
    SELECT A.COUNTRY,A.NAME,S.DUE_DATE
        ,NVL(S.AMOUNT_CHARGED - NVL(S.AMOUNT_PAID,0),0)
            AS   AMOUNT
        FROM ARTIST A JOIN STUDIOTIME S USING (ARTIST_ID)
        ORDER BY 1,2,3;
    AT90DAYS INTEGER DEFAULT 0;
    AT60DAYS INTEGER DEFAULT 0;
    AT30DAYS INTEGER DEFAULT 0;
    NOTDUE INTEGER DEFAULT 0;
BEGIN
/* Loop through all the rows, adding amounts to the
   4 variables. */
  FOR RSTUDIO IN CSTUDIO LOOP
      CASE
      WHEN TODAY - RSTUDIO.DUE_DATE > 90 THEN
          AT90DAYS := AT90DAYS + RSTUDIO.AMOUNT;
      WHEN TODAY - RSTUDIO.DUE_DATE > 60 THEN
          AT60DAYS := AT60DAYS + RSTUDIO.AMOUNT;
      WHEN TODAY - RSTUDIO.DUE_DATE > 30 THEN
          AT30DAYS := AT30DAYS + RSTUDIO.AMOUNT;
      ELSE
      NOTDUE := NOTDUE + RSTUDIO.AMOUNT;
      END CASE;
  END LOOP;
/* Print results now */
DBMS_OUTPUT.PUT_LINE('90 +  days:    '||TO_CHAR(AT90DAYS,'$999,999.99'));
DBMS_OUTPUT.PUT_LINE('60 - 89 days: '||TO_CHAR(AT60DAYS,'$999,999.99'));
DBMS_OUTPUT.PUT_LINE('30 - 59 days: '||TO_CHAR(AT30DAYS,'$999,999.99'));
DBMS_OUTPUT.PUT_LINE('< 30 days:    '||TO_CHAR(NOTDUE,'$999,999.99'));
END;
/
```

24.7.1.2.2 CASE Statement Selector and Expression

The next example shows the selector version of the CASE statement. Change the CASE statement code of the previous example. In this example, we have divided the output based on the COUNTRY column. Additionally, the ELSE clause is not used because we know we do not have any countries other than Canada, England, or the USA, and we have no null-valued countries as well. See the result in Figure 24.17.

```
SET SERVEROUTPUT ON
DECLARE
TODAY DATE DEFAULT '01-JUL-2001';
CURSOR CSTUDIO IS
    SELECT A.COUNTRY,A.NAME,S.DUE_DATE
        ,NVL(S.AMOUNT_CHARGED - NVL(S.AMOUNT_PAID,0),0)
            AS    AMOUNT
        FROM ARTIST A JOIN STUDIOTIME S USING (ARTIST_ID)
        ORDER BY 1,2,3;
    CANADA INTEGER DEFAULT 0;
    USA INTEGER DEFAULT 0;
    ENGLAND INTEGER DEFAULT 0;
    OTHER INTEGER DEFAULT 0;
BEGIN
/* Loop through all the rows, adding amounts to the
   4 variables. */
FOR RSTUDIO IN CSTUDIO LOOP
    CASE RSTUDIO.COUNTRY
    WHEN 'CAN' THEN CANADA:=CANADA+RSTUDIO.AMOUNT;
    WHEN 'England' THEN ENGLAND:=ENGLAND+RSTUDIO.AMOUNT;
    WHEN 'USA' THEN USA:=USA+RSTUDIO.AMOUNT;
    ELSE OTHER:=OTHER+RSTUDIO.AMOUNT;
    END CASE;
END LOOP;
/* Print results now */
    DBMS_OUTPUT.PUT_LINE(
            'Canada:  '||TO_CHAR(CANADA,'$999,999.99'));
    DBMS_OUTPUT.PUT_LINE(
            'USA:     '||TO_CHAR(USA,'$999,999.99'));
    DBMS_OUTPUT.PUT_LINE(
            'England: '||TO_CHAR(ENGLAND,'$999,999.99'));
    DBMS_OUTPUT.PUT_LINE(
            'Other:   '||TO_CHAR(OTHER,'$999,999.99'));
END;
/
```

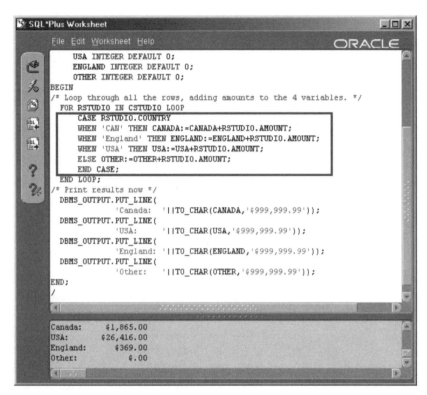

Figure 24.17
Splitting Results Using a Selector-type CASE Statement.

24.7.2 **Iteration or Repetition**

In programming, loops are either FOR loops, WHILE loops, or UNTIL loops:

- **FOR Loop**. Iterate through a known set of values.

- **WHILE Loop**. Iterate as long as a condition is true.

- **LOOP...END LOOP Construct**. A potentially infinite loop iterating without a condition on the loop statement. This construct can be used as an UNTIL loop (iterates until a condition is true) by placing an EXIT WHEN clause just before the END LOOP statement.

- **FORALL Command**. The FORALL command is exclusive to PL/SQL and is a collection iteration or looping command. It allows scanning through the elements of a VARRAY, nested table, or associative array. $(10g)$ There are improvements in Oracle Database 10g.

24.7.2.1   The FOR Loop

Loops a known number of times and can be aborted using the EXIT WHEN clause. The range values can be integers, variables containing integers, or expressions resulting in integer values. The syntax of the FOR loop is shown in Figure 24.18.

Following are some example FOR loops. Example screenshots are not included for these FOR loop examples. The first example counts forward from 1 to 5.

```
DECLARE
STEP INTEGER;
BEGIN
FOR STEP IN 1..5 LOOP
    DBMS_OUTPUT.PUT_LINE(TO_CHAR(STEP));
END LOOP;
END;
/
```

The second example counts in reverse from 2 back to –2. Note how even the reverse-counting loop places the lower-valued integer first and the higher-valued integer last. This is shown in the syntax diagram for the FOR loop in Figure 24.18.

Figure 24.18
*FOR Loop
Statement Syntax.*

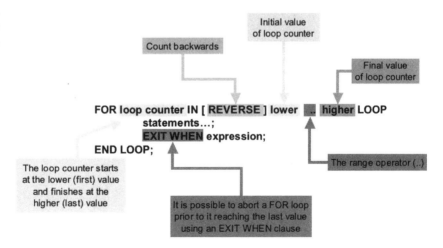

```
DECLARE
STEP INTEGER;
BEGIN
FOR STEP IN REVERSE -2..2 LOOP
    DBMS_OUTPUT.PUT_LINE(TO_CHAR(STEP));
END LOOP;
END;
/
```

The third example shows the use of variables and expressions in FOR loop range counters. The result is a FOR loop that iterates five times from 1 to 5.

```
DECLARE
    STEP INTEGER;
    J INTEGER DEFAULT 1;
    K INTEGER DEFAULT 1;
BEGIN
    FOR STEP IN J..(K+4) LOOP
        DBMS_OUTPUT.PUT_LINE(TO_CHAR(STEP));
    END LOOP;
END;
/
```

The last example shows use of labels and the loop EXIT command. Note how the EXIT command forces control out of two nested loops. This nested FOR loop will execute 10 times through the outer loop and from 1 to 10 times through the inner loop before being terminated by the EXIT command.

```
DECLARE
OUTER INTEGER;
INNER INTEGER;
BEGIN
DBMS_OUTPUT.PUT_LINE('Start of Nested FOR loops');
<<outerloop>>
FOR OUTER IN 1..10 LOOP
        FOR INNER IN 1..10 LOOP
            IF OUTER > INNER THEN
EXIT outerloop;
```

```
END IF;
DBMS_OUTPUT.PUT_LINE(TO_CHAR(OUTER)||' '||TO_CHAR(INNER));
      END LOOP;
END LOOP outerloop;
DBMS_OUTPUT.PUT_LINE('Done with nested FOR loops');
END;
/
```

Note: Forcing control out of a loop using an EXIT command is poor modular programming practice. Doing the same from more than a single nested loop level is worse, but it can be done in PL/SQL.

24.7.2.2   The WHILE Loop

The WHILE loop is executed as long as a condition at the start of the loop is false and can be aborted using the EXIT WHEN clause. WHILE loop syntax is shown in Figure 24.19.

The example WHILE loop following will iterate through the loop nine times. The variable STEP starts at 1 because of the DEFAULT 1 clause in the variable definition. When the WHILE loop condition reaches 10, the condition fails and control is passed to the line after the END LOOP state-

Figure 24.19
WHILE Loop
Statement Syntax.

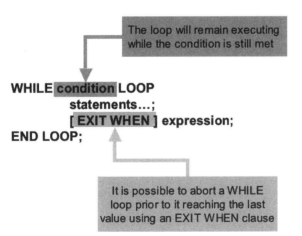

ment (the WHILE loop counts from 1 to 9). An example screenshot is not included for this example as with the FOR loop examples.

```
DECLARE
STEP INTEGER DEFAULT 1;
```

```
BEGIN
WHILE STEP < 10 LOOP
        DBMS_OUTPUT.PUT_LINE(TO_CHAR(STEP));
        STEP := STEP + 1;
END LOOP;
END;
/
```

Note: Note the presence of the counter (STEP := STEP + 1) in the WHILE loop example. A FOR loop counts automatically.

24.7.2.3   The LOOP...END LOOP Construct

This loop is usually called the Infinite Loop and is the simplest of all the looping constructs. The EXIT WHEN clause is used to abort the loop from anywhere within that loop. The syntax for the LOOP...END LOOP construct is shown in Figure 24.20.

Figure 24.20
*LOOP ... END
LOOP Statement
Syntax.*

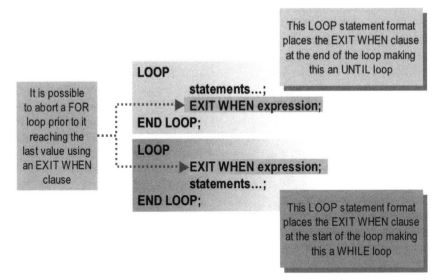

The following example counts forward from 1 to 5. An example screen-shot is not included for this LOOP...END LOOP example.

```
DECLARE
STEP INTEGER DEFAULT 1;
BEGIN
```

```
LOOP
        DBMS_OUTPUT.PUT_LINE(TO_CHAR(STEP));
        STEP := STEP + 1;
        IF STEP > 5 THEN EXIT; END IF;
END LOOP;
END;
/
```

Note: Note the presence of the counter (STEP := STEP + 1) in the WHILE loop example. A FOR loop counts automatically.

24.7.2.4 The FORALL Command

The syntax for the FORALL command is shown in Figure 24.21. The FORALL is essentially a loop, looping through and executing on the elements of a collection as opposed to a coded loop such as with a FOR loop.

24.7.3 Sequence Controls

- **The GOTO Statement**. Allows branching from one point in a block of code to another point where the target line is denoted by a label.

- **The NULL Statement**. This does nothing and passes control on to the following statement.

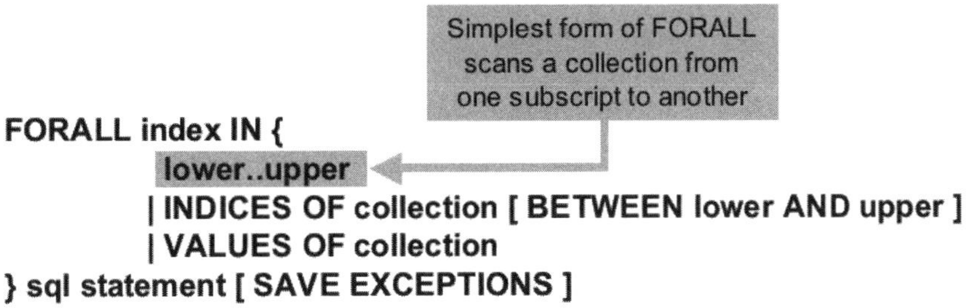

Figure 24.21
FORALL Command Syntax.

Simplest form of FORALL scans a collection from one subscript to another

FORALL index IN {
    lower..upper
    | INDICES OF collection [BETWEEN lower AND upper]
    | VALUES OF collection
} sql statement [SAVE EXCEPTIONS]

24.7.3.1 The GOTO Statement

A pseudocode example of use of the GOTO statement is shown as follows. Once again, please note that proper coding practices generally will never require the use of GOTO statements.

```
BEGIN
<<labelone>>
```

```
    statements…;
IF condition THEN GOTO labelone; END IF;
    statements…;
    IF condition THEN GOTO labeltwo; END IF;
    statements…;
    <<labeltwo>>
    statements…;
END;
```

24.7.3.2   The NULL Command

The NULL command does nothing. A common use for the NULL command is to ignore an error trap (no error is returned). In the following code sample, the SELECT statement will cause an SQL error because the ARTIST_ID value of 0 does not exist in the ARTIST table. The result is that the second DBMS_OUTPUT.PUT_LINE procedure will not be executed because control is passed out of the PL/SQL block. See the result in Figure 24.22.

```
DECLARE
    VNAME ARTIST.NAME%TYPE;
BEGIN
    DBMS_OUTPUT.PUT_LINE('Start');
    SELECT NAME INTO VNAME FROM ARTIST
    WHERE ARTIST_ID = 0;
    DBMS_OUTPUT.PUT_LINE('Finish');
EXCEPTION WHEN OTHERS THEN NULL;
END;
/
```

24.8   Objects and Methods

There is capability in PL/SQL for creation of classes and attached methods. Object-oriented PL/SQL code can be constructed. However, this area of PL/SQL coding is extremely complex and perhaps one arena that is a little beyond the scope of this book.

Figure 24.22
*Demonstrating the
Use of the NULL
Command.*

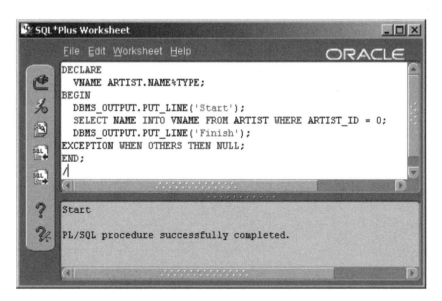

24.9   Oracle-Provided Packages

Oracle Database provides access to an enormous number of extra and
optional features. Many of these features are provided by add-on packaged
PL/SQL routines. A scant few of the more interesting and general-use packages are described as follows:

- **DBMS_REDEFINITION**. Online redefinition of tables.

- **DBMS_LOB**. Manipulate LOB objects.

- **DBMS_OUTPUT**. Can be used to produce output from PL/SQL
  blocks; often used for debugging.

- **DBMS_SQL**. Allows for coding of dynamically generated SQL code,
  superseded by the EXECUTE IMMEDIATE command.

- **UTL_FILE**. Output to files in the operating system from Oracle
  Database.

- **UTL_HTTP**. Similar type of function to UTL_FILE, except calls
  over an HTTP protocol from SQL and PL/SQL.

- **DBMS_PIPE**. A pipe permits interprocess communication, in the
  case of Oracle Database intersession communication.

- **DBMS_JOB**. Scheduling of jobs.

- (10g) **DBMS_WARNINGS**. Use this package to enable or disable PL/SQL compilation warnings. The PLSQL_WARNINGS database configuration parameter performs the same function.

- (10g) **UTL_COMPRESS**. Allows data compression.

- (10g) **UTL_MAIL**. Simplifies e-mail from within PL/SQL such that protocol detail is no longer required.

24.10 Metadata Views

This section simply describes metadata views applicable to PL/SQL objects. Chapter 19 describes the basis and detail of Oracle Database metadata views.

- **USER_OBJECTS**. Shows all object types. A good method of searching for PL/SQL objects such as procedures, functions, and triggers.

- **USER_PROCEDURES**. Shows procedure details.

- **USER_TRIGGERS**. Shows trigger details.

- **USER_TRIGGER_COLS**. Trigger column usage.

- **USER_SOURCE**. Stored blocks source code.

- **USER_ERRORS**. Most recent errors. When compiling a procedure with an error, either access USER_ERRORS or type the command SHOW ERRORS into SQL*Plus.

This chapter has described the basics of PL/SQL as a programming language for constructing database stored procedures. Additionally, this chapter ends this book covering Oracle SQL for Oracle Database 10g. I hope you have enjoyed reading this book as much as I have enjoyed writing it.

MUSIC schema scripts can be found from a simple menu on my website at the following URL, along with many other goodies including my resume.

```
http://www.oracledbaexpert.com/oracle/
OracleSQLJumpstartWithExamples/index.html.
```

A.1   MUSICMASTER.SQL

```
SET ECHO OFF
UNDEF DBNAME
PROMPT WHAT IS THE DATABASE OR NETWORK NAME? (SUCH AS: ORADB10)
ACCEPT DBNAME
PROMPT CONNECTING TO SYSTEM NOW.
CONNECT SYSTEM@&&DBNAME
@CREATEUSER.SQL
CONNECT MUSIC/MUSIC@&&DBNAME
@SCHEMAOLTP.SQL
@SEQUENCES.SQL
@INSTRUMENT.SQL
@ARTIST.SQL
@GENRE.SQL;
@MUSICCD.SQL
@SONGANDTRACK.SQL
@GUESTARTIST.SQL
@STUDIOTIME.SQL
@UPDATEDATA.SQL
@CHECKDATA.SQL
@SCHEMADW.SQL
@DIMENSIONS.SQL
@FACTS.SQL
EXIT;
```

A.2   CREATEUSER.SQL

```
SPOOL log/CREATEUSER.LOG;
DROP USER MUSIC CASCADE;
CREATE USER MUSIC IDENTIFIED BY MUSIC
DEFAULT TABLESPACE USERS
TEMPORARY TABLESPACE TEMP
QUOTA UNLIMITED ON USERS
QUOTA UNLIMITED ON TEMP;
GRANT CONNECT,RESOURCE TO MUSIC;
GRANT UNLIMITED TABLESPACE TO MUSIC;
SPOOL OFF;
```

A.3   SCHEMAOLTP.SQL

```
SPOOL log/SCHEMA_OLTP.LOG;

DROP TABLE INSTRUMENT CASCADE CONSTRAINTS;
CREATE TABLE INSTRUMENT
(
  INSTRUMENT_ID NUMBER NOT NULL
 ,SECTION_ID NUMBER NULL
 ,NAME VARCHAR2(32) NOT NULL
 ,CONSTRAINT XPKINSTRUMENT PRIMARY KEY (INSTRUMENT_ID)
 ,CONSTRAINT FKI_1 FOREIGN KEY (SECTION_ID) REFERENCES INSTRUMENT
);
CREATE UNIQUE INDEX XUK_INSTRUMENT_NAME ON INSTRUMENT (NAME);
CREATE INDEX XFK_I_1 ON INSTRUMENT (SECTION_ID);

DROP TABLE ARTIST CASCADE CONSTRAINTS;
CREATE OR REPLACE TYPE INSTRUMENTSCOLLECTION AS VARRAY(10) OF VARCHAR2(32);
/
CREATE TABLE ARTIST
(
  ARTIST_ID NUMBER NOT NULL
 ,NAME VARCHAR2(32) NOT NULL
 ,STREET VARCHAR2(32)
 ,POBOX CHAR(20)
 ,CITY VARCHAR2(32)
 ,STATE_PROVINCE VARCHAR2(32)
 ,COUNTRY VARCHAR2(32)
 ,ZIP CHAR(10)
 ,EMAIL VARCHAR2(32)
 ,INSTRUMENTS INSTRUMENTSCOLLECTION
```

```
 ,CONSTRAINT XPKARTIST PRIMARY KEY (ARTIST_ID)
);
CREATE UNIQUE INDEX XUK_ARTIST_NAME ON ARTIST (NAME);

DROP TABLE SONG CASCADE CONSTRAINTS;
CREATE TABLE SONG
(
  SONG_ID NUMBER NOT NULL
 ,ARTIST_ID NUMBER NOT NULL
 ,TITLE VARCHAR2(64) NOT NULL
 ,RECORDING_DATE DATE
 ,PLAYING_TIME CHAR(10)
 ,RECORDING BLOB
 ,CONSTRAINT XPKSONG PRIMARY KEY (SONG_ID)
 ,CONSTRAINT FKSONG_1 FOREIGN KEY (ARTIST_ID) REFERENCES ARTIST
);
CREATE INDEX XFK_SONG_1 ON SONG (ARTIST_ID);
CREATE UNIQUE INDEX XUK_SONG_TITLE ON SONG (TITLE);

DROP TABLE GUESTAPPEARANCE CASCADE CONSTRAINTS;
CREATE TABLE GUESTAPPEARANCE
(
  SONG_ID NUMBER NOT NULL
 ,GUESTARTIST_ID NUMBER NO NULL
 ,COMMENT_TEXT VARCHAR2(256)
 ,CONSTRAINT XPKGUESTAPPEARANCE PRIMARY KEY (SONG_ID,GUESTARTIST_ID)
 ,CONSTRAINT FKGUESTAPPEARANCE_1 FOREIGN KEY (GUESTARTIST_ID) REFERENCES ARTIST
 ,CONSTRAINT FKGUESTAPPEARANCE_2 FOREIGN KEY (SONG_ID) REFERENCES SONG
);
CREATE INDEX XFK_GUESTAPPEARANCE_1 ON GUESTAPPEARANCE (GUESTARTIST_ID);
CREATE INDEX XFK_GUESTAPPEARANCE_2 ON GUESTAPPEARANCE (SONG_ID);

DROP TABLE INSTRUMENTATION CASCADE CONSTRAINTS;
CREATE TABLE INSTRUMENTATION
(
  SONG_ID NUMBER NOT NULL
 ,GUESTARTIST_ID NUMBER NOT NULL
 ,INSTRUMENT_ID NUMBER NOT NULL
 ,COMMENT_TEXT VARCHAR2(256)
 ,CONSTRAINT XPKISG PRIMARY KEY (SONG_ID,GUESTARTIST_ID,INSTRUMENT_ID)
 ,CONSTRAINT FKISG_1 FOREIGN KEY (SONG_ID,GUESTARTIST_ID) REFERENCES GUESTAPPEARANCE
 ,CONSTRAINT FKISG_2 FOREIGN KEY (INSTRUMENT_ID) REFERENCES INSTRUMENT
);
CREATE INDEX XFK_ISG_1 ON INSTRUMENTATION (INSTRUMENT_ID);
CREATE INDEX XFK_ISG_2 ON INSTRUMENTATION (SONG_ID, GUESTARTIST_ID);
```

```
DROP TABLE GENRE CASCADE CONSTRAINTS;
CREATE TABLE GENRE
(
  GENRE_ID NUMBER NOT NULL
 ,STYLE_ID NUMBER
 ,GENRE VARCHAR2(32)
 ,CONSTRAINT XPKGENRE PRIMARY KEY (GENRE_ID)
 ,CONSTRAINT FKG_1 FOREIGN KEY (STYLE_ID) REFERENCES GENRE
);
CREATE INDEX XFK_G_1 ON GENRE (STYLE_ID);

DROP TABLE MUSICCD CASCADE CONSTRAINTS;
CREATE TABLE MUSICCD
(
  MUSICCD_ID NUMBER NOT NULL
 ,GENRE_ID NUMBER
 ,TITLE VARCHAR2(32)
 ,PRESSED_DATE DATE
 ,PLAYING_TIME CHAR(10)
 ,LIST_PRICE FLOAT
 ,CONSTRAINT XPKMUSICCD PRIMARY KEY (MUSICCD_ID)
 ,CONSTRAINT FKMCD_1 FOREIGN KEY (GENRE_ID) REFERENCES GENRE
);
CREATE UNIQUE INDEX XUK_MUSICCD_TITLE ON MUSICCD (TITLE);
CREATE INDEX XFK_MCD_1 ON MUSICCD (GENRE_ID);

DROP TABLE CDTRACK CASCADE CONSTRAINTS;
CREATE TABLE CDTRACK
(
  MUSICCD_ID NUMBER NOT NULL
 ,SONG_ID NUMBER NOT NULL
 ,TRACK_SEQ_NO NUMBER NOT NULL
 ,CONSTRAINT XPKCDTRACK PRIMARY KEY (MUSICCD_ID,SONG_ID)
 ,CONSTRAINT FKCDTRACK_1 FOREIGN KEY (SONG_ID) REFERENCES SONG
 ,CONSTRAINT FKCDTRACK_2 FOREIGN KEY (MUSICCD_ID) REFERENCES MUSICCD
);
CREATE INDEX XFK_CDTRACK_1 ON CDTRACK (SONG_ID);
CREATE INDEX XFK_CDTRACK_2 ON CDTRACK (MUSICCD_ID);
CREATE UNIQUE INDEX XAK_CDTRACK_TRACK ON CDTRACK (MUSICCD_ID,TRACK_SEQ_NO);

DROP TABLE STUDIOTIME CASCADE CONSTRAINTS;
CREATE TABLE STUDIOTIME
(
  STUDIOTIME_ID NUMBER NOT NULL
 ,ARTIST_ID NUMBER NOT NULL
```

```
,SESSION_DATE DATE
,MINUTES_USED NUMBER(10,2)
,DUE_DATE DATE
,AMOUNT_CHARGED NUMBER(10,2)
,AMOUNT_PAID NUMBER(10,2)
,CONSTRAINT XPKSTUDIOTIME PRIMARY KEY (STUDIOTIME_ID)
,CONSTRAINT FKSTUDIOTIME_1 FOREIGN KEY (ARTIST_ID) REFERENCES ARTIST
);
CREATE INDEX XFK_STUDIOTIME_1 ON STUDIOTIME (ARTIST_ID);

SPOOL OFF;
```

A.4   SEQUENCES.SQL

```
SPOOL log/SEQUENCES.LOG;
DROP SEQUENCE ARTIST_ID_SEQ;
DROP SEQUENCE SONG_ID_SEQ;
DROP SEQUENCE INSTRUMENT_ID_SEQ;
DROP SEQUENCE STUDIOTIME_ID_SEQ;
DROP SEQUENCE MUSICCD_ID_SEQ;
DROP SEQUENCE GENRE_ID_SEQ;
DROP SEQUENCE continent_ID_SEQ;
DROP SEQUENCE country_ID_SEQ;
DROP SEQUENCE retailer_ID_SEQ;
DROP SEQUENCE CUSTOMER_ID_SEQ;
DROP SEQUENCE SALES_ID_SEQ;
CREATE SEQUENCE ARTIST_ID_SEQ START WITH 1 INCREMENT BY 1 NOMAXVALUE NOCYCLE;
CREATE SEQUENCE SONG_ID_SEQ START WITH 1 INCREMENT BY 1 NOMAXVALUE NOCYCLE;
CREATE SEQUENCE INSTRUMENT_ID_SEQ START WITH 1 INCREMENT BY 1 NOMAXVALUE NOCYCLE;
CREATE SEQUENCE STUDIOTIME_ID_SEQ START WITH 1 INCREMENT BY 1 NOMAXVALUE NOCYCLE;
CREATE SEQUENCE MUSICCD_ID_SEQ START WITH 1 INCREMENT BY 1 NOMAXVALUE NOCYCLE;
CREATE SEQUENCE GENRE_ID_SEQ START WITH 1 INCREMENT BY 1 NOMAXVALUE NOCYCLE;
CREATE SEQUENCE continent_ID_SEQ START WITH 1 INCREMENT BY 1 NOMAXVALUE NOCYCLE;
CREATE SEQUENCE country_ID_SEQ START WITH 1 INCREMENT BY 1 NOMAXVALUE NOCYCLE;
CREATE SEQUENCE retailer_ID_SEQ START WITH 1 INCREMENT BY 1 NOMAXVALUE NOCYCLE;
CREATE SEQUENCE CUSTOMER_ID_SEQ START WITH 1 INCREMENT BY 1 NOMAXVALUE NOCYCLE;
CREATE SEQUENCE SALES_ID_SEQ START WITH 1 INCREMENT BY 1 NOMAXVALUE NOCYCLE;
SPOOL OFF;
```

A.5   INSTRUMENT.SQL

```
SPOOL log/INSTRUMENT.LOG;
```

```
INSERT INTO INSTRUMENT(INSTRUMENT_ID,SECTION_ID,NAME)
VALUES(INSTRUMENT_ID_SEQ.NEXTVAL,NULL,'Guitar');
INSERT INTO INSTRUMENT(INSTRUMENT_ID,SECTION_ID,NAME)
VALUES(INSTRUMENT_ID_SEQ.NEXTVAL,NULL,'General');
INSERT INTO INSTRUMENT(INSTRUMENT_ID,SECTION_ID,NAME)
VALUES(INSTRUMENT_ID_SEQ.NEXTVAL,NULL,'Percussion');
INSERT INTO INSTRUMENT(INSTRUMENT_ID,SECTION_ID,NAME)
VALUES(INSTRUMENT_ID_SEQ.NEXTVAL,NULL,'Piano');
INSERT INTO INSTRUMENT(INSTRUMENT_ID,SECTION_ID,NAME)
VALUES(INSTRUMENT_ID_SEQ.NEXTVAL,NULL,'String');
INSERT INTO INSTRUMENT(INSTRUMENT_ID,SECTION_ID,NAME)
VALUES(INSTRUMENT_ID_SEQ.NEXTVAL,NULL,'Vocals');
INSERT INTO INSTRUMENT(INSTRUMENT_ID,SECTION_ID,NAME)
VALUES(INSTRUMENT_ID_SEQ.NEXTVAL,NULL,'Wind');
INSERT INTO INSTRUMENT(INSTRUMENT_ID,SECTION_ID,NAME)
VALUES(INSTRUMENT_ID_SEQ.NEXTVAL,NULL,'Orchestra');


INSERT INTO INSTRUMENT(INSTRUMENT_ID,SECTION_ID,NAME)
VALUES(INSTRUMENT_ID_SEQ.NEXTVAL,(SELECT INSTRUMENT_ID FROM INSTRUMENT WHERE
NAME='Guitar') ,'Acoustic Guitar');
INSERT INTO INSTRUMENT(INSTRUMENT_ID,SECTION_ID,NAME)
VALUES(INSTRUMENT_ID_SEQ.NEXTVAL,(SELECT INSTRUMENT_ID FROM INSTRUMENT WHERE
NAME='Guitar') ,'Electric Guitar');
INSERT INTO INSTRUMENT(INSTRUMENT_ID,SECTION_ID,NAME)
VALUES(INSTRUMENT_ID_SEQ.NEXTVAL,(SELECT INSTRUMENT_ID FROM INSTRUMENT WHERE
NAME='Wind') ,'Brass');
INSERT INTO INSTRUMENT(INSTRUMENT_ID,SECTION_ID,NAME)
VALUES(INSTRUMENT_ID_SEQ.NEXTVAL,(SELECT INSTRUMENT_ID FROM INSTRUMENT WHERE
NAME='Wind'),'Woodwind');


INSERT INTO INSTRUMENT(INSTRUMENT_ID,SECTION_ID,NAME)
VALUES(INSTRUMENT_ID_SEQ.NEXTVAL,(SELECT INSTRUMENT_ID FROM INSTRUMENT WHERE
NAME='Woodwind'),'Alto Horn');
INSERT INTO INSTRUMENT(INSTRUMENT_ID,SECTION_ID,NAME)
VALUES(INSTRUMENT_ID_SEQ.NEXTVAL,(SELECT INSTRUMENT_ID FROM INSTRUMENT WHERE
NAME='Brass'),'Alto Saxophone');
INSERT INTO INSTRUMENT(INSTRUMENT_ID,SECTION_ID,NAME)
VALUES(INSTRUMENT_ID_SEQ.NEXTVAL,(SELECT INSTRUMENT_ID FROM INSTRUMENT WHERE
NAME='Vocals') ,'Background Vocals');
INSERT INTO INSTRUMENT(INSTRUMENT_ID,SECTION_ID,NAME)
VALUES(INSTRUMENT_ID_SEQ.NEXTVAL,(SELECT INSTRUMENT_ID FROM INSTRUMENT WHERE
NAME='Brass') ,'Baritone / Bass Saxophone');
INSERT INTO INSTRUMENT(INSTRUMENT_ID,SECTION_ID,NAME)
VALUES(INSTRUMENT_ID_SEQ.NEXTVAL,(SELECT INSTRUMENT_ID FROM INSTRUMENT WHERE
NAME='Woodwind') ,'Baritone Horn');
INSERT INTO INSTRUMENT(INSTRUMENT_ID,SECTION_ID,NAME)
VALUES(INSTRUMENT_ID_SEQ.NEXTVAL,(SELECT INSTRUMENT_ID FROM INSTRUMENT WHERE
NAME='Electric Guitar') ,'Bass Guitar');
```

```
INSERT INTO INSTRUMENT(INSTRUMENT_ID,SECTION_ID,NAME)
VALUES(INSTRUMENT_ID_SEQ.NEXTVAL,(SELECT INSTRUMENT_ID FROM INSTRUMENT WHERE
NAME='String') ,'Cello');
INSERT INTO INSTRUMENT(INSTRUMENT_ID,SECTION_ID,NAME)
VALUES(INSTRUMENT_ID_SEQ.NEXTVAL,(SELECT INSTRUMENT_ID FROM INSTRUMENT WHERE
NAME='Woodwind') ,'Clarinet');
INSERT INTO INSTRUMENT(INSTRUMENT_ID,SECTION_ID,NAME)
VALUES(INSTRUMENT_ID_SEQ.NEXTVAL,(SELECT INSTRUMENT_ID FROM INSTRUMENT WHERE
NAME='Percussion') ,'Cymbals');
INSERT INTO INSTRUMENT(INSTRUMENT_ID,SECTION_ID,NAME)
VALUES(INSTRUMENT_ID_SEQ.NEXTVAL,(SELECT INSTRUMENT_ID FROM INSTRUMENT WHERE
NAME='String') ,'Double Bass');
INSERT INTO INSTRUMENT(INSTRUMENT_ID,SECTION_ID,NAME)
VALUES(INSTRUMENT_ID_SEQ.NEXTVAL,(SELECT INSTRUMENT_ID FROM INSTRUMENT WHERE
NAME='General') ,'Double Reeds');
INSERT INTO INSTRUMENT(INSTRUMENT_ID,SECTION_ID,NAME)
VALUES(INSTRUMENT_ID_SEQ.NEXTVAL,(SELECT INSTRUMENT_ID FROM INSTRUMENT WHERE
NAME='Percussion') ,'Drum Machines');
INSERT INTO INSTRUMENT(INSTRUMENT_ID,SECTION_ID,NAME)
VALUES(INSTRUMENT_ID_SEQ.NEXTVAL,(SELECT INSTRUMENT_ID FROM INSTRUMENT WHERE
NAME='Percussion') ,'Drums');
INSERT INTO INSTRUMENT(INSTRUMENT_ID,SECTION_ID,NAME)
VALUES(INSTRUMENT_ID_SEQ.NEXTVAL,(SELECT INSTRUMENT_ID FROM INSTRUMENT WHERE
NAME='Percussion') ,'Electronic Drums');
INSERT INTO INSTRUMENT(INSTRUMENT_ID,SECTION_ID,NAME)
VALUES(INSTRUMENT_ID_SEQ.NEXTVAL,(SELECT INSTRUMENT_ID FROM INSTRUMENT WHERE
NAME='String') ,'Fiddle');
INSERT INTO INSTRUMENT(INSTRUMENT_ID,SECTION_ID,NAME)
VALUES(INSTRUMENT_ID_SEQ.NEXTVAL,(SELECT INSTRUMENT_ID FROM INSTRUMENT WHERE
NAME='Wind') ,'Flugelhorn');
INSERT INTO INSTRUMENT(INSTRUMENT_ID,SECTION_ID,NAME)
VALUES(INSTRUMENT_ID_SEQ.NEXTVAL,(SELECT INSTRUMENT_ID FROM INSTRUMENT WHERE
NAME='Wind') ,'Flute');
INSERT INTO INSTRUMENT(INSTRUMENT_ID,SECTION_ID,NAME)
VALUES(INSTRUMENT_ID_SEQ.NEXTVAL,(SELECT INSTRUMENT_ID FROM INSTRUMENT WHERE
NAME='Brass') ,'French Horn');
INSERT INTO INSTRUMENT(INSTRUMENT_ID,SECTION_ID,NAME)
VALUES(INSTRUMENT_ID_SEQ.NEXTVAL,(SELECT INSTRUMENT_ID FROM INSTRUMENT WHERE
NAME='Piano') ,'Keyboards');
INSERT INTO INSTRUMENT(INSTRUMENT_ID,SECTION_ID,NAME)
VALUES(INSTRUMENT_ID_SEQ.NEXTVAL,(SELECT INSTRUMENT_ID FROM INSTRUMENT WHERE
NAME='Percussion') ,'Latin Percussion');
INSERT INTO INSTRUMENT(INSTRUMENT_ID,SECTION_ID,NAME)
VALUES(INSTRUMENT_ID_SEQ.NEXTVAL,(SELECT INSTRUMENT_ID FROM INSTRUMENT WHERE
NAME='Electric Guitar') ,'Lead Guitar');
INSERT INTO INSTRUMENT(INSTRUMENT_ID,SECTION_ID,NAME)
VALUES(INSTRUMENT_ID_SEQ.NEXTVAL,(SELECT INSTRUMENT_ID FROM INSTRUMENT WHERE
NAME='General') ,'Mellophone');
INSERT INTO INSTRUMENT(INSTRUMENT_ID,SECTION_ID,NAME)
VALUES(INSTRUMENT_ID_SEQ.NEXTVAL,(SELECT INSTRUMENT_ID FROM INSTRUMENT WHERE
NAME='Wind') ,'Piccolo');
```

```
INSERT INTO INSTRUMENT(INSTRUMENT_ID,SECTION_ID,NAME)
VALUES(INSTRUMENT_ID_SEQ.NEXTVAL,(SELECT INSTRUMENT_ID FROM INSTRUMENT WHERE
NAME='Acoustic Guitar') ,'Rhythm Guitar');
INSERT INTO INSTRUMENT(INSTRUMENT_ID,SECTION_ID,NAME)
VALUES(INSTRUMENT_ID_SEQ.NEXTVAL,(SELECT INSTRUMENT_ID FROM INSTRUMENT WHERE
NAME='Brass') ,'Soprano Saxophone');
INSERT INTO INSTRUMENT(INSTRUMENT_ID,SECTION_ID,NAME)
VALUES(INSTRUMENT_ID_SEQ.NEXTVAL,(SELECT INSTRUMENT_ID FROM INSTRUMENT WHERE
NAME='Brass') ,'Sousaphone');
INSERT INTO INSTRUMENT(INSTRUMENT_ID,SECTION_ID,NAME)
VALUES(INSTRUMENT_ID_SEQ.NEXTVAL,(SELECT INSTRUMENT_ID FROM INSTRUMENT WHERE
NAME='Acoustic Guitar') ,'Steel Guitar');
INSERT INTO INSTRUMENT(INSTRUMENT_ID,SECTION_ID,NAME)
VALUES(INSTRUMENT_ID_SEQ.NEXTVAL,(SELECT INSTRUMENT_ID FROM INSTRUMENT WHERE
NAME='Brass') ,'Tenor Saxophone');
INSERT INTO INSTRUMENT(INSTRUMENT_ID,SECTION_ID,NAME)
VALUES(INSTRUMENT_ID_SEQ.NEXTVAL,(SELECT INSTRUMENT_ID FROM INSTRUMENT WHERE
NAME='Brass') ,'Trombone');
INSERT INTO INSTRUMENT(INSTRUMENT_ID,SECTION_ID,NAME)
VALUES(INSTRUMENT_ID_SEQ.NEXTVAL,(SELECT INSTRUMENT_ID FROM INSTRUMENT WHERE
NAME='Brass') ,'Trumpet');
INSERT INTO INSTRUMENT(INSTRUMENT_ID,SECTION_ID,NAME)
VALUES(INSTRUMENT_ID_SEQ.NEXTVAL,(SELECT INSTRUMENT_ID FROM INSTRUMENT WHERE
NAME='Brass') ,'Tuba');
INSERT INTO INSTRUMENT(INSTRUMENT_ID,SECTION_ID,NAME)
VALUES(INSTRUMENT_ID_SEQ.NEXTVAL,(SELECT INSTRUMENT_ID FROM INSTRUMENT WHERE
NAME='String') ,'Viola');
INSERT INTO INSTRUMENT(INSTRUMENT_ID,SECTION_ID,NAME)
VALUES(INSTRUMENT_ID_SEQ.NEXTVAL,(SELECT INSTRUMENT_ID FROM INSTRUMENT WHERE
NAME='String') ,'Violin');

COMMIT;
SPOOL OFF;
```

A.6   ARTIST.SQL

```
SPOOL log/ARTIST.LOG;
INSERT INTO ARTIST(ARTIST_ID,NAME,INSTRUMENTS)
VALUES(ARTIST_ID_SEQ.NEXTVAL,'Sheryl Crow'
,INSTRUMENTSCOLLECTION('Vocals','Acoustic Guitar','Electric Guitar'));
INSERT INTO ARTIST(ARTIST_ID,NAME,INSTRUMENTS)
VALUES(ARTIST_ID_SEQ.NEXTVAL,'Barry Manilow'
,INSTRUMENTSCOLLECTION('Vocals','Piano'));
INSERT INTO ARTIST(ARTIST_ID,NAME,INSTRUMENTS)
VALUES(ARTIST_ID_SEQ.NEXTVAL,'Avril Lavigne'
,INSTRUMENTSCOLLECTION('Vocals'));
INSERT INTO ARTIST(ARTIST_ID,NAME,INSTRUMENTS)
VALUES(ARTIST_ID_SEQ.NEXTVAL,'Goo Goo Dolls',null);
```

```
INSERT INTO ARTIST(ARTIST_ID,NAME,INSTRUMENTS)
VALUES(ARTIST_ID_SEQ.NEXTVAL,'Puddle of Mudd',null);
INSERT INTO ARTIST(ARTIST_ID,NAME,INSTRUMENTS)
VALUES(ARTIST_ID_SEQ.NEXTVAL,'Nickelback',null);
INSERT INTO ARTIST(ARTIST_ID,NAME,INSTRUMENTS)
VALUES(ARTIST_ID_SEQ.NEXTVAL,'Matchbox Twenty',null);
INSERT INTO ARTIST(ARTIST_ID,NAME,INSTRUMENTS) VALUES(ARTIST_ID_SEQ.NEXTVAL,'Jewel'
,INSTRUMENTSCOLLECTION('Vocals','Acoustic Guitar'));
INSERT INTO ARTIST(ARTIST_ID,NAME,INSTRUMENTS)
VALUES(ARTIST_ID_SEQ.NEXTVAL,'Mozart',NULL);
INSERT INTO ARTIST(ARTIST_ID,NAME,INSTRUMENTS) VALUES(ARTIST_ID_SEQ.NEXTVAL,'James
Taylor',INSTRUMENTSCOLLECTION('Vocals','Acoustic Guitar'));
COMMIT;
SPOOL OFF;
```

A.7   GENRE.SQL

```
SPOOL log/GENRE.LOG;
INSERT INTO GENRE (GENRE_ID,STYLE_ID,GENRE) VALUES
(GENRE_ID_SEQ.NEXTVAL,NULL,'Classical');
INSERT INTO GENRE (GENRE_ID,STYLE_ID,GENRE) VALUES
(GENRE_ID_SEQ.NEXTVAL,NULL,'Folk');
INSERT INTO GENRE (GENRE_ID,STYLE_ID,GENRE) VALUES
(GENRE_ID_SEQ.NEXTVAL,NULL,'Popular');
INSERT INTO GENRE (GENRE_ID,STYLE_ID,GENRE) VALUES (GENRE_ID_SEQ.NEXTVAL,(SELECT
GENRE_ID FROM GENRE WHERE genre='Popular'),'Rock');
INSERT INTO GENRE (GENRE_ID,STYLE_ID,GENRE) VALUES (GENRE_ID_SEQ.NEXTVAL,(SELECT
GENRE_ID FROM GENRE WHERE genre='Popular'),'Blues');
INSERT INTO GENRE (GENRE_ID,STYLE_ID,GENRE) VALUES (GENRE_ID_SEQ.NEXTVAL,(SELECT
GENRE_ID FROM GENRE WHERE genre='Popular'),'Contemporary');
INSERT INTO GENRE (GENRE_ID,STYLE_ID,GENRE) VALUES (GENRE_ID_SEQ.NEXTVAL,(SELECT
GENRE_ID FROM GENRE WHERE genre='Popular'),'Motown');
INSERT INTO GENRE (GENRE_ID,STYLE_ID,GENRE) VALUES (GENRE_ID_SEQ.NEXTVAL,(SELECT
GENRE_ID FROM GENRE WHERE genre='Popular'),'Reggae');
INSERT INTO GENRE (GENRE_ID,STYLE_ID,GENRE) VALUES (GENRE_ID_SEQ.NEXTVAL,(SELECT
GENRE_ID FROM GENRE WHERE genre='Rock'),'Heavy Rock');
INSERT INTO GENRE (GENRE_ID,STYLE_ID,GENRE) VALUES (GENRE_ID_SEQ.NEXTVAL,(SELECT
GENRE_ID FROM GENRE WHERE genre='Rock'),'Intellectual Rock');
INSERT INTO GENRE (GENRE_ID,STYLE_ID,GENRE) VALUES (GENRE_ID_SEQ.NEXTVAL,(SELECT
GENRE_ID FROM GENRE WHERE genre='Rock'),'Grunge');
INSERT INTO GENRE (GENRE_ID,STYLE_ID,GENRE) VALUES (GENRE_ID_SEQ.NEXTVAL,(SELECT
GENRE_ID FROM GENRE WHERE genre='Rock'),'American Soft Rock');
INSERT INTO GENRE (GENRE_ID,STYLE_ID,GENRE) VALUES (GENRE_ID_SEQ.NEXTVAL,(SELECT
GENRE_ID FROM GENRE WHERE genre='Rock'),'Weird Rock');
INSERT INTO GENRE (GENRE_ID,STYLE_ID,GENRE) VALUES (GENRE_ID_SEQ.NEXTVAL,(SELECT
GENRE_ID FROM GENRE WHERE genre='Rock'),'More Weird Rock');
```

```
INSERT INTO GENRE (GENRE_ID,STYLE_ID,GENRE) VALUES (GENRE_ID_SEQ.NEXTVAL,(SELECT
GENRE_ID FROM GENRE WHERE genre='Rock'),'Manic Rock');
COMMIT;
SPOOL OFF;
```

A.8   **MUSISCD.SQL**

```
SPOOL log/MUSICCD.LOG;
INSERT INTO MUSICCD (MUSICCD_ID,GENRE_ID,TITLE,PRESSED_DATE,LIST_PRICE)
VALUES (MUSICCD_ID_SEQ.NEXTVAL,(SELECT GENRE_ID FROM GENRE WHERE GENRE='American Soft
Rock'),'Soak Up the Sun','28-FEB-2001',9.99);
INSERT INTO MUSICCD (MUSICCD_ID,GENRE_ID,TITLE,PRESSED_DATE,LIST_PRICE)
VALUES (MUSICCD_ID_SEQ.NEXTVAL,(SELECT GENRE_ID FROM GENRE WHERE GENRE='Manic
Rock'),'Complicated','15-DEC-2001',19.99);
INSERT INTO MUSICCD (MUSICCD_ID,GENRE_ID,TITLE,PRESSED_DATE,LIST_PRICE)
VALUES (MUSICCD_ID_SEQ.NEXTVAL,(SELECT GENRE_ID FROM GENRE WHERE GENRE='Weird
Rock'),'Here Is Gone Pt.1','11-JUN-2002',14.99);
INSERT INTO MUSICCD (MUSICCD_ID,GENRE_ID,TITLE,PRESSED_DATE,LIST_PRICE)
VALUES (MUSICCD_ID_SEQ.NEXTVAL,(SELECT GENRE_ID FROM GENRE WHERE GENRE='More Weird
Rock'),'Here Is Gone Pt.2','15-NOV-2001',9.99);
INSERT INTO MUSICCD (MUSICCD_ID,GENRE_ID,TITLE,PRESSED_DATE,PLAYING_TIME,LIST_PRICE)
VALUES (MUSICCD_ID_SEQ.NEXTVAL,(SELECT GENRE_ID FROM GENRE WHERE GENRE='American Soft
Rock'),'C''mon, C''mon','23-JAN-2002','56:32',19.99);
INSERT INTO MUSICCD (MUSICCD_ID,GENRE_ID,TITLE,PRESSED_DATE,PLAYING_TIME,LIST_PRICE)
VALUES (MUSICCD_ID_SEQ.NEXTVAL,(SELECT GENRE_ID FROM GENRE WHERE
GENRE='Popular'),'Come Clean','09-JAN-02','48:03',14.99);
INSERT INTO MUSICCD (MUSICCD_ID,GENRE_ID,TITLE,PRESSED_DATE,PLAYING_TIME,LIST_PRICE)
VALUES (MUSICCD_ID_SEQ.NEXTVAL,(SELECT GENRE_ID FROM GENRE WHERE
GENRE='Rock'),'Silver Side Up','14-JUL-2002','39:08',9.99);
INSERT INTO MUSICCD (MUSICCD_ID,GENRE_ID,TITLE,PRESSED_DATE,PLAYING_TIME,LIST_PRICE)
VALUES (MUSICCD_ID_SEQ.NEXTVAL,(SELECT GENRE_ID FROM GENRE WHERE
GENRE='Contemporary'),'Ultimate Manilow','25-MAR-2002','77:43',19.99);
INSERT INTO MUSICCD (MUSICCD_ID,GENRE_ID,TITLE,LIST_PRICE)
VALUES (MUSICCD_ID_SEQ.NEXTVAL,(SELECT GENRE_ID FROM GENRE WHERE GENRE='Grunge'),'Mad
Season',14.99);
INSERT INTO MUSICCD (MUSICCD_ID,GENRE_ID,TITLE,PLAYING_TIME,LIST_PRICE)
VALUES (MUSICCD_ID_SEQ.NEXTVAL,(SELECT GENRE_ID FROM GENRE WHERE GENRE='Blues'),'This
Way','58:42',9.99);
INSERT INTO MUSICCD (MUSICCD_ID,GENRE_ID,TITLE,PRESSED_DATE,PLAYING_TIME,LIST_PRICE)
VALUES (MUSICCD_ID_SEQ.NEXTVAL,(SELECT GENRE_ID FROM GENRE WHERE GENRE='Intellectual
Rock'),'The Best of Sheryl Crow','15-SEP-02','44:54',19.99);
INSERT INTO MUSICCD (MUSICCD_ID,GENRE_ID,TITLE,PRESSED_DATE,LIST_PRICE)
VALUES (MUSICCD_ID_SEQ.NEXTVAL,(SELECT GENRE_ID FROM GENRE WHERE
GENRE='Classical'),'Requiem','16-MAY-90',7.98);
INSERT INTO MUSICCD (MUSICCD_ID,GENRE_ID,TITLE,PRESSED_DATE,LIST_PRICE)
VALUES (MUSICCD_ID_SEQ.NEXTVAL,(SELECT GENRE_ID FROM GENRE WHERE GENRE='Folk'),'Sweet
Baby James','25-OCT-90',10.99);
```

```
COMMIT;
SPOOL OFF;
```

A.9   SONGANDTRACK.SQL

```
SPOOL log/SONGANDTRACK.LOG;
SET ECHO OFF

--Soak up the Sun by Sheryl Crow
INSERT INTO SONG(SONG_ID,ARTIST_ID,TITLE, PLAYING_TIME)
VALUES(SONG_ID_SEQ.NEXTVAL
,(SELECT ARTIST_ID FROM ARTIST WHERE NAME='Sheryl Crow')
,'Soak Up The Sun (Album Version)','11:20');
INSERT INTO SONG(SONG_ID,ARTIST_ID,TITLE, PLAYING_TIME)
VALUES(SONG_ID_SEQ.NEXTVAL
,(SELECT ARTIST_ID FROM ARTIST WHERE NAME='Sheryl Crow')
,'Soak Up The Sun (Sunsweep Radio Mix)','3:20');
INSERT INTO SONG(SONG_ID,ARTIST_ID,TITLE,PLAYING_TIME)
VALUES(SONG_ID_SEQ.NEXTVAL
,(SELECT ARTIST_ID FROM ARTIST WHERE NAME='Sheryl Crow')
,'Soak Up The Sun (Sunsweep Club Mix)','22:30');
INSERT INTO SONG(SONG_ID,ARTIST_ID,TITLE, PLAYING_TIME)
VALUES(SONG_ID_SEQ.NEXTVAL
,(SELECT ARTIST_ID FROM ARTIST WHERE NAME='Sheryl Crow')
,'Soak Up The Sun (Sunsweep Dub)','15:30');
COMMIT;

INSERT INTO CDTRACK(MUSICCD_ID,SONG_ID,TRACK_SEQ_NO)
VALUES ((SELECT MUSICCD_ID FROM MUSICCD WHERE TITLE='Soak Up the Sun')
,(SELECT SONG_ID FROM SONG
WHERE TITLE='Soak Up The Sun (Album Version)'),1);
INSERT INTO CDTRACK(MUSICCD_ID,SONG_ID,TRACK_SEQ_NO)
VALUES ((SELECT MUSICCD_ID FROM MUSICCD WHERE TITLE='Soak Up the Sun')
,(SELECT SONG_ID FROM SONG
WHERE TITLE='Soak Up The Sun (Sunsweep Radio Mix)'),2);
INSERT INTO CDTRACK(MUSICCD_ID,SONG_ID,TRACK_SEQ_NO)
VALUES ((SELECT MUSICCD_ID FROM MUSICCD WHERE TITLE='Soak Up the Sun')
,(SELECT SONG_ID FROM SONG
WHERE TITLE='Soak Up The Sun (Sunsweep Club Mix)'),3);
INSERT INTO CDTRACK(MUSICCD_ID,SONG_ID,TRACK_SEQ_NO)
VALUES ((SELECT MUSICCD_ID FROM MUSICCD WHERE TITLE='Soak Up the Sun')
,(SELECT SONG_ID FROM SONG
WHERE TITLE='Soak Up The Sun (Sunsweep Dub)'),4);
COMMIT;
```

```
--Complicated by Avril Lavigne
INSERT INTO SONG(SONG_ID,ARTIST_ID,TITLE)
VALUES(SONG_ID_SEQ.NEXTVAL
,(SELECT ARTIST_ID FROM ARTIST
WHERE NAME='Avril Lavigne'),'Complicated');
COMMIT;


INSERT INTO CDTRACK(MUSICCD_ID,SONG_ID,TRACK_SEQ_NO)
VALUES ((SELECT MUSICCD_ID FROM MUSICCD WHERE TITLE='Complicated')
,(SELECT SONG_ID FROM SONG WHERE TITLE='Complicated'),1);
COMMIT;


--Here is Gone Pt.1 by Goo Goo Dolls
INSERT INTO SONG(SONG_ID,ARTIST_ID,TITLE)
VALUES(SONG_ID_SEQ.NEXTVAL
,(SELECT ARTIST_ID FROM ARTIST WHERE NAME='Goo Goo Dolls')
,'Here Is Gone');
INSERT INTO SONG(SONG_ID,ARTIST_ID,TITLE)
VALUES(SONG_ID_SEQ.NEXTVAL
,(SELECT ARTIST_ID FROM ARTIST WHERE NAME='Goo Goo Dolls')
,'We Are The Normal');
INSERT INTO SONG(SONG_ID,ARTIST_ID,TITLE)
VALUES(SONG_ID_SEQ.NEXTVAL
,(SELECT ARTIST_ID FROM ARTIST WHERE NAME='Goo Goo Dolls')
,'Burnin Up');
INSERT INTO SONG(SONG_ID,ARTIST_ID,TITLE)
VALUES(SONG_ID_SEQ.NEXTVAL
,(SELECT ARTIST_ID FROM ARTIST WHERE NAME='Goo Goo Dolls')
,'Video');
COMMIT;
INSERT INTO CDTRACK(MUSICCD_ID,SONG_ID,TRACK_SEQ_NO)
VALUES ((SELECT MUSICCD_ID FROM MUSICCD WHERE TITLE='Here Is Gone Pt.1')
,(SELECT SONG_ID FROM SONG WHERE TITLE='Here Is Gone'),1);
INSERT INTO CDTRACK(MUSICCD_ID,SONG_ID,TRACK_SEQ_NO)
VALUES ((SELECT MUSICCD_ID FROM MUSICCD WHERE TITLE='Here Is Gone Pt.1')
,(SELECT SONG_ID FROM SONG WHERE TITLE='We Are The Normal'),2);
INSERT INTO CDTRACK(MUSICCD_ID,SONG_ID,TRACK_SEQ_NO)
VALUES ((SELECT MUSICCD_ID FROM MUSICCD WHERE TITLE='Here Is Gone Pt.1')
,(SELECT SONG_ID FROM SONG WHERE TITLE='Burnin Up'),3);
INSERT INTO CDTRACK(MUSICCD_ID,SONG_ID,TRACK_SEQ_NO)
VALUES ((SELECT MUSICCD_ID FROM MUSICCD WHERE TITLE='Here Is Gone Pt.1')
,(SELECT SONG_ID FROM SONG WHERE TITLE='Video'),4);
COMMIT;
```

```
--Here is Gone Pt.2 by Goo Goo Dolls
INSERT INTO SONG(SONG_ID,ARTIST_ID,TITLE)
VALUES(SONG_ID_SEQ.NEXTVAL
,(SELECT ARTIST_ID FROM ARTIST WHERE NAME='Goo Goo Dolls')
,'Here Is Gone Reprise');
INSERT INTO SONG(SONG_ID,ARTIST_ID,TITLE)
VALUES(SONG_ID_SEQ.NEXTVAL
,(SELECT ARTIST_ID FROM ARTIST WHERE NAME='Goo Goo Dolls')
,'Two Days In February');
INSERT INTO SONG(SONG_ID,ARTIST_ID,TITLE)
VALUES(SONG_ID_SEQ.NEXTVAL
,(SELECT ARTIST_ID FROM ARTIST WHERE NAME='Goo Goo Dolls')
,'Girl Right Next To Me');
COMMIT;

INSERT INTO CDTRACK(MUSICCD_ID,SONG_ID,TRACK_SEQ_NO)
VALUES ((SELECT MUSICCD_ID FROM MUSICCD WHERE TITLE='Here Is Gone Pt.2')
,(SELECT SONG_ID FROM SONG WHERE TITLE='Here Is Gone Reprise'),1);
INSERT INTO CDTRACK(MUSICCD_ID,SONG_ID,TRACK_SEQ_NO)
VALUES ((SELECT MUSICCD_ID FROM MUSICCD WHERE TITLE='Here Is Gone Pt.2')
,(SELECT SONG_ID FROM SONG WHERE TITLE='Two Days In February'),2);
INSERT INTO CDTRACK(MUSICCD_ID,SONG_ID,TRACK_SEQ_NO)
VALUES ((SELECT MUSICCD_ID FROM MUSICCD WHERE TITLE='Here Is Gone Pt.2')
,(SELECT SONG_ID FROM SONG WHERE TITLE='Girl Right Next To Me'),3);
COMMIT;

--Cmon Cmon by Sheryl Crow
INSERT INTO SONG(SONG_ID,ARTIST_ID,TITLE,PLAYING_TIME)
VALUES(SONG_ID_SEQ.NEXTVAL
,(SELECT ARTIST_ID FROM ARTIST WHERE NAME='Sheryl Crow')
,'Steve McQueen','3:25');
INSERT INTO SONG(SONG_ID,ARTIST_ID,TITLE,PLAYING_TIME)
VALUES(SONG_ID_SEQ.NEXTVAL
,(SELECT ARTIST_ID FROM ARTIST WHERE NAME='Sheryl Crow')
,'Soak Up The Sun','4:52');
INSERT INTO SONG(SONG_ID,ARTIST_ID,TITLE,PLAYING_TIME)
VALUES(SONG_ID_SEQ.NEXTVAL
,(SELECT ARTIST_ID FROM ARTIST WHERE NAME='Sheryl Crow')
,'You''re An Original','4:18');
INSERT INTO SONG(SONG_ID,ARTIST_ID,TITLE,PLAYING_TIME)
VALUES(SONG_ID_SEQ.NEXTVAL
,(SELECT ARTIST_ID FROM ARTIST WHERE NAME='Sheryl Crow')
,'Safe And Sound','4:32');
INSERT INTO SONG(SONG_ID,ARTIST_ID,TITLE,PLAYING_TIME)
VALUES(SONG_ID_SEQ.NEXTVAL
```

```
,(SELECT ARTIST_ID FROM ARTIST WHERE NAME='Sheryl Crow')
,'C''mon, C''mon','4:45');
INSERT INTO SONG(SONG_ID,ARTIST_ID,TITLE,PLAYING_TIME)
VALUES(SONG_ID_SEQ.NEXTVAL
,(SELECT ARTIST_ID FROM ARTIST WHERE NAME='Sheryl Crow')
,'It''s So Easy','3:24');
INSERT INTO SONG(SONG_ID,ARTIST_ID,TITLE,PLAYING_TIME)
VALUES(SONG_ID_SEQ.NEXTVAL
,(SELECT ARTIST_ID FROM ARTIST WHERE NAME='Sheryl Crow')
,'Over You','4:38');
INSERT INTO SONG(SONG_ID,ARTIST_ID,TITLE,PLAYING_TIME)
VALUES(SONG_ID_SEQ.NEXTVAL
,(SELECT ARTIST_ID FROM ARTIST WHERE NAME='Sheryl Crow')
,'Lucky Kid','4:02');
INSERT INTO SONG(SONG_ID,ARTIST_ID,TITLE,PLAYING_TIME)
VALUES(SONG_ID_SEQ.NEXTVAL
,(SELECT ARTIST_ID FROM ARTIST WHERE NAME='Sheryl Crow')
,'Diamond Road','4:09');
INSERT INTO SONG(SONG_ID,ARTIST_ID,TITLE,PLAYING_TIME)
VALUES(SONG_ID_SEQ.NEXTVAL
,(SELECT ARTIST_ID FROM ARTIST WHERE NAME='Sheryl Crow')
,'It''s Only Love','5:05');
INSERT INTO SONG(SONG_ID,ARTIST_ID,TITLE,PLAYING_TIME)
VALUES(SONG_ID_SEQ.NEXTVAL
,(SELECT ARTIST_ID FROM ARTIST WHERE NAME='Sheryl Crow')
,'Abilene','4:05');
INSERT INTO SONG(SONG_ID,ARTIST_ID,TITLE,PLAYING_TIME)
VALUES(SONG_ID_SEQ.NEXTVAL
,(SELECT ARTIST_ID FROM ARTIST WHERE NAME='Sheryl Crow')
,'Hole In My Pocket','4:37');
INSERT INTO SONG(SONG_ID,ARTIST_ID,TITLE,PLAYING_TIME)
VALUES(SONG_ID_SEQ.NEXTVAL
,(SELECT ARTIST_ID FROM ARTIST WHERE NAME='Sheryl Crow')
,'Weather Channel','4:40');
COMMIT;


--Mozart: Requiem
INSERT INTO SONG(SONG_ID,ARTIST_ID,TITLE) VALUES(SONG_ID_SEQ.NEXTVAL,(SELECT
ARTIST_ID FROM ARTIST WHERE NAME='Mozart'),'Requiem in D Minor: I. Introitus -
Requiem');
INSERT INTO SONG(SONG_ID,ARTIST_ID,TITLE) VALUES(SONG_ID_SEQ.NEXTVAL,(SELECT
ARTIST_ID FROM ARTIST WHERE NAME='Mozart'),'Requiem in D Minor: II. Kyrie');
INSERT INTO SONG(SONG_ID,ARTIST_ID,TITLE) VALUES(SONG_ID_SEQ.NEXTVAL,(SELECT
ARTIST_ID FROM ARTIST WHERE NAME='Mozart'),'Requiem in D Minor: III. Sequenz - No.1 -
Dies irae');
```

```
INSERT INTO SONG(SONG_ID,ARTIST_ID,TITLE) VALUES(SONG_ID_SEQ.NEXTVAL,(SELECT
ARTIST_ID FROM ARTIST WHERE NAME='Mozart'),'Requiem in D Minor: III. Sequenz - No. 2
- Tuba mirum');
INSERT INTO SONG(SONG_ID,ARTIST_ID,TITLE) VALUES(SONG_ID_SEQ.NEXTVAL,(SELECT
ARTIST_ID FROM ARTIST WHERE NAME='Mozart'),'Requiem in D Minor: III. Sequenz - No. 3
- Rex tremendae');
INSERT INTO SONG(SONG_ID,ARTIST_ID,TITLE) VALUES(SONG_ID_SEQ.NEXTVAL,(SELECT
ARTIST_ID FROM ARTIST WHERE NAME='Mozart'),'Requiem in D Minor: III. Sequenz - No. 4
- Recordare');
INSERT INTO SONG(SONG_ID,ARTIST_ID,TITLE) VALUES(SONG_ID_SEQ.NEXTVAL,(SELECT
ARTIST_ID FROM ARTIST WHERE NAME='Mozart'),'Requiem in D Minor: III. Sequenz - No. 5
- Confutatis');
INSERT INTO SONG(SONG_ID,ARTIST_ID,TITLE) VALUES(SONG_ID_SEQ.NEXTVAL,(SELECT
ARTIST_ID FROM ARTIST WHERE NAME='Mozart'),'Requiem in D Minor: III. Sequenz - No. 6
- Lacrimosa');
INSERT INTO SONG(SONG_ID,ARTIST_ID,TITLE) VALUES(SONG_ID_SEQ.NEXTVAL,(SELECT
ARTIST_ID FROM ARTIST WHERE NAME='Mozart'),'Requiem in D Minor: IV. Offertorium - No.
1 - Domine Jesu');
INSERT INTO SONG(SONG_ID,ARTIST_ID,TITLE) VALUES(SONG_ID_SEQ.NEXTVAL,(SELECT
ARTIST_ID FROM ARTIST WHERE NAME='Mozart'),'Requiem in D Minor: IV. Offertorium - No.
2 - Hostias');
INSERT INTO SONG(SONG_ID,ARTIST_ID,TITLE) VALUES(SONG_ID_SEQ.NEXTVAL,(SELECT
ARTIST_ID FROM ARTIST WHERE NAME='Mozart'),'Requiem in D Minor: V. Sanctus');
INSERT INTO SONG(SONG_ID,ARTIST_ID,TITLE) VALUES(SONG_ID_SEQ.NEXTVAL,(SELECT
ARTIST_ID FROM ARTIST WHERE NAME='Mozart'),'Requiem in D Minor: VI. Benedictus');
INSERT INTO SONG(SONG_ID,ARTIST_ID,TITLE) VALUES(SONG_ID_SEQ.NEXTVAL,(SELECT
ARTIST_ID FROM ARTIST WHERE NAME='Mozart'),'Requiem in D Minor: VII. Agnus Dei');
INSERT INTO SONG(SONG_ID,ARTIST_ID,TITLE) VALUES(SONG_ID_SEQ.NEXTVAL,(SELECT
ARTIST_ID FROM ARTIST WHERE NAME='Mozart'),'Requiem in D Minor: VIII. Communio - Lux
aeterna');
COMMIT;


INSERT INTO SONG(SONG_ID,ARTIST_ID,TITLE) VALUES(SONG_ID_SEQ.NEXTVAL,(SELECT
ARTIST_ID FROM ARTIST WHERE NAME='James Taylor'),'Sweet Baby James');
INSERT INTO SONG(SONG_ID,ARTIST_ID,TITLE) VALUES(SONG_ID_SEQ.NEXTVAL,(SELECT
ARTIST_ID FROM ARTIST WHERE NAME='James Taylor'),'Lo and Behold');
INSERT INTO SONG(SONG_ID,ARTIST_ID,TITLE) VALUES(SONG_ID_SEQ.NEXTVAL,(SELECT
ARTIST_ID FROM ARTIST WHERE NAME='James Taylor'),'Sunny Skies');
INSERT INTO SONG(SONG_ID,ARTIST_ID,TITLE) VALUES(SONG_ID_SEQ.NEXTVAL,(SELECT
ARTIST_ID FROM ARTIST WHERE NAME='James Taylor'),'Steamroller');
INSERT INTO SONG(SONG_ID,ARTIST_ID,TITLE) VALUES(SONG_ID_SEQ.NEXTVAL,(SELECT
ARTIST_ID FROM ARTIST WHERE NAME='James Taylor'),'Country Road');
INSERT INTO SONG(SONG_ID,ARTIST_ID,TITLE) VALUES(SONG_ID_SEQ.NEXTVAL,(SELECT
ARTIST_ID FROM ARTIST WHERE NAME='James Taylor'),'Oh Susanna');
INSERT INTO SONG(SONG_ID,ARTIST_ID,TITLE) VALUES(SONG_ID_SEQ.NEXTVAL,(SELECT
ARTIST_ID FROM ARTIST WHERE NAME='James Taylor'),'Fire and Rain');
INSERT INTO SONG(SONG_ID,ARTIST_ID,TITLE) VALUES(SONG_ID_SEQ.NEXTVAL,(SELECT
ARTIST_ID FROM ARTIST WHERE NAME='James Taylor'),'Blossom');
INSERT INTO SONG(SONG_ID,ARTIST_ID,TITLE) VALUES(SONG_ID_SEQ.NEXTVAL,(SELECT
ARTIST_ID FROM ARTIST WHERE NAME='James Taylor'),'Anywhere Like Heaven');
```

```
INSERT INTO SONG(SONG_ID,ARTIST_ID,TITLE) VALUES(SONG_ID_SEQ.NEXTVAL,(SELECT
ARTIST_ID FROM ARTIST WHERE NAME='James Taylor'),'Oh Baby, Don''t You Loose Your Lip
on Me');
INSERT INTO SONG(SONG_ID,ARTIST_ID,TITLE) VALUES(SONG_ID_SEQ.NEXTVAL,(SELECT
ARTIST_ID FROM ARTIST WHERE NAME='James Taylor'),'Suite for 20 G');
COMMIT;


INSERT INTO CDTRACK(MUSICCD_ID,SONG_ID,TRACK_SEQ_NO)
VALUES ((SELECT MUSICCD_ID FROM MUSICCD WHERE TITLE='C''mon, C''mon')
,(SELECT SONG_ID FROM SONG WHERE TITLE='Steve McQueen'),1);
INSERT INTO CDTRACK(MUSICCD_ID,SONG_ID,TRACK_SEQ_NO)
VALUES ((SELECT MUSICCD_ID FROM MUSICCD WHERE TITLE='C''mon, C''mon')
,(SELECT SONG_ID FROM SONG WHERE TITLE='Soak Up The Sun'),2);
INSERT INTO CDTRACK(MUSICCD_ID,SONG_ID,TRACK_SEQ_NO)
VALUES ((SELECT MUSICCD_ID FROM MUSICCD WHERE TITLE='C''mon, C''mon')
,(SELECT SONG_ID FROM SONG WHERE TITLE='You''re An Original'),3);
INSERT INTO CDTRACK(MUSICCD_ID,SONG_ID,TRACK_SEQ_NO)
VALUES ((SELECT MUSICCD_ID FROM MUSICCD WHERE TITLE='C''mon, C''mon')
,(SELECT SONG_ID FROM SONG WHERE TITLE='Safe And Sound'),4);
INSERT INTO CDTRACK(MUSICCD_ID,SONG_ID,TRACK_SEQ_NO)
VALUES ((SELECT MUSICCD_ID FROM MUSICCD WHERE TITLE='C''mon, C''mon')
,(SELECT SONG_ID FROM SONG WHERE TITLE='C''mon, C''mon'),5);
INSERT INTO CDTRACK(MUSICCD_ID,SONG_ID,TRACK_SEQ_NO)
VALUES ((SELECT MUSICCD_ID FROM MUSICCD WHERE TITLE='C''mon, C''mon')
,(SELECT SONG_ID FROM SONG WHERE TITLE='It''s So Easy'),6);
INSERT INTO CDTRACK(MUSICCD_ID,SONG_ID,TRACK_SEQ_NO)
VALUES ((SELECT MUSICCD_ID FROM MUSICCD WHERE TITLE='C''mon, C''mon')
,(SELECT SONG_ID FROM SONG WHERE TITLE='Over You'),7);
INSERT INTO CDTRACK(MUSICCD_ID,SONG_ID,TRACK_SEQ_NO)
VALUES ((SELECT MUSICCD_ID FROM MUSICCD WHERE TITLE='C''mon, C''mon')
,(SELECT SONG_ID FROM SONG WHERE TITLE='Lucky Kid'),8);
INSERT INTO CDTRACK(MUSICCD_ID,SONG_ID,TRACK_SEQ_NO)
VALUES ((SELECT MUSICCD_ID FROM MUSICCD WHERE TITLE='C''mon, C''mon')
,(SELECT SONG_ID FROM SONG WHERE TITLE='Diamond Road'),9);
INSERT INTO CDTRACK(MUSICCD_ID,SONG_ID,TRACK_SEQ_NO)
VALUES ((SELECT MUSICCD_ID FROM MUSICCD WHERE TITLE='C''mon, C''mon')
,(SELECT SONG_ID FROM SONG WHERE TITLE='It''s Only Love'),10);
INSERT INTO CDTRACK(MUSICCD_ID,SONG_ID,TRACK_SEQ_NO)
VALUES ((SELECT MUSICCD_ID FROM MUSICCD WHERE TITLE='C''mon, C''mon')
,(SELECT SONG_ID FROM SONG WHERE TITLE='Abilene'),11);
INSERT INTO CDTRACK(MUSICCD_ID,SONG_ID,TRACK_SEQ_NO)
VALUES ((SELECT MUSICCD_ID FROM MUSICCD WHERE TITLE='C''mon, C''mon')
,(SELECT SONG_ID FROM SONG WHERE TITLE='Hole In My Pocket'),12);
INSERT INTO CDTRACK(MUSICCD_ID,SONG_ID,TRACK_SEQ_NO)
VALUES ((SELECT MUSICCD_ID FROM MUSICCD WHERE TITLE='C''mon, C''mon')
```

```
,(SELECT SONG_ID FROM SONG WHERE TITLE='Weather Channel'),13);
COMMIT;

--Come Clean by Puddle of Mudd
INSERT INTO SONG(SONG_ID,ARTIST_ID,TITLE,PLAYING_TIME)
VALUES(SONG_ID_SEQ.NEXTVAL
,(SELECT ARTIST_ID FROM ARTIST WHERE NAME='Puddle of Mudd')
,'Control','3:50');
INSERT INTO SONG(SONG_ID,ARTIST_ID,TITLE,PLAYING_TIME)
VALUES(SONG_ID_SEQ.NEXTVAL
,(SELECT ARTIST_ID FROM ARTIST WHERE NAME='Puddle of Mudd')
,'Drift and Die','4:25');
INSERT INTO SONG(SONG_ID,ARTIST_ID,TITLE,PLAYING_TIME)
VALUES(SONG_ID_SEQ.NEXTVAL
,(SELECT ARTIST_ID FROM ARTIST WHERE NAME='Puddle of Mudd')
,'Out Of My Head','3:43');
INSERT INTO SONG(SONG_ID,ARTIST_ID,TITLE,PLAYING_TIME)
VALUES(SONG_ID_SEQ.NEXTVAL
,(SELECT ARTIST_ID FROM ARTIST WHERE NAME='Puddle of Mudd')
,'Nobody Told Me','5:21');
INSERT INTO SONG(SONG_ID,ARTIST_ID,TITLE,PLAYING_TIME)
VALUES(SONG_ID_SEQ.NEXTVAL
,(SELECT ARTIST_ID FROM ARTIST WHERE NAME='Puddle of Mudd')
,'Blurry','5:04');
INSERT INTO SONG(SONG_ID,ARTIST_ID,TITLE,PLAYING_TIME)
VALUES(SONG_ID_SEQ.NEXTVAL
,(SELECT ARTIST_ID FROM ARTIST WHERE NAME='Puddle of Mudd')
,'She Hates Me','3:36');
INSERT INTO SONG(SONG_ID,ARTIST_ID,TITLE,PLAYING_TIME)
VALUES(SONG_ID_SEQ.NEXTVAL
,(SELECT ARTIST_ID FROM ARTIST WHERE NAME='Puddle of Mudd')
,'Bring Me Down','4:02');
INSERT INTO SONG(SONG_ID,ARTIST_ID,TITLE,PLAYING_TIME)
VALUES(SONG_ID_SEQ.NEXTVAL
,(SELECT ARTIST_ID FROM ARTIST WHERE NAME='Puddle of Mudd')
,'Never Change','3:58');
INSERT INTO SONG(SONG_ID,ARTIST_ID,TITLE,PLAYING_TIME)
VALUES(SONG_ID_SEQ.NEXTVAL
,(SELECT ARTIST_ID FROM ARTIST WHERE NAME='Puddle of Mudd')
,'Basement','4:21');
INSERT INTO SONG(SONG_ID,ARTIST_ID,TITLE,PLAYING_TIME)
VALUES(SONG_ID_SEQ.NEXTVAL
,(SELECT ARTIST_ID FROM ARTIST WHERE NAME='Puddle of Mudd')
,'Said','4:05');
INSERT INTO SONG(SONG_ID,ARTIST_ID,TITLE,PLAYING_TIME)
```

```
VALUES(SONG_ID_SEQ.NEXTVAL
,(SELECT ARTIST_ID FROM ARTIST WHERE NAME='Puddle of Mudd')
,'It All Away','5:38');
COMMIT;

INSERT INTO CDTRACK(MUSICCD_ID,SONG_ID,TRACK_SEQ_NO)
VALUES ((SELECT MUSICCD_ID FROM MUSICCD WHERE TITLE='Come Clean')
,(SELECT SONG_ID FROM SONG WHERE TITLE='Control'),1);
INSERT INTO CDTRACK(MUSICCD_ID,SONG_ID,TRACK_SEQ_NO)
VALUES ((SELECT MUSICCD_ID FROM MUSICCD WHERE TITLE='Come Clean')
,(SELECT SONG_ID FROM SONG WHERE TITLE='Drift and Die'),2);
INSERT INTO CDTRACK(MUSICCD_ID,SONG_ID,TRACK_SEQ_NO)
VALUES ((SELECT MUSICCD_ID FROM MUSICCD WHERE TITLE='Come Clean')
,(SELECT SONG_ID FROM SONG WHERE TITLE='Out Of My Head'),3);
INSERT INTO CDTRACK(MUSICCD_ID,SONG_ID,TRACK_SEQ_NO)
VALUES ((SELECT MUSICCD_ID FROM MUSICCD WHERE TITLE='Come Clean')
,(SELECT SONG_ID FROM SONG WHERE TITLE='Nobody Told Me'),4);
INSERT INTO CDTRACK(MUSICCD_ID,SONG_ID,TRACK_SEQ_NO)
VALUES ((SELECT MUSICCD_ID FROM MUSICCD WHERE TITLE='Come Clean')
,(SELECT SONG_ID FROM SONG WHERE TITLE='Blurry'),5);
INSERT INTO CDTRACK(MUSICCD_ID,SONG_ID,TRACK_SEQ_NO)
VALUES ((SELECT MUSICCD_ID FROM MUSICCD WHERE TITLE='Come Clean')
,(SELECT SONG_ID FROM SONG WHERE TITLE='She Hates Me'),6);
INSERT INTO CDTRACK(MUSICCD_ID,SONG_ID,TRACK_SEQ_NO)
VALUES ((SELECT MUSICCD_ID FROM MUSICCD WHERE TITLE='Come Clean')
,(SELECT SONG_ID FROM SONG WHERE TITLE='Bring Me Down'),7);
INSERT INTO CDTRACK(MUSICCD_ID,SONG_ID,TRACK_SEQ_NO)
VALUES ((SELECT MUSICCD_ID FROM MUSICCD WHERE TITLE='Come Clean')
,(SELECT SONG_ID FROM SONG WHERE TITLE='Never Change'),8);
INSERT INTO CDTRACK(MUSICCD_ID,SONG_ID,TRACK_SEQ_NO)
VALUES ((SELECT MUSICCD_ID FROM MUSICCD WHERE TITLE='Come Clean')
,(SELECT SONG_ID FROM SONG WHERE TITLE='Basement'),9);
INSERT INTO CDTRACK(MUSICCD_ID,SONG_ID,TRACK_SEQ_NO)
VALUES ((SELECT MUSICCD_ID FROM MUSICCD WHERE TITLE='Come Clean')
,(SELECT SONG_ID FROM SONG WHERE TITLE='Said'),10);
INSERT INTO CDTRACK(MUSICCD_ID,SONG_ID,TRACK_SEQ_NO)
VALUES ((SELECT MUSICCD_ID FROM MUSICCD WHERE TITLE='Come Clean')
,(SELECT SONG_ID FROM SONG WHERE TITLE='It All Away'),11);
COMMIT;

--Silver Side Up by Nickelback
INSERT INTO SONG(SONG_ID,ARTIST_ID,TITLE,PLAYING_TIME)
VALUES(SONG_ID_SEQ.NEXTVAL
,(SELECT ARTIST_ID FROM ARTIST WHERE NAME='Nickelback')
,'Never Again','4:20');
```

```
INSERT INTO SONG(SONG_ID,ARTIST_ID,TITLE,PLAYING_TIME)
VALUES(SONG_ID_SEQ.NEXTVAL
,(SELECT ARTIST_ID FROM ARTIST WHERE NAME='Nickelback')
,'How You Remind Me','3:43');
INSERT INTO SONG(SONG_ID,ARTIST_ID,TITLE,PLAYING_TIME)
VALUES(SONG_ID_SEQ.NEXTVAL
,(SELECT ARTIST_ID FROM ARTIST WHERE NAME='Nickelback')
,'Woke Up This Morning','3:50');
INSERT INTO SONG(SONG_ID,ARTIST_ID,TITLE,PLAYING_TIME)
VALUES(SONG_ID_SEQ.NEXTVAL
,(SELECT ARTIST_ID FROM ARTIST WHERE NAME='Nickelback')
,'Too Bad','3:52');
INSERT INTO SONG(SONG_ID,ARTIST_ID,TITLE,PLAYING_TIME)
VALUES(SONG_ID_SEQ.NEXTVAL
,(SELECT ARTIST_ID FROM ARTIST WHERE NAME='Nickelback')
,'Just For','4:03');
INSERT INTO SONG(SONG_ID,ARTIST_ID,TITLE,PLAYING_TIME)
VALUES(SONG_ID_SEQ.NEXTVAL
,(SELECT ARTIST_ID FROM ARTIST WHERE NAME='Nickelback')
,'Hollywood','3:04');
INSERT INTO SONG(SONG_ID,ARTIST_ID,TITLE,PLAYING_TIME)
VALUES(SONG_ID_SEQ.NEXTVAL
,(SELECT ARTIST_ID FROM ARTIST WHERE NAME='Nickelback')
,'Money Bought','3:24');
INSERT INTO SONG(SONG_ID,ARTIST_ID,TITLE,PLAYING_TIME)
VALUES(SONG_ID_SEQ.NEXTVAL
,(SELECT ARTIST_ID FROM ARTIST WHERE NAME='Nickelback')
,'Where Do I Hide','3:38');
INSERT INTO SONG(SONG_ID,ARTIST_ID,TITLE,PLAYING_TIME)
VALUES(SONG_ID_SEQ.NEXTVAL
,(SELECT ARTIST_ID FROM ARTIST WHERE NAME='Nickelback')
,'Hangnail','3:54');
INSERT INTO SONG(SONG_ID,ARTIST_ID,TITLE,PLAYING_TIME)
VALUES(SONG_ID_SEQ.NEXTVAL
,(SELECT ARTIST_ID FROM ARTIST WHERE NAME='Nickelback')
,'Good Times Gone','5:20');
COMMIT;

INSERT INTO CDTRACK(MUSICCD_ID,SONG_ID,TRACK_SEQ_NO)
VALUES ((SELECT MUSICCD_ID FROM MUSICCD WHERE TITLE='Silver Side Up')
,(SELECT SONG_ID FROM SONG WHERE TITLE='Never Again'),1);
INSERT INTO CDTRACK(MUSICCD_ID,SONG_ID,TRACK_SEQ_NO)
VALUES ((SELECT MUSICCD_ID FROM MUSICCD WHERE TITLE='Silver Side Up')
,(SELECT SONG_ID FROM SONG WHERE TITLE='How You Remind Me'),2);
INSERT INTO CDTRACK(MUSICCD_ID,SONG_ID,TRACK_SEQ_NO)
```

```
VALUES ((SELECT MUSICCD_ID FROM MUSICCD WHERE TITLE='Silver Side Up')
,(SELECT SONG_ID FROM SONG WHERE TITLE='Woke Up This Morning'),3);
INSERT INTO CDTRACK(MUSICCD_ID,SONG_ID,TRACK_SEQ_NO)
VALUES ((SELECT MUSICCD_ID FROM MUSICCD WHERE TITLE='Silver Side Up')
,(SELECT SONG_ID FROM SONG WHERE TITLE='Too Bad'),4);
INSERT INTO CDTRACK(MUSICCD_ID,SONG_ID,TRACK_SEQ_NO)
VALUES ((SELECT MUSICCD_ID FROM MUSICCD WHERE TITLE='Silver Side Up')
,(SELECT SONG_ID FROM SONG WHERE TITLE='Just For'),5);
INSERT INTO CDTRACK(MUSICCD_ID,SONG_ID,TRACK_SEQ_NO)
VALUES ((SELECT MUSICCD_ID FROM MUSICCD WHERE TITLE='Silver Side Up')
,(SELECT SONG_ID FROM SONG WHERE TITLE='Hollywood'),6);
INSERT INTO CDTRACK(MUSICCD_ID,SONG_ID,TRACK_SEQ_NO)
VALUES ((SELECT MUSICCD_ID FROM MUSICCD WHERE TITLE='Silver Side Up')
,(SELECT SONG_ID FROM SONG WHERE TITLE='Money Bought'),7);
INSERT INTO CDTRACK(MUSICCD_ID,SONG_ID,TRACK_SEQ_NO)
VALUES ((SELECT MUSICCD_ID FROM MUSICCD WHERE TITLE='Silver Side Up')
,(SELECT SONG_ID FROM SONG WHERE TITLE='Where Do I Hide'),8);
INSERT INTO CDTRACK(MUSICCD_ID,SONG_ID,TRACK_SEQ_NO)
VALUES ((SELECT MUSICCD_ID FROM MUSICCD WHERE TITLE='Silver Side Up')
,(SELECT SONG_ID FROM SONG WHERE TITLE='Hangnail'),9);
INSERT INTO CDTRACK(MUSICCD_ID,SONG_ID,TRACK_SEQ_NO)
VALUES ((SELECT MUSICCD_ID FROM MUSICCD WHERE TITLE='Silver Side Up')
,(SELECT SONG_ID FROM SONG WHERE TITLE='Good Times Gone'),10);
COMMIT;


--Ultimate Manilow by Barry Manilow
INSERT INTO SONG(SONG_ID,ARTIST_ID,TITLE,PLAYING_TIME)
VALUES(SONG_ID_SEQ.NEXTVAL
,(SELECT ARTIST_ID FROM ARTIST WHERE NAME='Barry Manilow')
,'Mandy','3:17');
INSERT INTO SONG(SONG_ID,ARTIST_ID,TITLE,PLAYING_TIME)
VALUES(SONG_ID_SEQ.NEXTVAL
,(SELECT ARTIST_ID FROM ARTIST WHERE NAME='Barry Manilow')
,'It''s A Miracle','3:51');
INSERT INTO SONG(SONG_ID,ARTIST_ID,TITLE,PLAYING_TIME)
VALUES(SONG_ID_SEQ.NEXTVAL
,(SELECT ARTIST_ID FROM ARTIST WHERE NAME='Barry Manilow')
,'Could It Be Magic','6:47');
INSERT INTO SONG(SONG_ID,ARTIST_ID,TITLE,PLAYING_TIME)
VALUES(SONG_ID_SEQ.NEXTVAL
,(SELECT ARTIST_ID FROM ARTIST WHERE NAME='Barry Manilow')
,'I Write The Songs','3:50');
INSERT INTO SONG(SONG_ID,ARTIST_ID,TITLE,PLAYING_TIME)
VALUES(SONG_ID_SEQ.NEXTVAL
,(SELECT ARTIST_ID FROM ARTIST WHERE NAME='Barry Manilow')
```

```
,'Bandstand Boogie','2:50');
INSERT INTO SONG(SONG_ID,ARTIST_ID,TITLE,PLAYING_TIME)
VALUES(SONG_ID_SEQ.NEXTVAL
,(SELECT ARTIST_ID FROM ARTIST WHERE NAME='Barry Manilow')
,'Tryin'' To Get The Feeling Again','3:50');
INSERT INTO SONG(SONG_ID,ARTIST_ID,TITLE,PLAYING_TIME)
VALUES(SONG_ID_SEQ.NEXTVAL
,(SELECT ARTIST_ID FROM ARTIST WHERE NAME='Barry Manilow')
,'This One''s For You','3:26');
INSERT INTO SONG(SONG_ID,ARTIST_ID,TITLE,PLAYING_TIME)
VALUES(SONG_ID_SEQ.NEXTVAL
,(SELECT ARTIST_ID FROM ARTIST WHERE NAME='Barry Manilow')
,'Weekend In New England','3:45');
INSERT INTO SONG(SONG_ID,ARTIST_ID,TITLE,PLAYING_TIME)
VALUES(SONG_ID_SEQ.NEXTVAL
,(SELECT ARTIST_ID FROM ARTIST WHERE NAME='Barry Manilow')
,'Looks Like We Made It','3:32');
INSERT INTO SONG(SONG_ID,ARTIST_ID,TITLE,PLAYING_TIME)
VALUES(SONG_ID_SEQ.NEXTVAL
,(SELECT ARTIST_ID FROM ARTIST WHERE NAME='Barry Manilow')
,'Daybreak','3:05');
INSERT INTO SONG(SONG_ID,ARTIST_ID,TITLE,PLAYING_TIME)
VALUES(SONG_ID_SEQ.NEXTVAL
,(SELECT ARTIST_ID FROM ARTIST WHERE NAME='Barry Manilow')
,'Can''t Smile Without You','3:07');
INSERT INTO SONG(SONG_ID,ARTIST_ID,TITLE,PLAYING_TIME)
VALUES(SONG_ID_SEQ.NEXTVAL
,(SELECT ARTIST_ID FROM ARTIST WHERE NAME='Barry Manilow')
,'Even Now','3:26');
INSERT INTO SONG(SONG_ID,ARTIST_ID,TITLE,PLAYING_TIME)
VALUES(SONG_ID_SEQ.NEXTVAL
,(SELECT ARTIST_ID FROM ARTIST WHERE NAME='Barry Manilow')
,'Copacabana (At The Copa)','5:40');
INSERT INTO SONG(SONG_ID,ARTIST_ID,TITLE,PLAYING_TIME)
VALUES(SONG_ID_SEQ.NEXTVAL
,(SELECT ARTIST_ID FROM ARTIST WHERE NAME='Barry Manilow')
,'Somewhere In The Night','3:23');
INSERT INTO SONG(SONG_ID,ARTIST_ID,TITLE,PLAYING_TIME)
VALUES(SONG_ID_SEQ.NEXTVAL
,(SELECT ARTIST_ID FROM ARTIST WHERE NAME='Barry Manilow')
,'Ready To Take A Chance','2:57');
INSERT INTO SONG(SONG_ID,ARTIST_ID,TITLE,PLAYING_TIME)
VALUES(SONG_ID_SEQ.NEXTVAL
,(SELECT ARTIST_ID FROM ARTIST WHERE NAME='Barry Manilow')
,'Ships','4:00');
```

```
INSERT INTO SONG(SONG_ID,ARTIST_ID,TITLE,PLAYING_TIME)
VALUES(SONG_ID_SEQ.NEXTVAL
,(SELECT ARTIST_ID FROM ARTIST WHERE NAME='Barry Manilow')
,'I Made It Through The Rain','4:19');
INSERT INTO SONG(SONG_ID,ARTIST_ID,TITLE,PLAYING_TIME)
VALUES(SONG_ID_SEQ.NEXTVAL
,(SELECT ARTIST_ID FROM ARTIST WHERE NAME='Barry Manilow')
,'The Old Songs','4:41');
INSERT INTO SONG(SONG_ID,ARTIST_ID,TITLE,PLAYING_TIME)
VALUES(SONG_ID_SEQ.NEXTVAL
,(SELECT ARTIST_ID FROM ARTIST WHERE NAME='Barry Manilow')
,'When October Goes','3:58');
INSERT INTO SONG(SONG_ID,ARTIST_ID,TITLE,PLAYING_TIME)
VALUES(SONG_ID_SEQ.NEXTVAL
,(SELECT ARTIST_ID FROM ARTIST WHERE NAME='Barry Manilow')
,'Somewhere Down The Road','3:59');
COMMIT;

INSERT INTO CDTRACK(MUSICCD_ID,SONG_ID,TRACK_SEQ_NO)
VALUES ((SELECT MUSICCD_ID FROM MUSICCD WHERE TITLE='Ultimate Manilow')
,(SELECT SONG_ID FROM SONG WHERE TITLE='Mandy'),1);
INSERT INTO CDTRACK(MUSICCD_ID,SONG_ID,TRACK_SEQ_NO)
VALUES ((SELECT MUSICCD_ID FROM MUSICCD WHERE TITLE='Ultimate Manilow')
,(SELECT SONG_ID FROM SONG WHERE TITLE='It''s A Miracle'),2);
INSERT INTO CDTRACK(MUSICCD_ID,SONG_ID,TRACK_SEQ_NO)
VALUES ((SELECT MUSICCD_ID FROM MUSICCD WHERE TITLE='Ultimate Manilow')
,(SELECT SONG_ID FROM SONG WHERE TITLE='Could It Be Magic'),3);
INSERT INTO CDTRACK(MUSICCD_ID,SONG_ID,TRACK_SEQ_NO)
VALUES ((SELECT MUSICCD_ID FROM MUSICCD WHERE TITLE='Ultimate Manilow')
,(SELECT SONG_ID FROM SONG WHERE TITLE='I Write The Songs'),4);
INSERT INTO CDTRACK(MUSICCD_ID,SONG_ID,TRACK_SEQ_NO)
VALUES ((SELECT MUSICCD_ID FROM MUSICCD WHERE TITLE='Ultimate Manilow')
,(SELECT SONG_ID FROM SONG WHERE TITLE='Bandstand Boogie'),5);
INSERT INTO CDTRACK(MUSICCD_ID,SONG_ID,TRACK_SEQ_NO)
VALUES ((SELECT MUSICCD_ID FROM MUSICCD WHERE TITLE='Ultimate Manilow')
,(SELECT SONG_ID FROM SONG
WHERE TITLE='Tryin'' To Get The Feeling Again'),6);
INSERT INTO CDTRACK(MUSICCD_ID,SONG_ID,TRACK_SEQ_NO)
VALUES ((SELECT MUSICCD_ID FROM MUSICCD WHERE TITLE='Ultimate Manilow')
,(SELECT SONG_ID FROM SONG WHERE TITLE='This One''s For You'),7);
INSERT INTO CDTRACK(MUSICCD_ID,SONG_ID,TRACK_SEQ_NO)
VALUES ((SELECT MUSICCD_ID FROM MUSICCD WHERE TITLE='Ultimate Manilow')
,(SELECT SONG_ID FROM SONG WHERE TITLE='Weekend In New England'),8);
INSERT INTO CDTRACK(MUSICCD_ID,SONG_ID,TRACK_SEQ_NO)
VALUES ((SELECT MUSICCD_ID FROM MUSICCD WHERE TITLE='Ultimate Manilow')
```

```
,(SELECT SONG_ID FROM SONG WHERE TITLE='Looks Like We Made It'),9);
INSERT INTO CDTRACK(MUSICCD_ID,SONG_ID,TRACK_SEQ_NO)
VALUES ((SELECT MUSICCD_ID FROM MUSICCD WHERE TITLE='Ultimate Manilow')
,(SELECT SONG_ID FROM SONG WHERE TITLE='Daybreak'),10);
INSERT INTO CDTRACK(MUSICCD_ID,SONG_ID,TRACK_SEQ_NO)
VALUES ((SELECT MUSICCD_ID FROM MUSICCD WHERE TITLE='Ultimate Manilow')
,(SELECT SONG_ID FROM SONG WHERE TITLE='Can''t Smile Without You'),11);
INSERT INTO CDTRACK(MUSICCD_ID,SONG_ID,TRACK_SEQ_NO)
VALUES ((SELECT MUSICCD_ID FROM MUSICCD WHERE TITLE='Ultimate Manilow')
,(SELECT SONG_ID FROM SONG WHERE TITLE='Even Now'),12);
INSERT INTO CDTRACK(MUSICCD_ID,SONG_ID,TRACK_SEQ_NO)
VALUES ((SELECT MUSICCD_ID FROM MUSICCD WHERE TITLE='Ultimate Manilow')
,(SELECT SONG_ID FROM SONG WHERE TITLE='Copacabana (At The Copa)'),13);
INSERT INTO CDTRACK(MUSICCD_ID,SONG_ID,TRACK_SEQ_NO)
VALUES ((SELECT MUSICCD_ID FROM MUSICCD WHERE TITLE='Ultimate Manilow')
,(SELECT SONG_ID FROM SONG WHERE TITLE='Somewhere In The Night'),14);
INSERT INTO CDTRACK(MUSICCD_ID,SONG_ID,TRACK_SEQ_NO)
VALUES ((SELECT MUSICCD_ID FROM MUSICCD WHERE TITLE='Ultimate Manilow')
,(SELECT SONG_ID FROM SONG WHERE TITLE='Ready To Take A Chance'),15);
INSERT INTO CDTRACK(MUSICCD_ID,SONG_ID,TRACK_SEQ_NO)
VALUES ((SELECT MUSICCD_ID FROM MUSICCD WHERE TITLE='Ultimate Manilow')
,(SELECT SONG_ID FROM SONG WHERE TITLE='Ships'),16);
INSERT INTO CDTRACK(MUSICCD_ID,SONG_ID,TRACK_SEQ_NO)
VALUES ((SELECT MUSICCD_ID FROM MUSICCD WHERE TITLE='Ultimate Manilow')
,(SELECT SONG_ID FROM SONG
WHERE TITLE='I Made It Through The Rain'),17);
INSERT INTO CDTRACK(MUSICCD_ID,SONG_ID,TRACK_SEQ_NO)
VALUES ((SELECT MUSICCD_ID FROM MUSICCD WHERE TITLE='Ultimate Manilow')
,(SELECT SONG_ID FROM SONG WHERE TITLE='The Old Songs'),18);
INSERT INTO CDTRACK(MUSICCD_ID,SONG_ID,TRACK_SEQ_NO)
VALUES ((SELECT MUSICCD_ID FROM MUSICCD WHERE TITLE='Ultimate Manilow')
,(SELECT SONG_ID FROM SONG WHERE TITLE='When October Goes'),19);
INSERT INTO CDTRACK(MUSICCD_ID,SONG_ID,TRACK_SEQ_NO)
VALUES ((SELECT MUSICCD_ID FROM MUSICCD WHERE TITLE='Ultimate Manilow')
,(SELECT SONG_ID FROM SONG WHERE TITLE='Somewhere Down The Road'),20);
COMMIT;

--Mad Season By Matchbox Twenty
INSERT INTO SONG(SONG_ID,ARTIST_ID,TITLE)
VALUES(SONG_ID_SEQ.NEXTVAL
,(SELECT ARTIST_ID FROM ARTIST WHERE NAME='Matchbox Twenty'),'Angry');
INSERT INTO SONG(SONG_ID,ARTIST_ID,TITLE)
VALUES(SONG_ID_SEQ.NEXTVAL
,(SELECT ARTIST_ID FROM ARTIST WHERE NAME='Matchbox Twenty')
,'Black and White People');
```

```sql
INSERT INTO SONG(SONG_ID,ARTIST_ID,TITLE)
VALUES(SONG_ID_SEQ.NEXTVAL
,(SELECT ARTIST_ID FROM ARTIST WHERE NAME='Matchbox Twenty'),'Crutch');
INSERT INTO SONG(SONG_ID,ARTIST_ID,TITLE)
VALUES(SONG_ID_SEQ.NEXTVAL
,(SELECT ARTIST_ID FROM ARTIST WHERE NAME='Matchbox Twenty')
,'Last Beautiful Girl');
INSERT INTO SONG(SONG_ID,ARTIST_ID,TITLE)
VALUES(SONG_ID_SEQ.NEXTVAL
,(SELECT ARTIST_ID FROM ARTIST WHERE NAME='Matchbox Twenty')
,'If You''re Gone');
INSERT INTO SONG(SONG_ID,ARTIST_ID,TITLE)
VALUES(SONG_ID_SEQ.NEXTVAL
,(SELECT ARTIST_ID FROM ARTIST WHERE NAME='Matchbox Twenty')
,'Mad Season');
INSERT INTO SONG(SONG_ID,ARTIST_ID,TITLE)
VALUES(SONG_ID_SEQ.NEXTVAL
,(SELECT ARTIST_ID FROM ARTIST WHERE NAME='Matchbox Twenty')
,'Rest Stop');
INSERT INTO SONG(SONG_ID,ARTIST_ID,TITLE)
VALUES(SONG_ID_SEQ.NEXTVAL
,(SELECT ARTIST_ID FROM ARTIST WHERE NAME='Matchbox Twenty')
,'The Burn');
INSERT INTO SONG(SONG_ID,ARTIST_ID,TITLE)
VALUES(SONG_ID_SEQ.NEXTVAL
,(SELECT ARTIST_ID FROM ARTIST WHERE NAME='Matchbox Twenty'),'Bent');
INSERT INTO SONG(SONG_ID,ARTIST_ID,TITLE)
VALUES(SONG_ID_SEQ.NEXTVAL
,(SELECT ARTIST_ID FROM ARTIST WHERE NAME='Matchbox Twenty')
,'Bed Of Lies');
INSERT INTO SONG(SONG_ID,ARTIST_ID,TITLE)
VALUES(SONG_ID_SEQ.NEXTVAL
,(SELECT ARTIST_ID FROM ARTIST WHERE NAME='Matchbox Twenty'),'Leave');
INSERT INTO SONG(SONG_ID,ARTIST_ID,TITLE)
VALUES(SONG_ID_SEQ.NEXTVAL
,(SELECT ARTIST_ID FROM ARTIST WHERE NAME='Matchbox Twenty'),'Stop');
INSERT INTO SONG(SONG_ID,ARTIST_ID,TITLE)
VALUES(SONG_ID_SEQ.NEXTVAL
,(SELECT ARTIST_ID FROM ARTIST WHERE NAME='Matchbox Twenty')
,'You Won''t Be Mine');
COMMIT;

INSERT INTO CDTRACK(MUSICCD_ID,SONG_ID,TRACK_SEQ_NO)
VALUES ((SELECT MUSICCD_ID FROM MUSICCD WHERE TITLE='Mad Season')
,(SELECT SONG_ID FROM SONG WHERE TITLE='Angry'),1);
```

```
INSERT INTO CDTRACK(MUSICCD_ID,SONG_ID,TRACK_SEQ_NO)
VALUES ((SELECT MUSICCD_ID FROM MUSICCD WHERE TITLE='Mad Season')
,(SELECT SONG_ID FROM SONG WHERE TITLE='Black and White People'),2);
INSERT INTO CDTRACK(MUSICCD_ID,SONG_ID,TRACK_SEQ_NO)
VALUES ((SELECT MUSICCD_ID FROM MUSICCD WHERE TITLE='Mad Season')
,(SELECT SONG_ID FROM SONG WHERE TITLE='Crutch'),3);
INSERT INTO CDTRACK(MUSICCD_ID,SONG_ID,TRACK_SEQ_NO)
VALUES ((SELECT MUSICCD_ID FROM MUSICCD WHERE TITLE='Mad Season')
,(SELECT SONG_ID FROM SONG WHERE TITLE='Last Beautiful Girl'),4);
INSERT INTO CDTRACK(MUSICCD_ID,SONG_ID,TRACK_SEQ_NO)
VALUES ((SELECT MUSICCD_ID FROM MUSICCD WHERE TITLE='Mad Season')
,(SELECT SONG_ID FROM SONG WHERE TITLE='If You''re Gone'),5);
INSERT INTO CDTRACK(MUSICCD_ID,SONG_ID,TRACK_SEQ_NO)
VALUES ((SELECT MUSICCD_ID FROM MUSICCD WHERE TITLE='Mad Season')
,(SELECT SONG_ID FROM SONG WHERE TITLE='Mad Season'),6);
INSERT INTO CDTRACK(MUSICCD_ID,SONG_ID,TRACK_SEQ_NO)
VALUES ((SELECT MUSICCD_ID FROM MUSICCD WHERE TITLE='Mad Season')
,(SELECT SONG_ID FROM SONG WHERE TITLE='Rest Stop'),7);
INSERT INTO CDTRACK(MUSICCD_ID,SONG_ID,TRACK_SEQ_NO)
VALUES ((SELECT MUSICCD_ID FROM MUSICCD WHERE TITLE='Mad Season')
,(SELECT SONG_ID FROM SONG WHERE TITLE='The Burn'),8);
INSERT INTO CDTRACK(MUSICCD_ID,SONG_ID,TRACK_SEQ_NO)
VALUES ((SELECT MUSICCD_ID FROM MUSICCD WHERE TITLE='Mad Season')
,(SELECT SONG_ID FROM SONG WHERE TITLE='Bent'),9);
INSERT INTO CDTRACK(MUSICCD_ID,SONG_ID,TRACK_SEQ_NO)
VALUES ((SELECT MUSICCD_ID FROM MUSICCD WHERE TITLE='Mad Season')
,(SELECT SONG_ID FROM SONG WHERE TITLE='Bed Of Lies'),10);
INSERT INTO CDTRACK(MUSICCD_ID,SONG_ID,TRACK_SEQ_NO)
VALUES ((SELECT MUSICCD_ID FROM MUSICCD WHERE TITLE='Mad Season')
,(SELECT SONG_ID FROM SONG WHERE TITLE='Leave'),11);
INSERT INTO CDTRACK(MUSICCD_ID,SONG_ID,TRACK_SEQ_NO)
VALUES ((SELECT MUSICCD_ID FROM MUSICCD WHERE TITLE='Mad Season')
,(SELECT SONG_ID FROM SONG WHERE TITLE='Stop'),12);
INSERT INTO CDTRACK(MUSICCD_ID,SONG_ID,TRACK_SEQ_NO)
VALUES ((SELECT MUSICCD_ID FROM MUSICCD WHERE TITLE='Mad Season')
,(SELECT SONG_ID FROM SONG WHERE TITLE='You Won''t Be Mine'),13);
COMMIT;

--This Way by Jewel
INSERT INTO SONG(SONG_ID,ARTIST_ID,TITLE,PLAYING_TIME)
VALUES(SONG_ID_SEQ.NEXTVAL
,(SELECT ARTIST_ID FROM ARTIST WHERE NAME='Jewel')
,'Standing Still','4:30');
INSERT INTO SONG(SONG_ID,ARTIST_ID,TITLE,PLAYING_TIME)
VALUES(SONG_ID_SEQ.NEXTVAL
```

```sql
,(SELECT ARTIST_ID FROM ARTIST WHERE NAME='Jewel')
,'Jesus Loves You','3:20');
INSERT INTO SONG(SONG_ID,ARTIST_ID,TITLE,PLAYING_TIME)
VALUES(SONG_ID_SEQ.NEXTVAL
,(SELECT ARTIST_ID FROM ARTIST WHERE NAME='Jewel')
,'Everybody Needs Someone Sometime','4:08');
INSERT INTO SONG(SONG_ID,ARTIST_ID,TITLE,PLAYING_TIME)
VALUES(SONG_ID_SEQ.NEXTVAL
,(SELECT ARTIST_ID FROM ARTIST WHERE NAME='Jewel'),'Break Me','4:04');
INSERT INTO SONG(SONG_ID,ARTIST_ID,TITLE,PLAYING_TIME)
VALUES(SONG_ID_SEQ.NEXTVAL
,(SELECT ARTIST_ID FROM ARTIST WHERE NAME='Jewel')
,'Do You Want To Play ?','2:55');
INSERT INTO SONG(SONG_ID,ARTIST_ID,TITLE,PLAYING_TIME)
VALUES(SONG_ID_SEQ.NEXTVAL
,(SELECT ARTIST_ID FROM ARTIST WHERE NAME='Jewel')
,'Till We Run Out Of Road','4:45');
INSERT INTO SONG(SONG_ID,ARTIST_ID,TITLE,PLAYING_TIME)
VALUES(SONG_ID_SEQ.NEXTVAL
,(SELECT ARTIST_ID FROM ARTIST WHERE NAME='Jewel')
,'Serve The Ego','4:57');
INSERT INTO SONG(SONG_ID,ARTIST_ID,TITLE,PLAYING_TIME)
VALUES(SONG_ID_SEQ.NEXTVAL
,(SELECT ARTIST_ID FROM ARTIST WHERE NAME='Jewel'),'This Way','4:16');
INSERT INTO SONG(SONG_ID,ARTIST_ID,TITLE,PLAYING_TIME)
VALUES(SONG_ID_SEQ.NEXTVAL
,(SELECT ARTIST_ID FROM ARTIST WHERE NAME='Jewel'),'Cleveland','4:09');
INSERT INTO SONG(SONG_ID,ARTIST_ID,TITLE,PLAYING_TIME)
VALUES(SONG_ID_SEQ.NEXTVAL
,(SELECT ARTIST_ID FROM ARTIST WHERE NAME='Jewel')
,'I Won''t Walk Away','4:45');
INSERT INTO SONG(SONG_ID,ARTIST_ID,TITLE,PLAYING_TIME)
VALUES(SONG_ID_SEQ.NEXTVAL
,(SELECT ARTIST_ID FROM ARTIST WHERE NAME='Jewel')
,'Love Me, Just Leave Me Alone','3:47');
INSERT INTO SONG(SONG_ID,ARTIST_ID,TITLE,PLAYING_TIME)
VALUES(SONG_ID_SEQ.NEXTVAL
,(SELECT ARTIST_ID FROM ARTIST WHERE NAME='Jewel')
,'The New Wild West','4:47');
INSERT INTO SONG(SONG_ID,ARTIST_ID,TITLE,PLAYING_TIME)
VALUES(SONG_ID_SEQ.NEXTVAL
,(SELECT ARTIST_ID FROM ARTIST WHERE NAME='Jewel')
,'Grey Matter (Live)','4:35');
INSERT INTO SONG(SONG_ID,ARTIST_ID,TITLE,PLAYING_TIME)
VALUES(SONG_ID_SEQ.NEXTVAL
```

```
,(SELECT ARTIST_ID FROM ARTIST WHERE NAME='Jewel')
,'Sometimes It Be That Way (Live)','3:44');
COMMIT;


INSERT INTO CDTRACK(MUSICCD_ID,SONG_ID,TRACK_SEQ_NO)
VALUES ((SELECT MUSICCD_ID FROM MUSICCD WHERE TITLE='This Way')
,(SELECT SONG_ID FROM SONG WHERE TITLE='Standing Still'),1);
INSERT INTO CDTRACK(MUSICCD_ID,SONG_ID,TRACK_SEQ_NO)
VALUES ((SELECT MUSICCD_ID FROM MUSICCD WHERE TITLE='This Way')
,(SELECT SONG_ID FROM SONG WHERE TITLE='Jesus Loves You'),2);
INSERT INTO CDTRACK(MUSICCD_ID,SONG_ID,TRACK_SEQ_NO)
VALUES ((SELECT MUSICCD_ID FROM MUSICCD WHERE TITLE='This Way')
,(SELECT SONG_ID FROM SONG
WHERE TITLE='Everybody Needs Someone Sometime'),3);
INSERT INTO CDTRACK(MUSICCD_ID,SONG_ID,TRACK_SEQ_NO)
VALUES ((SELECT MUSICCD_ID FROM MUSICCD WHERE TITLE='This Way')
,(SELECT SONG_ID FROM SONG WHERE TITLE='Break Me'),4);
INSERT INTO CDTRACK(MUSICCD_ID,SONG_ID,TRACK_SEQ_NO)
VALUES ((SELECT MUSICCD_ID FROM MUSICCD WHERE TITLE='This Way')
,(SELECT SONG_ID FROM SONG WHERE TITLE='Do You Want To Play ?'),5);
INSERT INTO CDTRACK(MUSICCD_ID,SONG_ID,TRACK_SEQ_NO)
VALUES ((SELECT MUSICCD_ID FROM MUSICCD WHERE TITLE='This Way')
,(SELECT SONG_ID FROM SONG WHERE TITLE='Till We Run Out Of Road'),6);
INSERT INTO CDTRACK(MUSICCD_ID,SONG_ID,TRACK_SEQ_NO)
VALUES ((SELECT MUSICCD_ID FROM MUSICCD WHERE TITLE='This Way')
,(SELECT SONG_ID FROM SONG WHERE TITLE='Serve The Ego'),7);
INSERT INTO CDTRACK(MUSICCD_ID,SONG_ID,TRACK_SEQ_NO)
VALUES ((SELECT MUSICCD_ID FROM MUSICCD WHERE TITLE='This Way')
,(SELECT SONG_ID FROM SONG WHERE TITLE='This Way'),8);
INSERT INTO CDTRACK(MUSICCD_ID,SONG_ID,TRACK_SEQ_NO)
VALUES ((SELECT MUSICCD_ID FROM MUSICCD WHERE TITLE='This Way')
,(SELECT SONG_ID FROM SONG WHERE TITLE='Cleveland'),9);
INSERT INTO CDTRACK(MUSICCD_ID,SONG_ID,TRACK_SEQ_NO)
VALUES ((SELECT MUSICCD_ID FROM MUSICCD WHERE TITLE='This Way')
,(SELECT SONG_ID FROM SONG WHERE TITLE='I Won''t Walk Away'),10);
INSERT INTO CDTRACK(MUSICCD_ID,SONG_ID,TRACK_SEQ_NO)
VALUES ((SELECT MUSICCD_ID FROM MUSICCD WHERE TITLE='This Way')
,(SELECT SONG_ID FROM SONG
WHERE TITLE='Love Me, Just Leave Me Alone'),11);
INSERT INTO CDTRACK(MUSICCD_ID,SONG_ID,TRACK_SEQ_NO)
VALUES ((SELECT MUSICCD_ID FROM MUSICCD WHERE TITLE='This Way')
,(SELECT SONG_ID FROM SONG WHERE TITLE='The New Wild West'),12);
INSERT INTO CDTRACK(MUSICCD_ID,SONG_ID,TRACK_SEQ_NO)
VALUES ((SELECT MUSICCD_ID FROM MUSICCD WHERE TITLE='This Way')
,(SELECT SONG_ID FROM SONG WHERE TITLE='Grey Matter (Live)'),13);
```

```
INSERT INTO CDTRACK(MUSICCD_ID,SONG_ID,TRACK_SEQ_NO)
VALUES ((SELECT MUSICCD_ID FROM MUSICCD WHERE TITLE='This Way'),
(SELECT SONG_ID FROM SONG WHERE TITLE='Sometimes It Be That Way (Live)'),14);
COMMIT;

INSERT INTO CDTRACK(MUSICCD_ID,SONG_ID,TRACK_SEQ_NO)
VALUES ((SELECT MUSICCD_ID FROM MUSICCD
WHERE TITLE='The Best of Sheryl Crow')
,(SELECT SONG_ID FROM SONG
WHERE TITLE='Soak Up The Sun (Album Version)'),1);
INSERT INTO CDTRACK(MUSICCD_ID,SONG_ID,TRACK_SEQ_NO)
VALUES ((SELECT MUSICCD_ID FROM MUSICCD
WHERE TITLE='The Best of Sheryl Crow')
,(SELECT SONG_ID FROM SONG
WHERE TITLE='Soak Up The Sun (Sunsweep Dub)'),2);
INSERT INTO CDTRACK(MUSICCD_ID,SONG_ID,TRACK_SEQ_NO)
VALUES ((SELECT MUSICCD_ID FROM MUSICCD
WHERE TITLE='The Best of Sheryl Crow')
,(SELECT SONG_ID FROM SONG WHERE TITLE='It''s So Easy'),3);
INSERT INTO CDTRACK(MUSICCD_ID,SONG_ID,TRACK_SEQ_NO)
VALUES ((SELECT MUSICCD_ID FROM MUSICCD
WHERE TITLE='The Best of Sheryl Crow')
,(SELECT SONG_ID FROM SONG WHERE TITLE='Over You'),4);
INSERT INTO CDTRACK(MUSICCD_ID,SONG_ID,TRACK_SEQ_NO)
VALUES ((SELECT MUSICCD_ID FROM MUSICCD
WHERE TITLE='The Best of Sheryl Crow')
,(SELECT SONG_ID FROM SONG WHERE TITLE='Diamond Road'),5);
INSERT INTO CDTRACK(MUSICCD_ID,SONG_ID,TRACK_SEQ_NO)
VALUES ((SELECT MUSICCD_ID FROM MUSICCD
WHERE TITLE='The Best of Sheryl Crow')
,(SELECT SONG_ID FROM SONG WHERE TITLE='Hole In My Pocket'),6);
INSERT INTO CDTRACK(MUSICCD_ID,SONG_ID,TRACK_SEQ_NO)
VALUES ((SELECT MUSICCD_ID FROM MUSICCD
WHERE TITLE='The Best of Sheryl Crow')
,(SELECT SONG_ID FROM SONG WHERE TITLE='Weather Channel'),7);
COMMIT;

INSERT INTO CDTRACK(MUSICCD_ID,SONG_ID,TRACK_SEQ_NO) VALUES ((SELECT MUSICCD_ID FROM
MUSICCD WHERE TITLE='Requiem'),(SELECT SONG_ID FROM SONG WHERE TITLE='Requiem in D
Minor: I. Introitus - Requiem'),1);
INSERT INTO CDTRACK(MUSICCD_ID,SONG_ID,TRACK_SEQ_NO) VALUES ((SELECT MUSICCD_ID FROM
MUSICCD WHERE TITLE='Requiem'),(SELECT SONG_ID FROM SONG WHERE TITLE='Requiem in D
Minor: II. Kyrie'),2);
INSERT INTO CDTRACK(MUSICCD_ID,SONG_ID,TRACK_SEQ_NO) VALUES ((SELECT MUSICCD_ID FROM
MUSICCD WHERE TITLE='Requiem'),(SELECT SONG_ID FROM SONG WHERE TITLE='Requiem in D
Minor: III. Sequenz - No.1 - Dies irae'),3);
```

```
INSERT INTO CDTRACK(MUSICCD_ID,SONG_ID,TRACK_SEQ_NO) VALUES ((SELECT MUSICCD_ID FROM
MUSICCD WHERE TITLE='Requiem'),(SELECT SONG_ID FROM SONG WHERE TITLE='Requiem in D
Minor: III. Sequenz - No. 2 - Tuba mirum'),4);

INSERT INTO CDTRACK(MUSICCD_ID,SONG_ID,TRACK_SEQ_NO) VALUES ((SELECT MUSICCD_ID FROM
MUSICCD WHERE TITLE='Requiem'),(SELECT SONG_ID FROM SONG WHERE TITLE='Requiem in D
Minor: III. Sequenz - No. 3 - Rex tremendae'),5);

INSERT INTO CDTRACK(MUSICCD_ID,SONG_ID,TRACK_SEQ_NO) VALUES ((SELECT MUSICCD_ID FROM
MUSICCD WHERE TITLE='Requiem'),(SELECT SONG_ID FROM SONG WHERE TITLE='Requiem in D
Minor: III. Sequenz - No. 4 - Recordare'),6);

INSERT INTO CDTRACK(MUSICCD_ID,SONG_ID,TRACK_SEQ_NO) VALUES ((SELECT MUSICCD_ID FROM
MUSICCD WHERE TITLE='Requiem'),(SELECT SONG_ID FROM SONG WHERE TITLE='Requiem in D
Minor: III. Sequenz - No. 5 - Confutatis'),7);

INSERT INTO CDTRACK(MUSICCD_ID,SONG_ID,TRACK_SEQ_NO) VALUES ((SELECT MUSICCD_ID FROM
MUSICCD WHERE TITLE='Requiem'),(SELECT SONG_ID FROM SONG WHERE TITLE='Requiem in D
Minor: III. Sequenz - No. 6 - Lacrimosa'),8);

INSERT INTO CDTRACK(MUSICCD_ID,SONG_ID,TRACK_SEQ_NO) VALUES ((SELECT MUSICCD_ID FROM
MUSICCD WHERE TITLE='Requiem'),(SELECT SONG_ID FROM SONG WHERE TITLE='Requiem in D
Minor: IV. Offertorium - No. 1 - Domine Jesu'),9);

INSERT INTO CDTRACK(MUSICCD_ID,SONG_ID,TRACK_SEQ_NO) VALUES ((SELECT MUSICCD_ID FROM
MUSICCD WHERE TITLE='Requiem'),(SELECT SONG_ID FROM SONG WHERE TITLE='Requiem in D
Minor: IV. Offertorium - No. 2 - Hostias'),10);

INSERT INTO CDTRACK(MUSICCD_ID,SONG_ID,TRACK_SEQ_NO) VALUES ((SELECT MUSICCD_ID FROM
MUSICCD WHERE TITLE='Requiem'),(SELECT SONG_ID FROM SONG WHERE TITLE='Requiem in D
Minor: V. Sanctus'),11);

INSERT INTO CDTRACK(MUSICCD_ID,SONG_ID,TRACK_SEQ_NO) VALUES ((SELECT MUSICCD_ID FROM
MUSICCD WHERE TITLE='Requiem'),(SELECT SONG_ID FROM SONG WHERE TITLE='Requiem in D
Minor: VI. Benedictus'),12);

INSERT INTO CDTRACK(MUSICCD_ID,SONG_ID,TRACK_SEQ_NO) VALUES ((SELECT MUSICCD_ID FROM
MUSICCD WHERE TITLE='Requiem'),(SELECT SONG_ID FROM SONG WHERE TITLE='Requiem in D
Minor: VII. Agnus Dei'),13);

INSERT INTO CDTRACK(MUSICCD_ID,SONG_ID,TRACK_SEQ_NO) VALUES ((SELECT MUSICCD_ID FROM
MUSICCD WHERE TITLE='Requiem'),(SELECT SONG_ID FROM SONG WHERE TITLE='Requiem in D
Minor: VIII. Communio - Lux aeterna'),14);

COMMIT;


INSERT INTO CDTRACK(MUSICCD_ID,SONG_ID,TRACK_SEQ_NO) VALUES ((SELECT MUSICCD_ID FROM
MUSICCD WHERE TITLE='Sweet Baby James'),(SELECT SONG_ID FROM SONG WHERE TITLE='Sweet
Baby James'),1);

INSERT INTO CDTRACK(MUSICCD_ID,SONG_ID,TRACK_SEQ_NO) VALUES ((SELECT MUSICCD_ID FROM
MUSICCD WHERE TITLE='Sweet Baby James'),(SELECT SONG_ID FROM SONG WHERE TITLE='Lo and
Behold'),2);

INSERT INTO CDTRACK(MUSICCD_ID,SONG_ID,TRACK_SEQ_NO) VALUES ((SELECT MUSICCD_ID FROM
MUSICCD WHERE TITLE='Sweet Baby James'),(SELECT SONG_ID FROM SONG WHERE TITLE='Sunny
Skies'),3);

INSERT INTO CDTRACK(MUSICCD_ID,SONG_ID,TRACK_SEQ_NO) VALUES ((SELECT MUSICCD_ID FROM
MUSICCD WHERE TITLE='Sweet Baby James'),(SELECT SONG_ID FROM SONG WHERE
TITLE='Steamroller'),4);

INSERT INTO CDTRACK(MUSICCD_ID,SONG_ID,TRACK_SEQ_NO) VALUES ((SELECT MUSICCD_ID FROM
MUSICCD WHERE TITLE='Sweet Baby James'),(SELECT SONG_ID FROM SONG WHERE
TITLE='Country Road'),5);
```

```
INSERT INTO CDTRACK(MUSICCD_ID,SONG_ID,TRACK_SEQ_NO) VALUES ((SELECT MUSICCD_ID FROM
MUSICCD WHERE TITLE='Sweet Baby James'),(SELECT SONG_ID FROM SONG WHERE TITLE='Oh
Susanna'),6);
INSERT INTO CDTRACK(MUSICCD_ID,SONG_ID,TRACK_SEQ_NO) VALUES ((SELECT MUSICCD_ID FROM
MUSICCD WHERE TITLE='Sweet Baby James'),(SELECT SONG_ID FROM SONG WHERE TITLE='Fire
and Rain'),7);
INSERT INTO CDTRACK(MUSICCD_ID,SONG_ID,TRACK_SEQ_NO) VALUES ((SELECT MUSICCD_ID FROM
MUSICCD WHERE TITLE='Sweet Baby James'),(SELECT SONG_ID FROM SONG WHERE
TITLE='Blossom'),8);
INSERT INTO CDTRACK(MUSICCD_ID,SONG_ID,TRACK_SEQ_NO) VALUES ((SELECT MUSICCD_ID FROM
MUSICCD WHERE TITLE='Sweet Baby James'),(SELECT SONG_ID FROM SONG WHERE
TITLE='Anywhere Like Heaven'),9);
INSERT INTO CDTRACK(MUSICCD_ID,SONG_ID,TRACK_SEQ_NO) VALUES ((SELECT MUSICCD_ID FROM
MUSICCD WHERE TITLE='Sweet Baby James'),(SELECT SONG_ID FROM SONG WHERE TITLE='Oh
Baby, Don''t You Loose Your Lip on Me'),10);
INSERT INTO CDTRACK(MUSICCD_ID,SONG_ID,TRACK_SEQ_NO) VALUES ((SELECT MUSICCD_ID FROM
MUSICCD WHERE TITLE='Sweet Baby James'),(SELECT SONG_ID FROM SONG WHERE TITLE='Suite
for 20 G'),11);
COMMIT;

SPOOL OFF;
```

A.10 GUESTARTIST.SQL

```
SPOOL log/GUESTARTIST.LOG;

INSERT INTO ARTIST(ARTIST_ID,NAME,INSTRUMENTS)
VALUES(ARTIST_ID_SEQ.NEXTVAL,'Angie Aparo'
,INSTRUMENTSCOLLECTION('Background Vocals'));
INSERT INTO ARTIST(ARTIST_ID,NAME,INSTRUMENTS)
VALUES(ARTIST_ID_SEQ.NEXTVAL,'Peter Stuart'
,INSTRUMENTSCOLLECTION('Background Vocals'));
INSERT INTO ARTIST(ARTIST_ID,NAME,INSTRUMENTS)
VALUES(ARTIST_ID_SEQ.NEXTVAL,'Sam Bacco'
,INSTRUMENTSCOLLECTION('Percussion'));
INSERT INTO ARTIST(ARTIST_ID,NAME,INSTRUMENTS)
VALUES(ARTIST_ID_SEQ.NEXTVAL,'Tony Adams'
,INSTRUMENTSCOLLECTION('Drums'));
INSERT INTO ARTIST(ARTIST_ID,NAME,INSTRUMENTS)
VALUES(ARTIST_ID_SEQ.NEXTVAL,'Paul Doucette'
,INSTRUMENTSCOLLECTION('Acoustic Guitar'));
COMMIT;

INSERT INTO GUESTAPPEARANCE(COMMENT_TEXT,SONG_ID,GUESTARTIST_ID) VALUES('Arrived
late'
,(SELECT SONG_ID FROM SONG WHERE TITLE='Stop')
,(SELECT ARTIST_ID FROM ARTIST WHERE NAME='Angie Aparo'));
```

```
INSERT INTO GUESTAPPEARANCE(COMMENT_TEXT,SONG_ID,GUESTARTIST_ID) VALUES('Very
professional when meeting with the band'
,(SELECT SONG_ID FROM SONG WHERE TITLE='The Burn')
,(SELECT ARTIST_ID FROM ARTIST WHERE NAME='Peter Stuart'));
INSERT INTO GUESTAPPEARANCE(SONG_ID,GUESTARTIST_ID)
VALUES((SELECT SONG_ID FROM SONG WHERE TITLE='Last Beautiful Girl')
,(SELECT ARTIST_ID FROM ARTIST WHERE NAME='Sam Bacco'));
INSERT INTO GUESTAPPEARANCE(SONG_ID,GUESTARTIST_ID)
VALUES((SELECT SONG_ID FROM SONG WHERE TITLE='Stop')
,(SELECT ARTIST_ID FROM ARTIST WHERE NAME='Tony Adams'));
INSERT INTO GUESTAPPEARANCE(COMMENT_TEXT, SONG_ID,GUESTARTIST_ID) VALUES('Agreed to
work on this song for free'
,(SELECT SONG_ID FROM SONG WHERE TITLE='Stop')
,(SELECT ARTIST_ID FROM ARTIST WHERE NAME='Paul Doucette'));
COMMIT;

INSERT INTO INSTRUMENTATION
(COMMENT_TEXT,SONG_ID,GUESTARTIST_ID,INSTRUMENT_ID)
VALUES('Best crooning on the CD'
,(SELECT SONG_ID FROM SONG WHERE TITLE='Stop')
,(SELECT ARTIST_ID FROM ARTIST WHERE NAME='Angie Aparo')
,(SELECT INSTRUMENT_ID FROM INSTRUMENT
WHERE NAME='Background Vocals'));
INSERT INTO INSTRUMENTATION
(SONG_ID,GUESTARTIST_ID,INSTRUMENT_ID)
VALUES((SELECT SONG_ID FROM SONG WHERE TITLE='The Burn')
,(SELECT ARTIST_ID FROM ARTIST WHERE NAME='Peter Stuart')
,(SELECT INSTRUMENT_ID FROM INSTRUMENT
WHERE NAME='Background Vocals'));
INSERT INTO INSTRUMENTATION(SONG_ID,GUESTARTIST_ID,INSTRUMENT_ID) VALUES((SELECT
SONG_ID FROM SONG WHERE TITLE='Last Beautiful Girl')
,(SELECT ARTIST_ID FROM ARTIST WHERE NAME='Sam Bacco')
,(SELECT INSTRUMENT_ID FROM INSTRUMENT WHERE NAME='Percussion'));
INSERT INTO INSTRUMENTATION
(COMMENT_TEXT,SONG_ID,GUESTARTIST_ID,INSTRUMENT_ID)
VALUES('This song would not have happened without Tony'
,(SELECT SONG_ID FROM SONG WHERE TITLE='Stop')
,(SELECT ARTIST_ID FROM ARTIST WHERE NAME='Tony Adams')
,(SELECT INSTRUMENT_ID FROM INSTRUMENT WHERE NAME='Drums'));
INSERT INTO INSTRUMENTATION
(COMMENT_TEXT,SONG_ID,GUESTARTIST_ID,INSTRUMENT_ID)
VALUES('Great guitar solo'
,(SELECT SONG_ID FROM SONG WHERE TITLE='Stop')
,(SELECT ARTIST_ID FROM ARTIST WHERE NAME='Paul Doucette')
,(SELECT INSTRUMENT_ID FROM INSTRUMENT WHERE NAME='Acoustic Guitar'));
```

```
COMMIT;

SPOOL OFF;
```

A.11 STUDIOTIME.SQL

```
SPOOL log/STUDIOTIME.LOG;

INSERT INTO STUDIOTIME
(STUDIOTIME_ID, ARTIST_ID, SESSION_DATE, DUE_DATE, MINUTES_USED)
VALUES (STUDIOTIME_ID_SEQ.NEXTVAL,4,'08-MAY-00','07-JUN-00',120);
INSERT INTO STUDIOTIME
(STUDIOTIME_ID, ARTIST_ID, SESSION_DATE, DUE_DATE, MINUTES_USED)
VALUES (STUDIOTIME_ID_SEQ.NEXTVAL,8,'08-MAY-00','07-JUN-00',280);
INSERT INTO STUDIOTIME
(STUDIOTIME_ID, ARTIST_ID, SESSION_DATE, DUE_DATE, MINUTES_USED)
VALUES (STUDIOTIME_ID_SEQ.NEXTVAL,1,'12-MAY-00','11-JUN-00',1200);
INSERT INTO STUDIOTIME
(STUDIOTIME_ID, ARTIST_ID, SESSION_DATE, DUE_DATE, MINUTES_USED)
VALUES (STUDIOTIME_ID_SEQ.NEXTVAL,1,'12-MAY-00','11-JUN-00',480);
INSERT INTO STUDIOTIME
(STUDIOTIME_ID, ARTIST_ID, SESSION_DATE, DUE_DATE, MINUTES_USED)
VALUES (STUDIOTIME_ID_SEQ.NEXTVAL,7,'12-MAY-00','11-JUN-00',348);
INSERT INTO STUDIOTIME
(STUDIOTIME_ID, ARTIST_ID, SESSION_DATE, DUE_DATE, MINUTES_USED)
VALUES (STUDIOTIME_ID_SEQ.NEXTVAL,7,'12-MAY-00','11-JUN-00',189);
INSERT INTO STUDIOTIME
(STUDIOTIME_ID, ARTIST_ID, SESSION_DATE, DUE_DATE, MINUTES_USED)
VALUES (STUDIOTIME_ID_SEQ.NEXTVAL,7,'13-MAY-00','12-JUN-00',548);
INSERT INTO STUDIOTIME
(STUDIOTIME_ID, ARTIST_ID, SESSION_DATE, DUE_DATE, MINUTES_USED)
VALUES (STUDIOTIME_ID_SEQ.NEXTVAL,1,'11-NOV-00','11-DEC-00',760);
INSERT INTO STUDIOTIME
(STUDIOTIME_ID, ARTIST_ID, SESSION_DATE, DUE_DATE, MINUTES_USED)
VALUES (STUDIOTIME_ID_SEQ.NEXTVAL,1,'15-DEC-00','14-JAN-01',885.5);
INSERT INTO STUDIOTIME
(STUDIOTIME_ID, ARTIST_ID, SESSION_DATE, DUE_DATE, MINUTES_USED)
VALUES (STUDIOTIME_ID_SEQ.NEXTVAL,5,'15-JAN-01','14-FEB-01',332.25);
INSERT INTO STUDIOTIME
(STUDIOTIME_ID, ARTIST_ID, SESSION_DATE, DUE_DATE, MINUTES_USED)
VALUES (STUDIOTIME_ID_SEQ.NEXTVAL,1,'19-JAN-01','18-FEB-01',110.5);
INSERT INTO STUDIOTIME
(STUDIOTIME_ID, ARTIST_ID, SESSION_DATE, DUE_DATE, MINUTES_USED)
VALUES (STUDIOTIME_ID_SEQ.NEXTVAL,5,'19-JAN-01','18-FEB-01',100);
```

```
INSERT INTO STUDIOTIME
(STUDIOTIME_ID, ARTIST_ID, SESSION_DATE, DUE_DATE, MINUTES_USED)
VALUES (STUDIOTIME_ID_SEQ.NEXTVAL,5,'20-JAN-01','19-FEB-01',230);
INSERT INTO STUDIOTIME
(STUDIOTIME_ID, ARTIST_ID, SESSION_DATE, DUE_DATE, MINUTES_USED)
VALUES (STUDIOTIME_ID_SEQ.NEXTVAL,5,'21-JAN-01','20-FEB-01',350);
INSERT INTO STUDIOTIME
(STUDIOTIME_ID, ARTIST_ID, SESSION_DATE, DUE_DATE, MINUTES_USED)
VALUES (STUDIOTIME_ID_SEQ.NEXTVAL,6,'21-JAN-01','20-FEB-01',567);
INSERT INTO STUDIOTIME
(STUDIOTIME_ID, ARTIST_ID, SESSION_DATE, DUE_DATE, MINUTES_USED)
VALUES (STUDIOTIME_ID_SEQ.NEXTVAL,6,'22-JAN-01','21-FEB-01',875);
INSERT INTO STUDIOTIME
(STUDIOTIME_ID, ARTIST_ID, SESSION_DATE, DUE_DATE, MINUTES_USED)
VALUES (STUDIOTIME_ID_SEQ.NEXTVAL,6,'22-JAN-01','21-FEB-01',125);
INSERT INTO STUDIOTIME
(STUDIOTIME_ID, ARTIST_ID, SESSION_DATE, DUE_DATE, MINUTES_USED)
VALUES (STUDIOTIME_ID_SEQ.NEXTVAL,6,'23-JAN-01','22-FEB-01',106);
INSERT INTO STUDIOTIME
(STUDIOTIME_ID, ARTIST_ID, SESSION_DATE, DUE_DATE, MINUTES_USED)
VALUES (STUDIOTIME_ID_SEQ.NEXTVAL,6,'23-JAN-01','22-FEB-01',600);
INSERT INTO STUDIOTIME
(STUDIOTIME_ID, ARTIST_ID, SESSION_DATE, DUE_DATE, MINUTES_USED)
VALUES (STUDIOTIME_ID_SEQ.NEXTVAL,6,'24-JAN-01','23-FEB-01',750.4);
INSERT INTO STUDIOTIME
(STUDIOTIME_ID, ARTIST_ID, SESSION_DATE, DUE_DATE, MINUTES_USED)
VALUES (STUDIOTIME_ID_SEQ.NEXTVAL,1,'01-FEB-01','03-MAR-01',800);
INSERT INTO STUDIOTIME
(STUDIOTIME_ID, ARTIST_ID, SESSION_DATE, DUE_DATE, MINUTES_USED)
VALUES (STUDIOTIME_ID_SEQ.NEXTVAL,1,'12-FEB-01','14-MAR-01',1000);
INSERT INTO STUDIOTIME
(STUDIOTIME_ID, ARTIST_ID, SESSION_DATE, DUE_DATE, MINUTES_USED)
VALUES (STUDIOTIME_ID_SEQ.NEXTVAL,7,'20-FEB-01','22-MAR-01',850.5);
INSERT INTO STUDIOTIME
(STUDIOTIME_ID, ARTIST_ID, SESSION_DATE, DUE_DATE, MINUTES_USED)
VALUES (STUDIOTIME_ID_SEQ.NEXTVAL,1,'11-MAR-01','10-APR-01',245);
INSERT INTO STUDIOTIME
(STUDIOTIME_ID, ARTIST_ID, SESSION_DATE, DUE_DATE, MINUTES_USED)
VALUES (STUDIOTIME_ID_SEQ.NEXTVAL,5,'11-MAR-01','10-APR-01',650);
INSERT INTO STUDIOTIME
(STUDIOTIME_ID, ARTIST_ID, SESSION_DATE, DUE_DATE, MINUTES_USED)
VALUES (STUDIOTIME_ID_SEQ.NEXTVAL,2,'11-MAR-01','10-APR-01',122);
INSERT INTO STUDIOTIME
(STUDIOTIME_ID, ARTIST_ID, SESSION_DATE, DUE_DATE, MINUTES_USED)
VALUES (STUDIOTIME_ID_SEQ.NEXTVAL,1,'13-MAR-01','12-APR-01',540);
```

```
INSERT INTO STUDIOTIME
(STUDIOTIME_ID, ARTIST_ID, SESSION_DATE, DUE_DATE, MINUTES_USED)
VALUES (STUDIOTIME_ID_SEQ.NEXTVAL,2,'13-MAR-01','12-APR-01',300);
INSERT INTO STUDIOTIME
(STUDIOTIME_ID, ARTIST_ID, SESSION_DATE, DUE_DATE, MINUTES_USED)
VALUES (STUDIOTIME_ID_SEQ.NEXTVAL,4,'17-MAR-01','16-APR-01',90);
INSERT INTO STUDIOTIME
(STUDIOTIME_ID, ARTIST_ID, SESSION_DATE, DUE_DATE, MINUTES_USED)
VALUES (STUDIOTIME_ID_SEQ.NEXTVAL,4,'17-MAR-01','16-APR-01',45.5);
INSERT INTO STUDIOTIME
(STUDIOTIME_ID, ARTIST_ID, SESSION_DATE, DUE_DATE, MINUTES_USED)
VALUES (STUDIOTIME_ID_SEQ.NEXTVAL,6,'01-MAY-01','31-MAY-01',900);
INSERT INTO STUDIOTIME
(STUDIOTIME_ID, ARTIST_ID, SESSION_DATE, DUE_DATE, MINUTES_USED)
VALUES (STUDIOTIME_ID_SEQ.NEXTVAL,2,'01-MAY-01','31-MAY-01',345);
INSERT INTO STUDIOTIME
(STUDIOTIME_ID, ARTIST_ID, SESSION_DATE, DUE_DATE, MINUTES_USED)
VALUES (STUDIOTIME_ID_SEQ.NEXTVAL,2,'04-MAY-01','03-JUN-01',450.5);
INSERT INTO STUDIOTIME
(STUDIOTIME_ID, ARTIST_ID, SESSION_DATE, DUE_DATE, MINUTES_USED)
VALUES (STUDIOTIME_ID_SEQ.NEXTVAL,2,'05-MAY-01','04-JUN-01',396);
INSERT INTO STUDIOTIME
(STUDIOTIME_ID, ARTIST_ID, SESSION_DATE, DUE_DATE, MINUTES_USED)
VALUES (STUDIOTIME_ID_SEQ.NEXTVAL,2,'06-MAY-01','05-JUN-01',200);
INSERT INTO STUDIOTIME
(STUDIOTIME_ID, ARTIST_ID, SESSION_DATE, DUE_DATE, MINUTES_USED)
VALUES (STUDIOTIME_ID_SEQ.NEXTVAL,2,'07-MAY-01','06-JUN-01',690);
INSERT INTO STUDIOTIME
(STUDIOTIME_ID, ARTIST_ID, SESSION_DATE, DUE_DATE, MINUTES_USED)
VALUES (STUDIOTIME_ID_SEQ.NEXTVAL,2,'18-MAY-01','17-JUN-01',400);
INSERT INTO STUDIOTIME
(STUDIOTIME_ID, ARTIST_ID, SESSION_DATE, DUE_DATE, MINUTES_USED)
VALUES (STUDIOTIME_ID_SEQ.NEXTVAL,5,'02-JUN-01','02-JUL-01',300);
INSERT INTO STUDIOTIME
(STUDIOTIME_ID, ARTIST_ID, SESSION_DATE, DUE_DATE, MINUTES_USED)
VALUES (STUDIOTIME_ID_SEQ.NEXTVAL,2,'11-JUN-01','11-JUL-01',441);
INSERT INTO STUDIOTIME
(STUDIOTIME_ID, ARTIST_ID, SESSION_DATE, DUE_DATE, MINUTES_USED)
VALUES (STUDIOTIME_ID_SEQ.NEXTVAL,2,'12-JUN-01','12-JUL-01',450);
INSERT INTO STUDIOTIME
(STUDIOTIME_ID, ARTIST_ID, SESSION_DATE, DUE_DATE, MINUTES_USED)
VALUES (STUDIOTIME_ID_SEQ.NEXTVAL,2,'13-JUN-01','13-JUL-01',200);
INSERT INTO STUDIOTIME
(STUDIOTIME_ID, ARTIST_ID, SESSION_DATE, DUE_DATE, MINUTES_USED)
VALUES (STUDIOTIME_ID_SEQ.NEXTVAL,2,'14-JUN-01','14-JUL-01',795.5);
```

```
INSERT INTO STUDIOTIME
(STUDIOTIME_ID, ARTIST_ID, SESSION_DATE, DUE_DATE, MINUTES_USED)
VALUES (STUDIOTIME_ID_SEQ.NEXTVAL,7,'15-JUN-01','15-JUL-01',328);
INSERT INTO STUDIOTIME
(STUDIOTIME_ID, ARTIST_ID, SESSION_DATE, DUE_DATE, MINUTES_USED)
VALUES (STUDIOTIME_ID_SEQ.NEXTVAL,7,'15-JUN-01','15-JUL-01',200);
INSERT INTO STUDIOTIME
(STUDIOTIME_ID, ARTIST_ID, SESSION_DATE, DUE_DATE, MINUTES_USED)
VALUES (STUDIOTIME_ID_SEQ.NEXTVAL,7,'16-JUN-01','16-JUL-01',440);
INSERT INTO STUDIOTIME
(STUDIOTIME_ID, ARTIST_ID, SESSION_DATE, DUE_DATE, MINUTES_USED)
VALUES (STUDIOTIME_ID_SEQ.NEXTVAL,1,'05-JUL-01','04-AUG-01',820);
INSERT INTO STUDIOTIME
(STUDIOTIME_ID, ARTIST_ID, SESSION_DATE, DUE_DATE, MINUTES_USED)
VALUES (STUDIOTIME_ID_SEQ.NEXTVAL,7,'05-JUL-01','04-AUG-01',100);
INSERT INTO STUDIOTIME
(STUDIOTIME_ID, ARTIST_ID, SESSION_DATE, DUE_DATE, MINUTES_USED)
VALUES (STUDIOTIME_ID_SEQ.NEXTVAL,1,'05-JUL-01','04-AUG-01',15);
INSERT INTO STUDIOTIME
(STUDIOTIME_ID, ARTIST_ID, SESSION_DATE, DUE_DATE, MINUTES_USED)
VALUES (STUDIOTIME_ID_SEQ.NEXTVAL,2,'09-AUG-01','08-SEP-01',1000);
INSERT INTO STUDIOTIME
(STUDIOTIME_ID, ARTIST_ID, SESSION_DATE, DUE_DATE, MINUTES_USED)
VALUES (STUDIOTIME_ID_SEQ.NEXTVAL,4,'30-AUG-01','29-SEP-01',460);
INSERT INTO STUDIOTIME
(STUDIOTIME_ID, ARTIST_ID, SESSION_DATE, DUE_DATE, MINUTES_USED)
VALUES (STUDIOTIME_ID_SEQ.NEXTVAL,4,'30-AUG-01','29-SEP-01',200);
INSERT INTO STUDIOTIME
(STUDIOTIME_ID, ARTIST_ID, SESSION_DATE, DUE_DATE, MINUTES_USED)
VALUES (STUDIOTIME_ID_SEQ.NEXTVAL,6,'30-AUG-01','29-SEP-01',30);
INSERT INTO STUDIOTIME
(STUDIOTIME_ID, ARTIST_ID, SESSION_DATE, DUE_DATE, MINUTES_USED)
VALUES (STUDIOTIME_ID_SEQ.NEXTVAL,8,'12-SEP-01','12-OCT-01',159);
INSERT INTO STUDIOTIME
(STUDIOTIME_ID, ARTIST_ID, SESSION_DATE, DUE_DATE, MINUTES_USED)
VALUES (STUDIOTIME_ID_SEQ.NEXTVAL,1,'15-SEP-01','15-OCT-01',345.45);
INSERT INTO STUDIOTIME
(STUDIOTIME_ID, ARTIST_ID, SESSION_DATE, DUE_DATE, MINUTES_USED)
VALUES (STUDIOTIME_ID_SEQ.NEXTVAL,5,'15-SEP-01','15-OCT-01',20.5);
INSERT INTO STUDIOTIME
(STUDIOTIME_ID, ARTIST_ID, SESSION_DATE, DUE_DATE, MINUTES_USED)
VALUES (STUDIOTIME_ID_SEQ.NEXTVAL,4,'25-SEP-01','25-OCT-01',340.25);
INSERT INTO STUDIOTIME
(STUDIOTIME_ID, ARTIST_ID, SESSION_DATE, DUE_DATE, MINUTES_USED)
VALUES (STUDIOTIME_ID_SEQ.NEXTVAL,5,'25-SEP-01','25-OCT-01',100.5);
```

```
INSERT INTO STUDIOTIME
(STUDIOTIME_ID, ARTIST_ID, SESSION_DATE, DUE_DATE, MINUTES_USED)
VALUES (STUDIOTIME_ID_SEQ.NEXTVAL,1,'25-SEP-01','25-OCT-01',223.25);
INSERT INTO STUDIOTIME
(STUDIOTIME_ID, ARTIST_ID, SESSION_DATE, DUE_DATE, MINUTES_USED)
VALUES (STUDIOTIME_ID_SEQ.NEXTVAL,3,'12-OCT-01','11-NOV-01',410);
INSERT INTO STUDIOTIME
(STUDIOTIME_ID, ARTIST_ID, SESSION_DATE, DUE_DATE, MINUTES_USED)
VALUES (STUDIOTIME_ID_SEQ.NEXTVAL,7,'14-OCT-01','13-NOV-01',210);
INSERT INTO STUDIOTIME
(STUDIOTIME_ID, ARTIST_ID, SESSION_DATE, DUE_DATE, MINUTES_USED)
VALUES (STUDIOTIME_ID_SEQ.NEXTVAL,7,'14-OCT-01','13-NOV-01',120.5);
INSERT INTO STUDIOTIME
(STUDIOTIME_ID, ARTIST_ID, SESSION_DATE, DUE_DATE, MINUTES_USED)
VALUES (STUDIOTIME_ID_SEQ.NEXTVAL,8,'15-OCT-01','14-NOV-01',1000);
INSERT INTO STUDIOTIME
(STUDIOTIME_ID, ARTIST_ID, SESSION_DATE, DUE_DATE, MINUTES_USED)
VALUES (STUDIOTIME_ID_SEQ.NEXTVAL,8,'16-OCT-01','15-NOV-01',100);
INSERT INTO STUDIOTIME
(STUDIOTIME_ID, ARTIST_ID, SESSION_DATE, DUE_DATE, MINUTES_USED)
VALUES (STUDIOTIME_ID_SEQ.NEXTVAL,8,'18-OCT-01','17-NOV-01',210);
INSERT INTO STUDIOTIME
(STUDIOTIME_ID, ARTIST_ID, SESSION_DATE, DUE_DATE, MINUTES_USED)
VALUES (STUDIOTIME_ID_SEQ.NEXTVAL,8,'19-OCT-01','18-NOV-01',90);
INSERT INTO STUDIOTIME
(STUDIOTIME_ID, ARTIST_ID, SESSION_DATE, DUE_DATE, MINUTES_USED)
VALUES (STUDIOTIME_ID_SEQ.NEXTVAL,8,'20-OCT-01','19-NOV-01',360);
INSERT INTO STUDIOTIME
(STUDIOTIME_ID, ARTIST_ID, SESSION_DATE, DUE_DATE, MINUTES_USED)
VALUES (STUDIOTIME_ID_SEQ.NEXTVAL,1,'21-OCT-01','20-NOV-01',250);
INSERT INTO STUDIOTIME
(STUDIOTIME_ID, ARTIST_ID, SESSION_DATE, DUE_DATE, MINUTES_USED)
VALUES (STUDIOTIME_ID_SEQ.NEXTVAL,2,'21-OCT-01','20-NOV-01',101.35);
INSERT INTO STUDIOTIME
(STUDIOTIME_ID, ARTIST_ID, SESSION_DATE, DUE_DATE, MINUTES_USED)
VALUES (STUDIOTIME_ID_SEQ.NEXTVAL,1,'21-OCT-01','20-NOV-01',90.25);
INSERT INTO STUDIOTIME
(STUDIOTIME_ID, ARTIST_ID, SESSION_DATE, DUE_DATE, MINUTES_USED)
VALUES (STUDIOTIME_ID_SEQ.NEXTVAL,8,'21-OCT-01','20-NOV-01',30);
INSERT INTO STUDIOTIME
(STUDIOTIME_ID, ARTIST_ID, SESSION_DATE, DUE_DATE, MINUTES_USED)
VALUES (STUDIOTIME_ID_SEQ.NEXTVAL,8,'22-OCT-01','21-NOV-01',458);
INSERT INTO STUDIOTIME
(STUDIOTIME_ID, ARTIST_ID, SESSION_DATE, DUE_DATE, MINUTES_USED)
VALUES (STUDIOTIME_ID_SEQ.NEXTVAL,8,'23-OCT-01','22-NOV-01',333.5);
```

```
INSERT INTO STUDIOTIME
(STUDIOTIME_ID, ARTIST_ID, SESSION_DATE, DUE_DATE, MINUTES_USED)
VALUES (STUDIOTIME_ID_SEQ.NEXTVAL,2,'17-NOV-01','17-DEC-01',249);
INSERT INTO STUDIOTIME
(STUDIOTIME_ID, ARTIST_ID, SESSION_DATE, DUE_DATE, MINUTES_USED)
VALUES (STUDIOTIME_ID_SEQ.NEXTVAL,5,'20-NOV-01','20-DEC-01',100);
INSERT INTO STUDIOTIME
(STUDIOTIME_ID, ARTIST_ID, SESSION_DATE, DUE_DATE, MINUTES_USED)
VALUES (STUDIOTIME_ID_SEQ.NEXTVAL,8,'25-NOV-01','25-DEC-01',120);
INSERT INTO STUDIOTIME
(STUDIOTIME_ID, ARTIST_ID, SESSION_DATE, DUE_DATE, MINUTES_USED)
VALUES (STUDIOTIME_ID_SEQ.NEXTVAL,1,'03-DEC-01','02-JAN-02',1200);
INSERT INTO STUDIOTIME
(STUDIOTIME_ID, ARTIST_ID, SESSION_DATE, DUE_DATE, MINUTES_USED)
VALUES (STUDIOTIME_ID_SEQ.NEXTVAL,8,'03-DEC-01','02-JAN-02',199);
INSERT INTO STUDIOTIME
(STUDIOTIME_ID, ARTIST_ID, SESSION_DATE, DUE_DATE, MINUTES_USED)
VALUES (STUDIOTIME_ID_SEQ.NEXTVAL,5,'03-DEC-01','02-JAN-02',439.26);
INSERT INTO STUDIOTIME
(STUDIOTIME_ID, ARTIST_ID, SESSION_DATE, DUE_DATE, MINUTES_USED)
VALUES (STUDIOTIME_ID_SEQ.NEXTVAL,2,'03-DEC-01','02-JAN-02',25);
INSERT INTO STUDIOTIME
(STUDIOTIME_ID, ARTIST_ID, SESSION_DATE, DUE_DATE, MINUTES_USED)
VALUES (STUDIOTIME_ID_SEQ.NEXTVAL,1,'19-DEC-01','18-JAN-02',230);
INSERT INTO STUDIOTIME
(STUDIOTIME_ID, ARTIST_ID, SESSION_DATE, DUE_DATE, MINUTES_USED)
VALUES (STUDIOTIME_ID_SEQ.NEXTVAL,7,'04-JAN-02','03-FEB-02',220);
INSERT INTO STUDIOTIME
(STUDIOTIME_ID, ARTIST_ID, SESSION_DATE, DUE_DATE, MINUTES_USED)
VALUES (STUDIOTIME_ID_SEQ.NEXTVAL,4,'11-JAN-02','10-FEB-02',450);
INSERT INTO STUDIOTIME
(STUDIOTIME_ID, ARTIST_ID, SESSION_DATE, DUE_DATE, MINUTES_USED)
VALUES (STUDIOTIME_ID_SEQ.NEXTVAL,7,'13-JAN-02','12-FEB-02',340);
INSERT INTO STUDIOTIME
(STUDIOTIME_ID, ARTIST_ID, SESSION_DATE, DUE_DATE, MINUTES_USED)
VALUES (STUDIOTIME_ID_SEQ.NEXTVAL,5,'08-JAN-02','07-FEB-02',224);
INSERT INTO STUDIOTIME
(STUDIOTIME_ID, ARTIST_ID, SESSION_DATE, DUE_DATE, MINUTES_USED)
VALUES (STUDIOTIME_ID_SEQ.NEXTVAL,8,'09-JAN-02','08-FEB-02',553);
INSERT INTO STUDIOTIME
(STUDIOTIME_ID, ARTIST_ID, SESSION_DATE, DUE_DATE, MINUTES_USED)
VALUES (STUDIOTIME_ID_SEQ.NEXTVAL,7,'29-DEC-01','29-JAN-02',100);
COMMIT;

SPOOL OFF;
```

A.12 UPDATEDATA.SQL

```
SPOOL log/UPDATES.LOG

PROMPT ARTIST

UPDATE MUSIC.ARTIST
 SET STREET = '122 North Wells' , CITY = 'Corvalis' ,
 STATE_PROVINCE = 'OR' , COUNTRY = 'USA' , ZIP = '99887'
 , EMAIL = 'ccc@sheryl.net'
 WHERE NAME='Sheryl Crow';
UPDATE MUSIC.ARTIST
 SET STREET = '102341 High Road' , POBOX = 'PO Box 195' ,
 CITY = 'West Palm Beach' , STATE_PROVINCE = 'FL' ,
 COUNTRY = 'USA' , ZIP = '21987' , EMAIL =
 'gogo@whoknew.org'
 WHERE NAME= 'Barry Manilow';
UPDATE MUSIC.ARTIST
 SET STREET = '5A North Queens Ave' , CITY = 'London' ,
 COUNTRY = 'England' , ZIP = '1A4-5RA' , EMAIL = 'wendsday@thursday.com'
 WHERE NAME= 'Avril Lavigne';
UPDATE MUSIC.ARTIST SET STREET = '400 West Hollywood Blvd' ,
 CITY = 'Hollywood' , STATE_PROVINCE = 'CA' , COUNTRY = 'USA' ,
 ZIP = '87654' , EMAIL = 'googoo@googoo.net'
 WHERE NAME= 'Goo Goo Dolls';
UPDATE MUSIC.ARTIST SET STREET = '3498 S. Barnes Rd.' ,
 POBOX = 'PO Box 982356' , CITY = 'Treeville' , STATE_PROVINCE = 'NH' ,
 COUNTRY = 'USA' , ZIP = '10098-4998' , EMAIL = 'pompom@mmm.org'
 WHERE NAME= 'Puddle of Mudd';
UPDATE MUSIC.ARTIST SET STREET = 'PO Box 332244', POBOX = 'PO Box 332244' , CITY =
'South Emery' ,
 STATE_PROVINCE = 'Quebec' , COUNTRY = 'CAN' , ZIP = '4DQ-A3E' ,
 EMAIL = 'buddy@pals.pal'
 WHERE NAME= 'Nickelback';
UPDATE MUSIC.ARTIST SET STREET = '4398 SE 415th Ave' , POBOX = 'Suite 134' ,
 CITY = 'Portland' , STATE_PROVINCE = 'OR' , COUNTRY = 'USA' ,
 ZIP = '98765-0134' , EMAIL = 'm20@matchesboxes.org'
 WHERE NAME= 'Matchbox Twenty';
UPDATE MUSIC.ARTIST SET STREET = '10049 Sunset Blvd' , CITY = 'Los Angeles' ,
 STATE_PROVINCE = 'CA' , COUNTRY = 'USA' , ZIP = '60292' ,
 EMAIL = 'jjjewel@jewel.hk'
 WHERE NAME= 'Jewel';
UPDATE MUSIC.ARTIST SET STREET = '539 Smithsonian Rd' , POBOX = 'Apt 400' ,
 CITY = 'New York' , STATE_PROVINCE = 'NY' , COUNTRY = 'USA' ,
 ZIP = '10022' , EMAIL = 'Angie@parao.tk'
```

```
 WHERE NAME= 'Angie Aparo';
UPDATE MUSIC.ARTIST SET STREET = '100 North Wells Place' ,
 POBOX = 'PO Box 100' , CITY = 'Dallas' , STATE_PROVINCE = 'TX' ,
 COUNTRY = 'USA' , ZIP = '43455' , EMAIL = 'pstuart@dallas.mr'
 WHERE NAME= 'Peter Stuart';
UPDATE MUSIC.ARTIST SET STREET = '98-B Hillside Lane' , CITY = 'Charlotte' ,
 STATE_PROVINCE = 'NC' , COUNTRY = 'USA' , ZIP = '54098' ,
 EMAIL = 'sambacco@shatsup.org'
 WHERE NAME= 'Sam Bacco';
UPDATE MUSIC.ARTIST
 SET STREET = '159 Browning Drive' , CITY = 'Madison' ,
 STATE_PROVINCE = 'WI' , COUNTRY = 'USA' , ZIP = '53998' ,
 EMAIL = 'tony@adamshouse.com'
 WHERE NAME= 'Tony Adams';
UPDATE MUSIC.ARTIST SET STREET = '544 156th Ave' , CITY = 'Seattle' ,
 STATE_PROVINCE = 'WA' , COUNTRY = 'USA' , ZIP = '96777' ,
 EMAIL = 'pdoucette@pdoucette.com'
 WHERE NAME= 'Paul Doucette';
UPDATE MUSIC.ARTIST SET STREET = 'The JT Fan Club' , CITY = 'Boston' ,
 STATE_PROVINCE = 'MA' , COUNTRY = 'USA' , ZIP = '' ,
 EMAIL = 'info@jamestaylor.com'
 WHERE NAME= 'James Taylor';
UPDATE MUSIC.ARTIST SET STREET = 'Wien Strasse' , CITY = 'Vienna' ,
 STATE_PROVINCE = '' , COUNTRY = 'Austria' , ZIP = '' ,
 EMAIL = 'info@friendsofmozart.com'
 WHERE NAME= 'Mozart';
COMMIT;

PROMPT STUDIOTIME

UPDATE STUDIOTIME
SET AMOUNT_CHARGED = MINUTES_USED*1.5,
 AMOUNT_PAID = MINUTES_USED*1.5*TO_NUMBER(SUBSTR(MINUTES_USED,1,1))*.1;
COMMIT;

PROMPT SONG
PROMPT UPDATE SONG
UPDATE MUSIC.SONG SET RECORDING_DATE='19-JAN-01' WHERE TITLE='Abilene';
UPDATE MUSIC.SONG SET RECORDING_DATE='20-FEB-01' WHERE TITLE='Angry';
UPDATE MUSIC.SONG SET RECORDING_DATE='11-MAR-01'
WHERE TITLE='Bandstand Boogie';
UPDATE MUSIC.SONG SET RECORDING_DATE='15-JAN-01' WHERE TITLE='Basement';
UPDATE MUSIC.SONG SET RECORDING_DATE='12-MAY-00' WHERE TITLE='Bed Of Lies';
UPDATE MUSIC.SONG SET RECORDING_DATE='04-JAN-02' WHERE TITLE='Bent';
UPDATE MUSIC.SONG SET RECORDING_DATE='05-JUL-01'
```

```
WHERE TITLE='Black and White People';
UPDATE MUSIC.SONG SET RECORDING_DATE='11-MAR-01' WHERE TITLE='Blurry';
UPDATE MUSIC.SONG SET RECORDING_DATE='25-NOV-01' WHERE TITLE='Break Me';
UPDATE MUSIC.SONG SET RECORDING_DATE='20-NOV-01' WHERE TITLE='Bring Me Down';
UPDATE MUSIC.SONG SET RECORDING_DATE='11-JAN-02' WHERE TITLE='Burnin Up';
UPDATE MUSIC.SONG SET RECORDING_DATE='19-DEC-01'
WHERE TITLE='C''mon, C''mon';
UPDATE MUSIC.SONG SET RECORDING_DATE='21-OCT-01'
WHERE TITLE='Can''t Smile Without You';
UPDATE MUSIC.SONG SET RECORDING_DATE='15-OCT-01' WHERE TITLE='Cleveland';
UPDATE MUSIC.SONG SET RECORDING_DATE='12-OCT-01' WHERE TITLE='Complicated';
UPDATE MUSIC.SONG SET RECORDING_DATE='02-JUN-01' WHERE TITLE='Control';
UPDATE MUSIC.SONG SET RECORDING_DATE='17-NOV-01'
WHERE TITLE='Copacabana (At The Copa)';
UPDATE MUSIC.SONG SET RECORDING_DATE='13-MAR-01'
WHERE TITLE='Could It Be Magic';
UPDATE MUSIC.SONG SET RECORDING_DATE='13-JAN-02' WHERE TITLE='Crutch';
UPDATE MUSIC.SONG SET RECORDING_DATE='03-DEC-01' WHERE TITLE='Daybreak';
UPDATE MUSIC.SONG SET RECORDING_DATE='15-SEP-01' WHERE TITLE='Diamond Road';
UPDATE MUSIC.SONG SET RECORDING_DATE='03-DEC-01'
WHERE TITLE='Do You Want To Play ?';
UPDATE MUSIC.SONG SET RECORDING_DATE='25-SEP-01' WHERE TITLE='Drift and Die';
UPDATE MUSIC.SONG SET RECORDING_DATE='09-AUG-01' WHERE TITLE='Even Now';
UPDATE MUSIC.SONG SET RECORDING_DATE='08-MAY-00'
WHERE TITLE='Everybody Needs Someone Sometime';
UPDATE MUSIC.SONG SET RECORDING_DATE='17-MAR-01'
WHERE TITLE='Girl Right Next To Me';
UPDATE MUSIC.SONG SET RECORDING_DATE='30-AUG-01'
WHERE TITLE='Good Times Gone';
UPDATE MUSIC.SONG SET RECORDING_DATE='12-SEP-01'
WHERE TITLE='Grey Matter (Live)';
UPDATE MUSIC.SONG SET RECORDING_DATE='01-MAY-01' WHERE TITLE='Hangnail';
UPDATE MUSIC.SONG SET RECORDING_DATE='08-MAY-00' WHERE TITLE='Here Is Gone';
UPDATE MUSIC.SONG SET RECORDING_DATE='30-AUG-01'
WHERE TITLE='Here Is Gone Reprise';
UPDATE MUSIC.SONG SET RECORDING_DATE='13-MAR-01'
WHERE TITLE='Hole In My Pocket';
UPDATE MUSIC.SONG SET RECORDING_DATE='24-JAN-01' WHERE TITLE='Hollywood';
UPDATE MUSIC.SONG SET RECORDING_DATE='22-JAN-01'
WHERE TITLE='How You Remind Me';
UPDATE MUSIC.SONG SET RECORDING_DATE='12-JUN-01'
WHERE TITLE='I Made It Through The Rain';
UPDATE MUSIC.SONG SET RECORDING_DATE='21-OCT-01'
WHERE TITLE='I Won''t Walk Away';
UPDATE MUSIC.SONG SET RECORDING_DATE='06-MAY-01'
```

```
WHERE TITLE='I Write The Songs';
UPDATE MUSIC.SONG SET RECORDING_DATE='15-JUN-01'
WHERE TITLE='If You''re Gone';
UPDATE MUSIC.SONG SET RECORDING_DATE='21-JAN-01' WHERE TITLE='It All Away';
UPDATE MUSIC.SONG SET RECORDING_DATE='05-MAY-01'
WHERE TITLE='It''s A Miracle';
UPDATE MUSIC.SONG SET RECORDING_DATE='21-OCT-01'
WHERE TITLE='It''s Only Love';
UPDATE MUSIC.SONG SET RECORDING_DATE='05-JUL-01' WHERE TITLE='It''s So Easy';
UPDATE MUSIC.SONG SET RECORDING_DATE='16-OCT-01'
WHERE TITLE='Jesus Loves You';
UPDATE MUSIC.SONG SET RECORDING_DATE='23-JAN-01' WHERE TITLE='Just For';
UPDATE MUSIC.SONG SET RECORDING_DATE='15-JUN-01'
WHERE TITLE='Last Beautiful Girl';
UPDATE MUSIC.SONG SET RECORDING_DATE='13-MAY-00' WHERE TITLE='Leave';
UPDATE MUSIC.SONG SET RECORDING_DATE='18-MAY-01'
WHERE TITLE='Looks Like We Made It';
UPDATE MUSIC.SONG SET RECORDING_DATE='22-OCT-01'
WHERE TITLE='Love Me, Just Leave Me Alone';
UPDATE MUSIC.SONG SET RECORDING_DATE='21-OCT-01' WHERE TITLE='Lucky Kid';
UPDATE MUSIC.SONG SET RECORDING_DATE='16-JUN-01' WHERE TITLE='Mad Season';
UPDATE MUSIC.SONG SET RECORDING_DATE='04-MAY-01' WHERE TITLE='Mandy';
UPDATE MUSIC.SONG SET RECORDING_DATE='01-MAY-01' WHERE TITLE='Money Bought';
UPDATE MUSIC.SONG SET RECORDING_DATE='21-JAN-01' WHERE TITLE='Never Again';
UPDATE MUSIC.SONG SET RECORDING_DATE='19-JAN-01' WHERE TITLE='Never Change';
UPDATE MUSIC.SONG SET RECORDING_DATE='03-DEC-01'
WHERE TITLE='Out Of My Head';
UPDATE MUSIC.SONG SET RECORDING_DATE='11-MAR-01' WHERE TITLE='Over You';
UPDATE MUSIC.SONG SET RECORDING_DATE='11-JUN-01'
WHERE TITLE='Ready To Take A Chance';
UPDATE MUSIC.SONG SET RECORDING_DATE='05-JUL-01'
WHERE TITLE='Safe And Sound';
UPDATE MUSIC.SONG SET RECORDING_DATE='20-JAN-01' WHERE TITLE='Said';
UPDATE MUSIC.SONG SET RECORDING_DATE='19-OCT-01' WHERE TITLE='Serve The Ego';
UPDATE MUSIC.SONG SET RECORDING_DATE='15-SEP-01' WHERE TITLE='She Hates Me';
UPDATE MUSIC.SONG SET RECORDING_DATE='11-JUN-01' WHERE TITLE='Ships';
UPDATE MUSIC.SONG SET RECORDING_DATE='12-MAY-00'
WHERE TITLE='Soak Up The Sun';
UPDATE MUSIC.SONG SET RECORDING_DATE='11-NOV-00'
WHERE TITLE='Soak Up The Sun (Album Version)';
UPDATE MUSIC.SONG SET RECORDING_DATE='01-FEB-01'
WHERE TITLE='Soak Up The Sun (Sunsweep Club Mix)';
UPDATE MUSIC.SONG SET RECORDING_DATE='12-FEB-01'
WHERE TITLE='Soak Up The Sun (Sunsweep Dub)';
UPDATE MUSIC.SONG SET RECORDING_DATE='15-DEC-00'
```

```
WHERE TITLE='Soak Up The Sun (Sunsweep Radio Mix)';
UPDATE MUSIC.SONG SET RECORDING_DATE='14-JUN-01'
WHERE TITLE='Somewhere Down The Road';
UPDATE MUSIC.SONG SET RECORDING_DATE='01-MAY-01'
WHERE TITLE='Somewhere In The Night';
UPDATE MUSIC.SONG SET RECORDING_DATE='15-OCT-01'
WHERE TITLE='Standing Still';
UPDATE MUSIC.SONG SET RECORDING_DATE='25-SEP-01' WHERE TITLE='Steve McQueen';
UPDATE MUSIC.SONG SET RECORDING_DATE='14-OCT-01' WHERE TITLE='Stop';
UPDATE MUSIC.SONG SET RECORDING_DATE='12-MAY-00' WHERE TITLE='The Burn';
UPDATE MUSIC.SONG SET RECORDING_DATE='23-OCT-01'
WHERE TITLE='The New Wild West';
UPDATE MUSIC.SONG SET RECORDING_DATE='11-JUN-01' WHERE TITLE='The Old Songs';
UPDATE MUSIC.SONG SET RECORDING_DATE='07-MAY-01'
WHERE TITLE='This One''s For You';
UPDATE MUSIC.SONG SET RECORDING_DATE='20-OCT-01' WHERE TITLE='This Way';
UPDATE MUSIC.SONG SET RECORDING_DATE='18-OCT-01'
WHERE TITLE='Till We Run Out Of Road';
UPDATE MUSIC.SONG SET RECORDING_DATE='23-JAN-01' WHERE TITLE='Too Bad';
UPDATE MUSIC.SONG SET RECORDING_DATE='07-MAY-01'
WHERE TITLE='Tryin'' To Get The Feeling Again';
UPDATE MUSIC.SONG SET RECORDING_DATE='25-SEP-01'
WHERE TITLE='Two Days In February';
UPDATE MUSIC.SONG SET RECORDING_DATE='30-AUG-01' WHERE TITLE='Video';
UPDATE MUSIC.SONG SET RECORDING_DATE='17-MAR-01'
WHERE TITLE='We Are The Normal';
UPDATE MUSIC.SONG SET RECORDING_DATE='03-DEC-01'
WHERE TITLE='Weather Channel';
UPDATE MUSIC.SONG SET RECORDING_DATE='01-MAY-01'
WHERE TITLE='Weekend In New England';
UPDATE MUSIC.SONG SET RECORDING_DATE='13-JUN-01'
WHERE TITLE='When October Goes';
UPDATE MUSIC.SONG SET RECORDING_DATE='01-MAY-01'
WHERE TITLE='Where Do I Hide';
UPDATE MUSIC.SONG SET RECORDING_DATE='22-JAN-01'
WHERE TITLE='Woke Up This Morning';
UPDATE MUSIC.SONG SET RECORDING_DATE='14-OCT-01'
WHERE TITLE='You Won''t Be Mine';
UPDATE MUSIC.SONG SET RECORDING_DATE='12-MAY-00'
WHERE TITLE='You''re An Original';
COMMIT;

SPOOL OFF;
```

A.13 CHECKDATA.SQL

```
SPOOL log/VIEW_DATA.LOG;
SET TIMING OFF LINESIZE 132 PAGESIZE 40;

SELECT INSTRUMENT_ID,NAME "Instrument" FROM INSTRUMENT ORDER BY NAME;

SELECT ARTIST_ID,NAME,INSTRUMENTS FROM ARTIST ORDER BY NAME;

SELECT S.SONG_ID,S.TITLE,S.PLAYING_TIME,A.NAME "Artist" FROM SONG S,ARTIST A
WHERE A.ARTIST_ID = S.ARTIST_ID ORDER BY A.NAME,S.TITLE;

SELECT * FROM MUSICCD;

SELECT M.TITLE,C.TRACK_SEQ_NO,S.TITLE FROM SONG S,MUSICCD M,CDTRACK C
WHERE S.SONG_ID = C.SONG_ID AND C.MUSICCD_ID = M.MUSICCD_ID ORDER BY 1,2;

SELECT A.NAME "GuestArtist",S.TITLE "Song Title",I.NAME "Instrument"
FROM ARTIST A, SONG S, GUESTAPPEARANCE SG,
INSTRUMENTATION ISG,INSTRUMENT I
WHERE A.ARTIST_ID = SG.GUESTARTIST_ID
AND S.SONG_ID = SG.SONG_ID
AND SG.GUESTARTIST_ID = ISG.GUESTARTIST_ID
AND SG.SONG_ID = ISG.SONG_ID
AND ISG.INSTRUMENT_ID = I.INSTRUMENT_ID;

SPOOL OFF;
```

A.14 SCHEMADW.SQL

```
SPOOL log/SCHEMA_DW.LOG;

--
--dimensions
--

DROP TABLE CONTINENT CASCADE CONSTRAINTS;
CREATE TABLE CONTINENT
(
  CONTINENT_ID NUMBER NOT NULL
 ,NAME VARCHAR2(32)
 ,CONSTRAINT XPKCONTINENT PRIMARY KEY (CONTINENT_ID)
);
CREATE UNIQUE INDEX XUK_CONTINENT_NAME ON CONTINENT(NAME);
```

```
DROP TABLE COUNTRY CASCADE CONSTRAINTS;
CREATE TABLE COUNTRY
(
  COUNTRY_ID NUMBER NOT NULL
 ,CONTINENT_ID NUMBER
 ,NAME VARCHAR2(32)
 ,CONSTRAINT XPKCOUNTRY PRIMARY KEY (COUNTRY_ID)
 ,CONSTRAINT FKCOUNTRY_1 FOREIGN KEY (CONTINENT_ID) REFERENCES CONTINENT
);
CREATE UNIQUE INDEX XUK_COUNTRY_NAME ON COUNTRY(NAME);
CREATE INDEX XFKCOUNTRY_1 ON COUNTRY (CONTINENT_ID);

DROP TABLE RETAILER CASCADE CONSTRAINTS;
CREATE TABLE RETAILER
(
  RETAILER_ID NUMBER NOT NULL
 ,NAME VARCHAR2(32)
 ,DISCOUNT FLOAT
 ,URL VARCHAR2(128)
 ,CONSTRAINT XPKRETAILER PRIMARY KEY (RETAILER_ID)
);
CREATE UNIQUE INDEX XUK_RETAILER_NAME ON RETAILER(NAME);

--
--dimension oltp links
--

CREATE OR REPLACE TYPE PREFERENCESCOLLECTION AS TABLE OF VARCHAR2(32);
/
DROP TABLE CUSTOMER CASCADE CONSTRAINTS;
CREATE TABLE CUSTOMER
(
  CUSTOMER_ID NUMBER NOT NULL
 ,NAME VARCHAR2(32) NOT NULL
 ,USERNAME CHAR(8)
 ,PASSWORD CHAR(8)
 ,SHIPPING_ADDRESS CLOB
 ,BILLING_ADDRESS CLOB
 ,CREDIT_CARD CLOB
 ,PREFERENCES PREFERENCESCOLLECTION
 ,CONSTRAINT XPKCUSTOMER PRIMARY KEY (CUSTOMER_ID)
) NESTED TABLE PREFERENCES STORE AS PREFERENCESTAB;
CREATE UNIQUE INDEX XUK_CUSTOMER_NAME ON CUSTOMER(NAME);
```

```
--ALTER TABLE CUSTOMER ADD(PREFERENCES PREFERENCESCOLLECTION) NESTED TABLE
PREFERENCES STORE AS PREFERENCES;


--
--facts
--

DROP TABLE SALES CASCADE CONSTRAINTS;
CREATE TABLE SALES
(
  SALES_ID NUMBER NOT NULL
 ,MUSICCD_ID NUMBER NOT NULL
 ,CUSTOMER_ID NUMBER NOT NULL
 ,RETAILER_ID NUMBER
 ,CONTINENT_ID NUMBER
 ,COUNTRY_ID NUMBER
 ,LIST_PRICE FLOAT
 ,DISCOUNT FLOAT
 ,SALE_PRICE FLOAT
 ,SALE_DATE DATE
 ,SALE_QTY NUMBER
 ,SHIPPING_COST FLOAT
 ,CONSTRAINT XPKSALES PRIMARY KEY (SALES_ID)
 ,CONSTRAINT FKSALES_1 FOREIGN KEY (RETAILER_ID) REFERENCES RETAILER
 ,CONSTRAINT FKSALES_2 FOREIGN KEY (CONTINENT_ID) REFERENCES CONTINENT
 ,CONSTRAINT FKSALES_3 FOREIGN KEY (COUNTRY_ID) REFERENCES COUNTRY
 ,CONSTRAINT FKSALES_4 FOREIGN KEY (CUSTOMER_ID) REFERENCES CUSTOMER
);
CREATE INDEX XFK_SALES_1 ON SALES (RETAILER_ID);
CREATE INDEX XFK_SALES_2 ON SALES (CONTINENT_ID);
CREATE INDEX XFK_SALES_3 ON SALES (COUNTRY_ID);
CREATE INDEX XFK_SALES_4 ON SALES (CUSTOMER_ID);

SPOOL OFF;
```

A.15 DIMENSIONS.SQL

```
SPOOL log/DIMENSIONS.LOG;


--continent

INSERT INTO CONTINENT(CONTINENT_ID,NAME) VALUES(CONTINENT_ID_SEQ.NEXTVAL,'North
America');
INSERT INTO CONTINENT(CONTINENT_ID,NAME) VALUES(CONTINENT_ID_SEQ.NEXTVAL,'Europe');
```

```
INSERT INTO CONTINENT(CONTINENT_ID,NAME) VALUES(CONTINENT_ID_SEQ.NEXTVAL,'Central
America');
INSERT INTO CONTINENT(CONTINENT_ID,NAME) VALUES(CONTINENT_ID_SEQ.NEXTVAL,'South
America');
INSERT INTO CONTINENT(CONTINENT_ID,NAME) VALUES(CONTINENT_ID_SEQ.NEXTVAL,'Oceania');
INSERT INTO CONTINENT(CONTINENT_ID,NAME) VALUES(CONTINENT_ID_SEQ.NEXTVAL,'Africa');
INSERT INTO CONTINENT(CONTINENT_ID,NAME) VALUES(CONTINENT_ID_SEQ.NEXTVAL,'Asia');
INSERT INTO CONTINENT(CONTINENT_ID,NAME)
VALUES(CONTINENT_ID_SEQ.NEXTVAL,'Australasia');
COMMIT;

--country

INSERT INTO COUNTRY(COUNTRY_ID,CONTINENT_ID,NAME)
VALUES(COUNTRY_ID_SEQ.NEXTVAL,(SELECT CONTINENT_ID FROM CONTINENT WHERE NAME='North
America'),'United States');
INSERT INTO COUNTRY(COUNTRY_ID,CONTINENT_ID,NAME)
VALUES(COUNTRY_ID_SEQ.NEXTVAL,(SELECT CONTINENT_ID FROM CONTINENT WHERE NAME='North
America'),'Canada');
INSERT INTO COUNTRY(COUNTRY_ID,CONTINENT_ID,NAME)
VALUES(COUNTRY_ID_SEQ.NEXTVAL,(SELECT CONTINENT_ID FROM CONTINENT WHERE NAME='North
America'),'Mexico');

INSERT INTO COUNTRY(COUNTRY_ID,CONTINENT_ID,NAME)
VALUES(COUNTRY_ID_SEQ.NEXTVAL,(SELECT CONTINENT_ID FROM CONTINENT WHERE
NAME='Europe'),'United Kingdom');
INSERT INTO COUNTRY(COUNTRY_ID,CONTINENT_ID,NAME)
VALUES(COUNTRY_ID_SEQ.NEXTVAL,(SELECT CONTINENT_ID FROM CONTINENT WHERE
NAME='Europe'),'France');
INSERT INTO COUNTRY(COUNTRY_ID,CONTINENT_ID,NAME)
VALUES(COUNTRY_ID_SEQ.NEXTVAL,(SELECT CONTINENT_ID FROM CONTINENT WHERE
NAME='Europe'),'Czech Republic');
INSERT INTO COUNTRY(COUNTRY_ID,CONTINENT_ID,NAME)
VALUES(COUNTRY_ID_SEQ.NEXTVAL,(SELECT CONTINENT_ID FROM CONTINENT WHERE
NAME='Europe'),'Germany');
INSERT INTO COUNTRY(COUNTRY_ID,CONTINENT_ID,NAME)
VALUES(COUNTRY_ID_SEQ.NEXTVAL,(SELECT CONTINENT_ID FROM CONTINENT WHERE
NAME='Europe'),'Netherlands');
INSERT INTO COUNTRY(COUNTRY_ID,CONTINENT_ID,NAME)
VALUES(COUNTRY_ID_SEQ.NEXTVAL,(SELECT CONTINENT_ID FROM CONTINENT WHERE
NAME='Europe'),'Spain');
INSERT INTO COUNTRY(COUNTRY_ID,CONTINENT_ID,NAME)
VALUES(COUNTRY_ID_SEQ.NEXTVAL,(SELECT CONTINENT_ID FROM CONTINENT WHERE
NAME='Europe'),'Sweden');

INSERT INTO COUNTRY(COUNTRY_ID,CONTINENT_ID,NAME)
VALUES(COUNTRY_ID_SEQ.NEXTVAL,(SELECT CONTINENT_ID FROM CONTINENT WHERE NAME='South
America'),'Argentina');
```

```
INSERT INTO COUNTRY(COUNTRY_ID,CONTINENT_ID,NAME)
VALUES(COUNTRY_ID_SEQ.NEXTVAL,(SELECT CONTINENT_ID FROM CONTINENT WHERE NAME='South
America'),'Brazil');
INSERT INTO COUNTRY(COUNTRY_ID,CONTINENT_ID,NAME)
VALUES(COUNTRY_ID_SEQ.NEXTVAL,(SELECT CONTINENT_ID FROM CONTINENT WHERE NAME='South
America'),'Chile');
INSERT INTO COUNTRY(COUNTRY_ID,CONTINENT_ID,NAME)
VALUES(COUNTRY_ID_SEQ.NEXTVAL,(SELECT CONTINENT_ID FROM CONTINENT WHERE NAME='South
America'),'Colombia');
INSERT INTO COUNTRY(COUNTRY_ID,CONTINENT_ID,NAME)
VALUES(COUNTRY_ID_SEQ.NEXTVAL,(SELECT CONTINENT_ID FROM CONTINENT WHERE NAME='South
America'),'Peru');
INSERT INTO COUNTRY(COUNTRY_ID,CONTINENT_ID,NAME)
VALUES(COUNTRY_ID_SEQ.NEXTVAL,(SELECT CONTINENT_ID FROM CONTINENT WHERE NAME='South
America'),'Venezuela');


INSERT INTO COUNTRY(COUNTRY_ID,CONTINENT_ID,NAME)
VALUES(COUNTRY_ID_SEQ.NEXTVAL,(SELECT CONTINENT_ID FROM CONTINENT WHERE
NAME='Asia'),'Singapore');
INSERT INTO COUNTRY(COUNTRY_ID,CONTINENT_ID,NAME)
VALUES(COUNTRY_ID_SEQ.NEXTVAL,(SELECT CONTINENT_ID FROM CONTINENT WHERE
NAME='Asia'),'South Korea');
INSERT INTO COUNTRY(COUNTRY_ID,CONTINENT_ID,NAME)
VALUES(COUNTRY_ID_SEQ.NEXTVAL,(SELECT CONTINENT_ID FROM CONTINENT WHERE
NAME='Asia'),'Taiwan');
INSERT INTO COUNTRY(COUNTRY_ID,CONTINENT_ID,NAME)
VALUES(COUNTRY_ID_SEQ.NEXTVAL,(SELECT CONTINENT_ID FROM CONTINENT WHERE
NAME='Asia'),'Israel');
INSERT INTO COUNTRY(COUNTRY_ID,CONTINENT_ID,NAME)
VALUES(COUNTRY_ID_SEQ.NEXTVAL,(SELECT CONTINENT_ID FROM CONTINENT WHERE
NAME='Asia'),'Kuwait');
INSERT INTO COUNTRY(COUNTRY_ID,CONTINENT_ID,NAME)
VALUES(COUNTRY_ID_SEQ.NEXTVAL,(SELECT CONTINENT_ID FROM CONTINENT WHERE
NAME='Asia'),'Qatar');
INSERT INTO COUNTRY(COUNTRY_ID,CONTINENT_ID,NAME)
VALUES(COUNTRY_ID_SEQ.NEXTVAL,(SELECT CONTINENT_ID FROM CONTINENT WHERE
NAME='Asia'),'United Arab Emirates');
INSERT INTO COUNTRY(COUNTRY_ID,CONTINENT_ID,NAME)
VALUES(COUNTRY_ID_SEQ.NEXTVAL,(SELECT CONTINENT_ID FROM CONTINENT WHERE
NAME='Asia'),'India');


INSERT INTO COUNTRY(COUNTRY_ID,CONTINENT_ID,NAME)
VALUES(COUNTRY_ID_SEQ.NEXTVAL,(SELECT CONTINENT_ID FROM CONTINENT WHERE
NAME='Australasia'),'Australia');
INSERT INTO COUNTRY(COUNTRY_ID,CONTINENT_ID,NAME)
VALUES(COUNTRY_ID_SEQ.NEXTVAL,(SELECT CONTINENT_ID FROM CONTINENT WHERE
NAME='Australasia'),'New Zealand');


COMMIT;
```

```
--retailer

INSERT INTO RETAILER(RETAILER_ID,NAME,DISCOUNT,URL)
VALUES(RETAILER_ID_SEQ.NEXTVAL,'Amazon',0.2,'http://www.amazon.com');
INSERT INTO RETAILER(RETAILER_ID,NAME,DISCOUNT,URL)
VALUES(RETAILER_ID_SEQ.NEXTVAL,'Barnes and Noble',0.05,'http://
www.barnesandnoble.com');
INSERT INTO RETAILER(RETAILER_ID,NAME,DISCOUNT,URL)
VALUES(RETAILER_ID_SEQ.NEXTVAL,'CD Shop',0,NULL);

COMMIT;

SPOOL OFF;
```

A.16 FACTS.SQL

```
SPOOL log/FACTS.LOG;

create or replace procedure delay(limit IN integer) as
 i integer;
begin
 for i in 1..limit loop
  null;
 end loop;
end;
/

create or replace function rand(n IN NUMBER DEFAULT 1) return integer is
 f float default 0;
 rand integer default 0;
begin
 --gives a random number between 1 and 1000000000
 select to_number(to_char(SYSTIMESTAMP,'FF9'))+1 into f from dual;
 f := (f*n)/1000000000;
 rand := ROUND(f,0);
 if rand = 0 then rand := 1; end if;
 if rand > n then rand := n; end if;
 return ROUND(rand,0);
exception when others then
 dbms_output.put_line('FUNC: rand '||SQLERRM(SQLCODE));
end;
/

@@lastname.sql;
@@firstname.sql;
```

```
create or replace function getRetailer return integer is
 i integer;
begin
 select max(retailer_id) into i from retailer;
 return (rand(i));
exception when others then
 dbms_output.put_line('FUNC: getRetailer '||SQLERRM(SQLCODE));
end;
/


create or replace function getMusicCDID return integer is
 i integer;
begin
 select max(musiccd_id) into i from musiccd;
 return (rand(i));
exception when others then
 dbms_output.put_line('FUNC: getMusicCDID '||SQLERRM(SQLCODE));
end;
/


create or replace function getGenreID (i IN integer) return integer is
 j integer;
begin
 select genre_id into j from musiccd where MUSICCD_ID = i;
 return (j);
exception when others then
 dbms_output.put_line('FUNC: getGenreID '||SQLERRM(SQLCODE));
end;
/


create or replace function getListPrice (i IN integer) return float is
 f float;
begin
 select list_price into f from musiccd where MUSICCD_ID = i;
 return (f);
exception when others then
 dbms_output.put_line('FUNC: getListPrice '||SQLERRM(SQLCODE));
end;
/


create or replace function getGenre (i IN integer) return varchar is
 v varchar2(32);
begin
 select genre into v from genre where GENRE_ID = i;
```

```
 return (v);
exception when others then
 dbms_output.put_line('FUNC: getGenre '||SQLERRM(SQLCODE));
end;
/


create or replace function getCountryID return integer is
 i integer;
begin
 select max(country_id) into i from country;
 return (rand(i));
exception when others then
 dbms_output.put_line('FUNC: getCountryID '||SQLERRM(SQLCODE));
end;
/


create or replace function getContinentID (i IN integer) return integer is
 j integer;
begin
 select continent_id into j from country where COUNTRY_ID = i;
 return (j);
exception when others then
 dbms_output.put_line('FUNC: getContinentID '||SQLERRM(SQLCODE));
end;
/


create or replace function getCustomerName return varchar2 is
 i integer;
 fname varchar2(32);
 lname varchar2(32);
begin
 select count(*) into i from firstname;
 select name into fname from firstname where ID = rand(i);
 select count(*) into i from lastname;
 select name into lname from lastname where ID = rand(i);
 return (fname||' '||lname);
exception when others then
 dbms_output.put_line('FUNC: getCustomerName '||SQLERRM(SQLCODE));
end;
/


create or replace function getDiscount (i IN integer) return float is
 f float;
begin
 select discount into f from retailer where RETAILER_ID = i;
```

```
 return (f);
exception when others then
 dbms_output.put_line('FUNC: getDiscount '||SQLERRM(SQLCODE));
end;
/


--customer
create or replace procedure factsGenerate as
 id integer;
 vmusiccd_id integer default 0;
 vgenre_id number;
 vlist_price float;
 vcustomer_id integer;
 vretailer_id integer;
 vcontinent_id integer;
 vcountry_id integer;
 vdiscount float;
 vgenre varchar2(32);
 vfullname varchar2(64);
 vPreferences PreferencesCollection;
 i integer;
 j integer default 0;
 dte date;
begin

 vmusiccd_id := getMusicCDID();
 vgenre_id := getGenreID(vmusiccd_id);
 vlist_price := getListPrice(vmusiccd_id);
 vgenre := getGenre(vgenre_id);
 vretailer_id := getRetailer();
 vcountry_id := getCountryID;

 vcontinent_id := getContinentID(vcountry_id);
 vdiscount := getDiscount(vretailer_id);
 vfullname := getCustomerName();

 begin
  select customer_id into id from customer where NAME = vfullname;
  select preferences into vPreferences from customer where CUSTOMER_ID = id;
  j := 0; for i in vPreferences.first..vPreferences.last loop
   if vPreferences(i) = vgenre then j := 1; end if;
  end loop;
  if j = 0 then
   insert into table(select preferences from customer where CUSTOMER_ID = id)
values(vgenre);
```

```
  end if;
exception when NO_DATA_FOUND then
  insert into customer(customer_id,name,preferences)
  values(customer_id_seq.nextval,vfullname,PREFERENCESCOLLECTION(vgenre))
  returning customer_id into id;
end;

vcustomer_id := id;

--dte := TO_DATE('31-12-2004','DD-MM-YYYY') - rand(500);
--dbms_output.put_line(to_char(vcountry_id));
dte := (SYSDATE + 300) - rand(500);
dbms_output.put_line(to_char(vcountry_id)||','||dte);

insert into sales
(
  sales_id
 ,musiccd_id
 ,customer_id
 ,retailer_id
 ,continent_id
 ,country_id
 ,list_price
 ,discount
 ,sale_price
 ,sale_date
 ,sale_qty
 ,shipping_cost
)
values
(
  sales_id_seq.nextval
 ,vmusiccd_id
 ,vcustomer_id
 ,vretailer_id
 ,vcontinent_id
 ,vcountry_id
 ,vlist_price
 ,vdiscount
 ,ROUND(vlist_price * (1 - vdiscount),2)
 ,dte
 ,1
 ,0
);
commit;
```

```
exception when others then
 dbms_output.put_line('PROC: factGenerate '||SQLERRM(SQLCODE));
 rollback;
end;
/

create or replace procedure facts (i IN integer) is
 j integer;
begin
 for j in 1..i loop
  factsGenerate;
  delay(10000000);
  --dbms_output.put_line('Facts: '||to_char(j));
 end loop;
end;
/

set serveroutput on;
exec dbms_output.enable(10000000);
set timing on;
truncate table sales;
exec facts(1000);
exec dbms_output.disable;
set serveroutput off;

declare
 cursor cSales is select * from sales order by sale_qty;
begin
 for rSales in cSales loop
  update sales set sale_date = (SYSDATE + 300) - rand(500);
  commit;
 end loop;
end;
/

SPOOL OFF;
```

B

Please note that these scripts should be tested before use in a production environment.

B.1   Tables

```
set wrap off linesize 132 pages 80
column tab format a20
column col format a15
column pos format 990
column typ format a10
column tbs format a25
BREAK ON tab NODUPLICATES SKIP 2 ON NAME NODUPLICATES
select t.table_name "Tab"
    ,c.column_name "Col"
    ,c.column_id "Pos"
    ,c.data_type "Typ"
    ,DECODE(c.nullable,'N','NOT NULL',NULL) "Null"
    ,t.tablespace_name "Tbs"
from user_tables t, user_tab_columns c
where t.table_name = c.table_name
order by t.table_name, c.column_id;
```

B.2   Constraints

```
set wrap off linesize 132 pages 80
column tab format a20
column key format a10
column cons format a20
column col format a10
```

```
column pos format 990
BREAK ON tab NODUPLICATES SKIP 2 ON NAME NODUPLICATES
select t.table_name "Tab"

,decode(t.constraint_type,'P','Primary','R','Foreign','U','Alternate','Unknown')
"Key"
    ,t.constraint_name "Cons"
    ,c.column_name "Col"
    ,c.position "Pos"
from user_constraints t, user_cons_columns c
where t.constraint_type in ('P','R','U')
and t.table_name = c.table_name
and t.constraint_name = c.constraint_name
order by t.table_name, t.constraint_type, c.position;
```

B.3　Indexes

```
set wrap off linesize 132 pages 80
column tab format a25
column typ format a5
column ind format a25
column col format a20
column pos format 990
column tbs format a25
BREAK ON tab NODUPLICATES SKIP 2 ON NAME NODUPLICATES
Select t.table_name "Tab"
    ,decode(t.index_type,'NORMAL','BTree','BITMAP','Bitmap','FUNCTION-BASED
NORMAL','Function-Based BTree',t.index_type) "Typ"
    ,t.index_name "Ind"
    ,c.column_name "Col"
    ,c.column_position "Pos"
    ,t.tablespace_name "Tbs"
from user_indexes t, user_ind_columns c
where t.table_name = c.table_name
and t.index_name = c.index_name
and t.index_type not in ('IOT - TOP','LOB')
order by t.table_name, t.index_name, c.column_position;
```

C

The authors of this book can be contacted at the following e-mail addresses:

- oracledbaexpert@earthlink.net
- carolmdieter@yahoo.com

Oracle Technology Network at http://technet.oracle.com or http://otn.oracle.com is an excellent source for entire Oracle reference documentation sets.

Metalink at http://metalink.oracle.com is also excellent and a source of current information from support calls, questions, and answers placed by both Oracle users and Oracle support staff. The information on this site is well worth the Oracle licensing fees required.

Search for a term such as "free buffer waits" in search engines such as www.yahoo.com. Be aware that not all information will be current and might be incorrect. Verify any information found on Oracle Technet. If no results are found using Yahoo, try the full detailed listings on www.google.com.

Try www.amazon.com and www.barnesandnoble.com, where many Oracle titles can be found.

C.1   Other titles by the authors:

Gavin Powell (www.oracledbaexpert.com)

Oracle Performance Tuning for 9*i* and 10*g* (ISBN: 1-555-58305-9).

Introduction to Oracle 9*i* and Beyond: SQL & PL/SQL (ISBN: 1-932-07224-1).

Oracle Database Administration Fundamentals I (ISBN: 1-932-07253-5).

Oracle Database Administration Fundamentals II (ISBN: 1-932-07284-5).

Oracle SQL Exam Cram 2 (ISBN: 0-789-73248-3).

Carol McCullough-Dieter

Oracle9i Database Administrator: Implementation and Administration (ISBN: 0-619-15900-6).

Oracle9i for Dummies (ISBN: 0-764-50880-6).

Oracle8i DBA Bible (ISBN: 0-764-54623-6).

Oracle8i for Dummies (ISBN: 0-764-50798-2).

Several other out-of-print books

MUSIC schema scripts can be found from a simple menu on my Web site at the following URL, along with many other goodies, including my resume:

```
www.oracledbaexpert.com/oracle/
OracleSQLJumpstartWithExamples/index.html
www.oracledbaexpert.com/resume/resume.doc
```

Software accreditations:

- Microsoft Word, Powerpoint, Excel, Win2K.
- ERWin.
- Paintshop.
- Oracle Database 10*g* and Oracle Database 9*i*.

Index